Site Planning Standards

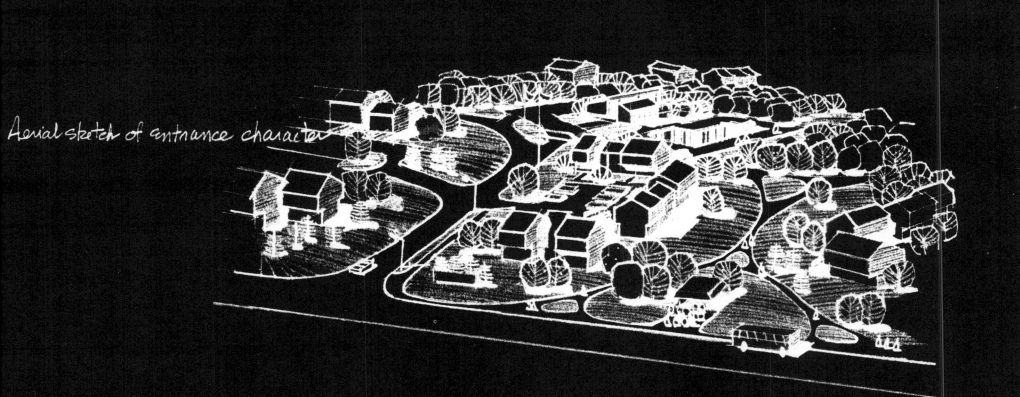

Aerial sketch of entrance character

Site Planning Standards

**Joseph De Chiara
Lee E. Koppelman**

McGraw-Hill Book Company

New York   St. Louis   San Francisco

Auckland   Bogotá   Düsseldorf   Johannesburg
London   Madrid   Mexico   Montreal   New Delhi   Panama
Paris   São Paulo   Singapore   Sydney   Tokyo   Toronto

Library of Congress Cataloging in Publication Data

De Chiara, Joseph, date.
Site planning standards.

Includes index.
1. Building sites.   I. Koppelman, Lee E., joint author.
II. Title.
NA2540.D4   721   77-9440
ISBN 0-07-016216-6

1234567890 HDBP 7654321098

The editors for this book were Jeremy Robinson and Tobia L. Worth, the designer was Edward J.
Fox, and the production supervisor was Frank P. Bellantoni. It was set in Helvetica by University
Graphics, Inc.

Printed by Halliday Lithograph Corporation and bound by The Book Press.

Contents

Factors Affecting Building
Location and Orientation, cont'd.

Section 4

Residential Site Development

Section 5

Layout of Recreational Facilities

Section 6

Typical Site Details

Typical Site Details, cont'd

Section 7

Illustrative Site Plans

Foreword

Site Planning Standards is an interdisciplinary handbook for any-one concerned with development. It pulls together in compact and easily accessible fashion geological, engineering, and environ-mental information essential to proper site planning. Especially helpful are the graphic representations of the subject matter.

The authors, Joseph De Chiara and Lee E. Koppelman, have pro-vided a most useful reference work and a valuable sequel to their *Urban Planning and Design Criteria* (1975), which has gained wide recognition.

John P. Keith, President
Regional Plan Association, Inc., New York

Preface

The general aim of this book is to afford those interested in site planning and design, whether they are students, teachers, practitioners, or public-agency planners, a graphic reference of current standards, design details, analytical methods, and design procedures. Most of the current literature on the subject is in written form. Since this book is meant to be a supplement to the theoretical and critical writings, emphasis is placed on graphical and pictorial presentation. Textual material is included only where clarity or exposition of the graphics is served.

One of the major problems in assembling a text on practice is the selection, within the constraints of a single volume, of the most appropriate standards from the wealth of available data. This difficulty is compounded by the needs of users whose concerns range in sophistication and magnitude from the elementary to those of great complexity. To resolve this problem, it was necessary to select material that would afford a balanced presentation. In some instances this meant the use of earlier standards and details that still have great utility. Therefore, the emphasis is on basic or general site criteria that will give designers and those who review or approve plans the yardsticks with which to measure specific proposals.

The authors caution users that the examples are generally applicable to typical conditions, reflecting planning principles and practices currently in vogue in the United States, and should not be followed automatically.

The format of the book follows the general path of the design process from the predesign stage of data inventory and ancillary surveys through the analysis of site conditions and into the design stages of plan alternatives with specific site details. Section 7 contains illustrative examples by current designers in the solution of a variety of site uses. Each example demonstrates the application of standards and analytical approaches in the earlier chapters.

We wish to acknowledge the generous support and courtesy of the many agencies, practitioners, and publications in allowing the use of their material. In particular, we are indebted to Wes Murray of Schnadelbach Associates, Arthur Middlestadt of Ward and Middlestadt, and Charles Barnett of the U.S. Department of Agriculture Soil Conservation Service.

Joseph De Chiara
Lee E. Koppelman

Site Planning Standards

Preliminary Site Investigation and Analysis

The process of site planning begins with the gathering of basic data relating specifically to the site under consideration and the surrounding areas. The data should include such items as master plans and studies, zoning ordinances, base and aerial maps, surveys, topographic data, geological information, the hydrology of the area, types of soils, vegetation, and existing easements.

After all the available information has been obtained, it must be examined and analyzed. One of the first objectives is to establish the site's advantages and limitations. On the basis of these conclusions, it is then possible to determine whether the land is suitable for the proposed use. If the land is found suitable, the data must be analyzed further to establish other specific parameters of the site. These include such items as the best areas for building locations because of soil conditions, areas to avoid because of steep slopes, areas with soil erosion problems because of drainage patterns, or areas to be left in their natural state because of vegetation.

The use of computer applications in site planning has arrived in the form of computer graphics. Such techniques enable site designers to depict quickly a land area for pictorial and analytical purposes. This tool is suitable for perspective and isometric depictions of topography, slope analysis, cut-and-fill calculations, watershed analysis, and simulation studies. Illustrations of these techniques are included in this section. Since this approach is usually prepared by specialized consultants, it may be economically feasible only for large projects.

Opposite: Grasslands Housing, Westchester
Development Corp. (Pokorny & Pertz)

1.1 Site Inventory and Resource Analysis

Developing an environment requires a thorough knowledge of natural-resource systems, cultural features, and other relevant data. Only when this information has been gathered and analyzed can one proceed to determine possible end use allocations. Although many systems have been developed to inventory and analyze natural resources, almost all share the following three basic purposes:

1. Development of an understanding of separate ecosystem components (soils, vegetation, hydrology, and others)
2. Development of an understanding of the interrelationship of the various ecosystem components (soil and water, climate, vegetation, soils, and others)
3. Determination of the suitability of resource elements and resource aggregates for specified land uses and functions

Illustrated below is a process for realizing these purposes in a logical, sequential fashion.

Resource Category Determination The first step in resource planning is to determine which resources should be investigated. There are several factors that influence this choice.

The resources to be investigated should be relevant to the functions or land uses (outputs) being considered. The factors (soil, water, vegetation canopy, and so on) that determine the suitability of a site for a particular function may be assumed to be the critical factors for which data must be collected, mapped, and evaluated. For instance, if a planner is interested in locating the best sites for wood duck production, the first step is to determine the resource factors that best express the suitability of a site for that particular function.

Listing relevant factors shows which resources need to be investigated and the degree or detail of the data that must be collected. The relation of assumed factors to the example of wood duck production suggests that the resource information presented in the accompanying table should be collected and mapped.

Resource Category Factors

Vegetation	1. Mature deciduous forest
	2. Medium-age deciduous forest
	3. Young deciduous forest
Shoreline features	1. Dense, overhanging woody vegetation
	2. Intermittent brush
	3. Emergent vegetation
Hydrology	1. Slow, meandering stream
	2. Slow- to medium-speed streams
	3. Ponds, 1 to 2 acres
	4. Ponds, 3 to 5 acres
	5. Large, open waters

This table shows that output factors greatly influence the sophistication of an inventory. If a planner is interested not only in locating optimum sites for wood duck production but also in locating optimum sites for interpretive centers, hiking trails, and automobile routes, the inventory will consist of all factors relating to the number of functions or outputs.

It is also imperative that resource planning activities be adjusted to respect local physiographic characteristics. Differences in terrain, climate, and vegetation greatly affect development constraints and opportunities. A function such as camping may be represented by one set of factors in the West and by another set in the Southeast. Thus no one set of factors can ever be used to represent accurately any function in all physiographic situations in the United States. All factors, however, may generally be accounted for within the framework of the following natural and cultural resource structure:

1. Soils
2. Vegetation
3. Hydrology
4. Climate
5. Topography
6. Aesthetics
7. Historical significance
8. Existing land use
9. Physiographic obstructions

Each of these structural components represents areas of major environmental influence

for most functions. The influence of each component naturally depends upon the type and intensity of the proposed function. It should also be emphasized that the type of information needed about each of the components depends upon the particular function or land uses being considered. An inventory of soils relating to a function such as a visitors' center may focus on engineering capabilities, whereas information required for locating specific habitat types may focus on a soil's ability to support a certain type of plant growth. The following statements regarding the individual components suggest their importance as locational factors.

The result of the resource category determination phase should be a rather extensive list of natural and cultural resource features for which data must be collected, mapped, and evaluated. Although most of the information presented in the resource inventory will relate to on-site resources, care should be taken to record any off-site or regional factors that influence on-site phenomena. Important migration routes, watersheds, and vegetation patterns far from the actual site boundaries may greatly affect on-site conditions.

Soils An understanding of soil development, which depends upon (1) parent material, (2) topography, (3) climate, (4) biotic forces, and (5) time, provides insight into many phenomena associated with natural resources. A knowledge of soils is important not only in terms of engineering capability but also in terms of its relevance to other natural-resource systems. An extensive knowledge of on-site soil conditions is helpful both in determining the suitability of a site to support buildings and roadways and in gaining an insight into existing plant communities and associated wildlife habitats. The following list presents soil information that could be considered part of the soil survey (example only).

SOURCE: *Planning for Wildlife and Man*, U.S. Department of the Interior, Fish and Wildlife Service, 1974.

1. Glacial till; shallow water table
2. Glacial till; deep, well drained
3. Glacial till; deep but pan
4. Glacial till; shallow bedrock, shallow water table
5. Stratified drift; deep, well drained
6. Stratified drift; shallow water table
7. Floodplain alluvium; shallow water table
8. Muck and peat
9. Floodplain alluvium; deep, well drained
10. Rock outcroppings

The following list represents soil inventory considerations.

1. Depth of horizon
2. Depth to seasonal high water
3. Depth to bedrock
4. Drainage characteristics
5. Suitability
   a. Septic tanks
   b. Excavation and grading
   c. Value as foundation material
6. Susceptibility to compaction
7. Susceptibility to erosion
8. pH rating
9. Soil fertility

RECOMMENDED SOURCES:
1. U.S. Department of Agriculture, Soil Conservation Service
2. On-site inspection

Vegetation Vegetative types and patterns represent a major visual, recreational, and ecological resource. Native vegetation types are closely related to soils as well as to microclimate, hydrology, and topography. This component is influential in determining the location of most natural-based outputs. The location of hiking trails, camping or picnicking sites, and, perhaps most important, wildlife habitats is greatly influenced by vegetation types and patterns. The following list presents vegetation features that might be studied as part of the vegetation survey (example only).

1. No vegetation
2. Emergent vegetation
3. Streamside and riverside vegetation
4. Vegetation beside ponds, lakes, and reservoirs
5. Wetlands; bog, and tree growth
6. Wetlands; brush growth

7. White pine and mixed northern hardwoods
8. White pine, northern hardwoods, and hemlock
9. Fir and spruce

The following list represents vegetation inventory considerations.

1. Density of canopy
2. Understory heights
3. Overstory heights

RECOMMENDED SOURCES:
1. Low-altitude photographs and photograph interpretation
2. Infrared photographs and photograph interpretation
3. On-site inspection
4. U.S. Geological Survey maps

Hydrology The type and quality of on-site water is a critical visual and recreational resource. Even more important is the overall consideration of the entire interlocking hydrological system. Surface water and drainage patterns greatly affect vegetation, wildlife, and even climatic systems. The capability of the hydrological system must be considered if it is to be utilized as a significant resource. The following list presents possible hydrological features that may be analyzed as part of the hydrology survey (example only).

1. Surface water
   a. First-order stream
   b. Second-order stream
   c. Third-order stream
   d. River
   e. Pond
   f. Lake
   g. Reservoir
2. Drainage basins (watersheds)
   a. First-order
   b. Second-order
   c. Third-order
3. Other
   a. Springs
   b. Pumping wells
   c. Artesian wells

The following list represents other hydrological considerations:

1. Runoff rates
2. Siltation
3. Oxygen content

4. Subsurface water characteristics

RECOMMENDED SOURCES:
1. U.S. Geological Survey
2. On-site inspection
3. State or county hydrological studies

Climate Overall precipitation and temperature variations affect the entire site, as do winds, cloud cover, and seasonal changes. It is important to consider both small- and large-scale climatic phenomena. Many on-site climatic changes are closely related to such on-site factors as changes in topography, slope orientation, vegetation, and the presence of water. Climatic conditions are interconnected with overall regional climatological patterns as well as with smaller site characteristics. The following list presents possible climatological features that may be analyzed as part of the climate survey (example only).

1. Temperature
   a. Annual average temperature range
   b. Temperature extremes
   c. Monthly temperature averages
2. Precipitation
   a. Annual precipitation
   b. Monthly precipitation
3. Wind
   a. Intensity and duration
   b. Seasonal direction
   c. Frequency of damaging storms
4. Snowfall
   a. Annual snowfall
   b. Monthly snowfall
5. Other
   a. Killing-frost dates
   b. Length of growing season
   c. Sun angles (azimuth)

RECOMMENDED SOURCE: National Weather Service.

Topography The basic land form or topographic structure of a site is a visual and aesthetic resource that strongly influences the

SOURCE: *Planning for Wildlife and Man,* U.S. Department of the Interior, Fish and Wildlife Service, 1974.

location of various land uses and recreational and interpretive functions. A complete understanding of the topographic structure not only gives an insight into the location of roadways and hiking trails but also helps reveal the spatial configuration of the site. This spatial structure is especially important when the visual aspects of the environment are being considered. The following list presents possible topographic features that may be analyzed as part of the topographic survey (example only).

1. Elevation above sea level
   a. 1520 to 1580 feet
   b. 1580 to 1620 feet
   c. 1620 to 1660 feet
   d. 1660 to 7700 feet
2. Topographic orientation
   a. Flat; less than 3 percent topographic slope
   b. East to southeast
   c. South to southwest
   d. North to northeast
   e. West to northwest
3. Topograhic slope
   a. 0 to 3 percent slope
   b. 3 to 8 percent slope
   c. 8 to 15 percent slope
   d. 15 to 25 percent slope
   e. 25 percent slope or higher

RECOMMENDED SOURCES:
   1. U.S. Geological Survey
   2. On-site inspection

Aesthetics   Aesthetic resources are largely responsible for locating sites for recreation and activities interpreting wildlife and wild land. These resources depend upon landform diversity, vegetation pattern, and surface waters as well as the spatial definition, views, vistas, and image of the site that stem from these features. The following list presents possible aesthetic features that may be analyzed as part of the aesthetic survey (example only).

1. Major spatial determinants. Landforms that serve as three-dimensional masses or barriers to define spaces from eye level
2. Promontory. Mountain peaks that serve as landmarks or points of reference; highly visible and identifiable landforms

3. Scenic vista. A visual panorama with particular scenic value illustrating a contrast between "closed views" and "open views" as found from an overlook or clearing
4. Orientation vista. A visual panorama with particular value as a locational reference for visitors; a site with a strong image
5. Tree cover. An area characterized by a dense vegetation canopy and limited views through woodlands
6. Flat grassland. An open expanse with long views and a high degree of exposure
7. Hilly grassland. An open expanse with short views and relatively hidden or concealed areas
8. Water image. A large area of surface water with a shallow shoreline profile and a strong sense of water

RECOMMENDED SOURCES:
   1. U.S. Geological Survey quadrant maps
   2. On-site inspection
   3. Aerial photographs

Historical Significance   Any given area generally has significant historical landmarks. A knowledge of the location and importance of these landmarks is valuable in interpreting the overall management area and in locating interpretive displays or exhibits that may focus on them. The following list presents possible historical features that may be analyzed as part of the historical significance survey (example only).

1. Historic trails or passageways
2. Historic buildings or structures
3. Sites of particular significance

RECOMMENDED SOURCES:
   1. Literature on local history
   2. Historical preservation society

Existing Land Use   A thorough knowledge of existing land uses on or adjacent to the site provides the planner with an understanding of constraints and opportunities. Existing land uses often represent significant expenditures and must be weighed accordingly. It is also important to document functions that are not considered land uses per se but are associated with certain land uses, that is, roads, fences,

and utilities. The following list presents possible existing land uses that may be analyzed as part of the land use survey (example only).

1. Conservation, forest, preservation
2. Recreation
3. Farm dwellings
4. Residences
5. Seasonal dwellings
6. Commercial use
7. Industrial use
8. Institutions
9. Air and railway facilities
10. Transmission lines
11. Water and sewage lines
12. Range fences
13. Transportation types
    a. Unimproved road
    b. Graded and drained road
    c. Gravel-surfaced road
    d. Bituminous-surfaced road
    e. Paved road
    f. Divided highway with partial control of access
    g. Divided highway with full control of access

RECOMMENDED SOURCES:
   1. U.S. Geological Survey maps
   2. City and county land use maps
   3. State and county highway maps
   4. On-site inspection

Physiographic Obstructions   Physiographic obstructions are natural elements that obstruct or are hazardous to certain types of development. The elements of an obstruction are related to the output or function being considered. Such conditions as earthquake faults and flash-flood zones are physiographic obstructions that seriously restrict almost all public-use activities that require buildings. Most other obstructions are less restrictive. Floodplain zones, which may be viewed as an obstruction for facilities requiring intensive development, are nevertheless usable for picnicking, hiking, or other functions that cannot damage or be

SOURCE: *Planning for Wildlife and Man,* U.S. Department of the Interior, Fish and Wildlife Service, 1974.

damaged by phenomena associated with such zones. The following list presents possible physiographic obstructions that may be analyzed as part of the physiographic obstruction survey (example only).

1. Fault zones
   a. Major fault zone
   b. Minor fault zone
2. Floodplains
   a. 10-year floodplains
   b. 50-year floodplains
   c. 100-year floodplains
3. Critical wildlife habitat areas
   a. Habitat of endangered or threatened species
   b. Critical migration routes
4. Aquifer recharge
5. Zones susceptible to storm damage
   a. Tornado
   b. Lightning
   c. Hurricane
6. Topography
   a. Low elevations susceptible to tidal inundation
   b. Area with a high water table
   c. Peat bogs
   d. Quicksand
7. Obstructions associated with wildlife or wild lands
   a. Poisonous snakes or reptiles
   b. Mosquitoes or other annoying insects
   c. Poison ivy, poison oak, and other poisonous plants

Data Collection   Pertinent data may be collected in a variety of ways. A thorough inquiry into the recommended sources cited above, in combination with a comprehensive review of the literature, is essential. Information thus gathered may be complemented by field study. Again, the data to be collected should be the total resource data indicated by the output factors.

Data Mapping   Most information on the location of natural and cultural resources will be represented on a variety of scales such as 1 inch = 400 feet or 1:24,000. An initial decision must be made on an appropriate scale for subsequent mapping. The determination of this scale generally depends upon the degree of

OUTPUT: WATERFOWL PRODUCTION—WOOD DUCKS

Factors	Characteristics		
	Optimum	Acceptable	Minimum
Tree cover (nesting)	Mature deciduous forest	Medium-age deciduous forest	Young deciduous forest
Brood ponds	Slow, meandering stream and ponds of 1 to 2 acres, or both	Faster-moving stream and ponds of 2 to 5 acres, or both	Large, open water
Shoreline features	Dense, overhanging woody vegetation and emergent vegetation	Intermittent brush and emergent vegetation	Void of brush or limited emergent vegetation, or both
Proximity of brood to nesting site	Adjacent	Within a half mile	Over a half mile

detail needed to evaluate the resource in terms of previously developed output factors. For instance, a cursory review of data and needs may suggest that a U.S. Geological Survey map of a scale of 1:24,000 is the best mapping scale. If this is so, resource data collected on a different scale must be transposed to the 1:24,000 scale. The transposition may be accomplished by a grid system or by photographic techniques. A standard technique for evaluating resource data requires that individual resources (soil, hydrology) be mapped on single sheets of paper. Once all locational data have been delineated on appropriate drawings on a consistent scale, the drawings can be converted through photographic techniques to transparent overlays. These techniques provide an opportunity to superimpose several individual resource overlays so that combinations of resources or resource aggregates can be evaluated.

Resource Evaluation   Once all the factors relating to the location of the proposed functions have been mapped and converted to transparent overlays, one can begin evaluating pertinent resources in terms of proposed functions or outputs. This process is accomplished by superimposing combinations of appropriate resource overlays to establish the locations of certain phenomena as well as to note pertinent relationships. For example, if a planner wants to locate a potential wood duck production

habitat, the first step is to extract the transparent resource overlays pertaining to the location of wood duck production. The planner's chosen criteria for wood duck production are shown in the accompanying table.

Each of the output factors can be mapped as part of a composite drawing (see Figure 1-1a and b). Once the mapping is complete, the resources can be evaluated in terms of the ability of specific resource aggregates to meet specific output criteria; that is, optimum, first class; acceptable, second class; minimum, third class.

The result of an individual output composite drawing should be a drawing of the entire site, with output locations indicated in terms of suitability (optimum, acceptable, minimum). Individual output composite drawings can, in turn, be used to determine other land use decisions. For instance, the need to determine the optimum location for a multipurpose public-use area may require the development of a composite formed of individual composites relating to picnicking, camping, hiking, and other outdoor activities.

It should be emphasized that determination of the optimum or acceptable suitability of a

SOURCE: *Planning for Wildlife and Man,* U.S. Department of the Interior, Fish and Wildlife Service, 1974.

particular site does not necessarily mean that the site should be developed for a given function. Suitability studies merely suggest the degree to which a site is suitable for a given function. For example, a site that may appear to be optimum for hiking may be located far from optimum camping facilities. If it is desirable to have camping and hiking facilities near each other, one must seek a lower-quality (acceptable or minimum) camping site near the hiking area, or vice versa. Decisions relating to the actual selection of final output locations can be made only after all relevant issues have been considered.

See also Figures 1-2, 1-3, and 1-4.

Figure 1-1a Map showing gross habitat types of wildlife areas. It is produced by superimposing the vegetation, soil, slope, and hydrology resource data.

Figure 1-1b Map showing suitable locations for four recreational activities. It is produced by superimposing the suitable resource overlays.

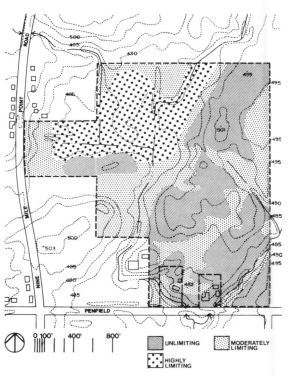

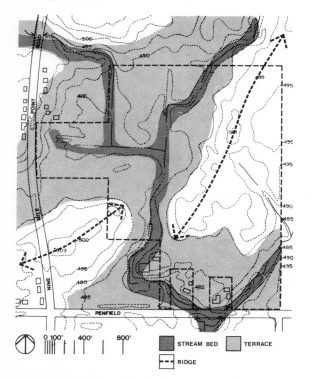

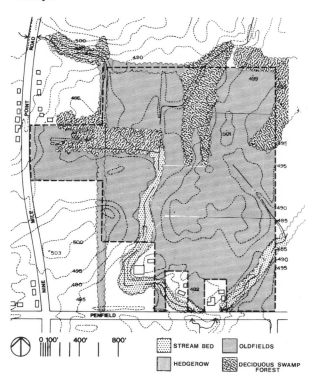

Figure 1-2 Landforms. [*Penfield road study; Schnadelbach Associates*]

Figure 1-3 Existing vegetation. [*Penfield road study; Schnadelbach Associates*]

Figure 1-4 Relative soil limitations. [*Penfield road study; Schnadelbach Associates*]

SOURCE: *Planning for Wildlife and Man*, U.S. Department of the Interior, Fish and Wildlife Service, 1974.

1.2 Survey Systems

Every legal description is based upon a survey of the land. To prepare a legal description of a parcel or tract of land, someone at some time must have walked on the parcel or tract and made some sort of survey.

Metes-and-Bounds Descriptions A metes-and-bounds description is the oldest-known manner of describing land. Literally it means the measurements and boundaries of a tract of land. This method consists of beginning at some point in the boundary of the tract to be described and then reciting the courses (the directions) and the distances from point to point entirely around the tract.

Two things are of prime importance in a metes-and-bounds description. First, the description must begin at some known point that can be readily identified; that is, the point must be substantial and so well established and witnessed that it can be relocated with certainty if the marker (or, as we say, the monument) that identifies the point is destroyed or removed. Second, the description must close; that is, if one follows the courses and distances of the description step by step from corner to corner, one must return to the place of beginning.

Monuments Monuments may be natural or artificial. Natural monuments are those created by nature, such as trees, rivers, and lakes. Artificial monuments are those created by man, such as highways, section corners, quarter corners, and boundaries or a stone or other permanent marker, properly located and witnessed.

Historical Background The metes-and-bounds method of description was followed by the settlers of the thirteen original colonies. An example of a legal description of property in Vermont contained in a deed of October 3, 1784, reads in part as follows: "Begin at the middle of a large white pine stump standing in the west side line of Simon Vender Cook's land and on the south side of the main road that leads to the new city,—and there is also a fence that stands a little to the west of Simon

Vender Cook's barn, which said fence if it was to run cross the said road southerly, would run to the middle of said stump; and running thence north 2 degrees east 19 chains and 50 links to a small white oak tree," and so on. This particular description continues with courses that run to trees and to stakes and piles of stones, and concludes with a course that reads "thence north 9 chains 16 links to the middle of the stump where it first begun."

Such a description, although probably sufficient, lacked permanence both as to the monument that identified the place of beginning and as to the monuments that marked the ends of the various courses. The destruction or removal of such monuments would make a resurvey of the property difficult if not impossible.

This description is typical of the early descriptions used in the colonial states. References to monuments that lacked permanence, surveying of large and irregular tracts without regard to system or uniformity, and the failure of the surveyors to make their survey notes a matter of public record gave rise to frequent disputes and litigation over boundary lines.

RECTANGULAR SURVEY SYSTEM

After the Revolutionary War and the adoption of the federal Constitution the greater part of the land in the United States outside the original thirteen colonies became the property of the federal government, either as a result of cession by the original thirteen states or by trades, purchase, or treaty.

The federal government found itself with vast tracts of undeveloped and uninhabited land that had few natural characteristics suitable for use as monuments in metes-and-bounds descriptions. In any case the metes-and-bounds system was not satisfactory, and it was necessary to devise a new standard system of describing land that would make parcels readily and permanently locatable and easily available for land office sales. Even before the adoption of the Constitution, a committee headed by Thomas Jefferson evolved a plan for dividing the land into a series of rectangles, which the Continental Congress adopted on April 26,

1785. The system adopted was truly American. Designated the "rectangular system" or the "government system" of survey, it is in use today in thirty of the fifty states of the Union. The other twenty states, which include the original colonial states and other states in the New England area carved from them, the Atlantic Coast states except Florida, and the states of Hawaii, West Virginia, Kentucky, Tennessee, and Texas, retained their direction of the surveys of lands within their boundaries upon their admission to the Union and did not adopt the rectangular system. Florida is the only Atlantic Coast state in which the system is used.

Those states and parts of states shown as shaded areas on the map in Figure 1-5, and also the State of Hawaii, are those that are not controlled by a rectangular survey system.

Meridians and Base Lines To understand the rectangular system of survey one must have an understanding of meridians and base lines, which form the framework upon which the system is built. There are thirty-five principal meridians and thirty-two base lines in the United States, as shown in Figure 1-5. A meridian is a line that runs straight north and south. The dictionary defines it as "an imaginary line on the surface of the earth extending from the north pole to the south pole." A base line is a line that runs straight east and west. The government system of survey is based on a series of meridians and base lines run astronomically by surveyors, that is, by the same methods used by navigators to locate ships at sea or planes in the air.

Principal Meridians Under the government system of survey, as under any other surveying system, surveyors first had to find a substantial landmark from which a start could be made. Usually they selected a place that could readily be referred to, such as the mouth of a river. From this point they ran a line due

SOURCE: John S. Hoag, *Fundamentals of Land Measurements,* Chicago Title Insurance Company, Chicago, 1971.

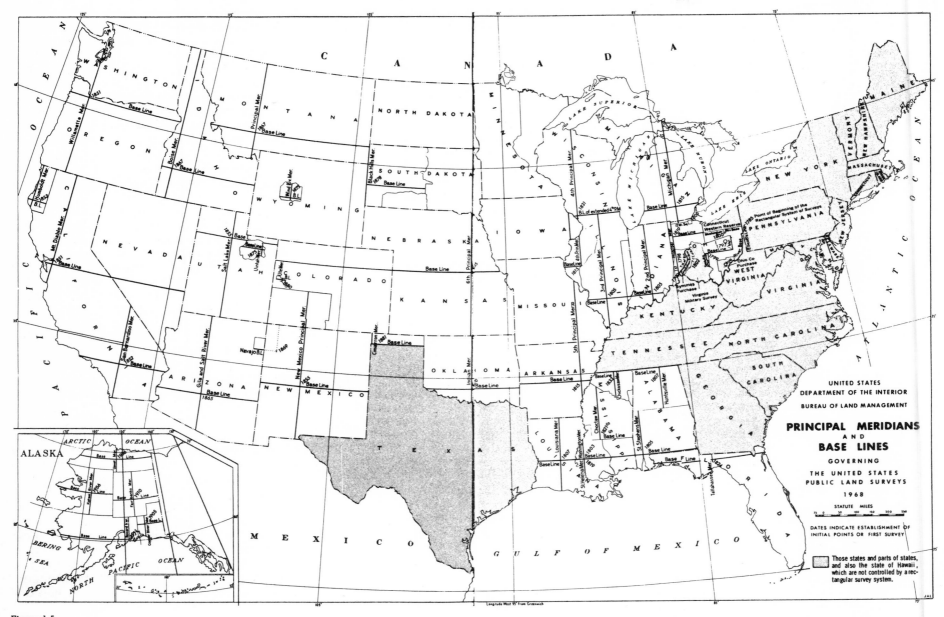

Figure 1-5

SOURCE: John S. Hoag, *Fundamentals of Land Measurements*, Chicago Title Insurance Company, Chicago, 1971.

north through the area to be surveyed. This north-and-south line was designated the principal meridian for that particular state or area. In addition to being marked and monumented, its location was fixed by a longitudinal reading, that is, as being so many degrees, minutes, and seconds west of the Greenwich meridian. As additional territories were opened and surveyed by the government, additional principal meridians were established, one being designated for each area so opened. Some of the principal meridians were numbered (first principal meridian, second principal meridian, and so on); while others were given names such as the Michigan meridian, which covers the survey of that state.

Base Lines Having fixed the line of the principal meridian (the north-and-south line) for a particular territory, the surveyors ascertained a point on the meridian from which they ran a line at right angles to the meridian, that is, a due east-and-west line. This line was designated the base line for the particular area, and its location (its latitude) was fixed astronomically as being so many degrees north of the equatorial line. In certain instances, when a new territory was opened up, the base line of an adjoining territory, previously surveyed, was extended to form the base line for the new territory. In Illinois, for example, the base line established for both the second principal meridian and the third principal meridian intersects the third principal meridian at a point about 10 miles south of Centralia and follows a parallel of latitude of 38 degrees, 28 minutes, and 20 seconds north of the equatorial line. The base line established for the fourth principal meridian follows a parallel of latitude of 40 degrees and 30 seconds north.

Correction Lines and Guide Meridians Having established a principal meridian and a base line, the surveyors proceeded with their survey, using the point of intersection of the principal meridian and the base line as their place of beginning. Their first step was to establish and locate east-and-west lines parallel to the base line at intervals of 24 miles measured along the meridian north and south

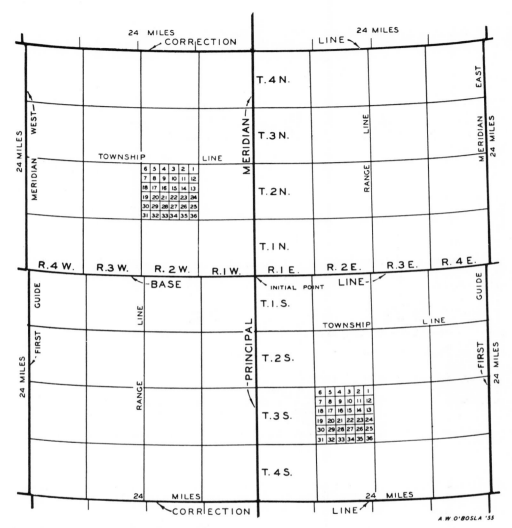

Figure 1-6 Correction lines and guide meridians.

of the base line. These lines were designated "correction lines."

Their next step consisted of establishing lines running due north and south at 24-mile intervals on each side of the principal meridian, commencing at the base line and extending to the first correction line. These lines were called "guide meridians." With the correction lines they divided the territory into squares measuring approximately 24 miles on each side. See Figure 1-6.

SOURCE: John S. Hoag, *Fundamentals of Land Measurements*, Chicago Title Insurance Company, Chicago, 1971.

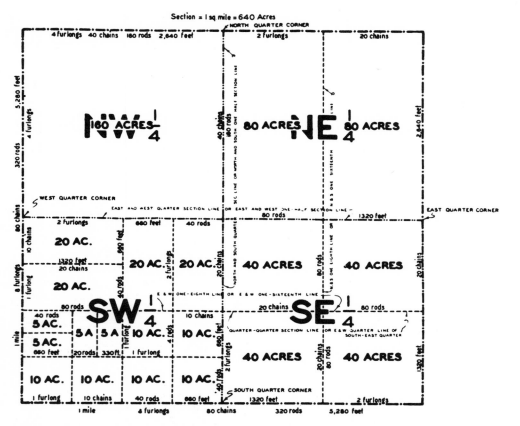

Figure 1-7 Section of land showing acreage and distances. 1 chain = 4 rods, or 66 feet; 1 mile = 320 rods, or 5280 feet; 1 section = 1 square mile, or 640 acres; 1 acre = 160 square rods, or 43,560 square feet.

Township and Range Lines The 24-mile squares were then divided into smaller tracts of land by running east-and-west lines, called "township lines," at 6-mile intervals parallel to the base line. At the same time, north-and-south lines, called "range lines," were run parallel to the principal meridian at regular 6-mile intervals. The result of this cross-hatching of lines was a grid of squares measuring approximately 6 miles on each side.

To locate a particular square in that grid, the government assigned to each square two numbers, a township number and a range number. To the first row of squares immediately adjacent to and parallel with the base line it

assigned "township 1"; to the second row it assigned "township 2," and so on. Thus each square in the first row north of the base line was called "township 1 north" of the base line; each in the second row, "township 2 north" of the base line, and so on. Likewise each square in the first row south of the base line was called "township 1 south"; each in the second row, "township 2 south," and so on.

In the same manner, the government assigned a range number to each row of squares in the rows running parallel to the principal meridian, starting the numbering with the principal meridian. Thus the squares in the first row east of the principal meridian were

numbered "range 1 east" of the particular principal meridian; those in the second row east, as "range 2 east," and so on. On the west side of the principal meridian those in the first row were numbered "range 1 west"; those in the second row, "range 2 west," and so on.

A glance at Figure 1-6, which shows a principal meridian, base line, correction lines, guide meridians, and township and range lines, makes it easy to understand the formation and numbering of townships and ranges, and the importance of these numbers in locating a particular tract of land.

Sections The act of 1785 creating the rectangular system of survey provided only for townships of 6 miles square; and in the early surveys only the outside boundaries of the townships were surveyed, although monuments were placed at every mile on the township lines. It soon became apparent that a 6-mile square was too large an area in which to describe and locate a given tract of land. Congress on May 18, 1796, passed an act directing that the townships theretofore surveyed be subdivided into thirty-six sections, each to be 1 mile square and containing "as nearly as may be" 640 acres; that each section corner be monumented; and that the sections be numbered consecutively from 1 to 36, beginning with 1 in the northeast corner of the township, proceeding west and east alternately through the township, and ending in the southeast corner with 36. This manner of numbering sections in a township has continued to the present time. See Figure 1-7.

By furnishing the section number, the township number north or south of the base line, and the range number east or west of the controlling principal meridian, a given tract of land can be located within the square mile of which it forms a part.

Purpose of Correction Lines You will recall that correction lines are east and west

SOURCE: John S. Hoag, *Fundamentals of Land Measurements*, Chicago Title Insurance Company, Chicago, 1971.

lines parallel to the base line and are established at intervals of 24 miles measured on the principal meridian. Each such correction line serves as a new base line for the townships that lie between it and the next correction line. It is necessary that such correction lines be established and used as new base lines if the townships and sections are to have substantially the size intended.

Because of the curvature of the earth it is necessary to compensate for the convergence of the meridians. If all the meridians were extended northward, they would meet at the north pole. The fact that they are constantly approaching each other is not observable from a point on the earth's surface without the aid of surveying instruments, but it is very real. An accurate survey of a township would show its north line to be about 50 feet shorter than its south line. Thus, in the case of the fourth township north of the base line, the difference is 4 times as great. The north line of the fourth township is 200.64 feet shorter than the south line of township 1.

To compensate for this convergence of the meridians, the south line of township 5 is measured the full distance of 6 miles on the correction line. The same practice is followed for every fourth township.

Subdivision of Sections   As time went on, Congress provided for the subdivision of sections into smaller units. An act passed in 1800 directed the subdivision of sections into east and west halves of 320 acres each "as nearly as may be" by running north-and-south lines through the center of the sections. Five years later, on February 11, 1805, Congress provided for the further division of sections into quarter sections by running east and west lines through the center of the sections and monumenting all quarter-section corners. This act further provided that all corners marked in the public surveys be established as the proper corners of the sections or quarter sections they were intended to designate and that "the boundary lines actually run and marked . . . shall be established as the proper boundary lines of the sections or subdivisions for which

they were intended, and the length of such lines as returned by . . . the surveyor-general . . . shall be held and considered as the true length thereof." In other words, the original corners established by the government surveyors must stand as the true corners whether or not they were in the place shown by the field notes.

In 1820, Congress directed the further division of sections into half-quarter sections by the running of north-and-south lines through all quarter sections. Finally, on April 5, 1832, it directed the subdivision of all public lands into quarter-quarter sections by running east-and-west lines through the quarter sections. The quarter-quarter section of 40 acres is the smallest statutory division of regular sections.

Figure 1-7 shows a section divided into the fractional parts most frequently found in legal descriptions. The measurements of each typical fraction are noted. A little time spent in study of the typical subdivisions of a section and their dimensions will help one to understand more quickly plats of survey and descriptions of parts of sections.

Legal Descriptions   Legal descriptions of land that follow the regular subdivisions of a regular section are easily understood and present few difficult problems. Care and accuracy are required so that the terms used actually refer to the land intended. The section, township, and range must be given to complete the description of each fraction; for example, the southwest quarter of the northeast quarter of **Section 6, Township 39, North, Range 13** east of the third principal meridian in Cook County, Illinois.

When one works with a description such as the north half of the northwest quarter of the southwest quarter of the southwest quarter of Section 6, it is somewhat easier to locate a tract of land if the description is read in reverse; that is, Section 6, southwest quarter, southwest quarter, northwest quarter, north half. Such a method must be used to avoid hopeless confusion.

A mental picture of a section or a chart such as Figure 1-7, together with familiarity with the

usual measurements and terms employed, plus care and thorough checking and rechecking, will produce descriptions that avoid trouble and loss of time.

Summary   The foregoing discussion has outlined the government survey. As a result of the survey, a large unmarked area has been reduced to a series of small squares; basic lines of survey have been established by astronomical measurements; markers or permanent monuments have been located on the ground by the surveyors to establish quarter-quarter section corners; and careful survey notes of the description and location of all markers have been made and filed with the government. It is readily seen that any tract of land in the government survey can be described with certainty and identified to the exclusion of all other tracts by the proper numbering or naming of the principal meridian, the fixing of the base line, and the proper numbering of the section, township, and range.

TYPICAL METES-AND-BOUNDS DESCRIPTION

A typical description will read as follows:

> Commencing at the northwest corner of Section 12, thence south along the section line 21 feet; thence east 10 feet for a place of beginning; thence continuing east 34 feet; thence south 62 degrees, 30 minutes, east 32 feet; thence southeasterly along a line forming an angle of 8 degrees, 4 minutes, to the right with a prolongation of the last-described course 29 feet; thence south 13 degrees, 0 minutes, to the left with a prolongation of the last-described line a distance of 49 feet; thence east to a line parallel with the west line of said section and 180 feet distant therefrom; thence south on the last-described line a distance of 65 feet; thence due west a distance of 82 feet to a point; thence north 1 degree west 39 feet; thence north 58 degrees west a distance of 49 feet; thence northwesterly along a line forming an angle of 163 degrees as measured from right to left with the last-described line a distance of 49 feet; thence north to the place of beginning.

SOURCE: John S. Hoag, *Fundamentals of Land Measurements*, Chicago Title Insurance Company, Chicago, 1971.

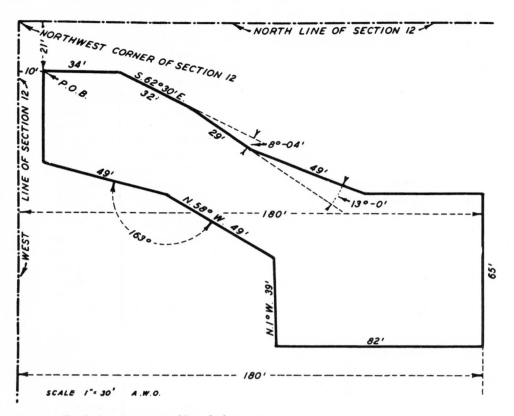

Figure 1-8 Sketch plat of a metes-and-bounds description.

Although today distances in the United States are generally expressed in feet and inches, land measure in the government survey is stated in chains, rods, and links, and these words should be understood.

A chain is 4 rods (66 feet) in length, divided into 100 links each 7.92 inches long. For years chain measurements were made with an actual metallic chain of 100 rings, or links, constructed in the early days from iron and later from heavy steel wire. Because the links tend to wear and stretch and the chain tends to twist and knot, accurate surveying often was diffi-

cult. Since about 1900 the surveyors have used steel ribbon tapes varying in length from 2 to 8 chains (from 166 to 528 feet).

A rod is 16½ feet. As the word implies, it was a pole of that length.

A link is the distance spanned by one loop of the chain formerly used by surveyors; it is 7.92 inches long.

SOURCE: John S. Hoag, *Fundamentals of Land Measurements*, Chicago Title Insurance Company, Chicago, 1971.

1.3 Soil Classification and Surveys

Soils are classified and named, just as plants and animals are. Plants are identified by such characteristics as the structure of the flower and the form of the leaf. Soils are identified by such characteristics as the kinds and numbers of horizons, or layers, that have developed in them. The texture (the relative amounts of stones, gravel, sand, silt, and clay), the kinds of minerals present and their amounts, and the presence of salts and alkali help distinguish the horizons.

Most of the characteristics that identify soils can be determined in the field. A few can be determined only in the laboratory, but even without laboratory tests you often can get an accurate knowledge of soil characteristics from standard works on soils and geology. For example, you can estimate the amount of sand in a soil from its feel when you rub it between your fingers, but for an accurate knowledge you must depend on laboratory analyses.

The type is the smallest unit in the natural classification of soils. One or a few types constitute a soil series. These are the common classification units seen on soil maps and survey reports.

A soil series is a group of soils having horizons that are essentially the same in the properties used to identify soils, with the exception of the texture of the surface soil and the kinds of layers that lie below what is considered the true soil. The names of soil series are taken from the towns or localities near the place where the soils were first defined.

The soil type, a subdivision of the soil series, is based on the texture of the surface soil. Stones, gravel, sand, silt, and clay have been defined as having the following diameters: gravel, from 3 inches down to 0.08 inch; sand, between 0.08 and 0.0002 inch; silt, between 0.0002 and 0.00008 inch; and clay, less than 0.00008 inch.

The full name of the soil type includes the name of the soil series and the textural class of the surface soil equivalent to the plow layer, that is, the upper 6 or 7 inches. Thus, if the surface of an area of the Fayette series is a silt loam, the name of the soil type is "Fayette silt-loam."

The soil phase is not a part of the natural classification. It can be a subdivision of the soil type, soil series, or one of the higher units in the classification. Phases shown on soil maps commonly are subdivisions of soil types and are based on characteristics of the soil significant to its use for agriculture. Phases shown on large-scale soil maps generally have reflected differences in slope, degree of erosion, and stoniness, but other bases for defining phases include drainage and flood protection, climate, and the presence of contrasting layers below the soil.

The legends that accompany soil maps generally include such names for the units on the map as "Sharpsburg silty clay loam, eroded rolling phase," or "Fayette silt loam, 8–14 percent slopes, eroded." These names identify the soil series, the soil type, and the phase. They represent names of the most specific kinds of soil, comparable to the name of a practical subdivision of a variety of a plant, such as "old Jonathan apple trees."

The word "Fayette" in the second soil name mentioned above designates the soil series. This word, plus the words "silt loam," identifies the soil type, and the phase is identified by the words "8–14 percent slopes, eroded." In this name, the word "phase" is not used but is understood.

Higher units in the classification system include families, great soil groups, suborders, and orders. They are seldom used on any but small-scale soil maps.

Soil series, types, and phases do not occur at random in the landscape. They have an orderly pattern related to the landform; the parent material from which the soil was formed; and the influence of the plants that grew on the soils, the animals that lived on them, and the way men have used them. On a given farm, the different kinds of soil commonly have a repeating pattern, which is associated with the slope.

The relationships between soils and landscapes vary in details in different parts of the country, but such relationships generally exist. Persons who are familiar with soils can visualize a landscape from a soil map; or if they see the landscape, they can predict where the boundaries are.

A soil survey includes determining which properties of soils are important, organizing the knowledge about the relations of soil properties and soil use, classifying soils into defined and described units, locating and plotting the boundaries of the units on maps, and preparing and publishing the maps and reports.

A soil survey report consists of a map that shows the distribution of soils in the area, descriptions of the soils, some suggestions as to their use and management, and general information about the area. Reports usually are prepared on the soils of one county, although a single report may cover several small counties or only parts of counties.

Soil surveys are made cooperatively by the Soil Conservation Service of the Department of Agriculture, agricultural experiment stations, and other state and federal agencies. Plans for the work in any area are developed jointly, and the reports are reviewed jointly before publication.

Soil maps have many uses, but generally they are made for one main purpose: to identify the soil as a basis for applying the results of research and experience to individual fields or parts of fields. Results from an experiment on a given soil can be applied directly to other areas of the same kind of soil with confidence. Two areas of the same kind of soil are no more identical than two oak trees, but they are so similar that, with comparable past management, they should respond to the same practices in a similar manner.

But many thousands of kinds of soil exist in the United States. Research can be conducted

SOURCE: Guy D. Smith and Andrew R. Aandahl, "Soil Classification and Survey," in *Soil: The Yearbook of Agriculture*, U.S. Department of Agriculture, 1957.

on only a few of them. The application of the research results must usually be based on the relationships of the properties of the soil on which the experiment was conducted to the properties of the soils shown on the maps. This can best be done by the soil classification system.

Significant properties that can be known from soil maps include physical properties, such as the amount of moisture that the soil will hold for plants, the rate at which air and water move through the soil, and the kinds and amounts of clays, all of which are important in drainage, irrigation, erosion control, maintenance of good tilth, and the choice of crops.

The soil map shows the distribution of specific kinds of soil and identifies them through the map legend. The legend is a list of the symbols used to identify the kinds of soil on the map. The commonest soil units shown on maps are the phases of soil types, but other kinds of units may also be shown.

Soil bodies, areas occupied by individual soil units, generally range from a few acres to a few hundred acres. Often within one soil body are small areas of other soils—series, types, or phases. If the included soils are similar, they are generally not identified unless they represent more than 10 to 15 percent of the soil body in which they are included. If the properties of the included soils differ markedly from those of the rest of the soil body, they usually are indicated by special symbols.

Occasionally the individual parts of a unit are so small and so mixed with other units that they cannot be shown. Then the legend indicates the area occupied by the intricate mixture as a soil complex if all the included units are present in nearly every area.

A complex may consist of two or more phases of a soil type, but commonly it consists of two or more series. The names of complexes may carry a hyphen between the names of two soil types or phases, such as "Barnes-Buse loams." If several series or types are included in the complex, the names of one or two of the most important series or types will be followed by the word "complex," for example, the "Clarinda-Lagonda complex."

Two other kinds of units are common on soil maps: the undifferentiated group and the miscellaneous land type.

Two or more recognized kinds of soil that are not regularly associated in the landscape may be combined if their separation is costly and the differences between them are not significant for the objective of the soil survey. This kind of undifferentiated group is shown in the legend with the names of the individual units connected by a conjunction, for example, "Downs or Fayette silt loams."

Miscellaneous land types are used for land that has little or no natural soil. The map units then are given descriptive names, such as "steep, stony land," "gullied land," and "mixed alluvial land."

The relationships between the units that appear on the maps and legends and the use and management alternatives are explained in the text that accompanies the soil survey report.

The Department of Agriculture began making soil surveys about 1900. The purposes of the work were the same then as now, but there was no body of knowledge of how soils are formed or how nutrients become available to plants. The early definitions of the soil series therefore failed to take into account some important properties and overemphasized some of the more obvious but less important ones, such as color.

As scientists learned more about the relationships between soils and plants, ideas about the importance of the properties originally used to distinguish between soil series and types changed. The first soil series was split into two or more series. These in turn were often subdivided. Consequently many of the names shown on the older maps have been changed. Changes will continue to be made as long as we continue to learn new things about soil-plant relationships.

Soil maps are made by experienced soil scientists who are graduates of state agricultural colleges or other colleges or universities that offer courses in soil science.

Ordinarily soil scientists use aerial photographs as a base for plotting soil boundaries. The scientists go over the land and dig with a spade or auger as often as necessary to determine and evaluate the important characteristics of the entire profile. They indentify the kind of soil, locate its boundaries in the field, plot the boundaries, and place the identification symbol of each soil mapping unit on the map.

In making detailed maps, they follow or see the boundaries between the kinds of soil through their entire length. In making reconnaissance surveys, they may not see the boundaries over their entire length; they merely identify one when they cross it and draw the boundary through to their next traverse, or crossing, on the basis of information obtained from aerial photographs.

Soil scientists make simple chemical tests in the field to determine the degree of acidity and the presence of lime, salts, and a few toxic compounds. They measure slopes with a hand level. Usually they take samples of a few representative soils during the survey and send them to the laboratory for detailed study. All stages of the work, from mapping to the contents of the report, are reviewed by the supervisors and representatives of the cooperating agencies.

Soil maps often are used before they are published. All cooperators of the soil conservation districts are furnished copies of the soil maps of their particular holdings.

County assessors and other users sometimes buy copies of such maps to use in their work before the publication of the completed survey. The local soils handbooks, available for reference at the Soil Conservation Service offices, give information needed to use and interpret the maps. Photographic copies of unpublished maps may be purchased through the Soil Conservation Service offices. These

SOURCE: Guy D. Smith and Andrew R. Aandahl, "Soil Classification and Surveys," in *Soil: The Yearbook of Agriculture*, U.S. Department of Agriculture, 1957.

offices are usually located in county seats.

Soil maps are published by the Soil Conservation Service for all states except Illinois. In Illinois the University of Illinois Agricultural Experiment Station publishes them.

Copies of available published maps and reports may be obtained through a state extension service or the Soil Conservation Service offices. Files of unpublished maps are maintained in the Soil Conservation Service offices and may be examined there.

Interpretations of soil maps are physical and economic analyses of the alternative opportunities available to the users of the land. They indicate the capabilities of the soils for agricultural use, adapted crops, estimated yields of crops under defined systems of management, the presence of specific soil management problems, opportunities and limitations for various management practices, and problems in nonagricultural use.

The main bases for interpretations are yield estimates, related to specific combinations of practices for soils in their climatic setting. Yield estimates for a soil are predictions of the average production of specific crops that a group of farmers can expect during the next 10 or 15 years if they follow the defined system of soil management. These estimates apply less closely to individual farmers, whose skills are variable, than to averages of groups. Sources of information are the results of research, the experiences of farmers, ranchers, and others who grow plants, and observations of plants growing on different kinds of soils.

The definitions and descriptions of the kinds of soil shown on maps provide information on their characteristics. These are used to infer the qualities of soils such as productivity and erosion hazard. Predictions can be made about a soil whose behavior is unknown by comparing its characteristics with those of soils about which such basic information is known. Basic principles of soil management are another tool to help extend predictions of soil behavior and responses to all kinds of soils.

THE USE OF SOIL MAPS

Soils may be grouped into land capability classes, subclasses, and units to help us use them properly. Of the eight classes, which normally do not all exist on any single farm or ranch, Classes I through IV are suited to cultivated crops, pasture or range, woodland, and wildlife. Classes V through VIII are suited to pasture or woodland and wildlife and are not generally recommended for cultivation. However, some kinds of soil in Classes V, VI, and VII may be cultivated safely with special management. Because several kinds of soil often occur in the same capability class on the same farm or ranch, the classes are divided into subclasses.

Four kinds of problems are recognized in the subclasses and are indicated by symbols: e—erosion and runoff; w—wetness and drainage; s—root zone and tillage limitations, such as shallowness, stoniness, droughtiness, and salinity; and c—climatic limitations. The subclass therefore provides more specific information about the kind and the degree of limitation for the use of soil than does the capability class. See Figure 1-9.

The land capability unit is the most detailed and specific soil grouping of the capability classification. Soils that can be used in the same way and will give about the same crop yield are grouped into a capability unit. This unit is used most commonly for planning in specific areas, for it groups soils which are nearly alike in the features that affect plant growth and in their response to management.

Other interpretative soil groupings also are used in conservation planning. In extensive range areas, the mapping units are grouped into range sites, which give information about

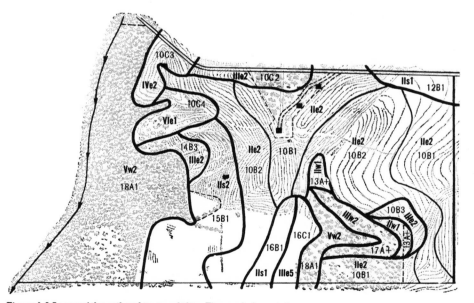

Figure 1-9 A map of the soil and its capability. The symbols pertain to various aspects of soil and topography. For example, 10B1 refers to the kind of soil, the number 10 to the soil type, the letter B to steepness of slope, and the number 1 to degree of erosion. The symbol IIe2 refers to the land capability unit, II designates the land capability class, e indicates the subclass, and 2 indicates the unit. Heavy lines indicate the boundaries of a capability unit.

SOURCE: A. M. Hedge and A. A. Klingebiel, "The Use of Soil Maps," in *Soil: The Yearbook of Agriculture,* U.S. Department of Agriculture, 1957.

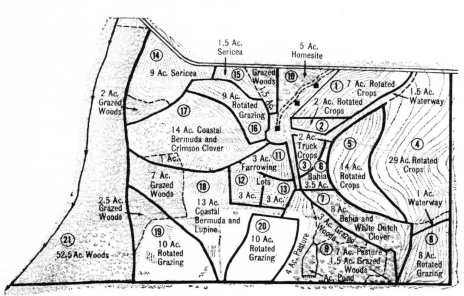

Figure 1-10 A conservation plan map. The decisions made by the farmer concerning the use and management of the land, together with the field unit arrangement, are recorded on this map. These decisions were based on the soil and capability map shown in Figure 1-9. The needs of the farmer relative to his farm enterprise also were considered.

the kind and amount of vegetation that the area will produce when it is in its best condition. This grouping, together with range conditions, provides the basis needed for sound range planning.

On farms or ranches that are to be used for woodland, range or pasture, and cropland, the soil map is interpreted to show the suitability of the land for these uses. For areas that are to be planned as woodland, the mapping units are grouped into woodland sites and interpreted in terms of the kinds and amounts of wood crops that can be produced. See Figure 1-10.

SOURCE: A. M. Hedge and A. A. Klingebiel, "The Use of Soil Maps," in *Soil: The Yearbook of Agriculture,* U.S. Department of Agriculture, 1957.

1.4 Geological Investigations

Geological investigations are made to determine the geologic conditions that affect the design, safety, effectiveness, and cost of a proposed project. Insufficient geological investigations and faulty interpretations of results have been responsible for costly contruction changes and could be the cause of the failure of a structure. The investigations are performed to determine the general geologic setting of the project, the geologic conditions that influence the selection of a site, the characteristics of the foundation soils and rocks, all other geologic conditions that influence design and construction, and sources of construction materials. The method employed for the investigations depends on the type of structures contemplated and on the character and degree of accuracy of the information required. The extent of the investigations depends on the magnitude of the project and the simplicity or complexity of local geology.

Research This phase of investigation includes a careful search of published and unpublished papers, reports, maps, and records and consultation with federal, state, and local geological authorities for information pertinent to the project or problem. Thorough utilization of this source of information during preliminary investigations of projects cannot be overemphasized. Publications of federal and state agencies, such as those of the various geological surveys, in many instances contain information pertinent to the geology of the area and of the project site as well as data on mineral resources. Annual bulletins of the U.S. Department of Commerce titled *United States Earthquakes* are good reference material on earthquakes. Many state geological surveys and university libraries have well-drilling data, groundwater data, logs, and information on rock outcrops that are available for examination and study. Some state highway departments have geological profiles for cuts along existing or proposed highways and possess records of borings and construction data that can be studied. Copies of such unpublished

data are obtainable in some instances. Exploration and construction data from work performed by private companies should be included in the research.

Maps Strictly speaking, the use of published maps in geologic investigations should fall under the category of research. It is discussed here separately for emphasis.

There are commonly available various types of published maps from which geologic information pertinent to a project can be obtained prior to exploration work. These include topographic maps, geologic maps, mineral resources maps, and soil maps. Such maps can be quite helpful for obtaining preliminary information and for planning subsequent reconnaissance and exploration.

Topographic Maps Most topographic maps published in the United States are prepared by the U.S. Geological Survey. These maps are available in 7½-minute quadrangle size plotted to scales of 1:24,000 and 1:31,680 and in 15-minute quadrangle size plotted to a scale of 1:62,500.

Topographic maps based on the United States military grid are published by the various agencies of the defense establishment, particularly the Army Map Service. Maps prepared by the Army Map Service are in 7½-minute quadrangle size plotted to a scale of 1:25,000, in 15-minute quadrangle size plotted to a scale of 1:50,000, and in 30-minute quadrangle size plotted to a scale of 1:125,000. Maps covering larger areas are prepared on scales of 1:250,000 and 1:500,000.

Certain information on engineering geology can be inferred from topographic maps by a proper interpretation of the landforms and drainage patterns shown on them. Topography tends to reflect the geologic structure and composition of the underlying rocks. Geologic features, however, are not equally apparent on all topographic maps, and considerable skill is required to arrive at geologic interpretations from maps of some areas. Information of engineering significance that may be obtained or inferred from topographic maps may be classified as follows:

Physiography
  Significant topographic features
  Physiographic history pertinent to engineering
General rock types
  Crystalline or noncrystalline
  Massive or thin-bedded
  Alternating hard and soft rocks
  Glacial terrain
Rock structure
  Dip and strike
  Folding
  Faults
  Joints
  Slide areas
Soil Types
  Glacial
  Alluvial
  Residual

Geologic Maps Geologic maps are published by the U.S. Geological Survey, by various state geological surveys or equivalent state agencies, and by some of the geological societies. A partial list of readily available sources follows:

1. U.S. Geological Survey
     Geologic map of the United States; scale, 1:2,500,000
     Folios of the *Geologic Atlas of the United States* (no longer published; many available in libraries)
     Geologic quadrangle maps, in publication since 1945; scale, 1:31,680, 1:62,500, and 1:125,000 (maps titled "Geology," "Bedrock Geology," "Surficial Geology," "Economic Geology," and "Engineering Geology" published in this series)
     Bulletins and professional papers
2. State geological surveys or equivalent state agencies
     Geologic maps of most states; scale, 1:500,000
     Bulletins, county reports, and monographs
3. Geological Society of America
     Glacial map of North America
     Glacial map of the United States east of the Rocky Mountains
     Map of Pleistocene eolian deposits of the United States, Alaska, and parts of Canada

SOURCE: *Geological Investigations,* U.S. Army Corps of Engineers, 1960.

The published geologic maps show the general geology of an area and provide information useful in preliminary planning of investigations.

Mineral Resources Maps   Mineral resources maps are published by the U.S. Geological Survey and by state geological surveys or equivalent agencies. These may be helpful and should be consulted in determining the effect of a proposed project on the mineral resources of the area.

Aerial Photographs   Aerial photographs may be either vertical or oblique views. Both are used effectively in geologic studies. Geologic interpretations for engineering are based on conventional principles of photointerpretation of landforms, drainage patterns, and other surface features. The procedure is similar to making geologic interpretations from topographic maps, with the exception that many more details can be seen on photographs than are shown on corresponding maps. Definite criteria for complete interpretation from aerial photographs, however, are difficult to set forth. Much depends upon the experience and ability of persons making the interpretation and upon their general geologic knowledge of the area. Analytical factors used in making systematic studies of aerial photographs include (1) topography, (2) drainage and erosion, (3) color tones, and (4) vegetative cover.

Aerial photographs are valuable tools for geologists, particularly in connection with field reconnaissance and preliminary studies. They present an overall view of the land surface and of the features of bedrock geology that otherwise may be seen only in piecemeal fashion or escape notice entirely. They also cover areas that have difficult or limited access by ground. Study of the pictures in many instances reveals features to which special attention should be given during reconnaissance or in later studies.

Field Reconnaissance   A geological field reconnaissance is a preliminary investigation involving one or more trips to the project site or area for the purpose of gathering such information as is obtainable without subsurface exploration or detailed study. Before plans for detailed surface and subsurface investigations are prepared, the geologist responsible for planning such investigations should have some advance knowledge of the geology, physiography, and cultural features of the area involved. Some of this knowledge will be obtained from a study of published reports and maps, but field reconnaissance is required to orient the published information with actual field conditions. During field reconnaissance, the geologist will study and record all topographic and geologic features that may have a significant bearing on the suitability of the site for an engineering project. It is essential to obtain at this time information on landforms, soil types and thickness, bedrock types and structure, groundwater conditions, construction materials, and mineral resources that can influence the type of structure or affect the cost of the project.

Geophysical Methods   Geophysical exploration consists of making certain physical measurements by the use of special instruments to obtain generalized subsurface geologic information. Geophysical observations in themselves are not geologic facts but are statistical and orderly measurements. The required geologic information is obtained indirectly through analysis or interpretation of these measurements and is not subject to direct visual verification. Geophysical explorations lack the degree of accuracy provided by core drilling; therefore, boreholes or other direct geological explorations are needed for reference and control of measurements when geophysical methods are used. Geophysical explorations are not a substitute for core drilling, test pits, or other direct methods of subsurface exploration. They are appropriate, however, for a rapid though roughly approximate determination of certain geologic conditions, such as the depth to bedrock, when supplemented by core boring or other reliable exploration methods. The cost of geophysical explorations is generally low compared with the cost of core borings or test pits, and considerable savings may often be effected by a judicious use of this exploration method in conjunction with other more reliable methods.

The six major geophysical exploration methods are the seismic, electrical resistivity, sonic, electrical logging, magnetic, and gravity methods.

Subsurface Borings   Borings of various kinds are the commonest methods of subsurface exploration. The boring methods most frequently used are discussed below.

Probings   Probings ordinarily consist of driving a steel rod into the ground and noting variations in penetration resistance. Probe rods may be of any size. They are generally round or hexagonal in cross section and about $\frac{5}{8}$ to $\frac{7}{8}$ inch in diameter. Most are pointed or have a driving point attached. Penetration may be accomplished by driving the rod by manual or mechanical hammers.

Probings generally are intended to determine the presence or absence of bedrock within prescribed depths. The resistance to penetration can be interpreted roughly in terms of the character of the material penetrated. Probings, however, are not reliable. Penetration refusal, which is often erroneously interpreted as bedrock, may actually prove to be a cobble, a boulder of a cemented soil condition. Probings should never be used for other than preliminary exploration purposes, and interpretations from them should always be checked by other boring methods.

Wash Borings   Wash boring consists essentially of forcing a wash pipe or a hollow drill rod through the overburden by chopping and jetting while water is pumped through the boring device. Usually, a chopping bit is attached to the bottom end of the wash pipe. The displaced soil is washed to the surface, where it may be caught in a bucket or other container for sampling. A casing is required in soft or loose soils, but it may not be needed in such materials as stiff clay or glacial till.

SOURCE: *Geological Investigations*, U.S. Army Corps of Engineers, 1960.

Wash borings are used principally to advance holes through overburden materials between zones of drive sampling or to obtain a bore through overburden to rock preparatory to rock drilling. They are not reliable for determining subsurface conditions, and the information obtained from them is nearly always misleading. Definite identification of soils cannot be made. Fine materials in the cuttings are lost in the wash water, and coarser materials, such as gravel or cobbles, either may not be forced up out of the hole or may be broken into fine chips that would not show in the cuttings. Boulders and cobbles may easily be taken for bedrock when arbitrary depths are selected for these borings.

Core Drilling   Core drilling involves the cutting and recovery of cylindrical cores of subsurface materials. The term includes certain methods of soil drilling and sampling but is most commonly applied to the drilling and recovery of continuous cores from bedrock.

Core drilling in bedrock is accomplished with rotary drills. These are obtainable in various sizes and models to meet different requirements related to drilling location, hole size and depth, and purpose of the borings. Drills may be post-, carriage-, skid-, or truck-mounted and may be powered by air or electric motors or by diesel or gasoline engines. For drills employed in cutting small-diameter cores, maintenance of pressure on and advancement of the bit are accomplished by a screw-feed or hydraulic-feed device in the swivel head of the drill.

Drilling is performed by rotating a tubular bit in a hole by means of a series of drill rods driven by a machine at the top of the hole. The cutting edge of the bit may be diamond- or alloy-set, or the bit may be of the calyx type or have alloy steel teeth. All coring bits are fastened to the bottom of a core barrel. The bit cuts an annular hole around a central core, and the barrel passes down over the core as the bit advances. The operation continues until the core barrel is filled, at which time the barrel with the core is recovered from the hole and the core samples are arranged in boxes for

logging. The drilling tools then are returned to the hole, and the drilling operation is resumed. Water or other drilling fluid is circulated through the drill rods and core barrel to the bit and thence back up the hole for the purpose of removing rock cuttings and keeping the bit cool.

Exploratory core borings are indispensable for determining the character of the overburden materials, the depth to bedrock, and the character and condition of bedrock materials. They should be employed on all foundation studies subsequent to preliminary examination, since the information obtained from them is more accurate than that obtained from most other exploration methods except excavation of test pits, shafts, trenches, and tunnels. Core drilling is the only practical method of sampling rock materials short of these more costly methods. Good core recovery, however, may be difficult in soft or weathered rock, in rock containing closely spaced fractures and cleavage planes, and in rock of widely varying hardness. As a general rule, the larger the diameter of the core, the higher the percentage of core recovered and the more accurate the geological observations on the character and condition of the rock.

Calyx Core Drilling   Calyx drilling differs from other coring methods chiefly in the type of bit used and in the means of obtaning the cutting action from the bit. The bit consists of a core barrel of soft steel with one or more slots cut in the bottom rim or of a short slotted tube of mild steel attached to the bottom edge of a single-tube core barrel. Steel shot, which is fed to the bottom edge of the barrel by drill water, is the cutting medium. Under the weight of the rotating barrel, the shot cuts an annular groove around the core without disturbing the wall of the borehole. Rock cuttings are removed by circulating water and are caught in a sludge barrel on top of the core barrel. Cores as small as 2 inches in diameter may be obtained by the calyx drilling method, but the greatest use of this method is for drilling large-diameter holes into which a person can be lowered to examine the rock in place. Such calyx holes usually are

36 inches or larger in diameter and afford opportunities to observe the actual condition of the rock through which the holes were drilled. Calyx drilling can be performed only in a vertically downward direction, because an even distribution of the shot at the base of the slotted bit cannot be achieved in inclined borings. Drilling progress is slow, and the drilling of large-diameter holes is expensive. Where extremely open or fractured water-bearing rocks are to be explored, rock voids must be consolidated by colored grout if inspection of the calyx hole is to be successful.

Borehole Photography   Borehole photography consists of photographing the interior surfaces of boreholes and studying the photographs to obtain information on the materials through which the borings have penetrated. The photographs are taken with special borehole cameras.

Borehole photography provides more extensive information from small-diameter borings than is obtainable from the cores alone and is much less expensive than the excavation of shafts and tunnels or the drilling of large-diameter calyx holes. The borehole photographs show existing conditions when no core is recovered or when the core is too badly broken to give reliable information. They show the conditions of weathering and the details and orientation of rock structures such as fractures, joints, and bedding planes. They can also show the effectiveness of pressure grouting of foundation openings.

Churn Drilling   This exploration method consists of drilling holes with cable tool drills or well drills. The hole is drilled by the impact and cutting action of a heavy chisel-edged drilling tool that is alternately raised and dropped by means of a cable. The up-and-down motion of the cable and the attached drilling bits may be accomplished by a tripod-winch-cathead arrangement or by a crank or spudding arm

SOURCE: *Geological Investigations*, U.S. Army Corps of Engineers, 1960.

that is operated by motorized units and used in conjuction with a hoisting mast. Such a drilling rig as the latter may be skid- or truck-mounted. The hole is kept partially filled with water during chopping, and the cuttings are cleaned from the hole periodically with a bailer at intervals of 5 or 10 feet. Casing is required when drilling through unstable materials.

Churn drilling is used principally in advancing holes through overburden to rock. The cuttings from churn drilling represent only the average disturbed composition of the materials penetrated, and an accurate determination of the undisturbed character of the subsurface materials is impossible. If the the character of the subsurface materials must be ascertained, undisturbed samples are taken with a soil-sampling head. Churn drilling has been used effectively for groundwater studies in regions where wells are needed to observe water table elevations and fluctuations in limestone formations.

Wagon and Jackhammer Drilling Wagon drills and jackhammers are percussion-type drills operated by compressed air or by a self-contained gasoline engine. As the name implies, the wagon drill is mounted on a wheeled carriage. The jackhammer drill is hand-held. Explorations with these drills consist of drilling holes into rock and observing the rate of and the resistance to penetration of the drill as well as the color of the cuttings from the hole. These observations are then interpreted in terms of bedrock condition.

Explorations with wagon drills or jackhammers may be useful as supplementary investigations for searching out shallow cavities, solution channels, and soft zones after the overburden has been stripped from foundation rock. Because such borings are extremely unreliable for determining either the composition or the engineering properties of subsurface materials, they cannot be substituted for core borings.

Test Pits, Trenches, and Tunnels

Test Pits Test pits are openings excavated vertically from the ground surface to expose the subsurface materials for examination in place. They may also be excavated to take undisturbed samples of soil materials. Their greatest use is in connection with soil exploration and testing. They may also be employed to study the character of the overburden bedrock contact and the position, character, and condition of the bedrock surface.

Trenches Trenches are functionally somewhat similar to test pits except that they are usually limited to relatively shallow depths below the ground surface. They are particularly useful for the continuous exploration, examination, and sampling of soil foundations of earth embankments and for examining and correlating bedrock surface conditions that elude accurate identification by conventional drilling and sampling methods. Combined with test pits, exploratory trenches are the only reliable method of determining the occurrence, composition, distribution, structure, and stability of unsatisfactory materials in deep alluvial and residual soil foundations for high dams.

Tunnels Tunnels and drifts are nearly horizontal underground passages or openings. They are excavated by common mining methods, which vary with the type of material being tunneled. Their principal function as an exploratory device is to permit detailed examination of the composition and geometry of such rock structures as joints, fractures, faults, shear zones, and solution channels when these conditions affect foundation excavation and treatment. Excavation of exploration tunnels generally is slow and expensive and should be used only when other methods are inadequate for supplying information. Tunnels are especially useful in the proper exploration of foundation conditions in the abutments of high concrete gravity and arch dams. Logs of exploration tunnels should be made concurrently with their excavation whenever possible. Sampling, if required, also should be done during the excavation.

Groundwater Observations Groundwater observations include observations and measurements of flows from springs and of water levels in existing wells, boreholes, selected observation wells, and piezometers. Such observations are made in connection with studies to determine water table elevations and profiles, fluctuations in water table elevations, the possible existence and location of perched water tables, depths of probable water-bearing horizons, artesian flow, and locations of possible leakage.

Springs The method employed for measuring the flow from natural springs generally depends on the size and location of the springs and on the shape of the outlet. Spring flow may be estimated when the quantity involved is too small to make measurements practicable, but in most instances actual measurements are practicable and should be made. Flows from small springs often are measured by directing the water into a container of known capacity and noting the time required to fill the container. Measurements also can be made by installing a weir across the channel along which the water flows from the spring. Flows are computed from measurements of the depths of water flowing over the notch in the weir by means of formulas that vary with the cross-sectional shape and size of the weir. Flows from large springs are computed from current velocity measurements in the outlet channel and from measurements of the size together with a consideration of the shape of the channel.

Existing Wells Water levels in existing wells usually are obtained from the well owners. If the owners do not have such information, measurements may be obtained by the methods described below.

Boreholes The depth to water level in a borehole may be determined by means of a chalked tape, a "plunker," or an electrical water-level indicator. Because of the influence of the drilling fluid on the water levels in the holes, time should elapse after the fluid circulation has stopped and the tools have been removed before measurements are made; the water in the hole can thus adjust to its static level. If measurements are desired before a hole is

---

SOURCE: *Geological Investigations*, U.S. Army Corps of Engineers, 1960.

completed, a common practice is to fill the hole with water at the end of the workday and to measure the depth to water level at the start of the next workday. Measurements after completion of a hole generally are made 24 hours or more after drilling has stopped. Numerous subsequent check readings often are required to obtain accurate water table elevations. Because of seasonal and other fluctuations in groundwater levels, all records of water-level measurements should contain the date on which the measurements were made. Records of measurements on uncompleted boreholes also should contain the time of day and the depth of hole at which the measurements were made in order that the measurements may be correlated with the progress of the borings.

Observation Wells These wells are employed when observations of groundwater levels are to be continued over a more or less prolonged period of time during which detailed observations are desired. Either existing wells and boreholes or holes drilled especially for groundwater observation purposes may be used. Although casing often is left in boreholes used as observation wells, the conversion of these holes to observation wells by the installation of piezometers or the use of specially constructed observation wells is preferable. Piezometers usually are composed of a well point or section of porous pipe attached to the lower end of a metal or plastic pipe. This is placed in a hole and surrounded by a filter of well-graded sand or gravel. A seal of compacted clay or bentonite is placed above the filter material in the annular space around the piezometer pipe to prevent the inflow of surface water and to seal off any portion of the hole above the zone for which waterhead observations are desired. Water-level measurements may be obtained by the same methods as described above under "Boreholes."

SOURCE: *Geological Investigations*, U.S. Army Corps of Engineers, 1960.

1.5 Unified Classification and Properties of Soils

The basic outline of the unified classification system is presented in Figure 1-11. The system has several outstanding features:

1. It is simple. There are twelve materials with which technicians are normally concerned: four coarse-grained materials, four fine-grained materials, and four combined materials. In addition, three organics require special attention, making a total of fifteen items.
2. It provides important physical characteristics, such as size, gradation, plasticity, strength, brittleness, and consolidation potential.
3. It is reliable. The engineering properties implied by the classification are realistic.

| | | IMPORTANT PROPERTIES | | | | | UNIFIED SOIL CLASSES |
| | | | | PERMEABILITY | | | |
TYPICAL NAMES	SHEAR STRENGTH	COMPRESS-IBILITY	WORKABILITY AS CONSTRUCTION MATERIAL	WHEN COMPACTED	K CM. PER SEC.	K FT. PER DAY	
Well graded gravels, gravel-sand mixtures, little or no fines.	Excellent	Negligible	Excellent	Pervious	$K > 10^{-2}$	$K > 30$	**GW**
Poorly graded gravels, gravel-sand mixtures, little or no fines.	Good	Negligible	Good	Very Pervious	$K > 10^{-2}$	$K > 30$	**GP**
Silty gravels, gravel-sand-silt mixtures.	Good to Fair	Negligible	Good	Semi-Pervious to Impervious	$K = 10^{-3}$ to 10^{-6}	$K = 3$ to 3×10^{-3}	**GM**
Clayey gravels, gravel-sand-clay mixtures.	Good	Very Low	Good	Impervious	$K = 10^{-6}$ to 10^{-8}	$K = 3 \times 10^{-3}$ to 3×10^{-5}	**GC**
Well graded sands, gravelly sands, little or no fines.	Excellent	Negligible	Excellent	Pervious	$K > 10^{-3}$	$K > 3$	**SW**
Poorly graded sands, gravelly sands, little or no fines.	Good	Very Low	Fair	Pervious	$K > 10^{-3}$	$K > 3$	**SP**
Silty sands, sand-silt mixtures	Good to Fair	Low	Fair	Semi-Pervious to Impervious	$K = 10^{-3}$ to 10^{-6}	$K = 3$ to 3×10^{-3}	**SM**
Clayey sands, sand-clay mixtures.	Good to Fair	Low	Good	Impervious	$K = 10^{-6}$ to 10^{-8}	$K = 3 \times 10^{-3}$ to 3×10^{-5}	**SC**
Inorganic silts and very fine sands, rock flour, silty or clayey fine sands or clayey silts with slight plasticity.	Fair	Medium to High	Fair	Semi-Pervious to Impervious	$K = 10^{-3}$ to 10^{-6}	$K = 3$ to 3×10^{-3}	**ML**
Inorganic clays of low to medium plasticity, gravelly clays, sandy clays, silty clays, lean clays.	Fair	Medium	Good to Fair	Impervious	$K = 10^{-6}$ to 10^{-8}	$K = 3 \times 10^{-3}$ to 3×10^{-5}	**CL**
Organic silts and organic silty clays of low plasticity.	Poor	Medium	Fair	Semi-Pervious to Impervious	$K = 10^{-4}$ to 10^{-6}	$K = 3 \times 10^{-1}$ to 3×10^{-3}	**OL**
Inorganic silts, micaceous or diatomaceous fine sandy or silty soils, elastic silts.	Fair to Poor	High	Poor	Semi-Pervious to Impervious	$K = 10^{-4}$ to 10^{-6}	$K = 3 \times 10^{-1}$ to 3×10^{-3}	**MH**
Inorganic clays of high plasticity, fat clays.	Poor	High to Very High	Poor	Impervious	$K = 10^{-6}$ to 10^{-8}	$K = 3 \times 10^{-3}$ to 3×10^{-5}	**CH**
Organic clays of medium to high plasticity, organic silts.	Poor	High	Poor	Impervious	$K = 10^{-6}$ to 10^{-8}	$K = 3 \times 10^{-3}$ to 3×10^{-5}	**OH**
Peat and other highly organic soils.	NOT SUITABLE FOR CONSTRUCTION						**Pt**

Figure 1-11 Unified classification system.

SOURCE: *Engineering Field Manual for Conservation Practices,* U.S. Department of Agriculture, Soil Conservation Service, 1969.

EMBANKMENTS								
COMPACTION CHARACTER-ISTICS	STANDARD PROCTER UNIT DENSITY LBS. PER CU. FT.	TYPE OF ROLLER DESIRABLE	RELATIVE CHARACTERISTICS: PERME-ABILITY	RELATIVE CHARACTERISTICS: COMPRESS-IBILITY	RESISTANCE TO PIPING	ABILITY TO TAKE PLASTIC DEFORMATION UNDER LOAD WITHOUT SHEARING	GENERAL DESCRIPTION & USE	UNIFIED SOIL CLASSES
Good	125-135	crawler tractor or steel wheeled & vibratory	High	Very Slight	Good	None	Very stable, pervious shells of dikes and dams.	GW
Good	115-125	crawler tractor or steel wheeled & vibratory	High	Very Slight	Good	None	Reasonably stable, pervious shells of dikes and dams.	GP
Good with close control	120-135	rubber-tired or sheepsfoot	Medium	Slight	Poor	Poor	Reasonably stable, not well suited to shells but may be used for impervious cores or blankets.	GM
Good	115-130	sheepsfoot or rubber-tired	Low	Slight	Good	Fair	Fairly stable, may be used for impervious core.	GC
Good	110-130	crawler tractor & vibratory or steel wheeled	High	Very Slight	Fair	None	Very stable, pervious sections, slope protection required.	SW
Good	100-120	crawler tractor & vibratory or steel wheeled	High	Very Slight	Fair to Poor	None	Reasonably stable, may be used in dike with flat slopes.	SP
Good with close control	110-125	rubber-tired or sheepsfoot	Medium	Slight	Poor to Very Poor	Poor	Fairly stable, not well suited to shells, but may be used for impervious cores or dikes.	SM
Good	105-125	sheepsfoot or rubber-tired	Low	Slight	Good	Fair	Fairly stable, use for impervious core for flood control structures.	SC
Good to Poor Close control essential	95-120	sheepsfoot	Medium	Medium	Poor to Very Poor	*Very Poor	Poor stability, may be used for embankments with proper control. *Varies with water content.	ML
Fair to Good	95-120	sheepsfoot	Low	Medium	Good to Fair	Good to Poor	Stable, impervious cores and blankets.	CL
Fair to Poor	80-100	sheepsfoot	Medium to Low	Medium to High	Good to Poor	Fair	Not suitable for embankments.	OL
Poor to Very Poor	70-95	sheepsfoot	Medium to Low	Very High	Good to Poor	Good	Poor stability, core of hydraulic fill dam, not desirable in rolled fill construction.	MH
Fair to Poor	75-105	sheepsfoot	Low	High	Excellent	Excellent	Fair stability with flat slopes, thin cores, blanket & dike sections.	CH
Poor to Very Poor	65-100	sheepsfoot	Medium to Low	Very High	Good to Poor	Good	Not suitable for embankments.	OH
DO NOT USE FOR EMBANKMENT CONSTRUCTION								Pt

Figure 1-11 Unified classification system. *(Continued)*

TENTATIVE FOR TRIAL USE ONLY

CHANNELS: LONG DURATION TO CONSTANT FLOWS.		FOUNDATION: FOUNDATION SOILS, BEING UNDISTURBED, ARE INFLUENCED TO A GREAT DEGREE BY THEIR GEOLOGIC ORIGIN. JUDGEMENT AND TESTING MUST BE USED IN ADDITION TO THESE GENERALIZATIONS.					
RELATIVE DESIRABILITY			RELATIVE DESIRABILITY		REQUIREMENTS FOR SEEPAGE CONTROL		
EROSION RESISTANCE	COMPACTED EARTH LINING	BEARING VALUE	SEEPAGE IMPORTANT	SEEPAGE NOT IMPORTANT	PERMANENT RESERVOIR	FLOODWATER RETARDING	UNIFIED SOIL CLASSES
1	-	Good	-	1	Positive cutoff or blanket	Control only within volume acceptable plus pressure relief if required.	GW
2	-	Good	-	3	Positive cutoff or blanket	Control only within volume acceptable plus pressure relief if required.	GP
4	4	Good	2	4	Core trench to none	None	GM
3	1	Good	1	6	None	None	GC
6	-	Good	-	2	Positive cutoff or upstream blanket & toe drains or wells.	Control only within volume acceptable plus pressure relief if required.	SW
7 if gravelly	-	Good to Poor depending upon density	-	5	Positive cutoff or upstream blanket & toe drains or wells.	Control only within volume acceptable plus pressure relief if required	SP
8 if gravelly	5 erosion critical	Good to Poor depending upon density	4	7	Upstream blanket & toe drains or wells	Sufficient control to prevent dangerous seepage piping.	SM
5	2	Good to Poor	3	8	None	None	SC
-	6 erosion critical	Very Poor, susceptible to liquefication	6, if saturated or pre-wetted	9	Positive cutoff or upstream blanket & toe drains or wells.	Sufficient control to prevent dangerous seepage piping.	ML
9	3	Good to Poor	5	10	None	None	CL
-	7 erosion critical	Fair to Poor, may have excessive settlement	7	11	None	None	OL
-	-	Poor	8	12	None	None	MH
10	8 volume change critical	Fair to Poor	9	13	None	None	CH
-	-	Very Poor	10	14	None	None	OH
-	-	REMOVE FROM FOUNDATION					Pt

No. 1 is best numerical rating.

SOURCE: *Engineering Field Manual for Conservation Practices*, U.S. Department of Agriculture, Soil Conservation Service, 1969.

1.6 Piles

Piles are used to transmit foundation loads to strata of adequate bearing capacity and to eliminate settlement from the consolidation of overlying materials. Figure 1-12 lists nine principal pile categories of the three structural materials: wood, steel, and concrete. No exact criteria for the applicability of the various pile types can be given. The selection of types should be based on factors listed in the figure and on comparative costs.

Pile type	Timber	Steel
Consider for length of....	30-60 ft	40-100 ft
Applicable material specifications.	TS-2P3	TS-P67
Maximum stresses.	Measured at most critical point, 1200 psi for Southern Pine and Douglas Fir. See U.S.D.A. Wood Handbook No. 72 for stress values of other species.	12,000 psi.
Consider for design loads of.	10-50 tons	40-120 tons.
Disadvantages.	Difficult to splice. Vulnerable to damage in hard driving. Vulnerable to decay unless treated, when piles are intermittently submerged.	Vulnerable to corrosion where exposed. BP section may be damaged or deflected by major obstructions.
Advantages..	Comparatively low initial cost. Permanently submerged piles are resistant to decay. Easy to handle.	Easy to splice. High capacity. Small displacement. Able to penetrate through light obstructions.
Remarks ...	Best suited for friction pile in granular material.	Best suited for endbearing on rock. Reduce allowable capacity for corrosive locations.
Typical illustrations.	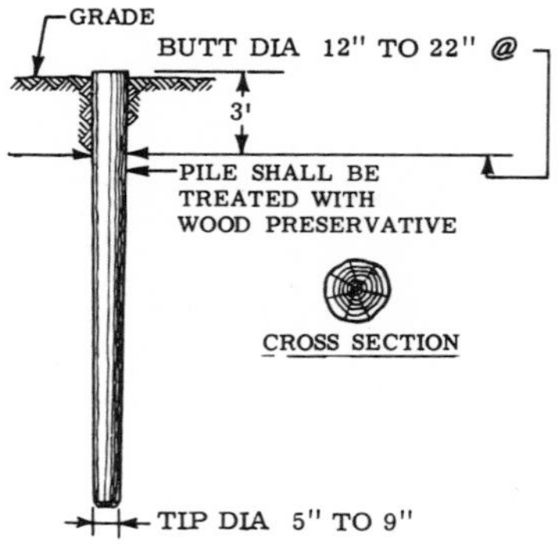 GRADE — BUTT DIA 12" TO 22" @ — 3' PILE SHALL BE TREATED WITH WOOD PRESERVATIVE CROSS SECTION TIP DIA 5" TO 9"	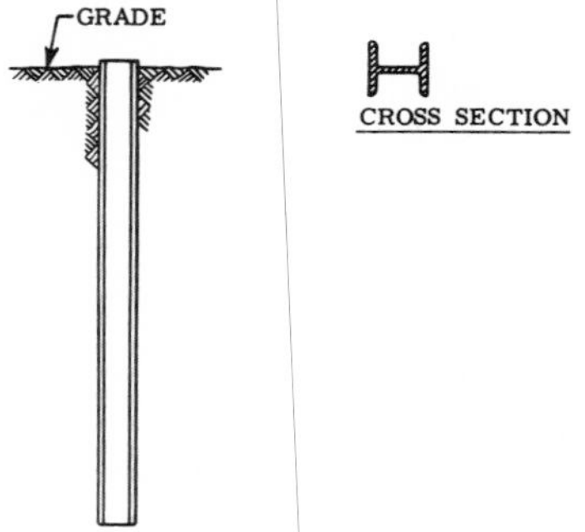 GRADE CROSS SECTION

See General Notes on last page of table.

Figure 1-12 Design criteria for bearing piles.

SOURCE: *Soil Mechanics, Foundations, and Earth Structures,* NAVFAC-DM-7, U.S. Department of the Navy.

Pile type	Precast concrete (including prestressed)	Cast-in-place concrete (thin shell driven with mandrel)
Consider for length of...	40-50 ft for precast. 60-100 ft for prestressed.	100 ft.
Applicable material specifications.	TS-P57	ACI Code 318—For Concrete.
Maximum stresses.	For precast—15% of 28-day strength of concrete, but no more than 700 psi. For prestressed—20% of 28-day strength of concrete, but no more than 1,000 psi in excess of prestress.	25% of 28-day strength of concrete with 1,000 psi maximum, measured at midpoint of length in bearing stratum.
Specifically designed for a wide range of loads.	. . . .	
Disadvantages.	Unless prestressed, vulnerable to handling. High initial cost. Considerable displacement. Prestressed difficult to splice.	Difficult to splice after concreting. Redriving not recommended. Thin shell vulnerable during driving. Considerable displacement.
Advantages..	High load capacities. Corrosion resistance can be attained. Hard driving possible.	Initial economy. Tapered sections provide higher bearing resistance in granular stratum.
Remarks ...	Cylinder piles in particular are suited for bending resistance.	Best suited for medium load friction piles in granular materials.
Typical illustrations.		
See General Notes on last page of table.		

Pile type	Cast-in-place concrete piles (shells driven without mandrel)	Pressure injected footings
Consider for length of...	30-80 ft	10 to 60 ft.
Applicable material specifications.	ACI Code 318	TS-F16.
Maximum stresses.	25% of 28-day strength of concrete with maximum of 1,000 psi measured at midpoint of length in bearing stratum. 9,000 psi in shell.	25% of 28-day strength of concrete, with a maximum of 1,000 psi. 9,000 psi for pipe shell if thickness greater than 1/8".
Consider for design loads of. . .	50-70 tons	60-120 tons.
Disadvantages.	Hard to splice after concreting. Considerable displacement.	*Base* of footing cannot be made in clay. When clay layers must be penetrated to reach suitable material, special precautions are required for *shafts* if in groups.
Advantages..	Can be redriven. Shell not easily damaged.	Provides means of placing high capacity footings on bearing stratum without necessity for excavation or dewatering. Required depths can be predicted accurately. High blow energy available for overcoming obstructions. Great uplift resistance if suitably reinforced.
Remarks ...	Best suited for friction piles of medium length.	Best suited for granular soils where bearing is achieved through compaction around base. Minimum spacing 4'-6" on center. For further design requirements see Philadelphia Building Code 4-1710.
Typical illustrations.		
See General Notes on last page of table.		

Figure 1-12 Design criteria for bearing piles. *(Continued)*

SOURCE: *Soil Mechanics, Foundations, and Earth Structures*, NAVFAC-DM-7, U.S. Department of the Navy.

Pile type	Concrete filled steel pipe piles	Composite piles	Pile type	Auger-placed, pressure-injected concrete piles	— General Notes —
Consider for length of...	40-120 ft	60-120 ft.	Consider for length of...	30-60 ft	1. Stresses given for steel piles are for noncorrosive locations. For corrosive locations, estimate possible reduction in steel cross section or provide protection from corrosion.
Applicable material specifications.	ASTM A7—for Core. ASTM A252—for Pipe. ACI Code 318—for Concrete.	ACI Code 318—for Concrete. ASTM-36—for Structural Section. ASTM A252—for Steel Pipe. TS-P2—for Timber.	Applicable material specifications.	TS-2P69........................	2. Lengths and loads indicated are for feasibility guidance only. They generally represent current practice.
Maximum stresses.	9,000 psi for pipe shell. 25% of 28-day strength of concrete with a maximum of 1,000 psi. 12,000 psi on Steel Cores.	25% of 28-day strength of concrete with 1,000 psi maximum. 9,000 psi for structural and pipe sections. Same as timber piles for wood composite.	Maximum stresses.	25% of 28-day strength of concrete with maximum of 1,000 psi.	3. Design load capacity should be determined by soil mechanics principles limiting stresses in piles and type and function of structure. See Section 3.
			Consider for design load of...	35-70 tons........................	
Consider for design load of...	80-120 tons without cores. 500-1,500 tons with cores.	30-80 tons.	Disadvantages.	More than average dependence on quality workmanship. Not suitable thru peat or similar highly compressible material.	
Disadvantages.	High initial cost. Displacement for closed end pipe.	Difficult to attain good joint between two materials.	Advantages..	Economy. Completely nondisplacement. No driving vibration to endanger adjacent structures. High skin friction. Good contact on rock for end bearing. Convenient for low-headroom underpinning work. Visual inspection of augered material. No splicing required.	
Advantages..	Best control during installation. No displacement for open end installation. Open end pipe best against obstructions. High load capacities. Easy to splice.	Considerable length can be provided at comparatively low cost.			
Remarks ...	Provides high bending resistance where unsupported length is loaded laterally.	The weakest of any material used shall govern allowable stresses and capacity.	Remarks ...	Process patented........................	
Typical illustrations.			Typical illustrations.		

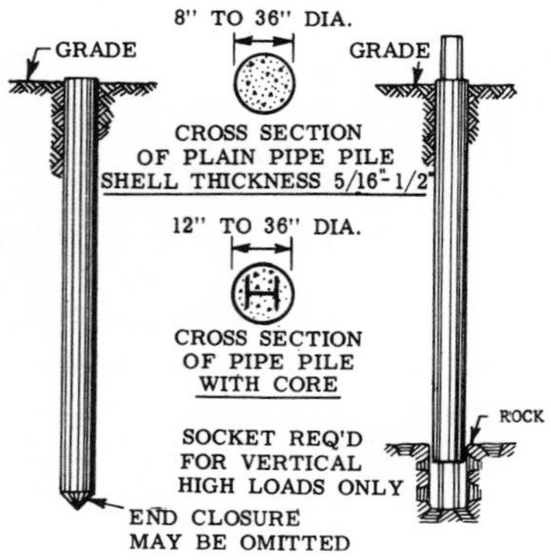

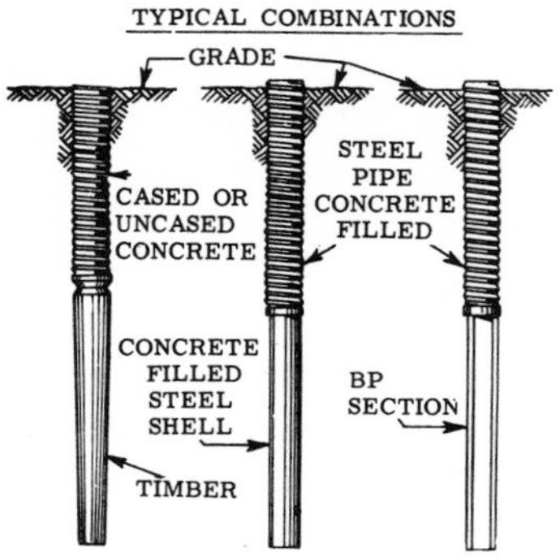

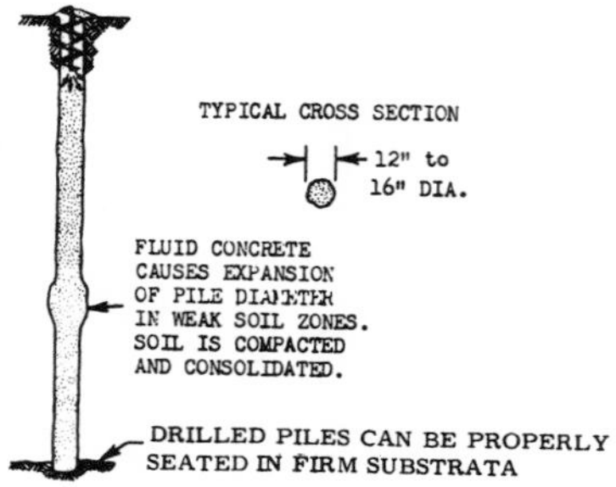

See General Notes on last page of table.

Figure 1-12 Design criteria for bearing piles. *(Continued)*

SOURCE: *Soil Mechanics, Foundations, and Earth Structures,* NAVFAC-DM-7, U.S. Department of the Navy.

1.7 Soil Bearing Values

The requirements for the determination of soil bearing values should be in accordance with the following data or with the American Standards Association's *Building Code Requirements for Excavations and Foundations.* Where the bearing value of soil is determined by field loading tests and where other bearing values are established by local practice and experience or because of special conditions, soil bearing values should not exceed those given in the accompanying table on undisturbed soil.

Modification of Bearing Value

Variation in Underlying Soils Where the bearing materials directly under a foundation overlie strata with a smaller allowable bearing value, such smaller value should not be exceeded at the top level of such strata. The computation of the vertical pressure in the bearing materials at any depth below a foundation should be made on the assumption that the load is spread uniformly at an angle of 1 horizontal to 2 vertical.

Loosened Bearing Materials Wherever bearing material is loosened or disturbed by a flow of water, the bearing value is to be reduced to the allowable bearing value of the loosened material, unless the loosened material is removed. Where the flow of water is controlled by well points or by another method so that the bearing material is not disturbed or loosened, the full bearing value of the unloosened material may be assumed.

Foundations on Laterally Supported Soil The presumptive unit bearing values given in the accompanying table may be increased for a load on soil where, because of the depth below ground level and permanent lateral support of the bearing soil, greater bearing values are justified.

Soil Bearing Load Test Tests should be made and interpreted so as to take into account all significant factors, such as the presence of soft underlying strata, variations in the size of footings, and the compressibility of the soils encountered. When the size of pro-

PRESUMPTIVE UNIT SOIL BEARING VALUES

Class	Material	Allowable bearing value, tons per square foot*
1	Massive crystalline bedrock, such as granite, gneiss, or traprock, in sound condition	100
2	Foliated rocks, such as schist and slate, in sound condition	40
3	Sedimentary rocks, such as hard shales, silt-stones, or sand-stones, in sound condition	15
4	Exceptionally compacted gravels or sands	10
5	Compact gravel sand-gravel mixtures	6
6	Loose gravel; compact coarse sand	4
7	Loose coarse sand; loose sand-gravel mixtures; compact fine sand; wet coarse sand (confined)	3
8	Loose fine sand; wet fine sand (confined)	2
9	Stiff clay	4
10	Medium-stiff clay	2
11	Soft clay	1
12	Fill, organic material, or silt	†

*Presumptive bearing values apply to loading at the surface or in cases where permanent lateral support for the bearing soil is not provided.

†Where, in the opinion of the enforcement officer, the bearing value is adequate for light frame structures, fill material, organic material, and silt are deemed to be without presumptive bearing value. The bearing value of such material may be fixed on the basis of tests or other satisfactory evidence.

posed footings varies substantially, loading tests should be made on several areas of different sizes as a guide in the determination of allowable bearing values for the various footing sizes.

Tests should be made where surface-water conditions and groundwater conditions are representative of the bearing soil and when the soil tested is free from frost. Tests should be made on leveled but otherwise undisturbed portions of foundation bearing material. Where tests are made materially below the ground level, any material immediately adjoining the test location should be removed to eliminate the effect of surcharge or reinforcing.

The test assembly should consist of a vertical timber or post, with or without braced timber footing, resting upon the soil to be tested and supporting a platform on which the test loads are to be placed. The exact area resting upon the soil should be ascertained; it should be not less than 1 square foot for bearing materials of Classes 1 to 4 inclusive as indicated in the table "Presumptive Unit Soil Bearing Values" and not less than 4 square feet for other bearing materials. The platform should be symmetrical in respect to the post and as close to the bearing soil as is practicable. The post should be maintained in a vertical position by guys or wedges. The load may be any convenient material that can be applied in the increments required, such as cement or sand in bags, or pig iron or steel in bars. In applying the load, precautions should be taken to prevent jarring or moving the post.

Settlement readings should be taken at least once every 24 hours at a point that should remain undisturbed during the test, and the settlement should be plotted against time. The proposed allowable load per square foot should be applied and allowed to remain undisturbed until there has been no settlement for 24 hours.

SOURCE: *Code Manual,* New York State Building Code Commission.

NOMINAL VALUES OF ALLOWABLE BEARING PRESSURES FOR SPREAD FOUNDATIONS

Type of bearing material	Consistency in place	Allowable bearing pressure (tons per square foot) Ordinary range	Allowable bearing pressure (tons per square foot) Recommended value for use
Massive crystalline igneous and metamorphic rock: granite, diorite, basalt, gneiss, thoroughly cemented conglomerate (sound condition allows minor cracks)	Hard, sound rock	60–100	80
Foliated metamorphic rock: slate, schist (sound condition allows minor cracks)	Medium-hard sound rock	30–40	35
Sedimentary rock: hard cemented shales, siltstone, sandstone, limestone without cavities	Medium-hard sound rock	15–25	20
Weathered or broken bedrock of any kind except highly argillaceous rock (shale)	Soft rock	8–12	10
Compaction shale or other highly argillaceous rock in sound condition	Soft rock	8–12	10
Well-graded mixture of fine- and coarse-grained soil: glacial till, hardpan, boulder clay (GW–GC, GC, SC)	Very compact	8–12	10
Gravel, gravel-sand mixtures, boulder-gravel mixtures (GW, GP, SW, SP)	Very compact	7–10	8
	Medium to compact	5–7	6
	Loose	3–6	4
Coarse to medium sand, sand with little gravel (SW, SP)	Very compact	4–6	4
	Medium to compact	3–4	3
	Loose	2–3	2
Fine to medium sand, silty or clayey medium to coarse sand (SW, SM, SC)	Very compact	3–5	3
	Medium to compact	2–4	2.5
	Loose	1–2	1.5
Fine sand, silty or clayey medium to fine sand (SP, SM, SC)	Very compact	3–4	3
	Medium to compact	2–3	2
	Loose	1–2	1.5
Homogeneous inorganic clay, sandy or silty clay (CL, CH)	Very stiff to hard	3–6	4
	Medium to stiff	1–3	2
	Soft	0.5–1	0.5
Inorganic silt, sandy or clayey silt, varved silt-clay–fine sand (ML, MH)	Very stiff to hard	2–4	3
	Medium to stiff	1–3	1.5
	Soft	0.5–1	0.5

NOTE: Under the Casagrande system of classification, C = clay, G = gravel, H = high compressibility, L = low to medium compressibility, M = silt, P = poorly graded, S = sand, and W = well graded.

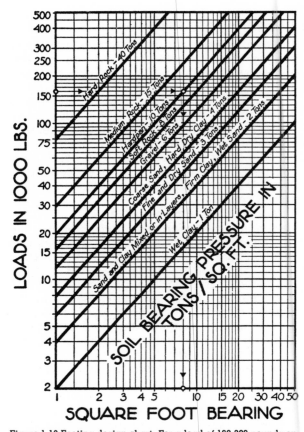

Figure 1-13 Footing design chart. For a load of 160,000 pounds on hardpan, the chart shows that a footing of 8 square feet would be required. The values given for various soils are averages and may not agree with local codes. Local requirements should be checked before this chart is used. Values falling between the diagonal lines can readily be interpolated.

FOOTING DESIGN CHART; FROST PENETRATION

The effect of freezing and thawing is much greater upon soil than upon other materials, such as brick or concrete. Footings should be carried below the frost line, the depth that frost penetrates below the grade. Many building codes require the footing to be carried 1 foot below the frost line. If the footings are above the frost line, they are likely to heave (move) as a result of soil pressures caused by extreme temperature change. It is evident from the map shown in Figure 1-14 that maximum frost penetration differs in various sections of the United States. Local building codes usually specify the footing depth. Depths below grade are deter-mined by the general drainage conditions and extreme temperatures in a locality.

UNDERPINNING, SHORING, AND SHEETPILING

Figures 1-15 and 1-16 demonstrate methods of underpinning abutting foundations and of pre-venting cave-ins in excavations by means of shoring and sheetpiling.

SOURCE: *Code Manual*, New York State Building Code Commission.

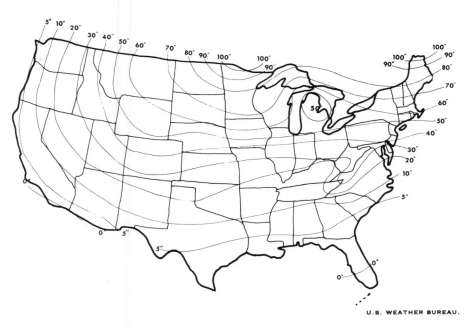

U.S. WEATHER BUREAU.

Figure 1-14 Maximum frost penetration in the United States.

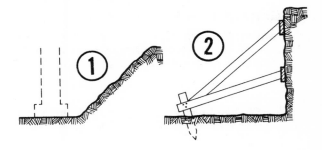

1. SLOPED BANK — In this type the earth takes its natural angle of repose where the soil lacks the stability to stand vertically when cut. Such excavation is undesirable and is frequently forbidden in specifications because the undisturbed earth remaining creates a bowl for the collection of water (both before and after the backfilling is done) and an undesirably large amount of soil removal and backfill is required.

2. BRACED BANK — If the soil has some stability but will not stand unaided, very simple bracing may be sufficient.

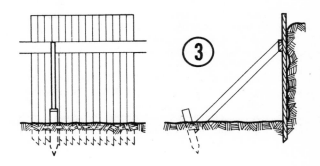

3. SHEET PILING — In very fluid soils sheet piling is driven and braced, and may be used as the outside form for poured foundations. Wood, steel, or concrete sheet piling are available.

Figure 1-16 Shoring and sheetpiling.
(1) *Sloped bank:* In this type of excavation the earth takes its natural angle of repose where the soil lacks the stability to stand vertically when cut. Such an excavation is undesirable and is frequently forbidden in specifications because the undisturbed earth remaining creates a bowl for the collection of water (both before and after backfilling) and an undesirably large amount of soil removal and backfilling is required.
(2) *Braced bank:* If the soil has some stability but will not stand unaided, very simple bracing may be sufficient.
(3) *Sheetpiling:* In very fluid soils sheetpiling is driven and braced and may be used as the outside form for poured foundations. Wood, steel, or concrete sheetpiling is available.

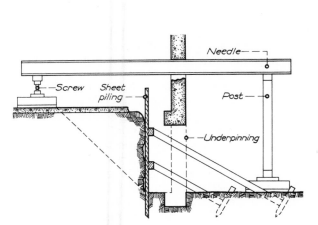

NEEDLING — Where old walls are in weak condition and/or the soil is not stable, the underpinning is accomplished with the aid of "needling." Shoring (*see below*) is usually necessary.

Figure 1-15 Underpinning abutting foundations.
(a) *Needling:* Where old walls are weak and the soil is not stable, or both, underpinning is accomplished with the aid of needling.
(b) *Shoring:* Sockets are cut in the old wall, and shores (also called "spur braces") are inserted. These rest on a crib of timbering. Shores prevent slipping and bulging and reduce the load to be

SHORING — Sockets are cut in the old wall and *shores*, also called *spur braces*, are inserted. These rest on a crib of timbering. Shores prevent slipping, bulging, and reduce the load to be supported while underpinning is placed.

SECTIONING — If the old walls are sound and the soil stable, a short excavation is made and a 6 ft. length of new wall is built under the old wall. When this new section will bear weight, another section is added, and so continued until the old wall has a continuous foundation under it.

supported while underpinning is placed.
(c) *Sectioning:* If the old walls are sound and the soil is stable, a short excavation is made and a 6-foot length of new wall is built under the old wall. When this new section will bear weight, another section is added, and the procedure is repeated until the old wall has a continuous foundation under it.

SOURCE: Donald T. Graf, *Don Graf's Data Sheets*, Reinhold Publishing Corporation, New York, 1949.

1.8 Grading (FHA Requirements)

Grading Design Grading design shall be considered in the early planning stages with the following principal objectives:

1. Development of attractive, suitable and economical building sites.
2. Provision of safe, convenient, and functional access to all areas for use and maintenance.
3. Disposal of surface runoff from the site area without erosion or sedimentation, or its collection as needed for water features, debris basins, or irrigation storage.
4. Diversion of surface and subsurface flow away from buildings and pavements to prevent undue saturation of the subgrade that could damage structures and weaken pavements.
5. Preservation of the natural character of the site by minimum disturbance of existing ground forms and meeting of satisfactory ground levels at existing trees to be saved.
6. Optimum on-site balance of cut and fill; stockpiling for reuse of existing topsoil suitable for the establishment of ground cover or planting.
7. Avoidance of filled areas that will add to the depth or instability of building foundations and pavement subgrades.
8. Avoidance of wavy profiles in streets and walks and of steps in walks.
9. Avoidance of earth banks requiring costly erosion control measures, except where these are needed in place of costly retaining walls.
10. Keeping finished grades as high as practicable where rock will be encountered close to the surface, thus reducing the cost of utility trenching and other excavation and improving growing conditions for vegetation.
11. Avoidance of runoff water over roadways. Ice forms during freezing weather and a hazardous driving situation results.

Areas Adjacent to Buildings Unpaved areas adjacent to buildings shall be sloped to direct surface water and roof drainage, including snowmelt, away from buildings at a minimum slope of 6 inches in the first 10 feet of horizontal distance and not across sidewalks. Surfaces paved with portland cement concrete shall have a slope of not less than 0.5 percent,

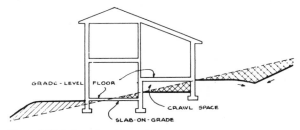

Figure 1-17 A three-level house that creates two levels at grade and involves a minimum of excavation.

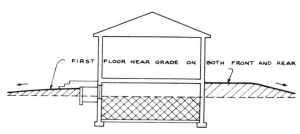

Figure 1-18 A house on level ground in which the excavated earth is reused to raise the grade immediately around the house. This procedure reduces required excavation and provides drainage away from the house.

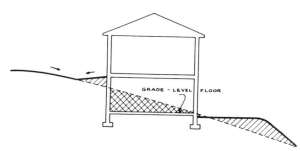

Figure 1-19 A house on a slope in which the slope is used to create a ground floor, the earth being reused to establish a level terrace and to care for the drainage.

and bituminous pavements a slope of not less than 1.5 percent, to assure adequate drainage without ponding or "birdbaths."

Unoccupied Site Areas Portions of the site not occupied by buildings or pavement shall have adequate continuous slopes to drain toward watercourses, drainage swales, roadways, and the minimum necessary storm drainage inlets. Drainage swales or channels shall be sized and sloped to accommodate design runoff. The runoff should be carried under walkways in pipes with diameters of not less than 8 inches or of larger sizes if clogging by debris or grass cuttings is a problem. Swales should be used to intercept water at the top and bottom of banks where large areas are drained. To provide positive drainage, a slope of not less than 2 percent for turfed areas is usually desirable, but more permeable soils may have adequate drainage with a lesser slope. Turf banks, where required, should be graded to permit the use of gang mowers, providing a maximum slope of 1 vertical to 3 horizontal and, if feasible, a slope of 1 vertical to 4 horizontal. The tops and bottoms of all slopes should be gently rounded in a transition curve for optimum appearance and ease of maintenance.

Grading Procedure The site areas shall be roughly graded to comply with the foregoing criteria on grading design and criteria on fine grading. The subgrade should be established parallel to the proposed finish grade and at elevations to allow for the thickness of topsoil or other surface. In fill areas, all topsoil, debris, and other noncompatible materials should be removed, and all tree stumps removed or cut out 18 inches below grade. On sloping areas to be filled, the original ground shall be scarified to provide bond for fill material where the original ground is clay. Fill material shall be free from debris and have a moisture content near the optimum when it is placed. Fill shall be compacted to a density that would avoid damaging settlement to drainage structures, walks, or other planned improvements.

See also Figures 1-17, 1-18, and 1-19.

SOURCE: *Minimum Property Standards,* Federal Housing Administration.

1.9 Cut and Fill

Cuts and fills to create the desired surface in land grading may be determined by the profile adjustment method or the plane method.

PROFILE ADJUSTMENT METHOD

This procedure for computing cuts and fills should be easier to follow than the plane method. Although it is not as accurate as the plane method, it should be adequate for surface drainage.

The field should be surveyed by the grid method. The size of the grids is not critical, but 100 feet is customary. Calculations are simpler when the first line of grid points in each direction is started at half the grid size from the boundaries (see Figure 1-20). Now each grid point becomes the center of a square, and the field is made up of such squares.

The elevations of the grid points should be plotted along each grid line on the direction of greatest slope or the direction in which row drainage is desired. A profile should be drawn for the existing land surface along the grid line. Limits within which the slope of the surface may be allowed to vary should be adopted. By the use of these limits, a new profile can be drawn in for each grid line so as to have more cutoff area than area to be filled in and thus allow for the cut-fill ratio. Existing topography should be followed as closely as possible to keep soil movement to a minimum.

When this has been done for each grid line, the cuts and fills should be added for each line. The total cuts and the total fills can then be calculated. The ratio

$$\frac{\text{Total cuts}}{\text{Total fills}} \times 100$$

can be determined. If this ratio is greater or smaller than that required for the soil, the cuts and fills must be adjusted by raising or lowering the new surface profiles by an amount that will give the desired cut-fill ratio.

The grid survey will probably have been done to the nearest 0.05 foot. This means that calculations to any greater accuracy than to the nearest 0.05 foot are time-wasting. Grid points should all be raised or lowered by 0.05 foot until the cut-fill ratio closest to the desired ratio is obtained. This is accurate enough for drainage work. If necessary, one grid line can be adjusted at a time until an overall cut-fill ratio close to that desired is achieved.

At this point the profiles across the field perpendicular to those already drawn should be plotted. This is a check to see whether the cross slopes exceed the limits that have been decided upon. These limits need not be the same as those chosen for the row grade; frequently greater variation is allowed for the cross slope than for the row grade. If the cross slopes do exceed the permissible variations, the row grade profiles must be further adjusted until the cross slopes are acceptable.

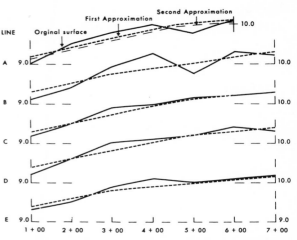

Figure 1-21 Profiles in row direction. The distance between horizontal lines is equal to 1 foot.

EXAMPLE:

Figure 1-20 is an example of a field which is to be graded and which has been surveyed on a 100-foot grid system. Profiles along the lines *A, B, C, D,* and *E* have been plotted and shown in Figure 1-21.

Assume that the row grade may vary between 0.05 and 0.3 percent and that the cross slope may vary by 0.5 percent. The cut-fill ratio is to be 150 percent. Now new profile lines are sketched in as shown.

The cuts and fills are determined for each station and put on the original survey sheet. These are the figures to the right and below each grid point in Figure 1-20. Now the cuts and fills are totaled.

The cut-fill ratio is

$$\frac{2.20}{1.65} \times 100 = 133 \text{ percent}$$

This is too low and therefore must be

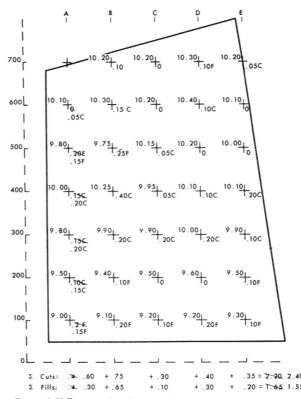

Σ Cuts: .60 + .75 + .30 + .40 + .35 = 2.40

Σ Fills: .30 + .65 + .10 + .30 + .20 = 1.55

Figure 1-20 Topographical survey sheet.

SOURCE: D. R. Coote and P. J. Zwerman, *Surface Drainage of Flat Lands,* New York State College of Agriculture at Cornell University, Ithaca, N.Y., 1970.

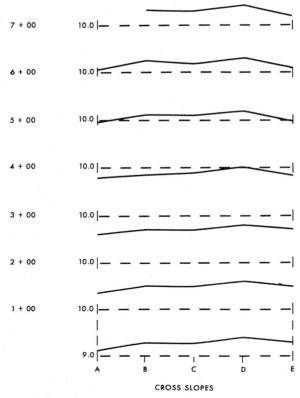

7 + 00   10.0

6 + 00   10.0

5 + 00   10.0

4 + 00   10.0

3 + 00   10.0

2 + 00   10.0

1 + 00   10.0

          9.0

          A   B   C   D   E

CROSS SLOPES

Figure 1-22 Cross-slope profiles. The distance between horizontal lines is equal to 1 foot.

increased. Line A is the only line in which cut does not exceed fill. Line A is now lowered by 0.05 foot, keeping to the same grade, and the new cuts and fills are totaled. Now the cut-fill ratio is

$$\frac{2.40}{1.55} = 154 \text{ percent}$$

No further adjustment is necessary.

The cross slopes have been plotted in Figure 1-22. They all are within the previously determined limits.

PLANE METHOD

As in the profile adjustment method, the field should be surveyed on a grid system. The size of the grids is not critical, but 100 feet is customary. Calculations are simpler when the first line of grid points in each direction is started at half the grid size from the boundaries, thus placing the "origin" outside the field by 50 feet in each direction.

The equation

$$E = a + S_x X + S_y Y$$

where E =   elevation at any point (X, Y)
a =   elevation of origin
S_x, S_y =   slope in X and Y directions respectively

will give the elevation of any point in a plane once S_x and S_y have been determined.

However, this equation will not give a plane that will balance the cut area with the fill or best fit the surface. To give equal cut and fill, the plane must pass through the centroid. The position of the centroid of the field can be determined as follows. Multiply the number of grid positions in each grid line by the distance of that line from the origin in each direction. Total these products in each direction and divide each figure thus obtained by the number of grid positions in that direction. This will give two figures, X_c and Y_c, representing the distance along each boundary from the origin, which will locate the centroid in the field.

The elevation of the centroid will be

$$E_c = \frac{\text{sum of all elevations}}{\text{total number of grid positions}}$$

The elevation of the origin will be

$$a = E_c - S_x X_c - S_y Y_c$$

With known X and Y slopes, the grid point elevation for any plane can be calculated so that total cut equals total fill. From the new elevations the cut and fill can be determined.

To avoid unnecessary earth moving, it is of value to know the best-fitting plane to any particular field. For rectangular fields the best-fitting slope in the X direction, S_x, can be found from

$$S_x = \frac{\Sigma(XE) - nX_c E_c}{\Sigma X^2 - nX_c^2}$$

where

n = number of grid positions (stations)
E = elevation at any station
X = station number in X direction
X_c = X distance of centroid

To find S_y, substitute Y and Y_c for X and X_c respectively.

For nonrectangular fields, the problem can be solved more accurately by using the following simultaneous equations:

$$S_x(\Sigma X^2 - nX_c^2) + S_y[\Sigma(XY) - nX_c Y_c] = \Sigma XE - nX_c E_c$$

$$S_y(\Sigma Y^2 - nY_c^2) + S_x[\Sigma(XY) - nX_c Y_c] = \Sigma YE - nY_c E_c.$$

EXAMPLE:

See Figure 1-23.

In the field in Figure 1-23, which is nonrectangular,

$$n = 34$$
$$X_c = \frac{104}{34} = 3.1$$
$$X_c^2 = 9.6$$
$$Y_c = \frac{133.0}{34} = 3.9$$
$$Y_c^2 = 15.2$$
$$E_c = \frac{335.2}{34} = 9.9$$

$\Sigma XY = 1(1 + 2 + 3 + 4 + 5 + 6) + 2(1 + 2 + 3 + 4 + 5 + 6 + 7) + \cdots + 7(1 + 2 + 3 + 4 + 5 + 6 + 7) = 413$

$\Sigma X^2 = 6(1) + 7(4) + 7(9) + 7(16) + 7(25) = 384$

$\Sigma Y^2 = 5(1) + 5(4) + 5(9) + 5(16) + 5(25) + 5(36) + 4(49) = 651$

$\Sigma XE = 58.2 + 2(68.9) + 3(69.2) + 4(69.8) + 5(69.1) = 1028.3$

$\Sigma YE = 45.8 + 2(47.5) + 3(49.5) + 4(50.4) + 5(49.5) + 6(51.1) + 7(41.0) = 1332$

SOURCE: D. R. Coote and P. J. Zwerman, *Surface Drainage of Flat Lands,* New York State College of Agriculture at Cornell University, Ithaca, N.Y., 1970.

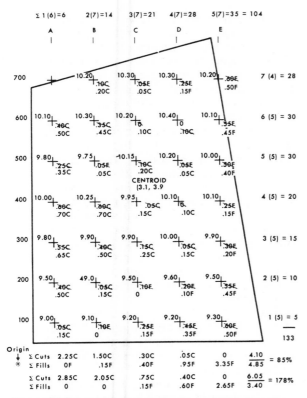

Figure 1-23 Cut-and-fill sheet for the plane method of grading.

Substitute these figures in the simultaneous equations

$S_x (384 - 326) + S_y (413 - 411) = 1028.3$
$\qquad\qquad\qquad\qquad - 1044.0 = -13.7$
$S_y (651 - 517) + S_x (413 - 411) = 1332.0$
$\qquad\qquad\qquad\qquad - 1312.0 = 20.0$
$58 S_x + 2 S_y = -13.7$
$2 S_x + 134 S_y = 20.0$
$58 S_x + 2 S_y = -13.7$
$58 S_x + 3890 S_y = 580$
$3888 S_y = 593.7$
$S_y = 0.153 \; foot/100 \; feet$
$S_x = 0.236 \; foot/100 \; feet$

If the slopes of the best-fitting plane are outside the limits imposed by erosion hazard, they will indicate at which end of the limits the slopes should be chosen. The best-fitting plane, once determined, can be varied or lowered until the difference between cut and fill volumes is appropriate to give the desired cut-fill ratio. Thus the best-fitting plane would have a slope in the Y direction of 0.15 foot/100 feet and a slope in the X direction of 0.24 foot/100 feet. Since the plane must pass through the centroid, the elevation of the origin can be computed:

$a = E_c - S_x X_c - S_y Y_c = 9.9$
$\qquad - (.24)(3.1) - (.15)(3.9) = 8.6$

Now the best-fitting plane is

$$E = 8.6 + 0.24 \, X + 0.15 \, Y$$

Each new elevation is computed, and the cut or fill is noted (see Figure 1-23).

The cuts and fills are totaled, and the ratio is determined:

$$\frac{\text{Total cuts}}{\text{Total fills}} = \frac{4.10}{4.85} = 85 \text{ percent}$$

The figure is not 100 percent because the numbers have been rounded off to the nearest 0.05 foot, which is the limit of accuracy for this work. However, we need a cut-fill ratio of 150 percent. If the whole plane is lowered by 0.05

foot, the new cuts and fills will give a ratio as follows:

$$\frac{5.00}{4.05} = 123 \text{ percent}$$

This is not adequate if we assume that a 150 percent cut-fill ratio is needed. Lowering the plane by a further 0.05 foot will give:

$$\frac{6.05}{3.40} = 178 \text{ percent.}$$

This is too much. For drainage work it is not necessary to maintain an exact plane; so simply lower half of the points by 0.10 foot and the remainder by 0.05 foot, which would result in the desired 150 percent. This should be done across the slope rather than along the length of the slope so as not to interfere with the desired row grade.

Earthwork Volume Calculations When grading land for drainage, it is almost impossible to determine precisely the volume of soil being moved. This is due to the degree of accuracy used in surveying.

When the grid points are positioned so that they are in the center of a square, the following formula is used:

Volume of cut (V_c)

$$= \frac{(\Sigma \; cuts) \times \text{area of grid square}}{27} \; \text{cubic yards}$$

By the profile adjustment method the volume of soil moved would be

$$V_c = \frac{2.40 \times 100 \times 100}{27} = 888 \text{ cubic yards}$$

By the plane method the volume would be

$$V_c = \frac{5.50 \times 100 \times 100}{27} = 2037 \text{ cubic yards}$$

SOURCE: D. R. Coote and P. J. Zwerman, *Surface Drainage of Flat Lands,* New York State College of Agriculture at Cornell University, Ithaca, N.Y., 1970.

1.10 Soil Erosion Control

There are two kinds of erosion and sediment control measures, mechanical and vegetative. The most widely used of these measures are discussed here from the standpoint of their general use and purpose. Detailed information and standards and specifications developed for local conditions can be obtained from local offices of the Soil Conservation Service (SCS) or from conservation districts. SCS can also give technical advice. Erosion control measures must be properly designed, installed, and maintained if they are to accomplish their intended purpose.

Mechanical Measures Mechanical measures are used to reshape the land to intercept, divert, convey, retard, or otherwise control runoff.

Land Grading Grading only areas going into immediate construction, as opposed to grading the entire site, helps immensely in controlling erosion. On large tracts, to avoid having a large area bare and unprotected, units of workable size can be graded one at a time. As construction is completed on one area, grading proceeds to another.

On some sites only the street rights-of-way are graded, until storm sewers have been installed. This leaves only limited areas exposed to erosion. Usually the adjacent undisturbed areas can be used as temporary outlets for diversions, or berms, built to protect the graded street rights-of-way. After the storm sewers have been installed, other areas can be graded and the runoff can be directed to the streets and storm sewers.

As a general rule, grading should be held to the minimum that makes the site suitable for its intended purpose without appreciably increasing runoff. Wherever possible, only undesirable trees should be removed. In some areas heavy cutting, filling, or reshaping of the natural topography is needed to increase the percentage of usable land. Heavy grading almost always increases erosion hazards and should be accompanied by the maximum use of appropriate erosion control measures.

The grading plan should show the location, slope, and elevation of the areas to be graded and the measures to be used for disposing of runoff and for erosion control. Constructed slopes should be limited to a degree of steepness that will provide stability and allow easy maintenance. Retaining walls may be required.

Stumps and other decayable material should not be used in fills. Soft, mushy soil material is not suitable for fills that are to be used to support buildings or other structures.

Bench Terraces Bench terraces constructed across the slope of the land and fitted to the natural terrain are used to break long slopes and slow the flow of runoff. In some areas the terraces are constructed wide enough to be used as residential sites. Since the cut-and-fill slopes of the bench terraces are always steeper than the natural slope of the land, landslides may be a threat. Engineering studies should always be made to guide the design of the slopes and ensure a reasonable degree of slope stability and safety.

Small bench terraces are sometimes used on the face of cut-and-fill slopes to help control runoff and erosion and establish vegetation.

Subsurface Drains Subsurface drains are sometimes required at the base of fill slopes to remove excess groundwater. In heavy grading it may be necessary to fill natural drainage channels; subsurface drains may have to be installed below the newly filled areas to prevent the accumulation of groundwater.

Subsurface drains may be needed in vegetated channels to lower a high water table that prevents establishing an effective plant cover.

Diversions Diversions intercept and divert runoff so that it will not cause damage; they consist of a channel and a ridge constructed across the slope. Diversions need a stable outlet to dispose of water safely.

In many places diversions are placed above critical slopes to divert runoff. Runoff over such slopes would cause serious erosion. Diversions can be used in the same way to protect construction areas. They can also be used on long slopes, in a series if necessary.

Permanent diversions should be seeded to the same grasses that cover the surrounding areas. If they are built to protect open spaces, they should blend into the landscape for both better appearance and ease of maintenance.

Berms Berms are a type of diversion. They are compacted earth ridges on a slight grade and have no channels, and they may be permanent or temporary.

Berms can be used to protect newly constructed slopes until the slopes are stabilized with permanent vegetation. They can be constructed across graded rights-of-way in a series and at intervals needed to intercept runoff. The side slopes of the berms are made flat enough to allow work vehicles to cross them.

Berms too must have stable outlets. Well-stabilized ungraded areas adjacent to the street rights-of-way are often used as temporary outlets. In many places half-channel flumes, sod, or other material can be used to make temporary outlets.

Storm Sewers Storm sewers dispose of runoff from the streets and adjacent lots. Temporary diversions may be needed to control runoff on the lots and convey it safely to the streets and storm sewers.

The use of storm sewers for runoff disposal does not prevent sediment from being deposited downstream. To reduce the sediment load carried by runoff through storm sewers during construction, some developers have improvised small sediment basins adjacent to sewer inlets. The sediment collected in the basins is removed following each runoff-producing rain.

Storm sewers should discharge at a place where the grade is stable. Generally an energy dissipater is needed to slow the force of the flow at the point of discharge.

Outlets Most outlets are grassed waterways, either natural or artificial, and serve to dispose safely of water from diversions and from parking lots, highways, and other areas. Natural waterways, or swales, can be improved by

SOURCE: *Controlling Erosion on Construction Sites*, U.S. Department of Agriculture, Soil Conservation Service, 1970.

grading, reshaping, and revegetating. Artificial outlets should have flat side slopes and a wide bottom so that they can be easily maintained. They should have adequate capacity.

Grass protects a channel against erosion by reducing the velocity of flow. The most suitable grass species are those that produce a dense uniform cover near the soil surface, are long-lived, can withstand small amounts of sedimentation, and provide protection during all seasons of the year. The species selected should be adapted to the locality and the site.

Jute netting or fiber glass can be used as a channel liner to protect the channel from erosion until vegetation becomes established. Liners may not be needed if the runoff can be diverted from the channel during the establishment period.

Waterway Stabilization Structures A waterway needs a stabilizing structure if its slope is so steep that the velocity of runoff exceeds the limit of protection that the vegetation alone gives. Grade stabilization structures, special culverts, and various kinds of pipe can be used in combination with vegetation. Energy dissipaters may be required. The structures should be designed and built to provide permanent stabilization.

Lined Channels The alternative to using vegetated waterways with grade stabilization structures is using lined channels. Such channels (paved ditches and valley gutters, for example) have many uses in urban areas where slopes are too steep or soils too unstable for control by vegetation alone. Fiber glass mats can be used as temporary lining for ditches and channels.

Sediment Basins The function of a sediment basin is to detain runoff and trap sediment, thus preventing damage to areas downstream. By detaining runoff, sediment basins also reduce peak flows. Basins can be excavated or formed by a combination of dam and excavation. Earth dams can be constructed across waterways to form basins. Under some conditions a highway embankment can serve as a dam. Sediment basins are almost always temporary structures. They are graded into the surrounding landscape after construction has been completed and the area has been stabilized. But they can be designed as permanent structures if there is a permanent need for them. Some industrial firms have preferred permanent basins that can be used later to protect downstream areas from accidentally released materials that would cause pollution.

The location, design, and construction of a sediment basin should be such that serious damage to areas downstream would be avoided if the basin failed. If the minimum storage requirement cannot be met, excavation to enlarge the basin and periodic cleanout may be necessary.

Sediment basins are constructed to discharge on stable ground below the dam. Emergency spillways should be added to increase safety. Exposed areas of the embankment and the emergency spillway should be protected by mulching and seeding.

Stream Channel and Bank Stabilization The increased runoff from construction sites may make it necessary to stabilize the stream channel below.

Stream channels can be stabilized by installing grade control structures or by paving. The undercutting of banks can be controlled by measures that withstand the flow, such as concrete structures or rock riprap built along the toe and lower facing of the bank, or by measures that dissipate the energy of the flow, such as jetties, piling, and fencing built into or along the channel. Realigning the channel may be desirable or necessary in many places, but it creates the risk of starting a new erosion cycle.

Stabilizing stream channels and stream banks is usually complex and costly. Control measures should be undertaken only on the basis of thorough engineering studies and plans. If a stream runs along or through a floodplain that is to be developed for parks and recreation, for example, aesthetic values may determine the methods of improvement.

Vegetative Measures Vegetative measures provide temporary cover to help control erosion during construction and permanent cover to stabilize the site after construction has been completed. The measures include the use of mulches and temporary and permanent cover crops.

Erosion can be controlled with less difficulty on some sites than on others during construction, and permanent cover is easy to establish on some sites and difficult on others. Establishing and maintaining good plant cover is easy in areas of fertile soil and moderate slopes. Usually such areas can be stabilized by using plants and cultural methods common in the community.

Sites that are difficult to stabilize because of exposed subsoil, steep slopes, a droughty exposure, and other conditions, require special treatment. Such sites are called critical areas because they erode severely and are the source of much sediment if they are not well stabilized.

Mulch Straw mulch can be used to protect constructed slopes and other areas brought to final grade at an unfavorable time for seeding. The areas can be seeded when the time is favorable without removing the mulch.

Mulch is essential in establishing good stands of grasses and legumes on steep cut-and-fill slopes and other areas where it is difficult to establish plants. By reducing runoff, mulch allows more water to infiltrate the soil. It also reduces the loss of soil moisture by evaporation, holds seed, lime, and fertilizer in place, and reduces seedling damage from the heaving of the soil caused by freezing and thawing.

The materials most widely used in mulching are small-grain straw, hay, and certain processed materials. Grain straw is easily applied and generally is more readily available than hay, and it costs less. In some places, certain hays are preferred because they are a source of seed of plants that can be used for stabilization. Straw and hay mulches are usually applied at the rate of $1\frac{1}{2}$ tons per acre.

A number of processed mulches are availa-

SOURCE: *Controlling Erosion on Construction Sites*, U.S. Department of Agriculture, Soil Conservation Service, 1970.

ble, and some show promise of greater use under specific conditions. Hydromulching, in which seed, fertilizer, and mulch are applied as a slurry, is a fast, all-in-one operation that requires little labor. Hydromulching may not be successful if it is carried out during a period of high-intensity storms.

Straw and hay mulches must be anchored to keep them from blowing or washing away. Anchoring methods include spraying the mulch with asphalt, tucking the mulch into the soil with a straight-blade disc, stapling netting over the mulch, and driving pegs into the mulched area at intervals of about 4 feet and interlacing them with twine.

Temporary Cover Temporary cover crops can be used when cover is needed for a few months or a year or two. If construction is delayed on a site that has been cleared and graded, temporary cover crops can be employed to protect the site from erosion. And they can be planted at a time of year that is unfavorable for seeding and establishing permanent cover.

Rapidly growing plants, such as annual rye grass, small grain, sudan grass, and millet, are most often used for temporary cover. Plants that are adapted to the locality and the season of the year during which protection is needed should always be used.

Permanent Cover Special care should be taken in selecting plants for permanent cover. There are many grasses and legumes, trees, shrubs, vines, and ground covers from which to choose in most humid areas of the United States, but only a few in most dry regions. Final choice should be based on the adaptation of the plants to the soils and climate, ease of establishment, suitability for a specific use, longevity or ability to self-reseed, maintenance requirements, aesthetic values, and other special qualities.

The best plants are those that are well adapted to the site and to the purpose for which they are to be used. For example, grasses used for waterway stabilization must be able to withstand submergence and provide a dense cover to prevent scouring of the channel. In play-

grounds, grasses must be able to withstand trampling. In some places, such as south-facing cut-and-fill slopes, the plants needed are those that are adapted to droughty areas. In other places, plants must be able to tolerate shade. Some plants can beautify as well as stabilize an area.

Maintenance may be the most important factor in selecting plants for permanent stabilization. Most tame grasses and legumes require much maintenance, and they gradually give way to native grasses, shrubs, and weedy plants if they are not mowed and fertilized regularly. In some areas native plants are preferred. On steep slopes and other inaccessible areas, it is preferable to select plants that require little or no maintenance. Sericea lespedeza, crown vetch, and honeysuckle, for example, are long-lived and provide good erosion control with a minimum of maintenance. Most native grasses, trees, and shrubs grow well with little or no maintenance.

Fibrous Materials A number of fibrous materials have special uses in erosion control. Jute netting, a coarse, open-mesh, weblike material, can be applied directly on the soil to protect newly seeded channels until vegetation becomes established. It can also be used in repairing outlets and diversions where gullies have cut the channel. In some places it can be used to hold down straw mulch. Cotton netting and paper netting are both lightweight; they can hold straw mulch in place and prevent it from blowing or washing away.

Solid, heavy-duty fiber glass matting can be used as a temporary channel liner where the water velocity is too high for the use of vegetation or where vegetation is not wanted. Impregnating the mat with asphalt prolongs its life. Perforated fiber glass matting can be used in the same way as jute netting to protect newly seeded channels. It can be used as a transition apron, lining the head of a channel to protect it from runoff, especially runoff from road culverts, which tends to cut a gully down the channel. And used as erosion stops, perforated matting can check rilling.

Fiber glass erosion stops have certain advan-

tages over rigid stops of masonry or wood. Soil often settles around rigid structures, causing a turbulent and erosive flow. The fiber glass stops are flexible and conform to the channel. Also, they are porous (water can seep through them), and subsurface drainage is improved.

Stabilizing Cut-and-Fill Slopes The first requirement in stabilizing cut-and-fill slopes is to prevent runoff from flowing over the face of the slopes. Temporary diversions, berms, shoulder dikes, or other measures should be used to intercept and divert the runoff. Permanent structures such as brow ditches and valley gutters are required where the areas contributing to runoff are large, for example, areas of highway construction. Small benches, interceptor ditches, or other measures can be used to protect long slopes from runoff originating on the slope itself.

Methods of establishing vegetation vary for different parts of the United States and depend on the plants used and on the soil and climate. In selecting plants and in getting them established, it is best to be guided by the methods commonly used and recommended in the particular area.

As a general rule, when seeding grasses and legumes it is advisable to prepare as good a seedbed as site conditions permit. Applications of lime and fertilizer should be based on local standards or on soil tests.

Usually a good stand can be obtained by broadcasting, drilling, or hydroseeding if other conditions are met. Mulching after seeding and then anchoring the mulch are essential in most areas. Irrigation is needed in many places.

Sodding is more costly than seeding, but it provides immediate protection. It should be used where the concentration of runoff is such that other methods of stabilization will not be effective. Sod can be laid whenever the soil is not frozen. Sod responds to a good seedbed and to lime and fertilizer. The strips of sod

SOURCE: *Controlling Erosion on Construction Sites*, U.S. Department of Agriculture, Soil Conservation Service, 1970.

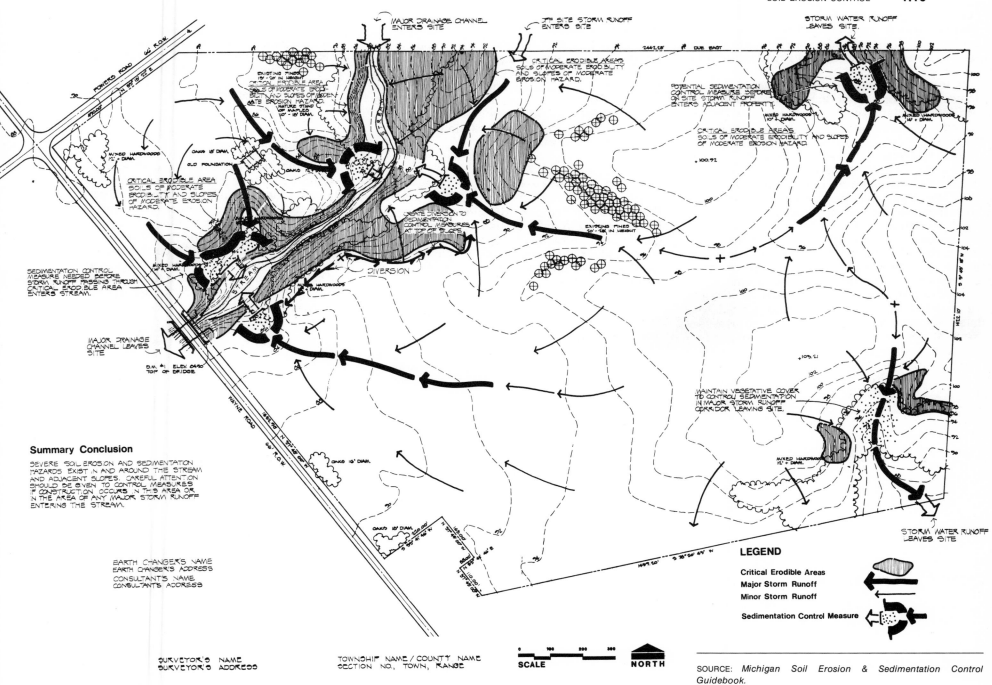

LEGEND

Critical Erodible Areas

Major Storm Runoff

Minor Storm Runoff

Sedimentation Control Measure

SCALE

NORTH

SOURCE: *Michigan Soil Erosion & Sedimentation Control Guidebook.*

Summary Conclusion

SEVERE SOIL EROSION AND SEDIMENTATION HAZARDS EXIST IN AND AROUND THE STREAM AND ADJACENT SLOPES. CAREFUL ATTENTION SHOULD BE GIVEN TO CONTROL MEASURES IF CONSTRUCTION OCCURS IN THIS AREA OR IN THE AREA OF ANY MAJOR STORM RUNOFF ENTERING THE STREAM.

EARTH CHANGER'S NAME
EARTH CHANGER'S ADDRESS
CONSULTANT'S NAME
CONSULTANT'S ADDRESS

SURVEYOR'S NAME
SURVEYOR'S ADDRESS

TOWNSHIP NAME / COUNTY NAME
SECTION NO., TOWN, RANGE

Figure 1-24 Site analysis.

should always be laid across the slope, anchored to the soil, and watered. Some grasses can be established by sprigging and chunk sodding.

If trees are used to stabilize steep slopes, they are usually planted in pure stands. Mulching is important. Vines are generally established by transplanting individual plants or crowns.

Site Analysis   The term "analysis" in this case means drawing conclusions about the information gathered during the site investigation. The objective of the analysis is to pinpoint site areas that are especially vulnerable to erosion or sedimentation because of existing topography, soils, vegetation, or drainage patterns. These characteristics must be interrelated in assessing the hazards of erosion and sedimentation for different site areas. The inventory and analysis information is of little value, however, if it is not used as a basis for later site planning decisions. After an assessment of erosion vulnerability has been made, an earth change plan can be developed so that the disturbance of vulnerable or critical areas

will be minimized.

The process of making specific conclusions about critically erodible areas involves interpretation of the inventory information already gathered for topography and soils (specifically, a slope interpretation and a soils survey). The following list illustrates the site conditions or combinations of conditions that determine critically erodible areas:

Condition 1: highly erodible soil   = critical area
Condition 2: high-erosion-hazard slope   = critical area
Condition 3: moderately erodible soil
             moderate erosion hazard slope = critical area

Conclusions   The considerations that should be addressed in an analysis of the site investigation information on topography, vegetation, soils, and existing drainage for site development are outlined below. Specific conclusions about these issues should be noted in the analysis.

1. Indicate where soils, topography, and vegetation combine to create critically erodible areas.
2. Indicate how the site or corridor relates to surrounding streams, drainageways, or other bodies of water. Assess the vulnerability to erosion

and sediment damage of these drainageways and surface waters and all off-site areas.
3. Indicate where storm-water runoff crosses the site boundaries. Indicate the potential options for disposing of storm-water runoff by including potential locations of sediment control structures.
4. Indicate how areas disturbed by construction might be protected from increasing surface storm-water runoff.

The map in Figure 1-24 provides a graphic example of what a site analysis might look like. By using the conclusions noted in the analysis above to guide the process of preparing an earth change plan, a plan that is strongly related to site conditions and minimizes soil erosion can be developed. An earth change plan developed in this way will be a direct response to soil erosion and sedimentation as well as other considerations of function, economics, engineering feasibility, and aesthetics.

SOURCE: _Michigan Soil Erosion & Sedimentation Control Guidebook._

1.11 Sources of Surveying and Geological Data

The governmental agencies in the accompanying table are sources of surveying and geological data.

GUIDE TO MAP SCALES

The table on page 40 is a guide to the conversion of map scales to linear and area measurements.

Agency	Nature of survey data
U.S. Geological Survey (USGS, Department of the interior)	Topographic maps and indexes; bench mark locations, level data, and tables of elevations; streamflow data; water resources; geologic maps; horizontal control data; monument location
National Ocean Survey (Department of Commerce)	Topographic maps; coastline charts; topographic and hydrographic studies of inland lakes and reservoirs; bench mark locations, level data, and tables of elevations; horizontal control data; state tables for lambert and transverse Mercator projections; tide and current tables; coast pilots' information; seismological studies; magnetic studies; aeronautical charts
Bureau of Land Management	Township plots, showing land divisions; state maps, showing public land and reservations; survey progress map of the United States, showing the progress of public-land surveys
Army Map Service (Department of the Army)	Topographic maps and charts
Corps of Engineers (Department of the Army)	Topographic maps; charts of Great Lakes and connecting waters
Board of Engineers for Rivers and Harbors (Department of the Army)	Maps and charts of ports and permits for construction of bridges, piers, and so on in navigable rivers and harbors
Coastal Engineering Research Center (Department of the Army)	Beach erosion data
Mississippi River Commission (Department of the Army)	Hydraulic studies and flood control information
Soil Conservation Service (SCS, Department of Agriculture)	Soil charts and maps; index
U.S. Forest Service (Department of Agriculture)	Forest reserve maps including topography and culture and vegetation classification
U.S. Postal Service	Rural free delivery maps by counties, showing roads, streams, and so on
Naval Oceanographic Office (Department of the Navy)	Nautical charts; navigational manuals; aeronautical charts
International Boundary Commission, United States and Canada	Topographic maps for ½ to 2½ miles on either side of the United States–Canadian boundaries
Local municipalities: county, town, village, city	Street maps; zoning maps, drainage maps; horizontal and vertical control data; utility maps

Scale	Feet per inch	Inches per 1000 feet	Inches per mile	Miles per inch	Meters per inch	Acres per square inch	Square inches per acre	Square miles per square inch
1:500	41.67	24.00	126.72	0.008	12.70	0.040	25.091	0.00006
1:600	50.00	20.00	105.60	0.009	15.24	0.057	17.424	0.00009
1:1,000	83.33	12.00	63.36	0.016	25.40	0.159	6.273	0.00025
1:1,200	100.00	10.00	52.80	0.019	30.48	0.230	4.356	0.00036
1:1,500	125.00	8.00	42.24	0.024	38.10	0.359	2.788	0.00056
1:2,000	166.67	6.00	31.68	0.032	50.80	0.638	1.568	0.00100
1:2,400	200.00	5.00	26.40	0.038	60.96	0.918	1.089	0.0014
1:2,500	208.33	4.80	25.34	0.039	63.50	0.996	1.004	0.0016
1:3,000	250.00	4.00	21.12	0.047	76.20	1.435	0.697	0.0022
1:4,000	333.33	3.00	15.84	0.063	101.60	2.551	0.392	0.0040
1:5,000	416.67	2.40	12.67	0.079	127.00	3.986	0.251	0.0062
1:6,000	500.00	2.00	10.56	0.095	152.40	5.739	0.174	0.0090
1:7,920	660.00	1.515	8.00	0.125	201.17	10.000	0.100	0.0156
1:8,000	666.67	1.500	7.92	0.126	203.20	10.203	0.098	0.0159
1:9,600	800.00	1.250	6.60	0.152	243.84	14.692	0.068	0.0230
1:10,000	833.33	1.200	6.336	0.158	254.00	15.942	0.063	0.0249
1:12,000	1,000.00	1.000	5.280	0.189	304.80	22.957	0.044	0.0359
1:15,000	1,250.00	0.800	4.224	0.237	381.00	35.870	0.028	0.0560
1:15,840	1,320.00	0.758	4.000	0.250	402.34	40.000	0.025	0.0625
1:19,200	1,600.00	0.625	3.300	0.303	487.68	58.770	0.017	0.0918
1:20,000	1,666.67	0.600	3.168	0.316	508.00	63.769	0.016	0.0996
1:21,120	1,760.00	0.568	3.000	0.333	536.45	71.111	0.014	0.1111
1:24,000	2,000.00	0.500	2.640	0.379	609.60	91.827	0.011	0.1435
1:25,000	2,083.33	0.480	2.534	0.395	635.00	99.639	0.010	0.1557
1:31,680	2,640.00	0.379	2.000	0.050	804.67	160.000	0.006	0.2500
1:48,000	4,000.00	0.250	1.320	0.758	1,219.20	367.309	0.003	0.5739
1:62,500	5,208.33	0.192	1.014	0.986	1,587.50	622.744	0.0016	0.9730
1:63,360	5,280.00	0.189	1.000	1.000	1,609.35	640.000	0.0016	1.00
1:100,000	8,333.33	0.120	0.634	1.578	2,540.00	1,594.225	0.0006	2.49
1:125,000	10,416.67	0.096	0.507	1.973	3175.01	2,490.980	0.0004	3.89
1:126,720	10,560.00	0.095	0.500	2.000	3,218.69	2,560.000	0.0004	4.00
1:250,000	20,833.33	0.048	0.253	3.946	6,350.01	9,963.907	0.0001	15.57
1:253,440	21,120.00	0.047	0.250	4.000	6,437.39	10,244.202	0.0001	16.00
1:500,000	41,666.67	0.024	0.127	7.891	12,700.02	39,855.627	$0.\overset{4}{-}25$	62.27
1:750,000	62,500.00	0.016	0.084	11.837	19,050.04	89,675.161	$0.\overset{4}{-}11$	140.12
1:1,000,000	83,333.33	0.012	0.063	15.783	25,400.05	159,422.507	$0.\overset{5}{-}62$	249.10
FORMULAS	$\dfrac{\text{Scale}}{12}$	$\dfrac{12,000}{\text{Scale}}$	$\dfrac{63,360}{\text{Scale}}$	$\dfrac{\text{Scale}}{63,360}$	Feet per inch $\times$ 0.3048006	$\dfrac{\text{Scale}^2}{43,560 \times 144}$	$\dfrac{43,560 \times 144}{\text{Scale}^2}$	$\dfrac{\text{Feet per inch}^2}{5,280^2}$

1.12 Mapping of Physical Environment

MASTER PLAN

Many basic data concerning the physical characteristics of a site can be obtained from local planning and assessors' offices. These include topographic, soil, climatic, and property maps (see Figure 1-25). Although the scale in some cases may not be readily suitable for small parcels, the maps nevertheless can help to establish boundary conditions around the site.

The following pages give examples of the most generally used sources and map forms.

TOPOGRAPHIC MAPS

The U.S. Geological Survey continues to publish the familiar and very widely used topographic maps on a variety of scales (see Figure 1-26). Quadrangles covering 7½ minutes of latitude and longitude are published on a scale of 1:24,000 (1 inch represents 2000 feet). Quadrangles covering 15 minutes of latitude and longitude are published on a scale of 1:62,500 (1 inch represents approximately 1 mile), and quadrangles covering 2 degrees of longitude by 1 degree of latitude are published on a scale of 1:250,000 (1 inch represents approximately 4 miles). Each quadrangle is designated by the name of a city, town, or prominent natural feature within it.

The maps are printed in five colors. The cultural features such as roads, railroads, and civil boundaries and lettering are in black. Water bodies are shown in blue. Green is used to identify areas of woodland. Red is used to identify developed urban areas and to classify roads. Features of terrain relief are shown by brown contour lines. The contour intervals differ according to the scale of the map and the amount of local relief.

Most topographic maps are available either with or without the green woodland overprint. Also, a special printing on which both green woodland tint and contours are omitted is available for certain quadrangles. These quadrangles are identified on the Geological Survey index maps.

As a means of reducing the time required to

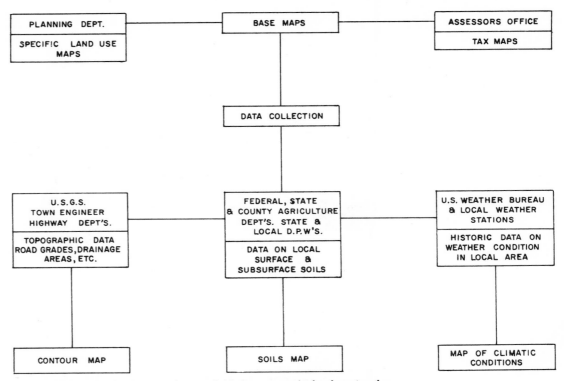

Figure 1-25 Source and type of site data available from maps of a local master plan.

revise its maps, the Geological Survey has begun a new type of map updating, called interim revision. Using this technique, revisions to published maps are compiled in the office from recent aerial photography and then are printed on the published map in a distinctive heliotrope color. No field checking is performed under this system, and production time is approximately one-sixth of that required for standard revision.

An index map identifying published maps and giving their publication date is published by the Geological Survey. This map contains details on other maps published by the Geological Survey as well as details on how to purchase maps. Free copies of the index map may be obtained from the Map Information Office, U.S. Geological Survey, Sunrise Valley Drive, Reston, Virginia 22092.

HYDROGRAPHIC CHARTS

The navigable waters in and around the United States are shown on a variety of maps and charts. The more common of these, such as topographic and county maps, generally do not include much detail on hydrographic features. Therefore, persons needing information on such features as navigational aids, underwater hazards, lights, and harbor facilities must consult specialized hydrographic charts. The principal agencies producing such charts are the National Ocean Survey and the Lake Survey Center.

SOURCE: *Mapnotes,* New York State Department of Transportation, 1971.

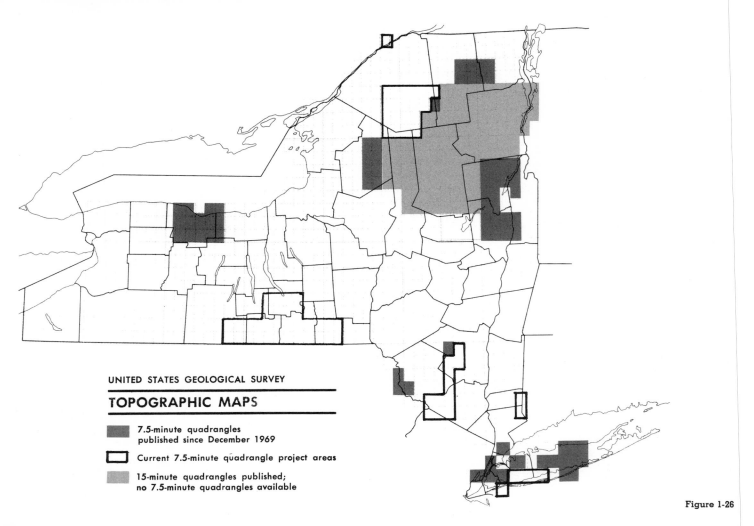

UNITED STATES GEOLOGICAL SURVEY

TOPOGRAPHIC MAPS

- 7.5-minute quadrangles published since December 1969
- Current 7.5-minute quadrangle project areas
- 15-minute quadrangles published; no 7.5-minute quadrangles available

Figure 1-26

National Ocean Survey The National Ocean Survey, previously known as the U.S. Coast and Geodetic Survey, publishes a wide variety of charts of United States coastal waters (see Figure 1-27).

Small Craft Charts These compact, accordion-folded charts are specifically designed for cockpit use and include special features such as large-scale harbor area insets, locations of facilities, lists of services and supplies, tide tables, current tabulations, weather data, course bearings, and illustrated whistle and distress signals. They are constructed from the same source material and to the same high standards as conventional charts and are issued with protective covers or jackets.

Harbor Charts These charts are intended for navigation and anchorage in harbors and smaller waterways and are published at scales of 1:50,000 and larger, depending on the size and importance of the harbor and the number and types of existing dangers.

Coast Charts These charts are intended for coastwise navigation inside offshore reefs and shoals, for entering bays and harbors of considerable size, and for navigating certain inland waterways. Their scales range from 1:50,000 to 1:100,000.

General Charts These charts are intended for the navigation of vessels whose positions can be fixed by landmarks, lights, buoys, and

SOURCE: *Mapnotes,* New York State Department of Transportation, 1971.

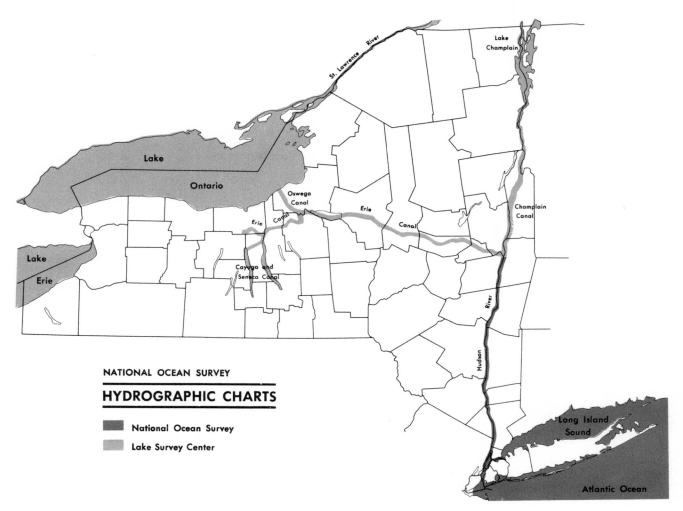

NATIONAL OCEAN SURVEY

HYDROGRAPHIC CHARTS

▮ National Ocean Survey

▮ Lake Survey Center

Figure 1-27

characteristic soundings but whose courses are well offshore. Their scales range from 1:100,000 to 1:600,000.

Sailing Charts These charts are plotting charts for offshore sailing between coastal ports and for approaching coasts from the open ocean. They are published at scales smaller than 1:600,000.

CENSUS MAPS

Population data published by the federal Bureau of the Census are summarized for many different types and sizes of areas. Many of the areas coincide with political boundaries, but these areas are frequently unsatisfactory for meaningful interpretation of the data. The Bureau of the Census therefore delineates areas that correlate more closely with settlement patterns and centers of activity.

To aid the census user in interpreting and using the various summaries of data, the Bureau of the Census publishes a variety of maps that delineate the limits of the statistical areas it uses. Figure 1-28 below summarizes

these maps and includes information on how to obtain copies. Some of the maps listed are published as part of census reports, and these are identified in the figure. Individual copies of the maps are usually available, but they generally cost more when they are purchased separately. Reproducible copies (either diazo

SOURCE: *Mapnotes,* New York State Department of Transportation, 1971.

MAP SERIES	SCALE	NUMBER OF MAP SHEETS	PRICE	SHEET SIZE	AVAILABILITY
US COUNTY OUTLINE MAP: Contains boundaries and names of all counties in the US. State boundaries are in black, county boundaries and names in black or blue.	1:5,000,000 (1" = approx. 79 mi.)	1 map sheet	$0.20 for black edition, $0.25 for black/blue edition	26" x 41"	Available from Government Printing Office
COUNTY SUBDIVISION MAPS: State maps showing 1970 boundaries of counties and county subdivisions, the location of all incorporated places and those unincorporated places for which population figures are published (Replaces Minor Civil Division Map)	Generally 1:750,000 (1" = approx. 12 mi.)	1 per state, except for each of the combinations noted below: Mass.-Conn.-R.I.-Vt.-N.H. D.C.-Del.-Md.	$0.20 per map ($9.40 for entire set)	36" x 48"	Available from Government Printing Office
COUNTY MAPS (Unpublished): Contain boundaries of MCD-CCD's, incorporated places, tracts (where established), and enumeration districts.	Generally 1" = 2 mi.	1 per county except for very large counties	$1.00 and up depending on map size	18" x 24" and larger	Available from Central Users' Service
TRACT OUTLINE MAPS: Show tract boundaries and incorporated limits for places over 25,000 population for each SMSA.	Varies depending on size and complexity of the area	1 to 4 per area	Varies depending on size of report	Varies	Available as part of tract reports (PHC(1) Series) from Government Printing Office. Preliminary maps may be obtained from the Central Users' Service
URBANIZED AREA MAPS: Show extent of and all areas included within 1970 Urbanized Areas.	1:250,000 (1" = approx. 4 miles)	1 to 6 per area	Varies	9" x 11⅓"	Available as part of final population reports (PC(1)A Series) from Government Printing Office
METROPOLITAN MAPS (MMS): Published for Urbanized Areas for which block statistics are available, contains all Census boundaries down to block level.	1" = 2000' with a few enlargements at 1" = 1000'	2 to 144 depending on size of area	Varies depending on size of area	18" x 24"	Available as part of Block Statistics reports (HC(3) Series) from Government Printing Office (Also available in microfiche form (4 maps to a sheet) from the National Technical Information Service, US Dept. of Commerce, Springfield, Va. 22151
PLACE MAPS (Unpublished): Prepared for incorporated and unincorporated places not shown on MMS, contains boundaries of tracts (where established), enumeration districts, and wards (where reported to the Bureau).	Varies with the size of the area, range from 1" = 400' to 1" = 1500'	Generally 1 per place	$1.50 and up depending on size of the map	Varies	Available from Central Users' Service

Figure 1-28 United States census maps available for public use.

mylars or photographic negatives or positives) are available for all census maps. The cost of these copies is higher than the cost of paper prints.

SANBORN MAPS

Utilization The Sanborn fire insurance map serves numerous diversified industries and purposes. This accurately scaled visual depiction of street layout, building location and construction, exposures, occupancies, fire hazards, and fire protection is a valuable guide to the fire and casualty underwriter. Fire insurance companies maintain complete nationwide files of Sanborn maps in their principal offices. These form a graphic record for review and underwriting of individual risks as well as block liability as daily reports are received from the field. See Figure 1-29 for a diagram of a residential block.

Mapping, the noting of liability on the face of the map, is an important function in underwriting. Insurance companies utilize the map as a source of original entry on individual risks, generally recording such information as policy numbers, expiration dates, amounts of net retention, and distribution of liability between buildings and contents, thus completing a visual record of current commitments.

Local fire insurance agents are equipped with Sanborn maps of their respective cities and towns. The maps' careful identification of risks by map volume, page, block, and house number on daily reports renders a helpful, timesaving service. Maps are kept up to date by correction slips made from periodic field surveys covering changes since the previous inspection of the territory.

Federal, state, county, and municipal governmental agencies rely on Sanborn maps to save costly field inspections and to keep a permanent record of valuable information. The

SOURCE: *The Sanborn Map*, Sanborn Map Company, Inc., Pelham, N.Y.

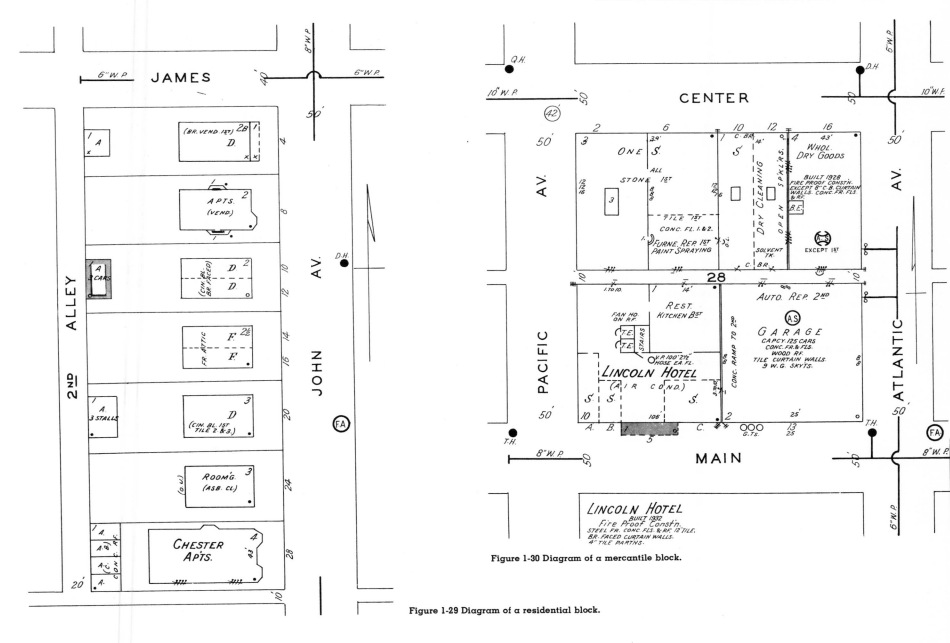

Figure 1-30 Diagram of a mercantile block.

Figure 1-29 Diagram of a residential block.

SOURCE: *The Sanborn Map*, Sanborn Map Company, Inc., Pelham, N.Y.

maps are widely used by municipal and county departments such as building, education, engineering, health and sanitation, highway, planning and zoning, public libraries, public works, sewer, tax assessment, and water and by city managers. Utility companies find them invaluable as an original record of their outside plant data. Banks and mortgage and life insurance companies utilize them in underwriting mortgage loans, recording their commitments much in the manner of the fire insurance companies.

In recent years the Sanborn Map Company has developed special market analysis maps, converting for marketing studies the wealth of detail of individual communities appearing in the standard fire insurance map. Sanborn's nationwide corps of field engineers and publishers has accumulated an unparalleled record of the physical growth and current status of municipalities throughout the United States. The facilities of the company are available for special surveys upon request.

Narrative Description of a Mercantile Block   The scale of the block shown in Figure 1-30 is 50 feet to the inch, and the direction is indicated by the meridian in the right margin.

The block is bounded on the north by Center Street, on the east by Atlantic Avenue, on the south by Main Street, and on the west by Pacific Avenue. All thoroughfares are 50 feet in width, as indicated by the figures at the extremity of each street. This block is elevated 42 feet above the city datum, as indicated by the figure in the circle at the intersection of Pacific Avenue and Center Street.

The number of the block is 28, as indicated by the prominent figure in the center of the 10-foot alley that divides the block into equal portions. This number represents the official designation for the block provided by the city or an arbitrary designation supplied by the Sanborn Map Company in the absence of a suitable official number.

5 Main Street   The size of the building is 100 by 100 feet. As indicated by the name, it is a hotel building.

On the first floor in the southwest corner of the building there is a drugstore *S,* the extent of which is indicated by a broken line, 50 by 15 feet. Adjoining this to east is a florist shop *S,* 30 by 15 feet. At the southeast corner there is a haberdashery *S,* 40 by 30 feet. In the northeast corner of the building there is a restaurant *Rest.,* 50 by 50 feet, the kitchen of which is located directly underneath in the basement, as indicated.

With the exception of the 50-by-50-foot section in the northeast corner, the main part of the building contains ten stories, as indicated by the figure in the southwest corner, and is 106 feet in height from the street level to the roof level, as indicated by the figure in the center of the Main Street side of the building.

The 50-by-50-foot section in the northeast corner of the building contains only one story, as indicated by the figure in the northwest corner of this section, and is 14 feet in height from the street level to the roof level.

SOURCE: *The Sanborn Map,* Sanborn Map Company, Inc., Pelham, N.Y.

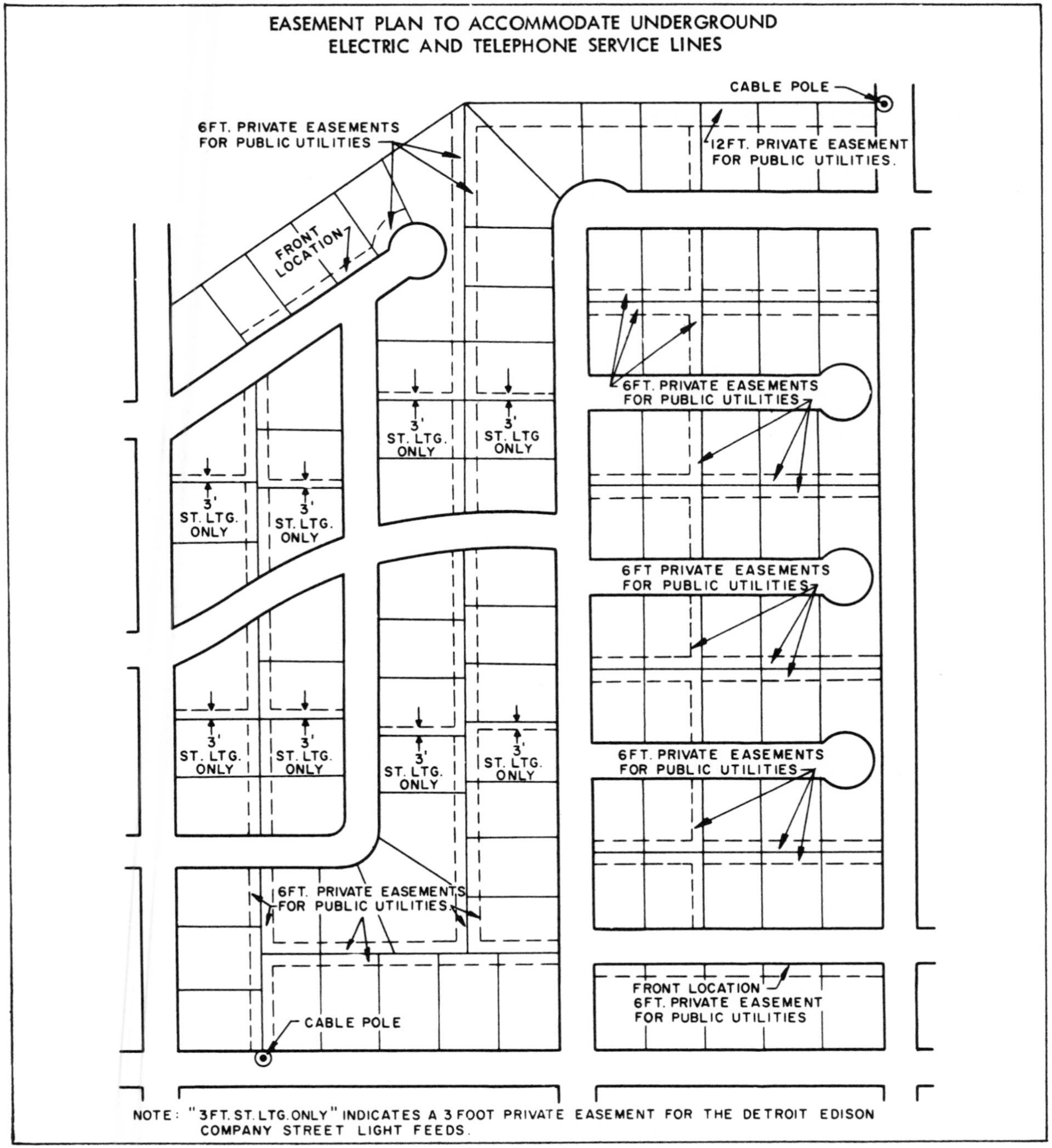

EASEMENT PLAN TO ACCOMMODATE UNDERGROUND
ELECTRIC AND TELEPHONE SERVICE LINES

NOTE: "3 FT. ST. LTG. ONLY" INDICATES A 3 FOOT PRIVATE EASEMENT FOR THE DETROIT EDISON
COMPANY STREET LIGHT FEEDS.

Figure 1-31

1.13 Utility Easements

Underground installations in new subdivisions are usually located within easements along rear lot lines. The easement plan in Figure 1-31, prepared by the Detroit Edison Company and the Michigan Bell Telephone Company, is typical. A utility easement guide prepared jointly by the two companies suggests the following design criteria for underground service lines:

In general, the locations of easements for underground service lines are similar to those required for overhead service lines, in that easements should be located along rear or side lot lines, or should be provided across lots in some cases. In addition, easements along front lot lines will be required at some locations.

Subdivision layout, topography, natural obstructions, and the use of these easements for water, sewer, and drainage facilities will influence the design of an easement system adequate for an underground distribution system.

SOURCE: *Easement Planning for Utility Services*, Detroit Edison Company–Michigan Bell Telephone Company, 1962.

1.14 Conversion Factors

Linear   Linear measure is used to express distances and to indicate the differences in elevation. The standard units of linear measure are the foot and the meter. In surveying operations, both units are frequently divided into tenths, hundredths, and thousandths for measurements. When long distances are involved, the foot is expanded into the statute mile, and the meter into the kilometer. The accompanying table shows the conversion factors for the most commonly used linear measurements.

1	Inches	Feet	Yards	Statute miles	Nautical miles	Millimeters
Inch	1	0.0833	0.0277			25.40
Foot	12	1	0.333			304.8
Yard	36	3	1	0.00056		914.4
Statute mile	63,360	5,280	1,760	1	0.8684	
Nautical mile	72,963	6,080	2,026	1.1516	1	
Millimeter	0.0394	0.0033	0.0011			1
Centimeter	0.3937	0.0328	0.0109			10
Decimeter	3.937	0.328	0.1093			100
Meter	39.37	3.2808	1.0936	0.0006	0.0005	1,000
Decameter	393.7	32.81	10.94	0.0062	0.0054	10,000
Hectometer	3,937	328.1	109.4	0.0621	0.0539	100,000
Kilometer	39,370	3,281	1,094	0.6214	0.5396	1,000,000
Myriameter	393,700	32,808	10,936	6.2137	5.3959	10,000,000

1	Centimeters	Decimeters	Meters	Decameters	Hectometers	Kilometers	Myriameters
Inch	2.540	0.2540	0.0254	0.0025	0.0003		
Foot	30.48	3.048	0.3048	0.0305	0.0030	0.0003	
Yard	91.44	9.144	0.9144	0.0914	0.0091	0.0009	
Statute mile	160,930	16,093	1,609	160.9	16.09	1.6093	0.1609
Nautical mile	185,325	18,532	1,853	185.3	18.53	1.8532	0.1853
Millimeter	0.1	0.01	0.001	0.0001			
Centimeter	1	0.1	0.01	0.001	0.0001		
Decimeter	10	1	0.1	0.01	0.001	0.0001	
Meter	100	10	1	0.1	0.01	0.001	0.0001
Decameter	1,000	100	10	1	0.1	0.01	0.001
Hectometer	10,000	1,000	100	10	1	0.1	0.01
Kilometer	100,000	10,000	1,000	100	10	1	0.1
Myriameter	1,000,000	100,000	10,000	1,000	100	10	1

Example 1:
Problem: Reduce 76 centimeters to ? inches
    76 cm × 0.3937 = 29 inches.
Answer: There are 29 inches in 76 centimeters.
Example 2:
Problem: How many feet are there in 2.74 meters?

$$\frac{2.74}{0.3048} = 9 \text{ feet}$$

Answer: There are approximately 9 feet in 2.74 meters.

Area Surveys are often made to obtain measured data from which area can be computed. The names of area units are frequently derived from the linear units, since area is the product of two linear measurements. The accompanying table shows the exact comparative values of some of the units. See also Figure 1-32.

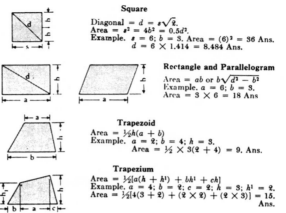

Square

Diagonal $= d = s\sqrt{2}$.
Area $= s^2 = 4b^2 = 0.5d^2$.
Example. $s = 6$; $b = 3$. Area $= (6)^2 = 36$ Ans.
$d = 6 \times 1.414 = 8.484$ Ans.

Rectangle and Parallelogram

Area $= ab$ or $b\sqrt{d^2 - b^2}$
Example. $a = 6$; $b = 3$.
Area $= 3 \times 6 = 18$ Ans

Trapezoid

Area $= \frac{1}{2}h(a + b)$
Example. $a = 2$; $b = 4$; $h = 3$.
Area $= \frac{1}{2} \times 3(2 + 4) = 9$. Ans.

Trapezium

Area $= \frac{1}{2}[a(h + h^1) + bh^1 + ch]$
Example. $a = 4$; $b = 2$; $c = 2$; $h = 3$; $h^1 = 2$.
Area $= \frac{1}{2}[4(3 + 2) + (2 \times 2) + (2 \times 3)] = 15$. Ans.

Triangles

Both formulas apply to both figures
Area $= \frac{1}{2}bh$.
Example. $h = 3$; $b = 5$.
Area $= \frac{1}{2}(3 \times 5) = 7\frac{1}{2}$. Ans.
Area $= \sqrt{S(S - a)(S - b)(S - c)}$ when $S = \frac{a + b + c}{2}$
Example. $a = 2$; $b = 3$; $c = 4$.
$S = \frac{2 + 3 + 4}{2} = 4.5$
Area $= \sqrt{4.5(4.5 - 2)(4.5 - 3)(4.5 - 4)} = 2.9$. Ans.

Circle

$\pi = 3.1416$; $A =$ area; $d =$ diameter; $p =$ circumference or periphery; $r =$ radius.
$p = \pi d = 3.1416d$. $\quad p = 2\sqrt{\pi A} = 3.54\sqrt{A}$
$p = 2\pi r = 6.2832r$. $\quad p = \frac{2A}{r} = \frac{4A}{d}$
$d = \frac{p}{\pi} = \frac{p}{3.1416}$ $\quad d = 2\sqrt{\frac{A}{\pi}} = 1.128\sqrt{A}$
$r = \frac{p}{2\pi} = \frac{p}{6.2832}$ $\quad r = \sqrt{\frac{A}{\pi}} = 0.564\sqrt{A}$
$A = \frac{\pi d^2}{4} = 0.7854d^2$ $\quad A = \frac{p^2}{4\pi} = \frac{p^2}{12.57}$
$A = \pi r^2 = 3.1416r^2$ $\quad A = \frac{pr}{2} = \frac{pd}{4}$

Figure 1-32 Areas of plane figures.

	Square inch	Square link	Square foot	Square vara (California)	Square vara (Texas)	Square yard	Square meter	Square rod, pole, or perch	Square chain	Rood	Acre	Square kilometer	Square mile (statute)
Square inch	1	0.01594	0.00694										
Square link	62.7264	1	0.4356	0.0576	0.05645	0.0484	0.04047	0.0016					
Square foot	144	2.29568	1	0.13223	0.1296	0.11111	0.0929	0.00367					
Square vara (California)	1089	17.3611	7.5625	1	0.9801	0.84028	0.70258	0.02778	0.00174				
Square vara (Texas)	1,111.11	17.7136	7.71605	1.0203	1	0.85734	0.71685	0.02834	0.00177				
Square yard	1,296	20.6612	9	1.19008	1.1664	1	0.83613	0.03306	0.00207				
Square meter	1,549.80	24.7104	10.7639	1.42332	1.395	1.19599	1	0.03954	0.00247				
Square rod, pole, or perch		625	272.25	36	35.2836	30.25	25.2930	1	0.0625	0.025	0.00625		
Square chain		10,000	4,356	576	564.538	484	404.687	16	1	0.4	0.1		
Rood		25,000	10,890	1,440	1,411.34	1,210	1,011.72	40	2.5	1	0.25	0.00101	
Acre		100,000	43,560	5,760	5,645.38	4,840	4,046.87	160	10	4	1	0.00405	0.00156
Square kilometer							1,000,000	39,536.7	2,471.044	988.418	247.104	1	0.3861
Square mile (statute)							102,400	6,400	2,560	640	2.59	1	

1.15 Graphic Analysis

VIEWS: VISUAL PERSPECTIVES AND ISOMETRICS

Computer-drawn illustrations can communicate the visual feelings of a land area. A given site can quickly be observed in a series of drawings shown from various directions of view. By using these drawings, an individual can extract and analyze a great deal of information in a short time.

Large land areas can easily be illustrated. Figure 1-33 is a ski resort in Park City, Utah. The visual perspective communicates a quick impression of the mountains and valleys and their distinct topographic values for skiing purposes.

The computer produces both two-dimensional and three-dimensional cross sections accurately and inexpensively. Sections, at any desired point or along any line, can easily be generated and plotted.

Figure 1-34 displays the proposed grading changes for a regional park, Prado Dam, in southern California. The visual effects of the proposed park are quickly communicated.

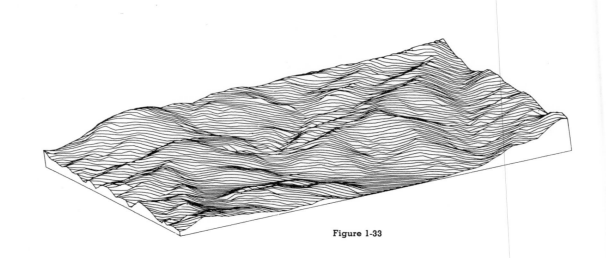

Figure 1-33

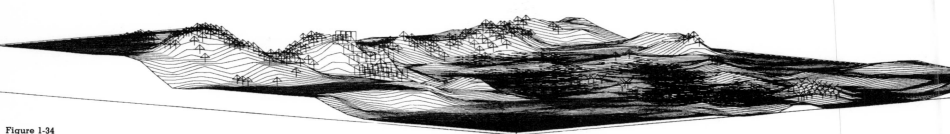

Figure 1-34

SOURCE: *Land Planning Tools,* Environmental Systems Research Institute, 14 North Fifth Street, Redlands, Calif.

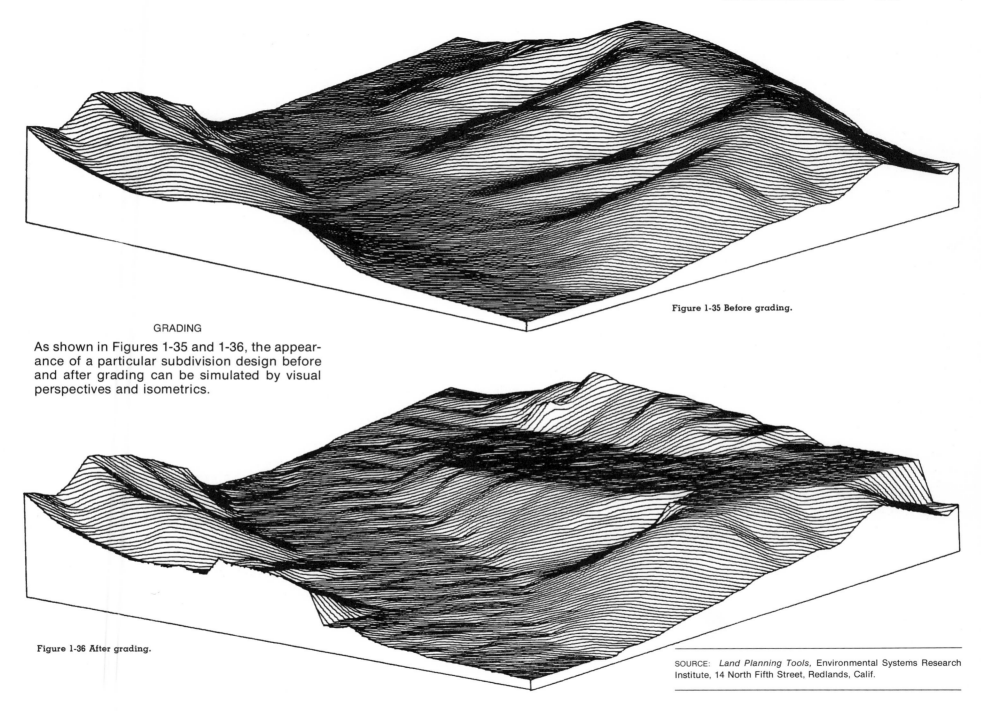

Figure 1-35 Before grading.

GRADING

As shown in Figures 1-35 and 1-36, the appearance of a particular subdivision design before and after grading can be simulated by visual perspectives and isometrics.

Figure 1-36 After grading.

SOURCE: *Land Planning Tools,* Environmental Systems Research Institute, 14 North Fifth Street, Redlands, Calif.

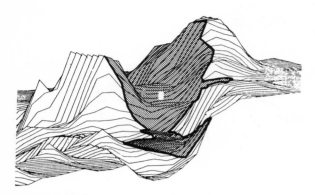

Figure 1-37 Dark areas are exposed.

EXPOSURE

The visual exposure of a single point or the relative exposure of a land area can be analyzed by the computer. Figure 1-37a is a single-point analysis that displays with dark grid cells areas that can be seen in 360 degrees when one is standing at a point of observation. This analysis of visual exposure for a given viewing point can be accomplished by using a standard computer data bank.

Figure 1-37b displays the relative visual exposure of a proposed park site near San Diego. In this example, the darker cells are more visible than the other cells, whereas the lighter shades of gray symbolize the less visible cells.

The single-point exposure has been used in locating vista points, restaurants, water towers, and refuse sites. The relative-exposure analysis is beneficial in the allocation of land uses. Open spaces might be located in high-exposure areas, while industry, power lines, and transportation might be located in low-exposure areas.

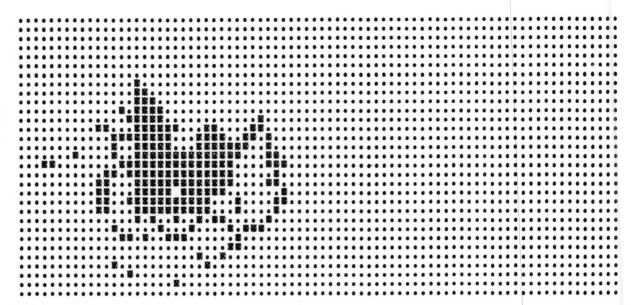

(a) Point exposure.

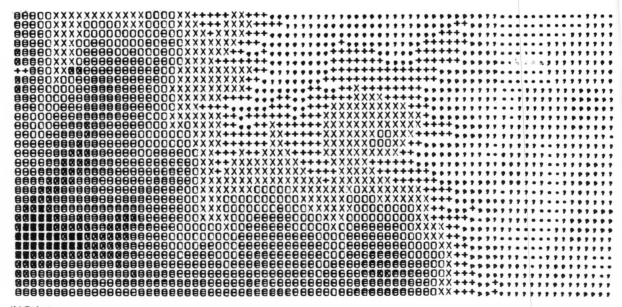

(b) Relative exposure.

SOURCE: *Land Planning Tools,* Environmental Systems Research Institute, 14 North Fifth Street, Redlands, Calif.

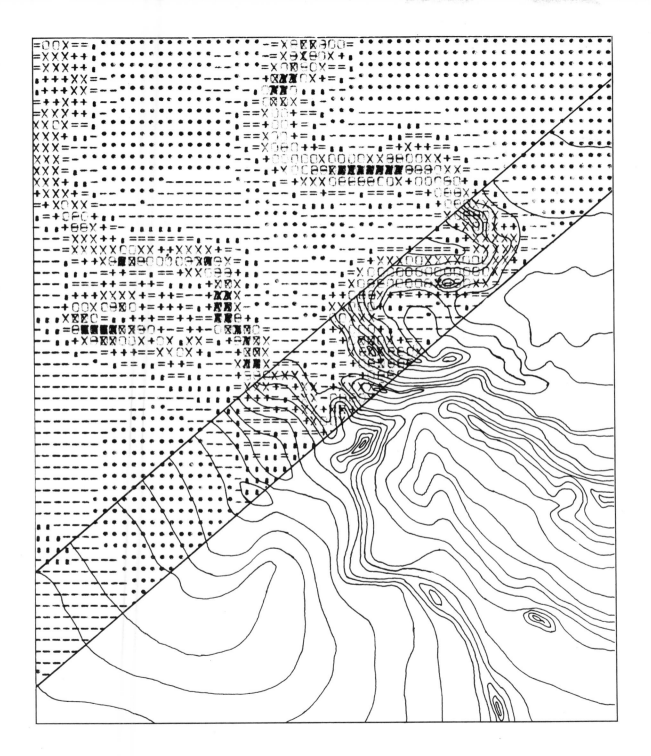

SLOPES

Topographic slope analysis is an important factor in land evaluation. This is an example of a computer service that analyzes graphically the relative percentage of slope for landscape terrain. This analysis has been extremely effective in evaluating the slope constraints on land developments and road designs. Normally, such an analysis is extremely time-consuming and suffers from inaccuracy. With the use of the computer technique, however, slopes can be rapidly located with a minimum of cost and effort.

Figure 1-38 compares a normal map of topography with a computer-produced slope map. Changes in tone represent changes in relative gradient. The key shows the gray tones that relate to the varying percentages of slope.

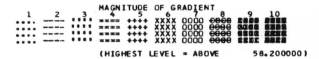

MAGNITUDE OF GRADIENT

(HIGHEST LEVEL = ABOVE 58.200000)

Figure 1-38

SOURCE: *Land Planning Tools,* Environmental Systems Research Institute, 14 North Fifth Street, Redlands, Calif.

CUT AND FILL

Accurate and inexpensive cut-and-fill analysis can be done by the computer. This analysis uses data banks of existing and proposed topography to calculate the differences in each grid cell (normally a 10-foot square). Five separate computer printouts are prepared:

1. Map of cut-and-fill areas
2. Map of relative cuts
3. Map of relative fills
4. Cut-and-fill balance
5. Elevation and volume differences at each grid cell

Two of the printouts are shown in Figure 1-39a and b.

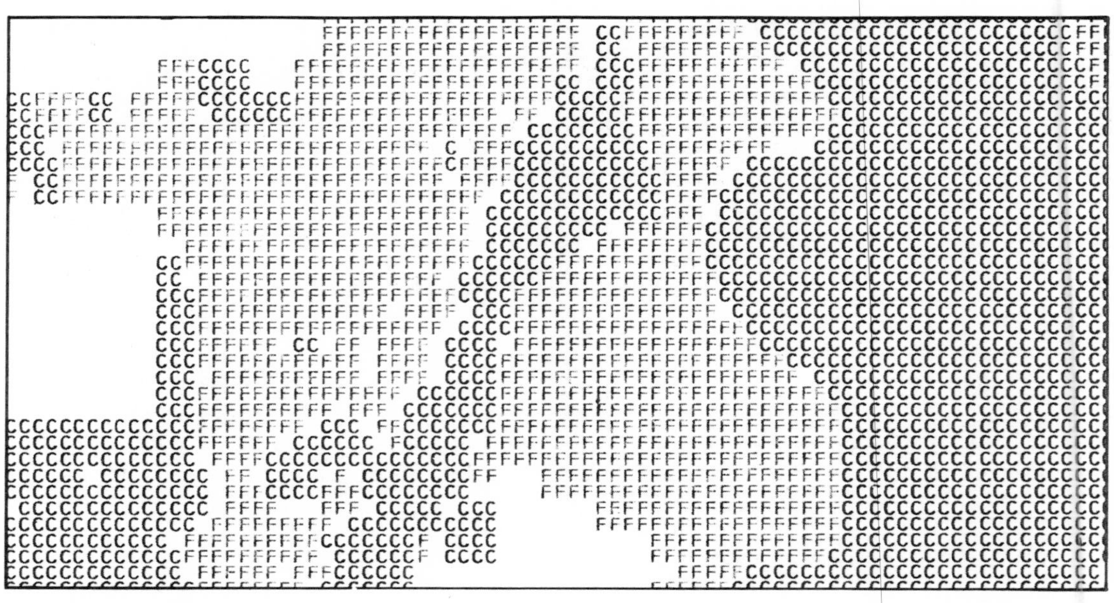

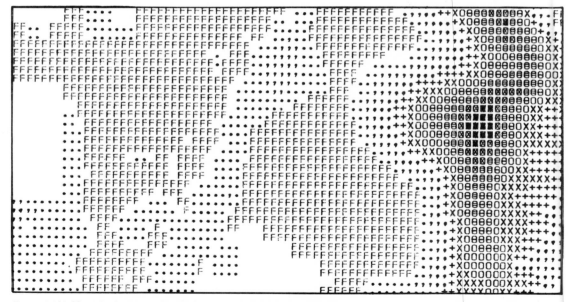

Figure 1-39a Map of cut-and-fill areas.

Figure 1-39b Map of relative cut (the darkest area indicates the greatest cut).

SOURCE: *Land Planning Tools*, Environmental Systems Research Institute, 14 North Fifth Street, Redlands, Calif.

Figure 1-40 Topographic map.

TOPOGRAPHIC MAPS

Extremely accurate topographic maps can be prepared from field survey data or other sources of point information. The computer program uses a highly advanced interpolation technique for producing contour lines. As shown in Figure 1-40, topographic elevations are indicated along given contour lines. A graphic and a numerical scale are displayed at the base of the drawing.

SOURCE: *Land Planning Tools,* Environmental Systems Research Institute, 14 North Fifth Street, Redlands, Calif.

WATERSHED AREAS

Land planning tools include a complete watershed analysis. This analysis provides statistical, schematic, and graphic information on natural boundaries and subwatersheds. Watershed analysis produces two separate outputs. The first is a printout of the general watershed areas illustrating graphically the ridgelines that separate them (see Figure 1-41a). The acreages for each watershed are calculated and included as part of the output. An example of this output appears in Figure 1-41b.

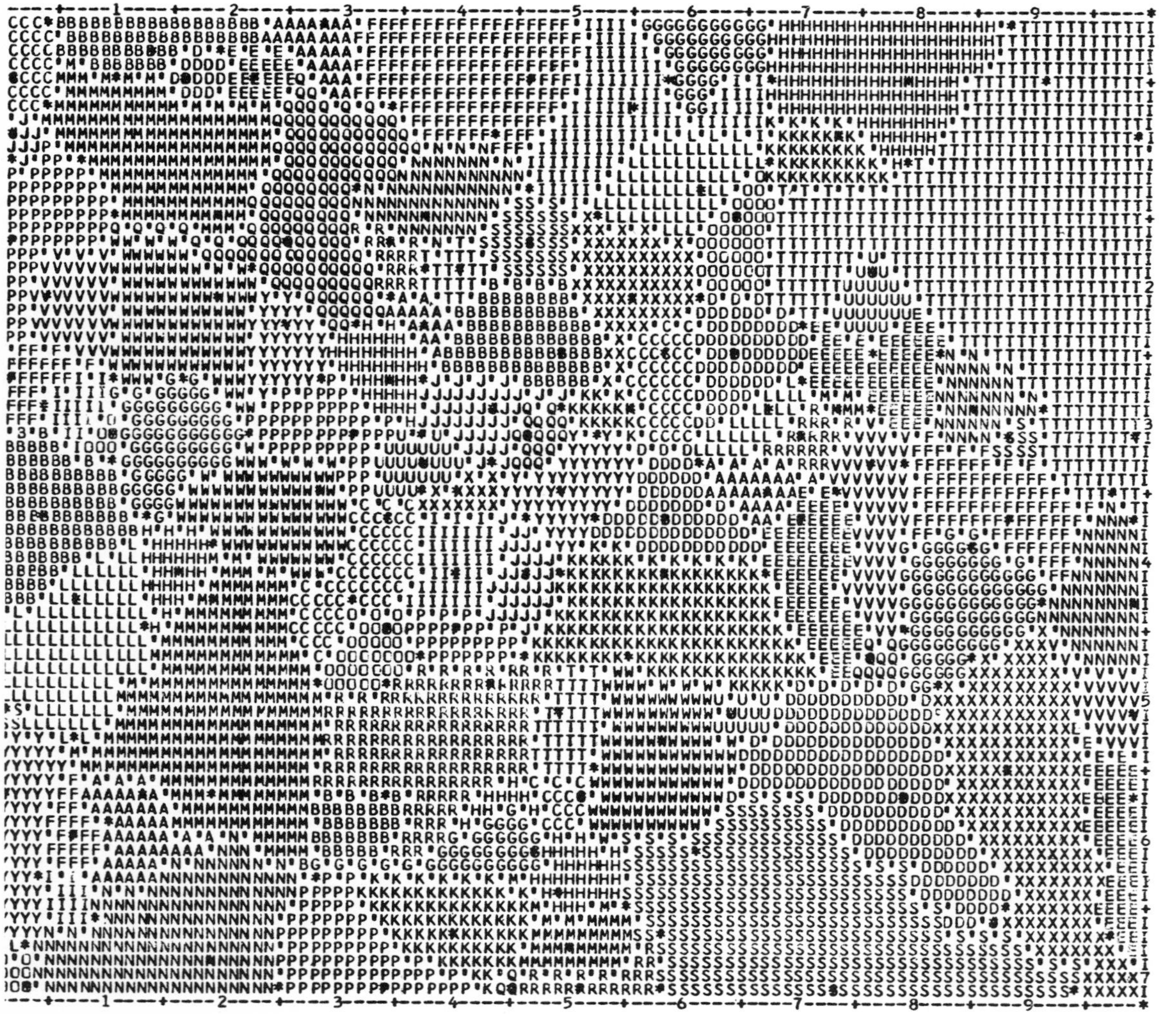

Figure 1-41a Subwatershed analysis.

LIST OF PITS

NUMBER	ROW	COLUMN	SYMBOL	AREA
1)	1	28	A	33
2)	3	13	B	54
3)	5	1	C	26
4)	5	16	D	16
5)	5	22	E	22
6)	5	46	F	155
7)	5	58	G	54
8)	7	79	H	149
9)	7	55	I	127
10)	9	1	J	10
11)	9	73	K	49
12)	13	61	L	80
13)	15	19	M	174
14)	15	37	N	74
15)	15	64	O	47
16)	17	1	P	71
17)	17	25	Q	185
18)	17	34	R	21
19)	17	46	S	44
20)	19	40	T	20
21)	19	76	U	33
22)	21	4	V	51
23)	21	18	W	127
24)	21	55	X	84
25)	23	25	Y	45
26)	23	37	Z	20
27)	25	49	A	94
28)	25	58	B	50
29)	25	64	C	71
30)	25	76	D	69
31)	27	1	E	29
32)	27	16	F	82
33)	27	34	G	43
34)	29	4	H	25
35)	29	43	I	55
36)	29	57	J	18
37)	29	73	K	29
38)	29	85	L	8
39)	29	10	M	46
40)	31	31	N	8
41)	31	46	O	64
42)	31	70	P	21
43)	31	88	Q	24
44)	31	95	R	11
45)	33	37	S	623
46)	33	76	T	29
47)	35	28	U	80
48)	35	40	V	104
49)	35	67	W	17
50)	35	67	X	63
51)	37	4	Y	36
52)	37	34	Z	101
53)	37	58	A	71
54)	37	70	B	70
55)	37	82	C	81
56)	39	85	D	104
57)	41	16	E	106
58)	41	40	F	37
59)	41	46	G	49
60)	41	58	H	41
61)	43	7	I	189
62)	43	19	J	132
63)	43	95	K	285
64)	45	34	L	74
65)	45	40	M	36
66)	47	76	N	32
67)	49	43	O	11
68)	51	1	P	178
69)	51	49	Q	4
70)	51	64	R	41
71)	51	99	S	17
72)	53	58	T	39
73)	55	82	U	130
74)	57	1	V	237
75)	57	13	W	66
76)	57	34	X	59
77)	57	51	Y	38
78)	57	79	Z	216
79)	57	99	A	18
80)	57	99	B	62

Figure 1-41b Acreage calculations.

SOURCE: *Land Planning Tools,* Environmental Systems Research Institute, 14 North Fifth Street, Redlands, Calif.

Figure 1-42 Watercourse map.

The computer also produces a pen-line drawing of water "courses" or "flows." An example of this drawing is presented in Figure 1-42. The asterisks represent the topographic peaks, whereas the boxes are topographic pits, and the arrows delineate the watercourse lines.

Some of the uses of this analysis are potential runoff calculations, flooding simulations, site analysis, and storm drain layout. Such analyses, although difficult to perform manually, are easily produced from the basic data bank.

SOURCE: *Land Planning Tools,* Environmental Systems Research Institute, 14 North Fifth Street, Redlands, Calif.

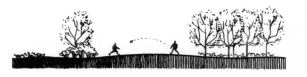

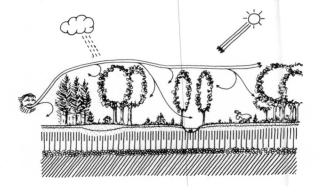

Environmental Considerations of the Site

Environmental considerations have always been an important aspect of the site design process. They may include the analysis of microclimates and macroclimates, ecosystems and their interrelationships, surface and subsurface hydrology, vegetation, and subsurface soil conditions. All these considerations require extensive and detailed study to produce meaningful conclusions. For sites that are strongly influenced by any of these factors, such studies are essential. Such sites most likely would include those on the shoreline, on mountainous terrain, or near floodplain areas. This section treats considerations dealing with climate, floodplains, flood control, drainage, and water supply.

Over the years, general criteria for the selection of sites for different kinds of uses have evolved from a variety of sources. These criteria encompass the total environment, both regional and local. With such a guide or checklist, it is possible to evaluate most proposed sites and determine their suitability for proposed uses. However, care should be used in applying these criteria. Few sites ever meet all the ideal conditions suggested by the criteria. Specific local considerations must be balanced with general requirements.

Included also in this section are a general discussion and some of the requirements for environmental impact satements. In recent years such statements have become extremely important, if not critical, for new large-scale developments of any kind.

2.1 United States Climatic Conditions

Figures 2-1, 2-2, 2-3, and 2-4 show the annual mean hours of sunshine, precipitation, number of days with a minimum temperature of 32 degrees Fahrenheit, and normal daily maximum temperature in July in all parts of the United States.

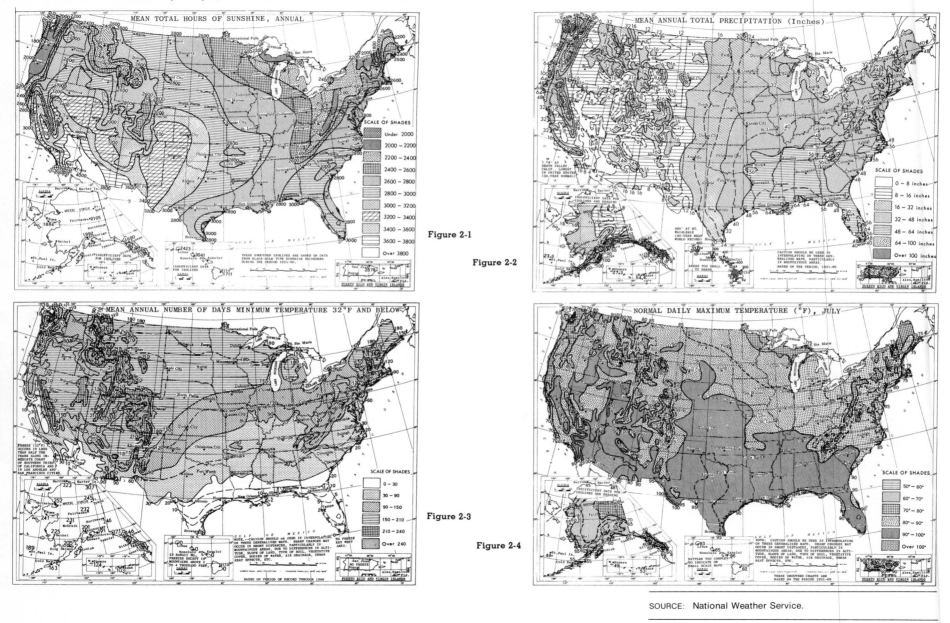

Figure 2-1

Figure 2-2

Figure 2-3

Figure 2-4

SOURCE: National Weather Service.

2.2 Floodplain Classification

Data on floods and their applicability to various areas and situations are presented in Figure 2-5.

SUMMARY OF FLOOD-DATA CLASSIFICATIONS AND APPLICABILITY

Classification	Determination of Three Hydraulic Factors Essential to Regulations			Desirable Areas of Application	Disadvantages	Advantages	Suggested Zoning Districts
	Profile	Floodway	Flood Plain				
Class A, Exact Flood Data Based on Hydraulic Calculations	Determined initially from engineering study	Determined initially from engineering study	Determined initially from engineering study	1) Areas of high development pressures for urban growth 2) Areas of intense existing development 3) Areas of high land values 4) Areas where zoning is the only management tool	Very costly and sometimes takes many years before studies are complete	1) Provide sound legal base for zoning 2) Expedites evaluation of proposed developments or amendments to adopted plans 3) Minimize hardships to applicant of proposed development 4) Contribute to flood emergency preparedness plan	1) Floodway 2) Flood fringe 3) Basement
Class B, Interpreted Flood Data Based on Known High-water Marks	Extrapolation from past floods records	Normal depth analysis (see footnote p. 35) on a case-by-case basis	Location by elevations from extrapolated profile on 1) topographic maps, 2) street-sewer maps that show ground elevations or 3) field surveys	1) Small amount of existing development affected 2) Little development pressure 3) Strong sanitary subdivision controls 4) Much land under public ownership 5) Ongoing program to acquire Class A data	1) Legal base questionable 2) Requires technical assistance to evaluate floodway 3) Applicant has greater burden to provide survey information	1) Low cost 2) Discourage land speculation 3) Valuable river basin 4) Guide to public facilities and transportation 5) Can be made available in short time to serve immediate need	1) General flood-plain district
Class C, Interpreted Flood Data Based on Nonhydraulic Calculations	Determined case-by-case (see footnote on hydraulic analysis p. 35)	Determined case-by-case (see footnote on hydraulic analysis p. 35)	Experienced flood maps, aerial photo examination, or detailed soil maps that have been correlated with engineering studies on similar streams	1) Rural areas little potential for development 2) Large portion of area under public ownership 3) Land-easement or acquisition program 4) Storng sanitary and subdivision regulations 5) Ongoing program to acquire Class A data	1) Frequency of mapped flood unknown 2) All 3 hydraulic factors unknown 3) Weak legal base 4) Source of technical assistance is needed 5) Burden to applicant to furnish surveys	1) Low cost 2) Readily expected by local people 3) Identifies pressure areas 4) Discourages land speculation	1) General flood-plain district

Figure 2-5

SOURCE: *Regulations for Flood Plains*, Report 277, American Society of Planning Officials, Planning Advisory Service, Chicago, 1972.

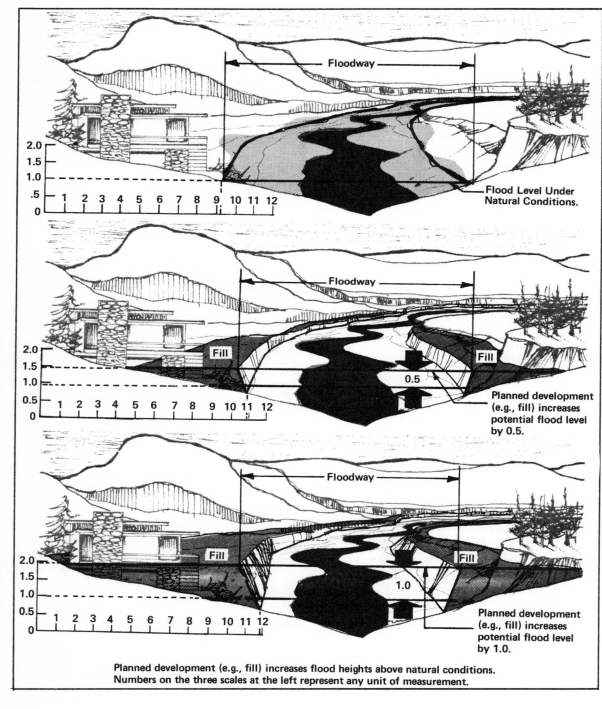

Planned development (e.g., fill) increases flood heights above natural conditions.
Numbers on the three scales at the left represent any unit of measurement.

2.3 Floodplain Districts

The three illustrations in Figure 2-6 show how a floodway can be developed to accommodate varying flood heights.

Plans for a single flood district and for two flood districts are shown in Figures 2-7 and 2-8.

Figure 2-6 Floodway planned for the same discharge with varying increases in flood heights.

SOURCE: *Regulations for Flood Plains,* Report 277, American Society of Planning Officials, Planning Advisory Service, Chicago, 1972.

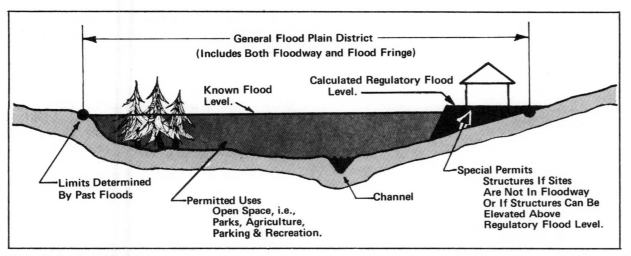

General Flood Plain District
(Includes Both Floodway and Flood Fringe)

Known Flood
Level.

Calculated Regulatory Flood
Level.

Limits Determined
By Past Floods

Permitted Uses
Open Space, i.e.,
Parks, Agriculture,
Parking & Recreation.

Channel

Special Permits
Structures If Sites
Are Not In Floodway
Or If Structures Can Be
Elevated Above
Regulatory Flood Level.

Figure 2-7 One floodplain district.

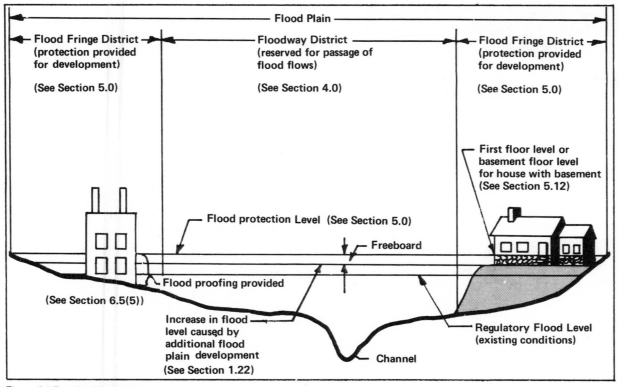

Flood Plain

Flood Fringe District
(protection provided
for development)

(See Section 5.0)

Floodway District
(reserved for passage of
flood flows)

(See Section 4.0)

Flood Fringe District
(protection provided
for development)

(See Section 5.0)

First floor level or
basement floor level
for house with basement
(See Section 5.12)

Flood protection Level (See Section 5.0)

Freeboard

Flood proofing provided

(See Section 6.5(5))

Increase in flood
level caused by
additional flood
plain development
(See Section 1.22)

Channel

Regulatory Flood Level
(existing conditions)

Figure 2-8 Two floodplain districts.

SOURCE: *Regulations for Flood Plains,* Report 277, American Society of Planning Officials, Planning Advisory Service, Chicago, 1972.

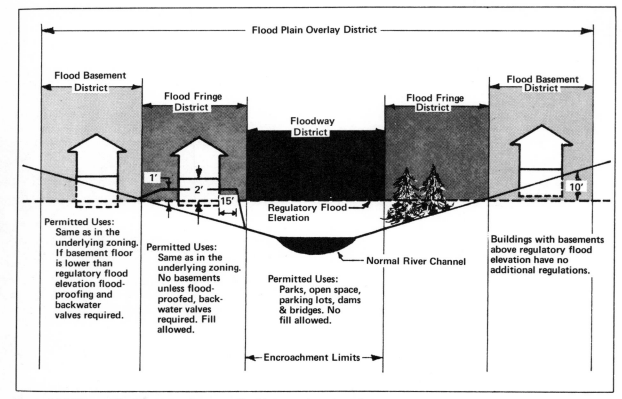

Addition of Flood Basement Distribution to Flood Fringe and Floodway Districts Figure 2-9 presents a three-district approach involving floodway, flood fringe, and flood basement districts for urban flood hazard areas with detailed engineering data that indicate serious basement flooding problems (Class A data). This approach is applicable to communities where soil conditions allow flood waters to seep into basements located beyond the floodplain, a problem usually caused by protracted floods.

Common Elements in Floodplain Regulations Floodplain regulations, whether they are included in comprehensive zoning ordinances or in a separate ordinance, should incorporate the following elements, which correspond approximately to those in the examples shown.

1. Finding of facts
2. Objectives
3. Establishment of floodplain zoning map
   a. Rules for the interpretation of district boundaries
   b. Warning and disclaimer of liability
4. Floodplain district regulations
   a. Floodway use standards
   b. Floodfringe use standards
5. Administrative provisions
   a. Variances
   b. Mapping disputes
   c. Special-use permits
      (1) Procedure to be followed in passing on special-use permits
      (2) Factors upon which decisions are to be based
      (3) Conditions attached
6. Nonconforming uses
7. Definitions

Figure 2-9 Addition of flood basement districts to flood fringe and floodway districts.

Flood Plain Overlay District

Flood Basement District

Flood Fringe District

Floodway District

Flood Fringe District

Flood Basement District

Regulatory Flood Elevation

Normal River Channel

Permitted Uses: Same as in the underlying zoning. If basement floor is lower than regulatory flood elevation flood-proofing and backwater valves required.

Permitted Uses: Same as in the underlying zoning. No basements unless flood-proofed, backwater valves required. Fill allowed.

Permitted Uses: Parks, open space, parking lots, dams & bridges. No fill allowed.

Buildings with basements above regulatory flood elevation have no additional regulations.

Encroachment Limits

1′ 2′ 15′ 10′

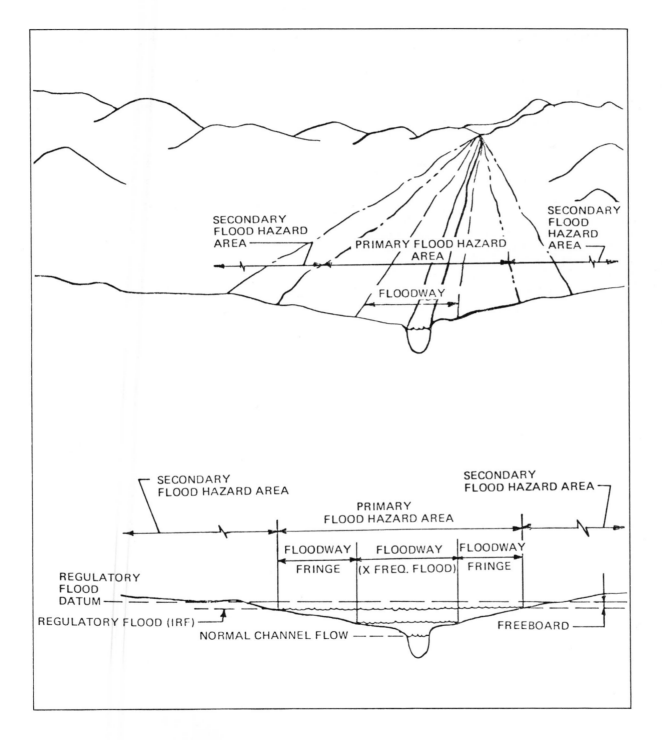

SECONDARY FLOOD HAZARD AREA

PRIMARY FLOOD HAZARD AREA

SECONDARY FLOOD HAZARD AREA

FLOODWAY

SECONDARY FLOOD HAZARD AREA

PRIMARY FLOOD HAZARD AREA

SECONDARY FLOOD HAZARD AREA

FLOODWAY FRINGE

FLOODWAY (X FREQ. FLOOD)

FLOODWAY FRINGE

REGULATORY FLOOD DATUM

REGULATORY FLOOD (IRF)

NORMAL CHANNEL FLOW

FREEBOARD

2.4 Floodproofing

Many thousands of structures and potential building sites are located in floodplains and thus are susceptible to flooding. Although flood control projects have partially protected some of these structures and building sites through reduction of the flood threat, the residual threat to these sites and the total threat to unprotected sites remain as major problems. Evidence of this situation is given every year by the millions of words and hundreds of headlines that dramatically describe floods and their resulting damage and loss of life. When floods strike developed areas, whole cities may be disrupted and their productive capacities impaired. Strategic transportation lines are cut. Public-service facilities are sapped, homes and crops are destroyed, and soils are eroded. Yet flood-vulnerable lands are the setting for continued urban growth in the United States.

Studies of floodplain use show that some encroachment is undertaken in ignorance of the hazard, some occurs in anticipation of increased federal protection, and some takes place because shifting the cost of the hazard to society makes it profitable for private owners to undertake such development. Even if full information on the flood hazard were available to all owners or users of floodplain property, there would still be conscious decisions for some reason or other to build in areas subject to flooding. To escape this dismal cycle of losses, partial protection, further induced development, and new unnecessary losses, old attitudes must be transformed into positive actions.

Primary among these actions is the revision of development policies and the enaction of a regulatory program to encourage the direction of growth or change necessary to achieve

Figure 2-10 Flood hazard areas and regulatory flood datum.

SOURCE: *Flood-proofing Regulations*, U.S. Army, Office of the Chief of Engineers, 1972.

floodplain management objectives. Information programs are essential to this revision. They foster the development of more appropriate policies and involve the gathering and dissemination of data on past floods, estimates of future floods, and alternative ways of dealing with flood losses in areas where intensive development has taken place or is anticipated. Such programs have led to an expanded approach to flood damage reduction and prevention that recognizes the need to control or regulate the use of lands adjacent to watercourses and the need to provide guidance in the design of floodplain structures through the planned management and development of the flood hazard areas.

Regulation of the use of floodplain lands is a responsibility of state and local governments and can be accomplished by a variety of means, such as the establishment of designated floodways and encroachment lines, zoning ordinances, subdivision regulations, and building codes. These land use controls, most often known as floodplain regulations, do not attempt to reduce or eliminate flooding but are intended to guide and regulate floodplain development to lessen the adverse effects of floods. Floodplain regulations are being adopted by communities and used as legal tools to control the extent and type of development permitted on floodplains.

Floodproofing standards applied through building codes and regulations to floodplain structures can permit economic development in the lower-risk areas by holding flood damages and other adverse effects within acceptable limits. Floodproofing requires adjustments both to structures and to building contents and involves keeping water out as well as reducing the effects of water entry. Such adjustments can be applied individually or as part of collective action either when buildings are under construction or during the remodeling or expansion of existing structures. They may be permanent or temporary.

Floodproofing, like other methods of adjusting to floods, has its limitations. For example, in addition to reducing loss potentials, a main purpose of floodproofing habitable structures is to provide for early return to normalcy after floods have receded rather than for continuous occupancy. See also Figure 2-10.

SOURCE: *Flood-proofing Regulations*, U.S. Army, Office of the Chief of Engineers, 1972.

2.5 Drainage (FHA Requirements)

Surface and subsurface drainage systems shall be provided, as appropriate, for the collection and disposal of storm drainage and subsurface water. These systems shall provide for the safety and convenience of occupants and the protection of dwellings, other improvements, and usable lot areas from water damage, flooding, and erosion. Where storm drainage flow is concentrated, permanently maintainable facilities shall be provided to prevent significant erosion and other damage or flooding on the site or on adjacent properties.

Drainage Design and Exposure to Flood Hazards Drainage shall be designed to accommodate storm runoff, calculated on the basis of the ultimate foreseeable developed conditions of contributory site and off-site drainage areas.

The minimum grades at buildings and at openings into basements shall be at elevations that will prevent adverse effects by water or water entering basements from flood levels equivalent to a 50-year return frequency. The floor elevations of all habitable space shall be above flood levels equivalent to a 100-year return frequency.

Provision shall be made for the best available routing of runoff water to assure that buildings or other important facilities will not be endangered by a major emergency flood runoff that would become active if the capacity of the site's storm drainage system were exceeded.

Streets shall be usable during runoff equivalent to a 10-year return frequency. Where drainage outfall is inadequate to prevent runoff equivalent to a 10-year return frequency from ponding more than 6 inches deep, streets shall be made passable for local commonly used emergency vehicles during runoff equivalent to a 25-year return frequency except where an alternate access street not subject to such ponding is available.

Site drainage shall be routed to permanent surface or subsurface outfall adequate to dispose of present and future anticipated runoff from the site and from contributing off-site watershed areas except where such water is necessary for controlled irrigation.

Drainage swales shall not carry runoff across walks in quantities that will make them undesirable to use. Walks shall not be designed as drainageways.

Developed portions of a site that can be adversely affected by a potentially high groundwater table shall be drained where possible by subsurface drainage facilities adequate for the disposal of excess groundwater.

Storm-water drainage shall be connected only to outfalls approved by the local jurisdiction.

Primary Storm Sewer The pipe size for the primary storm sewer system shall have an inside diameter based on design analysis but not less than 15 inches. The minimum gradient shall be selected to provide for self-scouring of the conduit under low-flow conditions and for the removal of foreseeable sediments from the drainage area.

Secondary Drains Pipe drains of adequate size from minor runoff concentration points shall be provided and connected to appropriate disposal lines when analysis indicates that they are necessary.

Drainage Swales and Gutters Paved gutters shall have a minimum grade of 0.5 percent. Paved gutters and unpaved drainage swales shall have adequate depth and width to accommodate the maximum foreseeable runoff without overflow. Swales and gutters shall be seeded, sodded, sprigged, or paved as appropriate to minimize potential erosion.

Open Channels Channels shall be protected from erosion by appropriate vegetative cover, lining, or other treatment indicated as necessary by analysis. Earthen channel side slopes shall be no steeper than 2 to 1 and shall be flatter to prevent erosion where analysis indicates the need.

Open channels with lining shall have a maximum gradient on side slopes of 67 percent ($1\frac{1}{2}$:1), with adequate provisions for weep hole drainage. Channel side slopes steeper than 67 percent shall be designed as structural retaining walls with provision for live and dead surcharge load.

SOURCE: *Minimum Property Standards*, Federal Housing Administration.

2.6 Drainage Systems

The following are four commonly used methods for providing site drainage:

1. Surface drainage system
2. Enclosed underground drainage system
3. Enclosed underground drainage system with on-site storage
4. Combination system with enclosed drainage for paved areas and surface drainage for unpaved areas

The selection of a particular drainage system has a direct effect on the control of erosion and sedimentation.

Surface Drainage System   Under this system the runoff from paved and unpaved areas is collected and conveyed off the site in surface drainage channels (see Figure 2-11). Channels must be designed so that channel erosion does not occur.

The surface roughness of the vegetative channel lining slows the velocity of the runoff. Such a reduction of velocity is desirable, but under certain conditions surface channels must be paved to prevent erosion within the

channel. The outlets of paved surface channels must control the runoff and sediment load at discharge sites. Where structural lining is necessary in only a small percentage of the total surface of the drainage system, cost advantages will make the use of a surface drainage system a preferred alternative.

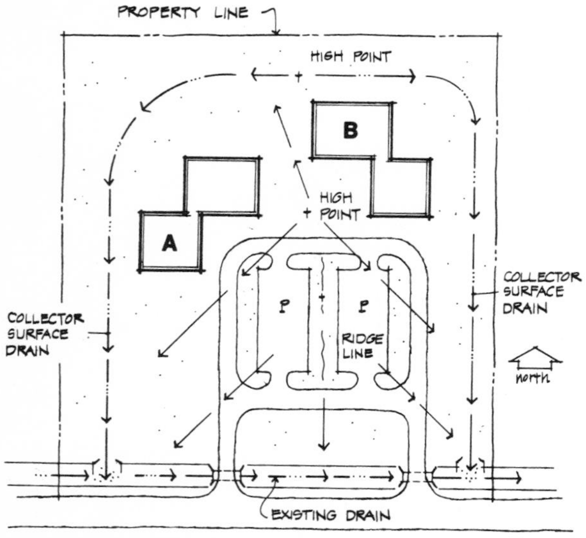

Surface drainage systems can release runoff to off-site surface drainageways or streams, to a street or municipal storm drainage system, or to an on-site sediment basin. In some cases, an on-site retention basin will be necessary to control the velocity of the runoff released from the site.

The principal disadvantage of the surface drainage system is its potential for on-site erosion. Such erosion will occur if channels are not adequately designed, stabilized, and maintained. Where the runoff flows from paved areas to grassy areas, the potential for erosion is high. Careful stabilization of the areas that will receive runoff from paved areas is necessary.

Enclosed Underground Drainage System   An enclosed drainage system intercepts runoff from both paved and unpaved areas and conveys it to an outlet at the edge of the site (surface drainageway or stream), a municipal storm drainage system, or an on-site sedimentation and storage basin (see Figure 2-12).

The major advantage of the enclosed drainage system is that the increased volume and velocity of runoff generated by development can be intercepted before runoff can cause on-site erosion damage. The principal disadvantage is that the velocity of runoff is increased and sediment often is not filtered from runoff. As a result, the points at which runoff is released from the system are subject to erosion and sedimentation. Thus, while the potential for erosion damage to the site itself is minimized, the erosion and sedimentation damage to off-site areas may be increased.

Where the enclosed drainage system empties into a municipal storm system, sediment must be removed before it reaches the municipal system outlet. Where the system outlet is at a site boundary or within the site, the potential

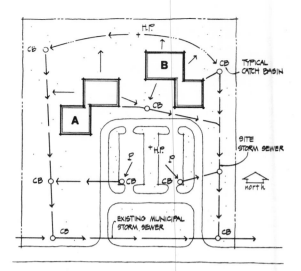

Figure 2-12 Enclosed underground drainage system.

for erosion and sedimentation damage that may be caused must be controlled by an earth changer. The velocity of runoff released at these outlets must be maintained at nonerosive levels. Sediment must be removed from runoff before it is released. An on-site storage and sediment basin may be included in the permanent erosion control plan if the enclosed drainage system within the site does not empty into an enclosed, underground municipal storm drainage system.

Enclosed Underground Drainage with On-Site Storage   This kind of alternative drainage system (see Figure 2-13) has the advantages of the enclosed drainage system of on-site erosion control; yet it avoids off-site damage. Instead of merely delaying the erosion and sedimentation impact of the enclosed drainage system, the on-site, storage-controlled runoff release system largely eliminates this impact.

SOURCE: *Michigan Soil Erosion & Sedimentation Control Guidebook.*

Figure 2-11 Surface drainage system.

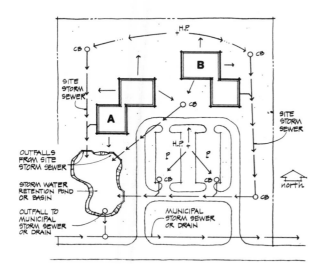

Figure 2-13 Enclosed underground drainage system with on-site storage.

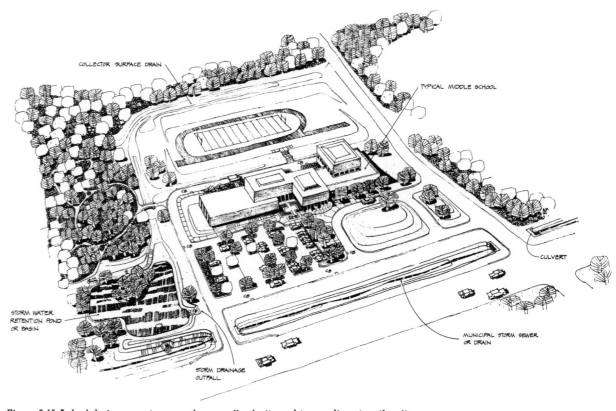

Figure 2-15 A dual drainage system can slow runoff velocity and trap sediment on the site.

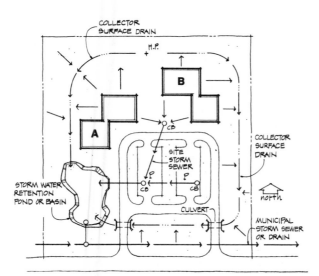

Figure 2-14 Combination drainage system.

Combination Drainage System Under this system runoff from open spaces is collected in surface drainageways, while runoff from paved areas is collected in an enclosed drainage system (see Figure 2-14). Because the enclosed drainage system intercepts runoff from only a limited area, the erosion and sedimentation risk at its outfall is likely to be less than if an enclosed system is used to drain the entire site. The runoff from the enclosed drainage system can be let out into the surface drainage system, and in some cases a permanent sediment basin may not be necessary. See Figure 2-15.

This system of dual drainage has the advantage of ensuring that no erosion will occur in vegetated areas adjacent to paved surfaces. Surface channels, especially if they must accommodate runoff released from the enclosed drainage system, must be carefully designed and stabilized to prevent channel erosion. A permanent sediment and storage basin will be required if either the content of runoff sediment or the runoff velocity is high. Careful design and maintenance are essential when this dual system is used.

SOURCE: *Michigan Soil Erosion & Sedimentation Control Guidebook.*

2.7 Water Supply

Quantity of Water   One of the first steps in the selection of a suitable water supply source is determining the demand that will be placed on it. The essential elements of water demand include the average daily water consumption and the peak rate of demand. The average daily water consumption must be estimated for these purposes:

1. To determine the ability of the water source to meet continuing demands over critical periods when surface flows are low and groundwater tables are at minimum elevations
2. To ascertain the quantities of stored water that will sustain demands during these critical periods

The peak demand rates must be estimated to determine plumbing and pipe sizing, pressure losses, and the storage facilities necessary to supply sufficient water during periods of peak demand.

Average Daily Water Use   Many factors influence water use for a given system. For example, the mere fact that water under pressure is available stimulates its use for watering lawns and gardens, for washing automobiles, for operating air-conditioning equipment, and for performing many other utility activities at home and on the farm. Modern kitchen and laundry appliances, such as food waste disposers and automatic dishwashers, contribute to a higher total water use and tend to increase peak demands. Since water requirements will influence all features of an individual development or improvement, they must figure prominently in plan preparation. The table "Planning Guide for Water Use" presents a summary of average water use as a guide in preparing estimates, local adaptations being made where necessary.

Peak Demands   The rate of water use for an individual water system will vary directly with activity in the home or with the operational farm program. Rates are generally highest in the home near mealtimes, during midmorning laundry periods, and shortly before bedtime. In the intervening daytime hours and at night,

PLANNING GUIDE FOR WATER USE

Types of establishments	Gallons per day
Airports (per passenger)	3 to 5
Apartments, multiple-family (per resident)	60
Bathhouses (per bather)	10
Camps:	
Construction, semipermanent (per worker)	50
Day with no meals served (per camper)	15
Luxury (per camper)	100 to 150
Resorts, day and night, with limited plumbing (per camper)	50
Tourist with central bath and toilet facilities (per person)	35
Cottages with seasonal occupancy (per resident)	50
Courts, tourist, with individual bath units (per person)	50
Clubs:	
Country (per resident member)	100
Country (per nonresident member present)	25
Dwellings:	
Boardinghouses (per boarder)	50
Additional kitchen requirements for nonresident boarders	10
Luxury (per person)	100 to 150
Multiple-family apartments (per resident)	40
Rooming houses (per resident)	60
Single-family (per resident)	50 to 75
Estates (per resident)	100 to 150
Factories (gallons per person per shift)	15 to 35
Highway rest areas (per person)	5
Hotels with private baths (two persons per room)	60
Hotels without private baths (per person)	50
Institutions other than hospitals (per person)	75 to 125
Hospitals (per bed)	250 to 400
Laundries, self-service (gallons per washing, that is, per customer)	50
Livestock (per animal):	
Cattle (drinking)	12
Dairy (drinking and servicing)	35
Goat (drinking)	2
Hog (drinking)	4
Horse (drinking)	12
Mule (drinking)	12
Sheep (drinking)	2
Steer (drinking)	12

(Continued)

Types of establishments	Gallons per day
Motels with bath, toilet, and kitchen facilities (per bed space)	50
With bed and toilet (per bed space)	40
Parks:	
Overnight with flush toilets (per camper)	25
Trailers with individual bath units, no sewer connection (per trailer)	25
Trailers with individual baths, connected to sewer (per person)	50
Picnic facilities:	
With bathhouses, showers, and flush toilets (per picnicker)	20
With toilet facilities only (gallons per picnicker)	10
Poultry:	
Chickens (per 100)	5 to 10
Turkeys (per 100)	10 to 18
Restaurants with toilet facilities (per patron)	7 to 10
Without toilet facilities (per person)	2½ to 3
With bars and cocktail lounge (additional quantity per patron)	2
Schools:	
Boarding (per pupil)	75 to 100
Day with cafeteria, gymnasiums, and showers (per pupil)	25
Day with cafeteria but no gymnasiums or showers (per pupil)	20
Day without cafeteria, gymnasiums, or showers (per pupil)	15
Service stations (per vehicle)	10
Stores (per toilet room)	400
Swimming pools (per swimmer)	10
Theaters:	
Drive-in (per car space)	5
Movie (per auditorium seat)	5
Workers:	
Construction (per person per shift)	50
Day (school or offices per person per shift)	15

SOURCE: *Manual of Individual Water Supply Systems,* Environmental Protection Agency, Water Supply Division, 1973.

RATES OF FLOW FOR CERTAIN PLUMBING, HOUSEHOLD, AND FARM FIXTURES

Location	Flow pressure* (pounds per square inch)	Flow rate (gallons per minute)
Ordinary basin faucet	8	2.0
Self-closing basin faucet	8	2.5
Sink faucet, ⅜-inch	8	4.5
Sink faucet, ½-inch	8	4.5
Bathtub faucet	8	6.0
Laundry tub faucet, ½-inch	8	5.0
Shower	8	5.0
Ball cock for closet	8	3.0
Flush valve for closet	15	15 to 40†
Flushometer valve for urinal	15	15.0
Garden hose (50 feet; ¾-inch sill cock)	30	5.0
Garden hose (50 feet; ⅝-inch outlet)	15	3.33
Drinking fountains	15	0.75
Fire hose (1½ inches; ½-inch nozzle)	30	40.0

*Flow pressure is the pressure in the supply near the faucet or water outlet while the faucet or water outlet is wide-open and flowing.
†The wide range is due to variations in the design and type of closet flush valves.

water use may be virtually nil. Thus, the total amount of water used by a household may be distributed over only a few hours of the day, during which the actual use is much greater than the average rate determined from the table "Planning Guide for Water Use."

Simultaneous operation of several plumbing fixtures will determine the maximum peak rate of water delivery for the home water system. For example, a shower, an automatic dishwasher, a lawn sprinkler system, and a flush-valve toilet all operated at the same time would probably produce a near-critical peak. It is true that not all these facilities are usually operated together; but if they exist on the same system, there is always a possibility that a critical combination may result, and for design purposes this method of calculation is sound. Rates of flow are summarized in the table "Rates of Flow for Certain Plumbing, Household, and Farm Fixtures."

Special Water Considerations

Lawn sprinkling. The amount of water required for lawn sprinkling depends upon the size of the lawn, the type of sprinkling equipment, climate, soil, and water control. In dry or arid areas the amount of water required may equal or exceed the total used for domestic or farmstead needs. For estimating purposes, a rate of approximately ½ inch per hour of surface area is reasonable. This amount of water can be applied by sprinkling 30 gallons of water per hour over each 100 square feet.

EXAMPLE:

$$\frac{1000}{100} \times 30 = 300 \text{ gallons per hour, or 5 gallons per minute}$$

A lawn of 1,000 square feet would require 300 gallons per hour.

When possible, the water system should have a minimum capacity of 500 to 600 gallons per hour. A water system of this size may be able to operate satisfactorily during a peak demand. Peak flows can be estimated by adding lawn sprinkling to peak domestic flows but not to fire flows.

Fire protection. In areas of individual water supply systems, effective fire fighting depends upon the facilities provided by the property owner. The National Fire Protection Association has prepared a report that outlines and describes ways to utilize available water supplies.[1]

The most important factors in successful fire fighting are early discovery and immediate action. For immediate protection, portable fire extinguishers are desirable. Such first-aid protection is designed only for the control of fires in the early stage; therefore, a water supply is desirable as a second line of defense.

The use of gravity water supplies for fire fighting presents certain basic problems. These include (1) the construction of a dam, farm pond, or storage tank to hold the water until needed and (2) the determination of the size of pipeline installed from the supply. The size of the pipe is dependent upon two factors, the total fall or head from the point of supply to the point of use and the length of pipeline required.

A properly constructed well tapping a good aquifer can be a dependable source for both domestic use and fire protection. If the well is to be relied upon for fire protection without supplemental storage, it should demonstrate, by a pumping test, a minimum capacity of 8 to 10 gallons per minute continously for a period of 2 hours during the driest time of the year.

An installation is more dependable when the motor, controls, and power lines are protected from fire. A high degree of protection is achieved when all the electrical elements are located outside at the well and a separate power line bypasses other buildings.

Numerous factors determine the amount of fire protection that should be built into a water system. Publications of the National Fire Pro-

[1]"Water Supply Systems for Rural Fire Protection," *National Fire Codes*, Vol. 8, National Fire Protection Association, Boston, 1969.

SOURCE: *Manual of Individual Water Supply Systems*, Environmental Protection Agency, Water Supply Division, 1973.

tection Association provide further information on this subject.

The smallest individual pressure systems commercially available provide about 210 gallons per hour (3½ gallons per minute). While this capacity will furnish a stream, through an ordinary garden hose, of some value in combating incipient fires or in wetting down adjacent buildings, it cannot be expected to be effective on a fire that has gained any headway. When such systems are already installed, connections and hose should be provided. When a new system is being planned or a replacement of equipment made, it is urged that a capacity of at least 500 gallons an hour (8⅓ gallons per minute) be specified and the supply increased to meet this demand. If necessary, storage should be added. The additional cost of the larger unit necessary for fire protection is offset partially by the increased quantities of water available for other uses.

Sanitary Survey The importance of a sanitary survey of water sources cannot be overemphasized. With a new supply, the sanitary survey should be made in conjunction with the collection of initial engineering data covering the development of a given source and its capacity to meet existing and future needs. The survey should include the detection of all health hazards and an assessment of their present and future importance. Persons trained and competent in public-health engineering and the epidemiology of waterborne diseases should conduct the sanitary survey. With an existing supply, the survey should be made as often as the control of health hazards and the maintenance of a good sanitary quality require.

The information furnished by the sanitary survey is essential to a complete interpretation of bacteriological and, frequently, chemical data. This information should always accompany the laboratory findings. The following outlines cover the essential factors to be investigated or considered in a sanitary survey. Not all the items are pertinent to any one supply, and items not on the lists would be important additions in some situations.

Groundwater Supplies

1. Character of local geology; slope of ground surface
2. Nature of soil and underlying porous strata; whether clay, sand, gravel, or rock (especially porous limestone); coarseness of sand or gravel; thickness of water-bearing stratum, depth to water table; location, log, and construction details of local wells
3. Slope of water table, preferably as determined from observational wells or as indicated, presumptively but not certainly, by slope of ground surface

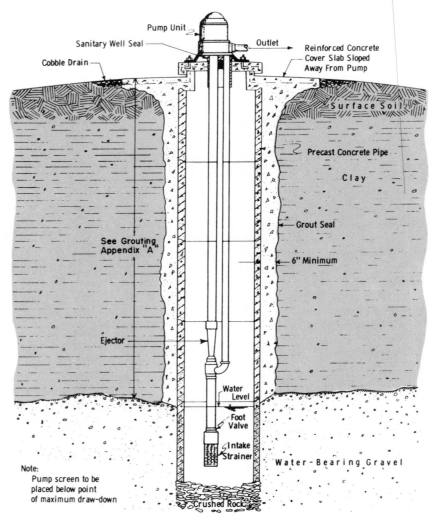

Figure 2-16 A dug well with a two-pipe jet pump installation

SOURCE: *Manual of Individual Water Supply Systems*, Environmental Protection Agency, Water Supply Division, 1973.

4. Extent of drainage area likely to contribute water to the supply
5. Nature, distance, and direction of local sources of pollution
6. Possibility of surface drainage water's entering the supply and of wells becoming flooded; methods of protection
7. Methods used for protecting the supply against pollution by means of sewage treatment, waste disposal, and the like
8. Well construction (see Figures 2-16, 2-17, and 2-18)
   a. Total depth of well
   b. Casing: diameter, wall thickness, material, and length from surface
   c. Screen or perforations: diameter, material, construction, locations, and lengths
   d. Formation seal: material (cement, sand, bentonite, and so on), depth intervals, annular thickness, and method of placement

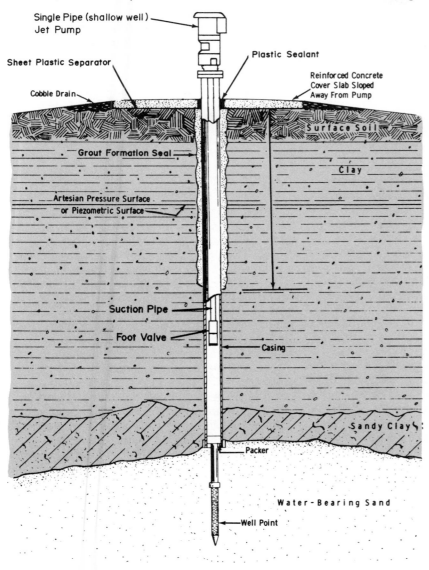

Figure 2-17 A hand-bored well with a driven well point and a "shallow well" jet pump.

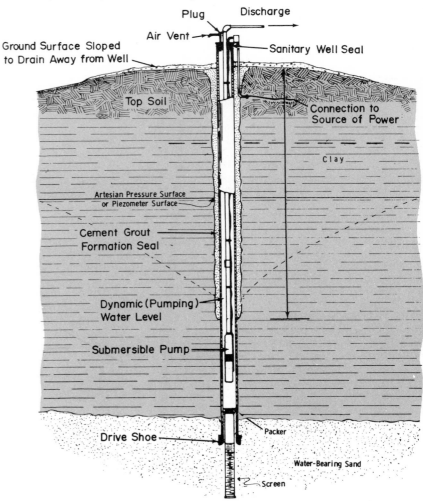

Figure 2-18 A drilled well with a submersible pump.

SOURCE: *Manual of Individual Water Supply Systems*, Environmental Protection Agency, Water Supply Division, 1973.

9. Protection of well at top: presence of sanitary well seal, casing height above ground, floor, or flood level, protection of well vent, protection of well from erosion and animals
10. Pump house construction (floors, drains, and so on), capacity of pumps, drawdown when pumps are in operation
11. Availability of an unsafe supply, usable in place of normal supply and hence involving danger to the public health
12. Disinfection: equipment, supervision, test kits, or other types of laboratory control

Surface-Water Supplies

1. Nature of surface geology: character of soils and rocks
2. Character of vegetation, forests, cultivated and irrigated land, including salinity, effect on irrigation water, and so on
3. Population and sewered population per square mile of catchment area
4. Methods of sewage disposal, whether by diversion from watershed or by treatment
5. Character and efficiency of sewage treatment works on watershed
6. Proximity of sources of fecal pollution to intake of water supply
7. Proximity, sources, and character of industrial wastes, oil field brines, acid mine waters, and so on
8. Adequacy of supply as to quantity
9. For lake or reservoir supplies: wind direction and velocity data, drift of pollution, sunshine data (algae)
10. Character and quality of raw water: coliform organisms, algae, turbidity, color, objectionable mineral constituents
11. Nominal period of detention in reservoir or storage basin
12. Probable minimum time required for water to flow from sources of pollution to reservoir and through reservoir intake
13. Shape of reservoir, with reference to possible currents of water, induced by wind or reservoir discharge, from inlet to water supply intake
14. Protective measures in connection with the use of watershed to control fishing, boating, landing of airplanes, swimming, wading, ice cutting, permitting of animals on marginal shore areas and in or upon the water, and so on
15. Efficiency and constancy of policing
16. Treatment of water: kind and adequacy of equipment, duplication of parts, effectiveness of treatment, adequacy of supervision and testing, contact period after disinfection, free chlorine residuals carried
17. Pumping facilities: pump house, pump capacity and standby units, and storage facilities

The selection and use of surface-water sources for individual water supply systems require the consideration of additional factors not usually associated with groundwater sources. When small streams, open ponds, lakes, or open reservoirs must be used as sources of water supply, the danger of contamination and of the consequent spread of enteric diseases such as typhoid fever and dysentery is increased. As a rule, surface water should be used only when groundwater sources are unavailable or inadequate. Clear water is not always safe, and the old saying that "running water purifies itself" to drinking-water quality within a stated distance is false. The physical and bacteriological contamination of surface water makes it necessary to regard such sources of supply as unsafe for domestic use unless reliable treatment, including filtration and disinfection, is provided.

The treatment of surface water to ensure a constant, safe supply requires diligent attention to operation and maintenance by the owner of the system. When groundwater sources are limited, consideration should be given to their development for domestic purposes only. Surface-water sources can then provide water needed for stock and poultry watering, gardening, fire fighting, and similar purposes. Treatment of surface water used for livestock is not generally considered essential. There is, however, a trend to provide stock and poultry with drinking water free from bacterial contamination and certain chemical elements.

Sources of Surface Water The principal sources of surface water that may be developed include controlled catchments, ponds or lakes, surface streams, and irrigation canals. Except for irrigation canals, where discharges depend on irrigation activity, these sources derive water from direct precipitation over the drainage area. Because of the complexities of the hydrological, geological, and meteorological factors affecting surface-water sources, it is recommended that in planning the development of natural catchment areas of more than a few acres, engineering advice be obtained.

To estimate the yield of the source, it is necessary to consider the following information pertaining to the drainage area:

1. Total annual precipitation
2. Seasonal distribution of precipitation
3. Annual or monthly variations of rainfall from normal levels
4. Annual and monthly evaporation and transpiration rates
5. Soil moisture requirements and infiltration rates
6. Runoff gauge information
7. All available local experience records

Much of the required data, particularly that concerning precipitation, can be obtained from publications of the National Weather Service. Essential data such as soil moisture and evapotranspiration requirements may be obtained from local soil conservation and agricultural agencies or from field tests conducted by hydrologists.

Controlled Catchments In some areas groundwater is almost inaccessible or is so highly mineralized that it is not satisfactory for domestic use. In these cases the use of controlled catchments and cisterns may be necessary. A properly located and constructed controlled catchment and cistern, augmented by a satisfactory filtration unit and adequate disinfection facilities, will provide safe water.

A controlled catchment is a defined surface area from which rainfall runoff is collected. It may be a roof or a paved ground surface. The collected water is stored in a constructed covered tank called a cistern or in a reservoir.

SOURCE: *Manual of Individual Water Supply Systems*, Environmental Protection Agency, Water Supply Division, 1973.

Ground surface catchments should be fenced to prevent unauthorized entrance by people or animals. There should be no possibility of the mixture of undesirable surface drainage and controlled runoff. An intercepting drainage ditch around the upper edge of the area and a raised curb around the surface will prevent the entry of any undesirable surface drainage.

For these controlled catchments, simple guidelines to determine water yield from rainfall totals can be established. When the controlled catchment area has a smooth surface or is paved and the runoff is collected in a cistern, water loss due to evaporation, replacement of soil moisture deficit, and infiltration is small. As a general rule, losses from ground catchments covered with smooth concrete or asphalt average less than 10 percent; for shingled roofs or tar and gravel surfaces losses should not exceed 15 percent, and for sheet metal roofs the loss is negligible.

A conservative design can be based on the assumption that the amount of water recoverable for use is three-fourths of the total annual rainfall. See Figure 2-19.

Location. A controlled catchment may be suitably located on a hillside near the edge of a natural bench. The catchment area can be placed on a moderate slope above the receiving cistern.

The location of the cistern should be governed by both convenience and quality protection. A cistern should be as close to the point of ultimate use as is practicable. It should not be placed closer than 50 feet from any part of a sewage disposal installation and should be on higher ground.

A cistern collecting water from a roof surface should be located adjacent to the building but not in a basement subject to flooding. It may be placed below the surface of the ground to keep the water from freezing in cold climates and to keep water temperatures low in warm climates, but it should be situated on the highest ground practicable, with the surrounding area graded to provide good drainage.

Size. The size of a cistern will depend on the size of the family and the length of time

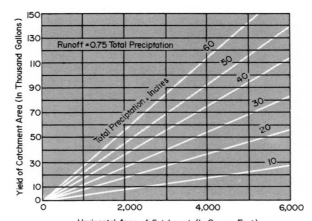

Figure 2-19 Yield of impervious catchment area.

between periods of heavy rainfall. Daily water requirements can be estimated from the table "Planning Guide for Water Use." The size of the catchment or roof will depend on the amount of rainfall and the character of the surface. It is desirable to allow a safety factor for lower-than-normal rainfall levels. Designing for two-thirds of the mean annual rainfall usually will result in a catchment area of adequate capacity.

The following example illustrates the procedure for determining the size of the cistern and required catchment area. Let us assume that the minimum drinking and culinary requirements of a family of four persons are 100 gallons per day[2] (4 persons × 25 gallons per day = 100 gallons) and that the effective period[3] between rainy periods is 150 days. The minimum volume of the cistern required will be 15,000 gallons (100 × 150). This volume could be held by a cistern 10 feet deep and 15 feet square. If the mean annual rainfall is 50 inches, then the total design rainfall is 33 inches (50 × ⅔). In Figure 2-19 the catchment area required to produce 36,500 gallons (365 days × 100 gallons per day), the total annual requirement, is 2400 square feet.

Construction. Cisterns should be of watertight construction with smooth interior sur-

faces. Manhole or other covers should be tight to prevent the entrance of light, dust, surface water, insects, and animals.

A manhole opening should have a watertight curb with edges projecting a minimum of 4 inches above the level of the surrounding surface. The edges of the manhole cover should overlap the curb and project downward a minimum of 2 inches. The cover should be provided with a lock to minimize the danger of contamination and accidents.

Provision can be made for diverting initial runoff from paved surfaces or rooftops before the runoff is allowed to enter the cistern, (see Figure 2-20). Inlet, outlet, and waste pipes should be effectively screened. Cistern drains and waste or sewer lines should not be connected.

Underground cisterns can be built of brick or stone, although reinforced concrete is preferable. If brick or stone is used, it must be low in permeability and laid with full portland cement mortar joints. Brick should be wet before laying. High-quality workmanship is required, and the use of unskilled labor for laying brick or stone is not advisable. Two ½-inch plaster coats of 1:3 portland cement mortar on the interior surface will aid in providing waterproofing. A hard, impervious surface can be made by troweling the final coat before it is fully hardened.

Figures 2-20 and 2-21 show a suggested design for a cistern of reinforced concrete. A dense concrete should be used to obtain watertightness and should be vibrated adequately during construction to eliminate honeycomb. All masonry cisterns should be allowed to wet-cure properly before being used.

---

[2]Twenty-five gallons per person per day if it is assumed that other uses are supplied by water of poorer quality.

[3]The effective period is the number of days between periods of rainfall during which there is negligible precipitation.

SOURCE: *Manual of Individual Water Supply Systems*, Environmental Protection Agency, Water Supply Division, 1973.

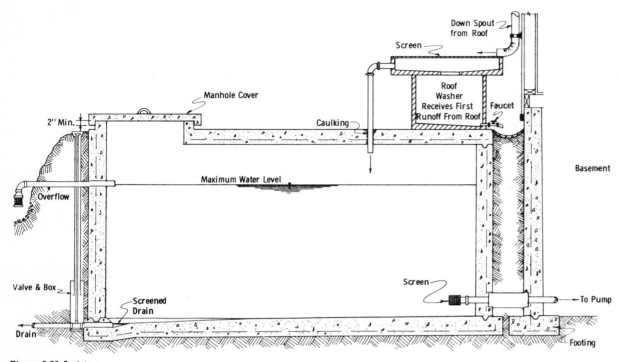

Figure 2-20 A cistern.

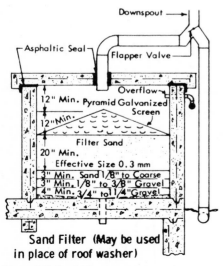

Sand Filter (May be used in place of roof washer)

Figure 2-21 Sand filter for a cistern.

entire water system. Local authorities may be able to furnish advice on pond development.

The value of a pond or lake development is its ability to store water during wet periods for use during periods of little or no rainfall. A pond should be capable of storing a minimum of a year's supply of water. It must be of sufficient capacity to meet water supply demands during periods of low rainfall with an additional allowance for seepage and evaporation losses. The drainage area (watershed) should be large enough to catch sufficient water to fill the pond or lake during wet seasons of the year.

Careful consideration of the location of the watershed and pond site reduces the possibility of chance contamination. The watershed should:

1. Be clean, preferably grassed
2. Be free from barns, septic tanks, privies, and soil absorption fields
3. Be effectively protected against erosion and drainage from livestock areas
4. Be fenced to exclude livestock

The pond should:

1. Be not less than 8 feet deep at the deepest point
2. Be designed to have the maximum possible water storage area more than 3 feet in depth
3. Be large enough to store at least a year's supply
4. Be fenced to keep out livestock
5. Be kept free of weeds, algae, and floating debris

In many instances pond development requires the construction of an embankment with an overflow or spillway. Assistance in designing a storage pond may be available from federal, state, or local health agencies, from the U.S. Soil Conservation Service, and in publications of state or county agricultural, geological, or soil conservation departments. For specific conditions, engineering or geological advice may be needed.

SOURCE: *Manual of Individual Water Supply Systems*, Environmental Protection Agency, Water Supply Division, 1973.

The cistern should be disinfected with chlorine solutions. Initial and periodic water samples should be taken to determine the bacteriological quality of the water supply. Chlorination may be required on a continuing basis if the bacteriological results indicate that the quality is unsatisfactory.

Ponds or Lakes A pond or a lake should be considered as a source of water supply only after groundwater sources and controlled catchment systems are found to be inadequate or unacceptable. The development of a pond as a supply source depends on several factors: (1) the selection of a watershed that permits only water of the highest quality to enter the pond, (2) usage of the best water collected in the pond, (3) filtration of the water to remove turbidity and reduce bacteria, (4) disinfection of filtered water, (5) proper storage of the treated water, and (6) proper maintenance of the

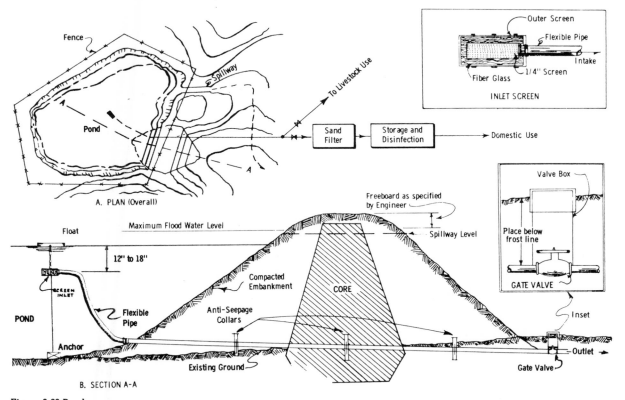

A. PLAN (Overall)

B. SECTION A-A

Figure 2-22 Pond.

Alum and other chemical aids speed the settling rate of suspended materials present in the water. This initial process helps to reduce the turbidity of the water to be passed through the filter. The addition of alum will lower the pH, which may have to be readjusted with lime if the distribution piping becomes corroded.

2. *Filtration unit.* After settling, the water moves to a second compartment, where it passes through a filter bed of sand and gravel. The suspended particles that have not been removed by settlement or flocculation are now removed.

3. *Clear water storage.* After the water leaves the filter, it drains into a clear well, cistern, or storage tank.

4. *Disinfection.* After the water has settled and has been filtered, it must be disinfected. Proper disinfection is the most important part of pond water treatment. The continuous operation and high-quality performance of the equipment are very important. When the water is chlorinated, livestock unaccustomed to chlorinated water may refuse to drink the water for several days, but they usually become accustomed to it within a short period of time.

Bacteriological examination. After the treatment and disinfection equipment have been checked and are operating satisfactorily, a bacteriological examination of a water sample should be made. Before a sample is collected, the examining laboratory should be asked to furnish recommendations. These recommendations should include the type of container to be used and the method and precautions to take during collection, handling, and mailing. Water should not be used for drinking and culinary purposes until the results of the bacteriological examination show it to be safe.

The frequency of subsequent bacteriological examinations should be based on any breakdown or changes made in the sanitary construction or protective measures associated

SOURCE: *Manual of Individual Water Supply Systems*, Environmental Protection Agency, Water Supply Division, 1973.

Intake. A pond intake must be properly located so that it may draw water of the highest possible quality. When the intake is placed too close to the pond bottom, it may draw turbid water or water containing decayed organic material. When it is placed too near the pond surface, the intake system may draw floating debris, algae, and aquatic plants. The depth at which it operates best varies with the season of the year and the layout of the pond. The most desirable water is usually obtained when the intake is located between 12 and 18 inches below the water surface. An intake located at the deepest point of the pond makes maximum use of stored water.

Pond intakes should be of the type illustrated in Figure 2-22. This is known as a floating intake. It consists of a flexible pipe attached to a rigid conduit that passes through the pond embankment.

In accordance with applicable specifications, gate valves should be installed on the main line below the dam and on any branch line to facilitate control of the rate of discharge.

Treatment. The pond water treatment facility consists of four general parts. See Figure 2-23.

1. *Settling basin.* The first unit is a settling basin. The purpose of the basin is to allow the large particles of turbidity to settle. This may be accomplished adequately in the pond. When this settling is not completely effective, a properly designed settling basin with provision for coagulation may be needed. The turbid water is mixed with a suitable chemical such as alum.

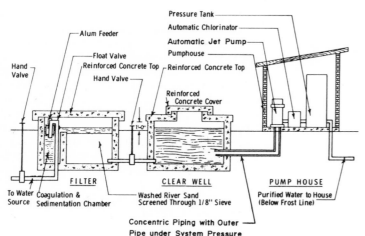

Figure 2-33 Schematic diagram of a pond water treatment system.

with the supply. A daily determination and record of the chlorine residual is recommended to ensure that proper disinfection is accomplished.

Plant maintenance. The treatment facility should be inspected daily. The disinfection equipment should be checked to make sure that it is operating satisfactorily. When chlorine disinfection is practiced, the chlorinator and the supply of chlorine solution should be checked. The water supply should be checked daily for its chlorine residual. The water may become turbid after heavy rains, and the quality may change. Increases in the amount of chlorine and coagulates used will then be required. The performance of the filter should be watched closely. When the water becomes turbid or the available quantity of water decreases, the filter should be cleaned or backwashed.

Protection from freezing. Protection from freezing must be provided unless the plant is not operated and is drained during freezing weather. In general, the filter and pump room should be located in a building that can be heated in winter. If the topography is suitable, the need for heat can be eliminated by placement of the pump room and filter underground on a hillside. Gravity drainage from the pump room must be possible to prevent flooding. No matter what the arrangement, the filter and

pump room must be easily accessible for maintenance and operation.

Tastes and odors. Surface water frequently develops musty or undesirable tastes and odors. These are generally caused by the presence of microscopic plants called algae. There are many kinds of algae. Some occur in long, threadlike filaments that are visible as large green masses of scum; others may be separately free-floating and entirely invisible to the unaided eye. Some varieties may grow in great quantities in the early spring, others in summer, and still others in the fall. Tastes and odors generally result from the decay of dead algae. This decay occurs naturally as plants pass through their life cycle.

Tastes and odors in water can usually be satisfactorily removed by passing the previously filtered and chlorinated surface water through activated carbon filters. These filters may be helpful in improving the taste of small quantities of previously treated water used for drinking or culinary purposes. They also absorb excess chlorine. Carbon filters are commercially available and require periodic servicing.

Carbon filters should not be expected to be a substitute for sand filtration and disinfection. Their area is insufficient to handle raw surface water, and they clog very rapidly when filtering turbid water.

Weed control. The growth of weeds around a pond should be controlled by cutting or pulling. Before weed killers are used, the advice of the local health department should be obtained, since herbicides often contain compounds that are highly toxic to humans and animals. Algae in the pond, particularly the blue-green types that produce scum and objectionable odors and that, in unusual instances, may harm livestock, should be controlled.

Streams Streams receiving runoff from large uncontrolled watersheds may be the only source of water supply. The physical and bacteriological quality of surface water varies and may impose unusually or abnormally high loads on the treatment facilities.

Stream intakes should be located upstream from sewer outlets or other sources of contamination. The water should be pumped when the silt load is low. A low-water stage usually means that the temperature of the water is higher than normal and that the water is of poor chemical quality. Maximum silt loads, however, occur during maximum runoff. High-water stages shortly after storms are usually the most favorable for diverting or pumping water to storage. These conditions vary, and the best time should be determined for the particular stream.

Irrigation Canals If properly treated, irrigation water may be used as a source of domestic water supply. Water obtained from irrigation canals should be treated like water from any other surface-water source.

When return irrigation (tail water) is practiced, the water may contain large concentrations of undesirable chemicals, including pesticides, herbicides, and fertilizers. Whenever water from return irrigation is used for domestic purposes, a periodic chemical analysis should be made. Because of the poor quality of this water, it should be used only if no other water source is available.

SOURCE: *Manual of Individual Water Supply Systems,* Environmental Protection Agency, Water Supply Division, 1973.

2.8. Types of Wells

Wells may be classified with respect to construction methods as dug, bored, driven, drilled, and jetted. Drilled wells may be drilled by either the rotary or the percussion method. Each type of well has distinguishing physical characteristics and is best adapted to meet particular water development requirements as shown in the accompanying table. The following factors should be considered when choosing the type of well to be constructed in a given situation.

1. Characteristics of the subsurface strata to be penetrated and their influence upon the method of construction
2. Hydrology of the specific situation and hydraulic properties of the aquifer; seasonal fluctuations of water levels
3. Degree of sanitary protection desired, particularly as this is affected by well depth
4. Cost of construction work and materials

WATER WELL CONSTRUCTION METHODS AND APPLICATIONS

Method	Materials for which the well is best suited	Water table depth for which best suited (feet)	Usual maximum depth (feet)	Usual diameter range	Usual casing material	Customary use	Yield* (gallons per minute)	Remarks
Driven wells: hand, air hammer	Silt, sand, gravel less than 2 inches	5 to 15	50	1¼ to 4 inches	Standard-weight pipe	Domestic, drainage	3 to 40	Limited to shallow water table; no large gravel
Jetted wells: light portable rig	Silt, sand, gravel less than 1 inch	5 to 15	50	1½ to 3 inches	Standard-weight pipe	Domestic, drainage	3 to 30	Limited to shallow water table; no large gravel
Drilled wells: cable tools	Unconsolidated and consolidated medium-hard and hard rock	Any depth	1500†	3 to 24 inches	Steel or wrought-iron pipe	All uses	3 to 3000	Effective for water exploration; requires casing in loose materials; mud scow and hollow rod bits developed for drilling unconsolidated fine to medium sediments
Hydraulic rotary	Silt, sand, gravel less than 1 inch; soft to hard consolidated rock	Any depth	1500†	3 to 18 inches	Steel or wrought-iron pipe	All uses	3 to 3000	Fastest method for all except hardest rock; casing usually not required during drilling; effective for gravel envelope wells
Reverse hydraulic rotary	Silt, sand, gravel, cobble	5 to 100	200	16 to 48 inches	Steel or wrought-iron pipe	Irrigation, industrial, municipal	500 to 4000	Effective for large-diameter holes in unconsolidated and partially consolidated deposits; requires large volume of water for drilling; effective for gravel envelope wells
Air rotary	Silt, sand, gravel less than 2 inches, soft to hard consolidated rock	Any depth	2000†	12 to 20 inches	Steel or wrought-iron pipe	Irrigation, industrial, municipal	500 to 3000	Now used in oil exploration; very fast drilling; combines rotary and percussion methods (air drilling); cuttings removed by air; would be economical for deep-water wells
Augering: hand auger	Clay, silt, sand, gravel less than 1 inch	5 to 30	35	2 to 8 inches	Sheet metal	Domestic, drainage	3 to 50	Most effective for penetrating and removing clay; limited by gravel over 1 inch; casing required if material is loose
Power auger	Clay, silt, sand, gravel less than 2 inches	5 to 50	75	6 to 36 inches	Concrete, steel, or wrought-iron pipe	Domestic, irrigation, drainage	3 to 100	Limited by gravel over 2 inches; otherwise the same as for hand auger

*Yield influenced primarily by geology and availability of groundwater.
†Greater depths reached with heavier equipment.

2.9 Types of Springs

The various types of springs and their characteristics are shown in the accompanying table.

TYPES OF SPRINGS AND THEIR CHARACTERISTIC FEATURES

Characteristic \ Type of spring	Gravity			Artesian	
	Depression springs	Contact springs	Fracture and tubular springs	Aquifer outcrop springs	Fault springs
Location	Along outcrop of the water table at the edges or in bottom of valleys, basins, and depressions in moraines filled with alluvium (stream deposits of gravel, sand, silt and clay) and in valleys cut in massive, permeable sandstone	Possibly present on hillsides or in valleys wherever the outcrop of an impermeable layer beneath a water-bearing permeable layer occurs	On hillsides or in valleys or wherever land surface is below the water table	Possibly present in any topographic position along outcrop of aquifer	Possibly present at any location along a fault or related fractures
Type of opening and water-bearing material	Irregular spaces between grains of the permeable material	Openings in sand or gravel irregular, intergranular spaces; openings in rocks joints or fractures; openings possibly tubular in limestone, gypsum, and basalt	Fractures in all kinds of rocks and sometimes tubular openings in limestone, gypsum, and lava Water-bearing material; fractured or jointed rocks	Depending upon nature of water-bearing material; if aquifer is sandstone, water possibly seeping from spaces between grains or from joints or tubular openings Water-bearing material; sandstone, limestone, or jointed basalt	Depending upon the nature of materials at the land surface; if surface is alluvium, water issuing from spaces between grains; if the surface is rock, water issuing from fractures Water-bearing material; possibly sandstone, limestone, or basalt; surface material may not indicate nature of the aquifer
Yield	Depending upon permeability of water-bearing material and size of tributary area; flow possibly ranging from less than 1 to several gallons per minute	Volume of flow possibly ranging from less than 1 gallon per minute to several thousand gallons per minute, depending upon permeability of the water-bearing material, the volume of aquifer tributary to the spring, and conditions of water intake	Flow possibly ranging from less than 1 to hundreds of gallons per minute, depending upon the extent of fracturing or joint system tributary to the opening	Flow possibly ranging from a few to several thousand gallon per minute	Volume of flow possibly ranging from a few to several thousand gallon per minute

(Continued)

TYPES OF SPRINGS AND THEIR CHARACTERISTIC FEATURES (Continued)

Type of spring / Characteristic	Gravity			Artesian	
	Depression springs	Contact springs	Fracture and tubular springs	Aquifer outcrop springs	Fault springs
Type of flow	May be either perennial or intermittent, depending upon rise or fall of the water table; if the contributing area is small, the flow will depend on local precipitation	Usually perennial for contact springs supplied by the area water table; if the contact spring is supplied by a perched water table, the flow possibly intermittent	Usually perennial; possibly fluctuating with precipitation if the contributing area is small	Perennial, usually constant; quickly affected by wells drawing from same aquifer; possibly affected by long droughts	Perennial, constant, and only affected by long periods of drought; quickly affected by pumping from wells drawing upon the source aquifer
Quality of water	Usually fair to excellent but may be mineralized if the aquifer contains soluble substances	Usually fair to excellent but may be mineralized if water-bearing material is soluble	Usually good to excellent; possibly hard, because of calcium carbonate if spring issues from or percolates through limestone	Usually good to excellent; water possibly hard if aquifer is limestone	Usually good to excellent; water possibly hard if aquifer is limestone
Features produced	Usually none in valleys; in windswept arid and semiarid basins the wetted area and the vegetation growing around the spring may cause deposition of material resulting in a mound of loess and organic matter	Travertine (calcium carbonate) deposited as described under "Fracture and tubular springs"	Travertine deposited about the spring opening if warmer than the mean annual temperature and has percolated through limestone on its way to the point of discharge; water from other materials usually producing no surface features	If water is from a limestone aquifer and is warmer than the mean annual temperature, travertine will be deposited; the reduction of pressure in an artesian aquifer that occurs as the water reaches the surface also causes deposition of dissolved solids about the spring opening	

2.10 Site Comparison: Checklist

Sites may be examined and compared with the following checklist.

1. Conformance with urban pattern
   a. Conformance with accepted urban development plans, tentative plans, or probable trends in land use
   b. Present zoning: possible changes
   c. Approval of city planning bodies
   d. Possibility of closing existing streets and dedicating new streets
   e. Effect of building codes and possibility of modification
2. Slum clearance considerations
   a. Number, character, and condition of existing buildings on site
   b. Number of families housed at present
   c. Relocation of present residents
   d. Equivalent elimination
3. Characteristics of site and environment
   a. Area of site compared with area needed for buildings and project facilities
   b. Shape of site, parcels necessarily excluded, deed restrictions, and easements
   c. Topography as it affects livability of the site plan; favorable features such as existing shade trees, pleasing outlook, and desirable slopes
   d. Quality of neighborhood: extent of nonresidential land use, suitability of neighborhood for dwelling type desired
   e. Effect of project on neighborhood
   f. Hazards: possibility of flooding, slides, or subsidence; proximity to railroads, high-speed trafficways, high embankments, unprotected bodies of water; presence of insect or rodent breeding places; high groundwater level that might cause dampness in building
   g. Nuisances: nearness to industrial plants, railroads, switchyards, heavy-traffic streets, airports, and so on, causing noise, smoke, dust, odor, or vibrations
4. Availability of special municipal services
   a. Garbage and rubbish collection
   b. Fire protection as affected by site location and street access
   c. Streets: lighting, cleaning, maintenance, snow removal, tree planting and maintenance, and so on
   d. Police protection and other municipal services
5. Civic and community facilities
   a. Public transportation facilities: means, routes, adequacy and expense of transportation to employment, schools, central business district, and so on
   b. Accessibility to paved thoroughfares
   c. Amount and character of employment within walking distance and within reasonable travel radius
   d. Stores and markets: kinds and locations; need for additional facilities as part of project development
   e. Schools (grade, junior high, and high): locations, capacities, adequacy; probability of enlargement if needed
   f. Parks and playgrounds: locations, facilities provided, adequacy, maintenance and supervision supplied; possible additions
   g. Churches, theaters, clinics
6. Appropriateness of project design to site, with reference to livability
   a. Type or types of dwellings
   b. Project density
   c. Utility selection
7. Elements of project development cost
   a. Land costs, including site acquisition, expense, and unpaid special assessments
   b. Effect of soil conditions, topographic features, project density appropriate to the neighborhood, availability of utilities, extent of existing street improvements, recreational facilities and additions to be provided by municipality or utility companies, and so on
   c. Building types, utility selection, site conditions, and requirements for nondwelling structures
8. Project maintenance and operating costs
   a. Differences in costs of utilities appropriate to the respective sites
   b. Differentials in grounds maintenance costs due to topography
   c. Differences in payments in lieu of taxes

2.11 Residential Site Selection

Controlling Importance of Site Selection The purpose of selecting a site for residential development may be summarized as follows: to procure a site which is suitable for physical development, including the installation of utilities, and for the provision of dwellings, a circulation system, and neighborhood community facilities in a well-planned relation (all within the economic means of a definitely visualized group of families), and which is free from any grossly unfavorable environmental factors.

The selection of a site for a neighborhood, housing project, or subdivision is an irrevocable step that often makes the difference between success and failure. It is for this reason that site selection assumes such critical importance.

The perfect site seldom exists. Judgment must be made, on the one hand, as to the limitations that wholly preclude satisfactory development and, on the other hand, as to the site defects that can be brought within satisfactory limits or must, in a given case, be accepted as minor but necessary evils. The lines of demarcation are not always definite, and much depends on cost. If adverse conditions make the choice doubtful, the developer must determine three fundamental conditions:

1. Are the necessary improvements technically feasible?
2. If remedial action is the responsibility of an outside agency, is there a guarantee that defects will be corrected within a reasonable period of time?
3. If such improvements fall upon the developer, are they feasible within the economic range of the projected development?

Many problems to be judged in the course of site selection will of course be evident to lay people on their first inspection of a site; others lie below the surface of the land and will be handled by proper specialists. A third type of problem, however, should be stressed: the problem that varies seasonally (or in any other cycle). A piece of land that is bone-dry in August may be regularly flooded by a rise of groundwater in March. The odors of a nearby hog farm may not be evident on a still day, but the prevailing summer breezes might waft them to every open window on the site.

Essential Physical Characteristics of the Site The following conditions for healthful development and maintenance must be borne in mind in the selection of a site.

Soil and Subsoil Conditions Soil and subsoil conditions must be suitable for excavation and site preparation, for the location of utility connections, and for grading and planting. Subsoil conditions should afford suitable bearing capacity for the economical construction of buildings of the types contemplated. Bearing capacity will be affected if the site contains muck, peat, poorly compacted fill, shifting sand, or quicksand. Test borings will normally be needed as a check on these and other characteristics. For economical construction subsoil should contain no ledge, hardpan, or other obstruction to efficient excavation for the necessary utilities, foundations, or basements.

Groundwater and Drainage Essential factors in site selection include a water table low enough to protect the buildings against basement flooding and interference with sewerage, the absence of swamps or marshes, and sufficient slope to permit surface drainage of normal rainfall and a free flow of sanitary sewers. Periodic flooding due to the high groundwater table should disqualify a site unless preventive measures can be applied.

If dwelling basements are contemplated, the groundwater table should be below basement floors. Even where basements are not used, high groundwater may cause dampness in crawl spaces beneath the buildings. Such dampness has caused serious problems and expense in many housing developments.

Flooding due to groundwater may occur not only through conditions on the site itself but also from present or future drainage onto the site from adjacent areas. Groundwater observation may be needed in several seasons, or the testimony of those familiar with the site throughout the year should be sought. In addition, possible future developments in adjoining areas should be taken into account.

Freedom From Surface Floods The development area should be free from danger of surface flooding by streams, lakes, or tidal waters. Significant floods are those that inundate buildings, make them unusable by drowning utilities, or impede circulation within or to and from the development area.

Ideally, no land should be included in a development area that has been flooded at any time of record unless flood control measures have subsequently removed the danger. As a practical matter, locally varying compromises may be made below this standard. It would seem reasonable to insist, however, that land be excluded from development areas if it shows a history of flooding at intervals of less than 25 years unless the source of the flood has subsequently been controlled.

Suitability for Siting of Projected Buildings Land should not be too steep for satisfactory grading in relation to dwelling construction. Building sites should not have elevations above those at which normal water pressure for domestic use and fire fighting can be obtained.

The orientation of slopes may affect the possibility of good development. Southerly slopes will favor exposure of dwellings to the winter sun (steep northerly slopes may be undesirable on this count alone).

Suitability for Access and Circulation Topography should permit adequate vehicular and pedestrian access to and circulation within the development area. It should permit grading so that streets and walks conform to grade standards.

Suitability for Development of Open Areas Land to be reserved for private yards or gardens, play lots, playgrounds, and neighborhood parks should permit grading and development in conformance with specifications.

SOURCE: *Planning the Neighborhood,* Public Administration Service, Chicago, 1960.

Freedom from Topographic Accident Hazards The development area should be free from, or the plan should assure correction of, topographic conditions that might be a serious cause of bodily accidents. Under this heading would come bluffs or precipices, open pits, and hazardous shorelines.

If there is a reasonable expectancy of a major earth movement that may cause loss of life or serious damage to structures or utilities, every attempt should be made to avoid sites within the area affected. If this is impossible, special consideration should be given to placing and constructing the buildings so as to reduce the hazard to a minimum. Hazards of this type include landslides, earth settlement above disused mine workings, and earthquake slippage along known geological fault lines.

Availability of Sanitary and Protective Services

Water Supply and Sanitary Sewage Disposal Without the assurance of water for their overnight needs, campers will not pitch their tents. A healthful neighborhood can be developed only on a site with a water supply that is adequate and certain as to amount, that will not be a means of conveying disease, and that is reasonably free from chemical and physical impurities. Equally important is the collection and ultimate disposal of human excreta without sanitary hazard.

Where an existing municipal water supply and sewerage system can be used, the needed safeguards will usually have been assured by local authorities. However, where a new supply must be developed or new disposal facilities provided, the usability of a site may be determined wholly by the problems of such an installation. Under no circumstances should a site lacking public water supply and sewerage systems be accepted without a binding assurance that these problems can be solved.

A point that can hardly be overstressed is that water and sewerage systems must be visualized as long-term sanitary services and not merely as physical installations. Advance approval by the proper health authorities is equally imperative for on-site sewage disposal

facilities and for proposed extensions of existing water or sewer lines to serve a site.

A public water supply, with assured maintenance of official health standards, is generally preferable to individual or community private supplies on grounds both of safety and of economy. Preference should therefore be given to a site having access to a public system. Where a public supply is unavailable, it is necessary to be certain that a local supply can be developed at a reasonable cost.

In any case, under standard conditions water of safe quality must be available in each dwelling under pressure, and the general supply must be adequate in amount to provide for fire fighting and other special needs. Under certain semirural conditions, it may temporarily be necessary to accept supplies of safe quality from individual wells.

Removal of bodily wastes from a dwelling by a water carriage system is accepted by urban and semiurban America as standard practice. From a public health standpoint, a public sewerage system that is properly designed and operated affords the greatest safety. A site will usually be suitable for development if every residence can be connected to a public sewerage system of sufficient capacity. In the absence of a public sewerage system, an on-site community system is generally safer than septic tanks or other individual installations, provided adequate maintenance is assured.

The technical considerations in the development and operation of water and sewer systems should be studied before any neighborhood site is selected, for even if public water and sewer systems exist near the site, they may be inadequate or unavailable.

Removal of Refuse It is essential that a projected site have facilities for the effective removal from the neighborhood of domestic wastes (notably garbage but also inflammable and noncombustible rubbish) or that ultimate disposal on the site can be provided without sanitary hazard. Garbage should be regularly collected at time intervals varying from daily in hot weather to weekly in cold weather. If rubbish is collected separately, it may be removed

at somewhat less frequent intervals.

If regular municipal collection services can be tapped, no site selection problem of this kind will generally exist. The necessity of facilities within or near the site for burial, incineration, or chemical reduction will call for study of precautionary measures. Major problems will be a segregated location for disposal, avoidance of wind-borne smoke or odors, and the use of disposal methods that eliminate rat harborage and insect breeding.

Power, Fuel, and Communications Electricity is essential in every home, but since electric service can usually be extended to any development of more than a few families and can even be generated on the site if necessary, it seldom offers a serious problem in site selection. Reasonable electricity rates, especially in outlying areas where, in the absence of gas, electricity may be used for cooking and water heating, may be an important factor in achieving a reasonable total housing cost.

Gas is not considered an essential utility. If a domestic gas supply is desired beyond the reach of distribution mains, portable high-pressure tanks may serve the need.

Telephone service, like electricity, can be extended to most sites offering a demand. Its availability is seldom important as a site selection factor.

Fire and Police Protection Since water requirements for fire fighting normally set the peak-load demand for a community supply, this factor in the adequacy of fire protection will automatically be checked as a part of other site selection judgments.

The availability of fire-fighting crews and equipment from the larger community will depend on both the location of the new neighborhood and the administrative relations between the two. When these facilities must be supplied on the site by the developer, they will be an important factor of operating cost.

SOURCE: *Planning the Neighborhood*, Public Administration Service, Chicago, 1960.

The feasibility of police protection is little affected by location, but like fire protection it may involve special costs in isolated neighborhoods.

Freedom from Local Hazards and Nuisances The site should be entirely free from grave hazards to life or health and as free as possible from minor hazards and nuisances. Adequate techniques for measuring the seriousness of specific nuisances and standards for site selection in regard to them do not exist. Research on this whole problem, especially on such factors as minimum distances of dwellings from railroad lines, is badly needed. Some guides to specific standards for new development can be obtained from the procedures for the evaluation of existing neighborhoods given in a standard housing appraisal method.[1]

Certain nuisances and hazards may not be apparent in a single inspection of the site. Investigation must take into account the fact that many nuisances depend on season of the year, the time of day, the wind direction, or other weather factors. Nuisances and hazards common to all parts of a city, such as smoke in Knoxville or steep hills in San Francisco, must naturally be tolerated except where the degree of seriousness is markedly above the citywide norm.

Accident Hazards Major accident hazards are collision with moving vehicles, fire and explosions, falls, and drowning. The chief causes of collision are street traffic and railroads, with crash landings of aircraft to be considered near an airport. Sources of fire and explosion hazards include bulk storage of petroleum, gasoline, or gas; rifle ranges and other places where firearms are used under potentially dangerous conditions; dumps and rubbish piles; large expanses of brushland or cutover woodland from which the slash has not been cleared, especially in dry climates; and certain industries. Falls and drowning may occur with unprotected bodies of water, quarries, pits, junkyards, and so on.

Housing should not be located within the influence range of fire and explosion hazards from industrial sources. Safe distances from airports, as specified in airport zoning ordinances, should be maintained.

With respect to fire and explosion hazards, the "safe" distance must be determined for each specific hazard. Fire hazards not involving explosions may be partially controlled by the provision of adequate firebreaks.

It is desirable for both safety and noise protection to avoid housing construction on sites adjacent to heavy street traffic or railroads. When this is impossible, the following precautions against accidents must be enforced:

1. No grade crossings of railroads in or near the development area without a 24-hour guard. Rail lines at grade or depressed should be completely fenced or otherwise closed off so that children cannot wander onto them.
2. Adequate control of traffic hazards on all streets.

Accident hazards such as quarries, junkyards, docks, swamps, or hidden ponds are particularly dangerous to children. Sites near or including these hazards should not be used for housing without fencing off such features.

Noise and Vibration Excessive noise, sometimes with appreciable vibration, is commonly produced by railroads, airports, street traffic, heavy industry, boat whistles, foghorns, and the like. The site and the surrounding area should be investigated for such potential sources of noise. Where they exist, their distance from the source of the site and the presence of sound barriers should be determined. In the case of an undeveloped site in open country, distant noise of moderate intensity will tend to be masked by the general noise level of the new development itself.

Persons concerned with the operation of nearby airports, railroads, or industry and persons familiar with the site should be consulted as to the timing of noises and the carrying effect of prevailing winds. In investigating railroads, the character of the railroad (frequency of passenger and freight service, existence of switchyards) and the design of rights-of-way (tracks depressed, at grade, or elevated) should be considered. For airports, the type of traffic (commercial, military, or private) and its frequency should be determined.

Street noise should be considered not only as to volume of traffic but as to traffic congestion and steep hills, or stop intersections that necessitate gear shifting, braking, and the use of horns.

Housing should not be located on sites where excessive and uncontrollable noise regularly occurs, especially at night. Steady noises of moderate intensity, such as those of a highway or a major traffic street, can sometimes be brought within tolerable limits by barrier planting or by deep setbacks of dwellings from the source.

Odors, Smoke, and Dust The commonest sources of objectionable odors are the following:

1. Industrial plants, especially slaughterhouses, tanneries, and other animal product factories; rubber, chemical, or fertilizer plants; textile dyeing, bleaching, and finishing plants; paper, soap, or paint factories; and gasworks
2. Refuse dumps, especially when the disposal process involves burning
3. Streams polluted by sewage, sewer outfalls, or poorly operated sewage disposal plants
4. Farm animals, especially pigs or goats when kept under crowded or insanitary conditions; also, under some circumstances, any farm animals, manure, and fertilizer
5. Fumes from heavy motor traffic and from coal-burning railroads

Common sources of smoke and dust include industry, railroads, dumps, and incinerators. Dust may also come from open untreated dirt such as vacant lots, unplanted farmland and recreation areas, or other large expanses of dirt.

---

[1] *An Appraisal Method for Measuring the Quality of Housing*, part 3, *Appraisal of Neighborhood Environment*, American Public Health Association, Committee on the Hygiene of Housing, New York, 1950.

SOURCE: *Planning the Neighborhood*, Public Administration Service, Chicago, 1960.

The seriousness of these nuisances will depend on their intensity and frequency. Investigation should cover not only the distance of the site from potential sources but the direction of winds prevailing in all seasons. Smoke, dust, and odors may be a serious nuisance without being evident in a single investigation of the site, owing to the absence of wind or the season or time of day. Inquiries should be made of impartial persons familiar with the site over a long period. If there is any doubt as to the seriousness of smoke, odors, or dust, public-health officials should be consulted.

Excessive localized smoke, odor, or dust, unless it can be controlled, should disqualify a site for residential use. Because standards for measuring smoke are inadequate for site selection purposes and standards for odors are nonexistent, decisions as to the seriousness of the nuisance must be based on the judgment of qualified investigators. It should be noted that a continuous low-intensity odor is less likely to be objectionable than a periodic odor of equal intensity. However, an odor with unpleasant associations (from sewage disposal or pigsty) causes greater annoyance than

stronger odors without unpleasant associations.

Control of smoke and industrial odors can usually be obtained only by legal regulation, perhaps on a citywide basis. When ordinances exist, enforcement for the protection of a particular site may be possible.

SOURCE: *Planning the Neighborhood,* Public Administration Service, Chicago, 1960.

2.12 Site Selection for Multifamily Housing

The following topics should be considered in analyzing sites for multifamily housing:

1. Marketability
   a. Demand for multifamily housing
      (1) At what rents?
      (2) Distribution (no bedroom or one, two, or three bedrooms)
      (3) Size of rooms
   b. Existing population and potential growth
   c. Type of existing tenants living in apartments
      (1) With children and how many?
      (2) Without children
      (3) Elderly
      (4) Single-occupancy
      (5) Income brackets
      (6) Age brackets
   d. Industries in the area and their future plans
2. Pertinent information of the surrounding area
   a. Existing street layout and how it may affect the parcel in question
   b. Proposed street changes
      (1) Widening
      (2) Elimination of streets
      (3) Map changes
   c. Location of main arteries (parkways, freeways, and highways)
   d. Mobility from site in all directions
   e. Zoning and proposed changes
   f. Kind of buildings
      (1) Single-family
      (2) Multifamily
      (3) Commercial and industrial
   g. Appearance and general character
      (1) Design of exteriors
      (2) Condition of buildings, grounds, and streets
   h. Off-street parking
      (1) Is the surrounding area provided with adequate off-street parking?
      (2) Are the existing streets wide enough for street parking and easy access for cars and service vehicles?
   i. Proximity of parks, public playgrounds, other recreation areas, and waterways, if any, to site
   j. Hazards
      (1) Noise

      (2) Proximity of airports, railroads, and trucking highways
      (3) Smoke and fumes
      (4) High-tension wires
      (5) Ravines
   k. General trend
      (1) Stability of area
      (2) Building expansion
      (3) Deterioration
3. Transportation available
   a. Other than automobile
      (1) Rapid transit
      (2) Bus
      (3) Railroad
      (4) Taxis and other vehicles, such as helicopters, hydrofoils, ferryboats, and airplanes
   b. Time of travel to center of city and to job location
   c. Automobile travel
      (1) To center city
      (2) To job location
   d. Cost of daily traveling
      (1) Daily fares
      (2) Gas and oil and parking charges if by car
   e. Schedule of transport services
4. Zoning of the site
   a. Density coverage, height, yard requirements, and parking
   b. Proposed changes, if any
5. Planning boards
   a. Rules and regulations that control land development other than zoning
6. Deed restrictions
7. Community facilities (distance from the site and methods of getting there)
   a. Schools
      (1) Public, parochial, or preschool
      (2) Elementary, junior high, and high school
   b. Shopping
      (1) Necessities
      (2) All others
   c. Religious buildings
      (1) Denominations
   d. Recreation
      (1) Theaters
      (2) Playgrounds, beaches, swimming pools, bowling alleys, and others
   e. Hospitals, medical centers, and clinics
   f. Cultural
      (1) Libraries, art galleries, museums, and

      other cultural facilities
8. Community services
   a. Garbage and refuse collection
   b. Police and fire protection
   c. Snow removal
   d. Street cleaning
   e. Street maintenance
   f. Street lighting
9. Size and shape
   a. If irregular, can plot be utilized efficiently?
   b. If small, can an economical project be built?
10. Topography
    a. Rugged, gently sloping, or flat terrain
    b. Rock exposure or filled-in land
    c. Type of surface soil
    d. Surface drainage and groundwater
    e. Natural features
       (1) Trees, streams, lakes, adjoining parks, and rock outcroppings
11. Subsurface conditions (information usually received from borings)
    a. Composition of soil
    b. Evidence of rock or filled-in land
    c. Soil bearing capacity (necessity of piling)
    d. Underground streams
    e. Water level
    f. Percolation of soil
12. Utilities
    a. Storm and sanitary
       (1) Combined or separate
       (2) Nearby body of water or drainage ditch
       (3) Depth of sewers
       (4) Adequacy of sizes and pitch for additional loads anticipated
       (5) Public or private
    b. Water supply
       (1) Pressure
       (2) Reservoir, well, or other
       (3) Rates
       (4) Who pays for installation (from what point to what point)?
    c. Gas
       (1) High- or low-pressure
       (2) Natural or manufactured
       (3) Rates
       (4) Who pays for installation (from what point to what point)?

SOURCE: Samuel Paul, *Apartments*, Van Nostrand Reinhold Company, New York, 1967.

d. Electricity
    (1) Overhead or underground
    (2) Current available
    (3) Rates
    (4) Who pays for installation (from what point to what point)?
e. Telephone service

13. Features
  a. Views
  b. Trees, streams, lakes, and parks

14. Cost of site
  a. Potential yield (number of families)
    (1) Land cost per family
    (2) Land cost per room
  b. Rent limitations for area
    (1) Rent per room per month
    (2) Relation of total rent to cost of site
  c. Cost of abnormal site conditions
    (1) Excessive fill and grading
    (2) Piling

    (3) Rock excavation
    (4) Possible retaining walls
    (5) Cost of bringing utilities to site

SOURCE: Samuel Paul, *Apartments,* Van Nostrand Reinhold Company, New York, 1967.

SCORECARD FOR SELECTION OF SCHOOL BUILDING SITES

Location of site under consideration_____

Item	Description	1	2
1. Present and future environment:			75
a. Nature of present surroundings		50	
(1) Character of nearby residential housing	General locality offering only the most favorable social influences		
(2) Freedom from business distractions	Not near commercial centers or shops that take on undesirable characteristics		
(3) Freedom from noise, odors, dust, and traffic of industry	Set distinctly apart from industry and its inconveniences; prevailing winds fully considered		
(4) Remoteness from railroads, landing fields, and docks	Without impact of disturbing conditions from these traffic centers		
(5) Remoteness from heavily traveled highways	Sufficiently protected from highway noises and hazards		
b. Protection from present and possible future air travel routes	Location approved after careful study of takeoff and landing practices	10	
c. Future prospect for surroundings	Conservation of an attractive community setting apparently assured	15	
2. Integration with community planning:			75
a. Acceptability in complete community plan	Satisfying requirements of the comprehensive community plan and contributing its share of values	50	
b. Noninterference with other community projects	Sufficiently remote from hospital, church, and other community zones so that they will suffer no disturbance from large groups of children	15	
c. Value for extensive community use	Accessible and readily adjusted to adult use	10	
3. Role in comprehensive school-building plan:			100
a. Scientific determination of location with respect to present and future population	Objective techniques used to measure population in all aspects contributing to best choice	25	
b. Integration with existing schools	Serving a territory without overlapping or duplication with existing schools that have the promise of permanence	25	
c. Place in ultimate school program	Permanent dedication to education insofar as foreseeable	25	
d. Official approval of general location	Satisfactory to board of education and approved by current faculty	25	
4. Size of site:			300
a. Conformity to present and future educational programs	Making for satisfactory educational use and for educational expansion	50	
b. Compliance with following suggestions as the minimum in each case:	The minimum to be met; characteristics of locality and costs affecting final decision	150	
(1) 10 acres for a primary or elementary school and 1 acre for each 100 pupils	15 acres not necessarily excessive		
(2) 20 acres for a middle or junior high school and 1 acre for each 100 pupils	A defensible minimum because of present and future middle or junior high school programs		
(3) 30 acres for a senior high school and 1 acre for each 100 pupils	Acreage in excess of this minimum usually a good purchase		
c. Safeguarding of future educational extensions	Vision in selection encompassing all foreseeable extension needs	50	

(Continued)

2.13 Site Selection for Schools

In choosing a school site from several parcels of land under consideration, school officials may wish to rate each site with the aid of a scorecard that carries the criteria found by experience to be most significant. Such a scorecard is shown in the accompanying table.

With the use of this scorecard, ratings for school sites under consideration may be given on a 1000-point scale. Although these ratings will reflect the subjective judgments of the scorers, they ought to fall within a fairly narrow range if the basic criteria for selection are accepted in equal degree by all the scorers. An average of three carefully worked-out scores may be expected to give a fair rating to a site. Sites with ratings below 750 to 800 points can be considered poor choices for a school. To rate a site, scores should be placed to the right of the numbers in column 1 representing the perfect or maximum scores for each item. The totals in each section should then be entered to the right of the ideal totals in column 2. The total of the column 2 scores represents the overall score for the site.

SOURCE: Nickolaus L. Engelhardt, *Complete Guide for Planning New Schools*, Parker Publishing Co., Inc., Englewood Cliffs, N.J., 1970.

SCORECARD FOR SELECTION OF SCHOOL BUILDING SITES (Continued)
Location of site under consideration

Item	Description	1	2
d. Provision for present and future play areas for all groups	Character of land and orientation ensuring play and recreational facilities for all	50	
5. Accessibility:			100
a. Accessibility for general public	Free from approach and exit hazards; no dangerous gradients	25	
b. Optimum travel distances for children		25	
(1) 1½ to 2 miles for senior high school	Based upon national practices and not in conflict with local traditions; distances measured as the crow flies; travel routes protected by traffic lights and with police cooperation (these distances usually make possible schools of acceptable enrollments)		
(2) 1 mile for junior high or middle school			
(3) ½ mile for elementary school			
(4) ¼ to ½ mile for home-school units			
c. Feasibility of approaches	Pedestrian and vehicular approaches possible without congestion	25	
(1) Pedestrian	Attractive and readily traversable		
(2) Bicycle	Minimum of intersections with other traffic		
(3) Automobile	Minimum of intersections and no excessive grades		
(4) School bus	Easy access to loading center possible		
d. Safety of approaches	Safety the first consideration	25	
(1) Freedom from hazardous crossroads	Entrance and exit routes unhampered by conflicting traffic		
(2) Provision of sidewalks and good roads	Assurance of sidewalks and preferred road approaches		
(3) Elimination of conflicting travel currents	Freedom from heavy travel at school opening and closing hours		
(4) Provision of underpasses and pedestrian bridges	Artificial protection from crossing heavy or through traffic lines		
6. Site characteristics:			200
a. Shape of site	Square or rectangular preferred over very irregular or "shoestring" sites	50	
b. Present utilization	Site to be free of structures involving high costs for removal	25	
c. Aesthetic value of site	Maximum capitalization of views at a distance and at close range	25	
d. Influence of site on building design	Stimulation of community-acceptable design through characteristics of site	10	
e. Possibility of preferred orientation for all rooms and all game areas	Dimensions of site offering no restriction to freedom of planning	25	

(Continued)

SOURCE: Nickolaus L. Engelhardt, *Complete Guide for Planning New Schools,* Parker Publishing Co., Inc., Englewood Cliffs, N.J., 1970.

SCORECARD FOR SELECTION OF SCHOOL BUILDING SITES (Continued)
Location of site under consideration

Item	Description	1	2
f. Prevalence of characteristics usable to educational advantage	Abundance of natural resources such as trees, water, and elevations	15	
g. Ease of surface adaptation for buildings, play areas, and parking	Surface and near-surface conditions offering no known handicap to planning	25	
h. Subsoil conditions	No excessive fill, rock, quicksand, or subsurface water conditions known	25	
7. Utility services:			50
a. Proximity of utility connections	Ready access to utilities possible	25	
(1) Water connections	Excessive trenching not required		
(2) Sewage connections	Reasonably near connections possible		
(3) Gas	Distance for gas connections reasonably short		
b. Feasibility of making serviceable utility connections	Freedom from undesirable subsurface conditions	25	
8. Costs:			100
a. Cost of land	Favorable comparison with other nearby land costs per acre	50	
b. Cost of site preparation	No unusual site features necessitating excessive costs	25	
(1) General adjustment of land contours for building and play areas	Site characteristics lending themselves to complete and distinctive planning		
(2) Sufficient elevation for safeguarding drainage at reasonable cost	Sufficiently commanding location for buildings and reasonable adjustment for play areas		
(3) Freedom from drainage from contiguous land	Proposed site, rather than adjoining land, controlling drainage problem		
(4) Ease of preparation of parking areas, entrances, and service roads	Parking areas feasible for teachers, visitors, and students; ready creation of roads possible		
(5) Additional charges for piling, rock excavation, tree removal, and the like	Site conditions causing no serious costs for these items		
(6) Removal or razing of existing buildings	Salvage value of existing structures establishing low cost		
c. Cost of utility connections	Reasonably low	15	
(1) Length of trench work necessary	Not excessive		
(2) Extent of pumping needs	Not beyond average expectation		
d. Cost of new improvements adjoining and approaching site	Much of this cost not chargeable to the school	10	
(1) New street paving required	Payment following local practice		
(2) New sidewalk installations	This requirement entailing costs chargeable to school building budget		
	Maximum possible score	1000	1000

NOTE: Use the second half of column 1 for the scores on the lettered subdivisions when a specific site is being rated. The second half of column 2 permits summation of these scores.

SOURCE: Nickolaus L. Engelhardt, *Complete Guide for Planning New Schools*, Parker Publishing Co., Inc., Englewood Cliffs, N.J., 1970.

2.14 Industrial Site Selection

Noncost Factor Evaluation Under normal location procedures, particularly for a small or medium-size installation, it is extremely difficult, if not impossible, to establish reliable cost values for all the factors applicable in the location study. For factors which it is desirable to consider relative to the plant location but for which, because of required expenditures, required time, or lack of facilities, it is impractical to establish reliable costs, a noncost evaluation system may be designed, and each location may be evaluated on the basis of the cumulative effect of the factor values for the particular location.

As with any situation requiring subjective evaluation, it is necessary to design an evaluation system whereby each factor is assigned a proportional value relative to all other factors under consideration, while at the same time providing a means whereby a value for each factor may be assigned to each location according to the degree or quality of that factor existing at the particular location under consideration. For plant location purposes, the steps by which to accomplish this are as follows:

1. Prepare a list of the factors considered important to the location of the individual plant that are not being evaluated on a cost basis. In the initial list all possible factors should be included. If after the start of the evaluation procedure it is found that certain factors tend to be insignificant, they can be eliminated.

2. Establish relative values for each factor. The relative value assigned to each factor should be based upon its value under the most desirable conditions. It is convenient to express such relative values in terms of assigned points. A percentage of total worth may be used under certain conditions, but when a large number of factors are being evaluated, the individual percentage values assigned are numerically so small that difficulties are created in later steps in the evaluation procedure. If desired, a predetermined total number of points to be distributed among the various factors can be established. This provides a convenient reference value during an evaluation but is not necessary.

3. Establish a number of degrees for each factor. Each factor which has been listed and for which relative values have been established may be present at any particular location in varying degrees. It is necessary to establish means of measuring variations in the presence of each factor at the various locations. Each degree represents a measured variation. The number of degrees assigned to each factor should vary from four to six. The use of four to six degrees permits relative evaluation of the factor present at individual locations without requiring unrealistic differentiation between slight variations in factor presence.

4. Define the degree. The definition of each degree is required so that all personnel involved in the evaluation use the same reference points in selecting the degree of presence of the factor at an individual location. The definition of the maximum degree for each factor would be identical to the definition of the desirable level of presence of the factor at an individual location, as established in step 2. The definition of the lowest degree of each factor will be "not present" or "present in insufficient amounts."

5. Assign point values to the degree. In step 4 we defined the maximum degree of each factor as that level for which the relative point values were assigned in step 2. Therefore, these relative point values can now be assigned as the maximum degree value for each factor. In step 4 we also defined the lowest degree of each factor as being either not present or present in insufficient amounts. Therefore, the value of this lowest degree for the location under consideration must be zero. This establishes the minimum and the maximum point values assignable to the individual factor. It is now possible by either linear or curvilinear methods to establish point values for the intermediate degrees. If curvilinear methods are used, the equation of the curve used for distribution should be the same for each factor. Linear assignment of degree values is the most common and can be accomplished in the following manner:

a. Prepare a table, listing each factor with columns for each degree.

b. Enter zero in the lowest degree column and the point values assigned in step 2 to the maximum degree for each factor.

c. Calculate degree point increments. Increment value is equal to the maximum point value assigned for the individual factor divided by the number of degrees for the factor minus 1. The second degree value will be equal to the degree increment, the third degree value equal to 2 times the degree increment, and so on for each factor.

6. Designate mandatory factors. There will be certain factors within the list whose presence at some level is mandatory at the final location. These factors and the factor degree that is mandatory (which will normally be the second degree) must be designated on the evaluation form. Later, during the course of the actual evaluation, if a particular location fails to have the factor present at the mandatory level, that location is immediately eliminated from further consideration.

7. Evaluate all locations. Considering each location individually, proceed through the list of factors, selecting for each factor the degree that best defines the presence of the factor at the individual location under consideration.

8. Assign points to each location factor. Using the degree evaluations as established in step 7, return to the point value table established in step 5, and enter on the location evaluation sheet the assignable point values for each degree. Summarize the factor points earned by each location under consideration.

9. Select the location. From the standpoint of location selection on the basis of noncost factors, the location which has the highest total number of points and which does not fail to have any of the mandatory factors is selected

SOURCE: Ruddell Reed, Jr., *Plant Layout*, Richard D. Irwin, Inc., Homewood, Ill., 1961.

as the best location for the particular installation.

The location selected on a noncost factor basis can now be compared with the location selected on a cost basis. If the location selected by the two methods agrees, there is a high degree of probability that the most advantageous location for the particular installation has been indicated. If the location selected by the noncost factors differs from that selected on a cost basis, it is normally wise to choose finally the location that offers cost advantages unless the differentiation of the cost advantage over the noncost evaluation is so slight as to be offset by noncost considerations. This, however, is the exception rather than the rule and must be treated as such.

Valuation of Noncost Factors The following is a sample noncost evaluation system. Twenty-one factors with degree definition and assigned degree point values are included. An evaluation of three alternative locations is made below in the table "Converta Speed-King Co.: Summary of Noncost Rating."

1. *Nearness to market.* This factor takes into consideration the speed with which orders can be received and filled. The speed of delivery is of primary importance in building and developing good customer relations.

Degree	Description	Point assignment
0	Very inaccessible to the market	0
1	All markets relatively far from the plant	56
2	Many of the markets relatively far from the plant	112
3	Various distances to the markets fairly well distributed as to being near or distant from the plant	168
4	Majority of the market areas relatively close to the plant	224
Maximum	Location such that weighted distances to the markets are minimized	280

2. *Nearness to unworked goods.* This factor is instrumental in production planning and scheduling. Unworked goods should be available when needed with minimum delay and cost.

Degree	Description	Point assignment
0	Unworked goods practically inaccessible because of excessive travel distance	0
1	All sources relatively far from the plant	44
2	Many sources relatively far from the plant	88
3	Various distances to the sources fairly well distributed as to being near or distant from the plant	132
4	Majority of sources relatively close to the plant	176
Maximum	Location such that weighted distances to the sources are minimized	220

3. *Availability of power.* Power should meet present and future needs. Interruptions to any extent should be nonexistent.

Degree	Description	Point assignment
0	Unavailable	0
1	Available but not of correct nature (DC, 220–110 AC, etc.)	6
2	Available and of correct nature but in insufficient quantity	12
3	Available and of correct nature and in sufficient quantity but not dependable and unable to meet future demands	18
4	Available and of correct nature and in sufficient quantity to meet all future proposed demands	24
Maximum	Available and of correct nature and in sufficient quantity to meet all future proposed demands; also excellent consulting service facilities	30

4. *Climate.* The climate provides a pleasant atmosphere for employees to live and work in.

Degree	Description	Point assignment
0	Unlivable or prohibitive to planned manufacture; corrective measures unable to change conditions	0
1	Extreme variations in climate conditions; susceptible to violent, destructive storms, floods, etc.	6
2	Wide climate variation; infrequent destructive climatic forces	12
3	Wide climate variation; little likelihood of destructive climatic forces	18
4	Moderate climatic variations; very livable; corrective measures needed for limited periods of the year	24
Maximum	Ideal for both living and manufacturing; limited climatic variations	30

5. *Availability of water.* Water is in sufficient amount and pressure to meet drinking, heating, cleaning, and sprinkler system requirements.

Degree	Description	Point assignment
0	Unavailable	0
1	Available in small quantities at premium prices; of dubious purity for manufacturing process	2
2	Available in sufficient quantities for households but not for manufacturing processes	4

(Continued)

SOURCE: Ruddell Reed, Jr., *Plant Layout,* Richard D. Irwin, Inc., Homewood, Ill., 1961.

Degree	Description	Point assignment
3	Available in sufficient quantities for manufacturing but highly treated	6
4	Available in sufficient quantities and pure enough for proposed manufacturing process	8
Maximum	Abundant for proposed usage; of a very pure nature	10

6. *Capital availability.* It is relatively easy to acquire capital for construction, expansion, mortgages, payroll, or other needs by loans or other means.

Degree	Description	Point assignment
0	Unavailable	0
1	Available but at exorbitant rates; very hard to obtain	12
2	Available at exorbitant rates	24
3	Equitable rates of return but hard to obtain	36
4	Equitable rates of return and relatively easy to obtain	48
Maximum	Available at low rates and in sufficient quantities to encourage location	60

7. *Momentum of early start.* There is prior availability of service facilities, markets, labor, materials, and capital, established by similar industries in the general area.

Degree	Description	Point assignment
0	No similar industry present and none coming	0
1	No similar industry present but some coming	2
2	Similar industry present	4
3	Similar industry present and more coming	6
4	Similar industry large portion of industry in area	8
Maximum	Center for given industry in consideration	10

8. *Fire protection.* Adequate facilities are available for protecting plant and employees against the hazard of fire, thereby allowing reduced insurance rates.

Degree	Description	Point assignment
0	No fire protection facilities and many fire hazards	0
1	Few fire protection facilities but no extreme hazards	2
2	Fire hazards present but excellent fire protection facilities existing	4
3	Excellent fire protection facilities available	6
4	Excellent fire protection facilities available; proposed plan to maintain protection at its present quality	8
Maximum	Excellent fire protection facilities available; proposed plan to maintain protection at its present quality; absence of fire hazards	10

9. *Police protection.* Protection is of such a nature as to prevent harm from theft or destruction of property.

Degree	Description	Point assignment
0	No police protection available; theft and property damage common	0
1	Little police protection available; theft and property damage common	4
2	Theft and property damage occurring but excellent police protection in existence	8
3	Excellent police protection available	12
4	Excellent police protection available; proposed plans to maintain this status	16
Maximum	Excellent police protection available; proposed plans to maintain this status; low crime rates	20

10. *Schools and colleges.* There are adequate educational facilities for employees' children of all ages, for continuing adult education, and for the provision of skilled labor.

Degree	Description	Point assignment
0	No schools	0
1	Only low-quality public schools through the high school level	4
2	Only low-quality public schools through the high school level but good private schools	8
3	High-quality public schools through the high school level	12
4	High-quality public schools through the high school level; excellent private, vocational, and junior colleges; colleges or universities very near	16
Maximum	High-quality public schools through the high school level; excellent private, vocational, and junior colleges; colleges or universities very near; comprehensive plan for further adult education available	20

11. *Union activity.* This factor includes the existence of unions and their methods of attaining goals, influence in the industry, general attitude, and influence in the locality.

Degree	Description	Point assignment
0	Powerful, aggressive unions organized through the national and international level	0
1	Powerful, aggressive local unions	12
2	Weak, aggressive local unions	24
3	Unions nonexistent	36
4	Weak cooperative unions	48
Maximum	Cooperative unions	60

SOURCE: Ruddell Reed, Jr., *Plant Layout,* Richard D. Irwin, Inc., Homewood, Ill., 1961.

12. *Churches and religious facilities.* These are provided for all denominations and faiths.

Degree	Description	Point assignment
0	Nonexistent	0
1	Few denominations or faiths	3
2	Variety of denominations and representative faiths	6
Maximum	Excellent facilities for all faiths	10

13. *Recreation opportunities.* Employees should have access to numerous kinds of recreation.

Degree	Description	Point assignment
0	Nonexistent	0
1	A few poor-quality facilities	5
2	A few poor-quality facilities and a few good-quality facilities	10
3	Many good-quality facilities and a few poor-quality facilities; would meet a large range of interests	15
Maximum	Many excellent facilities to meet almost any interest	20

14. *Housing.* Housing is available in various types and in sufficient quantities at reasonable costs.

Degree	Description	Point assignment
0	Nonexistent	0
1	Largely unavailable and of poor quality	2
2	Largely available but of poor quality	4
3	Available, of acceptable quality, and at reasonable rates	6
4	Of excellent quality, in a limited range of types, and at reasonable rates	8
Maximum	Of excellent quality, in a wide range of types, and at reasonable rates	10

15. *Vulnerability to air attack.* The site is near areas that might be considered primary targets by an aggressor force.

Degree	Description	Point assignment
0	Almost assured of being a target area in case of attack	0
1	Probable target area in case of attack	2
2	Possible target area in case of attack	5
3	Improbable target area if there is an attack	7
Maximum	Nonexistent present potential target	10

16. *Community attitude.* The community is willing to accept industry as part of the community; city officials should be receptive and helpful; the general attitude should not be parasitic.

Degree	Description	Point assignment
0	Hostile, bitter, and non-cooperative	0
1	Parasitic in nature	15
2	Noncooperative	30
3	Cooperative	45
Maximum	Friendly and more than co-operative	60

17. *Local ordinances.* Are existing or proposed ordinances likely to prevent planned operation of the plant? Do they impose undue costs in meeting their provisions?

Degree	Description	Point assignment
0	Of such a nature as to prohibit location	0
1	Very restrictive and burdensome	10
2	Enforced biasedly	20
3	Regulated with discretion	30
4	Regulated with discretion and not generally burdensome in nature	40
Maximum	Nonexistent or not burdensome	50

18. *Labor laws.* Do existing or proposed laws have any derogatory effect upon the functioning of labor regulations or proposed employment policies?

Degree	Description	Point assignment
0	Strict and rigidly enforced	0
1	Strict but not rigidly enforced	8
2	Working no hardship on employment policy	15
3	Very few and not troublesome	23
Maximum	Nonexistent or of such a nature as to be conducive to good relations	30

19. *Future growth of community.* Is it likely to parallel the firm's growth and development and provide for the firm's increased demands?

Degree	Description	Point assignment
0	Community dying	0
1	Community growth stagnant	6
2	Community growing very slowly	12
3	Community growing quite rapidly	18
4	Community growing quite rapidly and not experiencing growing pains	24
Maximum	Community prospering and growing in such a manner as to enhance location	30

20. *Medical facilities.* Facilities are adequate to meet and maintain a high overall level of health.

Degree	Description	Point assignment
0	Nonexistent	0
1	Few and of poor quality	2

(Continued)

SOURCE: Ruddell Reed, Jr., *Plant Layout,* Richard D. Irwin, Inc., Homewood, Ill., 1961.

Degree	Description	Point assignment
2	Adequate but of poor quality	4
3	Adequate and of good quality	6
4	Adequate and of good quality; proposed plans for mainte- nance of this high standard	8
Maximum	Full range of facilities at reason- able cost; proposed plans for maintenance of this standard	10

Degree	Description	Point assignment
0	Nonexistent	0
1	Of poor quality; little available	4
2	Of poor quality but variety of types available	8
3	A few good-quality transporta- tion facilities available and at reasonable rates	12
4	Many good-quality facilities available at reasonable rates; cooperative	16
Maximum	Almost any kind of facilities avail- able at reasonable rates; cooperative	20

21. *Employee transportation facilities.* Facili- ties allow the convenient and rapid movement of employees to and from work as needed.

CONVERTA SPEED-KING CO.: SUMMARY OF NONCOST RATING

Factor	Name	ATWN Rating	ATWN Points	CHO Rating	CHO Points	TEO Rating	TEO Points
1.	Nearness to market	3	168	3	168	maximum	280
2.	Nearness to unworked goods	1	44	2	88	4	176
3.	Availability of power	4	24	4	24	4	24
4.	Climate	3	18	3	18	3	18
5.	Availability of water	3	6	3	6	3	6
6.	Capital availability	4	48	4	48	maximum	60
7.	Momentum of early start	1	2	1	2	1	2
8.	Fire protection	4	8	3	6	4	8
9.	Police protection	3	12	3	12	3	12
10.	Schools and colleges	3	12	3	12	4	16
11.	Union activity	0	0	2	24	0	0
12.	Churches	maximum	10	2	6	maximum	10
13.	Recreation	maximum	20	3	15	maximum	20
14.	Housing	4	8	4	8	4	8
15.	Vulnerability to air attack	2	5	3	7	1	2
16.	Community attitude	maximum	60	maximum	60	maximum	60
17.	Local ordinances	3	30	3	30	3	30
18.	Labor laws	3	23	3	23	3	23
19.	Future growth of community	3	18	2	12	2	12
20.	Medical facilities	4	8	3	6	3	6
21.	Transportation facilities	4	16	3	12	maximum	20
	Totals		528		577		793

SOURCE: Ruddell Reed, Jr., *Plant Layout,* Richard D. Irwin, Inc., Homewood, Ill., 1961.

2.15 Conservation Measures for a Developing Area

Increasingly, farms, forests, and other open spaces are being converted to urban uses. Land disturbance associated with residential, industrial, and commercial developments and supporting activities (building streets, sewer lines, power transmission lines, and airports) contributes to a serious nationwide problem of soil erosion and sediment damage. More than 25,000 tons of soil may be eroded from a square mile of developing area and find its way into marshes, streams, ponds, rivers, lakes, and marine estuaries. Silted ponds, lakes, and reservoirs have less room to store storm water, and thus water supplies are damaged and flood hazards increased. Government and industry spend millions of dollars to remove sediment from water to be used in homes, hospitals, and factories. Sediment destroys spawning grounds for fish and is a health hazard because disease germs, pesticides, and other unwanted materials attached to it are transported from one community to another.

Many villages, towns, townships, cities, and counties are enacting ordinances or issuing rules and regulations designed to protect the public from unnecessary and destructive soil erosion and sedimentation. In many areas, conservation plans must be prepared by developers and approved by conservation districts before land-disturbing permits are granted. Such conservation plans show, for instance, how housing developers will use their land and control erosion and sedimentation during and after construction.

Soil surveys provide developers with information on the location and extent of the different kinds of soil in an area and show the soil limitations for selected uses. Once the soil limitations are known, streets, homes, utilities, and other kinds of construction often can be planned on selected soils that are stable, dry, and generally free of problems. In some places soils with moderate or severe limitations must be used. Soil interpretations show the kinds of soil problems so that engineers and developers can investigate them in detail and plan and design structures to reduce or overcome them. In this way decisions can be made early about selecting areas for specific uses, and maintenance costs can be held to a minimum. Constructing homes and other buildings on desirable soils increases opportunities for landscaping with a variety of plants, both for beauty and for erosion control.

A conservation plan shows the steep land that is to be protected with vegetation. Waterways are preserved and protected, and recreation areas are located on suitable sites. Land subject to overflow from streams also is preserved and protected to curtail flooding and to provide additional open space for wildlife and recreation.

Equally important, a conservation plan shows the location of conservation measures, such as dikes, water diversions, terraces, dams, reservoirs, water conduits, grassed waterways, and plantings of grass, trees, and shrubs. A plan accounts for the timing and sequence of installing conservation measures to provide maximum control of erosion and sedimentation.

Measures to Control Erosion and Sedimentation To control erosion and sedimentation in this area during and after construction, the developers agree to:

1. Disturb only the areas needed for construction. At the present time, natural vegetation covers this area, and there is little erosion. The stream bed and stream banks are stable. The vegetation on the floodplain and on the adjacent slopes will contribute to the aesthetic and environmental quality of the development.
2. Remove only those trees, shrubs, and grasses that must be removed for construction; protect the rest to preserve their aesthetic and erosion control values.
3. Stockpile topsoil, and protect it with anchored straw mulch.
4. Install sediment basins and diversion dikes before disturbing the land that drains into them. Diversion dikes in the central part of the development may be constructed after streets have been installed but before construction has been started on the lots that drain into them.
5. Install streets, curbs, water mains, electric and telephone cables, storm drains, and sewers in advance of home construction.
6. Install erosion and sediment control practices as indicated in the plan and according to soil conservation district standards and specifications. The practices are to be maintained in effective working condition during construction and until the drainage area has been permanently stabilized.
7. Temporarily stabilize each segment of graded or otherwise disturbed land, including the sediment control devices not otherwise stabilized, by seeding and mulching or by mulching alone. As construction is completed, permanently stabilize each segment with perennial vegetation and structural measures. Both temporary and permanent stabilization practices are to be installed according to soil conservation district standards and specifications.
8. "Loose-pile" material that is excavated for home construction purposes. Keep it loose-piled until it is used for foundation backfill or until the lot is ready for final grading and permanent vegetation.
9. Stabilize each lot within 4 months after work has been started on home construction.
10. Backfill, compact, seed, and mulch trenches within 15 days after they have been opened.
11. Level diversion dikes, sediment basins, and silt traps after areas that drain into them have been stabilized. Establish permanent vegetation on these areas. Sediment basins that are to be retained for storm-water detention may be seeded to permanent vegetation soon after they have been built.
12. Discharge water from outlet structures at nonerosive velocities.
13. Design and retain two debris basins as detention reservoirs so that peak runoff from the development area is no greater than the peak runoff before the development was established.

SOURCE: U.S. Department of Agriculture, Soil Conservation Service.

LEGEND AND SOIL DESCRIPTIONS

Symbol	Soil	Brief description
CrA CrB2	Crosby silt loam, 0 to 2 percent slopes Crosby silt loam, 2 to 6 percent slopes, eroded	Light-colored to moderately dark-colored, deep, somewhat poorly drained, slowly permeable soils on nearly level to gently sloping areas in uplands; developed from firm glacial till
Es	Eel silt loam	Moderately dark-colored, deep, moderately well drained, moderately permeable soils on nearly level areas in bottom lands; developed from friable alluvium
HeF	Hennepin soils, 18 to 35 percent slopes	Light-colored, deep, well-drained, moderately permeable soils on steep slopes in uplands; developed from firm glacial till
MnB2 MnC MnC2 MnD MnD2	Miami silt loam, 2 to 6 percent slopes, eroded Miami silt loam, 6 to 12 percent slopes Miami silt loam, 6 to 12 percent slopes, eroded Miami silt loam, 12 to 18 percent slopes Miami silt loam, 12 to 18 percent slopes, eroded	Light-colored, deep, well-drained, moderately permeable soils on gentle slopes to moderately steep slopes in uplands; developed from firm glacial till

SOIL INTERPRETATIONS

Symbol	Soil	Erosion hazard	Dwellings (three stories or less) With basement	Dwellings (three stories or less) Without basement	Septic tank absorption fields	Location of roads and streets	Parks or nature trails
CrA	Crosby	Slight	Severe; wetness	Moderate; wetness	Severe; wetness	Moderate; wetness	Moderate; wetness
CrB2	Crosby	Moderate; sheet erosion	Severe; wetness	Moderate; wetness	Severe; wetness	Moderate; wetness	Moderate; wetness
Es	Eel	Moderate; stream bank erosion	Severe; floods	Severe; floods	Severe; floods	Severe; floods	Moderate; floods
HeF	Hennepin	Severe; sheet and gully erosion	Severe; slope	Severe; slope	Severe; slope	Severe; slope	Severe; slope
MnB2	Miami	Moderate; sheet erosion	Slight	Slight	Slight	Slight	Slight
MnC, MnC2	Miami	Severe; sheet and gully erosion	Moderate; slope	Moderate; slope	Moderate; slope	Moderate; slope	Moderate; slope
MnD, MnD2	Miami	Severe; sheet and gully erosion	Severe; slope	Severe; slope	Severe; slope	Severe; slope	Severe; slope

NOTE: Soils rated as slight have few or no limitations for the use. Soils rated as moderate have limitations that reduce to some degree their desirability for the purpose being considered. They require some corrective measures. Soils rated as severe have unfavorable soil properties or features that severely restrict their use and desirability for the purpose. A severe rating does not mean that the soil cannot be used for a specific purpose because many of the problems can be corrected.

The accompanying tables interpret the data in the soil map shown in Figure 2-24.

Land Use The land use pattern proposed by these developers contributes to the control of erosion and sedimentation and to the maintenance of the environmental and aesthetic values of this area.

1. The floodplain and adjacent steep slopes are reserved for public use. Trails or other projects for recreation or environmental improvement may be developed by the local unit of government.
2. Public access lands connect each street with the open space dedicated to public use.
3. Storm sewers carry street and lot runoff to stable outlets or water detention reservoirs.
4. Street patterns conform to land contours and are designed for pedestrian safety and abatement of traffic noises.
5. Building lots are laid out to conform to the contours of the land in order to reduce land disturbance.
6. The area is platted so that a maximum number of lots share the wooded sectors.
7. Natural watercourses are preserved and protected.

The Plan This example of developers' conservation plans for a housing development provides for an attractive environment based on careful use of soil, water, and plant resources. The plan is based on interpretations of the soils in the area. A pictorial map (Figure 2-25) is used here to show the developers' plan. More often, however, a plat map that shows topography, lot measurements, street widths, and other features is used.

Detailed designs of conservation measures, although not shown in this example, are a necessary part of conservation plans. Designs must comply with standards and specifications adopted by the governmental entity that has responsibility for review and approval.

Conservation plans for developing areas that have different climate, soils, and topography

SOURCE: U.S. Department of Agriculture, Soil Conservation Service.

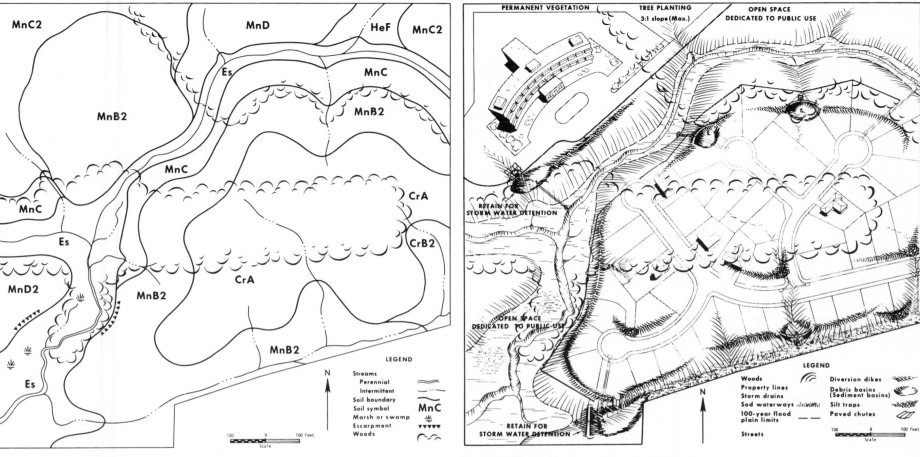

Figure 2-24 Soil map.

Figure 2-25 Planned land use and conservation treatment.

require different land use and conservation measures. For instance, in some areas a high water table is as great a problem as erosion and sedimentation.

Conservation plans can be prepared by engi-neers, developers, building contractors, or other technically qualified resource planners. If needed, Soil Conservation Service technical assistance can be made available through the local soil conservation district.

SOURCE: U.S. Department of Agriculture, Soil Conservation Service.

2.16 Environmental Impact Statements

General Content of an Environmental Impact Statement The following outline presents general topics usually required in an impact statement. Various topics may be expanded, modified, reduced, added, or eliminated to accommodate a specific project, to apply to a particular type of site, or to satisfy the guidelines of the particular agency to which the statement must be submitted.

Section 1. Existing condition of the region and the project site (resource inventory section)
The resource inventory is the most important phase of the environmental assessment process. Without a detailed, scientifically accurate analysis of the conditions of the site, there is no basis, or only a faulty one, for the subsequent decisions on the rational use of the site. Some of the general items to be included are:
  a. Landform, topography, physiography, location, and size
  b. Vegetation and land use
  c. Soils, geology, and groundwater
  d. Streams and water quality
  e. Wildlife
  f. Climatology
  g. Air quality
  h. Noise
  i. Socioeconomics, demography, transportation, utilities
  j. Archaeology and historic sites
Section 2. Description of the proposed project
In this section, which is the most important part of an environmental assessment, the proposed project is described in a semitechnical manner that emphasizes the way in which the project will interface with the environment. Some aspects to be included are:
  a. Need, public benefits, and economic feasibility
  b. Facilities to be placed on the site
  c. Gaseous, liquid, and solid wastes to be generated from project; project noise levels; ability to meet air and water quality standards and noise limitations
  d. Energy and water requirements
  e. Transportation requirements (raw material imports, product exports, employee traffic, and customer traffic)
  f. Manpower requirements (expected local recruitment, expected transfer of employees from other areas, and number of new employees to be attracted to the region)

Section 3. The environmental impact assessment
This section, which is the most important part of the process, is unique to each project. It is an evaluation based on an overlay of the proposed project on the resource inventory of the site and the region. One must determine the goodness of fit, identify environmental and socioeconomic conflicts, and compare project requirements with resource supplies.

In regard to air and water quality, for example, the applicant must consider and explain the direct and secondary impact of his or her project during construction and during operation, including anticipated rundown periods, during times of facility upsets, and in the event of accident. These considerations must include not only average conditions but also worst-case conditions of weather and facility performance. Such evaluations properly are a phase of careful environmental planning and usually result in minor to very major revisions in the project. The most suitable solutions should be reflected in the final proposed plan. Discarded concepts and less-than-best solutions may be listed in Section 4 as alternatives.
Section 4. Alternatives to the proposed project
  a. Alternative locations for project siting. What are the determinants in site selection (size of tract, transportation facilities, availability of large volumes of water or high-quality water, labor force, or others)? Why was the proposed site selected? What unique qualities does it provide for the project? What other sites were considered? Why were they rejected?
  b. Alternative processes or methods. In what other way can the goals of this project be achieved? Why was an alternative process or method not proposed? Can the proposed project be modified further to avoid or minimize some adverse impacts? If the project were an electric generating station powered by coal, one should explain why a nuclear or oil-fired generator was not proposed or whether hydroelectric generation is possible. If once-through water is proposed for cooling, the applicant must explain why evaporative cooling towers or dry towers cannot be used. In the case of a road crossing of a marshland, the alternatives of construction on fill, on piles, or on open structures of short and long spans should be discussed.
  c. Alternative configurations within the site. Sensitive areas on the site often can be preserved by a careful arrangement of facilities. A slight alteration of ingress and egress points may

reduce potential traffic problems. Aesthetic impacts may be reduced by shifting the positions of some components. These aspects should be explained in this subsection.
  d. The no-action alternative. What would be the consequences of not implementing the proposed project? What public benefits would be lost? What alternative use is likely to be made of the site? What adverse impacts would be avoided?
Section 5. Adverse impacts that cannot be avoided. In this summary section, the adverse environmental and socioeconomic effects of the proposed project are listed in the approximate order of magnitude and described briefly. No discussion of possible justifications, mitigations, or trade-offs should be included here.

This listing is intended to red-flag critical points for the consideration of regulatory agencies and other interested parties. It serves to focus the attention of reviewers who may be able to suggest methods to reduce the adverse effects.

Review, Comment, and Revision This is the heart of the environmental assessment process. It establishes an interface for the free exchange of information, criticisms, and suggestions between the following:

1. The applicant and his or her physical planners (engineers, architects, and so on)
2. Environmental and socioeconomic resource analysts
3. Regulatory agency personnel
4. Government organizations with jurisdiction or expertise, or both, citizen groups, and individuals

Most state and local ordinances, laws, or regulations establish an appointed official or a particular agency as the authority with the power to determine the acceptability of an environmental impact statement. This authority extends to the form, content, adequacy of anal-

SOURCE: *Proceedings of the Environmental Assessment and Impact Statements Conference,* presented by the Environmental Studies Institute, Center for Urban Research and Environmental Studies of Drexel University, Philadelphia, 1973.

ysis, and suitability of environmentally protective measures described in the statement.

Public informational meetings and public hearings are important components of the environmental assessment process. Especially in publicly financed projects, public informa-tional meetings should be initiated early, while project planning still is uncommitted and flexible. Interim meetings should be convened at critical moments in the planning process. These will provide forums to receive criticism, additional information, and new ideas.

SOURCE: *Proceedings of the Environmental Assessment and Impact and Statements Conference,* presented by the Environmental Studies Institute, Center for Urban Research and Environmental Studies of Drexel University, Philadelphia, 1973.

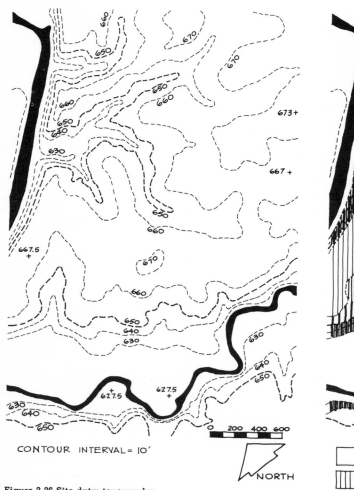

CONTOUR INTERVAL = 10'

Figure 2-26 Site data: topography.

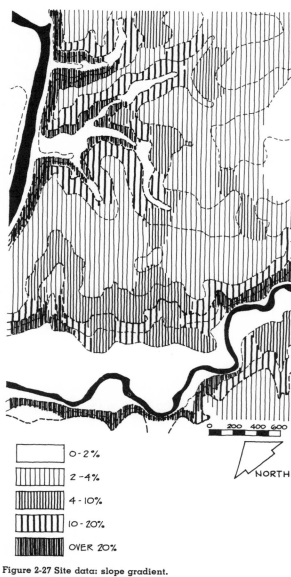

□	0 - 2 %
▥	2 - 4 %
▤	4 - 10 %
▥	10 - 20 %
▓	OVER 20 %

Figure 2-27 Site data: slope gradient.

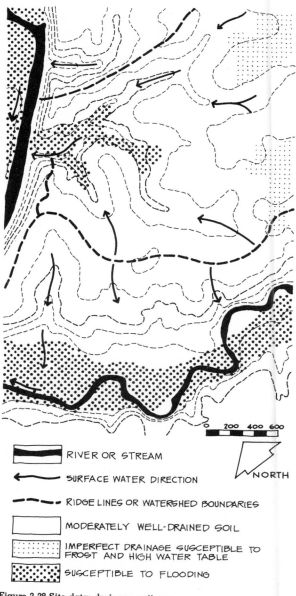

▬	RIVER OR STREAM
←	SURFACE WATER DIRECTION
– – –	RIDGE LINES OR WATERSHED BOUNDARIES
□	MODERATELY WELL-DRAINED SOIL
⠿	IMPERFECT DRAINAGE SUSCEPTIBLE TO FROST AND HIGH WATER TABLE
●	SUSCEPTIBLE TO FLOODING

Figure 2-28 Site data: drainage patterns.

SOURCE: A. J. Rutledge, *Anatomy of a Park,* copyright © 1971 by McGraw-Hill, Inc., used with permission of McGraw-Hill Book Company, New York.

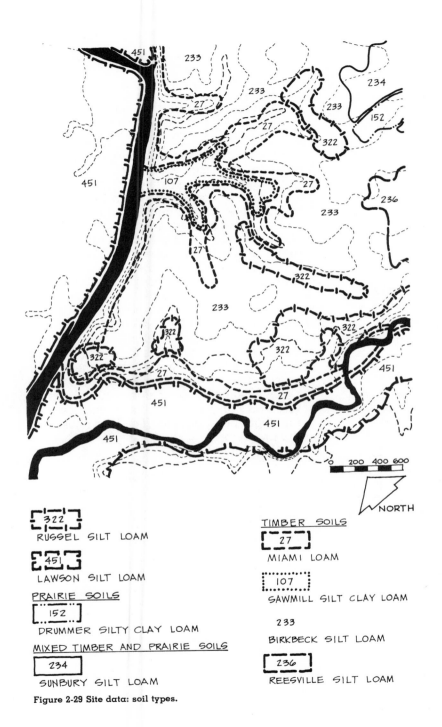

TIMBER SOILS

┌╌┐
│ 322 │
└╌┘
RUSSEL SILT LOAM

┌╌┐
│ 451 │
└╌┘
LAWSON SILT LOAM

┌╌┐
│ 27 │
└╌┘
MIAMI LOAM

PRAIRIE SOILS

┌┈┐
│ 152 │
└┈┘
DRUMMER SILTY CLAY LOAM

┌┈┐
│ 107 │
└┈┘
SAWMILL SILT CLAY LOAM

233

BIRKBECK SILT LOAM

MIXED TIMBER AND PRAIRIE SOILS

┌──┐
│ 234 │
└──┘
SUNBURY SILT LOAM

┌──┐
│ 236 │
└──┘
REESVILLE SILT LOAM

Figure 2-29 Site data: soil types.

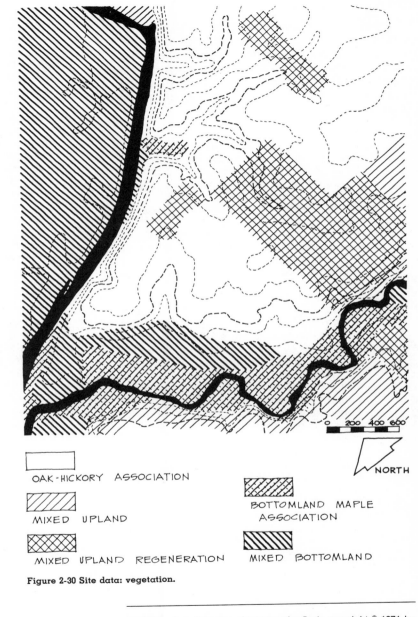

☐ OAK-HICKORY ASSOCIATION

▨ MIXED UPLAND

▦ MIXED UPLAND REGENERATION

▨ BOTTOMLAND MAPLE ASSOCIATION

▨ MIXED BOTTOMLAND

Figure 2-30 Site data: vegetation.

SOURCE: A. J. Rutledge, *Anatomy of a Park,* copyright © 1971 by McGraw-Hill, Inc., with permission of McGraw-Hill Book Company, New York.

2.17 Inventory of Site Data

Inventory of On-Site Factors   After the program has been thrashed out, the designer turns to gathering facts about the site, securing information from maps and personal inspections of the area under study. Such data could include the location of or knowledge about existing

1. Artificial elements
   a. Legal and physical boundaries, private holdings, and public easements
   b. Buildings, bridges, and other structures including those of historical and archaeological significance
   c. Roads, walks, and other transportation ways
   d. Electric lines, gas mains, and other utilities
   e. Land uses: agriculture, industrial, recreation, and so on
   f. Applicable ordinances such as zoning regulations and health codes
2. Natural resources
   a. Topography, including high and low points (Figure 2-26), gradients (Figure 2-27), and drainage patterns (Figure 2-28)
   b. Soil types, by name if available, for clues regarding ground surface permeability, stability, and fertility (Figure 2-29)
   c. Water bodies, including permanence, fluctuations, and other habits
   d. Subsurface matter: geology of the underlying rock including the existence of commercially or functionally valuable material such as sand and gravel, coal, and water
   e. Vegetation types (mixed hardwoods, pine forest, prairie grassland, and so on) and individual specimens of consequence (Figure 2-30)
   f. Wildlife including the existence of desirable habitat as low cover for pheasants, caves for bears, berries for birds, and so on
3. Natural forces (including both macroclimate as generally found over the entire site and microclimate characteristics or changes from the norm as experienced in isolated patches)
   a. Temperature (air and water), especially day, night, and seasonal norms, extremes, and their durations
   b. Sun angles at various seasons and times of the day
   c. Sun pockets such as may be found in forest clearings; frost pockets that may be in low places where the wind that sweeps away the morning dew is blocked
   d. Wind directions and intensities as they occur daily and seasonally
   e. Precipitation: rain, snow, and sleet seasons and accumulations; storm frequencies and intensities
4. Perceptual characteristics
   a. Views into and from the site; significant features
   b. Smells and sounds and their sources
   c. Spatial patterns
   d. Lines, forms, textures, and colors and scales that give the site its peculiar character
   e. General impressions regarding the experience potential of the site and its parts

Inventory of Off-Site Factors   The designer must also accumulate information about the artificial, natural, and perceptual elements on the properties that surround or otherwise affect the site. These might include both existing and anticipated

1. Land use patterns
2. Stream and drainage sources
3. Visuals, smells, and sounds
4. Neighboring aesthetic character
5. Public utility locations and capacities
6. Transportation ways and systems

Each step in the survey phase begins in isolation, the first facts collected being merely those that are immediately handy. Soon all steps become intertwined, each giving direction to another to turn general notions of what might be needed into specific requirements and ensure that nothing that could affect the design's outcome has been left out of consideration. Designers find themselves working back and forth between program and inventory. Program items suggest to them not only what information must be collected but also what is inconsequential. The fact that a playground is being dealt with sends the landscape architect after data about sun angles and the peripheral traffic situation. At the same time, it suggests little urgency to seek out a map showing the location of bear dens and pheasant cover. In a complementary fashion, data garnered might point out modifications necessary in the program.

SOURCE: A. J. Rutledge, *Anatomy of a Park*, copyright © 1971 by McGraw-Hill, Inc., with permission of McGraw-Hill Book Company, New York.

Factors Affecting Building Location and Orientation

3

The location of a building on a site or its relationship to other buildings is extremely important. If properly situated, the building achieves harmony with the topography, liveability is enhanced, drainage problems are minimized, and the building's functional efficiency is increased. If the building is not properly situated, many problems that cannot easily be corrected can and will ensue.

Orientation of the building to sun, wind, and vistas is a basic consideration. Under most conditions it is desirable to be protected from the hot summer sun and exposed to the sun's rays during the cold winter months. Taking advantage of summer breezes can reduce or eliminate the need for air conditioning. In winter maximum protection against northerly winds can substantially reduce heat loss and heating costs.

Siting a building to conform with its topography will result in a minimum of necessary grading, reduce initial construction costs, and eliminate continuous drainage problems.

Exposure of a site to noise pollution has become a serious problem in both urban and suburban areas. This problem can be controlled or minimized by the judicious placement of the structure on the site.

Plant materials, both trees and shrubs, are an integral part of site design. They serve not only as aesthetic elements but as buffer strips, screens, and dividers.

Creating greater physical security and street safety through site planning has become in the past few years a significant new development. The concept, which is known as "defensible space," deals with the placement of buildings, tight control of access to and egress from the site, and visual surveillance of all public areas.

Opposite: Dag Hammarskjold Plaza,
New York. (M. Paul Friedberg & Associates)

3.1 Sun Orientation

Orientation for sun and prevailing summer breezes always merits consideration. Latitude largely determines the former; local conditions, the latter. Orientation for sunlight is most successful when sunshine is made available in kitchens on winter mornings and when some sun reaches living rooms in afternoons. When ideal conditions cannot be secured, a desirable minimum is considered to be achieved if some sun is available in each room at some time of day.

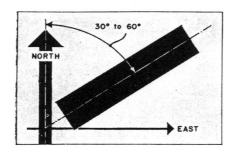

Figure 3-1a Orientation for sunlight in Northern states. The building angle approaches an east-west line as one goes south.

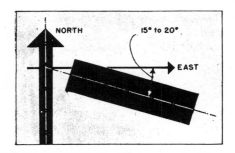

Figure 3-1b Secondary favorable zone giving good early-afternoon sun in winter and protection from afternoon sun in summer.

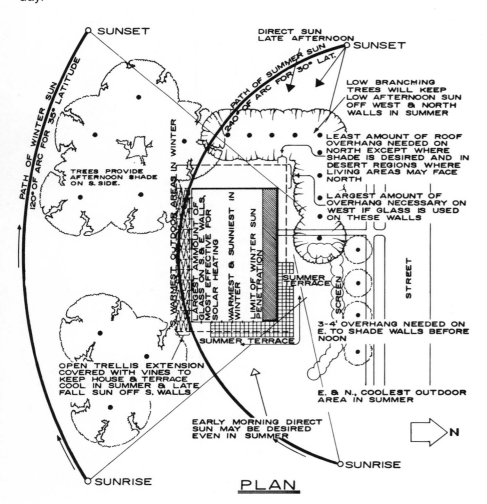

PLAN

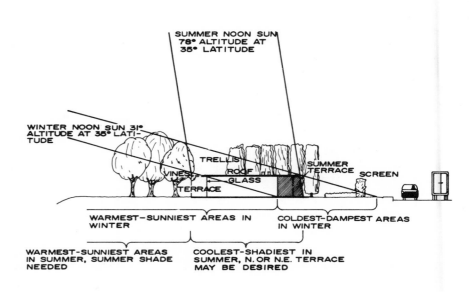

ELEVATION

Figure 3-2

SOURCE: *Landscape Development,* U.S. Department of the Interior, Field Technical Office, Littleton, Colo.

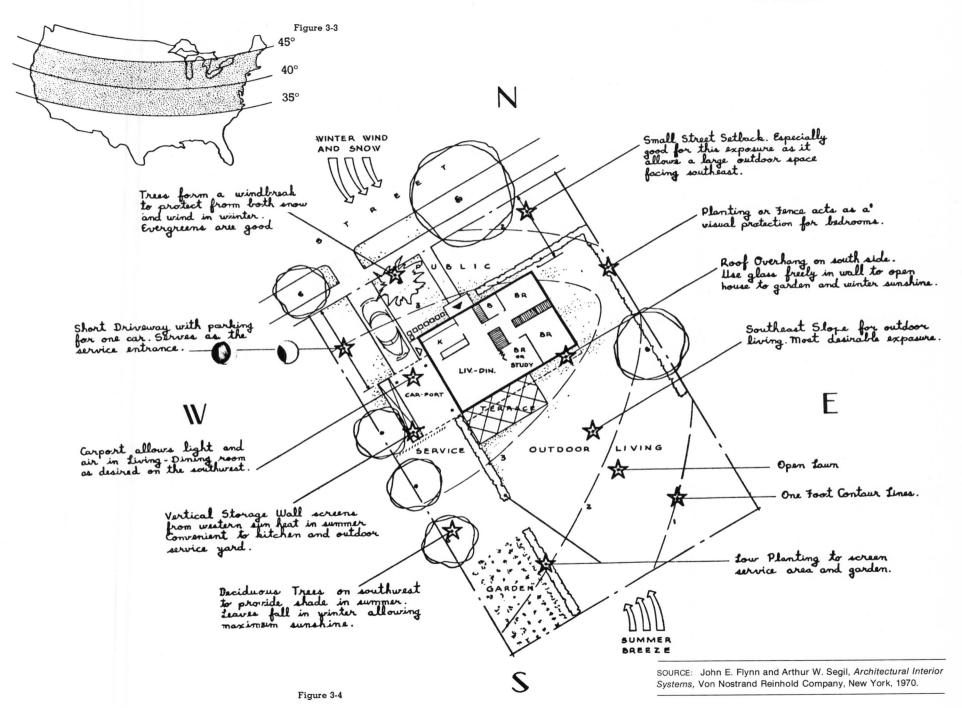

Figure 3-3

Figure 3-4

Trees form a windbreak to protect from both snow and wind in winter. Evergreens are good

Short Driveway with parking for one car. Serves as the service entrance.

Carport allows light and air in Living-Dining room as desired on the southwest.

Vertical Storage Wall screens from western sun heat in summer. Convenient to kitchen and outdoor service yard.

Deciduous Trees on southwest to provide shade in summer. Leaves fall in winter allowing maximum sunshine.

WINTER WIND AND SNOW

Small Street Setback. Especially good for this exposure as it allows a large outdoor space facing southeast.

Planting or Fence acts as a visual protection for bedrooms.

Roof Overhang on south side. Use glass freely in wall to open house to garden and winter sunshine.

Southeast Slope for outdoor living. Most desirable exposure.

Open Lawn

One Foot Contour Lines.

Low Planting to screen service area and garden.

SUMMER BREEZE

N

W

E

S

PUBLIC

SERVICE

OUTDOOR LIVING

GARDEN

LIV.-DIN.

CAR-PORT

TERRACE

BR

BR

K

BR or STUDY

SOURCE: John E. Flynn and Arthur W. Segil, *Architectural Interior Systems,* Von Nostrand Reinhold Company, New York, 1970.

Although no absolute rules can be laid down, it is generally recognized that in Northern states buildings should lie with their long axes running from northeast to southwest, at an angle of from 30 to 60 degrees off north (see Figure 3-1a). Such an orientation will enable some sun to melt snow and to dry ground on the northerly side of the building. Where winters are shorter and there is less snow, this approximate angle diminishes until, in the extreme South, a true east-west alignment is usually preferred.

Under some conditions insolation (the sun's heat) becomes important, both negatively in summer and positively at other seasons. This factor, considered alone, points to southerly exposures in winter, southwesterly in summer; the building is aligned from northwest to southeast. The axis should not swing more than from 15 to 20 degrees from an east-west line (see Figure 3-1b).

Local atmospheric conditions also affect orientation. In the vicinity of New York, for example, prevalent morning mists make southwesterly exposures the sunniest.

Satisfactory orientation for sunlight thus becomes a compromise between conflicting factors. Local conditions furnish the basis for choice or for evaluating one factor against another. See also Figure 3-2.

Although the study of orientation is a comprehensive and detailed science, the knowledge and use of even a few basic rules will mean comfort and economy for the homeowner and a better house for the developer. The latitude belt between 35 and 45 degrees across the United States includes many of the most densely populated areas (see Figure 3-3). This set of solar conditions thus has a wide application. In most locations below this latitude belt capturing summer breezes and protection from intense sun heat are the main consideration. Above the latitude belt shown in the map, protection from cold winter winds and utilization of the warming rays of the sun in winter are the prime objective. When the solar conditions of the belt between 35 and 45 degrees are used (except as noted), it is well to remember

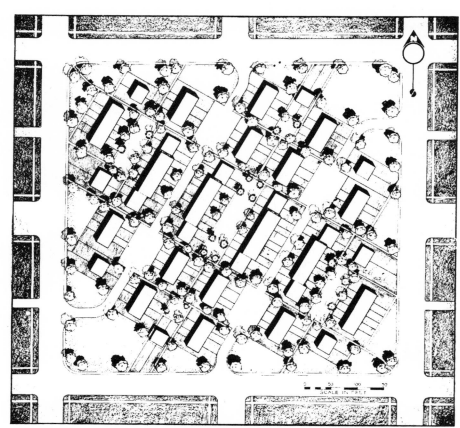

Figure 3-5 This site plan was developed for a project in a small Midwestern city. Since the ground is comparatively flat, orientation for sunlight was the principal consideration.

that the information presented in Figure 3-4 becomes more general and less exact as the distance increases from the midpoint of 40 degrees. See also Figure 3-5.

SOLAR HEAT ON BUILDINGS

In the north temperate zone, heavy radiation loads will act most decisively on the roof and on the east and west exposures during the summer. South exposures permit moderately significant heat gains during the summer, but they allow very significant heat gains during the winter. North exposures receive minimal radiation throughout the year. To be somewhat more specific:

1. If walls facing north of east or north of west receive direct radiation at all, they will tend to receive this radiation only in the late spring and early summer.
2. Walls facing south of east or south of west will tend to receive maximum direct radiation in the late fall and early winter.
3. Walls facing east of north or east of south will tend to receive maximum direct radiation at sunrise or during the morning hours.
4. Walls facing west of north or west of south will tend to receive maximum direct radiation during the afternoon hours or at sunset.

SOURCE: John E. Flynn and Arthur W. Segil, *Architectural Interior Systems,* Von Nostrand Reinhold Company, New York, 1970.

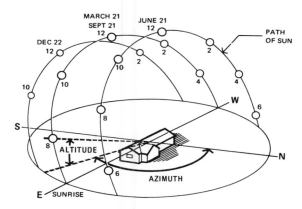

Figure 3-6 Azimith and altitude angles.

See Figure 3-6 for azimith and altitude angles and Figures 3-7 and 3-8 for the effects of solar heat through glassed openings in winter and summer.

LANDSCAPING FOR THERMAL CONTROL

Site vegetation and landforms can influence the immediate thermal environment of a building. These influences generally involve (1) the diversion of storm winds, (2) the channeling of cooling summer breezes, and (3) sun shading. The typical locations of basic landscape elements for thermal control on an open site are indicated in Figure 3-9. However, the optimum positioning of these elements may vary with local variations in prevailing wind patterns.

Under north temperate climatic conditions, it is desirable to follow these steps in utilizing sites:

1. To facilitate maximum exposure to the sun during prolonged winter periods, utilize warm slopes for building sites in colder regions.
2. Where it is desirable to provide natural summer cooling, utilize the lower portion of windward slopes. To induce penetration of prevailing summer breezes, openings should be placed to admit ventilation air on the windward side of the building, exhaust outlets being placed on the leeward side.

   As a related factor, to faciliate natural internal cooling action during warm periods, the blockage of prevailing summer breezes should be

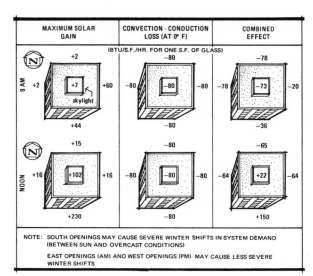

Figure 3-7 Effect of solar heat gain through glassed openings in peak winter periods.

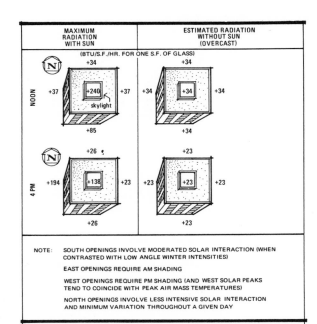

Figure 3-8 Effect of solar heat gain through glassed openings in peak summer periods.

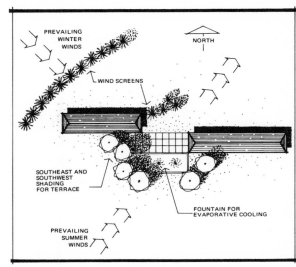

Figure 3-9 Landscape elements for thermal control.

minimized. Usually this means that dense site screening should be curtailed on the south and southwest exposures.

3. Wind screening is desirable on the windward side of the building during cold periods. Usually this consideration applies to north and northwest exposures.
4. Utilize evergreens for wind-screening purposes. Utilize deciduous trees for sun-shading purposes.
5. If possible, locate the building so that available fully developed shade trees will provide shading on the east and west sides of low buildings. Similar considerations apply to the location of outdoor living areas.
6. Paving should be minimized immediately adjacent to the building. Where possible, vegetation should be used in this location to absorb rather than reflect solar energy. The critical west and southwest exposures are the most likely to produce significant reflected energy during periods of peak solar heat gain.
7. Walks should be shielded from winter winds and summer sun.

SOURCE: John E. Flynn and Arthur W. Segil, *Architectural Interior Systems,* Von Nostrand Reinhold Company, New York, 1970.

3.2 Wind Orientation

Figures 3-10 and 3-11 show the effect of winds on various inland and shore homesites.

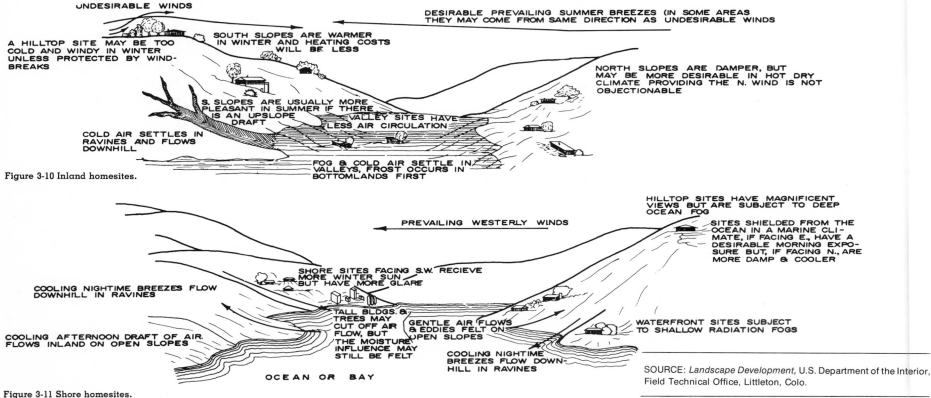

Figure 3-10 Inland homesites.

Figure 3-11 Shore homesites.

SOURCE: *Landscape Development,* U.S. Department of the Interior, Field Technical Office, Littleton, Colo.

WINDBREAKS

Control of Wind by Plants Basically, plants control wind by obstruction, guidance, deflection, and filtration. The differentiation is based not only on the degree of effectiveness of plants but on the techniques of placing them. There are books and articles that describe a number of ways in which plants control wind and their effectiveness in doing so. However, plants, as natural elements, are not always predictable in their size, shape, and growth rate and thus in their absolute effectiveness.

Obstruction with trees, as with all other barriers, reduces wind speed by increasing the resistance to wind flow. Coniferous and deciduous trees and shrubs used individually or in combination affect air movement. See Figure 3-12.

Plants may be used in conjunction with landforms and architectural materials to alter the airflow over the landscape and around or through buildings.

Deflection of wind over trees or shrubs is another method of wind control. Plants of varying heights, widths, species, and composition,

planted either individually or in rows, have varying degrees of effect on wind deflection.

Coniferous evergreens that branch to the ground are generally the most effective year-round plants for wind control; and deciduous shrubs and trees, when in leaf, are most effective in summer. Wind velocity is cut from 15 to 25 percent of the open-field velocity directly

SOURCE: *Plants, People, and Environmental Quality,* U.S. Department of the Interior, National Park Service, 1972.

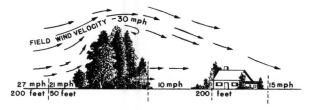

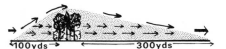

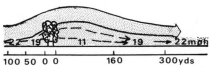

A 30ft. high shelterbelt affects wind speed for 100yds.in front of the trees and 300yds. down wind.

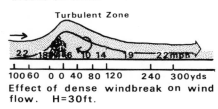

Effect of moderately penetrable windbreaks on wind.

Effect of dense windbreak on wind flow. H=30ft.

Figure 3-14

Figure 3-12 Windbreaks reduce wind currents. As shown here, part of the air current is diverted over the tops of the trees, and part filters through the trees.

leeward of a dense screen planting such as spruce or fir, while a loose barrier of Lombardy poplars reduces leeward wind velocity to 60 percent of the open-field velocity. Wind velocity is cut from 12 to 3 miles per hour for a distance of 40 feet leeward of a 20-foot Austrian pine.

Filtration of wind under or through plants is still another method of control. It is sometimes desirable to speed up or slow down wind in this way.

Height The zones of wind reduction on the leeward and windward sides of a barrier depend largely upon the height of the barrier. The taller the trees, the greater the number of rows of trees required for protection. With an increase in the height of the trees, shelterbelts become more open. Instead of reducing the wind, avenues of trees open at the bottom increase wind speed as the airstream is forced beneath the tree canopy and around the tree trunks.

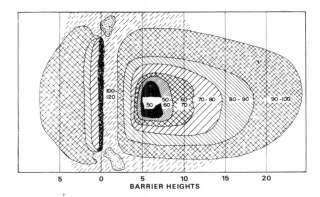

Figure 3-13

Width The field of effectiveness of a shelterbelt depends primarily on the shelterbelt's height and penetrability. The width of the planting is of secondary importance only insofar as it affects the degree of penetrability. The windbreak's width has a negligible influence on reducing wind velocity at its leeward edge, but it can cause a notable variation in the microclimate within the sheltered area. With a wide shelterbelt or forest, the maximum reduction in the velocity of the wind occurs within the shelterbelt or forest itself. Therefore, a wide shelterbelt or forest block actually consumes its own shelter to the extent that the wind velocity is reduced within the shelter itself.

An irregular windbreak, such as the tops of a picket fence, is more effective than a uniform one in breaking up a portion of the airstream deflected over it. A mixture of species and sizes of plants within the windbreak therefore produces a rough upper surface and is more effective in controlling wind.

Shelterbelts Studies have shown that shelterbelts and windbreaks are most effective when they are perpendicular to the prevailing winds. Wind velocity may be reduced by 50 percent for a distance of from 10 to 20 times the tree height downwind of a shelterbelt. The degree of protection and wind reduction depends upon the height, width, and penetrability of the plants used. See Figure 3-13.

Near a moderately dense shelterbelt, at the end of the windbreak wind speed is increased by more than 10 percent of the open-field velocity prior to its interception. The leeward sheltered zone is not confined within lines drawn perpendicular to the ends of the barrier

but is broader than the length of the barrier.

Wind speed is also affected within or on the windward side of a windbreak. For example, the speed is reduced for a distance of 100 yards on the windward or front side of a 30-foot-high shelterbelt and for a distance of 300 yards downwind or behind the shelterbelt. See Figure 3-14.

Partially penetrable windbreaks have effects on windflow that differ from those of dense windbreaks. Wind velocities immediately to the leeward of any windbreak are directly affected by the type of material or kinds of plants used.

The more penetrable the windbreak, the longer the distance that protection extends behind the windbreak. In passing through a penetrable windbreak, some wind retains some of its laminar flow characteristics at a reduced velocity, thus inhibiting turbulence behind it.

SOURCE: *Plants, People, and Environmental Quality,* U.S. Department of the Interior, National Park Service, 1972.

3.3 Topography: Slopes

To avoid costly construction and to make maximum use of grade variations, plans should always be studied in relation to accurately drawn topographical maps or sketches—if possible, directly over them.

Level Sites Even though project land may be so flat that topography does not control site planning, the grouping of buildings should be studied to devise a satisfactory system of drainage. Surfaces or recreation areas and yards

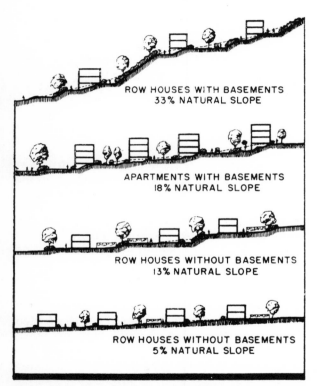

Figure 3-15 Cross sections showing treatments for varying degrees of slope. With a 33 percent slope, basement stories contain apartments, and buildings act as retaining walls. With an 18 percent slope, partially exposed basements contain apartments, laundries, and storage. With a 13 percent slope, buildings are fitted closely to the natural grade, and necessary adjustments are made between yards rather than near buildings. In all three of these cases walks are adjacent to buildings. In the bottom drawing (5 percent slope) buildings are also closely related to the natural grade, but walks and drives are midway between the buildings.

require some pitch for discharging water to surface inlets. The locations of these facilities and the economical placing of areas for cutting and filling are important.

Steep or Broken Sites If there are marked differences in elevation, correlating the site plan with the topography will produce economies of first cost and maintenance, particularly in relation to sewer and drainage lines. A careful use of topographical variations may give a site plan individuality.

Very steep or broken sites may cause excessive development costs. On even moderate slopes, the practice of placing buildings parallel to contours will eliminate much costly construction, grading, and filling. This advice holds particularly true when rock is encountered in excavating. If buildings must be placed on comparatively steep portions of the site, the buildings themselves may serve as retaining walls. By a study of topographical sections, it is possible to determine whether to draw buildings closely together along the entrance side, leaving the greater portion of the slope to be taken up in yards and gardens, or to concentrate all garden areas on one side of each row, leaving only sufficient room for access walks on the other side. Adjustments in grades are preferably taken up between yards rather than close to buildings.

See Figure 3-15 for treatment of differing slopes.

Walks and Roads On sites having steeper slopes, say, greater than 5 percent, it is common practice, where conditions permit, to locate walkways close to buildings to reduce further costs of cutting and filling. Depending upon the project, roads may be similarly laid out. Roads should run parallel to contours to avoid grading expense. Since steps are considered undesirable, walkways also should parallel contours. Abrupt changes in level may in some cases be overcome by the introduction of switchbacks.

Preservation of Trees and Buildings Topographical surveys should show existing trees. Efforts to preserve them may save time and expense in producing necessary shade

DESIRABLE SLOPES

	Percent of slope	
	Maximum	Minimum
Streets, service drives, and parking areas	8.0	0.5[a]
Collector and approach walks	10.0[b]	0.5
Entrance walks	4.0[c]	1.0
Ramps	15.0	...
Paved play and sitting areas	2.0	0.5
Paved gutters	...	0.5
Lawn areas	25.0[d]	1.0
Grassed playgrounds	4.0	0.5
Swales	10.0[e]	1.0[f]
Grassed banks	4:1 slope	
Planted banks	2:1 slope	
	(3:1 preferable)	

[a]0.75 percent for dished section.
[b]Less where icy conditions may occur frequently.
[c]Slopes up to 10 percent or more are satisfactory provided walks are long enough to employ a curved profile, so that a slope not exceeding 4 percent can be used adjoining the building platform. See note c.
[d]Steepest grade recommended for power mower.
[e]Less for drainage areas of more than approximately ½ acre.
[f]2 percent preferable in all cases, particularly if swales cross walks.

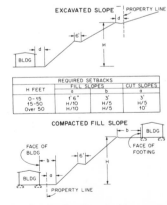

Figure 3-16 Required setbacks. After the *Uniform Building Code of 1964*, Sections 7013–7014, Figure 1.

SOURCE: Federal Housing Administration.

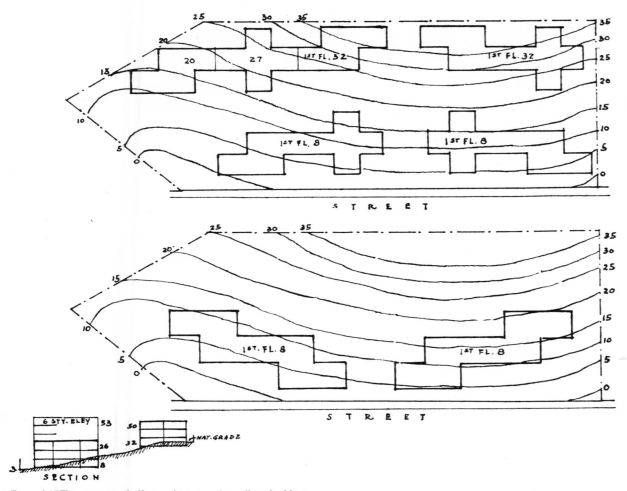

Figure 3-17 This site is too shallow and too steep for walk-up buildings.

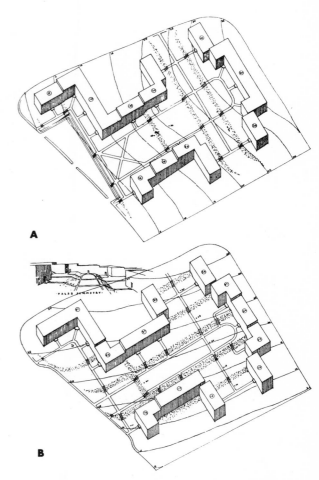

Fig. 3-18 (a) A symmetrical layout on sloping land when the axis of symmetry is perpendicular to the contours; (b) an axis of symmetry parallel to the contours.

besides adding charm. Slight variations in a plan to accommodate trees will help achieve a desirable informal appearance.

Desirable slope percentages are shown in the accompanying table, and required setbacks in Figure 3-16.

Figures 3-17 and 3-18 show suggested layouts for varying topography.

Relation of Buildings to Topography Few sites are entirely level; many are broken and steep, sometimes so much so as to be considered unbuildable. It is not good practice to fight against the land; yet many plans show evidence of this tendency. Level-land plans have been forced upon rugged sites, and occasionally planning that is characteristic of steep or rolling sites has been adapted artificially to level land. Although in some cases there may be justification for changing the fundamental character of the land, the basic idea is to follow the contours. However, this is a general principle only and not a rule to be accepted blindly.

Single houses can be dotted along a slope without much change in natural grade, but houses in long rows and large apartments can follow only the general sweep of the surface. If slopes are steep, the following schemes should be used:

SOURCE: Federal Housing Administration.

115

Figure 3-20 Construction problems and costs are compared for level and steep sites (a through d), and objections to sites containing soft, compacted fill are illustrated (e).

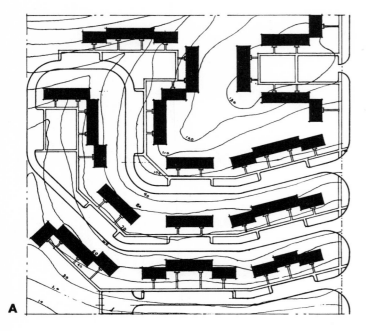

A

B

Figure 3-19 Contrasting access roads, cut and fill, and necessary surface drainage systems are shown for (a) a hilly site and (b) an almost level site.

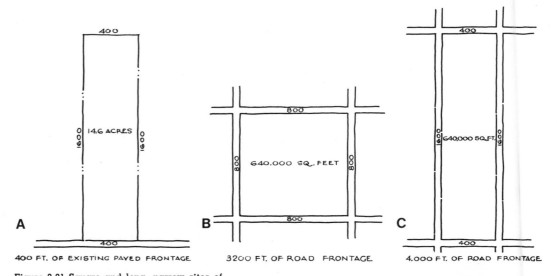

A

400 FT. OF EXISTING PAVED FRONTAGE

B

3200 FT. OF ROAD FRONTAGE

C

4,000 FT. OF ROAD FRONTAGE

Figure 3-21 Square and long, narrow sites of identical areas are compared. With the square site (b) the buildings may be serviced from peripheral streets, whereas the long, narrow site (a, c) requires interior roads. Where new peripheral roads, utilities, and so on must be provided at the project's expense, sites approaching square shapes have been found preferable.

1. Buildings are placed on nearly level terraces cut into the hillsides. Streets are either parallel to the buildings and substantially parallel to the contours, or they are as nearly perpendicular to the contours as the maximum practicable gradient permits.
2. Buildings are built in a series of steps following streets that oppose the contours.

The choice of a site may not always be a part of the architect's job. However, all other factors being equal, level or gently sloping sites present few serious topographical difficulties as compared with those of hilly sites. See Figures 3-19, 3-20, and 3-21.

SOURCE: Federal Housing Administration.

3.4 Gradients

Suggested gradient standards are shown in Figure 3-22 and in the accompanying table.

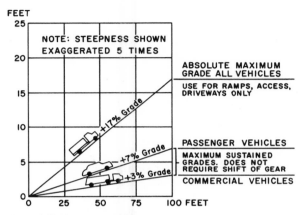

Figure 3-22 Maximum grades.

GRADIENTS
(In percentages[a])

Access and parking	Minimum		Maximum	
	Center line	Crown or cross slope	Center line	Crown or cross slope
Streets	0.5	1.0	14.0	5.0
Street intersections	0.5	1.0	5.0	5.0
Driveways[b]	0.5	1.0	14.0	5.0
Sidewalks[c]				
Concrete	0.5			
Bituminous	1.0			
Building entrances and				
short walks	1.0		12.0	5.0
Main walks	0.5		10.0	5.0
Adjoining steps			2.0	
Landings		1.0		2.0
Stepped ramp treads	1.0		2.0	
Parking		0.5	5.0	5.0
Slope Gradients				
Slope away from foundations:				
Pervious surfaces	5.0[d]		21.0[e]	
Impervious surfaces	1.0[d]		21.0[e]	
Slope to upper end of a drainage swale	2.5[d, f]			
Pervious surfaces:				
Ground frost areas	2.0			
Non-ground frost areas	1.0[g]			
Impervious surfaces	0.5			
Usable open area			5.0	
Other areas[h]:			50.0	(2:1)
Slopes to be maintained by machine			33.0	(3:1)

[a]Approximate equivalents: 0.5 percent = 1/16 inch per foot, 1.0 percent = 1/8 inch per foot, 2.0 percent = 1/4 inch per foot, 5.0 percent = 5/8 inch per foot, 10.0 percent = 1 1/4 inches per foot, 12.0 percent = 1 1/2 inches per foot, and 21 percent = 2 5/8 inches per foot.
[b]Vertical transitions shall prevent contact of car undercarriage or bumper with driveway surface.
[c]5.0 percent maximum for major use by elderly tenants.
[d]Minimum length, 10 feet or as limited by property lines.
[e]Minimum length, 4 feet.
[f]Can be used only where no steep adjacent slopes will contribute storm runoff.
[g]Areas having annual precipitation of more than 50 inches use a 2.0 percent gradient.
[h]After individual analysis the Department of Housing and Urban Development (HUD) may accept steeper slopes or require flatter slopes. See HUD technical study *Slope Protection for Residential Developments*.

SOURCE: *Minimum Property Standards*, Federal Housing Administration.

3.5 Noise

SITE EXPOSURE TO AIRCRAFT NOISE

To evaluate a site's exposure to aircraft noise, you will need to consider all airports, both commercial and military, within 15 miles of the site. The most likely sources for the information required for this evaluation are listed below.

1. Federal Aviation Administration (FAA) area office or military agency in charge of the airport. Are the noise exposure forecast (NEF) or composite noise rating (CNR) contours available? (These contours have not yet been constructed for all airports. When they are available, they are superimposed on a map with a marked scale.) Is there any available information about approved plans for runway changes (extensions or new runways).

2. FAA control tower or airport operator if NEF or CNR contours are not available. What is the number of nighttime jet operations (10 P.M.–7 A.M.)? What is the number of daytime jet operations (7 A.M.–10 P.M.)? Are there any supersonic jet operations? What are the flight paths of the major runways? Is there any available information about expected changes in airport traffic; for example, will the number of operations increase or decrease in the next 10 or 15 years? Are there any plans for supersonic jet traffic?

In making your evaluation, use the data for the heaviest traffic condition, whether present or future.

If NEF or CNR contours are available, locate the site by referring to the marked scale. Also locate a point roughly in the center of the area covered by the principal runways. If the site lies outside the NEF 30 (CNR 100) contour, draw a straight line to connect these two points. Measure along this line the distances between (1) the NEF 40 (CNR 115) and NEF 30 (CNR 100) contours and (2) the NEF 30 (CNR 100) contour and the site. Now use the table "Site Exposure to Aircraft Noise" to evaluate the site's exposure.

If NEF or CNR contours are not available, determine the effective number of operations for the airport as follows. Multiply the number of nighttime jet operations by 17. Then add the

Figure 3-23 Construction of approximate NEF contours with the use of the table "Distances for Approximate NEF Contours."

number of daytime jet operations to obtain an effective total. Any supersonic jet operation automatically places an airport in the largest category of the table "Distances for Approximate NEF Contours," which governs noise acceptability.

On a map of the area that shows the principal runways, mark the locations of the site and of the center of the area covered by these runways (see Figure 3-23). Then, using the distances in the second table, you can construct approximate NEF 40 and NEF 30 contours for the major runways and flight paths most likely to affect the site. Again use the first table to evaluate the site's exposure to aircraft noise.

EXAMPLE 1:

Figure 3-24 shows two sites located on a map that has NEF contours. We drew a line from each of these sites to a point roughly in the center of the area covered by the principal runways. Measuring along these lines, we find that site 1 lies outside the NEF 30 contour at a distance greater than that between the NEF 30 and NEF 40 contours and that site 2 lies outside the NEF 30 contour at a distance less than

SITE EXPOSURE TO AIRCRAFT NOISE

Distance from site to center of area covered by principal runways	Acceptability category
Outside NEF 30 (CNR 100) contour, at a distance greater than or equal to distance between NEF 30 and NEF 40 (CNR 100, CNR 115) contours	Clearly acceptable
Outside NEF 30 (CNR 100) contour, at a distance less than distance between NEF 30 and NEF 40 (CNR 100, CNR 115) contours	Normally acceptable
Between NEF 30 and NEF 40 (CNR 100, CNR 115) contours	Normally unacceptable
Within NEF 40 (CNR 115) Contour	Clearly unacceptable

DISTANCES FOR APPROXIMATE NEF CONTOURS

Effective number of operations	Distances to NEF 30 contour		Distances to NEF 40 contour	
	Distance 1	Distance 2	Distance 1	Distance 2
0–50	1000 feet	1 mile	0	0
51–500	½ mile	3 miles	1000 feet	1 mile
501–1300	1½ miles	6 miles	2000 feet	2½ miles
More than 1300 or any supersonic jet operations	2 miles	10 miles	3000 feet	4 miles

SOURCE: *Noise Assessment Guidelines*, U.S. Department of Housing and Urban Development, 1971.

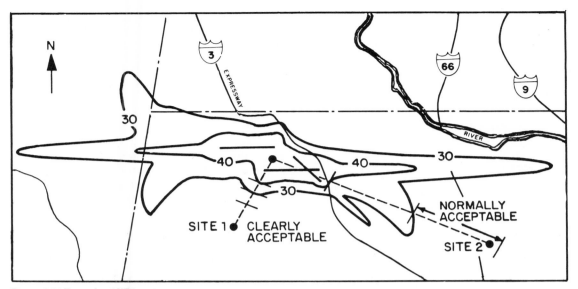

Figure 3-24 Example of NEF contours.

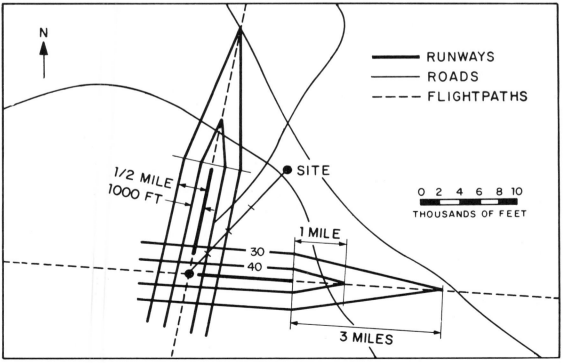

Figure 3-25 Example of approximate NEF contours drawn for an airport with an effective number of operations between 51 and 400.

that between the NEF 30 and NEF 40 contours. Therefore, the exposure of site 1 to aircraft noise is clearly acceptable, and the exposure of site 2 is normally acceptable.

EXAMPLE 2:

Figure 3-25 shows an airport for which NEF or CNR contours are not available. The airport has 20 nighttime and 125 daytime jet operations. There are no supersonic flights, and so we determine the effective number of operations as follows:

$$20 \text{ (nighttime)} \times 17 = 340$$

Add to this the actual number of daytime operations:

$$340 + 125 \text{ (daytime)} = 465$$

Using the distances in the table "Distances for Approximate NEF Contours," we construct approximate contours and then draw a line from the site to a point roughly in the center of the area covered by the principal runways. Measuring along this line, we find that the site lies outside the NEF 30 contour at a distance greater than that between the NEF 30 and NEF 40 contours. Therefore, the site's exposure to aircraft noise is clearly acceptable.

SITE EXPOSURE TO ROADWAY NOISE

To evaluate a site's exposure to roadway noise, you will need to consider all major roads within 1000 feet of the site. The most likely sources for information required for this evaluation are listed below. Before beginning the evaluation, you should try to obtain any available information about approved plans for roadway changes, such as widening existing roads or building new roads, and about expected changes in road traffic. For example, will the traffic on this road increase significantly in the next 10 or 15 years?

1. Area map, city (county) engineer, or both.

SOURCE: *Noise Assessment Guidelines*, U.S. Department of Housing and Urban Development, 1971.

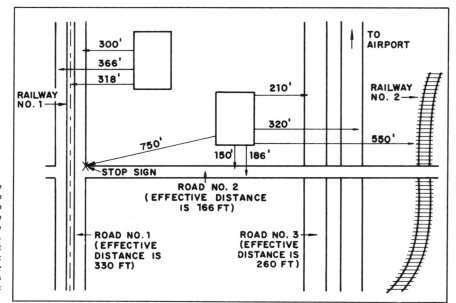

Figure 3-26 Plan view of a site showing how distances should be measured from the location of the dwelling nearest to the source. The site is exposed to noise from three major roads. Road 1 has four lanes, each 12 feet wide, and a 30-foot median strip that accommodates a rapid-transit line. Raod 2 has four lanes, each 12 feet wide. Road 3 has six lanes, each 15 feet wide, and a median strip 35 feet wide.

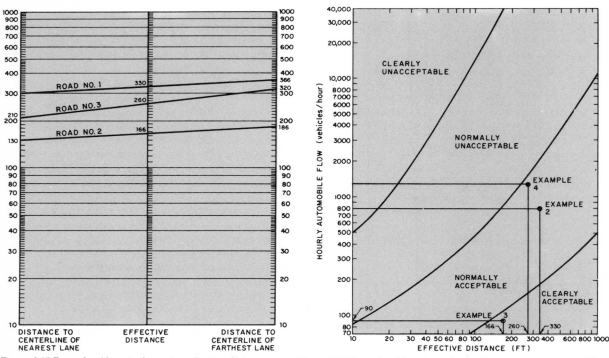

Figure 3-27 Example of how to determine effective distances.

Figure 3-28 Example of how to evaluate site exposure to automobile noise.

What are the distances from the site to the center lines of the nearest and farthest lanes of traffic?

2. City (county) director of traffic. What is the peak hourly automobile traffic flow in both directions combined? What is the peak number of trucks and buses (buses count as trucks) per hour in each direction? If the road has a gradient of 3 percent or more, record uphill and downhill numbers separately because these figures will be necessary later. If not, simply record the total number of trucks.

You may also need to make adjustments for the following circumstances:

A road gradient of 3 percent or more
Stop-and-go traffic
Mean speed
A barrier

The information required for these adjustments can be obtained from the city (county) director of traffic.

Traffic surveys show that the level of roadway noise depends on the percentage of trucks in the total traffic volume. To account for this effect, the guidelines discussed below provide for the separate evaluation of automobile and truck traffic.

Before proceeding with these separate evaluations, however, determine the effective distance from the site to each road by locating on Figure 3-27 the distances from the site to the center lines of the nearest and farthest lanes of traffic. (See also Figure 3-26; the distances in this figure are used for all roadway examples.)

Now lay a straightedge to connect these two distances and read off the value at the point where the straightedge crosses the middle scale. This value is the effective distance to the road.

Automobile Traffic The numbers in Figure 3-28, which is used to evaluate the site's exposure to automobile noise, were arrived at with the following assumptions:

SOURCE: *Noise Assessment Guidelines,* U.S. Department of Housing and Urban Development, 1971.

1. There is no traffic signal or stop sign within 800 feet of the site.
2. The mean automobile traffic speed is 60 miles per hour.
3. There is line-of-sight exposure from the site to the road; that is, there is no barrier that effectively shields the site from the road.

If a road meets these three conditions, proceed to Figure 3-28 for an immediate evaluation of the site's exposure to the automobile noise from that road. However, if any of these conditions are different, make the necessary adjustments and then use Figure 3-28 for the evaluation.

Adjustments for Stop-and-Go Traffic If there is a traffic signal or a stop sign within 800 feet of the site, multiply the total number of automobiles per hour by 0.1.

Adjustments for Mean Traffic Speed If there is no traffic signal or stop sign within 800 feet of the site and the mean automobile speed is other than 60 miles per hour, multiply the total number of automobiles by the adjustment factor shown in the accompanying table.

Barrier Adjustment This adjustment affects distance and applies equally to automobiles and to trucks on the same road. Therefore, instructions for this adjustment appear below after those for truck traffic.

EXAMPLE 1:

For road 1, the distance from the site to the center line of the nearest lane of traffic is 300

Mean traffic speed (miles per hour)	Adjustment factor
20	0.12
25	0.18
30	0.25
35	0.32
40	0.40
45	0.55
50	0.70
55	0.85
60	1.00
65	1.20
70	1.40

feet. The distance to the center line of the farthest lane of traffic is 366 feet. Figure 3-26 shows that the effective distance from the site to this road is 330 feet. For road 2, the distance to the center line of the nearest lane of traffic is 150 feet. The distance to the center line of the farthest lane of traffic is 186 feet. Figure 3-26 shows that the effective distance from the site to this road is 166 feet. For road 3, the distance to the center line of the nearest lane of traffic is 210 feet. The distance to the center line of the farthest lane of traffic is 320 feet. Figure 3-26 shows that the effective distance from the site to this road is 260 feet.

EXAMPLE 2:

Road 1 meets the three conditions that allow for an immediate evaluation. In obtaining the information necessary for this evaluation, we found that the hourly automobile flow is 800 vehicles. On Figure 3-28, we locate on the vertical scale the point representing 800 vehicles per hour and on the horizontal scale the point representing 330 feet (note that we must estimate the location of this point). Using a straightedge, we draw lines to connect these two values and find that the site's exposuré to automobile noise from this road is normally acceptable.

EXAMPLE 3:

Road 2 has a stop sign at 750 feet from the site. The hourly automobile flow is reported as 900 vehicles. We adjust for stop-and-go traffic:

$$900 \times 0.1 = 90 \text{ vehicles}$$

We find from Figure 3-28 that the exposure to automobile noise is clearly acceptable.

EXAMPLE 4:

Road 3 is a depressed highway. There is no traffic signal or stop sign and the mean speed is 60 miles per hour. The hourly automobile flow is 1200 vehicles. The road profile shields all residential levels of the housing from line-of-sight exposure to the traffic. The only adjustment that can be made is the barrier adjustment. This adjustment is necessary, however,

only when the site's exposure to noise has been found to be clearly or normally unacceptable. Figure 3-28 shows that the exposure to automobile noise is normally acceptable. Therefore, no adjustment for barrier is necessary.

Truck Traffic The numbers in Figure 3-29, which is used to evaluate the site's exposure to truck noise, were arrived at with the following assumptions:

1. There is a road gradient of less than 3 percent.
2. There is no traffic signal or stop sign within 800 feet of the site.
3. The mean truck traffic speed is 30 miles per hour.
4. There is line-of-sight exposure from the site to the road; that is, there is no barrier that effectively shields the site from the road.

If a road meets these four conditions, proceed to Figure 3-29 for an immediate evaluation of the site's exposure to truck noise from that road. However, if any of the conditions are different, make the necessary adjustments and then use Figure 3-29 for the evaluation.

Adjustments for Road Gradient If there is a gradient of 3 percent or more, multiply the number of trucks per hour in the uphill direction by the appropriate adjustment factor.

Add to this adjusted figure the number of trucks per hour in the downhill direction.

Percent of gradient	Adjustment factor
3–4	1.4
5–6	1.7
More than 6	2.5

Adjustments for Stop-and-Go Traffic If there is a traffic signal or a stop sign within 800 feet of the site, multiply by 5 the total number of trucks.

SOURCE: *Noise Assessment Guidelines*, U.S. Department of Housing and Urban Development, 1971.

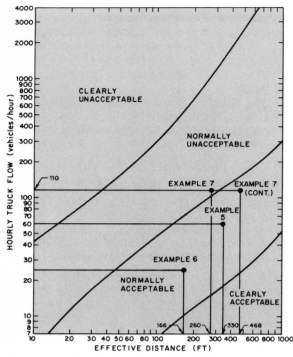

Figure 3-29 Example of how to evaluate the site's exposure to truck noise.

Adjustments for Mean Traffic Speed Make this adjustment only if there is no traffic signal or stop sign within 800 feet of the site and the mean speed is not 30 miles per hour. If the mean truck speed differs with direction, treat the uphill and downhill traffic separately. Multiply each by the appropriate adjustment factor below.

EXAMPLE 5:

Road 1 meets the four conditions that allow for an immediate evaluation. The hourly truck flow is 60 vehicles. Figure 3-29 shows that the site's exposure to truck noise from this road is normally acceptable.

EXAMPLE 6:

Road 2 has a stop sign at 750 feet from the site. There is also a road gradient of 4 percent.

No trucks are allowed on this road, but four buses per hour are scheduled (two in each direction).

We adjust first for gradient:

Uphill	$2 \times 1.4 =$	2.8 vehicles
Downhill		2.0 vehicles
Total flow		4.8 vehicles

We then adjust for stop-and-go traffic:

$$4.8 \times 5 = 24 \text{ vehicles per hour}$$

Figure 3-29 shows that the exposure to truck or bus noise from this road is normally acceptable.

Mean traffic speed (miles per hour)	Adjustment factor
20	1.60
25	1.20
30	1.00
35	0.88
40	0.75
45	0.69
50	0.63
55	0.57
60	0.50
65	0.46
70	0.43

EXAMPLE 7:

The profile of road 3 shields all residential levels of the housing from line-of-sight exposure to the traffic. The mean truck speed is 50 miles per hour. The hourly truck flow is 175 vehicles. We adjust for mean speed:

$$175 \times 0.63 = 110.24$$
$$= 110 \text{ vehicles}$$

We find from Figure 3-29 that exposure to truck noise is normally unacceptable. Therefore, we proceed with the barrier adjustment.

Road 3 has been depressed 25 feet from the 150-foot elevation of the natural terrain. The actual road elevation therefore is 125 feet. We find the effective road elevation to be

$$125 + 5 = 130 \text{ feet}$$

Six stories are planned for the housing, which is located at an elevation of 130 feet. The effective site elevation for the highest story is

$$6 \times 10 = 60 + 130 - 5 = 185 \text{ feet}$$

Barrier Adjustment A barrier may be formed by the road profile, by a solid wall or embankment, by a continuous row of buildings, or by the terrain itself. To be an effective shield, however, the barrier must block all residential levels of all buildings from line-of-sight exposure to the road, and it must not have any gaps that would allow noise to leak through. This adjustment is necessary only when the site's exposure to noise from a road has been found to be normally or clearly unacceptable.

Step 1. From the city (county) engineer obtain the elevation of the road. (Roads may be elevated above the natural terrain or may be depressed, as in our example. Make certain, therefore, that the figure you obtain for road elevation takes any such change into account.) Add 5 feet to this figure to obtain the effective road elevation.

Step 2. From the applicant obtain the ground elevation of the site and the number of stories

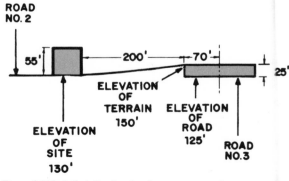

Figure 3-30 Detail of site showing the measurements necessary for a barrier adjustment.

SOURCE: *Noise Assessment Guidelines*, U.S. Department of Housing and Urban Development, 1971.

in the proposed housing. Multiply the number of stories by 10 feet. Add the site elevation, and then subtract 5 feet from this total to obtain the effective site elevation.

Step 3. From the city (county) engineer or a contour map obtain the elevation of the terrain where the barrier is located. Add the actual height of the barrier to obtain the effective barrier elevation. (Note that in some cases, as in our example, the barrier is formed by the road profile, and the elevation of the terrain is the effective barrier elevation.) To find the barrier adjustment factor, you will need Figure 3-31 and a straightedge. The example of barrier adjustment below explains how to use Figure 3-31.

When you have determined the barrier adjustment factor, multiply the effective distance by the factor to obtain the adjusted distance from the site to the road.

EXAMPLE 7 (CONTINUED):

The barrier, which is formed by the road profile, has no height other than the 150-foot elevation of the natural terrain. Thus, the effective barrier elevation is 150 feet. The difference in effective elevation between the site and the road is 55 feet, and between the barrier and the road is 20 feet. We now use Figure 3-31 to find the barrier adjustment factor.

EXAMPLE OF BARRIER ADJUSTMENT:

1. The distance from the site to the barrier is 200 feet.
2. The distance from the center of the road to the barrier is 70 feet.
3. The difference in effective elevation between the site and the road is 55 feet.
4. The difference in effective elevation between the barrier and the road is 20 feet.

On the vertical scale of Graph 1 in Figure 3-31, we mark 200 feet and draw a straight horizontal line to meet the curve marked 70 feet. Then we draw a vertical line down to Graph 2 to meet the point that represents 55 feet (note that we must guess the location) and a horizontal line over to Graph 3 to meet the curve marked 20 feet. (If the line from Graph 2 does not meet

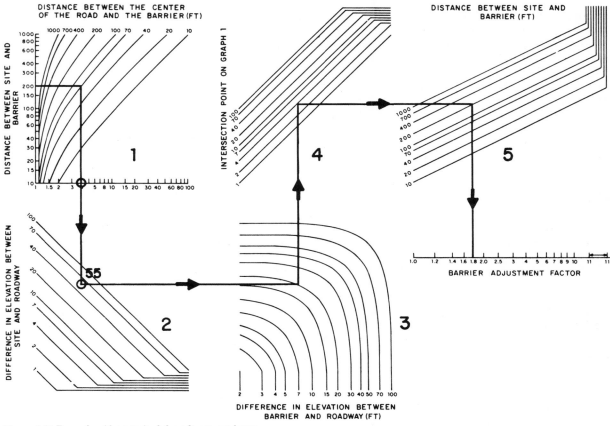

Figure 3-31 Example of how to find the adjustment factor.

the appropriate curve on Graph 3, the barrier is not an effective shield, and there is no adjustment.)

Next we draw a vertical line up to Graph 4 to meet the curve marked 4 (the number intersected by the line going from Graph 1 to Graph 2) and a horizontal line over to Graph 5 to meet the curve marked 200 feet. From Graph 5 we draw a vertical line down to the adjustment scale and find that our multiplier is 1.8.

Using this multiplier, we adjust the effective distance

$$260 \times 1.8 = 468 \text{ feet}$$

We find from Figure 3-29 that the site's expo-

sure to truck noise from this road is normally acceptable.

SITE EXPOSURE TO RAILWAY NOISE

To evaluate a site's exposure to railway noise, you will need to consider all aboveground rapid-transit lines and railroads within 3000 feet of the site. The most likely sources for information required for this evaluation are listed below. Before beginning the evaluation, you

SOURCE: *Noise Assessment Guidelines,* U.S. Department of Housing and Urban Development, 1971.

should record the information on a work sheet.

1. Area map, county engineer, or both. What is the distance from the site to the railway right-of-way? Does a barrier effectively shield the site from the railway? Remember that an effective barrier blocks all residential levels of all buildings from line-of-sight exposure to the railway and has no gaps that would allow noise to leak through.

2. Supervisor of customer relations for the railway. What is the number of nighttime railway operations (10 P.M.–7 A.M.)? Is there any available information about approved plans for changing the number of nighttime operations?

Distances in the table "Site Exposure to Railway Noise" were arrived at on the assumption that there are ten or more nighttime railway operations (10 P.M.–7 A.M.). If a railway has ten or more nighttime operations, proceed to the table for an immediate evaluation of the site's exposure to noise from that railway. However, if a railway has fewer than ten nighttime operations, multiply the distance from the site to that railway by the appropriate adjustment factor; then proceed to the table.

Number of nighttime railway operations	Adjustment factor
1–2	3.3
3–5	1.7
6–9	1.2

EXAMPLE 1:

The distance from the site to railway 1 is 318 feet. There are two nighttime operations, and there is direct line-of-sight exposure to the right-of-way. Since there are fewer than ten nighttime operations, we adjust the distance as follows:

$$318 \text{ feet} \times 3.3 = 1049 \text{ feet}$$

We then proceed to the table "Site Exposure to Railway Noise," where we find that exposure to noise from this railway is normally acceptable.

EXAMPLE 2:

The distance from the site to railway 2 is 550 feet. There are twenty nighttime railway operations, and the site is completely shielded from the right-of-way. Since there are more than ten nighttime operations, we proceed immediately to the table and find that the site's exposure to noise from this railway is clearly acceptable.

SITE EXPOSURE TO RAILWAY NOISE

Distance from site to right-of-way (possibly adjusted for number of nighttime operations)		Acceptability category
Line-of-sight exposure (feet)	Shielded exposure (feet)	
More than 3000	More than 500	Clearly acceptable
601–3000	101–500	Normally acceptable
101–600	51–100	Normally unacceptable
Less than 100	Less than 50	Clearly unacceptable

SOURCE: *Noise Assessment Guidelines,* U.S. Department of Housing and Urban Development, 1971.

LANDSCAPING FOR NOISE CONTROL

When external noise cannot be muffled at the source, landscape barriers can provide some control within the site. These barriers generally involve shielding or absorption, or both.

The combination of trees, low foliage, and ground cover provides noise attenuation when significant masses of such absorbing vegetation are involved. Generally, such foliage should be from 500 to 1000 feet deep to diminish properly the intensity of normal traffic noises. While relatively thin barriers serve effectively as a visual barrier or a sunscreen, a sonic barrier must be of much greater dimensions. See Figures 3-32 and 3-33.

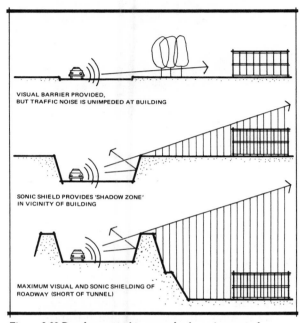

VISUAL BARRIER PROVIDED, BUT TRAFFIC NOISE IS UNIMPEDED AT BUILDING

SONIC SHIELD PROVIDES 'SHADOW ZONE' IN VICINITY OF BUILDING

MAXIMUM VISUAL AND SONIC SHIELDING OF ROADWAY (SHORT OF TUNNEL)

Figure 3-32 Development of topography for noise control.

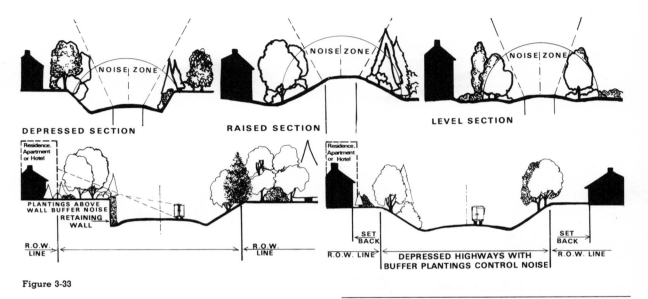

DEPRESSED SECTION   RAISED SECTION   LEVEL SECTION

Figure 3-33

SOURCE: John E. Flynn and Arthur W. Segil, *Architectural Interior Systems*, Van Nostrand Reinhold Company, New York, 1970.

3.6 Spatial Structure

Spatial structure is defined as the configuration of physical open space of a given site. Spatial structure is generally the result of topographic characteristics, vegetation massing, and topographic characteristics in conjunction with vegetation massing (see Figure 3-34).

Because these three elements determine the size and, to a great extent, the quality of a space, they may be referred to as spatial determinants.

As the spatial configuration of a landscape is documented, the information thus obtained can be transferred to a site drawing (see Figure 3-35).

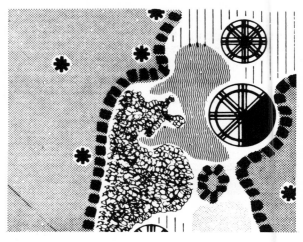

Figure 3-35 The aesthetic resources resulting from landform diversity, vegetation patterns, surface waters, and visual quality establish the major spatial definitions, high points, views and vistas, and site image.

Spatial Structure of Landscape After determining the spatial structure of a given landscape, one can establish the qualitative characteristics of a given space. An understanding of the overall spatial structure of a landscape, together with an understanding of the qualitative characteristics of the individual spaces, is extremely important in locating functions that are greatly influenced by visual factors, such as roadways, visitor centers, and walking and hiking trails.

Spatial Characteristics The spatial characteristics of a landscape generally depend upon three issues: size of space, degree of visual enclosure, and visual character.

Size of Space The size of a space is important in determining its total visual impact as well as its potential to absorb a given function. Size may be evaluated both in terms of acreage and in the relationship of its size to that of all other on-site spaces.

SOURCE: *Planning for Wildlife and Man*, U.S. Department of the Interior, Fish and Wildlife Service, 1974.

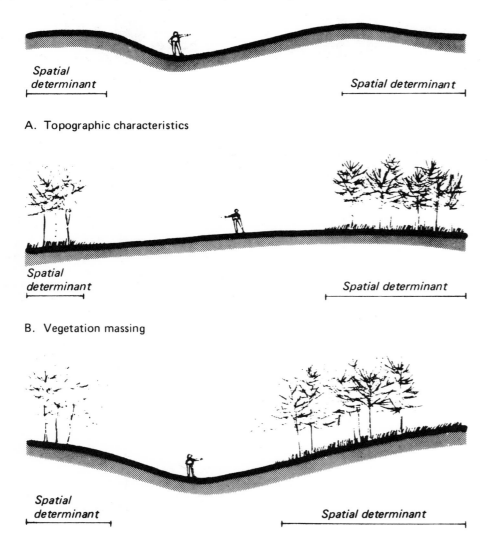

A.   Topographic characteristics

B.   Vegetation massing

Figure 3-34   C.   Topographic characteristics in conjunction with vegetation massing.

Degree of Visual Enclosure The degree of visual enclosure of a space is an important spatial factor, especially in locating functions that are greatly influenced by the need for circulation linkages (trails or roadways) or scenic views or vistas (scenic overlooks, visitor centers, or trails). Although the definition of space suggests enclosure, the spatial structure may be such as to evoke a feeling or image of one of the three diagrams in Figure 3-36.

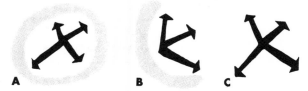

Figure 3-36 (a) Total enclosure. (b) Semiopen enclosure. (c) No enclosure.

Degree of enclosure is an important planning consideration not only in terms of spatial access but also in terms of visual form. For instance, a person near a topographic or vegetative mass will tend to look away from it (see Figure 3-37). This tendency may be used advantageously by the planner in directing the visitor to more promising views or to other important visual phenomena.

Yet another important consideration of spatial enclosure relates to the "harbor quality" of a space. Harbor quality is the ability of a space to invite or attract use. Many spaces offer such a strong attraction. As shown in Figure 3-37, these spaces can best be employed as entry points wherever a strong sense of invitation and arrival is important.

Perhaps the single most important aspect of spatial structure consists in locating and developing sites that can support various land uses. A knowledge of on-site spatial enclosures arms the planner with greater opportunities for placing aesthetically unappealing activities (storage, service, water tanks) in less readily observable sites (see Figure 3-38).

Figure 3-37

SOURCE: *Planning for Wildlife and Man,* U.S. Department of the Interior, Fish and Wildlife Service, 1974.

Figure 3-38

Figure 3-39

Visual Character In determining the visual characteristics of a space, one should carefully interpret the space in terms of the inherent visual images it presents. For instance, a certain space may have a heavy background of conifers and a strong view of distant mountains; yet a centrally located lake may be so visually dominant that the entire scene evokes an image of a waterscape. Here, the particular space might be noted as follows:

Space X
Major image: Lake and associated
water edge
Subordinate
images: Dense conifer forest
View of distant
mountains

A general listing of the natural or cultural features that may influence the visual characteristics of a space (example only) follows:

Natural features

1. Vegetation
   a. Dense conifer forest
   b. Grassland image
   c. Wetland image
2. Topography and geology
   a. Rock outcropping
   b. Scattered boulders
   c. Sand dunes
3. Hydrology
   a. Open lake
   b. Slow, meandering stream

Cultural features:

1. Land uses
   a. Agriculture
   b. Service and storage
2. Utilities
   a. Telephone utilities
   b. Gas pipes
3. Barriers
   a. Corrals
   b. Fences

The inherent visual quality of a site will greatly influence the type of activity that occurs on it. Dense and heavily screened spaces will naturally promote an entirely different feeling from that produced by open, gently rolling spaces. If the final plan is to be successful, the activities planned for various sites should reflect the inherent quality of the site, that is, running, jumping, or passive recreation, such as meditation (see Figure 3-39).

SOURCE: *Planning for Wildlife and Man,* U.S. Department of the Interior, Fish and Wildlife Service, 1974.

3.7 Landscaping Elements

PLANT MATERIALS, DENSITY, AND VOLUME

The factors that determine the selection of plant materials, their density, and their volume are illustrated in Figures 3-40, 3-41, and 3-42.

SELECTING PLANT MATERIALS

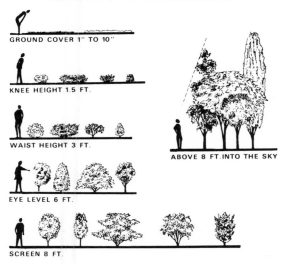

GROUND COVER 1" TO 10"

KNEE HEIGHT 1.5 FT.

WAIST HEIGHT 3 FT.

ABOVE 8 FT.INTO THE SKY

EYE LEVEL 6 FT.

SCREEN 8 FT.

PEOPLE

PEOPLE—THEIR LINE OF VISION DETERMINES WHETHER A FENCE WILL PROVIDE PRIVACY OR MERELY SEPARATION. THEIR HEIGHT MEASURES FENCES, SHRUBS, TREES AND ALL VERTICAL AND OVERHEAD ELEMENTS.

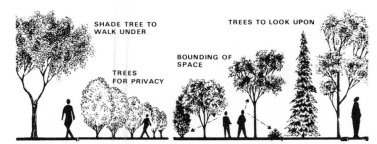

SHADE TREE TO WALK UNDER

TREES TO LOOK UPON

TREES FOR PRIVACY

BOUNDING OF SPACE

Figure 3-40

DENSITY

PETIOLE SIZE, SHAPE AND LENGTH

SOME PETIOLE SHAPES HAVE MORE STRUCTURAL STABILITY THAN DO OTHERS. ON PLANTS WITH MORE RIGID PETIOLES THERE IS LESS LEAF MOVEMENT, AND THE PLANT APPEARS MORE SOLID AND DENSE.

⬙ SQUARE
◎ CIRCULAR
○ OVAL
△ TRIANGULAR
⬡ OCTANGULAR

ARRANGEMENT OF LEAVES

LEAVES ARE ARRANGED IN GENERAL ORDER OF INCREASING COMPLEXITY OF FORM AND/OR MARGIN FROM LEFT TO RIGHT. THIS INCREASING COMPLEXITY COMBINED WITH VARIOUS BRANCHING FORMS WILL PRODUCE VARYING DEGREES OF DENSITY.

EVERGREEN

DECIDUOUS

Figure 3-41

VOLUME

BRANCHING PATTERN — BRANCHING SPACING — BRANCHING HEIGHT

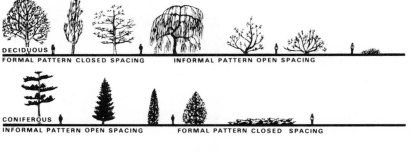

DECIDUOUS

FORMAL PATTERN CLOSED SPACING   INFORMAL PATTERN OPEN SPACING

CONIFEROUS

INFORMAL PATTERN OPEN SPACING   FORMAL PATTERN CLOSED SPACING

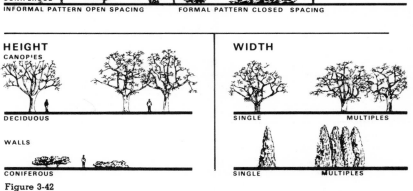

HEIGHT
CANOPIES

DECIDUOUS

WALLS

CONIFEROUS

Figure 3-42

WIDTH

SINGLE   MULTIPLES

SINGLE   MULTIPLES

SOURCE: *Plants, People, and Environmental Quality*, U.S. Department of the Interior, National Park Service, 1972.

WALLS, CEILINGS, AND FLOORS

Factors that determine the use of plant materials as walls, ceilings, and floors are illustrated in Figure 3-43.

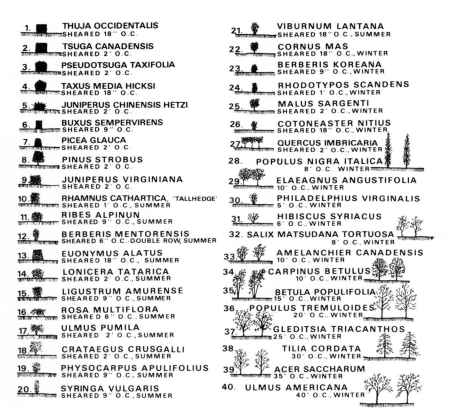

WALLS REPRESENTATIVE PLANTS INDICATING THE RELATIVE DEGREES OF VISUAL DENSITY. (AT LEAST 6' HIGH)

1. THUJA OCCIDENTALIS — SHEARED 18" O.C.
2. TSUGA CANADENSIS — SHEARED 2' O.C.
3. PSEUDOTSUGA TAXIFOLIA — SHEARED 2' O.C.
4. TAXUS MEDIA HICKSI — SHEARED 18" O.C.
5. JUNIPERUS CHINENSIS HETZI — SHEARED 2' O.C.
6. BUXUS SEMPERVIRENS — SHEARED 9" O.C.
7. PICEA GLAUCA — SHEARED 2' O.C.
8. PINUS STROBUS — SHEARED 2' O.C.
9. JUNIPERUS VIRGINIANA — SHEARED 2' O.C.
10. RHAMNUS CATHARTICA, 'TALLHEDGE' — SHEARED 1' O.C., SUMMER
11. RIBES ALPINUN — SHEARED 9" O.C., SUMMER
12. BERBERIS MENTORENSIS — SHEARED 6" O.C.-DOUBLE ROW, SUMMER
13. EUONYMUS ALATUS — SHEARED 18" O.C., SUMMER
14. LONICERA TATARICA — SHEARED 2' O.C., SUMMER
15. LIGUSTRUM AMURENSE — SHEARED 9" O.C., SUMMER
16. ROSA MULTIFLORA — SHEARED 6" O.C., SUMMER
17. ULMUS PUMILA — SHEARED 2' O.C., SUMMER
18. CRATAEGUS CRUSGALLI — SHEARED 2' O.C., SUMMER
19. PHYSOCARPUS APULIFOLIUS — SHEARED 9" O.C., SUMMER
20. SYRINGA VULGARIS — SHEARED 9" O.C., SUMMER
21. VIBURNUM LANTANA — SHEARED 18" O.C., SUMMER
22. CORNUS MAS — SHEARED 18" O.C., WINTER
23. BERBERIS KOREANA — SHEARED 9" O.C., WINTER
24. RHODOTYPOS SCANDENS — SHEARED 1' O.C., WINTER
25. MALUS SARGENTI — SHEARED 2' O.C., WINTER
26. COTONEASTER NITIUS — SHEARED 18" O.C., WINTER
27. QUERCUS IMBRICARIA — SHEARED 2' O.C., WINTER
28. POPULUS NIGRA ITALICA — 8' O.C. WINTER
29. ELAEAGNUS ANGUSTIFOLIA — 10' O.C., WINTER
30. PHILADELPHIUS VIRGINALIS — 5' O.C., WINTER
31. HIBISCUS SYRIACUS — 6' O.C., WINTER
32. SALIX MATSUDANA TORTUOSA — 8' O.C., WINTER
33. AMELANCHIER CANADENSIS — 10' O.C., WINTER
34. CARPINUS BETULUS — 10' O.C., WINTER
35. BETULA POPULIFOLIA — 15' O.C., WINTER
36. POPULUS TREMULOIDES — 20' O.C., WINTER
37. GLEDITSIA TRIACANTHOS — 25' O.C., WINTER
38. TILIA CORDATA — 30' O.C., WINTER
39. ACER SACCHARUM — 35' O.C., WINTER
40. ULMUS AMERICANA — 40' O.C., WINTER

CEILINGS REPRESENTATIVE PLANTS INDICATING THE RELATIVE DEGREES OF VISUAL DENSITY. (SPACED TO GIVE UNIFORM CEILING DENSITY.)

1. THUJA OCCIDENTALIS — AMERICAN ARBOR-VITAE
2. JUNIPERUS VIRGINIANA — EASTERN RED-CEDAR
3. PSEUDOTSUGA TAXIFOLIA — DOUGLAS-FIR
4. ACER PLATANOIDES — NORWAY MAPLE, SUMMER
5. LARIX DECIDUA — EUROPEAN LARCH, SUMMER
6. PICEA PUNGENS — COLORADO BLUE SPRUCE
7. QUERCUS ALBA — WHITE OAK, SUMMER
8. CELTIS OCCIDENTALIS — AMERICAN HACKBERRY, SUMMER
9. ULMUS AMERICANA — AMERICAN ELM, SUMMER
10. FRAXINUS PENNSYLVANICA LANCEOLATA — GREEN ASH, SUMMER
11. QUERCUS ALBA — WHITE OAK, WINTER
12. BETULA POPULIFOLIA — GREY BIRCH, WINTER
13. MACLURA POMIFERA — OSAGE-ORANGE, WINTER
14. QUERCUS PALUSTRIS — PIN OAK, WINTER
15. SORBUS AUCUPARIA — EUROPEAN MOUNTAIN ASH, WINTER
16. CLADRASTIS LUTEA — AMERICAN YELLOW-WOOD, WINTER
17. GINKGO BILOBA — GINKGO, WINTER
18. GLEDITSIA TRIACANTHOS — COMMON HONEY-LOCUST, WINTER
19. RHUS TYPHINA — STAGHORN SUMAC, WINTER
20. ROBINIA PSEUDOACACIA — BLACK LOCUST, WINTER

FLOORS OF EXTERIOR SPACES CREATED BY PLANT MATERIALS RATED BY THEIR ABILITY TO WITHSTAND FOOT TRAFFIC AND THE EASE WITH WHICH THEY ARE ABLE TO BE WALKED UPON.

1. POA PRATENSIS — KENTUCKY BLUEGRASS
2. THYMUS SERPYLLUM — THYME
3. ANENARIA VERNA CAESPITOSA — MOSS SANDWORT
4. ANTHEMIS NOBILIS — CAMOMILE
5. MATRICARIA TCHIHATCHEWII — TURFING DAISY
6. CERASTIUM TOMENTOSUM — SNOW-IN-SUMMER
7. HEDERA HELIX — ENGLISH IVY
8. AJUGA REPTANS — BUNGLEWEED
9. COTONEASTER ADPRESSA PRAECOX — CREEPING COTONEASTER
10. ROSA WICHURAIANA — MEMORIAL ROSE

SOURCE: *Plants, People, and Environmental Quality*, U.S. Department of the Interior, National Park Service, 1972.

Figure 3-43

FLOORSCAPE AND CEILINGSCAPE

Factors affecting the role of plant materials in the role of floorscape and ceilingscape are shown in Figure 3-44.

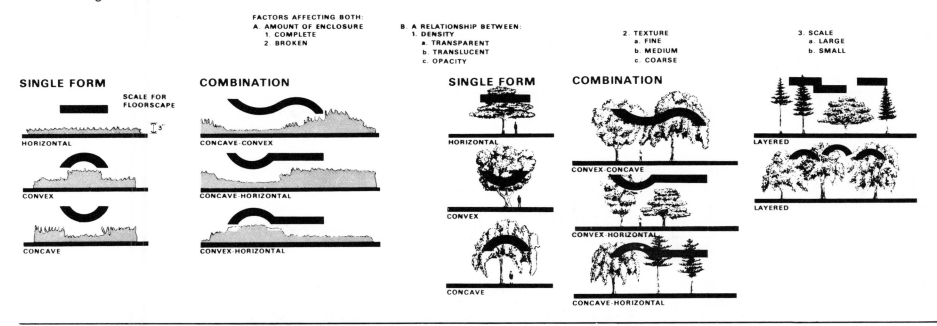

FLOORSCAPES AND CEILINGSCAPES ARE FORMED THROUGH APPLICATIONS OF: PLANT FORMS, PLANT SCALE, PLANT DENSITY, PLANT TEXTURE, PLANTS IN COMBINATION WITH PLANTS, AND PLANTS IN COMBINATION WITH LANDFORMS.

Figure 3-44 Floorscape and ceilingscape.

SOURCE: *Plants, People, and Environmental Quality*, U.S. Department of the Interior, National Park Service, 1972.

SPACE ARTICULATORS

The various ways in which plants can be used
to articulate space are shown in Figure 3-45.

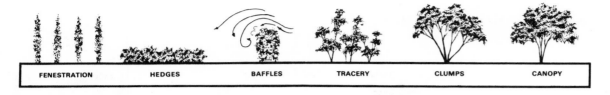

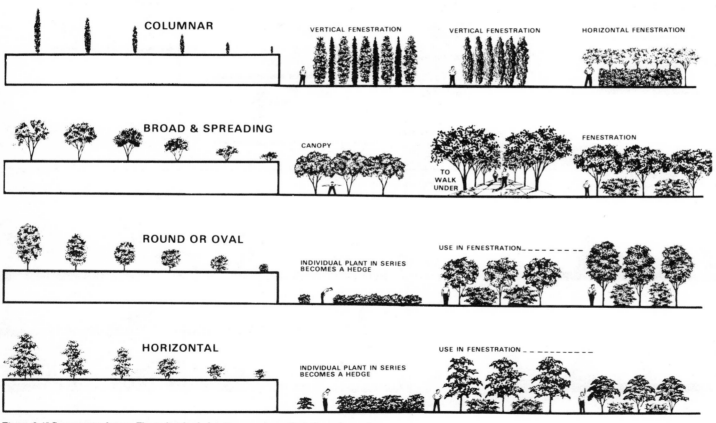

Figure 3-45 Space articulators. The individual plant is a specimen that, through spacing,
becomes fenestration, hedges, baffles, tracery, clumps, or canopy.

SOURCE: *Plants, People, and Environmental Quality*, U.S. Department of the Interior, National Park Service, 1972.

3.8 Regional Trees and Shrubs

Plant materials for each of the nine temperature regions of the United States are listed in the following pages. The correct list from which to select plants for a particular geographic location can be determined by examining the map in Figure 3-46, which shows the division of the United States into nine regions of average annual minimum temperature. Since extreme variations in altitude within the major regions or proximity to bodies of water may create somewhat colder or warmer areas within the particular regions, the experience of a local landscape architect familiar with the locality should be relied upon for a final judgment of a plant's hardiness in the area.

It should also be pointed out that although the plant materials listed for each region thrive best within that region, such plants are frequently usable in another region, thereby vastly increasing the number of plants from which a landscape architect can make a selection for a particular purpose.

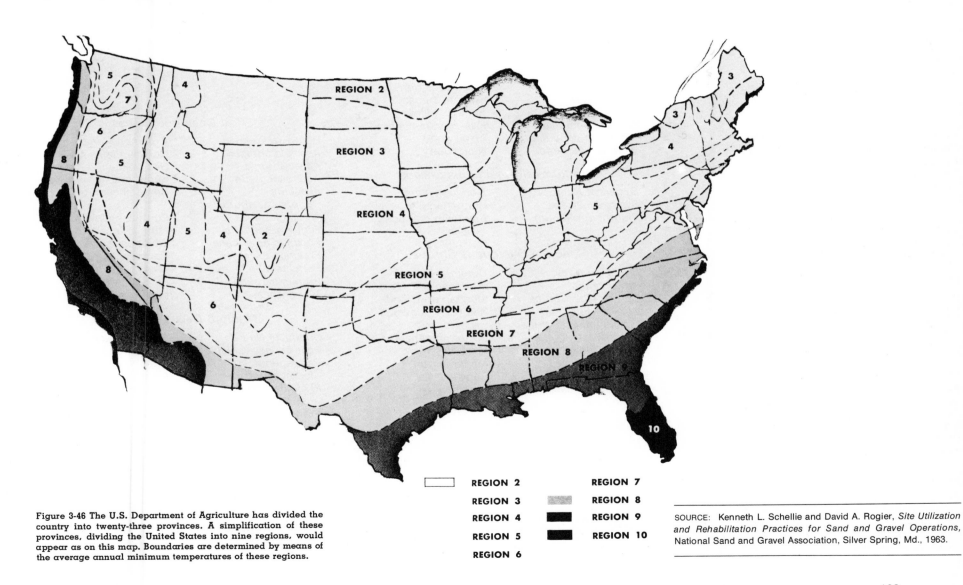

Figure 3-46 The U.S. Department of Agriculture has divided the country into twenty-three provinces. A simplification of these provinces, dividing the United States into nine regions, would appear as on this map. Boundaries are determined by means of the average annual minimum temperatures of these regions.

	REGION 2		REGION 7
	REGION 3		REGION 8
	REGION 4		REGION 9
	REGION 5		REGION 10
	REGION 6		

SOURCE: Kenneth L. Schellie and David A. Rogier, *Site Utilization and Rehabilitation Practices for Sand and Gravel Operations*, National Sand and Gravel Association, Silver Spring, Md., 1963.

Region 2

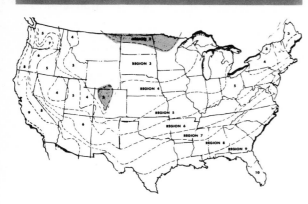

Tall Deciduous Trees

Botanical Name	Common Name
Betula papyrifera	Canoe birch
Populus deltoides	Cottonwood
Populus nigra italica	Lombardy poplar
Populus tremuloides	Quaking aspen

Medium Deciduous Trees

Botanical Name	Common Name
Acer negundo	Box elder
Alnus incana	Speckled alder
Betula pendula	European birch
Fraxinus pennsylvanica	Red ash
Malus baccata	Siberian crab apple
Populus simoni	Simon poplar
Salix alba	White willow
Sorbus aucuparia	European mountain ash

Low Deciduous Trees

Botanical Name	Common Name
Acer spicatum	Mountain maple
Carpinus caroliniana	American hornbeam
Elaeagnus angustifolia	Russian olive
Malus ioensis plena	Bechtel crab apple
Prunus pennsylvanica	Pin cherry

Tall Evergreen Trees

Botanical Name	Common Name
Juniperus virginiana	Eastern red cedar
Larix decidua	European larch
Larix laricina	Eastern larch
Picea engelmanni	Engelmann spruce
Picea pungens	Colorado spruce

Medium Evergreen Trees

Botanical Name	Common Name
Picea glauca	Black Hills spruce
Pinus banksiana	Jack pine
Pinus cembra	Swiss stone pine
Pinus flexilis	Limber pine
Pinus sylvestris	Scotch pine
Thuja occidentalis	American arborvitae

Tall Deciduous Shrubs

Botanical Name	Common Name
Acer ginnala	Amur maple
Alnus rugosa	Smooth alder
Caragana arborescens	Siberian pea tree
Lonicera maacki	Amur honeysuckle
Rhamnus frangula	Alder buckthorn
Rhus glabra	Smooth sumac
Salix lucida	Shining willow
Tamarix pentandra	Five-stamen tamarix
Viburnum dentatum	Arrowwood
Viburnum lentago	Nannyberry

Medium-tall Deciduous Shrubs

Botanical Name	Common Name
Syringa josikaea	Hungarian lilac
Viburnum trilobum	American cranberry bush

Medium Deciduous Shrubs

Botanical Name	Common Name
Alnus viridis	European green alder
Cornus alba sibirica	Siberian dogwood
Cornus stolonifera	Red osier dogwood
Myrica pennsylvanica	Bayberry
Physocarpus opulifolius	Eastern ninebark
Prunus tomentosa	Manchu cherry
Ribes alpinum	Alpine currant
Rosa rugosa	Rugosa rose
Shepherdia canadensis	Buffalo berry
Syringa villosa	Late lilac

Low-medium Deciduous Shrubs

Botanical Name	Common Name
Amorpha canescens	Leadplant
Comptonia peregrina	Sweet fern
Symphoricarpus orbiculatus	Indiana currant

Low Deciduous Shrubs

Botanical Name	Common Name
Genista tinctoria	Dyer's greenweed

Region 3

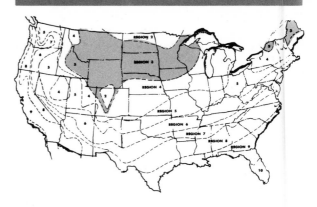

Tall Deciduous Trees

Botanical Name	Common Name
Acer platanoides	Norway maple
Acer rubrum	Red maple
Acer saccharum	Sugar maple
Aesculus hippocastanum	Horse chestnut
Alnus glutinosa	European alder
Fagus grandifolia	American beech
Fraxinus americana	White ash
Fraxinus excelsior	European ash
Populus alba	White poplar
Prunus serotina	Black cherry
Tilia cordata	Littleleaf linden

Medium Deciduous Trees

Botanical Name	Common Name
Acer pennsylvanicum	Moosewood
Betula lenta	Sweet birch
Cladrastis lutea	American Yellowwood
Phellodendron amurense	Amur cork tree
Prunus avium	Sweet cherry
Quercus bicolor	Swamp white oak
Robinia pseudoacacia	Black locust

SOURCE: Kenneth L. Schellie and David A. Rogier, *Site Utilization for Sand and Gravel Operations,* National Sand and Gravel Association, Silver Spring, Md., 1963.

Low Deciduous Trees

Botanical Name	Common Name
Aesculus glabra	Ohio buckeye
Prunus cerasifera atropurpurea	Pissard plum
Prunus cerasus	Sour cherry

Tall Evergreen trees

Botanical Name	Common Name
Abies veitchi	Veitchi fir
Chamaecyparis obtusa	Hinoki false cypress
Chamaecyparis pisifera	Sawara false cypress
Tsuga canadensis	Canada hemlock

Tall Deciduous Shrubs

Botanical Name	Common Name
Corylus avellana	European hazel
Euonymus europeus	Spindle tree
Hippophaë rhamnoides	Sea buckthorn
Ligustrum amurense	Amur privet
Rhus typhina	Staghorn sumac
Syringa vulgaris	Common lilac
Viburnum opulus	European cranberry bush
Viburnum prunifolium	Black haw

Medium-tall Deciduous Shrubs

Botanical Name	Common Name
Elaeagnus umbellata	Autumn elaeagnus
Sambucus canadensis	American elder
Vaccinium corymbosum	Highbush blueberry

Medium Deciduous Shrubs

Botanical Name	Common Name
Clethra alnifolia	Summer sweet
Cotoneaster racemiflora	Coin-leaf cotoneaster
Euonymus alatus	Winged burning bush
Lonicera tatarica	Tatarian honeysuckle
Symphoricarpus albus	Snowberry
Viburnum acerifolium	Mapleleaf viburnum
Viburnum cassinoides	Withe rod

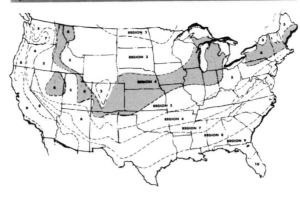

Region 4

Tall Deciduous Trees

Botanical Name	Common Name
Betula nigra	River birch
Carya cordiformis	Bitternut
Carya glabra	Pignut
Carya ovata	Shagbark hickory
Catalpa speciosa	Northern catalpa
Cercidiphyllum japonicum	Katsura tree
Fagus sylvatica	European beech
Ginkgo biloba	Ginkgo
Gleditsia triacanthos	Common honey locust
Gymnocladus dioicus	Kentucky Coffee tree
Juglans nigra	Eastern black walnut
Kalopanax pictus	Castor aralia
Liquidamber styraciflua	Sweet gum
Liriodendron tulipifera	Tulip tree
Magnolia acuminata	Cucumber tree
Nyssa sylvatica	Black tupelo
Quercus alba	White oak
Quercus velutina	Black oak
Tilia tomentosa	Silver linden

Medium Deciduous Trees

Botanical Name	Common Name
Ailanthus altissima	Tree of heaven
Amelanchier canadensis	Shadblow serviceberry
Castanea mollissima	Chinese chestnut
Catalpa bignonioides	Southern catalpa
Diospyros virginiana	Common persimmon
Juglans sieboldiana	Heartnut
Morus alba	White mulberry
Ostrya virginiana	Hop hornbeam
Oxydendrum arboreum	Sorrel tree

Quercus borealis	Red oak
Quercus coccinea	Scarlet oak
Quercus palustris	Pin oak
Sassafras albidum officinale	Sassafras
Sophora japonica	Japanese pagoda tree

Low Deciduous Trees

Botanical Name	Common Name
Carya tomentosa	Mockernut
Cercis canadensis	Eastern redbud
Cornus florida	Flowering dogwood
Cornus mas	Cornelian cherry
Crataegus crus-galli	Cockspur thorn
Crataegus phaenopyrum	Washington hawthorn
Halesia carolina	Carolina silver bell
Malus arnoldiana	Arnold crab apple
Malus coronaria charlottae	Charlotte crab apple
Malus floribunda	Japanese flowering crab apple
Malus hopa	Red flowering crab
Malus scheideckeri	Scheidecker crab apple
Malus spectabilis riversi	River's crab apple
Salix caprea	Goat willow
Syringa amurensis	Japanese tree lilac

Tall Evergreen Trees

Botanical Name	Common Name
Abies concolor	White fir
Abies homolepis	Nikko fir
Chamaecyparis nootkatensis	Nootka false cypress
Picea omorika	Serbian spruce
Pinus nigra	Austrian pine
Pseudotsuga taxifolia	Douglas fir
Taxodium distichum	Common bald cypress

Medium Evergreen Trees

Botanical Name	Common Name
Juniperus chinensis	Chinese juniper
Pinus bungeana	Lacebark pine
Pinus rigida	Pitch pine
Pinus virginiana	Scrub pine
Tsuga caroliniana	Carolina hemlock

SOURCE: Kenneth L. Schellie and David A. Rogier, *Site Utilization and Rehabilitation Practices for Sand and Gravel Operations*, National Sand and Gravel Association, Silver Spring, Md., 1963.

Tall Deciduous Shrubs

Botanical Name	Common Name
Cephalanthus occidentalis	Buttonbush
Chionanthus virginicus	Fringe tree
Cornus mas	Cornelian cherry
Cornus racemosa	Gray dogwood
Euonymus yedoensis	Yeddo euonymus
Hamamelis virginiana	Common Witch hazel
Hydrangea paniculata	Plumed hydrangea
Ligustrum vulgare	Common privet
Lindera benzoin	Spicebush
Photinia villosa	Oriental photinia
Rhus copallina	Shining sumac
Rosa setigera	Prairie rose
Syringa amurensis japonica	Japanese tree lilac
Tamarix parviflora	Small-flowered tamarix
Viburnum sieboldi	Siebold viburnum

Medium-tall Deciduous Shrubs

Botanical Name	Common Name
Aesculus parviflora	Bottlebrush buckeye
Kolkwitzia amabilis	Beauty bush
Ligustrum ibolium	Ibolium privet
Sambucus racemosa	European red elder

Medium Deciduous Shrubs

Botanical Name	Common Name
Acanthopanax sieboldianus	Five-fingered aralia
Calycanthus floridus	Carolina allspice
Chaenomeles lagenaria	Flowering quince
Deutzia lemoinei	Lemoine deutzia
Elaeagnus multiflora	Cherry elaeagnus
Lonicera bella	Belle honeysuckle
Lonicera morrowi	Morrow honeysuckle
Philadelphus coronarius	Sweet mock orange
Philadelphus grandiflorus	Big scentless mock orange
Ribes adoratum	Clove currant
Rosa eglanteria	Sweetbrier
Spiraea prunifolia	Bridal wreath spirea
Spiraea vanhouttei	Vanhoutte spirea
Stephanandra incisa	Cut-leaf stephanandra
Viburnum tomentosum	Double-file viburnum

Low-medium Deciduous Shrubs

Botanical Name	Common Name
Deutzia gracilis	Slender deutzia
Kerria japonica	Kerria

Spiraea arguta	Garland spirea
Spiraea thunbergi	Thunberg spirea
Viburnum carlesi	Fragrant viburnum

Low Deciduous Shrubs

Botanical Name	Common Name
Aronia melanocarpa	Black chokeberry
Ceanothus americanus	New Jersey tea
Chaenomeles japonica	Japanese quince
Cotoneaster horizontalis	Rock spray
Daphne mezereum	February daphne
Hydrangea arborescens	Smooth hydrangea
Hypericum prolificum	Shrubby Saint-John's-wort
Rosa carolina	Carolina rose
Spiraea tomentosa	Hardhack spirea

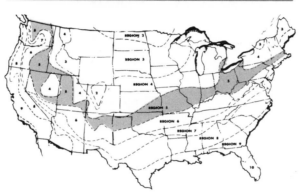

Region 5

Tall Deciduous Trees

Botanical Name	Common Name
Acer pseudoplatanus	Sycamore maple
Platanus acerifolia	London plane tree
Quercus imbricaria	Shingle oak
Quercus robur	English oak
Tilia petiolaris	Pendent silver linden
Zelkova serrata	Japanese zelkova

Medium Deciduous Trees

Botanical Name	Common Name
Asimina triloba	Pawpaw
Carpinus betulus	European hornbeam
Maclura pomifera	Osage orange
Paulownia tomentosa	Royal paulownia
Quercus phellos	Willow oak

| Tilia euchlora | Crimean linden |

Low Deciduous Trees

Botanical Name	Common Name
Acer campestre	Hedge maple
Acer palmatum	Japanese maple
Betula populifolia	Gray birch
Franklinia alatamaha	Franklinia
Koelreuteria paniculata	Goldenrain Tree
Magnolia soulangeana	Saucer magnolia
Prunus persica	Peach
Prunus subhirtella	Higan cherry

Tall Evergreen Trees

Botanical Name	Common Name
Cedrus libani	Cedar of Lebanon
Chamaecyparis lawsoniana	Lawson false cypress
Cryptomeria japonica	Cryptomeria
Picea polita	Tiger's-tail
Sciadopitys verticillata	Umbrella tree
Thuja plicata	Giant Arborvitae

Tall Deciduous Shrubs

Botanical Name	Common Name
Buddleia davidi	Butterfly bush
Cotinus coggygria	Smoke bush
Hibiscus syriacus	Shrub althea
Ligustrum ovalifolium	California privet
Magnolia stellata	Star magnolia
Prunus triloba	Flowering almond
Rhus chinensis	Chinese sumac
Spyringa chinensis	Chinese lilac
Xanthoceras sorbifolium	Shiny-leaf yellow horn

Medium-tall Deciduous Shrubs

Botanical Name	Common Name
Colutea arborescens	Bladder senna
Hamamelis vernalis	Vernal witchhazel
Lonicera korolkowi	Blue-leaf honeysuckle
Ribes sanguineum	Winter currant
Rosa multiflora	Japanese rose

Medium Deciduous Shrubs

Botanical Name	Common Name
Aronia arbutifolia	Red chokeberry

SOURCE: Kenneth L. Schellie and David A. Rogier, *Site Utilization and Rehabilitation Practices for Sand and Gravel Operations*, National Sand and Gravel Association, Silver Spring, Md., 1963.

Berberis thunbergi	Japanese barberry
Cornus amomum	Silky dogwood
Cotoneaster divaricata	Spreading cotoneaster
Cytisus scoparius	Scotch broom
Deutzia scabra	Snowflake deutzia
Forsythia intermedia	Golden bell
Forsythia suspensa	Weeping forsythia
Forsythia viridissima	Green-stem forsythia
Hydrangea quercifolia	Oak-leaved hydrangea
Lanicera fragrantissima	Winter honeysuckle
Rhodotypos scandens	Jetbead
Rosa hugonis	Father Hugo rose
Syringa persica	Persian lilac
Syringa sweginzowi	Chengtu lilac

Low-medium Deciduous Scrubs

Botanical Name	Common Name
Abeliophyllum distichum	Korean abelia leaf
Caryopteris incana	Bluebeard
Philadelphus lemoinei	Lemoine mock orange

Low Deciduous Shrubs

Botanical Name	Common Name
Berberis buxifolia	Dwarf Magellan barberry
Robinia hispida	Rose acacia
Weigela florida	Rose weigela

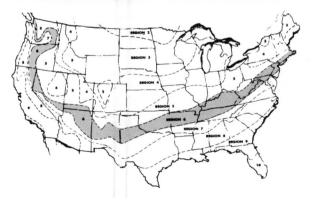

Region 6

Tall Deciduous Trees

Botanical Name	Common Name
Acer macrophyllum	Big-leaf maple
Celtis australis	European hackberry
Fraxinus oregona	Oregon ash

Juglans regia	English walnut
Platanus orientalis	Oriental plane tree
Quercus cerris	Turkey oak
Quercus garryana	Oregon white oak

Medium Deciduous Trees

Botanical Name	Common Name
Broussonetia papyrifera	Common paper mulberry
Cercis chinensis	Chinese redbud
Davidia involucrata	Dove tree
Quercus acutissima	Sawtooth oak
Quercus nigra	Water oak

Low Deciduous Trees

Botanical Name	Common Name
Cercis siliquastrum	Judas tree
Ficus carica	Common fig
Magnolia sieboldi	Oyama magnolia
Prunus amygdalus	Almond
Prunus conradinae semiplena	Double conradina cherry
Prunus mume	Japanese apricot
Quercus marilandica	Blackjack oak
Salix babylonica	Babylon weeping willow

Tall Evergreen Trees

Botanical Name	Common Name
Abies pinsapo	Spanish fir
Cedrus atlantica	Atlas cedar
Sequoia gigantea	Giant sequoia
Tsuga heterophylla	Western hemlock

Medium Evergreen Trees

Botanical Name	Common Name
Ilex aquifolium	English holly
Taxus baccata	English yew
Thuja orientalis	Oriental arborvitae

Low Evergreen Trees

Botanical Name	Common Name
Ilex pernyi	Perny holly
Laurus nobilis	Sweet bay
Myrica cerifera	Southern wax myrtle

Tall Deciduous Shrubs

Botanical Name	Common Name
Cercis chinensis	Chinese Judas tree
Clerodendron trichotomum	Harlequin glory-bower
Magnolia wilsoni	Wilson magnolia

Viburnum nudum	Smooth withe rod

Medium-tall Deciduous Shrubs

Botanical Name	Common Name
Aesculus splendens	Flame buckeye

Medium Deciduous Shrubs

Botanical Name	Common Name
Berberis beaniana	Bean's barberry
Cytisus dallimorei	Dallimore broom
Cytisus multiflorus	White Spanish broom
Euonymus americana	Strawberry bush
Garrya wrighti	Wright silk tassel
Ligustrum quihoui	Quihou privet
Magnolia liliflora nigra	Purple lily magnolia
Pyracantha coccinea	Scarlet fire thorn
Sorbaria aitchisoni	Kashmir false spirea
Vitex agnus-castus	Chaste tree

Low Deciduous Shrubs

Botanical Name	Common Name
Berberis concinna	Dainty barberry
Spiraea cantoniensis	Reeve's spirea

Tall Evergreen Shrubs

Botanical Name	Common Name
Ilex crenata	Japanese holly
Laurus nobilis	Laurel
Myrica cerifera	Wax myrtle
Osmanthus ilicifolius	Holly osmanthus
Prunus laurocerasus	Cherry laurel
Taxus baccata	English yew

Medium-tall Evergreen Shrubs

Botanical Name	Common Name
Mahonia beali	Leatherleaf mahonia

Medium Evergreen Shrubs

Botanical Name	Common Name
Phillyrea decora	Lance-leaf phillyrea
Rosmarinus officinalis	Rosemary

Low Evergreen Shrubs

Botanical Name	Common Name
Erica darleyensis	Darley heath

SOURCE: Kenneth L. Schellie and David A. Rogier, *Site Utilization and Rehabilitation Practices for Sand and Gravel Operations*, National Sand and Gravel Association, Silver Spring, Md., 1963.

Low Bamboos

Botanical Name	Common Name
Pseudosasa Japonica	Arrow bamboo
Sasa pumila	Ground bamboo
Sasa veitchi	Veitchi bamboo
Shibataea kumasaca	Kumasaca bamboo

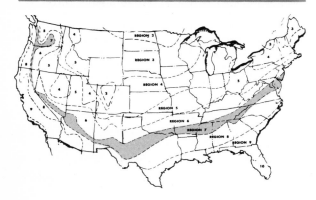

Region 7

Tall Deciduous Trees

Botanical Name	Common Name
Keteleeria fortunei	Fortune keteleeria
Platanus racemosa	California plane tree
Populus fremonti	Fremont cottonwood
Quercus kelloggi	California black oak

Medium Deciduous Trees

Botanical Name	Common Name
Clethra delavayi	Delavay clethra
Cornus nuttalli	Pacific dogwood
Diospyros kaki	Kaki persimmon
Fraxinus velutina	Velvet ash
Magnolia veitchi	Veitchi magnolia
Melia azedarach	Chinaberry
Podocarpus macrophyllus	Yew podocarpus
Quercus chrysolepis	Canyon live oak
Quercus laurifolia	Laurel oak
Quercus suber	Cork oak
Quercus virginiana	Live oak

Low Deciduous Trees

Botanical Name	Common Name
Albizzia julibrissin	Silk tree

Cercis racemosa	Raceme redbud
Prunus campanulata	Taiwan cherry
Prunus lusitanica	Portugal laurel

Tall Evergreen Trees

Botanical Name	Common Name
Araucaria araucana	Monkey-puzzle tree
Arbutus menziesi	Pacific madrone
Castanopsis chrysophylla	Giant evergreen chinquapin
Cedrus deodora	Deodar cedar
Cupressus macrocarpa	Monterey cypress
Cupressus sempervirens	Italian cypress
Magnolia grandiflora	Southern magnolia
Pinus coulteri	Big-cone pine
Pinus pinaster	Cluster pine
Sequoia sempervirens	Redwood

Medium Evergreen Trees

Botanical Name	Common Name
Camellia japonica	Common camellia
Cunninghamia lanceolata	Common China fir
Ilex latifolia	Luster-leaf holly
Juniperus drupacea	Syrian juniper
Juniperus excelsa	Greek juniper
Juniperus pachyphloea	Alligator juniper
Pinus radiata	Monterey pine
Umbellularia californica	California laurel

Low Evergreen Trees

Botanical Name	Common Name
Cupressus arizonica bonita	Smooth Arizona cypress
Ilex cassine	Dahoon
Myrica californica	California bayberry
Photinia serrulata	Chinese photinia

Tall Deciduous Shrubs

Botanical Name	Common Name
Chilopsis linearis	Desert willow
Cotoneaster frigida	Himalayan cotoneaster
Cudrania tricuspidata	Silkworm Tree
Lagerstroemia indica	Crape myrtle
Paliurus spina-christi	Christ's-thorn
Punica granatum	Pomegranate
Stewartia malacodendron	Virginia stewartia

Medium-tall Deciduous Shrubs

Botanical Name	Common Name
Corylopsis griffithi	Griffith winter hazel

Ligustrum sinense	Chinese privet
Spartium junceum	Spanish broom

Medium Deciduous Shrubs

Botanical Name	Common Name
Berberis potanini	Long-spine barberry
Chimonanthus praecox	Winter sweet
Hydrangea sargentiana	Sargent hydrangea
Leycesteria formosa	Formosa honeysuckle
Spiraea canescens	Hoary spirea
Styrax wilsoni	Wilson snowbell

Low-medium Deciduous Shrubs

Botanical Name	Common Name
Abelia schumanni	Schumann abelia

Low Deciduous Shrubs

Botanical Name	Common Name
Genista cinerea	Ashy woadwaxen

Tall Evergreen Shrubs

Botanical Name	Common Name
Aucuba japonica	Japanese aucuba
Camellia japonica	Common camellia
Camellia sasanqua	Sasanqua camellia
Ilex cassine	Dahoon
Ligustrum lucidum	Glossy privet
Michelia fuscata	Banana shrub
Myrica californica	California bayberry
Nerium oleander	Oleander
Nothopanax davidi	David false panax
Photinia serrulata	Chinese photinia
Rosa odorata	Tea rose

Medium-tall Evergreen Shrubs

Botanical Name	Common Name
Berberis darwini	Darwin barberry
Cotoneaster henryana	Henry cotoneaster
Elaeagnus pungens	Thorny elaeagnus
Ilex yunnanensis	Yunnan holly
Ligustrum henryi	Henry privet
Ligustrum japonicum	Japanese privet
Osmanthus fortunei	Fortune's osmanthus
Pieris formosa	Himalayan andromeda
Prunus lusitanica	Portugal laurel

SOURCE: Kenneth L. Schellie and David A. Rogier, *Site Utilization and Rehabilitation Practices for Sand and Gravel Operations*, National Sand and Gravel Association, Silver Spring, Md., 1963.

Pyracantha crenulata rogersiana — Rogers fire thorn

Vaccinium ovatum — Box blueberry

Viburnum tinus — Laurustine

Medium Evergreen Shrubs

Botanical Name	Common Name
Arctostaphylos stanfordiana	Stanford manzanita
Ceanothus delilianus	Delisle ceanothus
Choisya ternata	Mexican orange
Cistus albidus	White-leaf rockrose
Cistus cyprius	Spotted rockrose
Cistus laurifolius	Laurel rockrose
Cistus purpureus	Purple rockrose
Cotoneaster pannosa	Silverleaf cotoneaster
Hebe traversi	Travers hebe
Hypericum hookerianum	Hooker's Saint-John's-wort
Ilex cornuta	Chinese holly
Illicium floridanum	Florida anise tree
Lonicera nitida	Box honeysuckle
Nandina domestica	Nandina
Pieris taiwanensis	Formosa andromeda
Raphiolepsis umbellata	Yeddo hawthorn
Sarcococca ruscifolia	Fragrant sarcococca
Viburnum henryi	Henry viburnum
Viburnum japonicum	Japanese viburnum

Low-medium Evergreen Shrubs

Botanical Name	Common Name
Daphne odora	Winter daphne
Erica mediterranea	Mediterranean heath
Hebe buxifolia	Box-leaf hebe
Skimmia japonica	Japanese skimmia
Sophora secundiflora	Mescal bean

Low Evergreen Shrubs

Botanical Name	Common Name
Danae racemosa	Alexandrian laurel
Gaultheria veitchiana	Veitchi wintergreen
Ruscus aculeatus	Butcher's broom
Viburnum davidi	David viburnum

Region 8

Medium Deciduous Trees

Botanical Name	Common Name
Juglans hindsi	Hinds black walnut
Prosopis glandulosa	Honey mesquite

Tall Evergreen Trees

Botanical Name	Common Name
Pinus canariensis	Canary pine

Medium Evergreen Trees

Botanical Name	Common Name
Gordonia lasianthus	Loblolly bay gordonia
Pinus torreyana	Torrey pine

Low Evergreen Trees

Botanical Name	Common Name
Arbustus unedo	Strawberry tree

Medium-tall Deciduous Shrubs

Botanical Name	Common Name
Acacia farnesiana	Opopanax
Cassia corymbosa	Flowery senna

Medium Deciduous Shrubs

Botanical Name	Common Name
Severinia buxifolia	Chinese box orange

Low-medium Deciduous Shrubs

Botanical Name	Common Name
Ceratostigma willmottianum	Willmott blue leadwort

Tall Evergreen Shrubs

Botanical Name	Common Name
Arbutus unedo	Strawberry tree
Enonymus japonica	Evergreen enonymus

Medium-tall Evergreen Shrubs

Botanical Name	Common Name
Pittosporum tobira	Japanese pittosporum

Medium Evergreen Shrubs

Botanical Name	Common Name
Abelia floribunda	Mexican abelia
Carpenteria californica	Evergreen mock orange
Garrya elliptica	Silk tassel
Myrtus communis	Myrtle
Olearia haasti	New Zealand daisybush

Low-medium Evergreen Shrubs

Botanical Name	Common Name
Gardenia jasminoides	Gardenia

Low Evergreen Shrubs

Botanical Name	Common Name
Philesia magellanica	Magellan box lily

Tall Bamboos

Botanical Name	Common Name
Arundinaria simoni	Simon bamboo
Phyllostachys aurea	Golden bamboo
Phyllostachys bambusoides	Timber bamboo

SOURCE: Kenneth L. Schellie and David A. Rogier, *Site Utilization and Rehabilitation Practices for Sand and Gravel Operations,* National Sand and Gravel Association, Silver Spring, Md., 1963.

Region 9

Medium Deciduous Trees

Botanical Name	Common Name
Acacia decurrens dealbata	Silver wattle
Acer floridanum	Florida maple
Firmiana simplex	Chinese parasol tree
Pistacia chinensis	Chinese pistachio
Sapium sebiferum	Chinese tallow tree
Schinus molle	California pepper tree

Low Deciduous Trees

Botanical Name	Common Name
Parkinsonia aculeata	Jerusalem thorn

Tall Evergreen Trees

Botanical Name	Common Name
Pinus pinea	Italian stone pine
Quercus agrifolia	California live oak

Medium Evergreen Trees

Botanical Name	Common Name
Cinnamomum camphora	Camphor tree
Eugenia paniculata	Brush cherry eugenia
Juniperus lucayana	West Indies juniper
Lagunaria patersoni	Paterson Sugarplum tree
Pinus halepensis	Aleppo pine
Quercus ilex	Holly oak
Schinus terebinthifolius	Brazil pepper tree

Low Evergreen Trees

Botanical Name	Common Name
Leptospermum laevigatum	Australian tea tree
Maytenus boaria	Chile mayten tree
Olea europaea	Common olive

Tall Deciduous Shrubs

Botanical Name	Common Name
Hibiscus rosa-sinensis	Chinese hibiscus

Tall Evergreen Shrubs

Botanical Name	Common Name
Callistemon lanceolatus	Lemon bottlebrush
Carissa grandiflora	Natal plum

Medium-tall Evergreen Shrubs

Botanical Name	Common Name
Viburnum odoratissimum	Sweet viburnum

Medium Evergreen Shrubs

Botanical Name	Common Name
Heteromeles arbutifolia	Christmas berry
Viburnum suspensum	Sandankwa viburnum

Low Palms

Botanical Name	Common Name
Sabal minor	Dwarf palmetto
Serenoa repens	Saw palmetto

SOURCE: Kenneth L. Schellie and David A. Rogier, *Site Utilization and Rehabilitation Practices for Sand and Gravel Operations,* National Sand and Gravel Association, Silver Spring, Md., 1963.

Region 10

Tall Deciduous Trees

Botanical Name	Common Name
Ceiba pentandra	Silk cotton tree

Medium Deciduous Trees

Botanical Name	Common Name
Acacia decurrens mollis	Black wattle
Brachychiton acerifolium	Flame bottle tree
Delonix regia	Flame tree
Jacaranda acutifolia	Sharp-leaf jacaranda

Low Deciduous Trees

Botanical Name	Common Name
Acacia baileyana	Cootamundra wattle
Acacia longifolia floribunda	Gossamer Sydney acacia
Acacia pendula	Weeping boree acacia
Bauhinia variegata	Buddist bauhinia
Cassia fistula	Golden shower Senna

Tall Evergreen Trees

Botanical Name	Common Name
Araucaria excelsa	Norfolk Island pine
Grevillea robusta	Silk oak grevillea
Pittosporum rhombifolium	Diamond-leaf pittosporum
Podocarpus elongatus	Fern podocarpus

Medium Evergreen Trees

Botanical Name	Common Name
Castanospermum australe	Moreton Bay chestnut
Casuarina equisetifolia	Horsetail beefwood
Ceratonia siliqua	Carob
Ficus macrophylla	Moreton Bay fig
Hymenosporum flavum	Sweet shade
Melaleuca leucadendron	Cajeput tree
Pittosporum eugenioides	Tarata pittosporum

Botanical Name	Common Name
Quillaja saponaria	Soapbark tree
Spathodea campanulata	Bell flambeau tree

Low Evergreen Trees

Botanical Name	Common Name
Casuarina stricta	Coast beefwood
Leucadendron argenteum	Silver leucadendron
Macadamia ternifolia	Queensland nut

Tall Palms

Botanical Name	Common Name
Cocos nucifera	Coconut
Sabal palmetto	Palmetto
Washingtonia robusta	Mexican Washington palm

Medium Palms

Botanical Name	Common Name
Livistona australis	Australian pan palm
Roystonea regia	Royal palm

Low Palms

Botanical Name	Common Name
Erythea armata	Blue erythea
Phoenix reclinata	Senegal date palm
Ravenala madagascariensis	Madagascar traveler's-tree

SOURCE: Kenneth L. Schellie and David A. Rogier, *Site Utilization and Rehabilitation Practices for Sand and Gravel Operations*, National Sand and Gravel Association, Silver Spring, Md., 1963.

3.9 Regional Grasses

Listed below by four climatic zones are grasses suitable for planting within the United States. Since this is a rather general grouping of grasses and since climate and soil vary within these zones, the final selection of the best grass should be made by someone familiar with local soil and climatic conditions. The map in Figure 3-47 graphically displays the four zones into which the grasses have been tabulated.

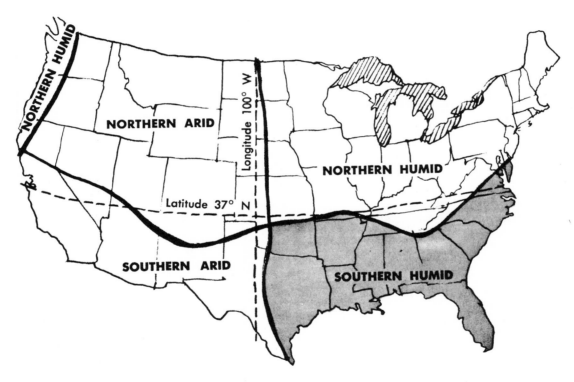

Figure 3-47 As shown on this map, grasses flourish differently in the four major climatic zones of the United States. Local soil and temperature conditions can cause some variation in growth.

SOURCE: Kenneth L. Schellie and David A. Rogier, *Site Utilization and Rehabilitation Practices for Sand and Gravel Operations,* National Sand and Gravel Association, Silver Spring, Md., 1963.

Grasses for the Northern Humid Zone

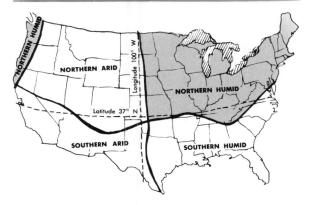

Canada bluegrass (Poa pratensis). Canada bluegrass has a rather shallow root system but can thrive on soils low in fertility. It is satisfactory for use where a dense turf is not essential.

Chewings fescue (Festuca rubra commutata). Chewings fescue is a fine-leaf grass that has a dense matted-root system. It is best suited to well-drained soils such as sandy loams. A clay soil, which has poor drainage characteristics, will not allow vigorous growth of this grass. Although chewings fescue can be used alone, it is frequently sown in combination with other grasses such as bluegrass or redtop.

Kentucky bluegrass (Poa pratensis). Kentucky bluegrass is the most widely used grass for lawns and other turfing within the northern humid region. Soil and climatic requirements for this grass are more exacting than for other grasses, for it does not grow well on sandy soils or on soils that are low in fertility, and it must have an abundance of moisture. Because Kentucky bluegrass germinates rather slowly and requires time to become completely established, it is normally sown in combination with other grasses such as chewings fescue.

Red fescue (Festuca rubra). Red fescue is similar to chewings fescue in its requirements for growth and use. It tends to creep more than does chewings fescue.

Redtop (Agrostis alba). Redtop is a temporary grass that will usually persist for 2 or 3 years. A fast-growing, vigorous strain, it is best used as a temporary cover crop in combination with a permanent grass such as Kentucky bluegrass. Redtop is frequently preferred over ryegrass as a cover crop in that it is not as strong a competitor of the permanent strain with which it is sown.

Ryegrass (Lolium multiflorum). Ryegrass is another temporary grass that normally will persist for only 3 or 4 years. Because of its initial fast growth, it is frequently used as a temporary cover crop in combination with permanent grasses that are slower in establishing themselves. Ryegrass will make the best growth on fertile, moist soils.

Smooth brome (Bromus inermis). Smooth brome is a rather coarse grass with strong, creeping rhizomes that makes it excellent for erosion and dust control. Fertile soil is required for its successful growth.

Grasses for the Southern Humid Zone

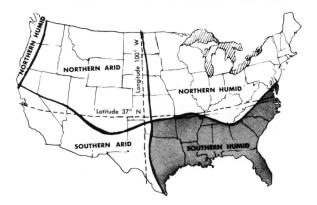

Bahia grass (Paspalum notatum). This grass is adaptable to sandy soils of the southern humid zone. Since it can also be grown on soils of low fertility and in climates with minimum rainfall, Bahia grass is quite useful. The stout rootstalks of this grass form a firm mat that is useful in dust and erosion control.

Bermuda grass (Cynodon dactylon). Bermuda grass is perhaps the best grass for use in the southern humid zone because of its tolerance of high temperatures and minimum rainfalls and its adaptability to a wide range of soils. It is sometimes considered a pest when used for individual lawns because of its invasive characteristic, which is difficult to restrain. Another disadvantage is that this grass will not grow satisfactorily in shaded areas.

Bluestem (Andropogon scoparius). Because of its deep root system, bluestem is primarily useful for erosion control. A perennial grass, bluestem is adaptable to a variety of soils.

Common carpet grass (Axonopus affinis). This grass is more adaptable to clay than it is to sandy soils. The growth of common carpet grass is generally limited to the southern half of the southern humid zone. Since it requires more moisture for survival than does Bermuda grass, it is less useful in most parts of the southern humid zone than Bermuda is.

Rhodes grass (Chloris gayana). Rhodes grass is a vigorous grass that spreads by means of runners. It is not completely adaptable to all parts of the southern humid zone.

Ryegrass (Lolium multiflorum). Ryegrass is a temporary grass that normally will persist for only 3 or 4 years. Because of its initial fast growth, it is frequently used as a temporary cover crop in combination with permanent grasses that are slower in establishing themselves. Ryegrass will make the best growth on fertile, moist soils and hence may not be suitable in sections of the southern humid zone.

Sudan grass (Sorghum vulgare sudanense). Sudan grass is an annual that is useful only as a temporary cover crop. It is probably one of the best temporary dust control grasses. Even though it is killed by the first hard frost, the stubble that remains provides some erosion control and furnishes a temporary cover in which to seed perennial species of grasses. Sudan grass is tolerant of a great variety of soil situations.

SOURCE: Kenneth L. Schellie and David A. Rogier, *Site Utilization and Rehabilitation Practices for Sand and Gravel Operations,* National Sand and Gravel Association, Silver Spring, Md., 1963.

Grasses for the Northern Arid Zone

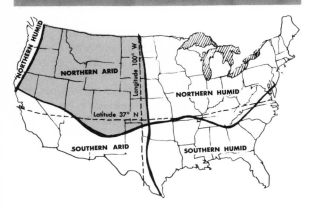

Alkali sacaton (Sporobolus airoides). This grass is best suited to heavy-textured soils such as clays. Alkali sacaton grows to a medium height and is a deep-rooted grass.

Blue grama (Bouteloua gracilis). Blue grama is a low-growing grass that adapts itself to a wide range of soil conditions. Thick stands of turf can be developed if the soil is of adequate fertility and the area is heavily seeded.

Buffalo grass (Buchloe dactyloides). Buffalo grass is not particularly adaptable to sandy soils, but it does thrive well on heavier, well-drained soils. It spreads rapidly by means of stolons and forms a dense, matted turf. Buffalo grass can withstand long periods of drought.

Sand dropseed (Sporobolus cryptandrus). Sand dropseed is generally adaptable in areas where blue grama and buffalo grass can be successfully grown. Its primary usefulness is for erosion and dust control.

Smooth brome (Bromus inermis). Smooth brome is a rather coarse grass with strong, creeping rhizomes that makes it excellent for erosion and dust control. Fertile soil is required for its successful growth.

Sudan grass (Sorghum vulgare sudanense). Sudan grass is an annual that is useful only as

a temporary cover crop. It is probably one of the best temporary dust control grasses. Even though it is killed by the first hard frost, the stubble that remains provides some erosion control and furnishes a temporary cover in which to seed perennial species of grasses. Sudan grass is tolerant of a great variety of soil situations.

Western wheatgrass (Agropyron smithii). Wheatgrass is a perennial grass with sod-forming fibrous roots and strong, creeping root-stalks. It can grow on a variety of soil types.

Grasses for the Southern Arid Zone

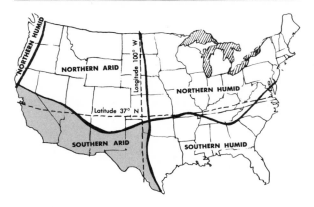

Alkali sacaton (Sporobolus airoides). This grass is best suited to heavy-textured soils such as clays. Alkali sacaton grows to a medium height and is a deep-rooted grass.

Bermuda grass (Cynodon dactylon). With irrigation Bermuda grass is an ideal grass for the southern arid zone because of its tolerance of high temperatures and its adaptability to a wide range of soils. It is sometimes considered a pest when used for individual lawns because of its invasive characteristic, which is difficult to restrain. Another disadvantage is that this grass will not grow well in shaded areas.

Blue grama (Bouteloua gracilis). Blue grama is a low-growing grass that adapts itself to a wide range of soil conditions. Thick stands of turf can be developed if the soil is of adequate fertility and the area is heavily seeded.

Buffalo grass (Buchloe dactyloides). Buffalo grass is not particularly adaptable to sandy soils, but it does thrive well on heavier, well-drained soils. It spreads rapidly by means of stolons and forms a dense, matted turf. Buffalo grass can withstand long periods of drought.

Rhodes grass (Chloris gayana). Rhodes grass is a vigorous grass that spreads by means of runners. In areas receiving less than 25 inches of annual rainfall, it is usually preferred to Bermuda grass.

Sand dropseed (Sporobolus cryptandrus). Sand dropseed is generally adaptable in areas where blue grama and buffalo grass can be successfully grown. Its primary usefulness is for erosion and dust control.

Sudan grass (Sorghum vulgare sudanense). Sudan grass is an annual that is useful only as a temporary cover crop. It is probably one of the best temporary dust control grasses. Even though it is killed by the first hard frost, the stubble that remains provides some erosion control and furnishes a temporary cover in which to seed perennial species of grasses. Sudan grass is tolerant of a great variety of soil situations.

Weeping love grass (Eragrostis curvula). Weeping love grass is a quick-growing perennial grass of chief value in controlling dust and erosion on infertile areas. It grows well on sandy soils if the area receives from 15 to 20 inches of rainfall annually.

SOURCE: Kenneth L. Schellie and David A. Rogier, *Site Utilization and Rehabilitation Practices for Sand and Gravel Operations,* National Sand and Gravel Association, Silver Spring, Md., 1963.

3.10 Site Security: Defensible Space

"Defensible space" is a term used to describe a series of physical design characteristics that maximize resident control of behavior, particularly crime, within a residential community. A residential environment designed under defensible-space guidelines clearly defines all areas as public, semiprivate, or private. In so doing, it determines who has the right to be in each space and allows residents to be confident in responding to any questionable activity or persons within their complex. The same design concepts improve the ability of police to monitor activities within the community.

Implementation of defensible space utilizes various elements of physical planning and architectural design such as site planning and the grouping and positioning of units, paths, windows, stairwells, doors, and elevators. Provision of defensible-space mechanisms is best achieved in a project's inception, as it involves major decisions with respect to the project.

However, a series of small-scale physical design techniques can be used to create defensible space and consequently to reduce crime in existing residential areas. These techniques consist of subdividing a project or building to limit access and improve neighbors' recognition, thus symbolically defining an area as coming under the sphere of influence of a particular group of inhabitants and improving the inhabitants' surveillance capacity.

The term "limiting access" refers to the use of physical design to prevent a potential criminal from entering certain spaces. Although no barrier is impregnable, physical barriers of this type are real and are relatively difficult to overcome.

In contrast, it is possible to use psychological or "symbolic" barriers that, while presenting no physical restriction, discourage criminal penetration by making an obvious distinction between stranger and intruder and bringing all activity under more intense surveillance. An intruder invading the space defined by such symbolic barriers becomes conspicuous to both residents and police.

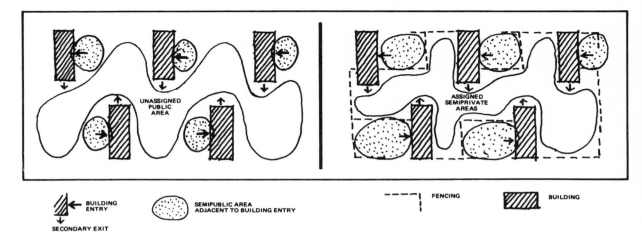

Figure 3-48 Alternative site plans with unassigned and assigned areas.

Improved neighbor recognition plays a key role in the functional workings of psychological barriers. If, by newly defining areas, neighbors can be made to recognize one another, the potential criminal then can not only be seen but also be perceived as an intruder. This subdivision of space also reinforces the feeling in residents that they have the right to intervene on their own behalf.

Creating Territorial Areas Residential developments consisting of large superblocks devoid of interior streets have been found to suffer higher crime rates than projects of comparable size and density in which existing city streets have been allowed to continue through the sites.

Housing sites larger than a city block are best subdivided by through streets. The small scale of neighboring city blocks should be maintained where possible. This directive runs contrary to site planning principles aimed at removing vehicular traffic from the interior of large projects to free areas for recreation. However, large areas of low- and moderate-income projects that have closed off city streets but permitted public access have been considered dangerous by inhabitants and have consequently received minimal use. Through streets bring safety for three reasons:

1. They facilitate direct access to all buildings in the project by car and bus.
2. They bring vehicular and pedestrian traffic into the project and so provide the important measure of safety that comes with the presence of people.
3. They facilitate patrolling by police, provide easy access, and are a means of identifying building locations. Much of the crime deterrence provided by police occurs while they pass through an area in a patrol car.

A project's site should be subdivided so that all of its areas are related to particular buildings or clusters of buildings. No area should be unassigned or simply left "public" (see Figure 3-48). Zones of influence should embrace all areas of a project, and the site plan should be so conceived. A "zone of influence" is an area surrounding a building, or preferably an area surrounded by a building, that is perceived by residents as an outdoor extension of their dwellings. As such, it comes under their con-

SOURCE: Center for Residential Security Design, New York, *A Design Guide for Improving Residential Security,* U.S. Department of Housing and Urban Development, Office of Policy Development and Research, Division of Building Technology, 1973.

tinued use and surveillance. Residents using these areas should feel that they are under natural observation by other project residents. A potential criminal should equally feel that any suspicious behavior will come under immediate scrutiny.

Grounds should be allocated to specific buildings or building clusters. This practice assigns responsibility and primary claim to certain residents. It also sets up an association between a building resident in his or her apartment and the grounds below.

Residents in projects that are subdivided have the opportunity of viewing a particular segment of the project as their own turf. When an incident occurs there, they are able to determine whether their area or another area is involved. When divisions do not exist within a project plan, an incident in one area is related to the complex and can create the impression of lack of safety in the entire project.

Defining Zones of Transition   Boundaries can be defined by either real or symbolic barriers. Real barriers require entrants to possess a mechanical opening device, a familiar face or voice, or some other means of identification to indicate their belonging prior to entry. That is, access to a residence through a real barrier is by the approval of its occupants only, whether through the issuance of a key or through acceptance by their agents or by electronic signal.

Symbolic barriers define areas or relate them to particular buildings without physically preventing intrusion (see Figure 3-49). The success of symbolic versus real barriers in restricting entry rests on four conditions:

1. The capacity of the intruder to read the symbols
2. The capacity of the inhabitants or their agents to maintain controls and reinforce the space definition as symbolically defined

Figure 3-50 Zones of transition between public street, project grounds, and building interior.

3. The capacity of the defined space to require the intruder to make obvious his or her intentions
4. The capacity of the inhabitants or their agents to challenge the presence of an intruder and to take subsequent action

Since many of these components work in concept, a successful symbolic barrier is one that provides the greatest likelihood of the presence of all these conditions. By employing a combination of symbolic barriers, it is possible to indicate to entrants that they are crossing a series of boundaries without employing literal barriers to define the spaces along the route.

These symbolic tools for restricting space usage assume particular importance in exist-

SOURCE: Center for Residential Security Design, New York, *A Design Guide for Improving Residential Security*, U.S. Department of Housing and Urban Development, Office of Policy Development and Research, Division of Building Technology, 1973.

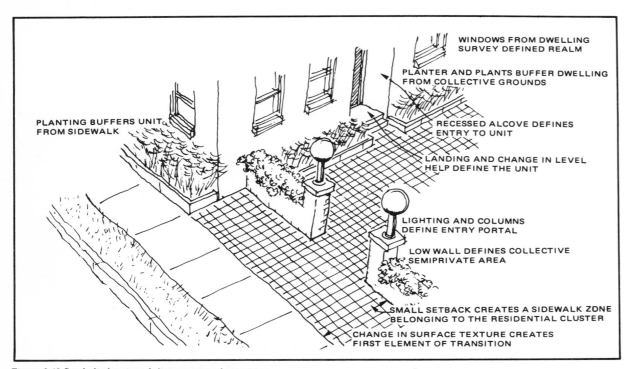

WINDOWS FROM DWELLING SURVEY DEFINED REALM

PLANTER AND PLANTS BUFFER DWELLING FROM COLLECTIVE GROUNDS

PLANTING BUFFERS UNIT FROM SIDEWALK

RECESSED ALCOVE DEFINES ENTRY TO UNIT

LANDING AND CHANGE IN LEVEL HELP DEFINE THE UNIT

LIGHTING AND COLUMNS DEFINE ENTRY PORTAL

LOW WALL DEFINES COLLECTIVE SEMIPRIVATE AREA

SMALL SETBACK CREATES A SIDEWALK ZONE BELONGING TO THE RESIDENTIAL CLUSTER

CHANGE IN SURFACE TEXTURE CREATES FIRST ELEMENT OF TRANSITION

Figure 3-49 Symbolic barriers defining zones of transition.

ing projects that cannot be subdivided into territorial areas. When it is still the intent to make space obey semiprivate rules and fall under the influence and control of inhabitants, the introduction of symbolic elements along paths of access can serve this function.

Opportunities for the use of symbolic barriers to define zones of transition are many. As illustrated in Figure 3-50, the barriers can occur in moving from the public street to the semipublic grounds of the project, in the transition from outdoors to indoors, and in the transition from the semipublic space of a building lobby to the corridors of each floor.

Symbolic barriers can also be used by residents as boundary lines to define areas of comparative safety. Parents may use symbolic barriers to delimit the areas where young children may play. Similarly, because symbolic barriers force outsiders to realize that they are intruding into a semiprivate domain, they can effectively restrict behavior to that which residents find acceptable.

Locating Amenities Recreational and open-space areas should serve the needs of different groups. An understanding of what different age groups desire of open-space and recreational facilities is essential to the successful use of such areas. The design and location of these areas within the residential environment should follow the demands, capabilities, and expectations of their eventual users.

All areas of the grounds should be defined

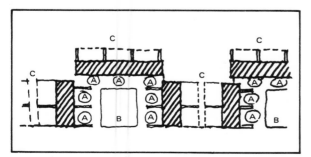

Figure 3-51 Ground areas assigned for particular uses.

for specific uses and designed to suit those uses. Figure 3-51 illustrates different uses and users. The areas adjacent to each entry, labeled *A,* have been allocated for the use of 1- to 5-year-olds, with seating for adults. The larger areas in the center of each entry compound, labeled *B,* are provided with play facilities serving 6- to 12-year-olds. The areas labeled *C* are intended for more passive activity and as decorative green areas. The *C* areas, accessible from the building interiors only, are provided with barbecuing facilities and some seating.

Well-designed recreation facilities improve the security of an area if they provide for activities of a particular group of residents and are adjacent to the residents' interior environs. So

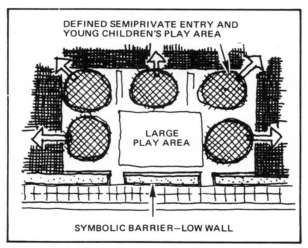

Figure 3-52 Common entry to a cluster of buildings.

designed, the facilities create outdoor zones that are effective extensions of the dwellings. By providing for outdoor activities adjacent to homes, these areas allow residents to assume a further realm of territory and further responsibility.

Children 1 to 5 years in age are most comfortable playing in an outdoor area immediately adjacent to their dwellings, preferably just outside the door in both single-family units and multiple dwellings. Figure 3-53 illustrates such

Figure 3-53 Play area defining a buffer to a multifamily building entry.

an area. The location of these facilities adjacent to the entry door to the unit and the inclusion of benches for adults further create a semiprivate buffer zone separating the private zone of the residential interior from the more public zones.

In the design of a multifamily residential complex serving many groups of families, each with its own entry to its own building, the buffers that demarcate each entry zone can also define a larger subcluster within the project.

Figure 3-52, which extends the concept shown in Figure 3-53, illustrates the common entry area of a cluster of buildings. Each entry zone is provided with its own tot play area and surrounding seating. The five entries share a common central play facility for the 5- to 12-year-olds that is large enough to accommodate more active play and sufficiently separated from the dwelling units to reduce noise penetration. The large play area is, however, still very much in view of every dwelling.

Play areas for 12- to 18-year-olds should not

SOURCE: Center for Residential Security Design, New York, *A Design Guide for Improving Residential Security,* U.S. Department of Housing and Urban Development, Office of Policy Development and Research, Division of Building Technology, 1973.

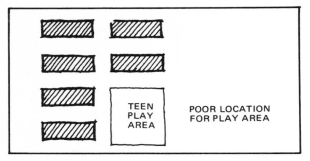

Figure 3-54 Teen play area located at the periphery of a project.

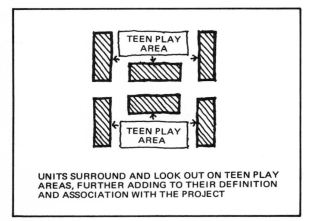

Figure 3-55 Teen play areas surrounded by buildings and their entries.

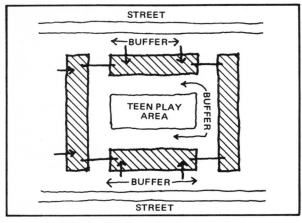

Figure 3-56 Teen play area located with a semiprivate zone.

Figure 3-57 Play areas adjacent to a decorative green.

be located immediately adjacent to home, but neither should they be too far away. They should be large enough to house activities of interest to this age group: basketball, football, handball, dancing.

These teen play areas should not be located in an isolated area of a development, disassociated from dwelling units. This is a common practice (see Figure 3-54) that results in the area's neglect, vandalization, or underuse. Rather, teen play areas should be bordered on three or four sides by the dwellings of residents, as illustrated in Figures 3-55 and 3-56.

The teen area should be provided with occasional benches bordering play areas. Benches allow children to gather and watch while only a few play. Children also use the benches for piling extra clothing and for resting after strenuous exercise. Benches give the play area a feeling of stability and containment. When such areas are defined in this way, they frequently are adopted for social uses in the evening.

Green areas unencumbered by play facilities are the pride of the elderly and usually the thorn in the side of 7- to 15-year-olds, who are prevented from using these areas for playfields. It is therefore important to provide such green areas with protection by judicious placement and use of shrubs and fences. However, as Figure 3-57 illustrates, the best guarantee that these green areas will be respected for their decorative purpose is the provision of adjacent and separate play areas and equipment.

SOURCE: Center for Residential Security Design, *A Design Guide for Improving Residential Security,* U.S. Department of Housing and Urban Development, Office of Policy Development and Research, Division of Building Technology, 1973.

Creating Surveillance Opportunities

Surveillance is a major crime deterrent and a major contributor to the image of a safe environment. By allowing tenants to monitor activities in the areas adjacent to their apartment buildings, tenants in areas outside their homes feel that they are observed by other project residents. Surveillance also makes obvious to potential criminals that any overt act or suspicious behavior will come under the scrutiny of project occupants.

The ability to observe criminal activity may not, however, impel an observer to respond with assistance to the person or defense of the property being victimized. The decision to act will depend on the presence of the following conditions:

1. The extent to which the observer has developed a sense of his or her personal and proprietary rights and is accustomed to defending them
2. The extent to which the activity observed is understood to be occurring in an area within the influence of the observer
3. Identification of the observed behavior as

Figure 3-58 Project designed to face surrounding streets and define interior areas as semiprivate.

being abnormal to the area
4. Identification on the part of the observer with either the victim or the property being vandalized or stolen
5. The extent to which the observer feels that he or she can effectively alter the course of events being observed

Linking opportunities for surveillance to ter-

ritorially defined areas will go a long way toward ensuring that many of these required conditions will be satisfied. Figure 3-58 illustrates a territorially defined site plan that is supported by surveillance opportunities.

Designers should position all public paths so that access from public streets to units is as direct as possible. Access arteries should be limited in number to ensure that they are well peopled. They should also be evenly lit. The paths through a project should be designed to allow prescanning before use. There should be no (or few) turns on any artery, and all points along access routes should be observed from the point of origin to the point of destination. When a building is located for the particular use of the elderly, front entrances should face the street and be within 50 feet of the street.

SOURCE: Center for Residential Security Design, *A Design Guide for Improving Residential Security,* U.S. Department of Housing and Urban Development, Office of Policy Development and Research, Division of Building Technology, 1973.

3.11 Sewage Disposal

GENERAL DESIGN

This subsection on sewage disposal will enable one to design private (self-contained) sewage disposal systems for residences, camps, summer cottages, schools, factories, hospitals, institutions, and the like for any number of occupants up to the equivalent of fifty persons in residence. For larger systems, a sanitation engineer should be consulted.

Past experience, engineering practice, and bacteriological research have proved that the old-time sewage cesspool is a menace to health and a nuisance. Sanitation engineers agree that all sewage disposal systems must include a septic tank, wherein sewage is changed by the action of anaerobic bacteria into gases and an effluent liquid, which is then rendered harmless by earth leaching, where aerobic bacteria oxidize all obnoxious components.

Influencing Factors A complete sewage disposal system, with all essential and optional elements is presented below (see Figure 3-60). The final design of a specific installation is influenced by (1) the amount of sewage handled, which is based on the equivalent occupancy, and (2) the character of the soil as expressed by its relative absorption. Both of these factors can be determined for any project by methods described here.

Equivalent Occupancy The amount of sewage to be handled is related to the type of building and its occupancy. The base is the normal amount of sewage obtained under residential conditions per person per 24 hours (see table "Equivalent Occupancy"). That is, in residential service 50 gallons of sewage per person must be treated each 24 hours. Other types of buildings are related to this base by means of a conversion factor. To find the equivalent occupancy in any project, multiply the number of persons occupying the type of building given in the table.

Equivalent occupancy governs the size of the septic tank and also influences the capacity required in the effluent disposal system. For

EQUIVALENT OCCUPANCY

Type of building	Gallons per person	Conversion factor
Residence	50	1
Camp	25	1/2
Summer cottages	40	4/5
Day schools without showers or kitchens	15	3/10
Factories without showers or kitchens	15	3/10
Day schools with showers and kitchens	30	3/5
Institutions except hospitals	100	2
Hospitals	200	4

NOTE: To find equivalent occupancy, multiply the number of persons occupying the type of building by the conversion factor.

convenience the table is repeated on each page where equivalent occupancy is a factor in design.

Relative Absorption The porosity or absorption of the soil is a vital factor in design. A simple field method of determining the characteristics of any soil in relation to effluent disposal consists of digging a pit of fixed dimensions and measuring the rate of outflow of water from the pit.

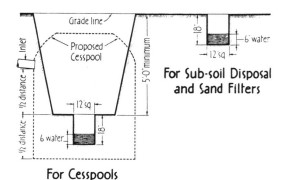

Figure 3-59 Test pits for relative absorption.

The depth below grade of this test pit varies according to the unit under consideration, as developed in detail under the headings "Leaching Cesspools," "Subsoil Disposal Beds," and "Sand Filters." The size of the pit in which the water test is made is always 12 inches square and 18 inches deep, as illustrated in Figure 3-59. Water to a depth of 6 inches (about 3¾ gallons) is poured quickly into this square test pit. The time required for the water to disappear is measured, and one-sixth of this time is taken as the average time for the water level to fall 1 inch. The latter time is the relative absorption factor for the soil, but for convenience it is expressed as rapid, medium, slow, semi-impervious, and impervious, as indicated in the table "Relative Absorption."

RELATIVE ABSORPTION

Time (1-inch drop in minutes)	Relative absorption
0–3	Rapid
3–5	Medium
5–30	Slow
30–60	Semi-impervious
60 and up	Impervious

Design Procedure A tentative layout of the proposed sewage disposal system similar to the diagrammatic plan in Figure 3-60, should be made over a topographic plot plan of the property. Test pits should be dug at the sites of any proposed leaching cesspool or other effluent disposal area and the relative absorption determined.

With these data on the equivalent occupancy known, reference should be made to the table "Selection of Effluent Sewage Disposal System" to select the type of system best adapted to project conditions.

SOURCE: *Time-Saver Standards*, 1st ed., F. W. Dodge Company, New York, 1946.

SELECTION OF EFFLUENT SEWAGE DISPOSAL SYSTEM

Conditions	Type of disposal system		
	Leaching cesspool	Subsoil drainage	Sand filter
Relative absorption:			
Rapid	Yes	Yes	No
Medium	Yes	Yes	No
Slow	Yes	Yes	No
Semi-impervious	No	Yes	No
Impervious	No	No	Yes
Available area:			
Large	Yes	Yes	Yes
Moderate	Yes	Yes	Yes
Small	Yes	No	No
Groundwater:			
Below Grade	8 feet minimum	2 feet minimum	2 feet minimum
Final disposal of effluent	Not necessary	Required only for semi-impervious soils	Always necessary
Relative initial cost	Low	Medium	High

Elements of Sewage Disposal Systems

House Sewer   The house sewer extends from the house main to the septic tank. The house main is a continuation of the cast-iron soil line to a minimum of 5 feet outside the foundation. No trap or fresh-air inlet is required in the house main. The house sewer may be solid, glazed clay tile, cement bell-and-spigot pipe, or, preferably, cast-iron pipe, laid with filled joints. Always use cast iron within 100 feet of any potable water supply and near trees. Never connect surface drainage lines to the sewage disposal system.

Requirements. Size: 6-inch preferable; minimum, 4-inch. Pitch: 1 inch in 8 feet for 6-inch pipe; 1 inch in 4 feet for 4-inch pipe. Grade: northern latitudes, 1 foot 6 inches minimum below surface; southern latitudes, sufficient depth to cover.

Grease-bearing waste and trap. These are optional elements, used to separate grease and oil from waste. When they are installed, run from the grease-carrying waste in building through a trap to the house sewer.

Septic Tank   This is the essential element of a sanitary disposal system. Locate it as far to leeward of building as possible. Its function is

Figure 3-60 At right, a key diagram of a sewage disposal system.

to retain the raw sewage out of contact with air until anaerobic bacteria can break down the solids into gases that escape through vents and an effluent liquid that is subsequently purified by oxidation. Some solids settle as sludge. Construction and operating details are given under the heading "Septic and Siphon Tanks."

Siphon tank. This tank is required in large installations and when a sand filter is used; it is desirable but not essential with small septic tanks. It functions to collect effluent from the septic tank and periodically to discharge it to the effluenct disposal system.

Sludge drain and pit. These elements are optional. They serve to draw sludge from the septic tank without interrupting its operation for cleaning. The drain is similar in construction to the house sewer. For details, see the section "Distribution Boxes."

Effluent Disposal   There are three principal types of effluent disposal systems, the choice being governed by soil conditions and topography. All are designed to permit the effluent to

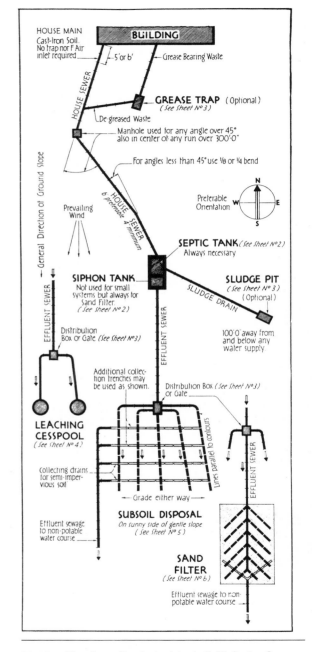

SOURCE: *Time-Saver Standards*, 1st ed., F. W. Dodge Company, New York, 1946.

come in contact with air and soil where it may be oxidized and rendered harmless by aerobic bacteria.

Effluent sewer. This element is common to all systems and is a closed sewerage line similar in construction and size to the house sewer, extending from the septic or siphon tank through a distribution box or gate to the chosen type of effluent disposal element. The minimum pitch may be 1 inch in 16 feet.

Distribution Box or Gate. This device serves to distribute the effluent to one part or another of the effluent disposal system in order to "rest" the part not in use. Details are given in the section "Distribution Boxes."

The choice of effluent disposal system is governed by factors included in the tables "Equivalent Occupancy" and "Relative Absorption." Selection is determined from the table "Selection of Effluent Sewage Disposal System" and from the sections "Leaching Cesspools," "Subsoil Disposal Beds," and "Sand Filters."

SEPTIC AND SIPHON TANKS

The septic and siphon tanks described here are of reinforced concrete and can be constructed by any competent contractor without requiring the use of any patented or manufactured element other than the automatic siphon, which is an essential part of a siphon tank. Septic tanks are made in commercial units and are available in all parts of the United States. They are built of steel, precast concrete, and other materials. The use of commercial septic and siphon tanks eliminates the need for detailed design of these units as presented here, but the selection of the proper size of a commercial unit is indicated by the data presented.

Operation Raw sewage from the house sewer enters the septic tank, where by a submerged intake it reaches the liquid in the tank below the overflow level. The liquid in the septic tank quickly forms three distinct layers: solid matter or sludge settles to the bottom, effluent sewage forms the main liquid content in the middle, and the upper stratum is a scum that serves to keep air out of contact with the

EQUIVALENT OCCUPANCY

Type of building	Gallons per person	Conversion factor
Residence	50	1
Camp	25	1/2
Summer cottages	40	4/5
Day schools without showers or kitchens	15	3/10
Factories without showers or kitchens	15	3/10
Day schools with showers and kitchens	30	3/5
Institutions except hospitals	100	2
Hospitals	200	4

SELECTION AND DESIGN OF SEPTIC AND SIPHON TANKS

Equivalent occupancy	Capacity (gallons)	Septic tank Length A	Septic tank Width B	Septic tank Air space C	Septic tank Liquid depth D	Siphon tank Length E	Siphon tank Width F	Siphon tank Depth G	Siphon Size L	Siphon Drawing depth M	Concrete thickness Walls J	Concrete thickness Top I	Concrete thickness Bottom K
1–4	325*	5'0"	2'6"	1'0"	3'6"	†							
5–9	450	6'0"	2'6"	1'0"	4'0"	3'0"†	2'6"†	3'0"†	3"	1'6"	6"	4"	6"
10–14	720	7'0"	3'6"	1'0"	4'0"	3'6"†	3'6"†	3'0"†	3'	1'6"	6"	4"	6"
15–20	1000	8'0"	4'0"	1'0"	4'0"	4'0"	4'0"	3'0"	4"	1'8"	6"	4"	6"
21–25	1250	9'0"	4'6"	1'0"	4'3"	4'6"	4'6"	3'0"	4"	1'8"	7"	5"	6"
26–30	1480	9'6"	4'8"	1'3"	4'6"	4'8"	4'8"	3'6"	4"	2'2"	8"	5"	6"
31–35	1720	10'0"	5'0"	1'3"	4'8"	5'0"	5'0"	3'6"	4"	2'2"	8"	5"	6"
36–40	1950	10'6"	5'3"	1'3"	4'9"	5'3"	5'3"	3'6"	4"	2'2"	9"	5"	6"
41–45	2174	11'0"	5'6"	1'3"	4'10"	5'6"	5'6"	3'6"	5"	2'2"	9"	5"	6"
46–50	2400	11'6"	5'9"	1'3"	5'0"	5'9"	5'9"	3'6"	5"	2'2"	9"	5"	6"

*Smallest size recommended.
†Siphon tank not essential for septic tanks under 1000-gallon capacity; rarely used on the smallest size.
NOTE: Capacity of tanks is based on 50 gallons per equivalent occupancy per 24 hours.

The sludge that forms at the bottom of the septic tank must be removed periodically to avoid filling the tank with solid matter. In large installations, where interruption of the operation of the septic tank for cleaning purposes is undesirable, a sludge drain and sludge pit should be provided to permit removal of sludge while the tank is in continuous operation.

When an effluent disposal system of the sand filter type is used, when the system is designed for 1000 gallons or more daily capacity, and preferably in all residences, the septic tank should be equipped with a siphon tank. However, this unit is not actually required in small installations using leaching cesspools or subsoil disposal beds.

The siphon tank functions to collect overflow from the septic tank and to discharge it periodically through the action of the automatic siphon into the effluent sewer and disposal system. This permits the disposal units to

effluent sewage and permits anaerobic bacterial action or septicization to take place. Most of the suspended solid matter is changed by this action into (1) gases that escape through vents provided for the purpose and (2) effluent sewage that overflows either directly or through the siphon tank into the effluent sewer and then to the effluent disposal system.

SOURCE: *Time-Saver Standards*, 1st ed., F. W. Dodge Company, New York, 1946.

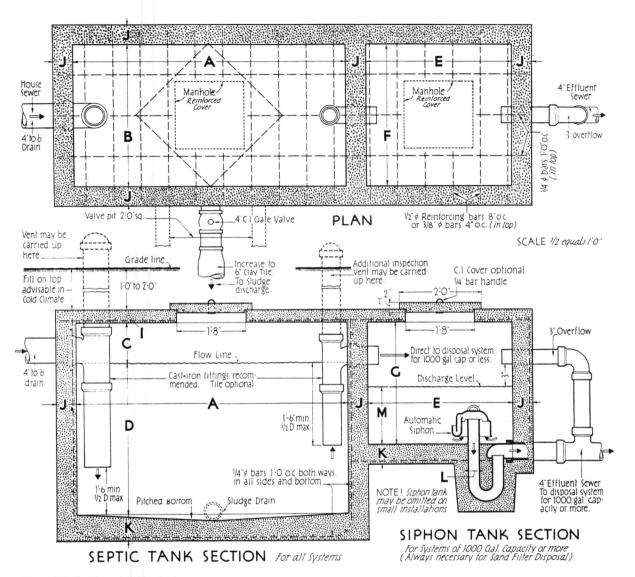

Figure 3-61 Septic and siphon tanks.

occupying the type of building by the conversion factor given in the table "Equivalent Occupancy."

Rule 2 To find the dimensions and construction details for any reinforced-concrete septic tank and siphon tank as detailed in Figure 3-61, refer to the table "Selection and Design of Septic and Siphon Tanks," and find in the first column the equivalent occupancy nearest to that calculated for the project. Read horizontally to the right for all dimensions not given directly on the drawings.

Rule 3 To ascertain the capacity of any commercial septic tank, proceed as in Rule 2 but find in the table the capacity in gallons that corresponds to the equivalent occupancy of the project and select a unit guaranteed by the manufacturer to treat that quantity of sewage per 24 hours. The siphon tank adapted to the manufactured septic tank will be indicated by the manufacturer's own data.

Location When a septic tank is equipped with a sludge drain and pit, it can be buried and its manhole cover identified merely by the position of the protruding vent or vents. However, the manhole for access to the sludge drain gate valve should be carried near the surface so that it can be exposed conveniently for operating the valve. When no sludge drain and pit are provided, the septic tank should be so located that the covering earth may be removed periodically without disfiguring the property. The same precautions also pertain to the manhole cover for the siphon tank.

Maintenance Data The owner of a septic tank should be provided by the designer with a written memorandum containing the following data: (1) A plan indicating the exact location of the septic and siphon tank manholes and sludge drain gate valve manhole, when used. (2) Advice for inspection of the septic tank each spring and fall by removing the vent caps and testing the depth of the sludge by means of a

absorb the effluent intermittently and prevents saturation of the disposal beds.

Design The size of a septic tank, and therefore the size of its related siphon tank, is governed wholly by the number of gallons of sewage to be treated per 24 hours. This can be

determined from the data relating to equivalent occupancy given in the section "General Design," which is repeated here for convenience.

Rule 1 To find the equivalent occupancy in any project, multiply the number of persons

SOURCE: *Time-Saver Standards*, 1st ed., F. W. Dodge Company, New York, 1946.

rod or a plumb bob. During severe weather the vents should be examined periodically to see that excess flowing on the interior has not obstructed their operation. (3) Instructions that whenever the sludge level appears to reach the low end of the intake or discharge pipes or there are any signs of flooding, the septic tank should be immediately cleaned or the sludge drawn off to the sludge pit. (4) Advice that whenever the siphon tank requires cleaning, the manhole cover of the tank should be removed and inspected and the automatic siphon cleaned.

DISTRIBUTION BOXES

This section provides data for the design of three types of units: grease traps, sludge pits, and distribution boxes. Of these, grease traps and sludge pits are optional units that may or may not be required by the system, according to the conditions defined in the preceding sections. Distribution boxes are required in almost all systems.

Grease Traps The function of a grease trap is to separate grease and oil from kitchen, laundry, and other specialized wastes and to prevent them from entering the sewage disposal system. Grease and oil may interfere with the formation of a proper scum in the septic tank and may clog or reduce the porosity of leaching cesspools, subsoil disposal beds, and sand filters. The use of a grease trap is therefore recommended in the majority of installations, but it is not a mandatory requirement in small installations where no great quantity of grease or oil occurs.

The grease traps described here are of concrete construction for use outside the house. Such a unit is not required if a metal grease trap has been installed indoors in waste lines carrying grease or oil. Indoor traps offer greater convenience for cleaning and may be used in small- or medium-size projects if the odor arising during their cleaning operation is not a serious objection.

Complete design data are contained in Figure 3-62. The size of the grease trap does not vary materially with the size of the building it

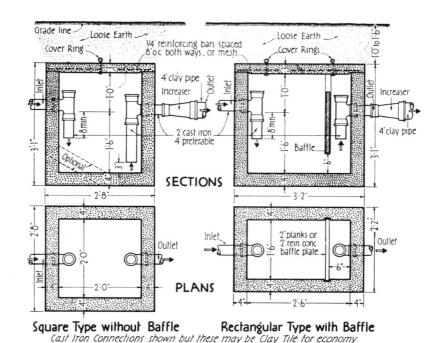

SECTIONS

PLANS

Square Type without Baffle · Rectangular Type with Baffle
Cast Iron Connections shown but these may be Clay Tile for economy

Figure 3-62 Grease traps.

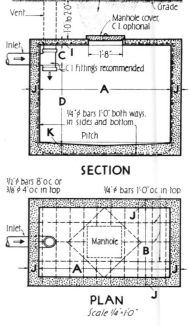

SECTION

PLAN
Scale 1/4"=1'0"

Figure 3-63 Sludge pit.

SLUDGE PIT DIMENSIONS

Equivalent occupancy	Capacity (gallons)	Length A	Width B	Air space C	Liquid depth D
1–4	325	5'0"	2'6"	1'0"	3'6"
5–9	450	6'0"	2'6"	1'0"	4'0"
10–14	720	7'0"	3'6"	1'0"	4'0"
15–20	1000	8'0"	4'0"	1'0"	4'0"
21–25	1250	9'0"	4'6"	1'0"	4'3"
26–30	1480	9'6"	4'8"	1'3"	4'6"
31–35	1720	10'0"	5'0"	1'3"	4'8"
36–40	1950	10'6"	5'3"	1'3"	4'9"
41–45	2175	11'0"	5'6"	1'3"	4'10"
46–50	2400	11'6"	5'9"	1'3"	5'0"

NOTE: Sludge pits should be of the same capacity as the septic tanks they serve.

serves. However, when the quantity of waste causes rapid flow, it is advisable to use a rectangular trap with a baffle.

SOURCE: *Time-Saver Standards*, 1st ed., F. W. Dodge Company, New York, 1946.

Owners should be advised to clean grease traps frequently. Therefore, the trap should be located at a point where the loose earth over the cover may be removed and replaced without unduly impairing the appearance of the property.

Within reason, the grease trap should be located as far as possible from the building and to leeward to minimize objections to the odor that always follows a grease trap–cleaning operation.

Sludge Pits As indicated in the section "General Design," the use of a sludge pit depends upon the need for cleaning septic tanks without interrupting their operation. The location of a sludge pit is indicated in Figure 3-60.

Since a sludge pit must be of such a size that it has a capacity equivalent to the septic tank it serves, refer to the section "General Design" for methods of determining the size required and to the table "Sludge Pit Dimen-

sions" for all dimensions not shown directly in Figure 3-63.

Distribution Boxes The location and general use of distribution boxes is indicated in Figure 3-60 and in the section "General Design," as well as in each of the following sections relating to effluent disposal methods.

Distribution boxes function to control and direct the flow of effluent sewage from the effluent sewage main to various parts of the effluent disposal system, permitting part of that system to enter while another part or parts is functioning. The type of box varies with the number of outlets and the manner in which the flow must be controlled. In every installation the distribution box should be designed to provide one or more outlets in addition to those contemplated in the initial installation in order to facilitate the extension, removal, or relocation of the effluent disposal units. Complete design data for concrete distribution boxes are contained in Figure 3-64.

LEACHING CESSPOOLS

This section gives complete design data on leaching cesspools, which constitute one of three types of effluent disposal methods from which the designer may choose. The choice is governed largely by soil conditions and the amount of land area available, as defined in detail in the section "General Design."

Application The advantages of the leaching cesspool are that it requires a minimum of land area, it can be used on a site of any slope, its initial cost is low, and it seldom requires cleaning at more frequent intervals than about 2 years. It can be used in all reasonably absorptive soils.

The limitations on the use of the leaching cesspool are that it can never be used in a soil rated as semi-impervious or impervious, it requires a location where the normal groundwater level is at least 8 feet below grade or 2 feet below the bottom of the cesspool, it should never be located within 100 feet or more of a potable water supply, and it should be situated at least 15 feet from the building it serves.

Leaching cesspools are limited in capacity; hence several units may be required to handle the effluent from large septic tanks. The spacing and the land area required by multiple leaching cesspools are indicated in Figure 3-65. It is recommended that when two or more cesspools are used, at least the first pair be connected through a distribution box for alternate operation rather than be installed in tandem. When more than two are employed, tandem operation is permissible for the first pair because the more remote cesspool takes the overflow of the nearer unit when loads are heavy.

Operation Leaching cesspools receive the effluent sewage from the septic tank or siphon tank and allow the liquid to be absorbed by the

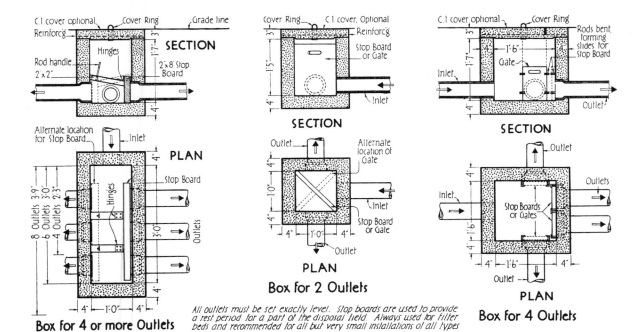

All outlets must be set exactly level. Stop boards are used to provide a rest period for a part of the disposal field. Always used for filter beds and recommended for all but very small installations of all types

Box for 4 or more Outlets

Box for 2 Outlets

Box for 4 Outlets

Figure 3-64 Distribution boxes.

SOURCE: *Time-Saver Standards*, 1st ed., F. W. Dodge Company, New York, 1946.

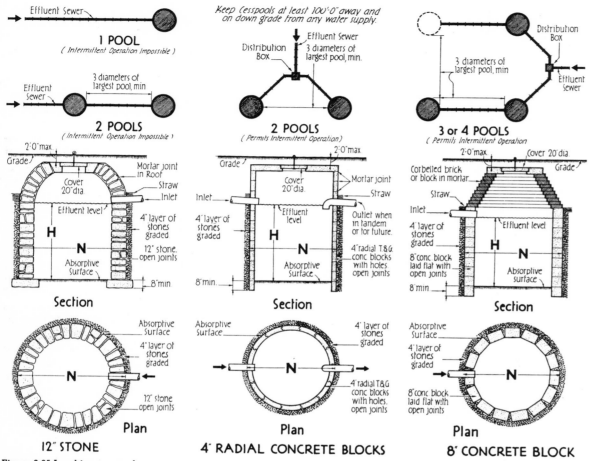

1 POOL
(Intermittent Operation Impossible)

Effluent Sewer

Keep Cesspools at least 100'-0" away and on down grade from any water supply.

2 POOLS
(Intermittent Operation Impossible)

3 diameters of largest pool, min.

Effluent Sewer

Distribution Box

Effluent Sewer 3 diameters of largest pool, min.

2 POOLS
(Permits Intermittent Operation)

Distribution Box

3 diameters of largest pool, min

Effluent Sewer

3 or 4 POOLS
(Permits Intermittent Operation)

Section — 12" STONE

Section — 4" RADIAL CONCRETE BLOCKS

Section — 8" CONCRETE BLOCK

Plan — 12" STONE

Plan — 4" RADIAL CONCRETE BLOCKS

Plan — 8" CONCRETE BLOCK

Figure 3-65 Leaching cesspools.

surrounding porous earth. The walls of the pool are laid up below the inlet with open seepage joints to allow the liquid to pass through these joints to a surrounding layer of broken stone and thence to the earth. The bottom of the pool is also an absorptive surface. All masonry above the inlet should be laid with tight mortar joints to minimize the entrance of surface water as well to achieve structural strength.

Design To determine the size and number of leaching cesspools required by any project, it is first necessary to determine the equivalent occupancy (which governs the amount of effluent to be treated) and the relative absorption of the soil (which influences the capacity of the individual units). Methods of determining these two factors are given in the section "General Design" in general terms, but they are repeated here for the reader's convenience.

Rule 1 To find the equivalent occupancy in any project, multiply the number of persons occupying the type of building by the conversion factor given in the table "Equivalent Occupancy."

EQUIVALENT OCCUPANCY

Type of building	Gallons per person	Conversion factor
Residence	50	1
Camp	25	1/2
Summer cottages	40	4/5
Day schools without showers or kitchens	15	3/10
Factories without showers or kitchens	15	3/10
Day schools with showers and kitchens	30	3/5
Institutions except hospitals	100	2
Hospitals	200	4

Rule 2 To find the relative absorption of the soil at the site of any leaching cesspool, excavate a test pit at the site selected for the cesspool to a depth approximately half the distance from the inlet level to the bottom of the proposed cesspool but never less than 5 feet below grade. Make this pit large enough to work in conveniently. At the bottom of the pit carefully excavate a rectangular pit 12 inches square and 18 inches deep. Pour water into

RELATIVE ABSORPTION

Time (1-inch drop in minutes)	Relative absorption
0–3	Rapid
3–5	Medium
5–30	Slow
30–60	Semi-impervious (do not use leaching cesspools)
60 and up	Impervious (do not use leaching cesspools)

SOURCE: *Time-Saver Standards*, 1st ed., F. W. Dodge Company, New York, 1946.

this small pit as quickly as possible, to a depth of 6 inches (requiring approximately 3¾ gallons). Note the time required for this 6 inches of water to be absorbed, and take one-sixth of this time as the average time for the water to fall 1 inch. Refer to the table "Relative Absorption" to find whether the absorption is rapid, medium, or slow. If the rate of absorption exceeds 30 minutes, the site is not suitable for leaching cesspools.

Rule 3 To find the dimensions of any cesspool and the number of cesspools required for a given equivalent occupancy and determined relative absorption, refer to the table "Selection and Design of Leaching Cesspools" and Figure 3-65. Note that the table is divided into three parts according to the type of soil and that in each part the first column indicates the number of cesspools required.

EQUIVALENT OCCUPANCY

Type of building	Gallons per person	Conversion factor
Residence	50	1
Camp	25	1/2
Summer cottages	40	4/5
Day schools without showers or kitchens	15	3/10
Factories without showers or kitchens	15	3/10
Day schools with showers and kitchens	30	3/5
Institutions except hospitals	100	2
Hospitals	200	4

SUBSOIL DISPOSAL BEDS

This section covers the design of subsoil disposal beds, which represent one of three methods for disposing of liquid effluent after it leaves the septic or siphon tank.

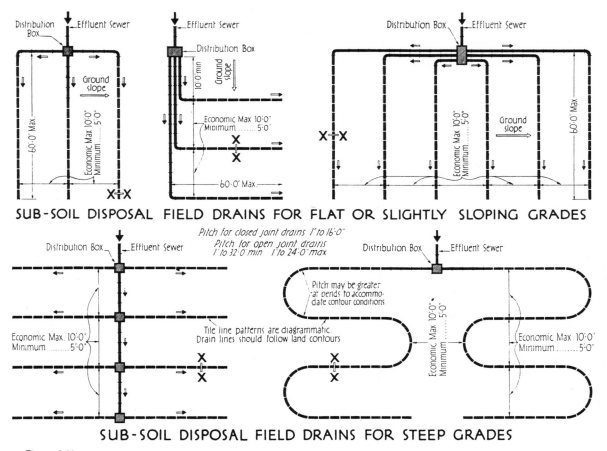

SUB-SOIL DISPOSAL FIELD DRAINS FOR FLAT OR SLIGHTLY SLOPING GRADES

SUB-SOIL DISPOSAL FIELD DRAINS FOR STEEP GRADES

Figure 3-66

Application The advantages of the subsoil disposal bed as compared with leaching cesspools or sand filters are that it may be used in any soil except that rated as impervious. When it is used in soils rated as rapid, medium, or slow, distribution drains only are required; but when it is used in soils rated as semi-impervious, both distribution and collection drains are needed, and the filtered effluent sewage from the collection drains must be disposed of to more absorptive soil or to a nonpotable watercourse. These beds may be located on ground that is level or slightly sloping or, occasionally, on relatively steep slopes by a proper arrangement of drainage lines, and they require little or no cleaning if the septic tank is kept in good operating condition. When possible, the disposal beds should be placed on a southern slope.

Limitations on the use of this method are that groundwater should be more than 2 feet below grade. The initial cost of subsoil disposal beds is usually greater than the cost of leach-

SOURCE: *Time-Saver Standards*, 1st ed., F. W. Dodge Company, New York, 1946.

SELECTION AND DESIGN OF LEACHING CESSPOOLS

| | Relative absorption | | | | | | | | | | | |
| | Rapid absorption; coarse sand or gravel | | | | Medium absorption; fine sand or sandy loam | | | | Slow absorption; clay with sand or loam | | | |
Equivalent occupancy	Number of cesspools	Diameter N	Depth H	Absorptive area per person (square feet)	Number of cesspools	Diameter N	Depth H	Absorptive area per person (square feet)	Number of cesspools	Diameter N	Depth H	Absorptive area per person (square feet)
1–4	1	5'	5'	24.5	1	6'	6'	35.0	2	5'	5'	49.0
5–9	1	6'	6'	15.7	2	6'	6'	31.3	2	8'	7'	48.0
10–14	1	8'	6'	14.4	2	8'	6'	28.7	2	10'	8'	46.7
15–20	2	6'	6'	14.1	2	9'	7'	26.14	3	10'	8'	49.5
21–25	2	7'	6'	13.6	2	10'	8'	27.1	4	9'	8'	46.4
26–30	2	8'	6'	13.4	3	9'	7'	26.14	4	10'	8'	43.6
31–35	1 1	8' 9'	7' 7'	13.6	1 2	9' 10'	7' 8'	26.1	5	10'	8'	46.7
36–40	1 1	9' 9'	7' 8'	13.7	4	9'	7'	26.1	4	12'	10'	48.9
41–45	3	8'	6'	13.4	4	9'	8'	25.7	5	12'	10'	54.3
46–50	2	10'	8'	13.0	4	10'	8'	26.1	5	12'	10'	48.9

ing cesspools though less than that of sand filters. The land area required is greater than that for either cesspools or sand filters.

Operation Subsoil disposal beds consist of a series of drain lines laid with tight joints where slopes are relatively steep, leading to continuations of these lines laid with open joints through which the effluent sewage filters into the surrounding soil. The open-joint lines are laid at slopes ranging from 1 inch in 24 feet to 1 inch in 32 feet, and therefore usually follow the contour lines. The arrangement of lines shown in Figure 3-66 is purely diagrammatic.

Design The capacity of a subsoil disposal bed is governed by the number of lineal feet of 4-inch drainage lines laid with open joints. Drain lines laid with tight joints to effect proper separation of the seepage lines are not counted in computing the capacity of the bed. Capacity is related to both the equivalent occupancy upon which the entire system is designed and to the relative absorption of the soil. Methods of determining these factors are covered in the section "General Design" but

are repeated here for convenience.

Rule 1 To find the equivalent occupancy in any project, multiply the number of persons occupying the type of building by the conversion factor given in the table "Equivalent Occupancy."

Rule 2 To determine the relative absorption, proceed as follows. At the site of the proposed bed excavate a rectangular pit 12 inches square and 18 inches deep below the finished surface grade of that area, shaping the sides for accurate measurements as carefully as possible. Into this pit quickly pour water to the depth of 6 inches (requiring approximately 3¾ gallons), and measure the time needed for the water to be completely absorbed by the soil. Take one-sixth of this time as the average time required for the soil to absorb 1 inch. Refer to the table "Relative Absorption" and find the relative absorption as rapid, medium, slow, or semi-impervious. If the time for a 1-inch drop exceeds 60 minutes, subsoil disposal beds should not be used. If the time for a 1-inch drop is from 30 to 60 minutes, design the bed with

RELATIVE ABSORPTION

Time (1-inch drop in minutes)	Relative Absorption
0–3	Rapid
3–5	Medium
5–30	Slow
30–60	Semi-impervious (use collection drains)
60 and up	Impervious (do not use subsoil disposal)

collection drains as indicated in Figure 3-66 and carry the collection line to a nonpotable watercourse or to a cesspool or second disposal bed in a more absorptive soil.

Rule 3 To determine the lineal feet of 4-inch open-joint tile drain required for any equivalent

SOURCE: *Time-Saver Standards*, 1st ed., F. W. Dodge Company, New York, 1946.

Round   Hexagon   Round Tile on Foundation Block   U-Tile on Hollow Foundation Blocks   Horse Shoe

TYPES OF DRAINAGE TILES

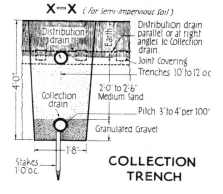

X–X *(For Semi-impervious Soil)*

Distribution drain

Collection drain

Earth

Distribution drain parallel or at right angles to Collection drain.

Joint Covering

Trenches 10' to 12' oc

2'-0" to 2'-6" Medium Sand

Pitch 3" to 4" per 100'

Granulated Gravel

Stakes 1'-0" oc

COLLECTION TRENCH

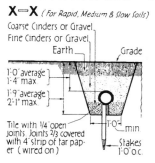

X–X *(For Rapid, Medium & Slow Soils)*

Coarse Cinders or Gravel
Fine Cinders or Gravel
Earth

Grade

1'-0" average
1'-4" max.

1'-9" average
2'-1" max.

Tile with 1/4" open joints. Joints 2/3 covered with 4" strip of tar paper (wired on)

1'-0" min.

Stakes 1'-0" o.c.

DRAIN TILE TRENCH

Tar paper, screening or burlap, covering 2/3 tile and tied on.

Metal Collars accurately space and hold tile 1/4" apart....... Used instead of bldg paper or burlap.

Perspective of patented Metal Collars

DRAIN TILE CONNECTORS

Figure 3-67

LENGTH OF SUBSOIL DRAINAGE LINES

Equivalent occupancy	Relative absorption		
	Rapid; coarse sand or gravel	Medium; fine sand or sandy loam	Slow or semi-impervious; clay with sand or loam
	Lineal feet of 4-inch open-joint tile drain required		
1–4	100	150	250
5–9	200	350	700
10–14	340	500	1000
15–20	475	650	1250
21–25	600	800	1500
26–30	725	1025	1800
31–35	850	1150	2100
36–40	975	1300	2400
41–45	1100	1450	2700
46–50	1200	1600	3000

occupancy and for any relative absorption up to impervious soils, refer to the table "Length of Subsoil Drainage Lines" and find the equivalent occupancy figure nearest to that determined for the project. Read to the right for the lineal feet of 4-inch open-joint drain tile in the column representing the relative absorption of the soil as determined by the preceding test. Note that the same number of lineal feet of tile is used for soils of slow absorption and those rated as semi-impervious, the difference in systems being reflected in the use of collection drains in semi-impervious soils.

Method of Laying Tile Complete data on the layout of subsoil disposal drains are contained in Figures 3-66 and 3-67, which also show accepted methods for protecting the open joints between tiles. It is suggested that stakes and boards be used for accurately aligning the slope of drainage lines. The choice of various types of drainage lines is governed largely by their local availability and cost and the ease of laying them under project conditions.

SAND FILTERS

This section gives complete design data on sand filters, which constitute the last of the three types of effluent disposal methods from which the designer may choose. The choice is governed largely by soil conditions because this type of system is the only method adaptable to soils rated as impervious; the other two methods, being less expensive, would normally be chosen for other soil conditions.

Application The sole advantage of sand filters lies in their adaptability to impervious soils. The limitations and disadvantages of this effluent disposal method are that collection drains must be used and the collected effluent be carried to a nonpotable watercourse or to leaching cesspools or subsoil disposal beds in more absorptive soils. The cost is relatively high because the entire area of the filter bed must be excavated and refilled with suitable filtering material, usually clean, coarse sand. The total area, however, is considerably less than the area of land required for subsoil disposal beds.

There are two types of sand filter. The closed type carries both the distribution and the collection drains underground in the filter bed, the upper layer of drains being covered with earth. These closed sand filters may be laid out in approximately rectangular or round patterns as indicated in Figure 3-68 or, when circumstances of site and capacity both permit, in the form of a long filter bed with a single pair of distribution and collection drains.

The open type is far less desirable because it exposes the effluent sewage and requires a filter bed free of any covering over the sand. In some instances it is less expensive to construct and may be adapted to institutions or large estates where the filter bed is removed from the building. The effluent sewage is conveyed in closed-joint drainage lines above the surface of the bed, with outlets discharging into wood troughs that serve as splashboards; they are laid out in the same manner as the lateral branches of the drain tile system.

Design The capacity of a sand filter is expressed in its surface area in square feet and is related to the equivalent occupancy of the

SOURCE: *Time-Saver Standards*, 1st ed., F. W. Dodge Company, New York, 1946.

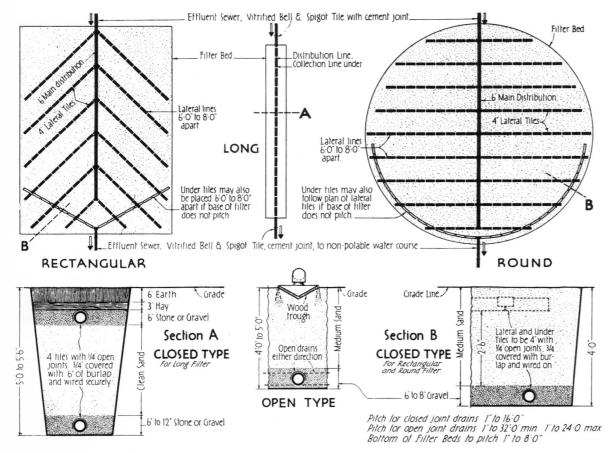

Figure 3-68 Sand filters.

EQUIVALENT OCCUPANCY

Type of building	Gallons per person	Conversion factor
Residence	50	1
Camp	25	1/2
Summer cottages	40	4/5
Day schools without showers or kitchens	15	3/10
Factories without showers or kitchens	15	3/10
Day schools with showers and kitchens	30	3/5
Institutions except hospitals	100	2
Hospitals	200	4

RELATIVE ABSORPTION

Time (1-inch drop in minutes)	Relative absorption
0–3	Rapid (do not use sand filter)
3–5	Medium (do not use sand filter)
5–30	Slow (do not use sand filter)
30–60	Semi-impervious (do not use sand filter)
60 and up	Impervious (use sand filter)

AREA OF FILTER BEDS

Equivalent occupancy	Area (square feet) Closed type	Area (square feet) Open type
1–4	200	100
5–9	900	450
10–14	1400	700
15–20	2000	1000
21–25	2500	1250
26–30	3000	1500
31–35	3500	1750
36–40	4000	2000
41–45	4500	2250
46–50	5000	2500

SOURCE: *Time-Saver Standards,* 1st ed., F. W. Dodge Company, New York, 1946.

building it serves. Since this system is normally used only in impervious soils, it is advisable also to determine the relative absorption of the soil on the site. Methods of determining these two factors are given in the section "General Design" but are repeated here for convenience.

Rule 1 To find the equivalent occupancy in any project, multiply the number of persons occupying the type of building by the conversion factor given in the table "Equivalent Occupancy."

Rule 2 To determine the relative absorption, proceed as follows. At the site of the proposed bed excavate a rectangular pit 12 inches square and 18 inches deep below the finished surface grade of that area, shaping the sides for accurate measurements as carefully as possible. Into this pit quickly pour water to the depth of 6 inches (requiring approximately 3¾ gallons), and measure the time required for the water to be completely absorbed by the soil. Take one-sixth of this time as the average time required for the soil to absorb 1 inch. Refer to the table "Relative Absorption" and find the relative absorption as rapid, medium, slow, or semi-impervious. If the time for a 1-inch drop exceeds 60 minutes, sand filters should be used.

Rule 3 To find the surface area of a sand filter bed required for a given equivalent occupancy refer to the table "Area of Filter Beds" and find the equivalent occupancy nearest to that computed for the project. Read to the right for the area in square feet of earth for closed or open types of sand filters.

The detailed design for sand filters is clearly indicated in Figure 3-68.

SOURCE: *Time-Saver Standards,* 1st ed., F. W. Dodge Company, New York, 1946.

Residential Development

Residential use is the largest single use of land in any community. Its successful design and development are essential for it to function efficiently and to be aesthetically pleasing. Almost all new residential development comes about through the subdivision of raw land. Such subdivision is the process whereby a relatively large tract of land is divided into blocks by streets that provide access. The blocks themselves are divided into lots for individual ownership. In the case of rental or cooperative development this division may not occur. Portions of the tract of land to be subdivided are reserved for parks or for schools. Adjacent areas normally contain shopping and other community facilities.

When this process occurs in a relatively undeveloped region, the result is generally referred to as a "new town" or a "new city." When it occurs adjacent to an existing built-up area, the development is generally considered simply as a subdivision or as an addition to the existing community. In both cases the process is basically the same.

This section deals with this residential development process and its various phases. The emphasis is on the physical development rather than on the administrative or legal aspects. The land use intensity standards provide a method of determining the maximum floor area of buildings on a given tract of land. They also determine the required amount of open space that must be provided for the specific floor area.

Types of streets and parking are important elements of any subdivision design. The street system must be laid out functionally and be appropriate for its particular use. It requires a separation, or classification, of local, collector, and major streets. Directly related to the street layout is the type of parking to be utilized. Open space and pedestrian circulation are other significant aspects of the subdivision process. Playgrounds and other recreational facilities are extensively covered in Section 5.

Opposite: Twin Parks West, Bronx, N.Y., New York State Urban Development Corp. (Prentice & Chan, Ohlhausen)

4.1 Land Use Intensity

Meaning of Land Use Intensity   In the *Minimum Property Standards for Multifamily Housing* (1965) of the Federal Housing Administration (FHA), land use intensity means the overall structural-mass and open-space relationship in a developed property. It correlates the amount of floor area, open space, livability space, recreation space, and car storage space of a property with the size of its site, or land area.

Land use intensity is somewhat similar to density: living units or people per acre. But its approach is different; it covers a broader field of planning factors and correlates them.

Why and When the FHA Makes an Intensity Rating   In analyzing certain housing developments, the FHA determines a land use intensity rating (LIR) of the site in order to apply the site planning standards of the *Minimum Property Standards for Multifamily Housing* (MPS). The rating ascribes to the site a set of interrelated standards for land area, floor area, open space, livability space, recreation space, and car storage capacity.

The rating of land use intensity is one of the most crucial steps in the preliminary consideration of a housing proposal. Correctly done, it establishes a workable basis for the planning, construction, and operation of a successful housing project—a project that is successful both as to market absorption and as to long-term values, successful whether the project is for rental or for home sales in a planned-unit development.

An unwarranted low rating tends to affect the project adversely through underuse of the land. An unwarranted high rating tends to affect the project adversely by lowering its livability beneath the level appropriate for its location in the community and thereby lowering its rentability or marketability. Of the two, the latter has the most detrimental effect, for an overly high intensity lowers the comfort, convenience, and appeal of the entire project, and this is reflected in the lower market appeal or lower rentals of the project during its life.

For the purpose of determining the FHA land use intensity rating of a site, data are gathered and analyzed. In some cases the market analyst, architect, site engineer, and sanitary engineer participate in the determining. They consider not only current conditions but also the future insofar as it can reasonably be anticipated.

Community Patterns   The basic intent of the land use intensity ratios provided in the multifamily MPS is to establish the intensity for the housing development so that it will be appropriate to the characteristics of the site and its location in the anticipated community pattern. Although the characteristics of the site (steepness, shape, and so on) may affect the site intensity, the principal determinant of intensity is the location of the site in the anticipated community pattern. It is therefore necessary for the rating of site intensity to consider community patterns thoroughly.

The land use patterns of a community have the following primary dimensions:

1. Width and length, including the space arrangement of various land uses located near to each other, such as the dividing line between a town house area and a detached-home area
2. The intensity range of land uses in the community, ranging upward from very low urban residential uses, such as small houses on 2-acre lots
3. The time factor of the land use, the growth stages through which the community progresses through time, such as the rapidity of suburban development in a booming metropolis

Space Arrangement of Land Uses   Community patterns have a great variety of space arrangements. Common arrangements are as follows:

1. A concentric pattern of development, typical of the medieval town and often found in small urban areas in the Plains states and elsewhere where topographic features do not shape community land usage
2. A string type of development where intensive uses are located in linear form, as along a main highway in a small town
3. A radial pattern, like the spokes of a wheel,

which is often seen in modern cities, with the hub as the city center or highly intensive land use area and other intensive land uses ranging out along transportation lines, radial boulevards, and other arteries

As an urban area grows, these and other patterns frequently develop numerous subcenters extending from the center of the city or metropolitan area. These minor centers of growth and development combine to form a many-centered pattern of land use that is very common in large metropolitan areas.

The land use intensity rating of a site for housing varies substantially with the location of the site in the community's space pattern. This is true even in a relatively small community. The intensity is highest, of course, in the center of the community and lowest in the general outlying area. In the transitional areas

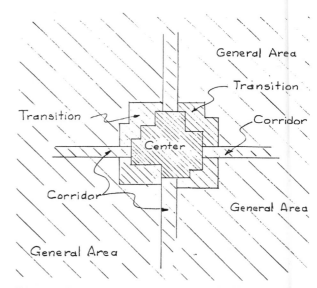

Figure 4-1 Typical community pattern. There is no intent to force this pattern or any other pattern on the growth of communities.

SOURCE: *Land Use Intensity Rating*, Land Planning Bulletin No. 7, Federal Housing Administration, 1966.

between the two are intermediate intensities. The site might also be located along a corridor connecting the center to another urban area. In rating the land use intensity of a proposed site, it is therefore necessary to understand the present and prospective space arrangement of the land use pattern of the community and to identify the position of the subject site in that arrangement of land uses. See Figure 4.1.

Intensity Range of Land Use Intensity of land use is markedly affected by the relationship of the size of the total long-term demand for land for urban use and the size of the supply of usable land. In the proper rating of a site in a specific community, it is therefore necessary to reach an understanding regarding the immediate and potential demand and supply factors of land use. The amount of land available to meet the present and prospective demand, as well as the opportunities and limitations of its physical development, can usually be determined by examination of the area. Long-term economic factors are not so easily determined, and they are of major importance.

Data related to land economics are usually available from local planning commissions. Other statistics necessary to intelligent land use rating are available from surveys and forecasts of industrial and other economic activity, population size, and anticipated growth.

It is possible to reach general conclusions on the total range of intensities appropriate to the land in the community currently and for the foreseeable future from the data obtained and from consideration of the present size, rate of growth, and probable ultimate size of the community. A very small community with a very slow growth rate and prospective small ultimate size will have a much narrower and lower range of land use intensity ratings than a larger community will. For instance, an isolated town of less than 2000 population with slow growth will have a much lower upper limit to its range of land use intensities than will a well-located, rapidly developing suburb in a metropolitan area.

Time Stages of Land Use Intensity A community's growth through time is one of the most significant dimensions of its land use pattern. In some cases, the intensity pattern as related to time is static. In others, as in a rapidly expanding metropolitan area, it may be characterized as explosive. The land use intensity may be recessive in depressed communities or in depressed sections of a community. The intensity pattern may be regenerative in cases such as a successful redevelopment area that revitalizes the economic activity of an entire community area or a major portion of it.

When the time pattern is static, the rating of land use intensity follows very closely the intensities of existing development. This may be true either of the community as a whole or of substantial static portions of it. An example is a conservation area, where properties are being conserved rather than rebuilt.

With an explosive community pattern, the proper rating of land use intensity in fringe areas and satellite developments presents very difficult problems. It is necessary to forecast the emerging and future intensity pattern. Many fast-developing residential areas follow a normally predictable pattern. New stimuli or changed conditions, however, may warrant more intensive land use in the future development pattern. Where this is the case, a higher land use intensity than that currently present in the area is appropriate for a project. To determine the presence of such a situation and the appropriate degree of higher land use intensity, the space arrangement and intensity range are carefully studied in conjunction with the following:

1. A thorough study of the probable effect of higher densities on existing development in the area and on adjacent undeveloped areas
2. Consultation with planning, zoning, and engineering officials having jurisdiction in the community
3. Consultation with realtors and mortgage lenders active in the area

Such determinations are preceded by a complete documentation of the file with all facts, opinions, and judgments justifying a higher land use intensity rating.

With a recessive community pattern, special care must be taken to determine not only the presence of a need for additional housing but also the proper intensity level. The proper level may well be lower than that of existing development, inasmuch as the demand for land is receding and the greater livability of lower intensity may be essential for successful marketing.

In the regenerative community pattern, which usually involves a redevelopment area, the existing land uses and intensities are given little consideration, the prime focus being on future needs and the anticipated pattern. In this regard the analysis resembles that of the explosive community pattern, and the same thorough analysis is made prior to determination of appropriate land use intensity.

Land Use Intensity Compared with Density The term "density" as commonly used in land use planning, zoning, and site planning means the number of living units or the number of people per unit of land area. Because the size of living units and the number of occupants of units of any given size vary widely, density is a rather crude measure of the degree of land use. This is why the FHA no longer uses density directly as a land use measure in its multifamily MPS.

In place of density the FHA now uses land use intensity, which is less variable and thus more reliable. The concept of land use intensity as employed here starts with the overall structural-mass and open-space relationships of a developed property, as explained below. It begins with and is directly related to the floor area ratio, which is the relation of the floor area to the land area. Thus, it is a measure of the total permitted floor area on a site of a given size.

In residential property, of course, total floor area roughly determines the number of living units and the number of people. Thus, land use intensity ratings based on floor and land areas

SOURCE: *Land Use Intensity Rating*, Land Planning Bulletin No. 7, Federal Housing Administration, 1966.

$FAR = \dfrac{FA}{LA}$ $\dfrac{FA}{LA} \times LA = FA$ $.5 \times 100 = 500$

LAND USE INTENSITY RELATED TO FLOOR AREA AND DENSITY

Land use intensity (LIR) (1)	Floor area ratio (FAR) (2)	Floor area per gross acre (square feet) (3)	Density in living units per gross acre	
			1089 square feet per living unit (4)	871.2 square feet per living unit (5)
0.0	0.0125	544.5	0.5	0.625
1.0	0.025	1,089	1.0	1.25
2.0	0.05	2,178	2.0	2.5
3.0	0.1	4,356	4.0	5.0
4.0	0.2	8,712	8.0	10.0
5.0	0.4	17,424	16.0	20.0
6.0	0.8	34,848	32.0	40.0
7.0	1.6	69,696	64.0	80.0
8.0	3.2	139,392	128.0	160.0

have some general relationships to density ratings based on living units and land area. Because density is unresponsive to wide variables in living-unit size and household size, density ratings can be compared with land use intensity ratings only in general terms and at the risk of gross misinterpretation. A valid comparison can be made, however, if the living-unit size or household size (the variable in density) is kept as a constant at some specific size. Some comparisons of this kind are made in the following subsections.

Floor Area: A Base for the Rating Scale To rate or measure, it is necessary to have a measurement scale. For land use intensity, the rating scale is based first and most directly on the relationship of total floor area to total land area, that is, on the floor area ratio as defined in the multifamily MPS.

The rating scale appears in column 1 of the table "Land Use Intensity Related to Floor Area and Density." It starts at a floor area ratio (FAR) of 0.0125. This is arbitrarily called 0.0 on the scale of land use intensity rating (LIR 0.0). Since the FAR multiplied by the land area (LA) equals the floor area (FA), FAR 0.0125 times the 43,560 square feet in an acre equals 544.5 square feet of floor area per acre at LIR 0.0. To visualize LIR 0.0, this floor area per acre can be converted to living units per gross acre. For

example, 544.5 square feet per acre equals one modest home with a floor area of 1089 square feet (2 × 544.5) with 2 acres of land. This is shown on the first line of the table. Each full unit on the intensity scale is equal to a 100 percent increase in the FAR. This increases the FA by 100 percent as related to the LA, thus doubling the number of living units of any given size for each full unit on the intensity scale, as illustrated in the table.

This doubling on the intensity scale and its origin at LIR 0.0 with FAR 0.0125 makes it easy to remember and visualize the entire scale. Note in line 2 and columns 3 and 4 of the table that LIR 1.0 means 1089 square feet of floor area or one house of that modest size per acre

LIR	Living units per acre for living units of 1089 square feet
1	1
2	2
3	4
4	8
5	16
6	32
7	64
8	128

of land. Remember that LIR 1.0 equals one living unit per 1 acre for a house of a little over 1000 square feet. Also remember the doubling of the intensity scale. Then it is easy to remember this table that visualizes the scale:

Memorizing another point on the scale is also helpful. LIR 3.0 is FAR 0.1. By starting from this, it is easy to find any FAR value through doubling:

LIR	FAR
3.0	0.1
4.0	0.2
5.0	0.4
6.0	0.8
7.0	1.6
8.0	3.2

Gross Land Area: Another Base for the Rating Scale We have noted that the FHA does not use density directly as a measure in its multifamily MPS. A comparison of the land base of density ratings will be helpful, however, as a preliminary to considering land as a base in the rating of intensity.

In density ratings, the number of living units is sometimes related to all the land that benefits or is used by the development, including on-site streets and half of bordering streets. This is the gross land area, or gross acres; the resultant is gross density. Sometimes street areas are not counted in the land area; the resultant is net density. At times public streets are not counted in the area while privately owned streets are counted; the resultant is another variety of net density, an ambivalent measure of doubtful meaning. In recent years the FHA has used the latter variety of net density. The confusion mounts when paved parking areas in bays along streets are not counted

SOURCE: *Land Use Intensity Rating,* Land Planning Bulletin No. 7, Federal Housing Administration, 1966.

in the net area but similar areas in stub compounds are counted.

Wiping the slate clean of such ambivalence and confusion, the FHA multifamily MPS now takes the gross land area as the firm base for the land use intensity rating. The intensity rating scale refers to the gross acres of all land benefiting a project. Within certain limits for land area (LA) established in the multifamily MPS, one-half of any abutting street right-of-way is included in the gross acreage. Also included in the LA for the intensity rating is one-half of any abutting park, river, or other beneficial open space that has a reasonable expectancy of perpetuity. Because the gross acreage of the total LA (all the area benefiting the project) is used in the rating, the land use intensity measures are more realistic and more reliable than are data based on net acres.

If existing information based on net area is used in site analysis, it is necessary to convert it to gross area for comparison with land use intensity ratings on the FHA's MPS-M intensity rating scale. Net area customarily excludes all street rights-of-way. These usually range from 15 to 30 percent of the total LA.

Gross area is converted to net area by subtracting the percentage of street area from 100 percent and multiplying the gross area by the difference.

EXAMPLE

If we know that the gross area is 125 gross acres and the street area is 20 percent of the gross area, what is the net area?

(100 − 20 percent)
× 125 gross acres = 100 net acres

Net area is converted to gross area by subtracting the percentage of street area from 100 percent and dividing the net area by the difference.

EXAMPLE:

If we know that the net area is 100 net acres and the street area is 20 percent of the gross area, what is the gross area?

100 net acres ÷ (100
− 20 percent) = 125 gross acres

Gross density is converted to net density by dividing the number of living units per gross acre by the difference between 100 percent and the percentage of street area.

EXAMPLE:

If we know that there are four living units per gross acre and the street area is 20 percent of the gross area, how many living units are there per net acre?

4 ÷ (100 − 20 percent)
= 5 living units per net acre

Net density is converted to gross density by multiplying the number of living units per net acre by the difference between 100 percent and the percentage of street area.

EXAMPLE:

If we know that there are five living units per net acre and the streets are 20 percent of the gross area, how many living units are there per gross acre?

5 × (100 − 20 percent)
= 4 living units per gross acre

Other Elements of the Rating Scale   As we have mentioned, the land use intensity rating not only relates floor area to land area but also correlates other planning elements. The other elements are open space, livability space, recreation space, occupant car storage, and total car storage including guest cars. These planning elements are described and defined in the multifamily MPS.

Open space, livability space, and recreation space are expressed in the intensity rating system in terms of the open-space ratio (OSR), livability space ratio (LSR), and recreation space ratio (RSR). The ratio is simply the total area of the open space, livability (outside nonvehicular) space, or large recreation space divided by the total floor area. In the rating system, car storage capacity is expressed in terms of the car ratio, which is the number of cars divided by the number of living units.

We have seen that the floor area ratio (FAR) as a base for the intensity rating scale has a very simple mathematical relationship to the scale: it doubles with each unit of the LIR. These other elements of the rating scale, however, have a more complex relationship to the rating scale of land use intensity. This is seen in the ratio chart in Figure 4-2, reproduced from the multifamily MPS. The established ratios for these elements represent appropriate relationships readily attainable by proper planning. Good design can surpass them substantially while attaining the total floor area at a given intensity rating.

These other elements in the rating system are of importance in determining a proper intensity rating for a proposed housing site. Their relationship to the intensity rating scale deserves careful study (see Figure 4-2).

How Many Living Units?   In the table "Land Use Intensity Related to Floor Area and Density" and the preceding discussion, we have seen that the rating scale for land use intensity is related directly to the floor area ratio and to the floor area and that the number of living units per acre is not related directly to an intensity rating because the size of living units varies. Columns 4 and 5 of the table show the great magnitude of this variation for living units of 1089 and 871.2 square feet. We have also seen that the rating of land use intensity is related to the amount of open space of several kinds, including livability space and recreation space, as well as to total open space.

Thus it becomes clear that the land use intensity rating scale is a measure of overall relationships of structural mass and open space. In the intensity rating these complex relationships are distilled into a single numerical scale. Grossly oversimplified, the intensity scale may be said to run from LIR 0.0 for very

SOURCE: *Land Use Intensity Rating*, Land Planning Bulletin No. 7, Federal Housing Administration, 1966.

low rural-type land use, through LIR 3.0 for suburban-type land use at about four modest houses per gross acre, to LIR 8.0 for very intensive urban land use for high-rise apartments. Actually, at each unit number of decimal subdivision of the intensity scale, there is a precise meaning of a definite degree of intensity of land use in terms of the relationships of maximum floor area for the land area and in terms of a minimum for open space, livability space, and recreation space for the floor area.

A natural question at this point is "How do the sponsors of a proposed development find out how many living units they can get on their site?" If it is an FHA development, the sponsors determine the number of living units acceptable to the FHA on the site by (1) obtaining the land use intensity rating of the site from the FHA and (2) then preparing a project planning program and project design properly related to the assigned site rating. An illustration of a simple approach to developing a planning program for a project starting with the intensity rating is in the multifamily MPS. The FHA provides blank forms of the illustrated method for the use of sponsors and their design professionals.

A more important question is "How would a higher land use intensity affect the financial soundness of the proposed project?" If the livability offered by a property is lower than the level appropriate for its location in the community pattern, the property is at a disadvantage in competition with others in comparable locations. Consequently it will suffer in rentability and marketability. The ratio lines of Figure 4-2 show how livability decreases very rapidly as land use intensity increases.

Too high a land use intensity is a false economy. Let us consider the case of Developer A and Developer B, assuming that each developer has a land cost of $8000 per acre and $11,200 for all other costs to produce 1089-square-foot town houses on similar tracts. Developer A develops the property at a land use intensity of 4.0; Developer B develops the property at a land use intensity of 5.0, with results as shown in the accompanying table.

| | LIR | Living units | Land per living unit | Land difference per LIR unit | Total cost per living unit* | FHA 203b home loan† | | |
						Down payment	Monthly payment	Difference per LIR unit
A	4.0	8	$1000		$12,200	$400	$70.14	
				$500				$2.97
B	5.0	16	500		11,700	400	67.17	

*$11,200 per living unit is assumed as the cost for building, land improvements, and other costs except raw land costs.
†Based on a 30-year mortgage at 5¼ percent interest plus ½ percent FHA premium.

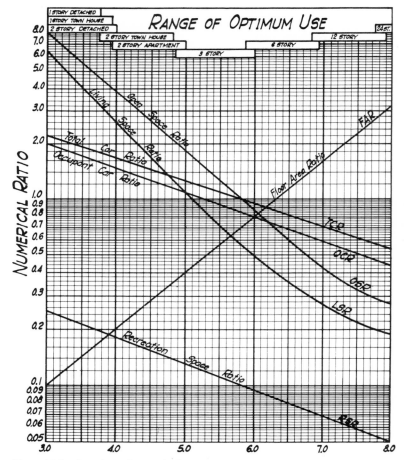

Figure 4-2 Land use intensity standards.

SOURCE: *Land Use Intensity Rating*, Land Planning Bulletin No. 7, Federal Housing Administration, 1966.

Note that Developer A, with a lower LIR of 4.0, offers a much more desirable property with only half the density of B's project, giving twice the amount of exterior livability space. A sells properties with an added cost of only $500 (4.3 percent), which the home buyer carries for an additional monthly payment of only $2.97.

Since raw land is a low-percentage component of the total housing cost, great reductions in total package costs cannot come from squeezing the land. We have seen that intensification of land use produces relatively small cost savings at the sacrifice of very great amounts of livability space. Because livability affects marketability and rentability, it is clear that an inappropriate intensification of land use is financially very hazardous. In determining the intensity rating of a specific site, an economic comparison of the type illustrated above can be prepared with applicable local data to aid in avoiding excessive intensity and its accompanying false economy.

To the extent practicable, FHA personnel participating in the intensity rating of a site inspect the site together, pool all collected data, analyze the data in consultation with each other, and coordinate their findings and recommendations. This is accomplished under the direction of the chief underwriter with the objective of reaching a concurrence of all participants. In any event, the intensity rating is made by the FHA chief underwriter after considering all data and recommendations.

How the Assigned Rating Is Used The land use intensity rating assigned by the FHA to a proposed housing site tells the project sponsor and his or her design professionals the maximum land use intensity that the FHA will accept for a development of the site with FHA-insured financing. In essence, the FHA, by assigning its intensity rating to a site, ascribes to the site a selected set of land use standards consisting of the maximum floor area ratio and minimum ratios for open space, livability space, recreation space, and car storage. These are found in Figure 4-2 by locating the assigned intensity rating on the scale at the bottom and following its vertical line to intersections with the ratio lines. The ratios and their application in the site planning of the project are defined and illustrated in the FHA *Minimum Property Standards for Multifamily Housing.*

SOURCE: *Land Use Intensity Rating,* Land Planning Bulletin No. 7, Federal Housing Administration, 1966.

4.2 Street Patterns

Modified Grids   It is possible to avoid the monotony of the grid system (see Figure 4-3) by modifying the street pattern. A few simple street alterations can provide interesting grouping possibilities that not only eliminate the tediousness of the straight street but even provide opportunities for green areas within the groups.

The first arrangement (Figure 4-4) has a central loop that not only creates interesting grouping possibilities but also relieves the traffic load by setting up a resistance to through traffic. The problem of grouping is much less critical because there are no long, unarrested views. If the center section of the loop is retained as a green area, the grouping of surrounding houses should be governed by the fact that the park is the main focal feature. Every house should be sited to take advantage of the pleasant open space. The lot planting and house layout should stress the visual enclosure of the green.

The second arrangement (Figure 4-5) suggests another design for the same six-block area. In this case, instead of a center loop, two outside loops have been formed. The grouping problem is very similar to that in the first arrangement.

Cul-de-Sac   With this type of street the grouping of houses presents a far less difficult problem than that of the straight street. A cul-de-sac is shaped so that the fronting houses automatically create an enclosed space.

A cul-de-sac that is longer than 500 feet may be too long to be effective for grouping purposes. It loses its compact shape and may have to be designed as a straight street with a distinct grouping of houses at the turnaround. The compactness of the shorter cul-de-sac usually permits a unified grouping of all the houses.

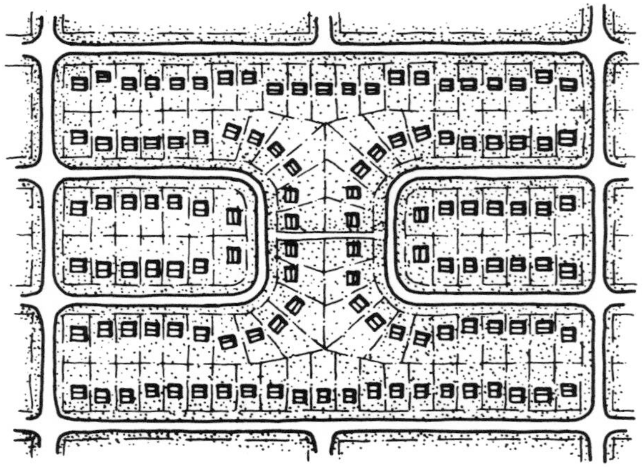

The more effective the enclosure of space at the circle, the more successful the house grouping. Some plans may look well on paper but in actuality may neither express the street shape nor enclose the space at the turnaround. This enclosure of space can be achieved by linking houses with screen walls or by carefully locating trees and hedges so that the space is defined.

Grouping 1 (Figure 4-6) uses two groups, one down the leg of the cul-de-sac and the other at the turning circle. The latter does not echo the street pattern; the houses are grouped to enclose a square terminating space.

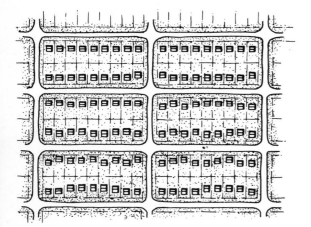

Figure 4-3 A typical grid pattern.

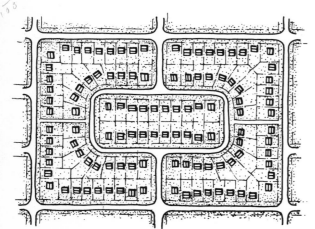

Figure 4-4 Modified grid 1.

Figure 4-5 Modified grid 2.

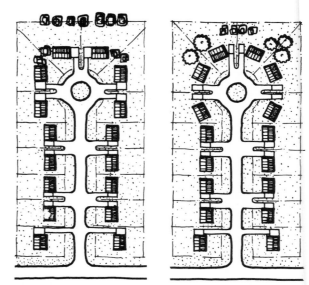

Figure 4-6 Grouping 1.   Figure 4-7 Grouping 2.

SOURCE: *Principles of Small House Grouping,* Central Mortgage and Housing Corporation, Ottawa, Canada, 1957.

In Grouping 2 (Figure 4-7) all the houses are illustrated as a single group. Their unbroken building line encloses a large symmetrical space that becomes the focal point of the group.

Grouping 3 (Figure 4-8) illustrates a recommended maximum-length cul-de-sac; the houses are treated as two groups. The space down the leg of the cul-de-sac has been emphasized by a definite setback, and to give the second group at the turning circle greater definition semidetached houses have been used to surround the space.

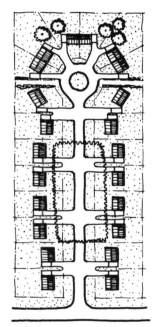

Figure 4-8 Grouping 3.

Loops Good opportunities exist for varied and interesting house groups on lots flanking looped streets. However, the typical loop arrangement (Figure 4-9) lacks design in both lot arrangement and house location. The narrow width at the building line of lots 5, 6, 7, 12, 13, and 14 is caused by the alignment of these

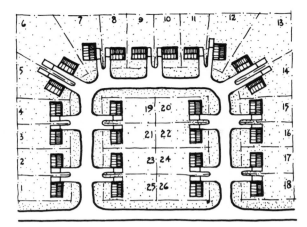

Figure 4-9 A typical loop.

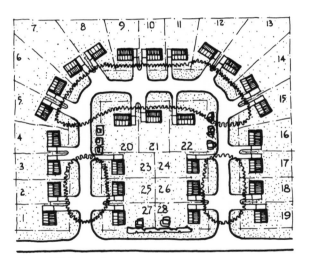

Figure 4-10 Layout 1.

lots on the radii of the looping road. The view from lots 8, 9, 10, and 11 is of backyard areas. The arrangement of houses is unsatisfactory since there is nothing to attract or arrest attention.

In Loop layout 1 (Figure 4-10) lots 5, 6, 7, 8, 12, 13, 14, and 15 have been enlarged. The

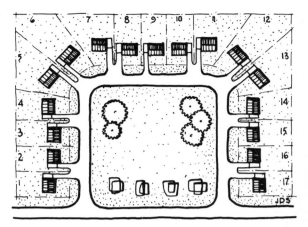

Figure 4-11 Layout 2.

interior arrangement of lots has been changed so that lots 20, 21, and 22 face the end of the loop. This improves the outlook for all the houses at the head of the loop. A particularly pleasing feature is the openness that has been achieved by the recession of houses on lots 5 to 8 and 12 to 15. From either direction of the loop there are satisfactory focal points that can be further improved by skillful planting and landscaping.

The feature of the third layout (Figure 4-11) is the central green, which provides all the houses with a pleasant outlook. If a uniform setback is adhered to for all the houses surrounding the green, it will give strong definition to the space enclosed. Alternatively, the houses on the corner lots can be set back to give some variety to the whole group. All the houses surrounding the green should be related so that they present a unified grouping with the green as the focal point. Houses 1 and 17 act as the terminating elements.

SOURCE: *Principles of Small House Grouping*, Central Mortgage and Housing Corporation, Ottawa, Canada, 1957.

4.3 Street Classification

The overall street system for a housing development must conform to the circulation requirements of the master plan for the community. This will provide maximum accessibility to all parts of the community and ensure proper coordination with proposed circulation changes.

Direct access to a major arterial highway is essential. Such intersections must be adequately controlled with lights or other means. The practical minimum distance between intersections on the major arterial highway should be 800 to 1000 feet. No through streets should be provided. All circulation should be directed around the periphery of the development to the major arterial highway.

Each lane of traffic will carry from 600 to 800 cars per hour. Horizontal alignment of all collector, minor, loop, and access streets (see Figure 4-12) should provide for a minimum of 200 feet in clear sight distance. The vertical alignment should not exceed a grade differential of 6 to 8 percent. Sidewalks, when used, should be a minimum of 4 feet wide. When trees are planted between the curb and the sidewalk, the sidewalk should be set back approximately 8 feet. If no trees are used, the setback should be 4 feet.

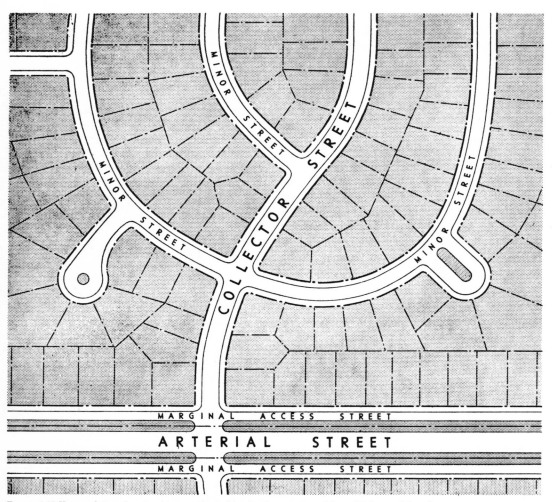

Figure 4-12 Nomenclature for street types adopted by the Association of State Highway Officials.

SOURCE: *Control of Land Subdivision,* New York State Department of Commerce, Albany, N.Y.

4.4 Types of Streets

Types of streets are described in the accompanying table and illustrated in Figure 4-13.

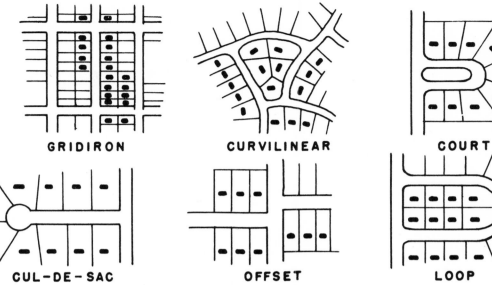

GRIDIRON   CURVILINEAR   COURT

CUL-DE-SAC   OFFSET   LOOP

Figure 4-13 Street patterns.

Type of street	Purpose	Interval for intersections	Width of right-of-way	Paved width	Grade (percent)	Traffic (miles per hour)	Sidewalks, etc.
Major roads (major arterials)	Provide unity throughout contiguous urban area; usually form boundaries for neighborhoods. Minor access control; channelized intersection; parking generally prohibited.	1½–2 miles	120–150 feet	84 feet maximum for four lanes, parking, and median strip	4	35–45	Require 5-foot-wide detached sidewalks in urban areas, planting strips (5 to 10 feet wide or wider), and adequate building setback lines (30 feet for buildings fronting on street and 60 feet for buildings backing on street).
Secondary roads (minor arterials)	Main feeder streets. Signals where needed; stop signs on side streets. Occasionally form boundaries for neighborhoods.	¾–1 mile	80 feet	60 feet	5	35–40	Require 5-foot-wide detached sidewalks, planting strips between sidewalks and curb (5 feet to 10 feet or wider), and adequate building setback lines (30 feet).
Collector streets	Main interior streets. Stop signs on side streets.	¼–½ mile	64 feet	44 feet (two 12-foot traffic lanes and two 10-foot parking lanes)	5	30	Require at least 4-foot-wide detached sidewalks; vertical curbs. Planting strips are desirable. Building setback lines are 30 feet from right-of-way.
Local streets	Local service streets; nonconducive to through traffic.	At blocks	50 feet	36 feet where street parking is permitted	6	25	Sidewalks at least 4 feet in width for densities greater than 1 dwelling unit per acre; curbs and gutters.
Cul-de-sac	Street open at only one end with provision for a practical turnaround at the other.	Only wherever practical	50 feet (90-foot-diameter turnaround)	30 to 36 feet (75-foot turnaround)	5		Should not have a length greater than 500 feet.

SOURCE: *Control of Land Subdivision*, New York State Department of Commerce, Albany, N.Y.

4.5 Typical Sections of Streets and Roads

STREETS

Typical street profiles for four types of streets are shown in Figure 4-14.

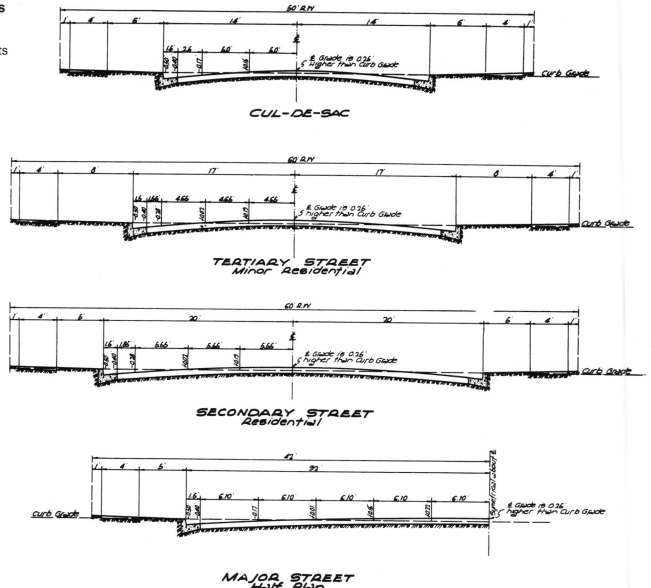

Figure 4-14 Street profiles.

SOURCE: *Land Subdivision Manual,* Planning Commission, Monterey County, California, 1957.

ROADS

Road sections used on projects constructed within the National Park Service are designated as Types I, II, III, and IV. Type I sections are used on main circulatory roads carrying heavy volumes of traffic. The paved driving surface is 22 feet in width. Cut sections are to have a bituminous paved ditch 4 feet wide on a 5:1 slope and a uniform 1-foot paved or bituminous-treated shoulder. Fill sections shall have a uniform 3-foot paved or bituminous-treated shoulder. Shoulders and paved ditch shall be given a seal coat and chips, colored and textured to delineate the driving surface clearly. Transitions from the 1-foot shoulders in cuts to the 3-foot shoulders in fills should be carefully studied to provide for proper blending of the two shoulder widths into the roadway.

Type II sections are used on main circulatory roads carrying moderate traffic volumes. Design criteria conform to Type I sections except that the driving surface shall be 20 feet. Typical sections for Types I and II are shown in Figure 4-15.

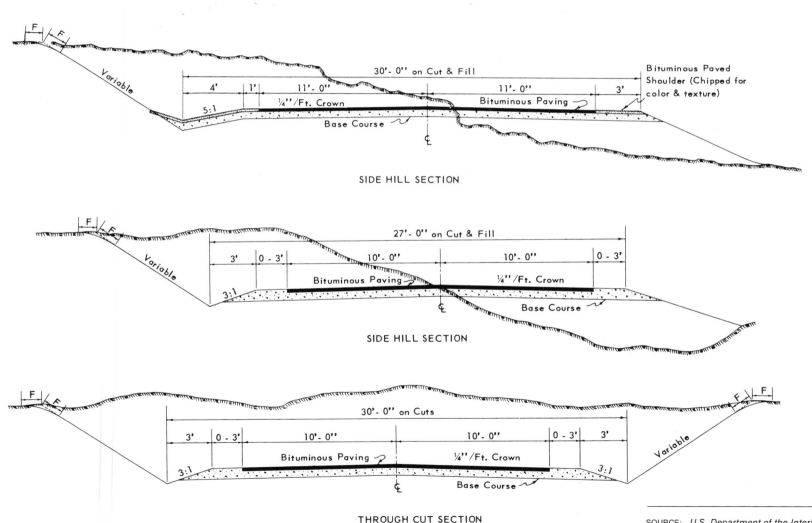

SIDE HILL SECTION

SIDE HILL SECTION

THROUGH CUT SECTION

Figure 4-15

SOURCE: *U.S. Department of the Interior,* National Park Service.

Type III sections may be used in lieu of Type II sections in dry and arid areas where drainage is a minor factor in design. They should be used on all secondary two-way circulatory roads such as campground and trailer access roads, picnic area access roads, residential and utility access and circulatory roads, access and circulatory roads in lodge and cabin areas, and loops and spurs serving overlooks, scenic viewpoints, interpretive features, and scenic overlooks. The driving surface of the Type III section is 20 feet wide. The shoulders may vary from 0 to 3 feet in width, depending upon the intended use and facility to be served. It is desirable that shoulders be gravel or grass.

In general, the ditch sections are 3 feet wide and 1 foot deep, but this specification may be modified to meet special requirements such as curbs and gutters. Ditches are paved only when special drainage problems are encountered.

Type IV sections are used for all one-way circulatory roads (see Figure 4-16). The paved surface is to be 12 feet wide. One-foot grass or gravel shoulders are to be provided, unless the

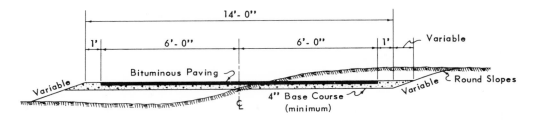

**ONE-WAY ROAD
TYPICAL SECTION**

NOTE: Surface to be Warped to Provide Drainage

Figure 4-16

SLOPE CHART

Fill (feet)	Slope	Cut (feet)	Slope	F
0–2	4:1	0–2	3:1	1
2–4	3:1	2–6	2:1	2
4–6	2:1	Over 6	1½:1	3
Over 6	1½:1	. . .	. . .	. . .

shoulders are used in conjunction with curbs, barriers, and so on, when the shoulder may be eliminated. In general, ditches shall not be used, and the surface should be warped to provide adequate drainage. See also accompanying slope chart.

SOURCE: *U.S. Department of the Interior,* National Park Service.

4.6 Subdivisions

VICINITY MAP

Figure 4-17 shows a vicinity map of appropriate scale that covers sufficient adjoining territory to indicate clearly nearby street patterns, property lines, other adjacent properties in the subdivider's ownership, and other significant features that will have a bearing upon the subdivision.

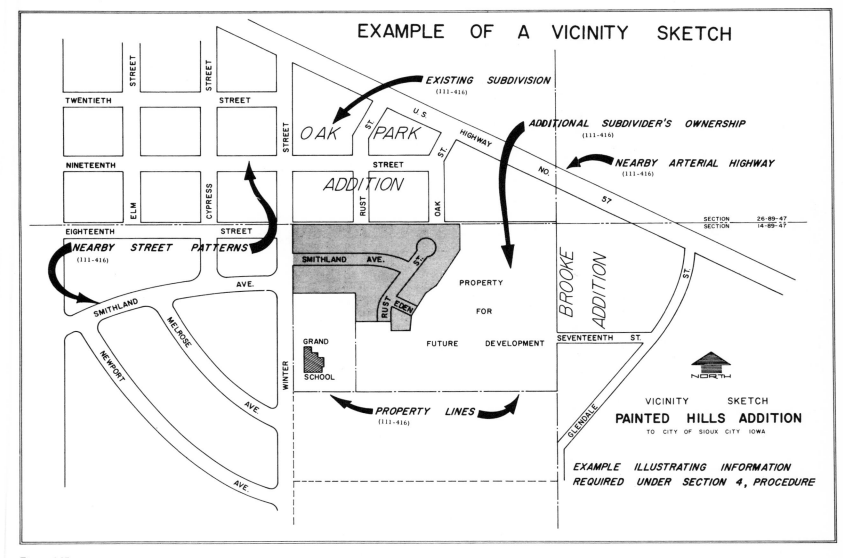

EXAMPLE OF A VICINITY SKETCH

EXISTING SUBDIVISION (111-416)

ADDITIONAL SUBDIVIDER'S OWNERSHIP (111-416)

NEARBY ARTERIAL HIGHWAY (111-416)

OAK PARK ADDITION

NEARBY STREET PATTERNS (111-416)

PROPERTY FOR FUTURE DEVELOPMENT

PROPERTY LINES (111-416)

SECTION 26-89-47
SECTION 14-89-47

BROOKE ADDITION

NORTH

VICINITY SKETCH
PAINTED HILLS ADDITION
TO CITY OF SIOUX CITY IOWA

EXAMPLE ILLUSTRATING INFORMATION REQUIRED UNDER SECTION 4, PROCEDURE

Figure 4-17

SOURCE: *Subdivision Regulations Manual*, Sioux City, Iowa.

CONTOUR MAP

Figure 4-18 shows a contour map of the parcel that has been made with suitable engineering accuracy and with contour intervals for determining general street and utility requirements. A contour map shall show existing substantial buildings, significant trees that should be preserved, watercourses, drainage ditches, storm or sanitary sewers with size and flow-line elevation, manholes, culverts, water lines, gas lines, power lines, permanent easements, streets, and other features that will have a bearing upon the design of the subdivision or on the provision of utilities.

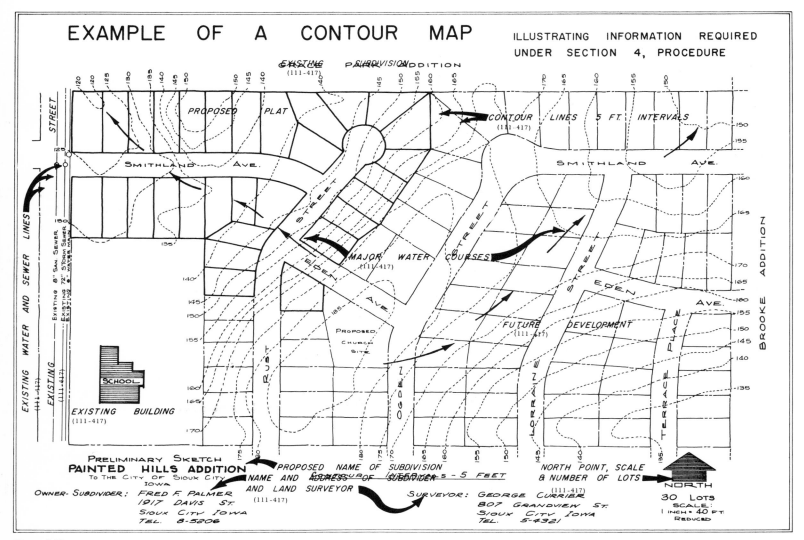

Figure 4-18

SOURCE: *Subdivision Regulations Manual*, Sioux City, Iowa.

PRELIMINARY SKETCH

Figure 4-19 shows a sketch to designated scale of the proposed layout or alternative layouts of streets, proposed street names, lots and blocks with numbering, utility easements, storm and sanitary sewers, drainage courses, and water mains.

Streets and lots shall be dimensioned to the nearest scaled foot. The sketch may be executed upon the contour map if the features required on the map are sparse enough to provide a legible and uncluttered result. The scale, north point, and total number of lots shall be indicated.

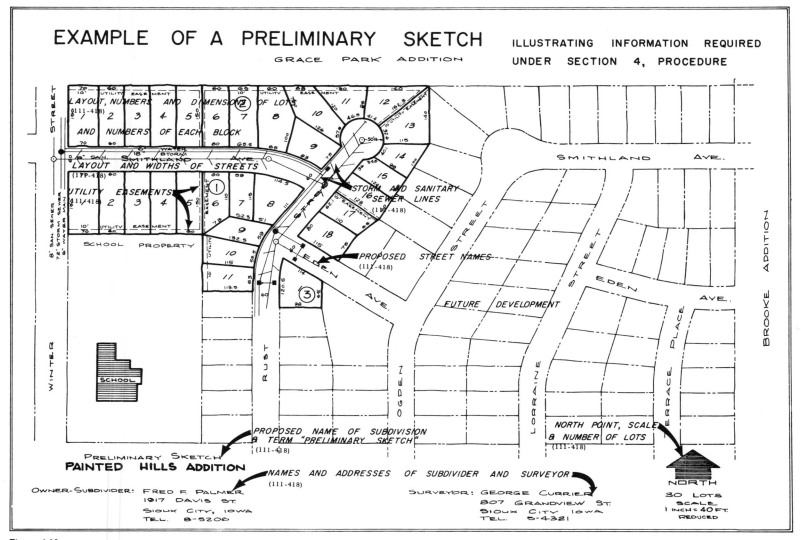

Figure 4-19

GRADING PLAN

Figure 4-20 shows plans and specifications prepared for the grading plan, which shall be sufficiently complete and of such engineering accuracy that they may be approved and used as final plans and specifications for rough grading.

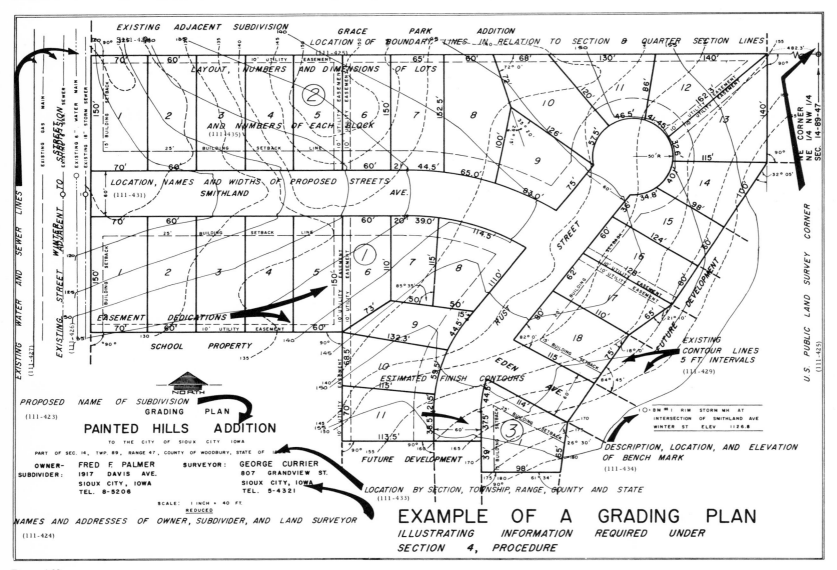

Figure 4-20

SOURCE: *Subdivision Regulations Manual*, Sioux City, Iowa.

STREET PROFILES

In selecting grades of proposed streets, consideration shall be given to topography with a view to securing safe and easy grades and avoiding unsightly and expensive cuts and fills. The subdivider shall furnish profiles of all proposed streets in the subdivisions (see Figure 4-21). The horizontal scale shall be 40 feet to the inch and the vertical scale 4 feet to the inch for grades over 2 percent and 2 feet to the inch for grades of less than 2 percent.

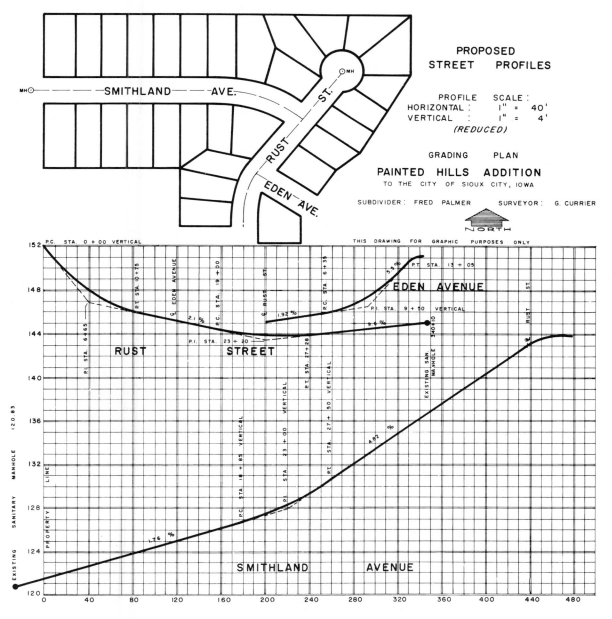

PROPOSED
STREET PROFILES

PROFILE SCALE:
HORIZONTAL: 1" = 40'
VERTICAL: 1" = 4'
(REDUCED)

GRADING PLAN
PAINTED HILLS ADDITION
TO THE CITY OF SIOUX CITY, IOWA

SUBDIVIDER: FRED PALMER   SURVEYOR: G. CURRIER

Figure 4-21 Example of a street profile, to be submitted with the grading plan.

SOURCE: *Subdivision Regulations Manual*, Sioux City, Iowa.

SANITARY SEWERS

A profile of sanitary sewers is shown in Figure 4-22.

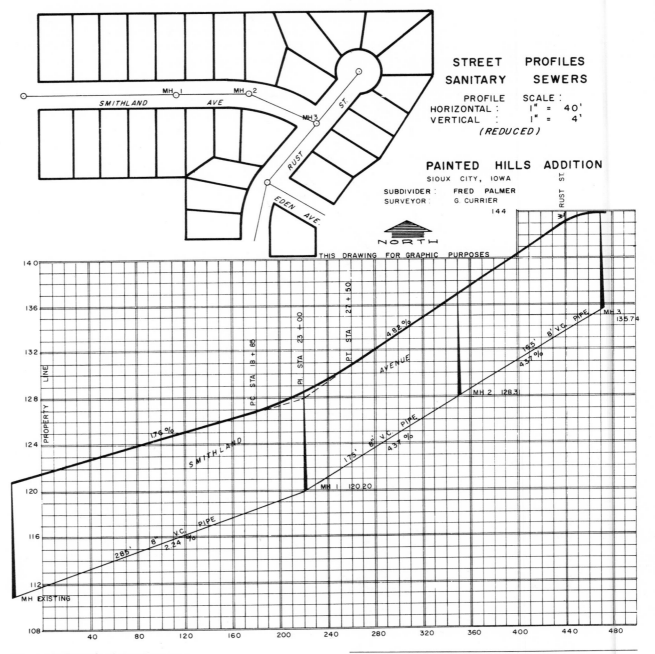

Figure 4-22 Example of sanitary sewers.

SOURCE: *Subdivision Regulations Manual*, Sioux City, Iowa.

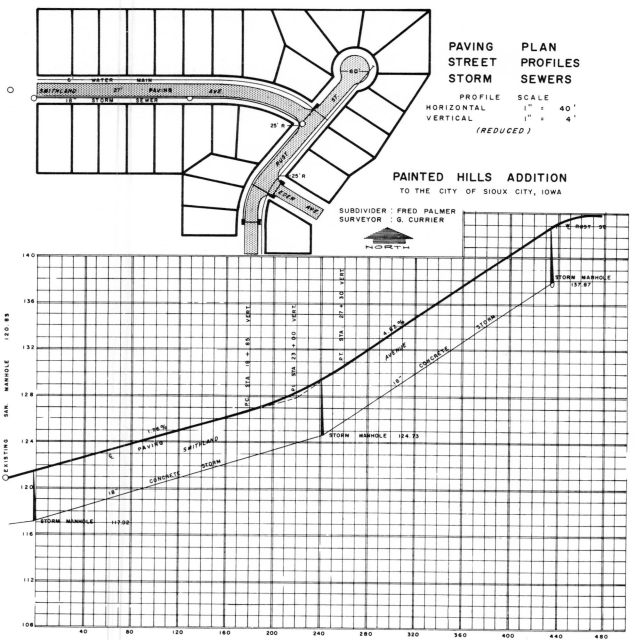

Figure 4-23 Example of storm sewers.

STORM SEWERS

A profile of storm sewers is shown in Figure 4-23.

SOURCE: *Subdivision Regulations Manual*, Sioux City, Iowa.

FINAL PLAT

The final plat (Figure 4-24) shall portray the following information:

1. The name of the subdivision, the points of the compass, the scale of the plat, the name of the subdivider, the date, and the name, address, and seal of the surveyor; also the location of boundary lines in relation to section and quarter section, all of which comprises a legal description of the property. All locations shall be tied to a United States public-land survey corner.
2. The lines of all streets and alleys and other lands to be dedicated with their widths and names.
3. All lot lines and dimensions and the numbering of lots and blocks on a uniform system.
4. An indication of building lines with dimensions if desired.
5. Easements for any right-of-way provided for public use, drainage, services, or utilities, showing dimensions and purpose.
6. All dimensions, both linear and angular, necessary for locating the lines of lots, tracts, or parcels of land, streets, alleys, easements, and the boundaries of the subdivision. The linear dimensions are to be expressed in feet and decimals of a foot. The plat shall show all curve data necessary to reconstruct on the ground all curvilinear boundaries and lines and the radii of all rounded corners.

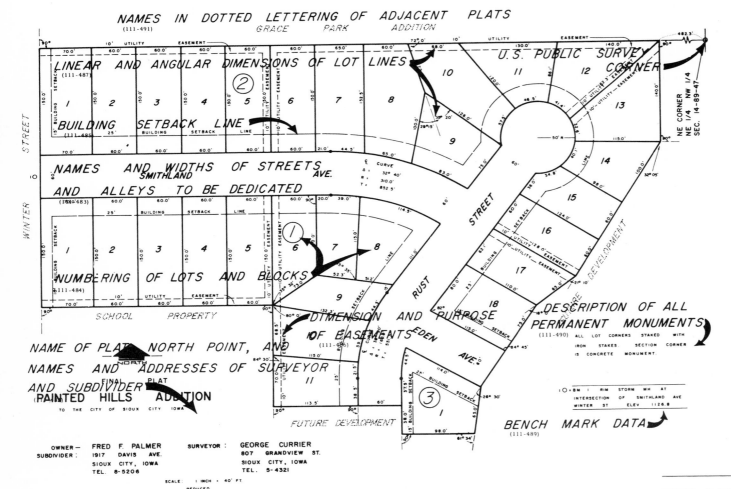

Figure 4-24 Example of a final plat.

SOURCE: *Subdivision Regulations Manual*, Sioux City, Iowa.

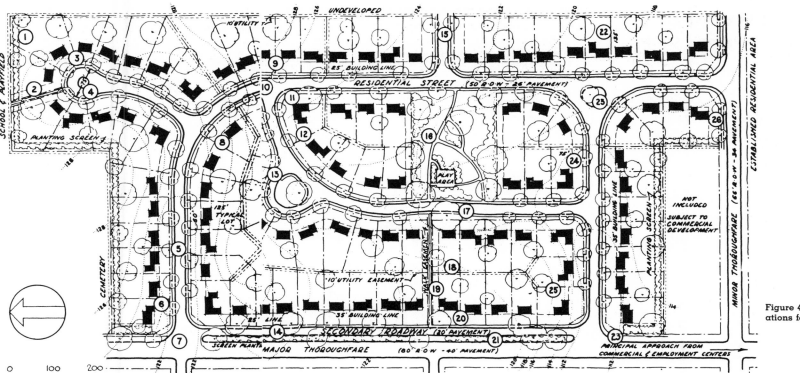

Figure 4-25 Design considerations for subdivisions

DESIGN CONSIDERATIONS

In Figure 4-25 various design considerations for subdivisions are illustrated. Keyed to the illustration are twenty-six important points:

1. A 15-foot easement for a planting screen provides protection from nonresidential use.
2. A 10-foot walk easement gives access to the school.
3. A cul-de-sac utilizes an odd parcel of land to advantage.
4. A turnaround right-of-way is 100 feet in diameter.
5. Street trees are planted approximately 50 feet apart where no trees exist.
6. An additional building setback improves the subdivision entrance.
7. Street intersections at right angles reduce hazards.
8. The lot side line is centered on the street end to avoid car lights' shining into residences.
9. Residences opposite the street end are set back farther to reduce glare from car lights.
10. Three-way intersections reduce hazards.
11. Property lines are on 30-foot radii at corners.
12. Lot lines are perpendicular to street right-of-way lines.
13. An "eyebrow" provides frontage for additional lots in a deeper portion of the block.
14. A secondary roadway eliminates the hazard of entering a major thoroughfare from individual driveways.
15. There is provision for access to land now undeveloped.
16. A neighborhood park is located near the center of the tract. Adjacent lots are wider to allow for a 15-foot protective side-line setback.
17. The pavement is shifted within the right-of-way to preserve existing trees.
18. Aboveground utilities are in rear-line easements.
19. A 10-foot walk easement provides access to a park. Adjacent lots are wider to allow for a 15-foot protective side-line setback.
20. Variation of the building line along a straight street creates interest.
21. Screen planting gives protection from noise and lights on the thoroughfare.
22. Lots backing to uncontrolled land are given greater depth for additional protection.
23. Low planting at street intersections permits clear vision.
24. A wider corner lot permits equal building setbacks on each street.
25. Platting of the block end avoids siding properties to residences across the street.
26. Lots are sided to the boundary street where land use across the street is nonconforming.

SOURCE: *Subdivision Planning Standards*, Federal Housing Administration, Land Planning Division.

4.7 Diagram of Gross Lots per Acre

When a site is studied for a possible subdivision, a critical determination is the number of lots per acre and the amount of open space for streets and park areas. The diagram in Figure 4-26 provides a quick means of determining the relationship of the number of lots per gross acre and percentages of open space. It is assumed that the site is level and entirely buildable, without steep slopes, marshy land, or other obstructions.

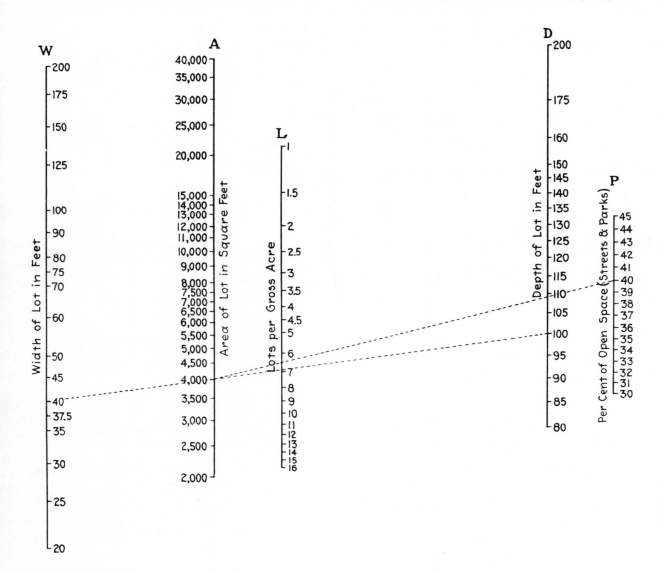

Figure 4-26 Diagram for determining lots per gross acre for varying lot sizes and percentages of open space in streets and parks. To use the diagram, start with values on the *W* and *D* scales. Lay a straightedge between them and read the area of the lot on the *A* scale; then choose a value on the *P* scale. Lay a straightedge between this value and the determined value on the *A* scale. Read the required answer on the *L* scale. In the example shown, *W* = 40 feet; hence *A* = 4000 square feet. With *P* = 40 percent, *L* = 6.5 lots per gross acre.

SOURCE: *New York Regional Survey of New York and Its Environs,* 1929.

4.8 Open-Space Alternatives

Seven alternative designs for the use of open space are shown in Figure 4-27.

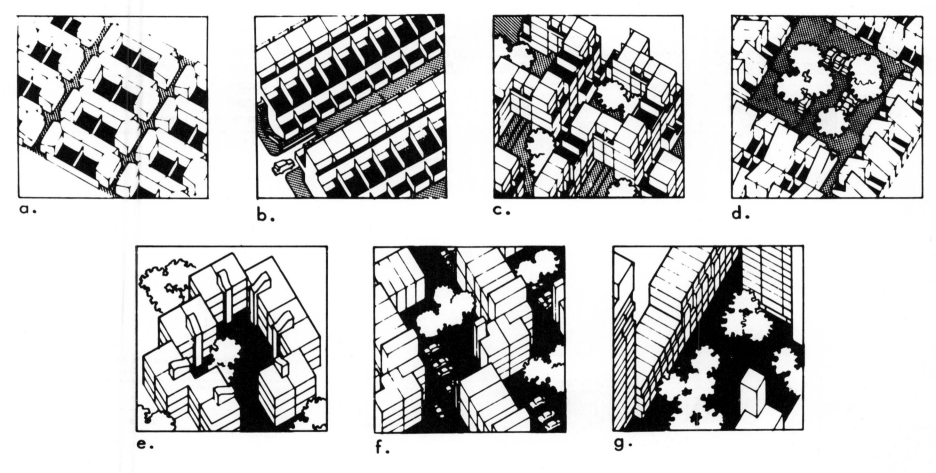

Figure 4-27

(a) Private open space on grade adjacent to dwelling unit; common open space reduced to access.

(b) Private open space on or in building structure adjacent to dwelling unit; common open space reduced to access.

(c) Private open space on grade or on or in building structure adjacent to dwelling unit; common open space shared by groups of dwelling units.

(d) Private open space on grade or on or in building structure adjacent to dwelling unit; common open space integrated with parking shared by groups of dwelling units.

(e) Common open space shared by groups of dwelling units.

(f) Common open space integrated with parking and shared by groups of dwelling units.

(g) Common open space shared by all dwelling units.

SOURCE: *Planning and Design Workbook for Community Participation,* Prepared for the New Jersey Department of Community Affairs by Princeton University, School of Architecture, Research Center for Urban and Environmental Planning.

4.9 Location and Type of Parking

Four types of parking facilities are shown in Figures 4-28, 4-29, 4-30, and 4-31.

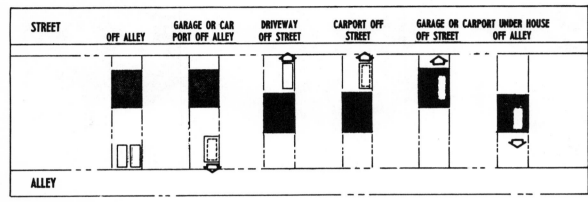

Figure 4-28 Parking on private lot.

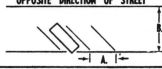

TO CURB	ANGLE	DIM. A IN FT.	DIM. B IN FT.	NO. CARS PER 100' OF CURB
PARALLEL	0°	23	18.5	4.3
DIAGONAL	30°	18	22	5.5
DIAGONAL	45°	12.8	25	7.8
DIAGONAL	60°	10.3	30	9.7
PERPENDICULAR	90°	9	35	11.1

Figure 4-30

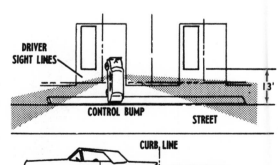

Figure 4-31

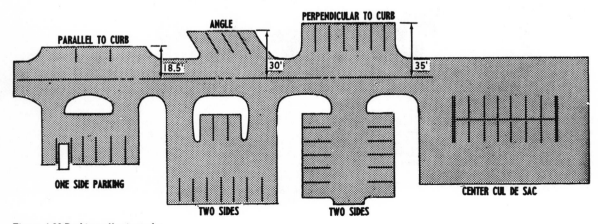

Figure 4-29 Parking off private lot.

SOURCE: *Eastwick New House Study,* Philadelphia Redevelopment Authority, 1957.

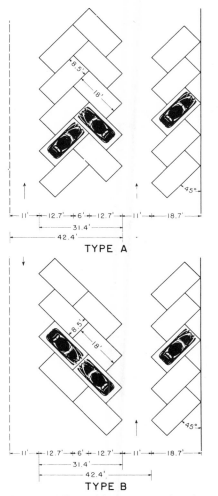

Figure 4-32 Herringbone-pattern parking layouts.

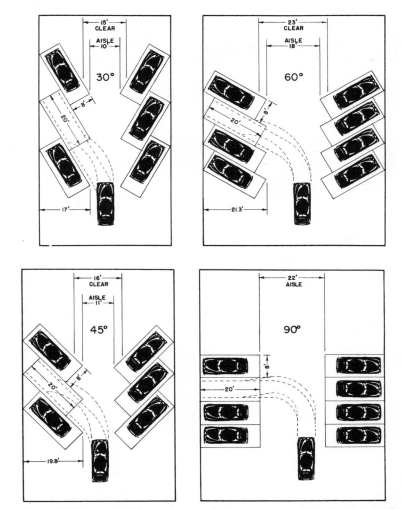

Figure 4-33 Space and aisle requirements for lot or garage parking at various angles.

PARKING LOT LAYOUTS

Various types of layouts for parking lots are shown in Figures 4-32 and 4-33.

The, herringbone pattern, shown in two variations in Figure 4-32, permits economies in some cases where space limitations prevent 90-degree parking. It will be noted that both patterns call for one-way aisles (unless cars are backed into stalls) but that type *A* requires the same direction of travel in all aisles while type *B* requires opposite directions in alternate aisles. The selection will depend upon the plan for circulation and the positions of entrances and exits. It will also be noted that either pattern is more economical of space than plain angle parking, which is used when only one aisle or row is possible.

Figure 4-33 shows the stall and aisle dimensions required for several different angles of parking, in each case giving an aisle wide enough to permit direct entrance without maneuvering for more than 75 percent of the cars. For any parking pattern, particularly one in which any angle other than 90 degrees is used, stall marking lines or curbs are necessary to achieve safety and to maintain the planned capacity.

SOURCE: *Parking Guide for Cities,* U.S. Department of Commerce, Bureau of Public Roads, 1956.

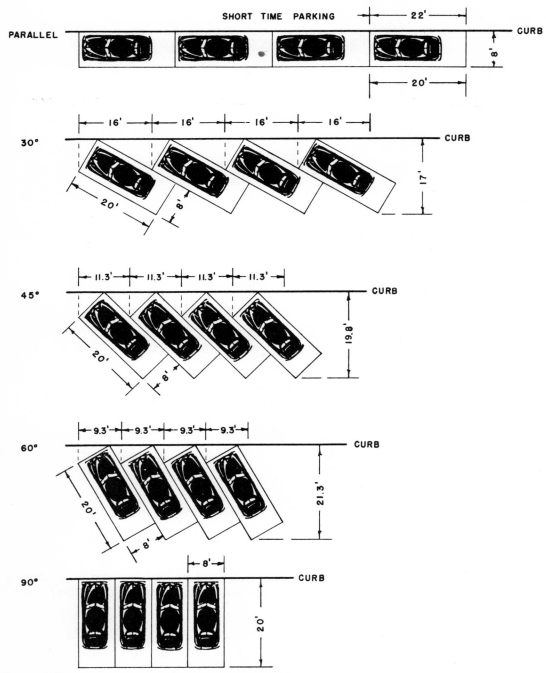

Figure 4-34 Space requirements for curb parking at various angles.

CURB PARKING

Parking spaces, whether at the curb, in a lot, or in a garage, may be parallel, at an acute angle, or at right angles to the curb, wall, or aisle. The choice depends upon the shape and dimensions of the available area. At the curb, parallel parking is the rule unless traffic is extremely light or the street is extremely wide. Figure 4-34 shows the curb and street space required for various angles of parking. Spaces for parallel parking should be at least 20 feet long (preferably 22 feet); if the allowed parking period is short (say, 15 minutes), such spaces should be 22 feet long or longer so that the parking operation of entering or leaving the stall may be completed in one maneuver.

The normal and usually the most efficient layout in larger lots is to place the stalls at right angles to the aisles for as much of the area as possible. This permits entrance or exit in either direction and is the most economical use of space. With stalls 8 feet 6 inches wide and aisles 25 feet wide, the stalls may easily be entered by a driver-parker without maneuvering. Acute-angle parking gives fewer stalls for a given length of curb or aisle than right-angle parking does, and it requires one-way aisles; but entrance is easier for drivers, and the aisle may be narrower, thus permitting the use of a lot too narrow for right-angle parking.

SOURCE: *Parking Guide for Cities,* U.S. Department of Commerce, Bureau of Public Roads, 1956.

4.10 Block and Lot Grading

The raw land that forms the site for building houses should be converted to its new use in accordance with a design that employs natural topography to the best advantage. The levels of streets and buildings must be established so that the surface of the land may be shaped and stabilized to provide for the runoff of rain and melting snow. Permanent features such as driveways, retaining walls, trees, and hedges are part of the landscape design.

Drainage The principal objective in shaping the ground is to provide satisfactory surface drainage so that water will flow away from buildings and be carried off by storm sewers or ditches. Areas that are not covered by buildings or paving must be provided with a permanent surface of grass or other material that will not be eroded by water and wind. For this reason there are great advantages in locating houses and streets so that the existing topsoil and trees are disturbed as little as possible. The replacement of this permanent ground cover is in itself an expensive landscape operation.

The most desirable topographical condition exists when the highest land forms a ridge along the rear lot lines of a block with a gentle slope toward the street on each side. Water will then flow toward the streets. Protective slopes are required to drain surface water away from the walls of buildings and from backfilled areas. To maintain the flow of surface water between buildings and to prevent pools from collecting in the rear of buildings, drainage swales are needed; these are formed by a slight dishing of the ground to provide natural channels. Grading layout 1 in Figure 4-35 illustrates such a grading plan by which water is moved from the rear yard and finally to the street for disposal.

For relatively flat land, as in grading layout 2, the surface water from the back-garden areas of lots can be drained to a rear swale, possibly designed as an easement, along the rear lot lines. In such an instance, the drainage divide occurs along the back edge of the landscaping plinth or protective slopes around the dwellings. All the remaining portion of the lot, including the front garden, is drained out to the street.

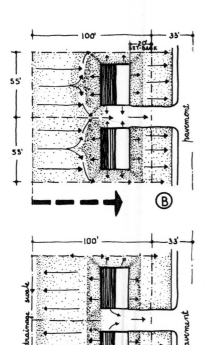

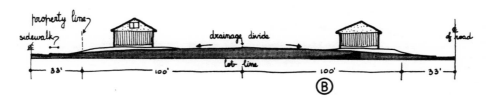

GRADING LAYOUT 1— Drainage to the street from **the rear of** the lot

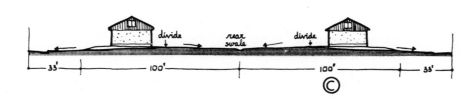

GRADING LAYOUT 2— Drainage to the street and to a rear swale

Figure 4-35

SOURCE: *Principles of Small House Grouping,* Central Mortgage and Housing Corporation, Ottawa, Canada, 1957.

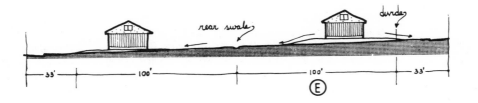

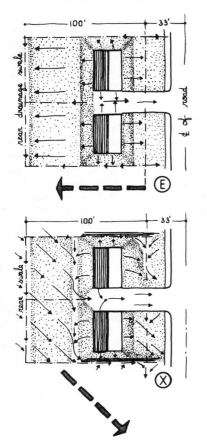

GRADING LAYOUT 3— Draining a lot which is highest on the street side

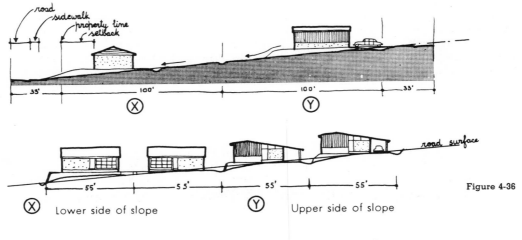

Figure 4-36

GRADING LAYOUT 4— Draining a lot with a cross slope

The slope across a block of houses may be such that lots on one side are higher than those on the other. In this instance, grading layout 3 (Figure 4-36), the drainage divide may occur along the front property line of the higher-level lots, with all drainage behind this line being directed between the dwellings and across the rear gardens. Intercepting drainage swales or easements must be provided along the rear lot lines or at intermediate locations leading out to the lower-level street. Such drainage easements must be permanently established by proper legal methods with continuous maintenance assured. Lots on the lower side of the block should be drained out to the street.

In another very common situation, a cross slope runs diagonally across a block and hence diagonally across each individual lot, either from back to front or from front to back. Grading layout 4 (Figure 4-36) shows such a situation. Drainage of these lots is more complicated, and special attention is needed to ensure that the width of individual lots is adequate to allow for protective slopes on either side of the dwelling, for the ground to fall away following the line of the slope, and for side swales. Small retaining walls or steep banks may be necessary along side lot lines, and these should be carefully carried out so that the stepping up of the slope as seen from the lower end of the street does not have a jerky and disorganized appearance.

The most important factor in lot grading and drainage is the relationship of house floor elevation to street elevation. If the floor elevation is too low in relation to adjoining street grades, adequate protective slopes and drainage swales cannot be provided to drain the lot satisfactorily. If the floor elevation is too high, unnecessary terracing and outside stairs will be required, and the house will appear to be dissociated from the natural lie of the land.

SOURCE: *Principles of Small House Grouping*, Central Mortgage and Housing Corporation, Ottawa, Canada, 1957.

LOT GRADING

Two types of lot grading, one in which all drainage is to the street and the other in which drainage is both to the rear and to the street, are shown in Figures 4-37 and 4-38.

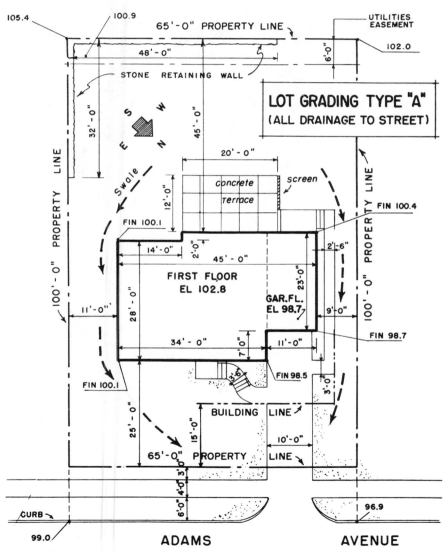

Figure 4-37

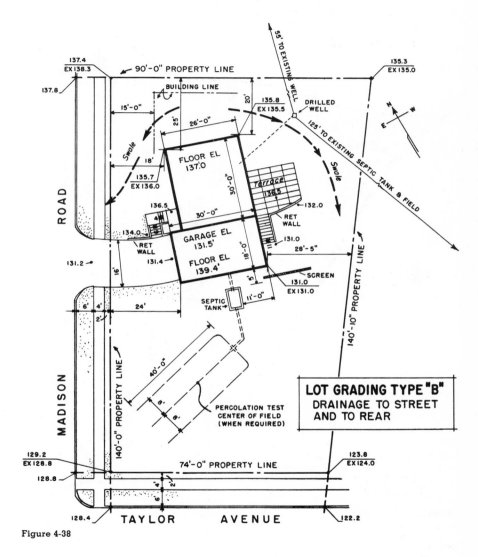

Figure 4-38

SOURCE: *Minimum Property Standards for 1 and 2 Living Units,* Federal Housing Administration, 1974.

4.11 Comparison of Site Development Proposals

Four types of site development are shown in Figures 4-39, 4-40, 4-41, and 4-42.

SINGLE DETACHED

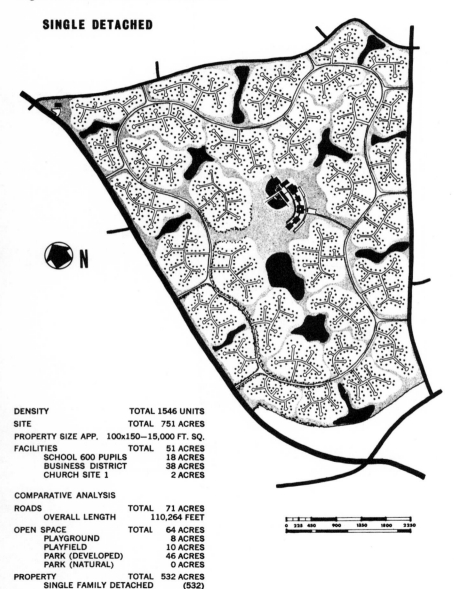

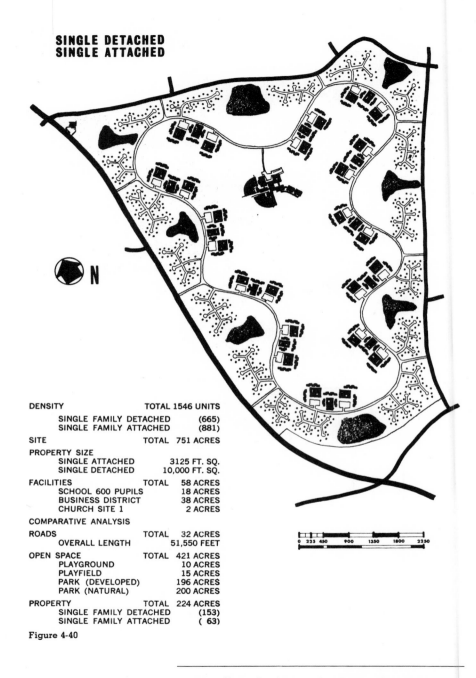

SINGLE DETACHED
SINGLE ATTACHED

DENSITY		TOTAL 1546 UNITS
	SINGLE FAMILY DETACHED	(665)
	SINGLE FAMILY ATTACHED	(881)
SITE		TOTAL 751 ACRES
PROPERTY SIZE		
	SINGLE ATTACHED	3125 FT. SQ.
	SINGLE DETACHED	10,000 FT. SQ.
FACILITIES	TOTAL	58 ACRES
	SCHOOL 600 PUPILS	18 ACRES
	BUSINESS DISTRICT	38 ACRES
	CHURCH SITE 1	2 ACRES
COMPARATIVE ANALYSIS		
ROADS	TOTAL	32 ACRES
	OVERALL LENGTH	51,550 FEET
OPEN SPACE	TOTAL	421 ACRES
	PLAYGROUND	10 ACRES
	PLAYFIELD	15 ACRES
	PARK (DEVELOPED)	196 ACRES
	PARK (NATURAL)	200 ACRES
PROPERTY	TOTAL	224 ACRES
	SINGLE FAMILY DETACHED	(153)
	SINGLE FAMILY ATTACHED	(63)

Figure 4-40

DENSITY		TOTAL 1546 UNITS
SITE		TOTAL 751 ACRES
PROPERTY SIZE APP.	100x150—15,000 FT. SQ.	
FACILITIES	TOTAL	51 ACRES
	SCHOOL 600 PUPILS	18 ACRES
	BUSINESS DISTRICT	38 ACRES
	CHURCH SITE 1	2 ACRES
COMPARATIVE ANALYSIS		
ROADS	TOTAL	71 ACRES
	OVERALL LENGTH	110,264 FEET
OPEN SPACE	TOTAL	64 ACRES
	PLAYGROUND	8 ACRES
	PLAYFIELD	10 ACRES
	PARK (DEVELOPED)	46 ACRES
	PARK (NATURAL)	0 ACRES
PROPERTY	TOTAL	532 ACRES
	SINGLE FAMILY DETACHED	(532)

Figure 4-39

SOURCE: *Cluster Development,* Pratt Institute, School of Architecture, Brooklyn, N.Y., n.d.

SINGLE DETACHED
SINGLE ATTACHED
APARTMENT TOWER

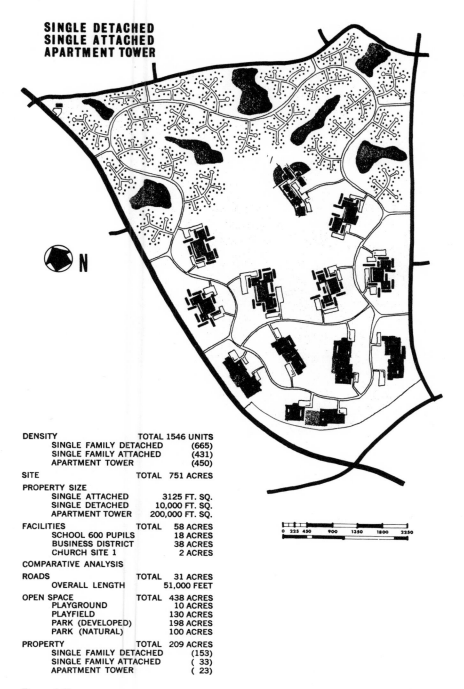

DENSITY   TOTAL 1546 UNITS
    SINGLE FAMILY DETACHED   (665)
    SINGLE FAMILY ATTACHED   (431)
    APARTMENT TOWER   (450)
SITE   TOTAL 751 ACRES
PROPERTY SIZE
    SINGLE ATTACHED   3125 FT. SQ.
    SINGLE DETACHED   10,000 FT. SQ.
    APARTMENT TOWER   200,000 FT. SQ.
FACILITIES   TOTAL   58 ACRES
    SCHOOL 600 PUPILS   18 ACRES
    BUSINESS DISTRICT   38 ACRES
    CHURCH SITE 1   2 ACRES
COMPARATIVE ANALYSIS
ROADS   TOTAL   31 ACRES
    OVERALL LENGTH   51,000 FEET
OPEN SPACE   TOTAL   438 ACRES
    PLAYGROUND   10 ACRES
    PLAYFIELD   130 ACRES
    PARK (DEVELOPED)   198 ACRES
    PARK (NATURAL)   100 ACRES
PROPERTY   TOTAL   209 ACRES
    SINGLE FAMILY DETACHED   (153)
    SINGLE FAMILY ATTACHED   (33)
    APARTMENT TOWER   (23)

Figure 4-41

SINGLE DETACHED

GRID

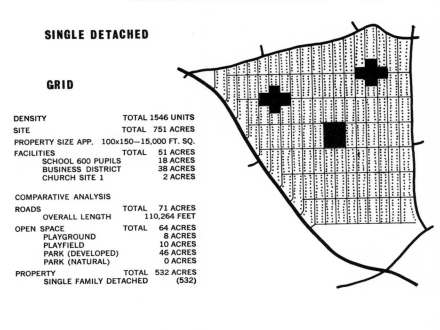

DENSITY   TOTAL 1546 UNITS
SITE   TOTAL 751 ACRES
PROPERTY SIZE APP.   100x150—15,000 FT. SQ.
FACILITIES   TOTAL   51 ACRES
    SCHOOL 600 PUPILS   18 ACRES
    BUSINESS DISTRICT   38 ACRES
    CHURCH SITE 1   2 ACRES

COMPARATIVE ANALYSIS
ROADS   TOTAL   71 ACRES
    OVERALL LENGTH   110,264 FEET
OPEN SPACE   TOTAL   64 ACRES
    PLAYGROUND   8 ACRES
    PLAYFIELD   10 ACRES
    PARK (DEVELOPED)   46 ACRES
    PARK (NATURAL)   0 ACRES
PROPERTY   TOTAL 532 ACRES
    SINGLE FAMILY DETACHED   (532)

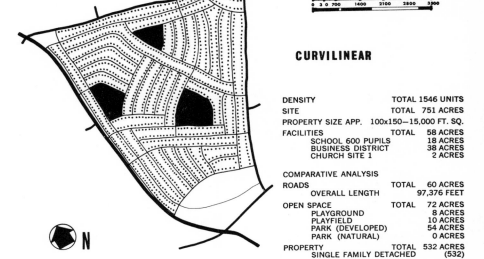

CURVILINEAR

DENSITY   TOTAL 1546 UNITS
SITE   TOTAL 751 ACRES
PROPERTY SIZE APP.   100x150—15,000 FT. SQ.
FACILITIES   TOTAL   58 ACRES
    SCHOOL 600 PUPILS   18 ACRES
    BUSINESS DISTRICT   38 ACRES
    CHURCH SITE 1   2 ACRES

COMPARATIVE ANALYSIS
ROADS   TOTAL   60 ACRES
    OVERALL LENGTH   97,376 FEET
OPEN SPACE   TOTAL   72 ACRES
    PLAYGROUND   8 ACRES
    PLAYFIELD   10 ACRES
    PARK (DEVELOPED)   54 ACRES
    PARK (NATURAL)   0 ACRES
PROPERTY   TOTAL 532 ACRES
    SINGLE FAMILY DETACHED   (532)

Figure 4-42

SOURCE: *Cluster Development,* Pratt Institute, School of Architecture, Brooklyn, N.Y., n.d.

Three site plans are illustrated in Figures 4-43, 4-44, and 4-45.

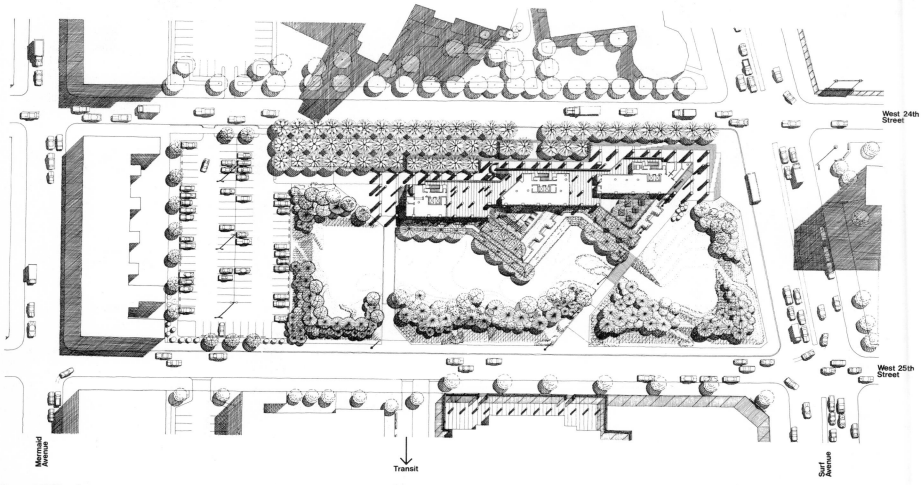

West 24th Street

West 25th Street

Mermaid Avenue

Transit

Surf Avenue

Figure 4-43 Site plan.

SOURCE: R. T. Schnadelbach, Landscape and Ecological Consultants, Philadelphia.

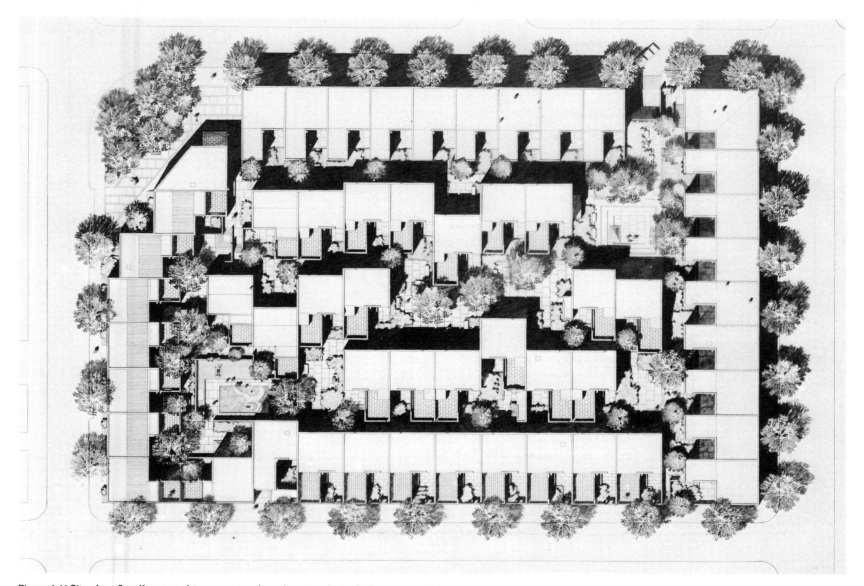

Figure 4-44 Site plan. A well-protected inner courtyard can be entered at only three secured places.

SOURCE: Penn Landing Square, Louis Sauer Associates, Architects, Philadelphia.

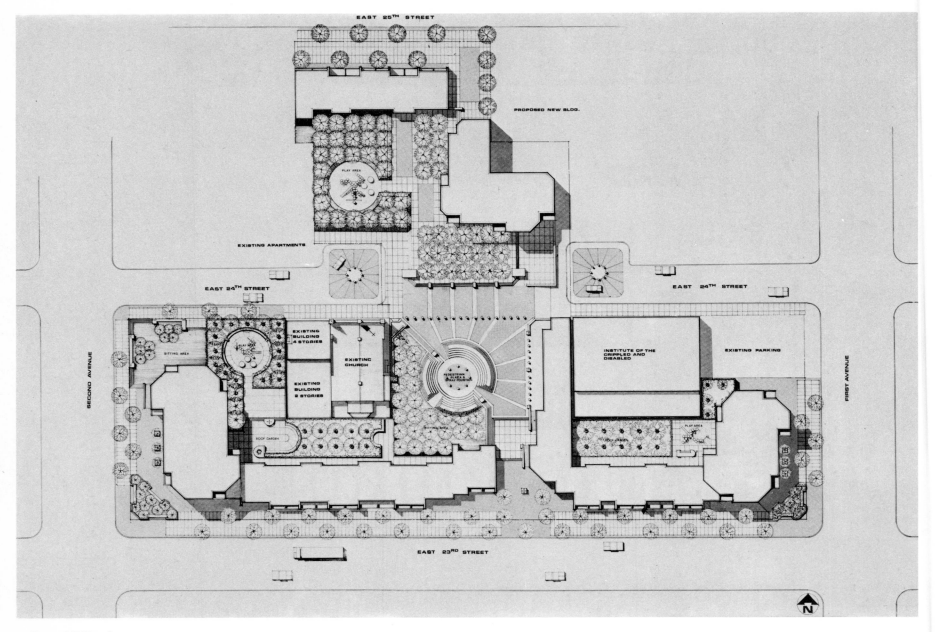

Figure 4-45 Site plan.

SOURCE: Genesee Crossroads, Louis Sauer Associates, Architects, Philadelphia.

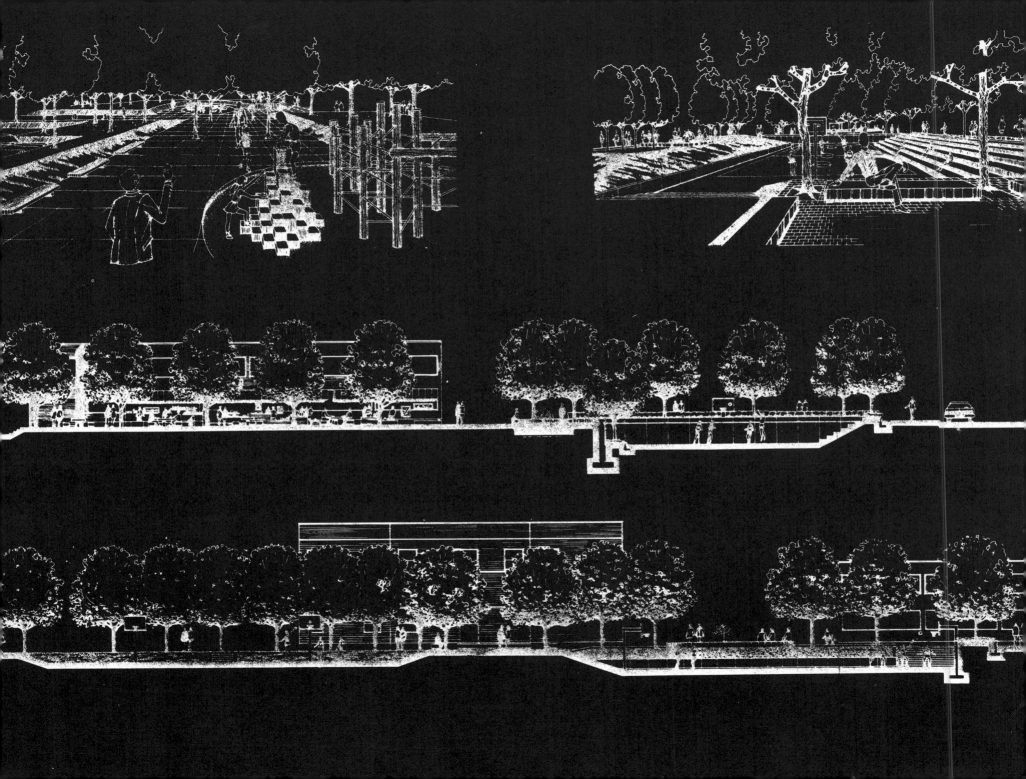

Layout of Recreational Facilities

Recreational facilities are common to all kinds of site development. They constitute major elements in the complexes of all schools, from elementary schools to universities. A wide range of recreational facilities is an essential accessory use for most residential developments, especially cooperatives and condominiums. In fact, many newer communities are designed around specialized recreational activities such as golf courses, tennis courts, and marinas. Even industrial parks today provide selective recreational amenities within their boundaries.

Recreational areas are planned and designed to provide proper facilities for games and sports. Each activity requires a specific area and layout for its best utilization. This section includes the layouts of the most popular games and sports as recommended by the various athletic associations. Since each activity is specific as to layout, the site must be prepared to its requirements of area, grading, and orientation.

After selecting the individual activities to be included within a particular site development, the site designer should take great care

1. To avoid conflicts or dangerous conditions in the juxtapositioning of the various activities
2. To provide physical and visual barriers between the recreational facilities and adjacent uses, such as residential or community facilities
3. To provide adequate parking areas to accommodate both participants and spectators
4. To provide proper access to the facilities for service and maintenance

Opposite: Woodlawn Park. (M. Paul Friedberg and Associates, Landscape Architects)

5.1 General Area Requirements for Games and Sports

Area requirements for popular games and sports are shown in the accompanying table.

Activity	Play area (feet)	Total area		Number of players
		Dimensions	Square feet	
Archery	Length; 90–300	50 (minimum) × 450 (maximum)		
Badminton	Single; 17 × 44	25 × 60	1,500	2
	Double; 20 × 44	30 × 60	1,800	4
Baseball	Diamond; 90 × 90	300 × 300 (minimum)	90,000	18
		350 × 350 (average)	122,500	
Basketball (men)	Minimum; 42 × 74	60 × 100 (average)	6,000	10
	Maximum; 50 × 94			
Basketball (women)	45 × 90	55 × 100 (average)	5,500	12–18
Bocci	18 × 62	30 × 80	2,400	2–4
Bowling (lawn)*	One alley; 14 × 100	120 × 120 (eight alleys)	14,400	32–64
Box hockey	4 × 10	16 × 20	320	2
Box lacrosse	Minimum; 60 × 160	85 × 185 (average)	15,725	14
	Maximum; 90 × 200			
Clock golf	Circle; 20–24 in diameter	30-foot circle	706	2–8
Cricket	Between wickets; 66	420 × 420	176,400	22
Croquet	30 × 60	30 × 60	1,800	2–8
Curling	Between hacks; 138	14 × 150	2,100	8
Deck tennis	Single; 12 × 40	20 × 50	1,000	2
	Double; 18 × 40	26 × 50	1,300	4
Field ball	180 × 300	210 × 340	71,400	22
Field hockey	Minimum; 150 × 270	200 × 350 (average)	70,000	22
	Maximum; 180 × 300			
Football	195 × 300; plus end zones	195 × 480	93,600	24
Handball	20 × 34	30 × 45	1,350	2 or 4
Hand tennis	16 × 40	25 × 60	1,500	2 or 4
Horseshoes (men)	Between stakes; 40	12 × 50	600	2 or 4
Horseshoes (women)	Between stakes; 30	12 × 40	480	2 or 4
Ice hockey	Minimum; 65 × 165	85 × 185 (average)	15,725	12
	Maximum; 85 × 200			
Lacrosse	Minimum; 210 × 450	260 × 500 (average)	130,000	24
Paddle tennis	Single; 16 × 44	28 × 70	1,960	2
	Double; 20 × 44	32 × 70	2,240	4
Polo	Maximum; 600 × 960	600 × 960	576,000	8
Quoits	Between stakes; 54	25 × 80	2,000	2 or 4
Roque	30 × 60	30 × 60	1,800	4

(Continued)

SOURCE: Standards and Definition of Terms, Ontario Department of Education, Community Programs Division.

Activity	Play area (feet)	Total area		Number of players
		Dimensions	Square feet	
Shuffleboard	6 × 52	10 × 64	640	2 or 4
Soccer (men)	Minimum; 150 × 300	240 × 360 (average)	86,400	22
	Maximum; 300 × 390			
Soccer (women)	Minimum; 120 × 240	200 × 320	64,000	22
	Maximum; 180 × 300			
Softball	Diamond; 60 × 60	250 × 250 (minimum)	62,500	20
Speedball (men)	Minimum; 160 × 240	180 × 300	54,000	22
	Maximum; 160 × 360	180 × 420	75,600	
Swimming (pool)†	75 × 45		4–8 lanes	
Competitive	165 × 7		4–8 lanes	
Synchronized	50 meters × 45 feet			
Table tennis	5 × 9	12 × 20	240	2 or 4
Tennis	Single; 27 × 78	50 × 120	6,000	2
	Double; 36 × 78	60 × 120	7,200	2 or 4
Tether tennis	Circle; 6 in diameter	20 × 20	400	2
Touch football	160 × 300	175 × 330	57,750	22
Volley ball	30 × 60	50 × 80	4,000	12–16
Water polo	55 yards × 15 yards × 6 feet			

*Most bowling greens in public recreation areas measure 120 × 120 feet and provide for eight alleys. The amount of space required for a single alley would be 20 by 120 feet.

†A 1-meter diving board requires a 9-foot depth of water; a 3-meter board requires 12 feet of water; a 10-meter diving platform requires 16 feet of water.

SOURCE: Standards and Definition of Terms, Ontario Department of Education, Community Programs Division.

5.2 Layout of Games and Sports Activities

RUNNING TRACK; FOOTBALL FIELD

Layouts of a running track and a football field are shown in Figures 5-1 and 5-2.

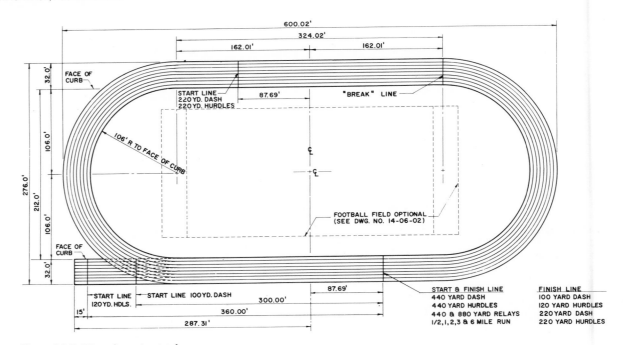

Figure 5-1 A 440-yard running track.

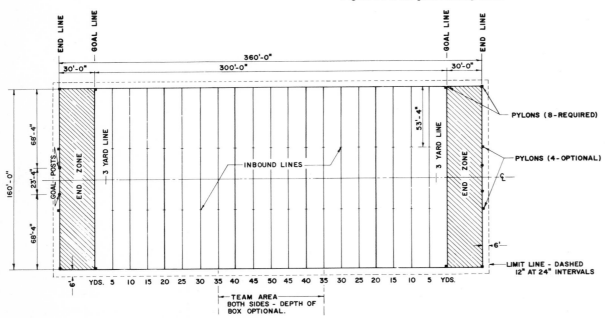

Figure 5-2 An eleven-man football field.

SOURCE: U.S. Department of the Army, Office of the Chief of Engineers.

FIELD AND TRACK

Layouts for the high jump, javelin throw, pole vault, combination long jump and triple jump, discus throw, and shot put and hammer throw are shown in Figures 5-3 through 5-8.

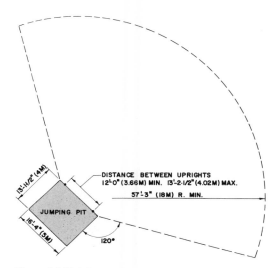

Figure 5-3 High jump.

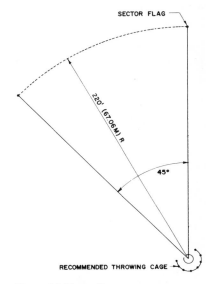

Figure 5-7 Discus throw.

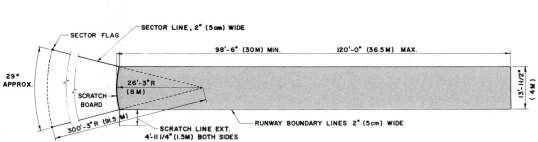

Figure 5-4 Javelin throw.

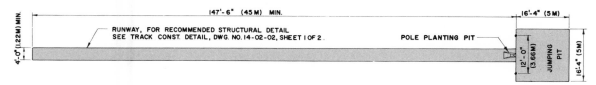

Figure 5-5 Pole vault.

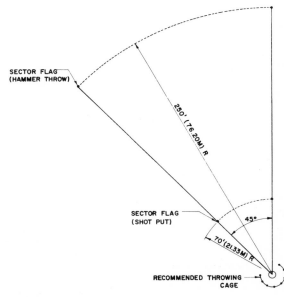

Figure 5-8 Shot put and hammer throw.

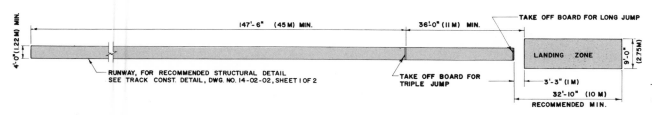

Figure 5-6 Combination long jump and triple jump.

SOURCE: U.S. Department of the Army, Office of the Chief of Engineers.

BASEBALL

Suggested layouts for a baseball diamond and for home and pitcher's plates are shown in Figures 5-9 and 5-10.

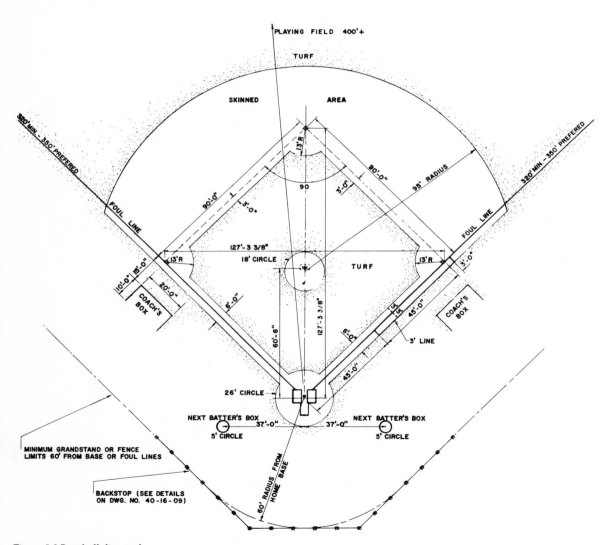

Figure 5-9 Baseball diamond.

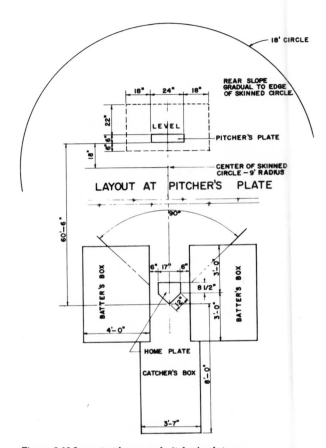

Figure 5-10 Layout at home and pitcher's plates.

SOURCE: U.S. Department of the Army, Office of the Chief of Engineers.

BOYS' BASEBALL; SPORTS FIELD

Diagrams for three boys' baseball fields and for multiple sports fields are shown in Figures 5-11, 5-12, 5-13, and 5-14.

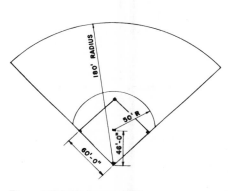

Figure 5-11 Little League field.

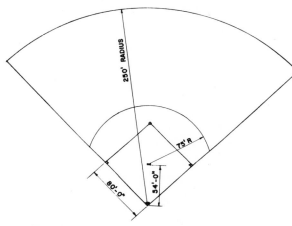

Figure 5-12 Pony League field.

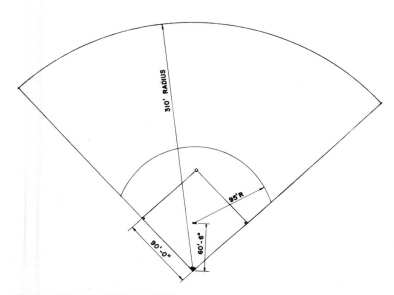

Figure 5-13 Babe Ruth League field.

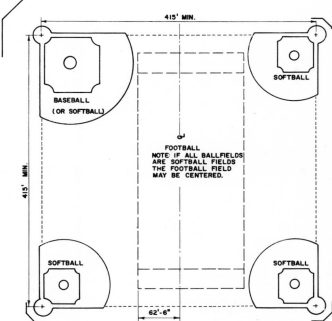

Figure 5-14 Multiple sports fields.

SOURCE: U.S. Department of the Army, Office of the Chief of Engineers.

SOFTBALL

Figures 5-15 and 5-16 show layouts of a softball diamond and of home base.

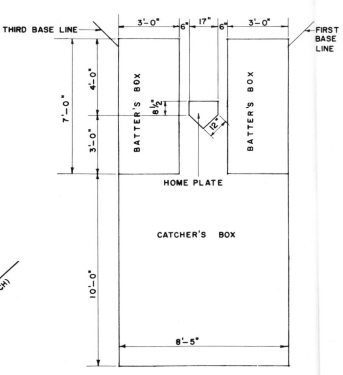

Figure 5-16 Layout at home base.

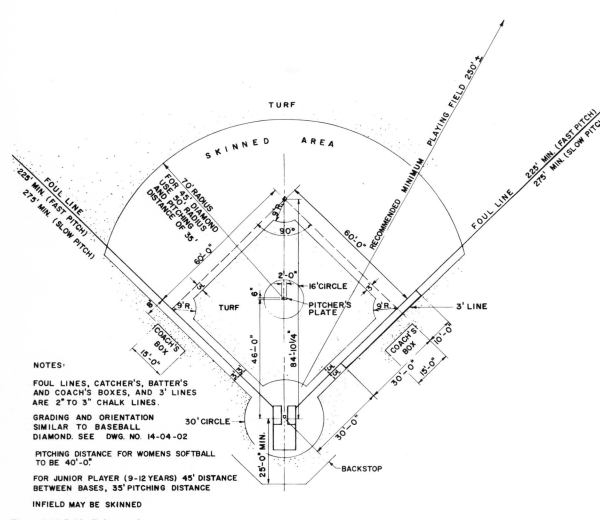

NOTES:

FOUL LINES, CATCHER'S, BATTER'S AND COACH'S BOXES, AND 3' LINES ARE 2" TO 3" CHALK LINES.

GRADING AND ORIENTATION SIMILAR TO BASEBALL DIAMOND. SEE DWG. NO. 14-04-02

PITCHING DISTANCE FOR WOMENS SOFTBALL TO BE 40'-0".

FOR JUNIOR PLAYER (9-12 YEARS) 45' DISTANCE BETWEEN BASES, 35' PITCHING DISTANCE

INFIELD MAY BE SKINNED

Figure 5-15 Softball diamond.

SOURCE: U.S. Department of the Army, Office of the Chief of Engineers.

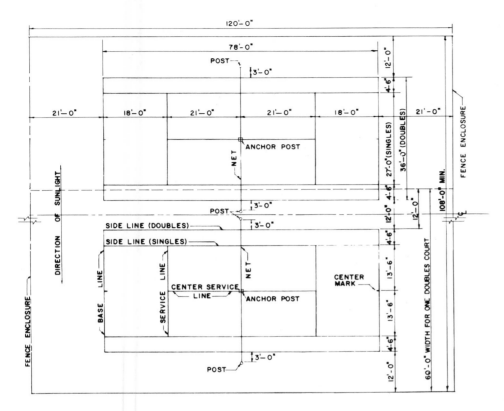

Figure 5-17 Tennis courts.

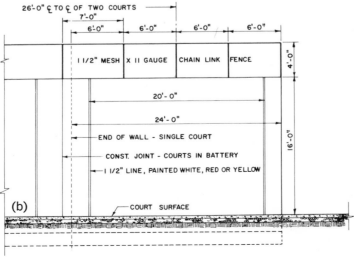

TENNIS; HANDBALL

A layout for two tennis courts is shown in Figure 5-17, and a layout and an elevation for a handball court are illustrated in Figure 5-18*a* and *b*.

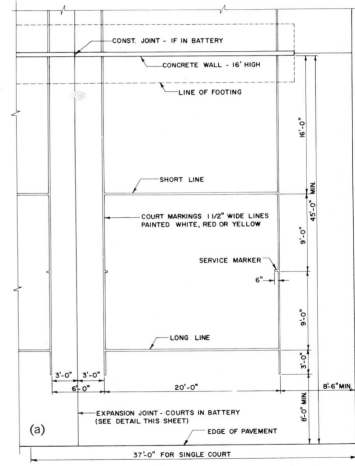

Figure 5-18 One-wall handball court. (*a*) Plan. (*b*) Elevation.

SOURCE: U.S. Department of the Army, Office of the Chief of Engineers.

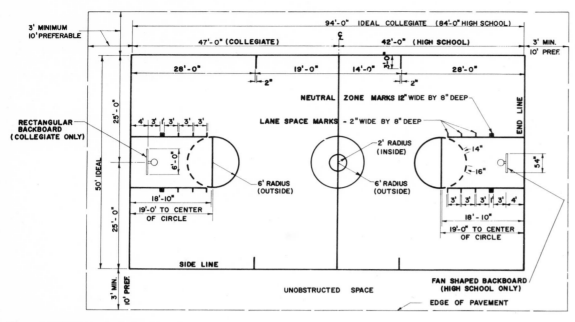

Figure 5-19 NCAA basketball court.

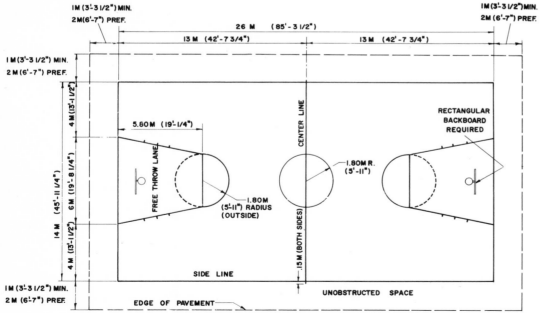

Figure 5-20 AAU basketball court.

NOTE: ALL LINES TO BE .05M (2") WIDE

BASKETBALL

Layouts of National Collegiate Athletic Association and Amateur Athletic Union basketball courts are shown in Figures 5-19 and 5-20. Two types of backboards appear in Figure 5-21.

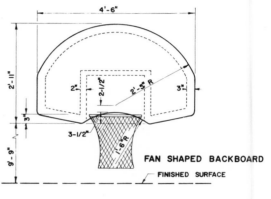

FAN SHAPED BACKBOARD

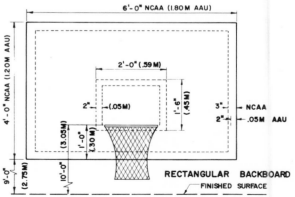

RECTANGULAR BACKBOARD

Figure 5-21

SOURCE: U.S. Department of the Army, Office of the Chief of Engineers.

VOLLEYBALL; BADMINTON; PADDLE TENNIS; POLO

Courts for volleyball, badminton, and paddle tennis are shown in Figures 5-22, 5-23, and 5-24; a polo field is illustrated in Figure 5-25.

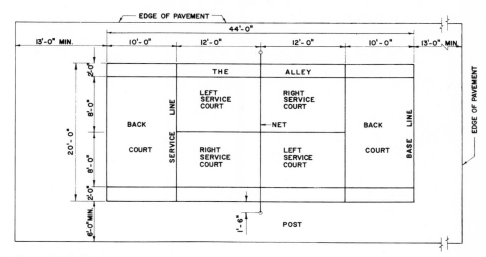

Figure 5-24 Paddle tennis court.

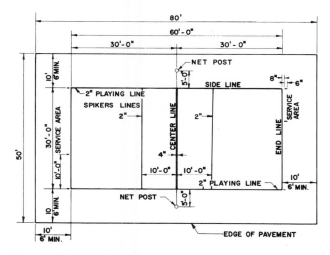

Figure 5-22 Volleyball court.

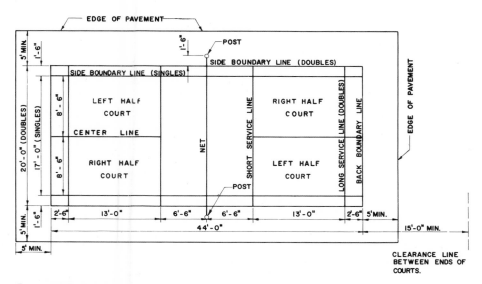

Figure 5-23 Badminton court.

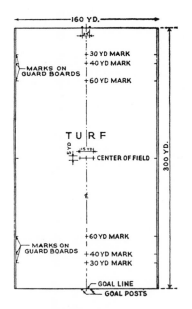

Figure 5-25 Polo field.

SOURCE: U.S. Department of the Army, Office of the Chief of Engineers.

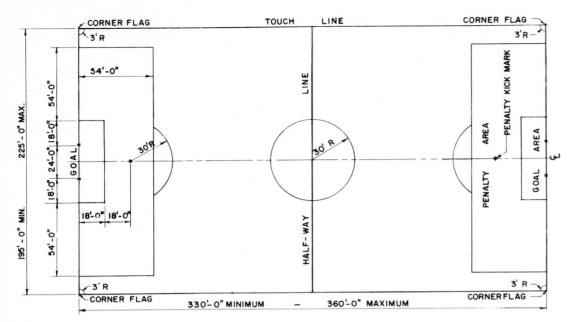

Figure 5-26 Soccer field.

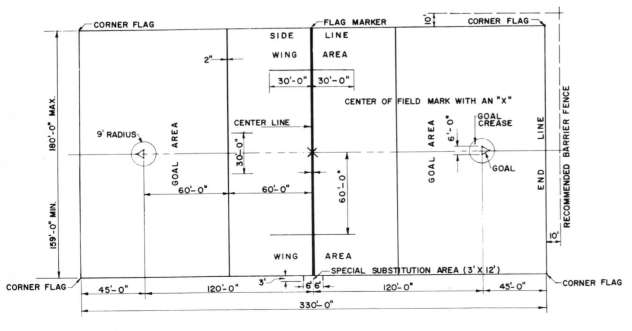

Figure 5-27 Lacrosse field.

SOCCER; LACROSSE

Figures 5-26 and 5-27 illustrate layouts for soccer and lacrosse fields.

SOURCE: U.S. Department of the Army, Office of the Chief of Engineers.

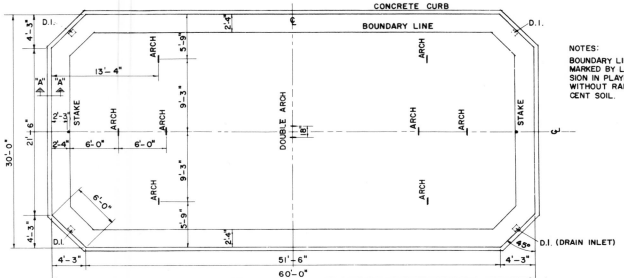

PLAYING SURFACE SHOULD BE HARD, SMOOTH, AND LEVEL SAND - CLAY.

NOTES:
BOUNDARY LINES ARE
MARKED BY LIGHT DEPRES-
SION IN PLAYING SURFACE
WITHOUT RAISING ADJA-
CENT SOIL.

FACILITY DRAWINGS AND DETAILS FOR ROQUE CONFORM TO 1973
PLAYING RULES PROVIDED BY THE "AMERICAN ROQUE LEAGUE INC."

Figure 5-18 Roque court.

ROQUE; CROQUET

Courts for roque and American croquet are
illustrated in Figures 5-28 and 5-29.

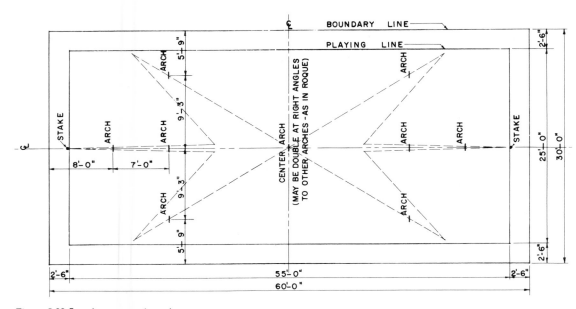

Figure 5-29 American croquet court.

SOURCE: U.S. Department of the Army, Office of the Chief of
Engineers.

213

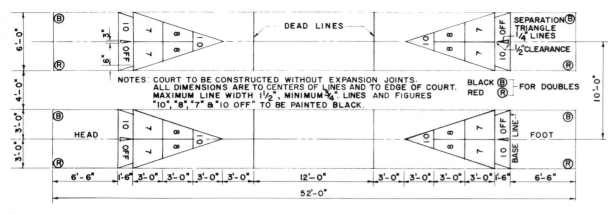

Figure 5-30 Shuffleboard court.

Figures 5-30 and 5-31 show courts for shuffleboard and horseshoes; Figures 5-32 and 5-33 illustrate an archery range and the design for a target.

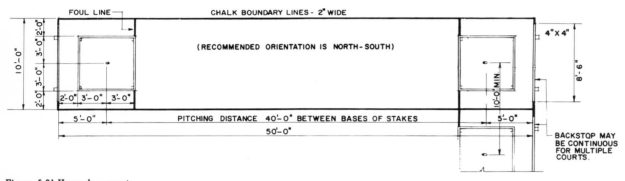

Figure 5-31 Horseshoe court.

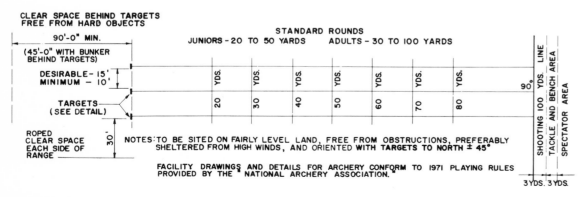

Figure 5-32 Archery range.

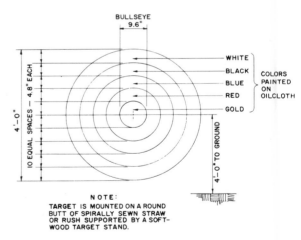

Figure 5-33 Target detail.

SOURCE: U.S. Department of the Army, Office of the Chief of Engineers.

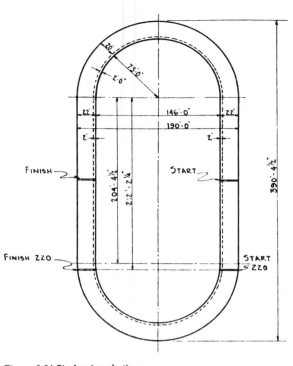

Figure 5-34 Six-lap ice skating.

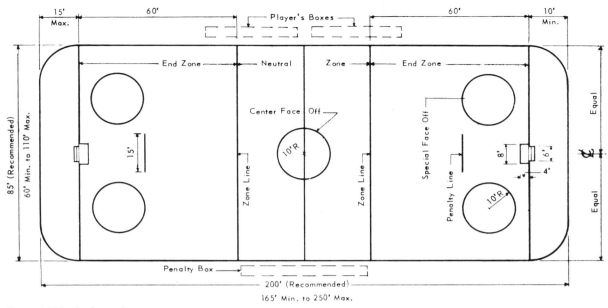

Figure 5-36 Ice hockey rink.

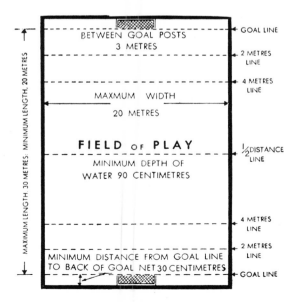

Figure 5-35 Water polo field.

WATER POLO; ICE HOCKEY; ICE SKATING; RUGBY

Layouts of facilities for water polo, ice hockey, six-lap ice skating, and rugby are depicted in Figures 5-34, 5-35, 5-36, and 5-37.

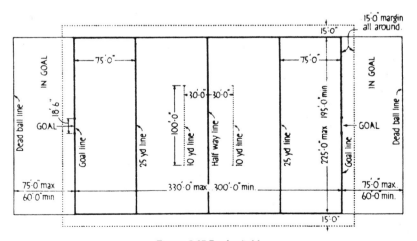

Figure 5-37 Rugby field.

SOURCE: U.S. Department of the Army, Office of the Chief of Engineers.

5.3 Play Lots

Play lots should be provided for preschool children up to 6 years of age primarily in conjunction with multifamily (town house and apartment) developments and, where desirable, in single-family neighborhoods remote from elementary schools. They are a necessary element of such developments to complement common open-space areas. Play lots may include (1) an enclosed area for play equipment and such special facilities as a sand area and a spray pool, (2) an open turfed area for active play, and (3) a shaded area for quiet activities.

Location Play lots should be included as an integral part of the housing area design and be located within 300 to 400 feet of each living unit served. They should be accessible without crossing any street, and walkways leading to them should have easy gradients for pushing strollers and carriages. Play lots may be included in playgrounds close to housing areas to serve the preschool age group in the adjoining neighborhood.

Size The enclosed area for play equipment and special facilities should be based on a minimum of 70 square feet per child, which is equivalent to 21 square feet per family on the average basis of 0.3 preschool child per family. A minimum enclosed area of approximately 2000 square feet will serve some thirty preschool children (about 100 families). Such a size will accommodate only a limited selection of play equipment. To accommodate a full range of equipment and special facilities, including a spray pool, the minimum enclosed area should be about 4000 square feet, which will serve up to fifty preschool children (about 165 families).

Additional space is required to accommodate the elements of the play lot outside the enclosed area. A turfed area at least 40 feet square should be provided for active games.

Activity Spaces and Elements A play lot should comprise the following basic activity spaces and elements:

1. An enclosed area with play equipment and special facilities including
   a. Play equipment such as climbers, slides, swing sets, play walls and playhouses, and play sculpture
   b. A sand area
   c. A spray pool
2. An open turfed area for running and active play
3. A shaded area for quiet activities
4. Miscellaneous elements including benches for supervising parents; walks and other paved areas wide enough for strollers, carriages, tricycles, wagons, and so on; and play space dividers (fences, walks, trees, and shrubs), a step-up drinking fountain, trash containers, and landscape planting

Layout The specific layout and shape of each play lot will be governed by existing site conditions and the facilities to be provided. The general layout principles are as follows:

1. The intensively used part of the play lot with play equipment and special facilities should be surrounded by a low enclosure with supplemental planting and provided with one entrance-exit. This design will discourage intrusion by animals or older children, provide adequate and safe control over the children, and prevent the area from becoming a thoroughfare. Adequate drainage should be provided.
2. Equipment should be selected and arranged with adequate surrounding space in small, natural play groups. Traffic flow should be planned to encourage movement throughout the play lot in a safe, orderly manner. This traffic flow may be facilitated by walks, plantings, low walls, and benches.
3. Equipment that enables large numbers of children to play without taking turns (climbers, play sculpture) should be located near the entrance, yet positioned so that it will not cause congestion. With such an arrangement,

children will tend to move more slowly to equipment that limits participation and requires turns (swings, slides), thus modifying the load factor and reducing conflicts.
4. Sand areas, play walls, playhouses, and play sculpture should be located away from such pieces of equipment as swings and slides for safety and to promote a creative atmosphere for the child's world of make-believe, Artificial or natural shade is desirable over the sedentary play pieces, where children will play on hot days without immediate supervision. Play sculpture may be placed in the sand area to enhance its value by providing a greater variety of play opportunities. A portion of the area should be maintained free of equipment for general sand play that is not in conflict with traffic flow.
5. Swings or other moving equipment should be located near the outside of the equipment area and should be sufficiently separated by walls or fences to discourage children from walking into them while the equipment is moving. Swings should be oriented toward the best view and away from the sun. Sliding equipment should preferably face north, away from the summer sun. Equipment with metal surfaces should be located in available shade.
6. Spray pools should be centrally located, and step-up drinking fountains strategically placed for convenience and economy in relation to water supply and waste disposal lines.
7. The open turfed area for running and active play and the shaded area for such quiet activities as reading and storytelling should be closely related to the enclosed equipment area and serve as buffer space around it.
8. Nonmovable benches should be conveniently located to assure good visibility and protection of the children at play. Durable trash containers should be provided and conveniently located to maintain a neat, orderly appearance.

SOURCE: *Children's Play Areas and Equipment,* U.S. Departments of the Army, the Navy, and the Air Force, 1969.

5.4 Playgrounds

ADVENTURE PLAYGROUND

Plans for an adventure playground in Freeport, New York, are shown in Figure 5-38.

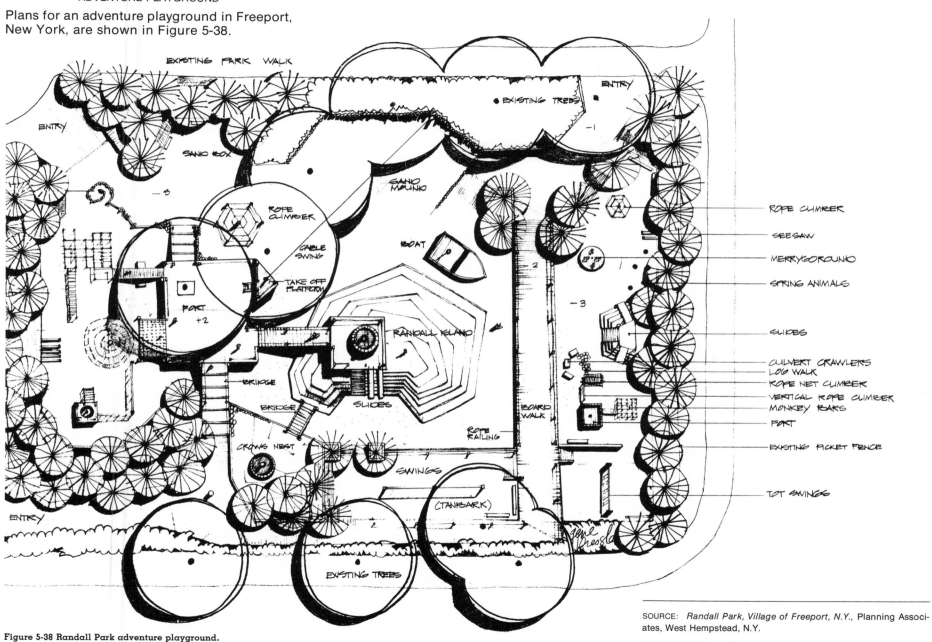

Figure 5-38 Randall Park adventure playground.

SOURCE: *Randall Park, Village of Freeport, N.Y.*, Planning Associates, West Hempstead, N.Y.

PLAYGROUND REQUIREMENTS

The playground is the chief center of outdoor play for children from 5 to 12 years of age. It also offers some opportunities for recreation for young people and adults.

At every elementary school the playground should be of sufficient size and design and be properly maintained to serve both the elementary educational program and the recreational needs of all age groups in the neighborhood. Since education and recreation programs complement each other in many ways, unnecessary duplication of essential outdoor recreational facilities should be avoided. Only where this joint function is not feasible should a separate playground be developed.

A playground may include (1) a play lot for preschool children, (2) an enclosed playground equipment area for elementary school children, (3) an open turfed area for active games, (4) shaded areas for quiet activities, (5) a paved multipurpose area, (6) an area for field games, and (7) circulation and buffer space.

Location A playground is an integral part of a complete elementary school development. School playgrounds and other playgrounds should be readily accessible from and conveniently related to the housing area served. There should be a playground within ¼ to ½ mile of every family housing unit.

Size and Number The recommended size of a playground is a minimum of 6 to 8 acres, which will serve approximately 1000 to 1500 families. The smallest playground that will accommodate essential activity spaces is about 3 acres, serving approximately 250 families (about 110 elementary school children). This minimum area should be increased at the rate of 0.2 to 0.4 acre for each additional 50 families. More than one playground should be provided where (1) a complete school playground is not feasible, (2) the population to be served exceeds 1500 families, or (3) the distance from some housing units is too great.

Activity Spaces and Elements A playground should contain the following basic activity space and elements:

1. A play lot
2. An enclosed playground equipment area with supplemental planting for elementary school children
3. An open turfed area for informal active games for elementary school children
4. Shaded areas for quiet activities such as reading, storytelling, quiet games, handicrafts, picnicking, and horseshoe pitching for both children and adults
5. A paved and well-lighted multipurpose area large enough for
   a. Activities such as roller skating, dancing, hopscotch, foursquare, and captain ball
   b. Games requiring specific courts, such as basketball, volleyball, tennis, handball, badminton, paddle tennis, and shuffleboard
6. An area for field games (including softball, junior baseball, touch or flag football, soccer, track and field activities, and other games), preferably well lighted, that will also serve for informal play of field sports and kite flying and be used occasionally for pageants, field days, and other community activities
7. Miscellaneous elements such as public shelters, storage space, toilet facilities, drinking fountains, walks, benches, trash containers, and buffer zones with planting

Layout The layout of a playground will vary with the size of the available site and its topography and the specific activities desired. It should fit the site with maximum preservation of the existing terrain and such natural features as large shade trees, interesting ground forms, rock outcrops, and streams. These features should be integrated into the layout to the maximum extent feasible for appropriate activity spaces, as natural divisions of various use areas, and for landscape interest. Grading should be kept to a minimum consistent with activity needs, adequate drainage, and erosion control.

The general principles of layout are as follows:

1. The play lot and the playground equipment area should be located adjacent to the school and to each other.
2. An open turfed area for informal active play should be located close to the play lot and the playground equipment area for convenient use by all elementary school children.
3. Areas for quiet activities for children and adults should be somewhat removed from active play spaces and be close to tree-shaded areas and other natural features of the site.
4. The paved multipurpose area should be set off from other areas by planting and be located near the school gymnasium so that it may be used for physical education without disturbing other school classes. All posts or net supports required on the courts should be constructed with sleeves and caps that will permit removal of the posts and supports.
5. The area for field games should be located on fairly level, well-drained land with finished grades not in excess of 2.5 percent. A minimum grade of 1 percent is acceptable on pervious soils having good percolation for proper drainage.
6. In general, the area of a playground may be divided as follows:
   a. Approximately half of the area should be parklike, including the open turfed areas for active play, the shaded areas for quiet activities, and the miscellaneous elements as described in paragraph 7.
   b. The other half of the area should include ¾ to 1 acre for the play lot, the playground equipment area, and the paved multipurpose area and 1¾ acres (for softball) to 4 acres (for baseball) for the field games area.
7. The playground site should be fully developed with landscape planting for activity control and traffic control and for attractiveness. This site also should have accessible public shelters, storage for maintenance and recreation equipment, toilet facilities, drinking fountains, walks wide enough for strollers and carriages, bicycle paths, benches for adults and children, and trash containers.

PLAYGROUND EQUIPMENT

Basic Play Equipment Play equipment may include swings, slides, and merry-go-rounds; various types of climbers; balancing equipment such as balance beams, conduits,

SOURCE: *Children's Play Areas and Equipment*, U.S. Departments of the Army, the Navy, and the Air Force, 1969.

leaping posts, and boxes; hanging equipment such as parallel bars, horizontal bars, and ladders; play walls and playhouses; and a variety of play sculpture forms. Different types of play equipment should be provided for preschool children and for elementary school children to meet the developmental and recreational needs of the two age groups.

Play Lot Equipment for Preschool Children The accompanying table indicates the types, quantities, and minimum play space requirements for various kinds of equipment totaling about 2800 square feet. This area, plus additional space for circulation and play space dividers, will accommodate a full range of play lot equipment serving a neighborhood containing approximately fifty preschool children (about 165 families).

Equipment	Number of pieces	Play space requirements (feet)
Climber	1	10 × 25
Junior swing set (four swings)	1	16 × 32
Play sculpture	1	10 × 10
Play wall or playhouse	1	15 × 15
Sand area	1	15 × 15
Slide	1	10 × 25
Spray pool (including deck)	1	36 × 36

Smaller play lots may be developed to serve a neighborhood containing about thirty children (about 100 families), using a limited selection of equipment with play space requirements totaling about 1200 square feet. This area, plus additional space for circulation and play space dividers, should be planned with the following desirable priorities: (1) a sand area, (2) a climbing device such as a climber, a play wall or a piece of play sculpture, (3) a slide, and (4) a swing set. If several play lots are provided, the equipment selections should be complementary rather than of the same type. For example, one play lot may include play walls or a playhouse, while another may provide a piece of play sculpture. Also, such a costly but popu-

lar item as a spray pool may be justified in only one out of every two or three play lots provided.

Playground Equipment for Elementary School Children The accompanying table indicates types, quantities, and minimum play space requirements totaling about 6600 square feet. This area, plus additional space for circulation, miscellaneous elements, and buffer zones, will accommodate a full range of playground equipment serving approximately fifty children at one time.

Equipment	Number of pieces	Play space requirements (feet)
Balance beam	1	15 × 30
Climbers	3	21 × 50
Climbing poles	3	10 × 20
Horizontal bars	3	15 × 30
Horizontal ladder	1	15 × 30
Merry-go-round	1	40 × 40
Parallel bars	1	15 × 30
Senior swing set (six swings)	1	30 × 45
Slide	1	12 × 35

Surfacing The selection of suitable surfacing materials for each type of play area and for circulation paths or walks, roads, and parking areas should be based on the following considerations:

1. *Function.* The surface should suit the purpose and the specific function of the area, such as surfaces for court games or field games and surfaces under play equipment. Choice of the surface should also depend on whether the area is multipurpose or single-purpose and whether it is intended for seasonal or year-round usage.

2. *Economy.* The factors of economy are the initial cost, replacement cost, and maintenance cost. Often an initially more expensive surfacing is the least expensive in the long run because of reduced maintenance.

3. *Durability.* The durability of the surface should be evaluated in the light of its resis-

tance to the general wear caused by the participants and of its resistance to extended periods of outdoor weathering such as sunlight, rain, freezing, sand, and dust.

4. *Cleanliness.* The surface should be clean and attractive to participants, it should not attract or harbor insects or rodents, and it should not track into adjacent buildings or discolor children's clothing.

5. *Maintenance.* Maintenance must be evaluated in the light not only of cost but also of the time when the facility is not available for use because of repair or upkeep.

6. *Safety.* The safety of participants is a primary consideration in selecting a play surface and should not be compromised for the sake of economy.

7. *Appearance.* A surface that has an attractive appearance and harmonizes with its surroundings is very desirable. Surfacing materials should encourage optimum use and enjoyment by all participants, and channel the activities in an orderly manner by providing visual contrasts.

Evaluation of Surfacing Materials The various types of surfacing material have their advantages and disadvantages.

1. *Turf.* This material is generally considered to be the best surface for many of the recreation activities carried on at play lots and playgrounds. Although turf is not feasible for heavily used play areas, most park and recreation authorities recommend using it wherever practicable. Underground irrigation sprinkler systems with rubber-top valves should be specified in areas with inadequate seasonal rainfall to maintain a turf cover. The major reasons for using turf are that it is relatively soft, providing greater safety than other surfaces, and that it has a pleasing, restful appearance with great appeal to participants. A turf surface is especially suitable for open and informal play areas for younger children and the large field game

SOURCE: *Children's Play Areas and Equipment,* U.S. Departments of the Army, the Navy, and the Air Force, 1969.

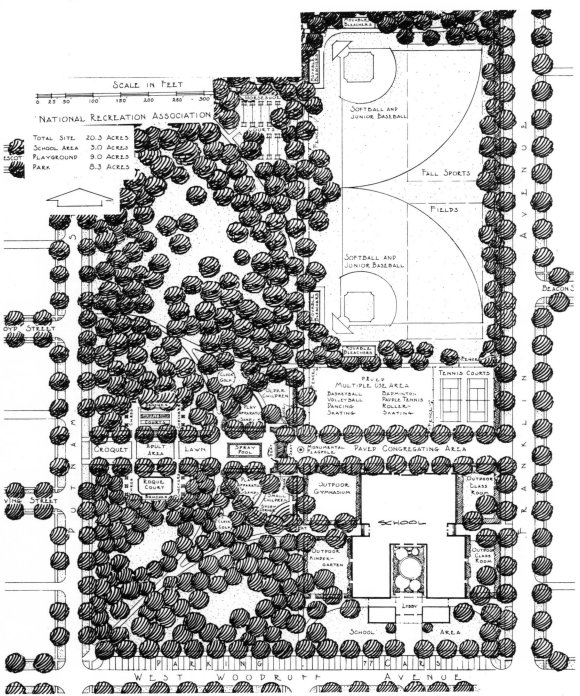

SCALE IN FEET

0 25 50 100' 150 200 250 300

NATIONAL RECREATION ASSOCIATION

TOTAL SITE   20.3 ACRES
SCHOOL AREA   3.0 ACRES
PLAYGROUND   9.0 ACRES
PARK   8.3 ACRES

areas for sports and general recreation use.

2. *Bituminous concrete.* This flexible paving material is the most generally used material for paving play areas. The designer should note that various asphalt grades and mixes, as well as color coatings to improve appearance and maintenance, are available. A suitable mix and careful grade control should be used to obtain a smooth, even surface, economical construction, and little or no maintenance. Bituminous concrete pavement is especially useful for paved multipurpose areas, for tennis, basketball, and volleyball courts, for roller-skating and ice-skating rinks, and for walks, roads, and parking areas.

3. *Portland cement concrete.* This rigid paving material is the most favored type of surface for use in specialized areas where permanence is desired. It provides uniformity, maximum durability, and little or no maintenance. A portland cement concrete surface is especially useful for court games requiring a true, even surface, such as tennis and handball, for shuffleboard courts, for roller-skating and ice-skating rinks, and for walks, curbs, roads, and parking areas.

Portland cement concrete and bituminous concrete surfaces are generally considered for many of the same uses. Choice of either one should include appropriateness for the purpose intended, initial cost, and long-term cost.

4. *Synthetic materials.* Synthetic materials that have a cushioning effect are being used by some school, park, and recreation departments, primarily for safety, under play equipment. Several companies have developed successful resilient materials that provide excellent safety surfaces; these have been more expensive than the other materials discussed here. A number of cities have conducted studies using these surfaces.

Figure 5-39

SOURCE: *Children's Play Areas and Equipment,* U.S. Departments of the Army, the Navy, and the Air Force, 1969.

ADVANTAGES AND DISADVANTAGES OF VARIOUS SURFACINGS FOR RECREATION AREAS

Surfacing type	Advantages	Disadvantages
Turf	Soft surface, ideal for many play purposes; low first cost	Cannot be used in wet weather; difficult to maintain
Natural soil	Low first cost; soft surface	Muddy in wet weather; dusty in dry weather
Gravel	Low first cost; pleasing appearance	Thrown about by children to such extent that it is unsuitable for any use as surfacing in housing developments
Sand-clay and clay-gravel	Low cost when suitable material is available; reasonably soft surface	Difficult to get properly proportioned mixture
Brick on sand cushion	Attractive appearance	Initial cost relatively high
Stone paving blocks on sand cushion or natural soil	Low cost when salvaged from old pavements; satisfactory appearance; durability	Surface too rough for play use; maintenance cost relatively high
Precast concrete slabs on sand or natural soil	Year-round utility; satisfactory appearance	
Flagstones on sand or natural soil	Year-round utility; pleasing appearance; durability	
Bituminous concrete	Good surface for most play purposes when properly specified and laid; not so hard on feet as portland cement concrete; year-round utility	Rough and abrasive unless properly specified and constructed (competent inspection essential for good workmanship); hot for bare feet; possibility of becoming soft; unattractive in large areas
Cork asphalt	Resiliency; excellent surface for many play purposes; year-round utility; satisfactory appearance	Comparatively high cost; (competent inspection essential for good workmanship); softening in very hot weather
Portland cement concrete	Year-round utility; minimum maintenance expense; good surface for wheeled toys, roller skating, and some court games	Lack of resiliency; initial cost relatively high; large areas requiring expansion joints; whiteness and glare of large areas unattractive

5. *Miscellaneous materials.* Materials used for specific areas include sand, sawdust, tanbark, or wood chips around and under play equipment, earth on baseball diamond infields, and brick, flagstone, or tile on walks and terraces.

See Figure 5-39 for a playground design and the accompanying table for a comparison of various surfacings.

SOURCE: *Public Housing Design,* National Housing Agency, Federal Public Housing Authority, 1946.

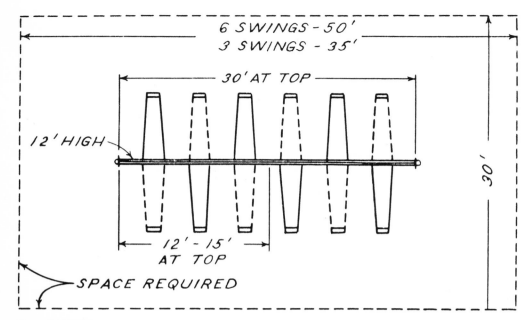

Figure 5-40 Swings.

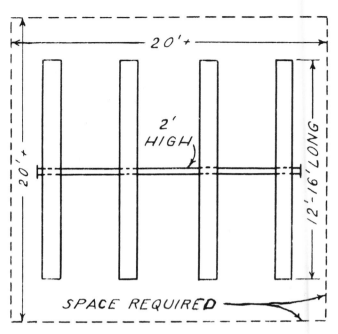

Figure 5-43 Seesaws.

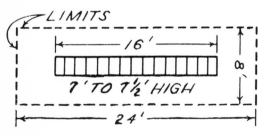

Figure 5-41 Horizontal ladder.

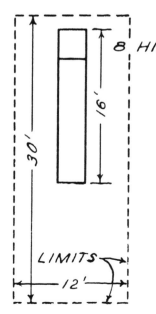

Figure 5-44 Slides.

Space requirements for various types of playground equipment are shown in Figures 5-40, 5-41, 5-42, 5-43, and 5-44.

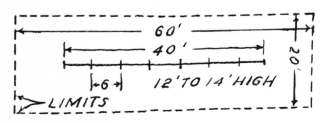

Figure 5-42 Traveling rings.

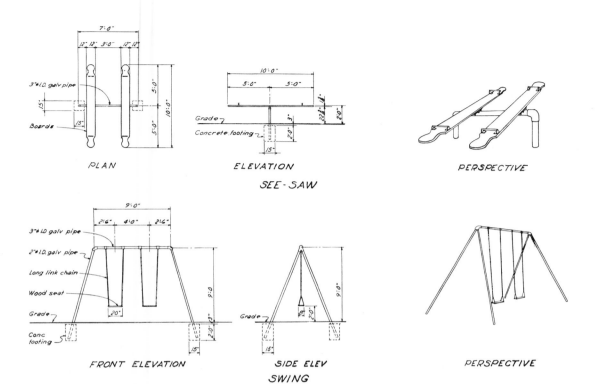

PLAN   ELEVATION   PERSPECTIVE

SEE-SAW

FRONT ELEVATION   SIDE ELEV   PERSPECTIVE

SWING

AREAS FOR CHILDREN'S GAMES

Space requirements for seesaws and swings are shown in Figure 5-45, and areas for a number of games are given in the accompanying table.

CHILDREN'S AREAS

Name	Dimensions of game areas (feet)	Use dimensions (feet)	Space required (square feet)	Number of players
Archery	60–150 in length; targets 15 feet apart	50 × 135 (minimum) 50 × 235 (maximum)	6,750 11,750	2 or more
Baseball	75-foot diamond 82-foot diamond	250 × 250	62,500	18
Basketball	40 × 60	50 × 70	3,500	10
Field hockey	120 × 200 (maximum)	150 × 250 (maximum)	37,500	22
Hopscotch	5 × 12½	10 × 20	200	2 or 4
Horseshoes	Stakes 25 feet apart	12 × 40	480	2 or 4
Marbles	10-foot diameter	18 × 18	324	2–6
Paddle tennis	13½ × 39 (singles) 18 × 39 (doubles)	25 × 60 30 × 60	1,500 1,800	2 4
Soccer	100 × 200	125 × 240	30,000	22
Softball	45-foot diamond	175 × 175 (average)	30,625	18
Speedball	120 × 220	150 × 260	39,000	22
Team dodge ball:				
Boys	Circle 40 feet in diameter	60 × 60	3,600	20
Girls	Circle 35 feet in diameter	50 × 50	2,500	20
Touch football	120 × 240	140 × 280	39,200	18–22
Volleyball	25 × 50	40 × 70	2,800	12–16

SOURCE: Table—H. S. Conover, *Public Grounds Maintenance Handbook,* Tennessee Valley Authority, Knoxville, Tenn., 1953.

5.5 Outdoor Swimming Pools

PUBLIC SWIMMING POOLS

In the development of any outdoor swimming pool and related facilities, there should first be a master plan of the area in which the pool is to be located. A swimming pool by itself is never as successful as a pool planned in conjunction with other recreational facilities, such as baseball diamonds, tennis courts, volleyball courts, a craft center, and a community center building. One activity complements another, and a pool thus related to other recreational facilities will be much more successful and easier to administer.

Residential pools and pools designed for hotels and motor courts are used almost exclusively for recreational swimming and sunbathing. On the other hand, pools at private clubs, city parks, and recreation areas are normally used for both recreational and competitive swimming. Competitive swimming is the impetus for wide usage of the pools by youths and young adults.

Publicly owned and operated pools probably constitute the largest market today for outdoor pools. An increasing number of public pools are being built each year. The private swimming-club–pool idea is fast expanding. The club pool meets a great need and is an excellent idea, but it generally will not take care of the needs of a community. The vast majority of potential swimmers come from families that cannot afford a family membership in a public pool, or an individual membership, or a daily gate fee. Therefore, the building of swimming pools for the general public today is largely a governmental responsibility, whether it be municipal, county, state, or federal.

Classification of Outdoor Pools

Public Pools   Public pools are ordinarily those owned and operated by municipalities, counties, schools, park districts, states (as in state parks), and the federal government (as in a national park).

Privately Owned Pools   The second category of sponsorship is the privately owned pool that serves the public. The YMCA, YWCA, boys'

clubs, YMHA, and other organizations build outdoor pools or indoor-outdoor pools that serve both winter and summer needs.

At most country clubs today, an outdoor swimming pool is considered a necessity if the club is to be a family-type club rather than just a golf club. These pools must be attractively designed, well built, and expertly operated. The private swimming club is expanding and serves a real need, particularly in suburban areas.

Most apartment houses are including a swimming pool in their complexes because they realize that this is a necessity if the apartment units are to be rented at capacity. Rooftop pools are no longer unique.

Many public housing projects are including swimming pools. These are publicly owned but are considered private since use of a pool is restricted to the occupants of a particular housing project.

Hotels are fast coming to realize that they must have a pool, and the outdoor pool is the usual thing. In many northern communities, the pool has been enclosed by either a permanent or a semipermanent structure.

Pools are included as a necessary attraction at resorts and resort hotels and motels. Motels for transients must also include a pool, even though some of them seem to be satisfied with the smallest pool that will answer the purpose: in many instances a pool measuring only 20 by 40 feet is installed.

Some motels have become aware of the non-use of the pools by their guests in the middle of the day, and the pools are being made available to community groups during this slack period. In several instances, the pools have been opened to underprivileged or low-income groups that lack other swimming facilities.

Commercial Pools   Commercial pools are those operated for a profit by an individual owner or corporation. These pools are usually separate and independent of other recreational facilities. Many such pools have been built in the past 25 or 30 years, but experience has proved that a pool by itself is not as good a business proposition as a pool with other recreational facilities. Such facilities can include a

par-3 golf course, a golf driving range, a miniature golf course, a bowling lane, a skating rink, or a group picnicking area.

Types of Pools by Design   A rectangle was probably the original pool shape, and a great many rectangular pools are still being built. Some of the first pools measured 50 by 100 feet or even 100 by 200 feet. Many indoor pools measured 30 by 60 feet and, in some few cases, 35 by 75 feet. A rectangular pool measuring 45 by 75 feet is quite acceptable today both indoors and outdoors, since it includes the 25-yard short course for competitive swimming. In some cases, a pool 60 feet wide, or preferably 75 feet (25-yard short course), and 50 meters (164 feet ½ inch) long is also quite acceptable.

The rectangular pool has a comparatively low construction cost and is easy to supervise. However, in small pools there is a low percentage of shallow water, and only one competitive activity can take place at a time. The rectangular pool is a traditional type of pool, but it is not as dramatic or as interesting as some of the free-form pools, which can easily include the proper competitive swimming lengths, make possible larger deck areas, offer an interesting shape that fits into the landscape, and give variety and interest to the activities.

The T-shaped pool was probably one of the first pools to break away from the rectangular shape, and it is today a very fine shape for a pool. The top of the T can be 45 feet by 164 feet ½ inch, preferably 60 feet by 164 feet ½ inch, and sometimes 75 feet by 164 feet ½ inch, thereby providing both short and long courses and an entire area of so-called shallow water that is 3 feet 3 inches to 5 feet in depth.

The lower part of the T should be reserved for the diving area and be separated from the top of the T by a float line. This is probably one of the most popular pool designs, although the L-shaped pool includes the same features,

SOURCE: *Planning Areas and Facilities for Health, Physical Education, and Recreation,* Athletic Institute and American Association for Health, Physical Education, and Recreation, Washington, 1965.

except that the deep area is placed at one end rather than in the middle.

The Z-shaped pool is also extremely functional, having the competitive swimming lengths and general swimming area in the center of the Z, the diving area offset from the main part on one side, and the extremely shallow area (extending to 2 feet) off the other side of the general swimming area. In this shape the swimming area could be the 25-yard or 50-meter distance. In some cases, the Z-shaped pool can include both the 25-yard and the 50-meter lengths. Although recreational swimming is the prime objective, the objectives of a good recreational area and competitive swimming lengths can be combined in such a pool. The most obvious advantages in the T-, L-, and Z-shaped pools are the separation of divers and swimmers, tending to eliminate the danger of collisions; and the provision of a larger shallow-water area. These shapes do, however, present some supervision problems.

The multiple-pool idea is an extremely good one, especially if funds are not available to build all the swimming facilities desired at one time. The program can be phased so that one pool is built at a time.

In a country club where there is need to spread out the use of the pool area and have pools for different groups (adults and juniors), a competitive pool, a diving pool, and a play pool for small children will be found most advantageous. The adult pool has been conceived to provide a special area for adults only. This is particularly desirable in a country club setting where alcoholic beverages are served around a pool.

The junior pool is a pool ranging from 2 to 3 feet in depth where swimming instruction can be conducted for children up to the age of 10.

The tots' play pool, more commonly known as the wading pool, has a water depth of from 0 to 15 or 18 inches. It is designed for the comfort and convenience of youngsters below the age of 6. The more completely equipped tots' play pool includes a 6- to 10-foot walk surrounding the pool; the entire area is enclosed with a barrier, such as a 3-foot chain link fence

(knuckle-finish top and bottom) or a masonry sitting wall for parents or others accompanying the children.

The separate diving pool has many advantages. Since there is usually a conflict between swimmers and divers, the safety feature is a good justification for the separation of the main pool from the diving pool.

There are advantages, certainly, to separate pools, safety being the principal one. However, separate pools cost more, require a greater number of lifeguards, need more extensive mechanical and water treatment systems, and occupy more space.

Free-form pools are ordinarily restricted to use as resort pools and residential pools. This shape is not favored for the public or institutional types of pool.

The spray pool is popular in many communities. In some instances, the water goes to waste, and in other locations the spray pool is combined with a wading area. Spray pools measuring 30 to 40 feet in diameter have been designed to serve also as dance and roller-skating areas. In the majority of cases, the pool with a wading area has proved more popular than the spray pool.

Recommended Sizes for Outdoor Pools It has been customary for cities to construct large pools. A large pool may sometimes be desirable. Most authorities agree, however, that a pool 50 meters long and 45, 60, or 75 feet wide, with a diving area to one side (as is possible in the T or L shapes), is as large a pool as any community needs. If a pool of this size does not adequately serve the needs of the community, it would probably be advantageous to have a second pool in another location. A pool is usually more popular and more successful if children and adults do not have to travel out of their own neighborhood.

In cities where a pool with 25-yard and 50-meter competitive swimming lengths and a large recreational swimming area can be justified, this may be the most desirable method of providing swimming facilities. As this pool is outgrown or as the need for additional swimming facilities is evident, it may be that the next

pool or next group of pools should be what is ordinarily called the neighborhood pool. This is a rectangular or fan-shaped pool measuring approximately 45 by 75 feet. An L-shaped pool with a swimming area of 45 by 75 feet and a diving area of 40 by 42 feet would be even better. The neighborhood pool has the advantage of making it possible for persons to put on their bathing suits at home. It also enables them to swim with their friends.

In designing a pool for a neighborhood or a community, the size of the pool should be in direct proportion to the number of people to be served. In cities of 30,000 population or less, the daily average attendance may be expected to be from 5 to 6 percent of the population, about one-third of whom will be at the pool at any one time during the day. On peak days the pool may be used by as much as 10 percent of the population.

General Planning Considerations Adequate area is needed around a pool not only to dignify its setting and location but to serve as a buffer from nearby streets and residences. Space must also be provided for parking and for other recreational areas and facilities.

A pool should not be located in a low spot. Water from the surrounding area will drain into the pool, and unless precautions are taken for proper drainage around the edge of the pool, considerable water will penetrate the area under the deck and floor and be a source of constant annoyance and engineering problems.

A pool should not be located in a grove of trees. Leaves fall into the pool and keep it dirty, clog filters and the hair and lint catcher, and in many ways leave a pool in an unsatisfactory condition. Trees also keep the sun away from the pool, and to be successful a pool area must have sunshine. The pool should be located so

SOURCE: *Planning Areas and Facilities for Health, Physical Education, and Recreation,* Athletic Institute and American Association for Health, Physical Education, and Recreation, Washington, 1965.

that buildings and trees to the west are at such a distance that they will not shade the pool in the late afternoon.

Location in relation to streets is most important. A pool must be near main traffic arteries for good circulation and for accessibility, but the pool itself should not be too near a busy street. The dirt from the street will blow into the pool and give considerable trouble in the filtration system. If possible, the pool should be set back from 200 to 300 feet or more from the street.

Recreation facilities supplementing a swimming pool can consist of recreation buildings or community centers, softball and baseball diamonds, a football field, pitch-and-putt, par-3, or regulation golf courses, a multiple-use paved area, an area for playground equipment for both small children and older groups, and parking areas. Games and sports such as tennis, croquet, shuffleboard, badminton, handball, horseshoes, paddle tennis, table tennis, deck tennis, roller skating, and volleyball can also be included.

Pools are often built in an area just large enough for the pool, no provision being made for other facilities. A swimming pool should be a part of an overall recreational development whenever possible. If circumstances will permit, the bathhouse should be designed as a section of a community recreation center. This is especially true when the building includes a gymnasium, the same dressing rooms serving the swimming pool during the summer and the gymnasium in the winter. It is quite possible that the dressing rooms will require a little more space, but this will certainly be more economical than designing multiple dressing areas. The bathhouse can be used the year around rather than just during the summer months. Relating the pool to the community center reduces the cost of administration and operation.

If the pool and a community recreation building are not related, a separate bathhouse is required. Of the many new ideas in bathhouse design, one of the most interesting is the bathhouse without a roof other than the roof cover-ing the immediate dressing space around the wall and the toilet facilities. Showers are usually out in the middle in the sunshine, and, in some cases flowers and grass areas have been incorporated in the interior of the bathhouse. The clothes checkroom is, of course, completely covered and can be secured. This type of design is economical to build, and while it will probably require more space, it is the kind of bathhouse that is ventilated. It is, however, subject to vandalism to a greater extent than the closed bathhouse.

When space is at a premium, a roof is essential for either a summer or a year-round bathhouse. The best plan is a roof with sky domes to permit natural light. All windows can be omitted since adequate light will come in through the sky domes. Vent domes and exhaust fans can be used for circulating the air. This will provide a bathhouse that is vandalproof, economical to construct, and easily maintained. Rest rooms and dressing rooms should be kept to a minimum size, and construction should be simple so that the cost will be minimized.

The pool and deck area should be completely surrounded with a chain link fence at least 7 feet high with knuckle-finish top and bottom. This fence is a safety feature for those using the pool and contributes to maintaining proper control of the facility. Plantings on both sides of the fence are desirable. The wading pool or play pool and space for the smaller children, usually located immediately adjacent to the swimming pool, should be separated from it by a fence and a gate.

Prevailing winds are an important consideration. When the water is cool, swimmers do not want the wind to dry them off too fast, thereby causing them to become chilled. Therefore, swimmers should be protected from prevailing winds by a proper orientation of the pool and bathhouse so that the bathhouse is on the side of the prevailing wind. A canvas may be hung on the fence, a plastic or glass panel may be provided, or a masonry wall may be installed to shield bathers from the wind. In northern climates windbreaks are almost essential.

For a pool to receive full usage, overhead and underwater lights should be provided for night use. Overhead lighting should be a minimum of 1.2 to 3 watts per square foot of pool surface. Championship meets require a 30-footcandle level of illumination 3 feet above the water surface. Overhead lighting can be provided by overhead floodlights mounted on 30-foot-high steel poles.

The underwater lighting of a pool should be planned with great care. If possible, the lights should be placed on the sidewalls rather than on the end walls. If they are placed on the end walls, they should be on a separate electrical circuit so that they can be turned off during swimming meets. Otherwise, the swimmers will be looking directly into the lights. Underwater lights placed on the end walls also present difficulties in that swimmers, in making flip turns at the ends of the swimming lanes, might kick and break the glass lenses. The lights should be placed near the bottom of the pool and should be located directly under the float lines and away from the centers of the swimming lanes so that swimmers will not kick the lights in turning. Underwater lights are valuable for safety and for aesthetics. It is recommended that 2 to 2.5 watts per square foot of water area be provided.

Construction and Design Factors

Water Depth Pools used for both recreational and competitive swimming often have a water depth in the shallow end of only 3 or 3½ feet, but provisions are made for flooding the gutters to secure extra depth during swimming meets. The water depth at the shallow end of a pool, as recommended by the Amateur Athletic Union (AAU), should be 4 feet. This depth will enable swimmers to make turns. Between 75 and 85 percent of the water area of a pool should have a depth of less than 5 feet. This is important because more than 85 percent of the

SOURCE: *Planning Areas and Facilities for Health, Physical Education, and Recreation,* Athletic Institute and American Association for Health, Physical Education, and Recreation, Washington, 1965.

swimmers will use the shallow water; only a small percentage will be in the deep water at one time.

Diving Facilities Nothing adds more to the attractiveness of a swimming pool, from the standpoint of both the swimmers and the spectators, than good diving facilities. While 1- and 3-meter boards have long been in use, many pools are now installing diving towers with 3-, 5-, 7½, and 10-meter diving platforms.

For the 10-meter platform, which is 32 feet 10 inches above the water surface, the minimum depth of the water must be 16 feet at a point 7 feet from the back wall of the pool. The hopper bottom should be at least 20 feet wide, and it should rise gradually to a water depth of 14 feet at a point 42 feet from the back wall of the pool. The overall diving area should extend a minimum length of 60 feet to a water depth of 6 feet, and the minimum width of the diving area should be 45 feet.

The 5-meter platform should be 16 feet 5 inches above the water surface, with a minimum water depth of 12½ feet, although a 14-foot depth is recommended. The 3-meter board should be 10 feet above the water surface, and the minimum depth of the water should be 12 feet. The board is installed so that the end of the board is 5 feet beyond the edge of the pool wall. The 1-meter board is similarly installed, the board being 39.37 inches above the surface of the water and the depth of the water being 9 feet.

The diving platforms will provide facilities for practice for various events and for official AAU and accredited Olympic tryouts and meets. The diving towers should preferably be constructed of reinforced concrete.

Pool Finishes It is the generally accepted practice that outdoor pool walls and floor be painted with a good pool paint. A pool should be painted pure white and not an off-color white. A good reason for this practice is that dirt or silt in the pool is immediately evident and attracts the attention of those responsible for keeping the pool clean. More important is the safety feature, since objects on the bottom of the pool are easily visible in a pure-white pool. Then, too, the appearance of the pool water is improved by using a pure-white background, which brings out the natural blue color of the clear water. A pool should never be painted with blue or green paint.

A very fine pool finish is obtained by using plaster of white marble dust, which should be applied during the construction period; however, it may be applied to an old pool. This finish is more durable than paint and, if cared for properly, will last eight years or more. For the finish to be successful, it must be applied by qualified technicians.

The finish of the floor and walls of a pool should be neither too rough nor too smooth. If the floor is too smooth (for instance, glazed tile), the swimmer will slide down. If it is too rough, the swimmer's feet will be scratched and hurt, and the pool will be difficult to keep clean.

Water Temperature Water temperature is important in a swimming pool. If the water is too cold, as is often the case when its source is a deep well or a spring, it is not comfortable for swimming. The most desirable temperature for water in an outdoor pool will vary with the region of the country and the atmospheric temperature. The colder the air temperature, the warmer the water, and vice versa. In colder climates, water temperatures of 78 to 80 degrees Fahrenheit should be maintained, and in air temperatures of 90 degrees Fahrenheit or more, the pool water should be maintained at 72 to 74 degrees to be comfortable for the bathers.

Deck Space It is important that the maximum amount of deck space be provided for the outdoor pool because this space greatly increases the pool's capacity. Surveys have shown that approximately one-third to one-half of the total number of swimmers in the pool area are in the water at one time. The cost per square foot of the walk or deck around a pool will usually be less than 10 percent of the cost per square foot of the water area. In addition, the deck area, if it is of sufficient width, can be used by the swimmers for sunbathing and lounging. If possible, the deck area should exceed by 100 percent the square footage of the water area of a pool and should be raised from 6 to 9 inches above the surface of the water.

SOURCE: *Planning Areas and Facilities for Health, Physical Education, and Recreation,* Athletic Institute and American Association for Health, Physical Education, and Recreation, Washington, 1965.

RECOMMENDED SWIMMING POOL DIMENSIONS

Size	A	B	C	D	E	F	G	H	J	K	L	Length of springboard	Overhang	Height of diving board stand
12 × 28	1' 6"	7' 0"	7' 0"	6' 6"	6' 0"		2' 6"	3' 0"	4' 6"	6' 6"	5' 0"	0	0	None
12 × 30	1' 6"	7' 0"	9' 0"	6' 6"	6' 0"		2' 6"	3' 0"	4' 6"	6' 6"	5' 0"	0	0	None
12 × 32	1' 6"	7' 0"	9' 0"	8' 6"	6' 0"		3' 0"	3' 6"	5' 0"	7' 6"	6' 0"	8' 0"	1' 6"	Deck level
15 × 30	1' 6"	7' 0"	8' 6"	7' 0"	6' 0"		3' 0"	3' 6"	5' 0"	7' 6"	6' 0"	8' 0"	1' 6"	Deck level
15 × 32	1' 6"	7' 0"	9' 0"	8' 6"	6' 0"		3' 0"	3' 6"	5' 0"	7' 6"	6' 0"	8' 0"	1' 6"	Deck level
15 × 35	2' 0"	8' 0"	10' 6"	8' 6"	6' 0"		3' 0"	3' 6"	5' 0"	8' 6"	7' 0"	10' 0"	2' 0"	Deck level to 12"
16 × 35	2' 0"	8' 0"	10' 6"	8' 6"	6' 0"		3' 0"	3' 6"	5' 0"	8' 6"	7' 0"	10' 0"	2' 0"	Deck level to 12"
16 × 40	2' 0"	8' 0"	10' 6"	13' 6"	6' 0"		3' 0"	3' 6"	5' 0"	8' 6"	7' 0"	10' 0"	2' 6"	12" to 18"
18 × 38	2' 0"	8' 0"	12' 6"	9' 6"	6' 0"		3' 0"	3' 6"	5' 0"	8' 6"	7' 0"	10' 0"	3' 0"	12" to 18"
18 × 40	3' 0"	9' 0"	11' 6"			16' 6"	3' 0"	See Note A	5' 0"	9' 0"	7' 6"	12' 0"	3' 0"	12" to 39"
20 × 40	3' 0"	9' 0"	11' 6"			16' 6"	3' 0"	See Note A	5' 0"	9' 0"	7' 6"	12' 0"	3' 0"	12" to 39"

NOTE A: Floor is to slope from 3 feet deep to a uniform slope to the 5-foot depth.
NOTE B: Provide about 30 square feet of floor space for filtration equipment (preferably inside the building).
NOTE C: Slope walks away from pool at ¼ inch per foot; provide drains as required.
NOTE D: Provide self-closing, self-latching gates capable of being locked.

Figure 5-46 Residential pool. (a) Plan. (b) Typical section.

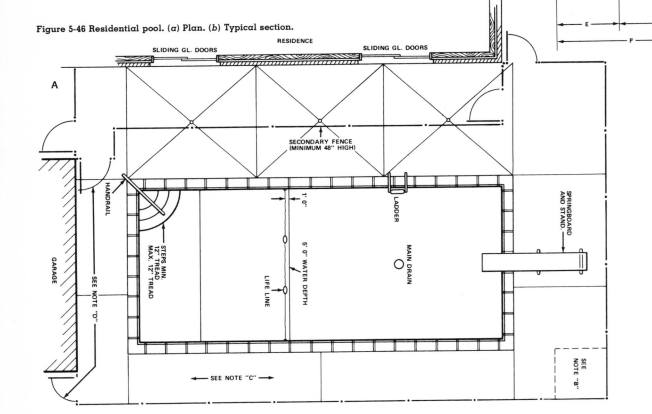

SWIMMING POOL SIZES

Figure 5-46 shows a plan (a) and a typical section (b) for a residential swimming pool. Data in the illustrations are elaborated in the accompanying table.

SOURCE: *Design Guide for Home Safety,* U.S. Department of Housing and Urban Development, 1972.

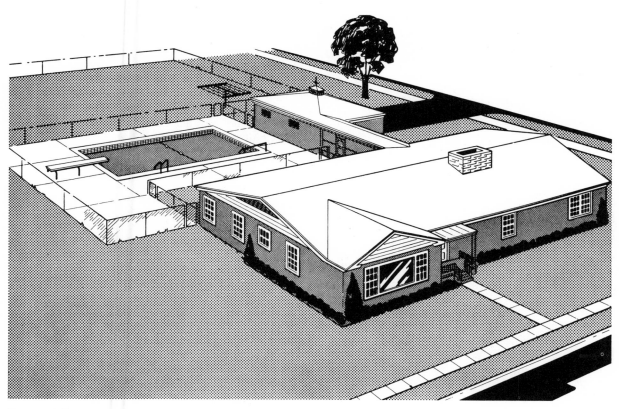

Figure 5-47 A residential swimming pool and its enclosure.

SWIMMING POOL ENCLOSURE

The following guidelines, recommendations, and suggestions for the design and construction of a protective enclosure will help to make a residential pool safer:

1. Substantial fence or protective barrier with a minimum height of 6 feet
2. Fence bracing and framing on the pool side
3. Fencing material with vertical segments or close mesh to minimize footholds and handholds
4. Fence flush with hard deck surface; 6 inches below ground level if installed on dirt surface
5. No solid fencing on living-area side
6. Secondary fence 48 inches high if the pool is contiguous with the home or another building
7. All openings equipped with self-closing, self-latching gates with provisions for locking
8. Gate latch located 3½ to 4 feet above the walking surface
9. Gate material and construction the same as that of fencing

A residential swimming pool and its enclosure are illustrated in Figure 5-47.

SOURCE: *Design Guide for Home Safety*, U.S. Department of Housing and Urban Development, 1972.

5.6 Waterfront Development

SWIMMING

In the following discussion of the location and construction of waterfront facilities, natural and artificial waterfronts are discussed separately.

Planning the Waterfront Location

Criteria for Natural Waterfronts The natural waterfront site should have certain characteristics to make it desirable for use in aquatic programs. The recommended criteria for the selection of waterfront or beach sites are discussed below. Helpful checklists have also been provided.

Water characteristics. The water content should be of a sanitary quality affording safe usage. The health conditions of a site are judged primarily by a careful examination of both its surrounding environs and its water content. The first is accomplished by a careful field analysis; the second, by a laboratory analysis. Both examinations can indicate the bacterial quality and physical clarity of the water.

CHECKLIST:

1. Surrounding water source
2. Water quality (bacterial content)
3. Water clarity (visibility test)

Water condition characteristics. The circulation of the water through the potential waterfront site should be examined. Slow-moving water can produce swampy or built-up mud conditions, while fast-moving water can produce undercurrents and erosive conditions.

The ideal water temperature for swimming ranges from 72 to 78 degrees Fahrenheit, depending upon the air temperature. The American Public Health Association indicates that less than 500 gallons of additional water per bather per day is too small a diluting volume unless there is sufficient application of disinfection.

CHECKLIST:

1. Rate of water flow
2. Rate of water turnover

3. Water-level fluctuation
4. Water constancy
5. Availability of water
6. Types of currents and undertow
7. Outlet for water
8. Eddies, floods, waves, or wash
9. Weeds, fungi, mold, or slime
10. Parasites, fish, and animals
11. Debris, broken glass, and so on
12. Oil slick
13. Odor, color, and taste

Bottom characteristics. The waterfront bottom should be unobstructed and clear of debris, rock, muck, mulch, peat, and mud. The waterfront should not be in an area where the channel shifts or silt builds up. The most desirable bottom is white sand with a gradual pitch sloping from the shallow to the deep end. The bottom should not be precipitous or too shallow or have holes, pots, channels, bars, or islands.

The bottom should be of gravel, sand, or stable hard ground to afford firm and secure footing. Soundings should be taken in a boat, and an actual underwater survey should be undertaken before a final decision is made on the location of the waterfront.

CHECKLIST:

1. Bottom movement
2. Amount of holes and debris
3. Slope of subsurface
4. Amount of area
5. Condition of soil
6. Porosity of bottom
7. Average depth and various depths
8. Bottom color

Climatic characteristics. Continuous dry spells or numerous rainy seasons raise water retention problems. Dangerous storms, including tornadoes, lightning, hurricanes, and northeasters, create extremely dangerous waterfront conditions. The severity of the winter can also affect the waterfront. Ice and ice movement can cause damage to waterfront facilities and bottom. The ideal is a south-southeast exposure, in which maximum benefit is derived from the sun and there is the least

exposure to the force of the wind.

CHECKLIST:

1. Number of storms and type
2. Prevailing winds
3. Amount of ice
4. Change of air temperature
5. Amount of precipitation
6. Fluctuation of temperature
7. Sun exposure

Environmental characteristics. The locale of the waterfront should be carefully examined for all influences on its construction and utilization. Zoning regulations, building codes, insurance restrictions, health ordinances, title covenants, and many other legal restrictions by the Coast Guard, conservation department, water resources commission, public works agencies, and fire department should be studied. The arrangement of land uses and their compatibility to the project, transportation, utilities, community facilities, population, and area economics should also be considered.

CHECKLIST:

1. Ownership and riparian rights
2. Availability of water supply
3. Zoning and deed restrictions
4. Local, state, and federal regulations
5. Adjacent ownerships
6. Water patrol and a control agency

Program characteristics. The waterfront should be so situated that it can be protected by a fence or other controlled access, particularly in a camp, marina, or other small area. It should also be internally segregated; that is, bathing should be separated from boating, boating from fishing, and so on. The site should also have storage room for waterfront equipment, a safety area near the lifeguard station or post, and ready access to a road.

SOURCE: *Planning Areas and Facilities for Health, Physical Education, and Recreation,* Athletic Institute and American Association for Health, Physical Education, and Recreation, Washington, 1965.

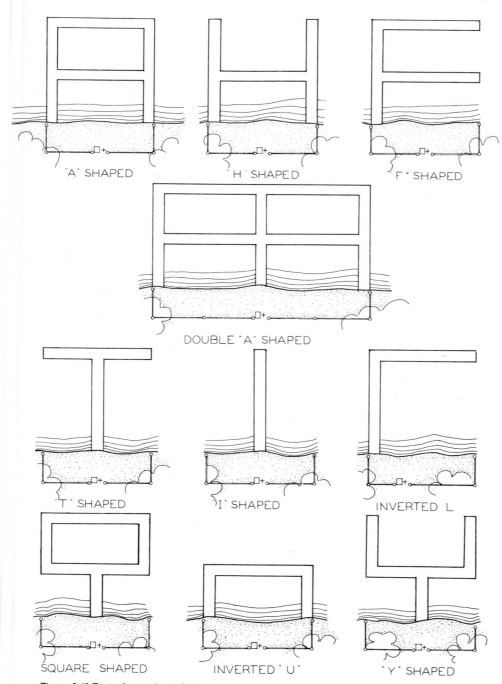

"A" SHAPED

"H" SHAPED

"F" SHAPED

DOUBLE "A" SHAPED

"T" SHAPED

"I" SHAPED

INVERTED "L"

SQUARE SHAPED

INVERTED "U"

"Y" SHAPED

Figure 5-48 Typical waterfront shapes.

CHECKLIST:

1. Distance of waterfront from other areas
2. Access road
3. Separation of waterfront activities
4. Area for unity of controls
5. Space available for adjunct activities

Access characteristics. The waterfront facility must be accessible by transportation available to the user. There should always be a means of vehicular access for emergency or maintenance use. The site around the waterfront and along its approach should be free of poison ivy, sumac, poison oak, burdock thistle, and other irritating plants.

CHECKLIST:

1. Location for access road
2. Poisonous plants
3. Area accessible yet controllable

Area characteristics. The waterfront bathing area should allow for at least 50 square feet for each user. There should be areas for instruction, recreation, and competition. The depth of the area to be used primarily for the instruction of nonswimmers should not exceed 3 feet. The area to be used for intermediate swimmers should not exceed 5½ feet (primarily for competition). Smaller or larger areas may be designed if users are divided differently.

The minimum recommended size for a camp swimming area is 60 by 30 feet, and the desirable size is 75 by 45 feet, providing a 25-yard short course.

CHECKLIST:

1. Space for bathing
2. Capacity of waterfront
3. Water depths
4. Division of bathing area into stations
5. Size of boating area
6. Size of fishing area

SOURCE: *Planning Areas and Facilities for Health, Physical Education, and Recreation,* Athletic Institute and American Association for Health, Physical Education, and Recreation, Washington, 1965.

Shore characteristics. The shoreline for the waterfront facility should be free of irregular rocks, stumps, debris, and obstructions. It should be a minimum of 100 feet long for bathing in a camp area and can be many miles long in a park beach.

There should be trees adjacent to waterfront areas to provide shade and wind protection. Large, high trees should be eliminated because they attract lightning, and moldy trees have many decayed overhanging branches. Too many deciduous trees create mucky shores and water bottoms because of their autumn leaves. Coniferous trees cause fewer problems.

CHECKLIST:

1. Surrounding vegetation
2. Slope of the shore
3. Existing beach
4. Extent of clearing
5. Amount of debris

Criteria for Artificial Waterfronts In locating and considering an artificial waterfront, most of the characteristics described for natural areas should be examined. Additional criteria to be considered are outlined below.

Environmental characteristics. If all available bodies of water are being utilized, artificial-waterfront facilities must be developed. In some cases, waterfront locations are unsatisfactory or unavailable for new camps or resorts. Thus, consideration must be given to utilizing undeveloped sites with sufficient watershed (runoff water), water table (underground water), and water bodies (surface water) for lakes, pools, or impoundments.

Water characteristics. Before any site is selected, the perculation rate and, in particular, the permeability of the soil should be carefully checked to make sure that water will be retained. The stability and structure of the soil must also be determined (from test borings or test pits, or both) because of the various types of dams, pump houses, dikes, pools, berms, spillways, and other structures that must be built.

Water content characteristics. Unlike the content of natural bodies of water, the content of artificial bodies can be controlled by chlorination and filtration. Runoff water obtained from storms and contained in a pond or lake should be collected by diversion ditches and fed to a reservoir and chlorination plant. This water can then be recirculated until potable water is obtained.

Underground water that is obtained from wells or springs can also be contained in a pond. This type of artificial water body usually has a continuous flow and thus would need only a simple filtration system plus chlorination.

Surface water that is obtained from running streams is usually contained in a bypass pond or in a pond in the stream itself. Both methods require the construction of a dam. These artificial water bodies have continuous running water. However, gate valves and floodgates are required, especially during storms, when there is a large flow of water to control. Unless there is a constant turnover or supply of clean water, these impoundments will require a filtration and chlorination system.

Climatic characteristics. Climatic considerations are very important in developing artificial bodies of water and waterfronts. In most cases, natural bodies of water fluctuate very little because of weather conditions. On the other hand, artificial bodies are solely dependent upon the climate because the water table, runoff, and streamflow depend on the amount and time of rainfall. All other climatic considerations mentioned for natural waterfronts generally apply to artificial waterfronts as well.

Drainage characteristics. A low-lying area, regardless of its appeal, is not a good location for a pool or pond. Adequate drainage is essential so that surface and deck water will drain away from the water body and the water body itself can be emptied without pumping. Groundwater and frost action resulting from improper drainage can undermine a foundation by causing it to heave and settle.

Waterfront Construction
Criteria for Natural Waterfronts A natural waterfront facility should have features that make it both safe and usable. The following criteria are suggested as a basis for the construction of such a facility.

Bottom characteristics. Most swimming facilities around natural bodies of water require the dragging and grading of the bottom subsurfaces to eliminate hazards. In many cases where definite improvement of the bottom is requried, mat, mesh, or plastic sheets must be laid down on top of muck and staked down. Once these sheets have been laid, sand must be spread over the mat surface. When the bottom is firm, sand can be spread 6 inches thick on top of ice in the crib area during winter. As the ice melts, the sand will fall fairly evenly over the bottom. However, this can only be accomplished when the ice does not shift or break and float away.

Shore characteristics. When a beach is constructed, a gentle slope of from 6 to 12 feet in 100 feet should be maintained. If the waterfront requires a great deal of construction, a dock shoreline is recommended rather than trying to maintain an unstable beach. The ground above the water can then be developed with turf, terraces, decks, and boardwalks, depending upon the nature of the project. When the bottom drops off very quickly, the shore can be dug out to the grade desired underwater. This forms a crescent-shaped waterfront with an excellent beach.

Access characteristics. If possible, access roads and streets around waterfront areas should be acquired by the owner to keep the area buffered from conflicting uses. These roads should be made durable and be attractively maintained. Access roads should have clear horizontal and vertical vision so that pedestrian and vehicular conflict can be prevented.

Program characteristics. The waterfront in small recreation areas, such as camps or

SOURCE: *Planning Areas and Facilities for Health, Physical Education, and Recreation,* Athletic Institute and American Association for Health, Physical Education, and Recreation, Washington, 1965.

resorts, should be completely enclosed by planting or fencing. There should be a central control for ingress and exit. Many facilities require the use of boards for checking in and out, tickets, and similar devices for controlling the use of the area. The waterfront bathing, boating, and fishing facilities should be separated, each with its own control.

Criteria for Artificial Waterfronts Both artificial and natural waterfronts should have features that make them safe and usable. In improving and developing an artificial waterfront, most of the same points should be considered as illustrated for the natural waterfront. The following additional criteria should be carefully considered in providing an artificial waterfront.

Bottom characteristics. When an artificial beach is constructed, the grade should be the same as that recommended for natural shores: 6 to 12 feet in 100 feet. For reservoirs and ponds, there should be a minimum of 9 inches of large crushed stones, then 4 inches of well-graded, smooth gravel to fill in the voids, and finally 9 inches of washed medium sand. If the sand beach terminates at a depth of approximately 7 feet of water, it is recommended that riprapping be established to resist the tendency of the beach sand to move down the slope. The area above the beach should be ditched where the natural slope of the ground exceeds that of the beach. Thus, the slopes of the beach should be approximately 6 percent below the water and 10 percent above it. For areas in tidal waters, a maximum slope of 1 foot for 15 feet can be established for the bottom below the waterline.

For pools, bottoms are usually concrete, with the sides of concrete, welded steel, or aluminum plate. Such innovations as precast concrete slabs, plastic, and rubber are being tried.

Shore characteristics. In creating a shoreline for artificial bodies of water, there should be either a berm or a dike if the water is to be confined. A steep slope to eliminate shallow areas is usually required to prevent weeds and

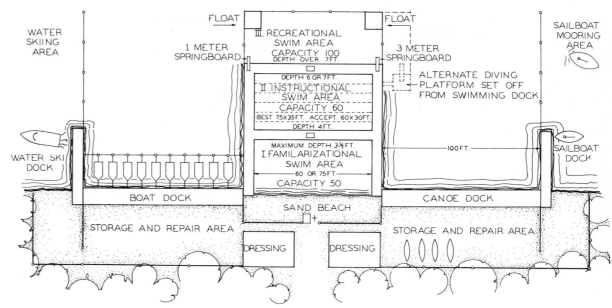

Figure 5-49 Typical waterfront layout.

other plant materials from growing in the water.

If the soil conditions will not allow a steep slope underwater (3 feet deep to retard water plant growth), bulkheads or docks will be required. Otherwise only a limited beach can be provided.

Typical waterfront shapes are shown in Figure 5-48, and a typical waterfront layout in Figure 5-49.

DOCKS AND FLOATS

Permanent structures are usually set on concrete, wood, or steel foundations or on piers or piles. The decks should be made in sections of 10 to 20 feet for ease in removing for repairs or winter storage. The dock should be constructed with at least a 1-foot air space between deck and water. Underwater braces and other crossbeams should be limited to prevent swimmers from becoming entangled in them. When water levels change, allowances should be made for

piers to be outside the deck limits so that the deck can move up and down on sleeves or brackets. Walkways or decks should be a minimum of 6 feet wide and preferably 8 or 10 feet wide. They should be cross-planked so that swimmers will avoid splinters. The planking should not be less than 2 inches thick by 4 to 6 inches wide. Boards should be spaced a maximum of ¼ inch apart to prevent toe stubbing. The deck should be treated with a non-creosote-based preservative, since creosote will burn feet, plus a plastic nonlead paint that is not heat-absorbing. The paint should be white with a blue or green tint to reduce the glare and aid in reflection.

SOURCE: *Planning Areas and Facilities for Health, Physical Education, and Recreation,* Athletic Institute and American Association for Health, Physical Education, and Recreation, Washington, 1965.

BOAT BASIN; MARINA

A design for a typical pleasure boat basin is shown in Figure 5-50.

The accompanying table should be used in conjunction with Figure 5-51 to obtain the widths of slips, the lengths of catwalks, and the locations of stern anchor piles. The table is based on the use of traveler irons.

DIMENSIONS FOR SLIPS AND CATWALKS

Length group for yachts (feet)	Beam to be provided for	Minimum clearance for beam	Minimum clear width of slip	Allowance for half anchor pile	Allowance for half of catwalk	Gross slip width: Type A	Gross slip width: Type B	Gross slip width: Type C	Gross slip width: Type D	Usuable width of catwalk	First catwalk span: length E	Second catwalk span: length F	Third catwalk span: length G	Total length of catwalk	Distance J to anchor pile
20–25	7' 6"	3' 0"	10' 6"	10"	1' 1"	12' 5"	12' 2"	12' 5"	...	2' 0"	10' 0"	8' 0"	...	18' 0"	28' 0"
	8' 6"	3' 0"	11' 6"	10"	1' 1"	13' 5"	13' 2"	13' 5"	...	2' 0"	10' 0"	8' 0"	...	18' 0"	28' 0"
25–30	7' 6"	3' 0"	10' 6"	10"	1' 1"	12' 5"	12' 2"	12' 5"	...	2' 0"	10' 0"	10' 0"	...	20' 0"	33' 0"
	9' 6"	3' 0"	12' 6"	10"	1' 1"	14' 5"	14' 2"	14' 5"	...	2' 0"	10' 0"	10' 0"	...	20' 0"	33' 0"
30–35	8' 6"	3' 0"	11' 6"	10"	1' 1"	13' 2"	13' 2"	13' 5"	...	2' 0"	12' 0"	10' 0"	...	22' 0"	38' 0"
	11' 6"	3' 0"	14' 6"	10"	1' 1"	16' 5"	16' 2"	16' 5"	...	2' 0"	12' 0"	10' 0"	...	22' 0"	38' 0"
35–40	9' 6"	3' 6"	13' 0"	10"	1' 1"	14' 11"	14' 8"	14' 11"	...	2' 0"	12' 0"	12' 0"	...	24' 0"	42' 0"
	12' 0"	3' 6"	15' 6"	10"	1' 1"	17' 5"	17' 2"	17' 5"	...	2' 0"	12' 0"	12' 0"	...	24' 0"	42' 0"
40–45	9' 6"	4' 0"	13' 6"	10"	1' 1"	15' 5"	15' 2"	15' 5"	...	2' 0"	14' 0"	12' 0"	...	26' 0"	47' 0"
	12' 6"	4' 0"	16' 6"	10"	1' 1"	18' 5"	18' 2"	18' 5"	...	2' 0"	14' 0"	12' 0"	...	26' 0"	47' 0"
45–50	10' 6"	4' 0"	14' 6"	10"	1' 1"	16' 5"	16' 2"	18' 5"	...	2' 0"	9' 0"	9' 0"	10' 0"	28' 0"	52' 0"
	13' 6"	4' 0"	17' 6"	10"	1' 1"	19' 5"	19' 2"	19' 5"	...	2' 0"	9' 0"	9' 0"	10' 0"	28' 0"	52' 0"
50–60	11' 6"	5' 0"	16' 6"	1' 7"	1' 1"	19' 2"	18' 11"	18' 5"	...	2' 0"	11' 0"	11' 0"	12' 0"	34' 0"	61' 0"
	14' 6"	5' 0"	19' 6"	1' 7"	1' 1"	22' 2"	21' 11"	21' 5"	...	2' 0"	11' 0"	11' 0"	12' 0"	34' 0"	61' 0"
60–70	12' 6"	5' 0"	17' 6"	1' 7"	2' 10"	21' 11"	19' 11"	21' 2"	...	4' 0"	11' 0"	11' 0"	12' 0"	34' 0"	72' 0"
	14' 6"	5' 0"	19' 6"	1' 7"	2' 10"	23' 11"	21' 11"	23' 2"	...	4' 0"	11' 0"	11' 0"	12' 0"	34' 0"	72' 0"
	16' 0"	5' 0"	21' 0"	1' 7"	2' 10"	25' 5"	23' 8"	24' 8"	...	4' 0"	11' 0"	11' 0"	12' 0"	34' 0"	72' 0"
70–80	13' 0"	5' 0"	18' 0"	1' 7"	2' 10"	22' 5"	20' 5"	21' 8"	...	4' 0"	11' 0"	11' 0"	12' 0"	34' 0"	82' 0"
	16' 6"	5' 0"	21' 6"	1' 7"	2' 10"	25' 11"	24' 11"	26' 2"	24' 7"	4' 0"	11' 0"	11' 0"	12' 0"	34' 0"	82' 0"

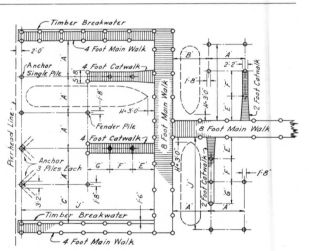

Figure 5-51 Dimension diagram for slips and catwalks for a typical pleasure boat basin.

SOURCE: *Marinas*, National Association of Engine and Boat Manufacturers, New York, 1947.

SOURCE: Charles A. Chaney, *Marinas: Recommendations for Design, Construction, and Maintenance*, 2d ed., National Association of Engine and Boat Manufacturers, New York, 1961.

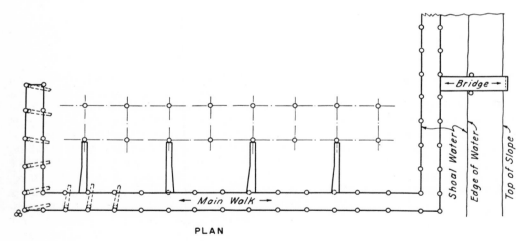

PLAN

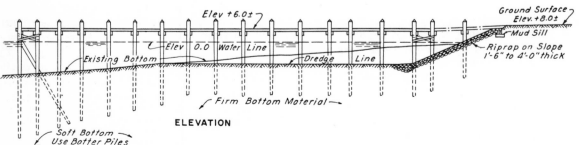

ELEVATION

Figure 5-50 Section through slope revetment for a marina without a bulkhead wall; a typical pleasure boat basin.

5.7 Ponds

Types of Ponds Farm ponds and reservoirs may be divided into two general types, embankment ponds and excavated ponds. An embankment pond is a body of water created by constructing a dam across a stream or a watercourse. It is usually built in an area where the land slope ranges from gentle to moderately steep and where the stream valley is sufficiently depressed to permit the storage of water to a considerable depth.

An excavated pond is a body of water created by excavating a pit or a dugout. It is usually constructed in a relatively level area. The fact that its capacity is obtained almost entirely by excavation limits its use to a location where only a small supply of water is required.

Ponds are also built in gentle to moderately sloping areas where capacity is obtained by both excavation and the construction of a dam. For the purpose of classification, these are considered to be embankment-type ponds if the depth of water impounded against the embankment exceeds 3 feet.

Selecting the Pond Site The selection of a suitable pond site should begin with preliminary studies of possible sites. If more than one site is available, each should be studied separately with a view of selecting the most practical and economical site.

From an economic point of view, a pond should be located where the largest storage volume can be obtained with the least amount of earth fill. This condition generally occurs at a site where the valley is narrow, side slopes are relatively steep, and the slope of the valley floor permits a large, deep basin. Such a site tends to minimize the area of shallow water, but it should be examined carefully for adverse geologic conditions. Unless the pond is to be used for wildlife, large areas of shallow water should be avoided because of excessive evaporation losses and the growth of noxious aquatic plants.

If water must be conveyed for use elsewhere, as for irrigation or fire protection, the pond should be located as close to the point of use as is practical.

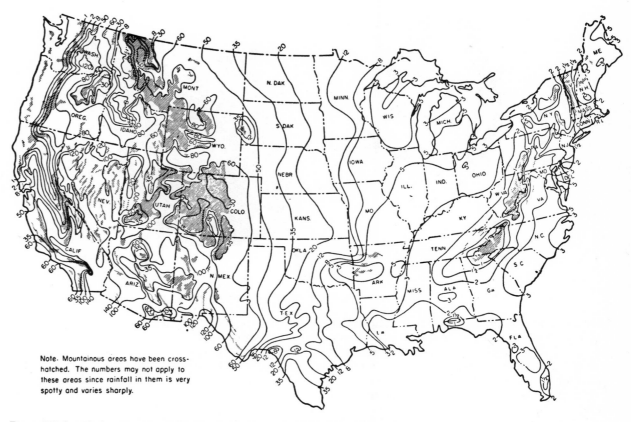

Note. Mountainous areas have been crosshatched. The numbers may not apply to these areas since rainfall in them is very spotty and varies sharply.

Figure 5-52 A guide for estimating the approximate size of the drainage area (in acres) required for each acre-foot of storage in an embankment or excavated pond.

Ponds to be used for fishing, boating, swimming, and other forms of recreation should be readily accessible by automobile. This is particularly true when the general public is charged a fee for use of the pond. The success of such an income-producing enterprise may well depend on the accessibility of the pond.

Pollution of farm pond water should be avoided by selecting a site where drainage from farmsteads, feeding lots, corrals, sewage lines, mine dumps, and similar areas will not reach the pond. Where this cannot be done practically, the drainage from such areas should be diverted from the pond.

The pond should not be located where a sudden release of the water because of failure of the dam would result in loss of life, injury to persons or livestock, damage to residences or industrial buildings, railroads, or highways, or interruption of use or service of public utilities.

Preliminary Site Studies In addition to the considerations mentioned for the selection of a pond location, other physical characteristics of the drainage area and the pond site should be investigated before the final selection is made.

SOURCE: *Ponds,* U.S. Department of Agriculture, Soil Conservation Service, 1971.

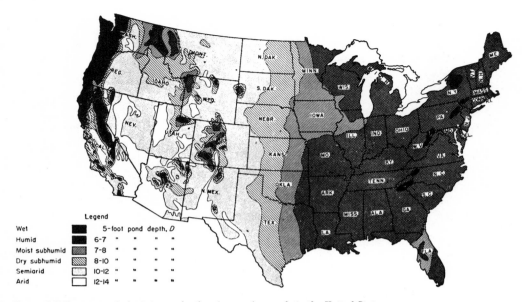

Figure 5-53 Recommended minimum depths of water for ponds in the United States.

Legend

Wet	5-foot pond depth, D
Humid	6–7 " "
Moist subhumid	7–8 " " " "
Dry subhumid	8–10 " " " "
Semiarid	10–12 " " " "
Arid	12–14 " " " "

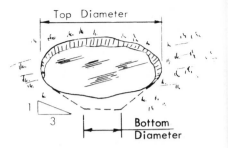

Figure 5-54 A circular pond.

Adequacy of the Drainage Area Where surface runoff is the main source of water supply, the contributing drainage area should be large enough to yield sufficient runoff to maintain the water supply in the pond during all periods of intended use. The drainage area should not be so large, however, as to require large and expensive overflow structures to bypass the runoff safely.

The amount of runoff that can be expected annually from a watershed of a given area depends on so many factors that no set rule can be given for its determination. The physical characteristics of the watershed that have a direct effect on the yield of water are land slopes, soil infiltration, vegetal cover, and surface storage. Storm characteristics such as the amount, intensity, and duration of rainfall also affect water yield. All these characteristics vary widely throughout the United States. Figure 5-52 can be used as a general guide for estimating the size of a watershed required for each acre-foot of capacity in a pond or reservoir to maintain normal pool level if more precise local data are not available.

Minimum Pond Depth For a permanent water supply, it is necessary to provide sufficient water depth to meet the intended use and to offset seepage and evaporation losses. Such losses vary in different sections of the United States and also from year to year in a given section. Figure 5-53 shows recommended minimum depths of water for farm ponds if normal seepage and evaporation losses are assumed. Greater depths are desirable when a year-round water supply is essential or when seepage losses may exceed 3 inches per month. See state standards and specifications for local minimum depths.

RECOMMENDED MINIMUM DEPTHS OF PONDS AND RESERVOIRS

Climate	Annual rainfall (inches)	Minimum water depth over 25 percent of the area (feet)
Superhumid	Over 60	6
Humid	40–60	8
Subhumid: moist	30–40	9
Subhumid: dry	20–30	10
Semiarid	10–20	12
Arid	Under 10	14

Drainage Area Protection To maintain the required depth and capacity of a farm pond, it is necessary that the inflow be reasonably free from sediment. The best protection is adequate erosion control on the contributing drainage area. Land under a cover of permanent vegetation, such as trees or grasses, makes the most desirable drainage area. If such an area is not available, cultivated areas that are protected by necessary conservation practices, such as terracing, contour tillage, strip cropping, conservation cropping systems, vegetated desilting areas, and other soil improvement practices, may be utilized as a last resort. Allowance should be made for the expected sedimentation during the effective life of the structure.

Figure 5-54 shows the design of a circular pond. The capacity of ponds of this type is given in the accompanying table.

CAPACITY OF CIRCULAR PONDS (BANK SLOPES OF 3:1)

Water depth (feet)	Top diameter (feet)	Bottom diameter (feet)	Capacity (gallons)
8	75	27	131,000
8	100	52	281,000
12	100	28	320,000
12	150	78	947,000
16	150	54	1,051,000

SOURCE: *Ponds*, U.S. Department of Agriculture, Soil Conservation Service, 1971.

5.8 Golf Courses

Par The United States Golf Association has set a general standard for par in relation to the yardage of any given hole: "'Par' is the score that an expert golfer would be expected to make for a given hole. Par means errorless play without flukes and under ordinary weather conditions allowing two strokes on the putting green." The method for computing par on any hole is shown in the accompanying table.[1]

DISTANCE (YARDS)

Men	Women	Par
Up to 250	Up to 210	3
251–470	211–400	4
471 and over	401–575	5
	576 and over	6

Regulation Golf Course In most cases a regulation golf course has a par of 70, 71, or 72 (occasionally 69 or 73). Many older courses built in the United States play to a total par of 70. However, in recent years par 72 has become the standard of excellence in the minds of many developers and golfers. It should be stressed, however, that the size and natural characteristics of a site determine what the total par should be; therefore, many courses are built outside the standard par 72. In many cases the golf course architect will determine that a shorter par-70 course may be much better than a forced par 72 because it is more demanding and natural. Neither par nor total yardage should be the criterion of quality, for the objectives of the recreational development golf course should be that it is fair and enjoyable to play.

A regulation golf course comprises eighteen holes with a combination of par 3s, 4s, and 5s, the sum of which equals pars 70 to 73. The standard mix for a par-72 golf course is ten par 4s, four par 3s, and four par 5s. Par-71 courses generally drop a par 4 and replace it with a par

3 or drop a par 5 and replace is with a par 4. A par-70 golf course generally has either six par 3s, eight par 4s, and four par 5s or four par 3s, twelve par 4s, and two par 5s. A par-73 golf course generally has an additional par 5 in place of a par 4. It is these combinations of pars that comprise what is considered to be the norm to qualify a course as regulation in the minds of golfers. However, it is neither total yardage nor par that determines the amount of area used, the quantity of lot frontage, and the cost of maintenance and control of the golf facility once it has been built. The needs of the project, the shape of the total property, and the physical characteristics of the site all have an influence on how and where the golf course architect, planner, and owner decide to lay out a regulation golf course.

Basic Golf Course Designs There are five basic golf course design types, with several possible options each, that can facilitate the particular needs of an individual development. After a feasible location has been determined by studying the topography and the natural site characteristics, the developer and design team can determine which type or combination of types would be most appropriate for the project from every standpoint.

The five basic prototypal configurations for an eighteen-hole regulation golf course are (1) a single-fairway eighteen-hole course with returning nines, (2) a single-fairway continuous eighteen-hole course, (3) a double-fairway eighteen-hole course with returning nines, (4) a double-fairway continuous eighteen-hole course, and (5) an eighteen-hole core golf course. (See below, Figures 5-58, 5-59, 5-60, 5-61, and 5-62.)

In the following discussion, hypothetical diagrams illustrate the five basic golf course designs. For ease of comparison, each diagram is shown with a 10-acre clubhouse site. All five layouts are 72 par, and each includes four par-5 holes of 500 yards, four par-3 holes of 200 yards, and ten par-4 holes of 420 yards, totaling 7000 yards in length. The diagrams are laid out on the same scale to facilitate visual and mathematical comparison of golf course

areas, real estate frontage, and function within a particular development.

It should be noted that any of these illustrative layouts, when applied to an existing site, will vary in area and configuration from the figures and plans shown to accommodate irregularities in property boundaries and topographic features. In addition, the architect may choose to combine the characteristics of several of the basic formats to serve best the requirements of the development and the dictates of the site. Site characteristics and topography must be accommodated before striving for good frontage figures.

The diagrams and dimensions of the five prototypal configurations are merely illustrations. The figures given for acreage and length of frontage were computed for comparative purposes, not for use as a rigid standard. The acreage figures for each prototype are slightly greater than would be necessary in most actual situations. Boundaries adjacent to tees can be from 75 to 90 feet closer to the center line than they must be in the target areas. The boundary must then be gradually angled away from the center line to the 150-foot distance at a point 450 to 500 feet from the back of the tee, as shown in Figure 5-55. If this is done on single- and double-row courses, the total acreage figure would decrease markedly. The acreage in a core course, with its fewer boundaries, will decrease minimally. The length of frontage for each prototype should also be regarded as the

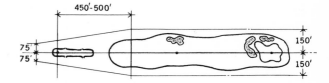

Figure 5-55 Conserving land in the tee areas.

SOURCE: Rees L. Jones and Guy L. Rando, *Golf Course Developments,* Technical Bulletin No. 70, Urban Land Institute, Washington, 1974.

[1] *Golf Committee Manual and USGA Golf Handicap System,* United States Golf Association, New York, 1969.

maximum figure because all features were sep-arated as much as was feasible to achieve the maximum frontage possible.

Different types of golf holes and bunker loca-tions are shown in Figures 5-56 and 5-57.

The five basic golf course designs are shown in Figures 5-58, 5-59, 5-60, 5-61, and 5-62.

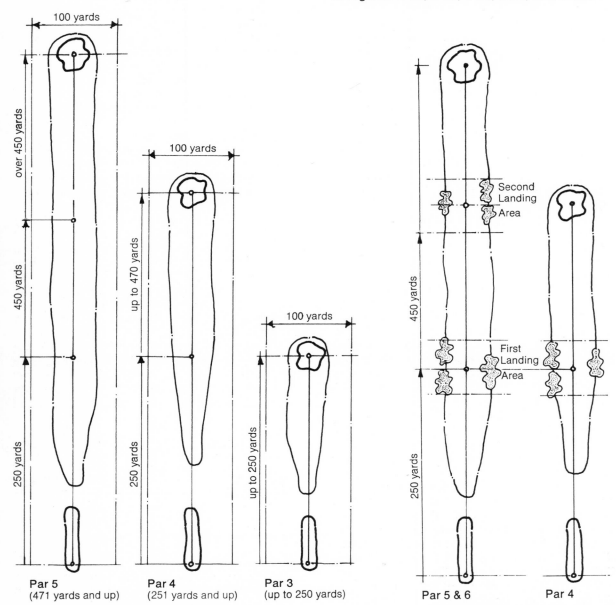

Figure 5-56 Different types of golf holes in relation to par.

Par 5
(471 yards and up)

Par 4
(251 yards and up)

Par 3
(up to 250 yards)

Par 5 & 6

Par 4

Figure 5-57 Strategic fairway bunker locations.

SOURCE: Rees L. Jones and Guy L. Rando, *Golf Course Develop-ments,* Technical Bulletin No. 70, Urban Land Institute, Washington, 1974.

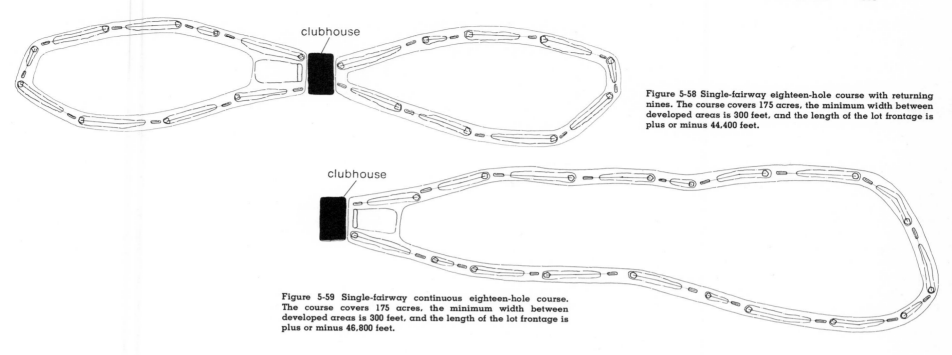

clubhouse

Figure 5-58 Single-fairway eighteen-hole course with returning nines. The course covers 175 acres, the minimum width between developed areas is 300 feet, and the length of the lot frontage is plus or minus 44,400 feet.

clubhouse

Figure 5-59 Single-fairway continuous eighteen-hole course. The course covers 175 acres, the minimum width between developed areas is 300 feet, and the length of the lot frontage is plus or minus 46,800 feet.

clubhouse

Figure 5-60 Double-fairway eighteen-hole course with returning nines. The course covers 150 acres, the minimum width between developed areas is 500 feet, and the length of the lot frontage is plus or minus 24,200 feet.

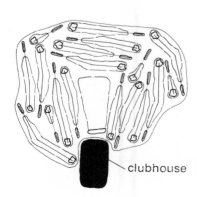

clubhouse

clubhouse

Figure 5-61 Double-fairway continuous eighteen-hole course. The course covers 150 acres, the minimum width between developed areas is 500 feet, and the length of the lot frontage is plus or minus 25,000 feet.

Figure 5-62 Core golf course. The course covers 140 acres, the minimum width between developed areas is zero feet, and the length of the lot frontage is plus or minus 10,000 feet.

SOURCE: Rees L. Jones and Guy L. Rando, *Golf Course Developments*, Technical Bulletin No. 70, Urban Land Institute, Washington, 1974.

Selection of Course Site The golf architect usually considers a number of prospective sites for a course and selects the one that, at a reasonable cost of land, can be converted into a good course at a minimum construction cost and can be maintained properly at minimum expense.

The size of the property is important, 50 acres for a nine-hole course and 110 acres for eighteen holes generally being considered the minimum. Even these areas involve risk of injury to players playing parallel holes. For better courses, 80 acres for a nine-hole course and 160 acres for eighteen holes are about right. Irregularly shaped plots often afford opportunities for most interesting course design.

The land should not be too rugged. A gently rolling area with some trees is preferable. Land that is too hilly is tiring on players, usually necessitates too many blind shots, and is more costly to keep well turfed.

The course should have a practice fairway area close to the clubhouse. Some public and daily-fee courses have installed practice ranges, lighted for night use, adjoining their courses and on highways. From these ranges they derive considerable income and develop golfers for day play on the courses.

The usual experience of a golf club that leases its land with an option to buy is that the installation of a course increases the value of the land enough to make the option an excellent investment when it is exercised. When finances permit and the community's prospects warrant, it also is well to tie up enough land so that property bordering on the course may be sold for residential sites and the proceeds used to pay off the club's loans. Frequently reference to this increase in value of surrounding property due to establishment of a golf club is so attractive to landowners that enough property exclusively for course use becomes available at a bargain price. The owners correctly surmise that not only is the net value of their entire holdings increased by the location of the golf course but that their property surrounding the course is more readily salable.

Accessibility Unless absolutely unavoidable, a golf course should not be off the beaten track. This is especially important in the case of a small-town course for which greens fees from transients are counted on to help to meet maintenance costs. Locate your course along the main highway into town. All other things being equal, design the course so that one or two holes parallel the highway; it is good advertising.

Another reason for not locating the course in an out-of-the-way spot is that the club should have good transportation for the members. It should be as near to town as possible, the cost of land being taken into consideration, and the main highway from town to the club should be one that is kept in good condition and not merely a country lane, unpaved and liable to become impassable with every heavy rain.

Soil Factors The condition of the soil is extremely important because the better the stand of turf raised on fairways and greens, the more satisfactory and more popular the course will be. The ideal golf course soil is a sandy loam. It is not impossible but is expensive to grow a good stand of grass on a heavy clay. Be sure to take the character of the soil into consideration when choosing a site.

Soil analysis of areas of the golf course site will be made at low cost by state agricultural departments or county agents. Considerable helpful information can be supplied by state agricultural experiment stations and county agents in determining the most desirable site from the viewpoint of a good possibility of golf turf development and in recommending the grass seeding, growing, and maintenance program.

Past Use Closely linked with soil factors is the use to which the land has been put in the past. Is the plot a run-down farm with soil from which a large part of the plant food has been removed, or is the soil rich in the elements that will be necessary for the successful cultivation of turf? Has the land lain idle for many years, or has it been intensively cultivated by its farmer owner without plant food being returned to the soil?

The selection of property that has been well kept up as pastureland is highly advisable. Much money is saved in putting the course into excellent condition. For instance, one southern Ohio club built its course on property that had been in bluegrass for about 30 years, and for that reason its fairways cost practically nothing. Frequently the scenic attractions of a site are such that to the susceptible and uninformed organizers of a golf club they totally outweigh soil conditions. A happy balance should be maintained between soil and scenic factors. Pick a site that will offer no serious handicaps to the attempts of the club to grow a stand of grass and maintain it thereafter.

Power and Water Availability Water and power are absolute necessities for any modern golf course. Even in the smallest communities, grass-green courses with a clubhouse are being built. To water only greens and tees or the whole course and to operate a clubhouse, you must have power and water.

The source of water should be close to the site and be reliable and pure enough to drink and to irrigate fine turf. It may be a city system, wells, a lake, a river, or some combination of these. The cost of connections to water and power supplies must be included in your plans.

How Much Clearing? Consider next the amount of clearing that must be done in building the course. Will it be necessary to move many trees or grub out many stumps? Will removing stones from the soil be expensive? Are there large swamp areas that must be filled in or drained? Do not misunderstand the question about clearing out trees. A golf course should, if possible, have patches of woodland, as trees offer one of the best natural hazards if properly placed with reference to the course. However, it is an expensive matter to remove large growing trees, and the site selected should not have too many of these in the portions that are intended to be fairways.

SOURCE: *Planning and Building the Golf Course*, National Golf Foundation, Chicago, 1967.

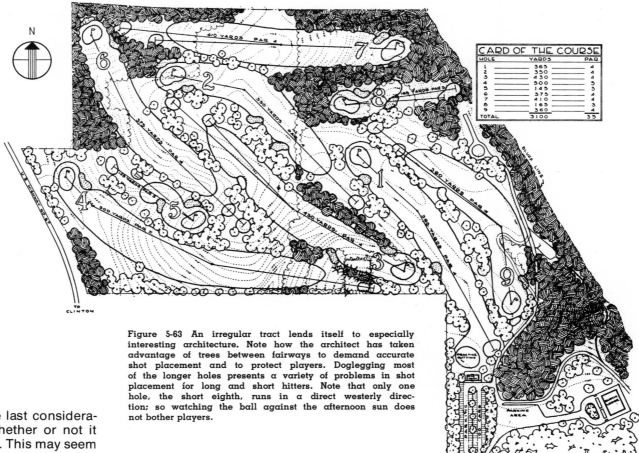

CARD OF THE COURSE

HOLE	YARDS	PAR
1	365	4
2	350	4
3	430	5
4	500	5
5	145	3
6	375	4
7	410	4
8	165	3
9	360	4
TOTAL	3100	35

Figure 5-63 An irregular tract lends itself to especially interesting architecture. Note how the architect has taken advantage of trees between fairways to demand accurate shot placement and to protect players. Doglegging most of the longer holes presents a variety of problems in shot placement for long and short hitters. Note that only one hole, the short eighth, runs in a direct westerly direction; so watching the ball against the afternoon sun does not bother players.

Natural Golf Features The last consideration in selecting the site is whether or not it possesses natural golf features. This may seem to the uninitiated the first and most important thing to look for, but natural golf features, while extremely desirable, are not nearly as important as the character of the soil and the site location. Rolling terrain, creek valleys, woodlands, ravines, ponds, and the like make the job of designing an interesting course much easier, but all these features or a substitute for them can be secured through artificial hazards. For this reason, the presence or absence of natural golf features is perhaps less important than any of the other factors mentioned above.

Figures 5-63, 5-64, 5-65, 5-66, 5-67, and 5-68 show desirable and undesirable golf course designs.

SOURCE: *Planning and Building the Golf Course,* National Golf Foundation, Chicago, 1967.

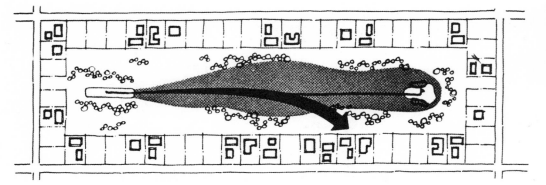

Figure 5-64 Single fairways are an expensive way to get frontage. Although they permit the maximum number of fairway lots, they present the greatest danger of golf balls flying into backyards. For safety's sake, single fairways should be at least 100 yards wide in the landing area, which extends from 150 to 250 yards from the tee. This width can be reduced if there are plenty of trees in the landing area.

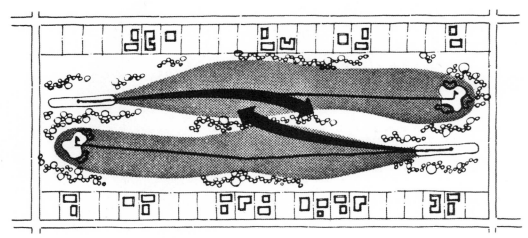

Figure 5-65 Double fairways require a smaller safety margin. They are laid out so that a sliced drive from either tee will go into the adjacent fairway. As a result, the combined width of the two landing areas need be only 150 yards. The double fairway thus requires 25 percent less maintenance. Since a ball sliced into another fairway is easier to find than one sliced into a border area or a house lot, play is speeded up.

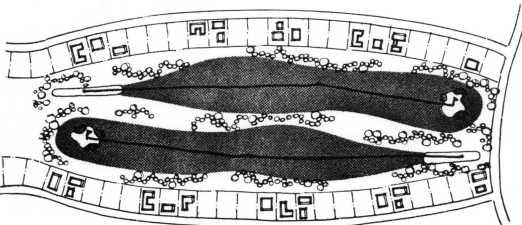

Figure 5-66 A curved building line saves even more land. Here is a good example of the need for coordinating course and housing. Tees and greens require less of a buffer zone around them than does the landing area, and the combined tee and green area at either end of this double fairway can be as narrow as 100 yards. If the adjacent building land and streets can be curved to fit this pattern, the result will be further saving of land, a deeper cut in maintenance costs, and, from the housing point of view, a more interesting subdivision.

SOURCE: *House and Home*, June 1968.

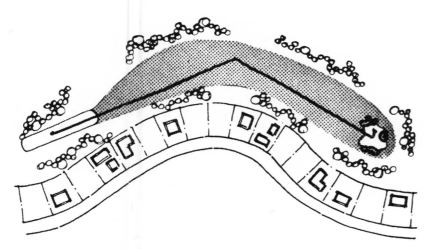

Figure 67*a* This dogleg layout is dangerous. Golfers always take the short route on a dogleg, and they will try to drive over a greenhouse if this will give them a shorter second shot. On this hole seven or eight lots are in the danger zone.

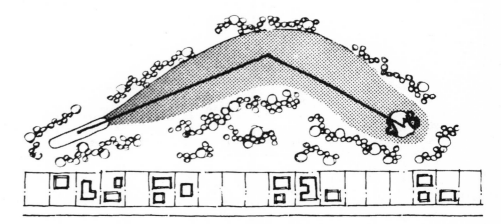

Figure 67*b* This dogleg layout wastes land. Houses near this hole are relatively safe from bombardment, and they have a very nice view. But the developer has lost a big piece of land—enough for half a dozen or so lots. And unless the wasted area is carefully manicured (which means extra maintenance), many golf balls could be lost in this area.

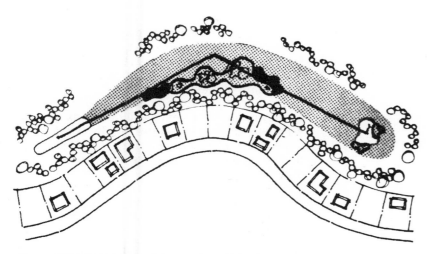

Figure 5-68*a* This dogleg plan is better. Golfers will think twice before they cut this corner. Trees are planted along the lot lines, including the area next to the tee. Traps and water hazards are placed on the right-hand side of the land area. As a result, the golfer who tries to go the short way is almost sure to get into trouble.

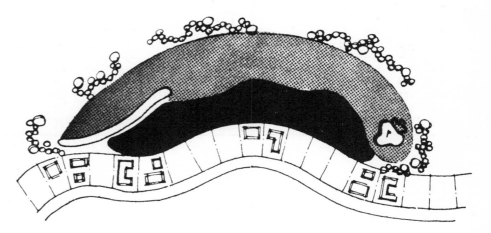

Figure 5-68*b* This dogleg is safe and beautiful. A lake has been built on the inside of the dogleg, protecting the houses. Golfers are forced to keep their drives away from them. The lake makes a challenging hole; the closer the drive to the water, the shorter the second shot. And it creates premium, high-priced lots for houses, town houses, or apartments that command a view of both fairway and water.

SOURCE: *House and Home*, June 1968.

a	b	c	d	e	f¹	f²
parking angle	stall width	stall to curb [19' long stall]	aisle width	curb length per car	center-to-center width of two-row bin with access road between curb-to-curb	overlap c-c
0°	8'0"	8.0	12.0	23.0	28.0	—
	8'6"	8.5	12.0	23.0	29.0	—
	9'0"	9.0	12.0	23.0	30.0	—
	9'6"	9.5	12.0	23.0	31.0	—
	10'0"	10.0	12.0	23.0	32.0	—
20°	8'0"	14.0	11.0	23.4	39.0	31.5
	8'6"	14.5	11.0	24.9	40.0	32.0
	9'0"	15.0	11.0	26.3	41.0	32.5
	9'6"	15.5	11.0	27.8	42.0	33.1
	10'0"	15.9	11.0	29.2	42.8	33.4
30°	8'0"	16.5	11.0	16.0	44.0	37.1
	8'6"	16.9	11.0	17.0	44.8	37.4
	9'0"	17.3	11.0	18.0	45.6	37.8
	9'6"	17.8	11.0	19.0	46.6	38.4
	10'0"	18.2	11.0	20.0	47.4	38.7
40°	8'0"	18.3	13.0	12.4	49.6	43.5
	8'6"	18.7	12.0	13.2	49.4	42.9
	9'0"	19.1	12.0	14.0	50.2	43.3
	9'6"	19.5	12.0	14.8	51.0	43.7
	10'0"	19.9	12.0	15.6	51.8	44.1
45°	8'0"	19.1	14.0	11.3	52.2	46.5
	8'6"	19.4	13.5	12.0	52.3	46.3
	9'0"	19.8	13.0	12.7	52.6	46.2
	9'6"	20.1	13.0	13.4	53.2	46.5
	10'0"	20.5	13.0	14.1	54.0	46.9

a	b	c	d	e	f¹	f²
parking angle	stall width	stall to curb [19' long stall]	aisle width	curb length per car	center-to-center width of two-row bin with access road between curb-to-curb	overlap c-c
50°	8'0"	19.7	14.0	10.5	53.4	48.3
	8'6"	20.0	12.5	11.1	52.5	47.0
	9'0"	20.4	12.0	11.7	52.8	47.0
	9'6"	20.7	12.0	12.4	53.4	47.3
	10'0"	21.0	12.0	13.1	54.0	47.6
60°	8'0"	20.4	19.0	9.2	59.8	55.8
	8'6"	20.7	18.5	9.8	59.9	55.6
	9'0"	21.0	18.0	10.4	60.0	55.5
	9'6"	21.2	18.0	11.0	60.4	55.6
	10'0"	21.5	18.0	11.5	61.0	56.0
70°	8'0"	20.6	20.0	8.5	61.2	58.5
	8'6"	20.8	19.5	9.0	61.1	58.2
	9'0"	21.0	19.0	9.6	61.0	57.9
	9'6"	21.2	18.5	10.1	60.9	57.7
	10'0"	21.2	18.0	10.6	60.4	57.0
80°	8'0"	20.1	25.0*	8.1	65.2	63.8
	8'6"	20.2	24.0*	8.6	64.4	62.9
	9'0"	20.3	24.0*	9.1	64.3	62.7
	9'6"	20.4	24.0*	9.6	64.4	62.7
	10'0"	20.5	24.0*	10.2	65.0	63.3
90°	8'0"	19.0	26.0*	8.0	64.0	—
	8'6"	19.0	25.0*	8.5	63.0	—
	9'0"	19.0	24.0*	9.0	62.0	—
	9'6"	19.0	24.0*	9.5	62.0	—
	10'0"	19.0	24.0*	10.0	62.0	—
90° Back in†	8'0"	18.5	22.0*	8.0	59.0	—
	8'6"	18.5	21.0*	8.5	58.0	—
	9'0"	18.5	20.0*	9.0	57.0	—

* Two-way circulation.
† For attendant parking only. Two-way traffic in aisles possible, but not desirable.

Figure 5-69

5.9 Tables for Parking-Lot Sizes

The series of quick-reference tables presented here simplifies the design of parking layouts. These tables (Figures 5-69, 5-70, 5-71, 5-72, and 5-73) will immediately answer the two questions that most commonly arise when a parking layout is being planned: (1) What parking pattern can be most advantageously fitted to this particular site? (2) If a certain parking angle has been specified, how many parking stalls at this angle can be imposed upon this site, or, alternatively, how big a site will be needed to accommodate a given number of cars parked at a specified angle?

In each table figures are given for five different stall widths from the utmost (and, we believe, shortsighted) economy of 8 feet to the new luxury standard of 10 feet. To fit the site without waste and the maximum number of stalls, a different parking angle may be used in one or both boundary rows. A table in each group shows the effect of these adjustments on the overall width.

Finally, for those who already know what they want and how to arrive at it, the tables can save a great deal of tiresome figuring. We have found them particularly useful for testing a number of alternative proposals in the early discussion stages of design.

The parking pattern is always considered to be viewed (as it normally will be by the designer) when looking along the length of the parking aisles, which should point toward the direction in which most parkers want to go when they leave their cars.

The large gray arrows on each page of tables refer to length and width as shown in the drawing on this page. Figures in the width tables always include the necessary aisles. The length tables do not include the circulation road along the row ends. The minimum width of this road might be taken as 24 feet.

SOURCE: From Geoffrey Baker and Bruno Funaro, *Parking*, © by Litton Educational Publishing, reprinted by permission of Van Nostrand Reinhold Company.

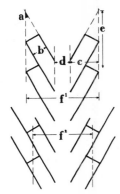

a	b	c	d	e	f¹	f²
parking angle	stall width	stall to curb [19' long stall]	aisle width	curb length per car	center-to-center width of two-row bin with access road between curb-to-curb	overlap c-c
30° 8'0"	16.5	11.0	16.0	44.0	37.1
8'6"	16.9	11.0	17.0	44.8	37.4
9'0"	17.3	11.0	18.0	45.6	37.8
9'6"	17.8	11.0	19.0	46.6	38.4
10'0"	18.2	11.0	20.0	47.4	38.7

ALTERNATE END ROWS FOR 30°
Change in overall width of parking:

With one end row of:	WIDTH OF STALL (same in end row as in rest of parking)				
	8'0"	8'6"	9'0"	9'6"	10'0"
0°	— 7'6"	— 7'6"	— 7'6"	— 7'6"	— 7'0"
45°	+ 5'6"	+ 5'0"	+ 4'6"	+ 4'6"	+ 4'6"
60°	+12'0"	+11'6"	+11'0"	+10'6"	+10'6"
90°	+17'6"	+16'0"	+14'6"	+14'0"	+14'0"

All dimensions in feet and inches are to nearest 6 inches

TOTAL LENGTH

NO. OF STALLS	SINGLE ROW WIDTH OF STALL:					OVERLAP				
	8'0"	8'6"	9'0"	9'6"	10'0"	8'0"	8'6"	9'0"	9'6"	10'0"
1	20'6"	20'6"	21'0"	21'0"	21'6"					
2	36'6"	37'6"	39'0"	40'0"	41'6"	20'0"	21'6"	22'6"	24'0"	25'0"
3	52'6"	54'6"	57'0"	59'0"	61'6"	36'6"	38'0"	39'0"	40'6"	41'6"
4	68'6"	71'6"	75'0"	78'0"	81'6"	36'0"	38'6"	40'6"	43'0"	45'0"
5	84'6"	88'6"	93'0"	97'0"	101'6"	52'6"	55'0"	57'0"	59'6"	61'6"
6	100'6"	105'6"	111'0"	116'0"	121'6"	52'0"	55'6"	58'6"	62'0"	65'0"
7	116'6"	122'6"	129'0"	135'0"	141'6"	68'6"	72'0"	75'0"	78'6"	81'6"
8	132'6"	139'6"	147'0"	154'0"	161'6"	68'0"	72'6"	76'6"	81'0"	85'0"
9	148'6"	156'6"	165'0"	173'0"	181'6"	84'6"	89'0"	93'0"	97'6"	101'6"
10	164'6"	173'6"	183'0"	192'0"	201'6"	84'0"	89'6"	94'6"	100'0"	105'0"
11	180'6"	190'6"	201'0"	211'0"	221'6"	100'6"	106'0"	111'0"	116'6"	121'6"
12	196'6"	207'6"	219'0"	230'0"	241'6"	100'0"	106'6"	112'6"	119'0"	125'0"
13	212'6"	224'6"	237'0"	249'0"	261'6"	116'6"	123'0"	129'0"	135'6"	141'6"
14	228'6"	241'6"	255'0"	268'0"	281'6"	116'0"	123'6"	130'6"	138'0"	145'0"
15	244'6"	258'6"	273'0"	287'0"	301'6"	132'6"	140'0"	147'0"	154'6"	161'6"
16	260'6"	275'6"	291'0"	306'0"	321'6"	132'0"	140'6"	148'6"	157'0"	165'0"
17	276'6"	292'6"	309'0"	325'0"	341'6"	148'6"	157'0"	165'0"	173'6"	181'6"
18	292'6"	309'6"	327'0"	344'0"	361'6"	148'0"	157'6"	166'6"	176'0"	185'0"
19	308'6"	326'6"	345'0"	363'0"	381'6"	164'6"	174'0"	183'0"	192'6"	201'6"
20	324'6"	343'6"	363'0"	382'0"	401'6"	164'0"	174'6"	184'6"	195'0"	205'0"

TOTAL WIDTH (including access roads)

STALL WIDTH	AISLE WIDTH	NUMBER OF ROWS 1	2	3	4	5	6	7	8	9	10	11	12	13	14	15	16	17	18	19	20
8'0"	11'0"	27'6"	44'0"	64'6"	81'0"	101'6"	118'0"	139'0"	155'6"	176'0"	192'6"	213'0"	229'6"	250'0"	266'6"	287'0"	303'6"	324'0"	341'0"	361'6"	378'0"
8'6"	11'0"	28'0"	45'0"	65'6"	82'0"	102'6"	119'6"	140'0"	157'0"	177'6"	194'6"	215'0"	232'0"	252'6"	269'0"	290'0"	306'0"	327'0"	344'0"	364'6"	381'6"
9'0"	11'0"	28'6"	45'6"	66'0"	83'6"	104'0"	121'0"	142'0"	159'0"	179'6"	197'0"	217'6"	234'6"	255'0"	272'6"	293'0"	310'6"	330'0"	348'0"	368'6"	385'0"
9'6"	11'0"	29'0"	46'6"	67'0"	85'0"	105'6"	123'6"	144'0"	162'0"	182'6"	200'0"	221'0"	238'6"	259'0"	277'0"	297'6"	315'6"	336'0"	354'0"	374'6"	392'0"
10'0"	11'0"	29'0"	47'6"	68'0"	86'0"	106'6"	125'0"	145'6"	163'6"	184'0"	202'0"	223'0"	241'0"	261'6"	279'6"	300'0"	318'6"	339'0"	357'0"	377'6"	395'6"

Figure 5-70 Tables for 30-degree parking.

Width of aisle and width of stall are interrelated. With self-parking particularly, a narrower stall will often require a wider aisle if the drivers are to turn into a stall in a single sweep without damage or delay. For this reason, as the tables show, a narrow stall may actually take more space per unit than one more generously proportioned. Stall width has a comparatively slight effect on the overall area.

Complete tables are given for 30-, 45-, 60-,

SOURCE: From Geoffrey Baker and Bruno Funaro, *Parking*, © by Litton Educational Publishing, reprinted by permission of Van Nostrand Reinhold Company.

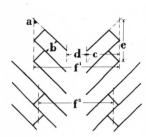

a	b	c	d	e	f¹	f²
parking angle	stall width	stall to curb [19' long stall]	aisle width	curb length per car	center-to-center width of two-row bin with access road between — curb-to-curb	overlap c-c
45° 8'0"	19.1	14.0	11.3		52.2	46.5
8'6"	19.4	13.5	12.0		52.3	46.3
9'0"	19.8	13.0	12.7		52.6	46.2
9'6"	20.1	13.0	13.4		53.2	46.5
10'0"	20.5	13.0	14.1		54.0	46.9

ALTERNATE END ROWS FOR 45°.
Change in overall width of parking:

With one end row of:	WIDTH OF STALL (same in end row as in rest of parking) 8'0"	8'6"	9'0"	9'6"	10'0"
0°	—11'0"	—11'0"	—11'0"	—10'6"	—10'6"
30°	—2'6"	—2'6"	—2'6"	—2'6"	—2'6"
60°	+6'6"	+6'6"	+6'0"	+6'0"	+6'0"
90°	+12'0"	+11'0"	+10'0"	+10'0"	+9'6"

All dimensions in feet and inches are to nearest 6 inches

HERRINGBONE for odd number of stalls = same as overlap table, opposite page

	WIDTH OF STALL: 8'0"	8'6"	9'0"	9'6"	10'0"
for even number of stalls add to overlap table:	+7'6"	+7'6"	+7'0"	+6'6"	+6'0"

TOTAL LENGTH

NO. OF STALLS	SINGLE ROW WIDTH OF STALL: 8'0"	8'6"	9'0"	9'6"	10'0"	OVERLAP 8'0"	8'6"	9'0"	9'6"	10'0"
1	19'0"	19'6"	19'6"	20'0"	20'6"					
2	30'6"	31'6"	32'6"	33'6"	34'6"	17'0"	18'0"	19'0"	20'0"	21'0"
3	41'6"	43'6"	45'0"	47'0"	48'6"	30'6"	31'6"	32'6"	33'6"	34'6"
4	53'0"	55'6"	58'0"	60'6"	62'6"	28'6"	30'0"	32'0"	33'6"	35'6"
5	64'0"	67'6"	70'6"	73'6"	77'0"	41'6"	43'6"	45'0"	47'0"	48'6"
6	75'6"	79'6"	83'0"	87'0"	91'0"	39'6"	42'0"	44'6"	47'0"	49'6"
7	87'0"	91'6"	96'0"	100'6"	105'0"	53'0"	55'6"	58'0"	60'6"	63'0"
8	98'0"	103'6"	108'6"	114'0"	119'0"	51'0"	54'0"	57'0"	60'6"	63'6"
9	109'6"	115'6"	121'6"	127'6"	133'0"	64'6"	67'6"	70'6"	73'6"	77'0"
10	120'6"	127'6"	134'0"	140'6"	147'6"	62'0"	66'0"	70'0"	73'6"	77'6"
11	132'0"	139'6"	146'6"	154'0"	161'6"	75'6"	79'6"	83'6"	87'0"	91'0"
12	143'6"	151'6"	159'6"	167'6"	175'6"	73'6"	78'0"	82'6"	87'0"	91'6"
13	154'6"	163'6"	172'0"	181'0"	189'6"	87'0"	91'6"	96'0"	100'6"	105'0"
14	166'0"	175'6"	185'0"	194'6"	203'6"	85'0"	90'0"	95'6"	100'6"	106'0"
15	177'0"	187'6"	197'6"	207'6"	218'0"	98'0"	103'6"	108'6"	114'0"	119'0"
16	188'6"	199'6"	210'0"	221'0"	232'0"	96'0"	102'0"	108'0"	114'0"	120'0"
17	200'0"	211'6"	223'0"	234'6"	246'0"	109'6"	115'6"	121'6"	127'6"	133'6"
18	211'0"	223'6"	235'6"	248'0"	260'0"	107'6"	114'0"	120'6"	127'6"	134'0"
19	222'6"	235'6"	248'6"	261'6"	274'0"	121'0"	127'6"	134'0"	140'6"	147'6"
20	233'6"	247'6"	261'0"	274'6"	288'6"	118'6"	126'0"	133'6"	140'6"	148'0"

TOTAL WIDTH (including access roads)

STALL WIDTH	AISLE WIDTH	NUMBER OF ROWS 1	2	3	4	5	6	7	8	9	10	11	12	13	14	15	16	17	18	19	20
8'0"	14'0"	33'0"	52'0"	79'6"	98'6"	126'0"	145'0"	172'6"	191'6"	219'0"	238'0"	265'6"	284'6"	312'0"	331'0"	358'6"	377'6"	405'0"	424'0"	451'6"	471'0"
8'6"	13'6"	33'0"	52'6"	79'0"	98'6"	125'6"	145'0"	172'0"	191'0"	218'0"	237'6"	264'6"	284'0"	310'6"	330'0"	357'0"	376'6"	403'6"	422'6"	449'6"	469'0"
9'0"	13'0"	33'0"	52'6"	79'0"	99'0"	125'0"	145'0"	171'6"	191'0"	217'6"	237'6"	264'0"	283'6"	310'0"	330'0"	356'0"	376'0"	402'6"	422'0"	448'6"	468'6"
9'6"	13'0"	33'0"	53'0"	79'6"	99'6"	126'0"	146'0"	172'6"	192'6"	219'0"	239'0"	265'6"	285'0"	312'0"	332'0"	358'6"	378'6"	405'0"	425'0"	451'6"	471'6"
10'0"	13'0"	33'6"	54'0"	80'6"	101'0"	127'6"	148'0"	174'0"	194'6"	221'0"	241'6"	268'0"	288'6"	315'0"	335'6"	362'0"	382'6"	408'6"	429'0"	455'6"	476'0"

Figure 5-71 Tables for 45-degree parking.

and 90-degree parking. For those who wish to investigate the subject more extensively, basic dimensions for every 10 degrees appear in Figure 5-69. One subtlety that cannot be shown in a table is an advantageous way of improving the 0-degree (parallel) parking pattern by pairing the stalls, as shown in the small drawing on this page. The allowance per car, 23 feet in

SOURCE: From Geoffrey Baker and Bruno Funaro, *Parking*, © by Litton Educational Publishing, reprinted by permission of Van Nostrand Reinhold Company.

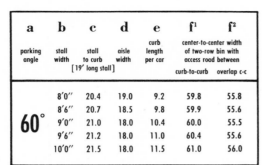

a	b	c	d	e	f¹	f²
parking angle	stall width	stall to curb [19' long stall]	aisle width	curb length per car	center-to-center width of two-row bin with access road between	
					curb-to-curb	overlap c-c
60° 8'0"	20.4	19.0	9.2	59.8	55.8	
8'6"	20.7	18.5	9.8	59.9	55.6	
9'0"	21.0	18.0	10.4	60.0	55.5	
9'6"	21.2	18.0	11.0	60.4	55.6	
10'0"	21.5	18.0	11.5	61.0	56.0	

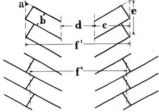

TOTAL LENGTH

NO. OF STALLS	SINGLE ROW					OVERLAP				
	WIDTH OF STALL: 8'0"	8'6"	9'0"	9'6"	10'0"	8'0"	8'6"	9'0"	9'6"	10'0"
1	16'6"	17'0"	17'6"	17'6"	18'0"					
2	25'6"	26'6"	27'6"	28'6"	29'6"	16'0"	17'0"	18'0"	19'0"	20'0"
3	35'0"	36'6"	38'0"	39'6"	41'0"	25'6"	26'6"	27'6"	28'6"	29'6"
4	44'0"	46'6"	48'6"	50'6"	52'6"	25'6"	27'0"	28'6"	30'0"	31'6"
5	53'0"	56'0"	59'0"	61'6"	64'0"	35'0"	36'6"	38'0"	39'6"	41'0"
6	62'6"	66'0"	69'6"	72'6"	75'6"	34'6"	37'0"	39'0"	41'0"	43'0"
7	71'6"	75'6"	79'6"	83'6"	87'0"	44'0"	46'6"	48'6"	50'6"	52'6"
8	81'0"	85'6"	90'0"	94'6"	98'6"	43'6"	46'6"	49'6"	52.0"	54'6"
9	90'0"	95'6"	100'6"	105'6"	110'0"	53'6"	56'0"	59'0"	61'6"	64'0"
10	99'0"	105'0"	111'0"	116'6"	121'6"	53'0"	56'6"	60'0"	63'0"	66'0"
11	108'6"	115'0"	121'6"	127'6"	133'0"	62'6"	66'0"	69'6"	72'6"	75'6"
12	117'6"	124'6"	131'6"	138'6"	144'6"	62'0"	66'0"	70'0"	74'0"	77'6"
13	127'0"	134'6"	142'0"	149'6"	156'0"	71'6"	75'6"	79'6"	83'6"	87'0"
14	136'0"	144'6"	152'6"	160'6"	167'6"	71'6"	76'0"	80'6"	85'0"	89'0"
15	145'0"	154'0"	163'0"	171'6"	179'0"	81'0"	85'6"	90'0"	94'6"	98'6"
16	154'6"	164'0"	173'6"	182'6"	190'6"	80'6"	86'0"	91'0"	96'0"	100'6"
17	163'6"	173'6"	183'6"	193'6"	202'0"	90'0"	95'6"	100'6"	105'6"	110'0"
18	173'0"	183'6"	194'0"	204'6"	213'6"	89'6"	95'6"	101'6"	107'0"	112'0"
19	182'0"	193'6"	204'6"	215'6"	225'0"	99'0"	105'0"	111'0"	116'6"	121'6"
20	191'0"	203'0"	215'0"	226'6"	236'6"	99'0"	105'6"	112'0"	118'0"	123'6"

ALTERNATE END ROWS FOR 60°.
Change in overall width of parking:

With one end row of:	WIDTH OF STALL (same in end row as in rest of parking) 8'0"	8'6"	9'0"	9'6"	10'0"
0°	—12'6"	—12'0"	—12'0"	—11'6"	—11'6"
30°	—4'0"	—4'0"	—3'6"	—3'6"	—3'6"
45°	—1'6"	—1'6"	—1'0"	—1'0"	—1'0"
90°	+5'6"	+5'6"	+4'0"	+4'0"	+3'6"

All dimensions in feet and inches are to nearest 6 inches

TOTAL WIDTH (including access roads)

STALL WIDTH	AISLE WIDTH	NUMBER OF ROWS 1	2	3	4	5	6	7	8	9	10	11	12	13	14	15	16	17	18	19	20
8'0"	19'0"	39'6"	60'0"	95'0"	115'6"	151'0"	171'6"	207'0"	227'0"	262'6"	283'0"	318'6"	339'0"	374'0"	394'6"	430'0"	450'6"	486'0"	506'0"	541'6"	562'0"
8'6"	18'6"	39'0"	60'0"	95'0"	115'6"	150'6"	171'6"	206'6"	227'0"	262'0"	282'6"	317'6"	338'6"	373'6"	394'0"	429'0"	450'0"	485'0"	505'6"	540'6"	561'0"
9'0"	18'0"	39'0"	60'0"	94'6"	115'6"	150'0"	171'0"	205'6"	226'6"	261'0"	282'0"	316'6"	337'6"	372'0"	393'0"	427'6"	448'6"	483'0"	504'0"	538'6"	559'6"
9'6"	18'0"	39'0"	60'6"	95'0"	116'0"	150'6"	172'0"	206'0"	227'6"	262'0"	283'0"	317'6"	339'0"	373'6"	394'6"	429'0"	450'6"	485'0"	506'0"	540'6"	561'6"
10'0"	18'0"	39'6"	61'0"	95'6"	117'0"	151'6"	173'0"	207'6"	229'0"	263'6"	285'0"	319'6"²	341'0"	375'6"	397'0"	431'6"	453'0"	487'6"	509'0"	543'6"	565'0"

Figure 5-72 Tables for 60-degree parking.

length, remains the same, but cars can park and unpark more quickly, and with less traffic delay on the street; and pedestrians can pass through the line of parked cars.

Figure 5-70 shows tables for 30-degree parking.

Figure 5-71 shows tables for 45-degree parking.

SOURCE: From Geoffrey Baker and Bruno Funaro, *Parking*, © by Litton Educational Publishing, reprinted by permission of Van Nostrand Reinhold Company.

a parking angle	b stall width	c stall to curb [19′ long stall]	d aisle width	e curb length per car	f¹ center-to-center width of two-row bin with access road between curb-to-curb	f² overlap c-c
90°	8′0″	19.0	26.0*	8.0	64.0	—
	8′6″	19.0	25.0*	8.5	63.0	—
	9′0″	19.0	24.0*	9.0	62.0	—
	9′6″	19.0	24.0*	9.5	62.0	—
	10′0″	19.0	24.0*	10.0	62.0	—

ALTERNATE END ROWS FOR 90°.
Change in overall width of parking:

With one end row of:	WIDTH OF STALL (same in end row as in rest of parking) 8′0″	8′6″	9′0″	9′6″	10′0″
0°	—11′0″	—10′6″	—10′0″	— 9′6″	— 9′0″
30°	— 2′6″	— 2′0″	— 1′6″	— 1′0″	— 1′0″
45°, 60°	Fewer cars in more width, so not worth consideration.				

All dimensions in feet and inches are to nearest 6 inches

TOTAL LENGTH

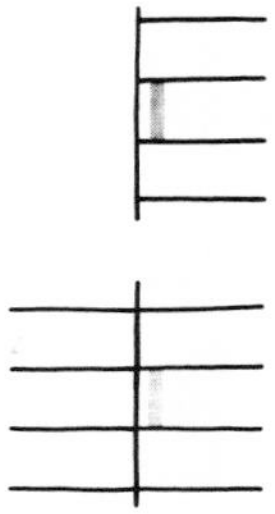

90° BACK IN*
Total length is
same as ordinary

NO. OF STALLS	WIDTH OF STALL: 8′0″	8′6″	9′0″	9′6″	10′0″
1	8′0″	8′6″	9′0″	9′6″	10′0″
2	16′0″	17′0″	18′0″	19′0″	20′0″
3	24′0″	25′6″	27′0″	28′6″	30′0″
4	32′0″	34′0″	36′0″	38′0″	40′0″
5	40′0″	42′6″	45′0″	47′6″	50′0″
6	48′0″	51′0″	54′0″	57′0″	60′0″
7	56′0″	59′6″	63′0″	66′6″	70′0″
8	64′0″	68′0″	72′0″	76′0″	80′0″
9	72′0″	76′6″	81′0″	85′6″	90′0″
10	80′0″	85′0″	90′0″	95′0″	100′0″
11	88′0″	93′6″	99′0″	104′6″	110′0″
12	96′0″	102′0″	108′0″	114′0″	120′0″
13	104′0″	110′6″	117′0″	123′6″	130′0″
14	112′0″	119′0″	126′0″	133′0″	140′0″
15	120′0″	127′6″	135′0″	142′6″	150′0″
16	128′0″	136′0″	144′0″	152′0″	160′0″
17	136′0″	144′6″	153′0″	161′6″	170′0″
18	144′0″	153′0″	162′0″	171′0″	180′0″
19	152′0″	161′6″	171′0″	180′6″	190′0″
20	160′0″	170′0″	180′0″	190′0″	200′0″

TOTAL WIDTH (including access roads)

	STALL WIDTH	AISLE WIDTH	NUMBER OF ROWS 1	2	3	4	5	6	7	8	9	10	11	12	13	14	15	16	17	18	19	20
	8′0″	26′0″	45′0″	64′0″	109′0″	128′0″	173′0″	192′0″	237′0″	256′0″	301′0″	320′0″	365′0″	384′0″	429′0″	448′0″	493′0″	512′0″	557′0″	576′0″	621′0″	640′0″
	8′6″	25′0″	44′0″	63′0″	107′0″	126′0″	170′0″	189′0″	233′0″	252′0″	296′0″	315′0″	359′0″	378′0″	422′0″	441′0″	485′0″	504′0″	548′0″	567′0″	611′0″	630′0″
	9′0″	24′0″	43′0″	62′0″	105′0″	124′0″	167′0″	186′0″	229′0″	248′0″	291′0″	310′0″	353′0″	372′0″	415′0″	434′0″	477′0″	496′0″	539′0″	558′0″	601′0″	620′0″
	9′6″	24′0″	43′0″	62′0″	105′0″	124′0″	167′0″	186′0″	229′0″	248′0″	291′0″	310′0″	353′0″	372′0″	415′0″	434′0″	477′0″	496′0″	539′0″	558′0″	601′0″	620′0″
	10′0″	24′0″	43′0″	62′0″	105′0″	124′0″	167′0″	186′0″	229′0″	248′0″	291′0″	310′0″	353′0″	372′0″	415′0″	434′0″	477′0″	496′0″	539′0″	558′0″	601′0″	620′0″
90° BACK IN*	8″′0	22′0″	40′6″	59′0″	99′6″	118′0″	158′6″	177′0″	217′6″	236′0″	276′6″	295′0″	335′6″	354′0″	394′6″	413′0″	453′6″	472′0″	512′6″	531′0″	571′6″	590′0″
	8′6″	21′0″	39′6″	58′0″	97′6″	116′0″	155′6″	174′0″	213′6″	232′0″	271′6″	290′0″	329′6″	348′0″	387′6″	406′0″	445′6″	464′0″	503′6″	522′0″	561′6″	580′0″
	9′0″	20′0″	38′6″	57′0″	95′6″	114′0″	152′6″	171′0″	209′6″	228′0″	266′6″	285′0″	323′6″	342′0″	380′6″	399′0″	437′6″	456′0″	594′6″	513′0″	551′6″	570′0″

* For attendant parking only

Figure 5-73 Tables for 90-degree parking.

Figure 5-72 shows tables for 60-degree parking.
Figure 5-73 shows tables for 90-degree parking.

SOURCE: From Geoffrey Baker and Bruno Funaro, *Parking*, © by Litton Educational Publishing, reprinted by permission of Van Nostrand Reinhold Company.

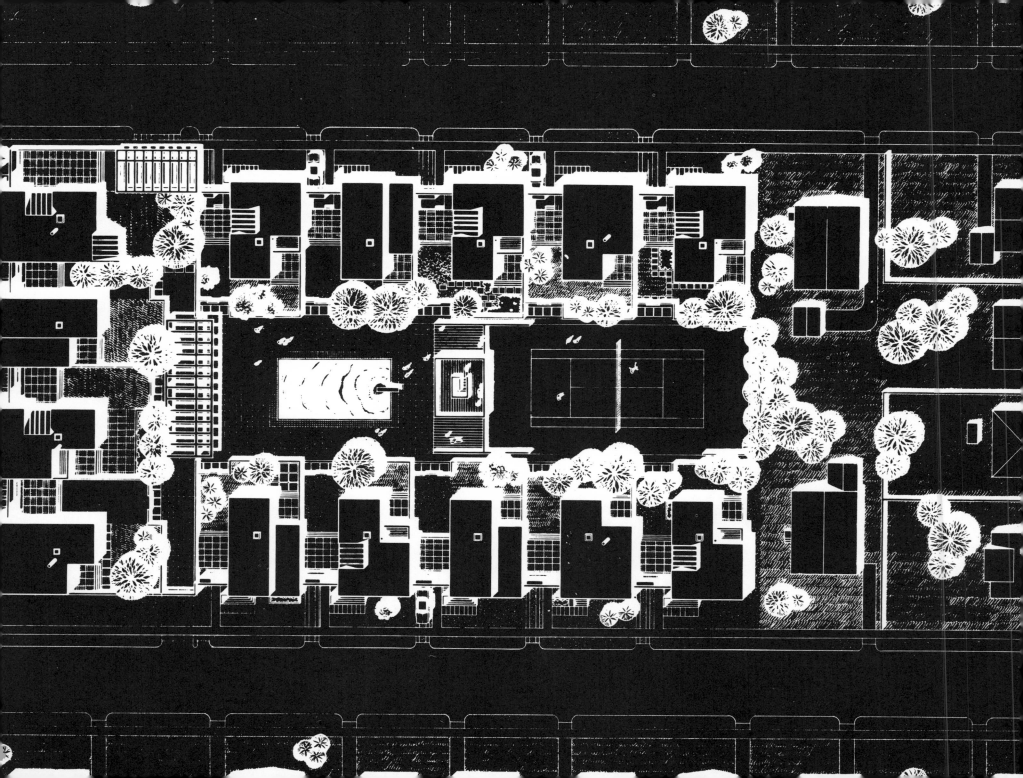

Typical Site Details

6

After the preparation of the overall site plan, many design details must be developed to show specific methods of construction. These details are an integral part of the design process and serve two important purposes. First, they stipulate the aesthetic and structural elements of the plan; and second, they provide the basis for costing the project.

This section offers a wide range of representative details of the various aspects of site development. Even though the scope of the details presented may seem extensive, they are only a very small segment of the available data. It is assumed that these details will act as a guide to assist site designers in solving their particular problems. The section is not intended to present aesthetic or design solutions but to indicate how others have handled similar technological difficulties. It should be emphasized that none of these details should be followed to the letter. Those that are more general in scope should be reviewed carefully against their anticipated use. Other details, which require structural or mechanical expertise, must be reviewed by appropriate professional engineers for their conformance with current codes and standards.

Opposite: Seascape, Avalon, N.J.
(Louis Sauer Associates, Architects)

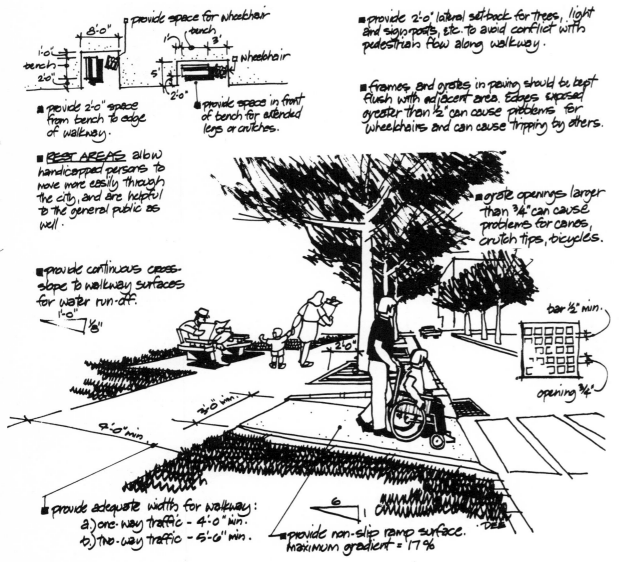

provide space for wheelchair
bench

8'-0"
1'-0"
bench
2'-0"

wheelchair

■ provide 2'-0" space from bench to edge of walkway.

provide space in front of bench for extended legs or crutches.

■ provide 2'-0" lateral setback for trees, light and sign posts, etc. to avoid conflict with pedestrian flow along walkway.

■ frames and grates in paving should be kept flush with adjacent area. Edges exposed greater than ½" can cause problems for wheelchairs and can cause tripping by others.

■ REST AREAS allow handicapped persons to move more easily through the city, and are helpful to the general public as well.

■ grate openings larger than ¾" can cause problems for canes, crutch tips, bicycles.

■ provide continuous cross-slope to walkway surfaces for water run-off.
1'-0"
⅛"

bar ½" min.

opening ¾"

2'-0"

2'-0" min.

3'-0" min.

4'-0" min.

■ provide adequate width for walkway:
a.) one-way traffic - 4'-0" min.
b.) two-way traffic - 5'-0" min.

6
1

■ provide non-slip ramp surface. maximum gradient = 17%

Figure 6-1 General dimensions of walks.

6.1 Walks

Walks should be designed to allow the greatest diversity of people to move safely, independently, and unhindered through the exterior environment (see Figure 6-1). Items to consider in the design or modification of walk systems are discussed in the following paragraphs.

Surfaces The surface of walks should be stable and firm, be relatively smooth in texture, and have a nonslip quality. The use of expansion and contraction joints should be minimized, and they should be as small as possible, preferably under ½ inch in width. Figure 6-2 shows the characteristics of different types of materials when used as walkway surfaces.

Rest Areas Occasional rest areas off the traveled path are enjoyable and helpful for all pedestrians and especially for those with handicaps that make walking long distances exhausting.

Gradients Pedestrian paths with gradients under 5 percent are considered walks. Walks with gradients in excess of 5 percent are considered ramps and have special design requirements. Routes with gradients up to 5 percent can be negotiated independently by the average wheelchair user, but sustained grades of 4 percent and 5 percent should have short (5-foot) level areas approximately every 100 feet to allow a chair-bound person using the walk to stop and rest. Gradients up to 3 percent are preferable where their use is practical.

SOURCE: *Barrier-free Site Design,* U.S. Department of Housing and Urban Development, 1975.

Lighting Lighting along walkways should vary from ½ to 5 footcandles, depending on the intensity of pedestrian use, the hazards present, and the relative need for personal safety.

Maintenance Proper maintenance of walks is imperative. If walks are deteriorating, repairs should be made to eliminate any conditions that may cause injury.

Curb Ramps Changes in grade from street to sidewalk and from sidewalk to building entrances create the most numerous problems for people with physical handicaps. To facilitate movement over low barriers, a curb ramp should be installed. Surfaces should be non-slip but not corrugated, for grooves may fill with water, freeze, and cause the ramp to become slippery.

Drainage Structures Improperly designed, constructed, or installed drainage structures may be hazardous to people who must move over them. They should be placed flush with the surface on which they occur, and grates having narrow parallel bars or patterns with openings larger than ¾ inch should not be used. Grates should be kept clean so as not to lessen the efficiency of the overall storm system. Obviously, a surface buildup of water, especially in winter, may present a hazard. For this reason, drainage structures should not be located between a curb ramp and the corner of a street or immediately downgrade from a curb ramp.

Dimensions Walkways vary in width according to the amount and type of traffic using them. They should be a minimum of 4 feet wide, with 5 feet 6 inches (6 feet preferred) being the minimum for moderate two-way traffic.

Wheel Stops Wheel stops are necessary where wheeled vehicles may roll into a hazardous area. They should be 2 to 3 inches high and 6 inches wide and should have breaks in them every 5 to 10 feet to allow water drainage off the walk.

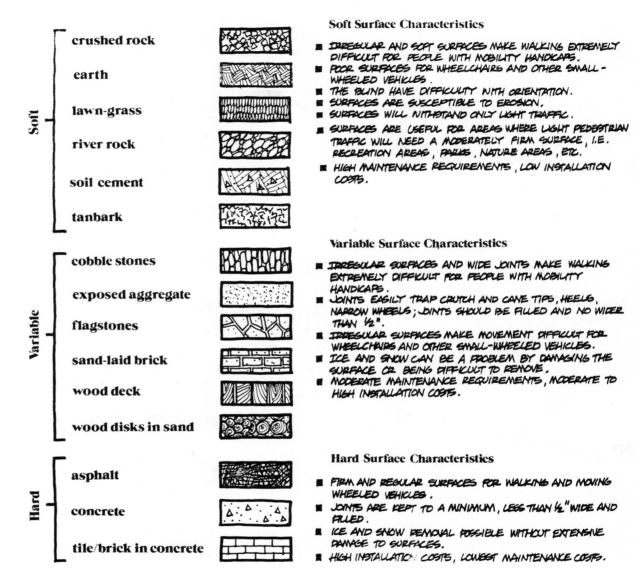

Figure 6-2 Surfaces for walkways.

Soft Surface Characteristics

- IRREGULAR AND SOFT SURFACES MAKE WALKING EXTREMELY DIFFICULT FOR PEOPLE WITH MOBILITY HANDICAPS.
- POOR SURFACES FOR WHEELCHAIRS AND OTHER SMALL-WHEELED VEHICLES.
- THE BLIND HAVE DIFFICULTY WITH ORIENTATION.
- SURFACES ARE SUSCEPTIBLE TO EROSION.
- SURFACES WILL WITHSTAND ONLY LIGHT TRAFFIC.
- SURFACES ARE USEFUL FOR AREAS WHERE LIGHT PEDESTRIAN TRAFFIC WILL NEED A MODERATELY FIRM SURFACE, I.E. RECREATION AREAS, PARKS, NATURE AREAS, ETC.
- HIGH MAINTENANCE REQUIREMENTS, LOW INSTALLATION COSTS.

Variable Surface Characteristics

- IRREGULAR SURFACES AND WIDE JOINTS MAKE WALKING EXTREMELY DIFFICULT FOR PEOPLE WITH MOBILITY HANDICAPS.
- JOINTS EASILY TRAP CRUTCH AND CANE TIPS, HEELS, NARROW WHEELS; JOINTS SHOULD BE FILLED AND NO WIDER THAN ½".
- IRREGULAR SURFACES MAKE MOVEMENT DIFFICULT FOR WHEELCHAIRS AND OTHER SMALL-WHEELED VEHICLES.
- ICE AND SNOW CAN BE A PROBLEM BY DAMAGING THE SURFACE OR BEING DIFFICULT TO REMOVE.
- MODERATE MAINTENANCE REQUIREMENTS, MODERATE TO HIGH INSTALLATION COSTS.

Hard Surface Characteristics

- FIRM AND REGULAR SURFACES FOR WALKING AND MOVING WHEELED VEHICLES.
- JOINTS ARE KEPT TO A MINIMUM, LESS THAN ½" WIDE AND FILLED.
- ICE AND SNOW REMOVAL POSSIBLE WITHOUT EXTENSIVE DAMAGE TO SURFACES.
- HIGH INSTALLATION COSTS, LOWEST MAINTENANCE COSTS.

SOURCE: *Barrier-free Site Design*, U.S. Department of Housing and Urban Development, 1975.

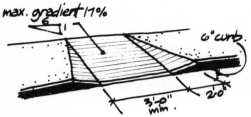

■ avoid "lip" greater than ½" wherever ramp meets adjacent paving at top or bottom.

max. gradient 17%

6" curb.

3'-0" min.   2'-0"

1. Flared Ramp

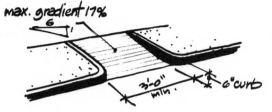

■ corrugated lines in ramps should be avoided since they can hold water in freezing weather and become icy.

max. gradient 17%

3'-0" min.   6" curb

2. Ramp With Continuous Curb

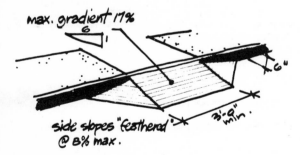

■ use of this type often interferes with curb-side storm drainage & snow plowing.

max. gradient 17%

6"

side slopes "feathered" @ 8% max.   3'-0" min.

3. Extended Ramp

Figure 6-3 Curb ramps.

■ locate handrail to avoid conflict with adjacent pedestrian walkway.

max. gradient 17%

3'-6" min.   5'-0" min.

STREET

6" curb

4. Parallel Ramp

CURB RAMPS

Curbing, though a commonly specified element on most sites, is one of the most neglected items with regard to the physical barriers it creates. The problem is twofold. It stems, first, from the attitude of most designers that 6 inch concrete curbs are an unavoidable necessity and, second, from municipalites that aggravate the problem by writing in curbing clauses to building ordinances for no reason other than that they have always been a requirement. While this subsection by no means advocates the retraction of municipal curbing requirements, it does seem that viable alternatives should be allowed where they would reduce potential barriers and hazards while satisfying existing requirements.

When specifying the use of conventional curbing, the designer should be aware of the following considerations:

1. Curbing should not create any unnecessary barriers to physically handicapped individuals. Where barriers have been created, previously laid curbs should either be removed or be ramped. See Figure 6-3.
2. Curbing, if necessary, should never be higher than the maximum height of one step, or 6½ inches. This is particularly important where there is any pedestrian traffic crossing over or vehicles parking adjacent to the curb.
3. Double, or stepped, curbs are difficult for the handicapped to negotiate and in darkness are hazardous to all pedestrians. Their use should be limited if not restricted.

SOURCE: *Barrier-free Site Design*, U.S. Department of Housing and Urban Development, 1975.

WALKWAYS

Various types of walkway construction are shown in Figure 6-4, and drainage in Figure 6-5.

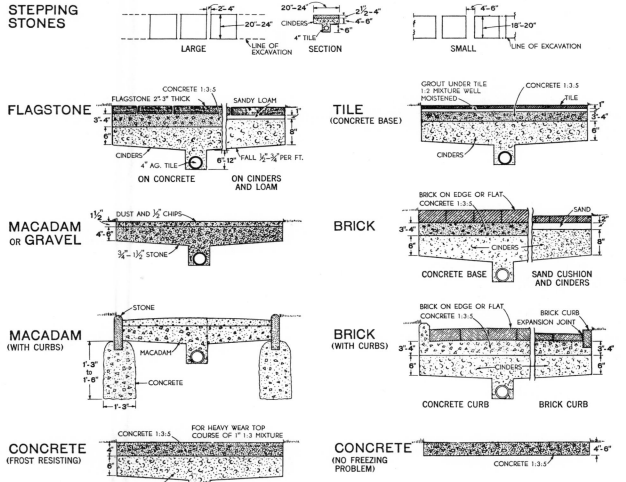

Figure 6-4 Walkway construction.

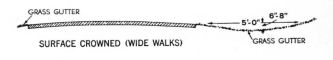

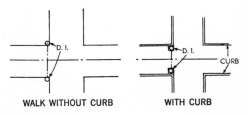

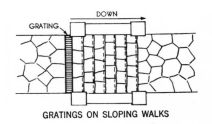

Figure 6-5 Walk drainage.

SOURCE: *Time-Saver Standards*, 1st ed., F. W. Dodge Company, New York, 1946.

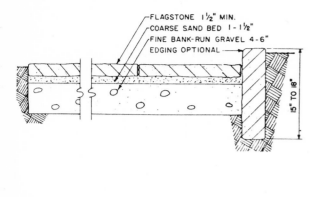

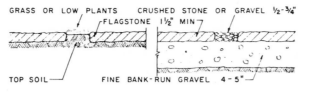

Methods of construction for walks and terraces of different types are shown in Figures 6-6, 6-7, 6-8, 6-9, and 6-10.

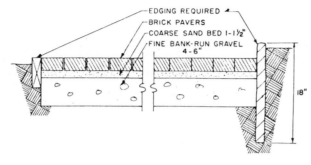

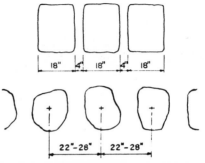

Figure 6-8 Stepping-stones: *(top)* rectangular; *(bottom)* irregular. Stones should be not less than 1½ inches thick. Common rectangular sizes are 12 by 15, 15 by 20, 18 by 24, 20 by 30, and 24 by 36 inches.

Figure 6-6 Dry construction. *(upper left)* Flagstone with tight joints. Edging may be Belgian block, granite, or flagstone. *(upper right)* Flagstone with gravel or grass joints. The type shown to the left will heave with frost. Grass or low plants in joints are hard to maintain. *(lower left)* Gravel. Edging may be 1-inch or thicker flagstone 18 inches deep or ³⁄₁₆- by 5-inch metal: or Belgian block, granite, or precast concrete

curb may be used. In frost-free zones, bricks on edge, ⅛- by 4-inch metal, or 1- by 6-inch redwood with 1- by 3- by 18-inch stakes 4 feet on center may be used. Metal edging should be used for curved walks. *(lower right)* Brick with tight joints. Edging may be 1- by 8-inch redwood, 1½- by 18-inch flagstone, or ¼- by 5-inch metal.

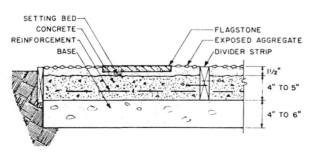

Figure 6-7 Frost-resisting construction. The base should be coarse bank-run gravel or slag or 1- to 3-inch crushed stone; it must be well drained. Concrete should have asphaltic expansion joints

every 20 feet. The top surface should be rough for bond to the setting bed. Reinforcement should be 6- by 6-inch welded wire mesh. Joints should be ¾ inch or narrower and be grouted; care

must be taken to keep grout from the face of the paving at all times. Edgings are required only during construction. In frost-free zones, the base and reinforcement may be omitted. *(left)* Flagstone or other paving units. Brick, quarry tile, slate, marble, Belgian block, or asphalt block may be set to the same details. There must be total contact, with no air pockets, between paving stone and cement setting bed. *(right)* Exposed aggregate concrete. Exposed aggregate ⅜ inch to 1 inch in size is set in natural or colored cement, with or without flagstones. If desired, dividers of 2- by 6-inch redwood may be used, with 4-inch galvanized spikes 12 inches on center to prevent heaving.

SOURCE: Joseph De Chiara and J. H. Callender, *Time-Saver Standards for Building Types*, McGraw-Hill Book Company, New York, 1973.

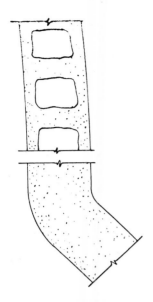

Figure 6-9 Gravel path with or without stepping-stones; width: single, 1 foot 6 inches to 3 feet; double, 3 feet 6 inches to 5 feet. Edging is required.

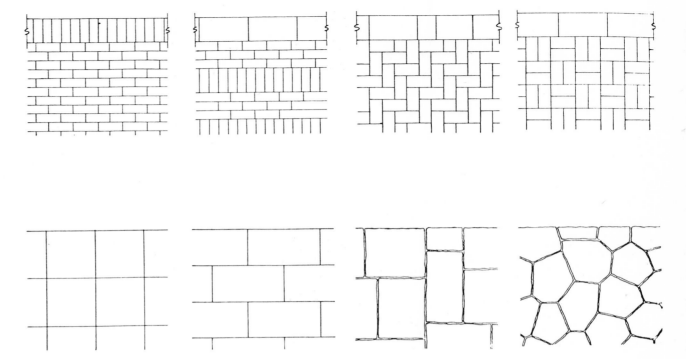

Figure 6-10 *(top row, left to right)* Brick pavement patterns: running bond; running-bond variation; herringbone; basket weave. Borders may be brick or stone. Edging is required with dry construction. *(center row, left to right)* Flagstone pavement patterns: squares; regular rectangular; random rectangular; irregular or polygonal. All joints should be tight. Some standard patterns are available in random irregular (for this pattern, joints should be broken every three stones or oftener). Square and rectangular shapes are also available in precast concrete. *(lower row, left to right)* Precast concrete in gravel or exposed aggregate concrete; flagstone or other paving blocks in exposed aggregate concrete; log sections in gravel. For logs, use cypress, redwood, chestnut, locust, or other durable wood, 6 inches thick; spacing is optional. Tanbark or low plants may be used instead of gravel.

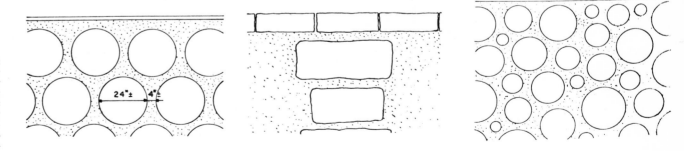

SOURCE: Joseph De Chiara and J. H. Callender, *Time-Saver Standards for Building Types,* McGraw-Hill Book Company, New York, 1973.

6.2 Steps

Figures 6-11, 6-12, 6-13, and 6-14 illustrate various types of step construction. Riser-tread ratios should be as follows: 4-inch riser, tread 16 to 18 inches; 5-inch riser, tread 14 to 16 inches; 6-inch riser, tread 12 to 14 inches. All treads should be pitched slightly for drainage. If ramps are used, their slope should not exceed 10 and must not exceed 12 percent.

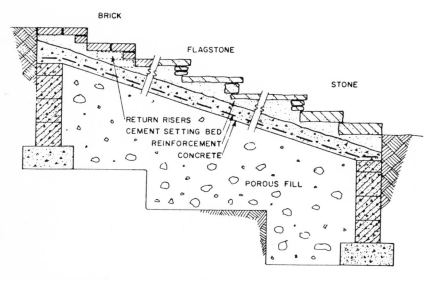

Figure 6-11 Steps of bonded frost-resistant construction. Treads may be brick, flagstone, or cut stone. Brick joints should not be wider than ⅜ inch. Flagstone treads should be 1½ to 2 inches thick. Risers may be brick, flagstone strips 4 inches wide, or selected flat stones with recessed joints. Visible joints should be rodded concave. Care must be taken not to get mortar on masonry faces. Risers must be returned at the sides if cheek wall is not used. Cut-stone treads should have some overlap for support. Concrete slab should be 5 to 6 inches thick with suitable reinforcement; the top surface is roughened for good bond with the setting bed. Foundations must extend below the frost line.

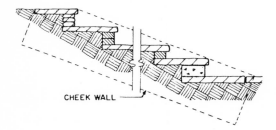

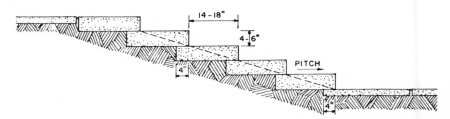

Figure 6-13 Cut-stone steps of dry construction. The treads should overlap 4 inches for support. The steps are set dry on soil fill; no sand.

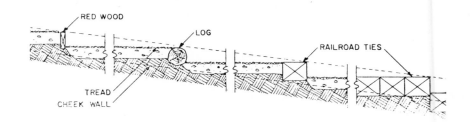

Figure 6-14 Variations of wood-and-gravel steps. Risers may be (1) redwood, 2 by 6 inches minimum, with cheek walls 2 by 8 inches and aluminum or stainless-steel nails; (2) logs, 6 inches or more in diameter, of cypress, juniper, arborvitae, black locust, or other decay-resistant wood; or (3) railroad ties. Treads may be (1) tanbark or ⅜-inch crushed stone 1 inch thick over a 4-inch base of bank-run gravel; or (2) railroad ties (also for cheek walls). Risers should have a maximum height of 4 inches; treads should measure 16, 40, or 64 inches.

Figure 6-12 Steps of dry construction with flagstone treads. The treads are 16 to 20 inches long and 1½ to 2 inches thick. The risers may be brick, flagstone strips 4 to 5 inches wide, stone, or concrete block, set dry on treads. Cheek wall is recommended; it may be flagstone 2 to 3 inches thick by 18 inches deep. The steps are set dry on soil fill; no sand.

SOURCE: Joseph De Chiara and J. H. Callender, *Time-Saver Standards for Building Types*, McGraw-Hill Book Company, New York, 1973.

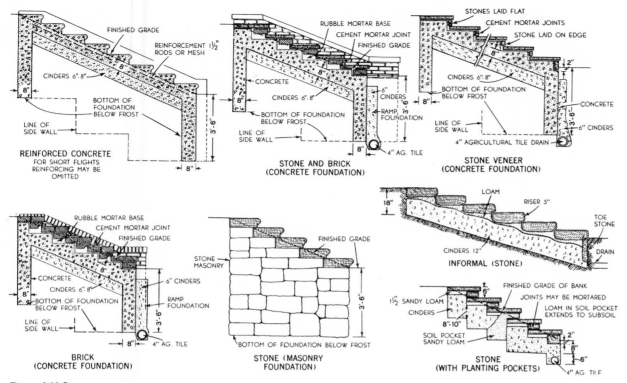

Figure 6-15 Steps.

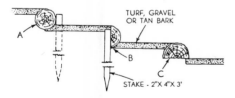

LOGS ALTERNATE METHODS

STONE

Prepared by A. D. TAYLOR LANDSCAPE ARCHITECT

Figure 6-16 Perrons.

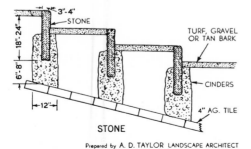

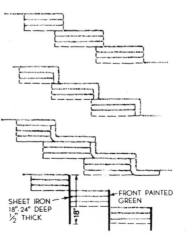

Figure 6-17 Turf steps: alternative methods.

STEPS AND PERRONS

The construction of various types of steps, ramps, and perrons is shown in Figures 6-15, 6-16, 6-17, 6-18, and 6-19.

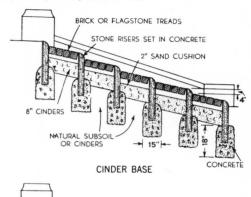

CINDER BASE

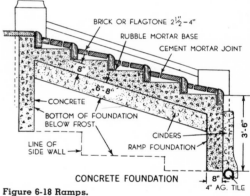

CONCRETE FOUNDATION

Figure 6-18 Ramps.

Figure 6-19 Wash-on steps.

SOURCE: *Time-Saver Standards*, 1st ed., F. W. Dodge Company, New York, 1946.

WOOD STEPS

The construction of wood steps and decks is illustrated in Figure 6-20. Redwood or cypress with fastenings of aluminum or stainless steel should be used for all exterior wood construction.

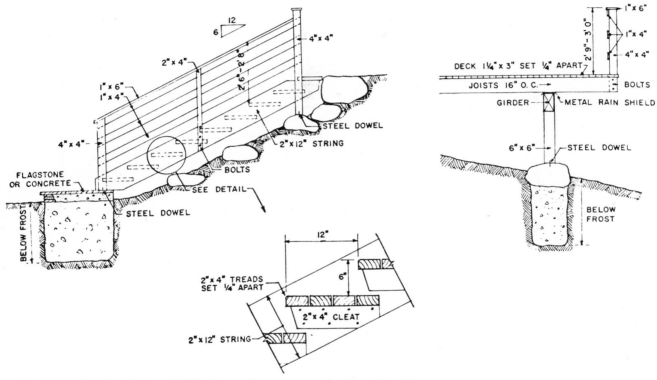

Figure 6-20 Wood decks and steps. *(left)* Wood steps. If steps are more than 30 inches wide, add a center carriage member. *(center)* Detail of stair treads. *(right)* Elevated wood deck.

SOURCE: Joseph De Chiara and J. H. Callender, *Time-Saver Standards for Building Types,* McGraw-Hill Book Company, New York, 1973.

RAMPS AND STEPPED RAMPS

Ramps and stepped ramps present a slipping hazard similar to that of stairs. Therefore, they should have a natural or applied slip-resistant surface. Broom-finished concrete, rough brick or stone, or the application of slip-resistant safety strips or cleats would reduce the slipping hazard.

For safety in negotiating changes of elevation in exterior applications, the design of ramps and stepped ramps should incorporate the following characteristics:

1. Ramps
   a. Preferable slope of 7 to 15 degrees; maximum, 20 degrees
2. Stepped ramps
   a. Maximum riser height, 5 inches
   b. Minimum tread width, 15 inches
   c. Ramp gradient: maximum, 1 degree (¼ inch per foot, or 2 percent); minimum, ½ degree (⅛ inch per foot, or 1 percent)
   d. Ramp length: one or three easy strides (3 or 6 feet suggested)
   e. Overall gradient: 15 degrees (3¼ inches per foot, or 27.1 percent) or as low as 10 degrees (2⅛ inches per foot, or 17.7 percent), with 4-inch risers and 1 percent treads

Recommended designs are shown in Figure 6-21.

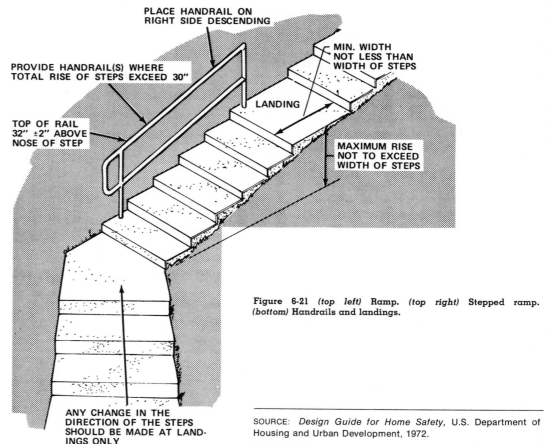

PLACE HANDRAIL ON RIGHT SIDE DESCENDING

PROVIDE HANDRAIL(S) WHERE TOTAL RISE OF STEPS EXCEED 30"

MIN. WIDTH NOT LESS THAN WIDTH OF STEPS

LANDING

TOP OF RAIL 32" ±2" ABOVE NOSE OF STEP

MAXIMUM RISE NOT TO EXCEED WIDTH OF STEPS

ANY CHANGE IN THE DIRECTION OF THE STEPS SHOULD BE MADE AT LANDINGS ONLY

Figure 6-21 *(top left)* Ramp. *(top right)* Stepped ramp. *(bottom)* Handrails and landings.

SOURCE: *Design Guide for Home Safety*, U.S. Department of Housing and Urban Development, 1972.

6.3 Benches and Tables

Suggested designs for benches and tables are
shown in Figures 6-22 through 6-30.

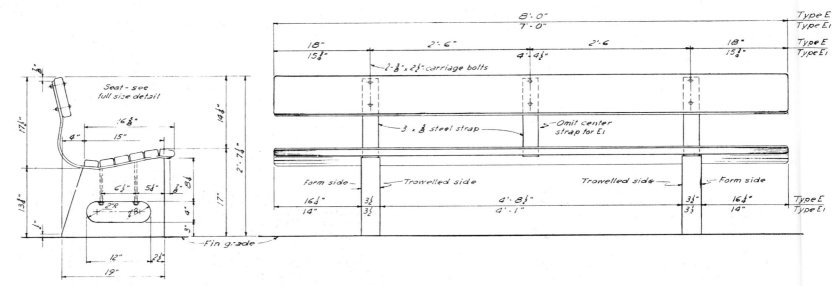

Figure 6-22 Bench.

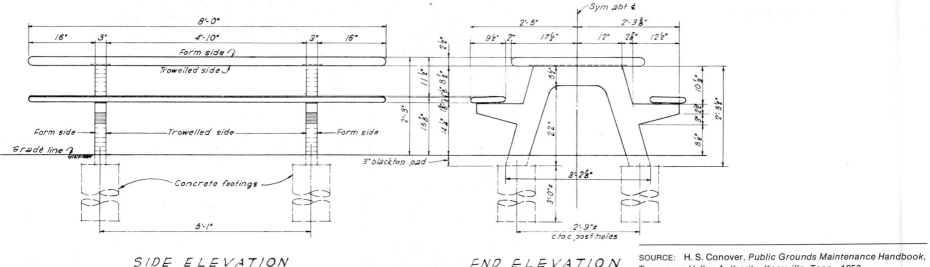

SIDE ELEVATION

END ELEVATION

SOURCE: H. S. Conover, *Public Grounds Maintenance Handbook,*
Tennessee Valley Authority, Knoxville, Tenn., 1953.

Figure 6-23 Table.

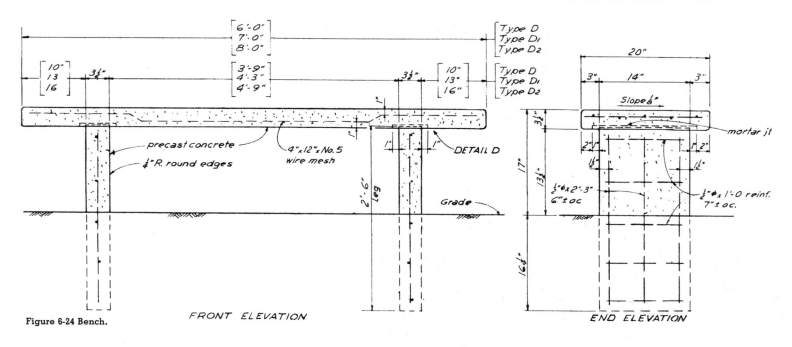

Figure 6-24 Bench.

FRONT ELEVATION

END ELEVATION

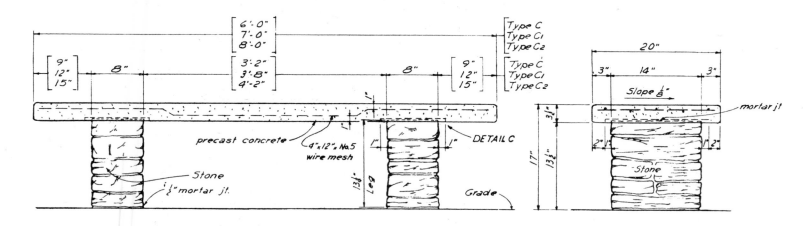

Figure 6-25 Bench.

FRONT ELEVATION

SOURCE: H. S. Conover, *Public Grounds Maintenance Handbook,* Tennessee Valley Authority, Knoxville, Tenn., 1953.

263

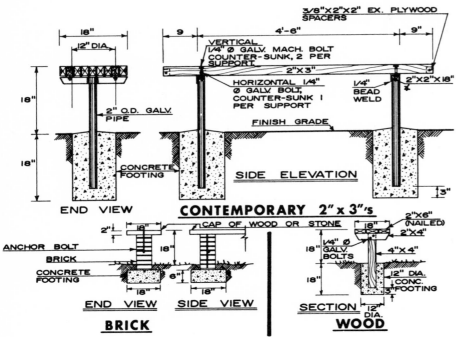

Figure 6-26 Benches.

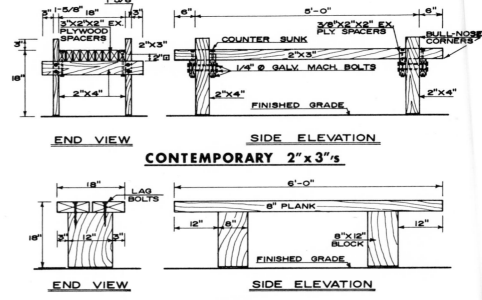

Figure 6-27 Benches.

SOURCE: *Landscape Development,* U.S. Department of the Interior, Field Technical Office, Littleton, Colo.

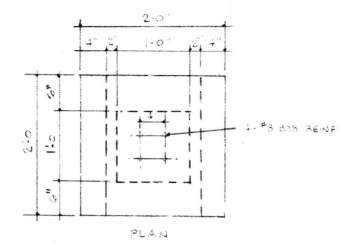

PLAN

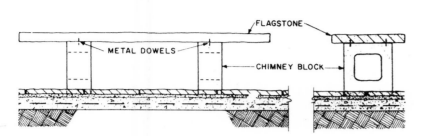

Figure 6-28 Bench. The seat may be flagstone or concrete, 2 to 3 inches thick and 18 to 24 inches wide; height is 14 to 18 inches. Supports are concrete chimney block, 8 by 16 by 16 inches.

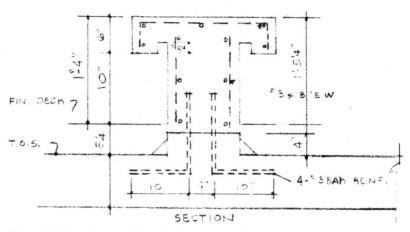

SECTION

Figure 6-30 Precast concrete bench. All surfaces should be sandblast-finished.

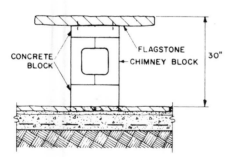

Figure 6-29 Table. The top may be flagstone, slate, or concrete, 1½ to 3 inches thick. Supports are a combination of concrete blocks 4 by 8 by 16 inches and 8 by 8 by 16 inches and chimney block 8 by 16 by 16 inches to obtain a height of 29 to 30 inches.

SOURCE: (Figures 6-28 and 6-29) Joseph De Chiara and J. H. Callender, *Time-Saver Standards for Building Types,* McGraw-Hill Book Company, New York, 1973.

6.4 Guardrails and Fences

PARKING BARRIER

Complete pressure treatment of all posts and rails is recommended for long life. A piece of tarred felt placed in the notch section is valu- able in reducing deterioration at that critical point.

Since parking barriers are more subject to vehicle impact than are parallel roadside guardrails (although not often so violently), a log segment laid in the ground a few feet in front of the barrier minimizes this possible damage by serving as a curbing.

All hardware should be galvanized.

See Figures 6-31 and 6-32 for diagrams of guardrails and a parking barrier.

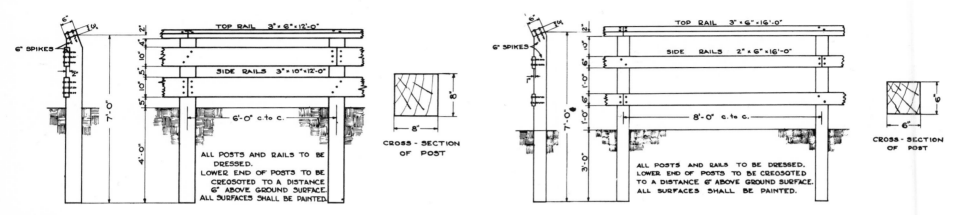

Figure 6-31 Guardrails.

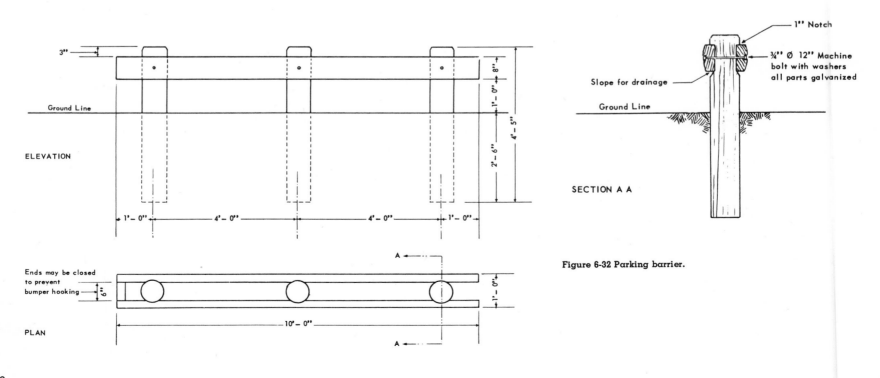

Figure 6-32 Parking barrier.

FENCES

Various types of fences are illustrated in Figures 6-33 and 6-34.

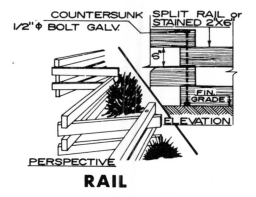

RAIL

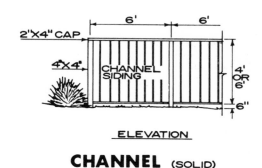

CHANNEL (SOLID)

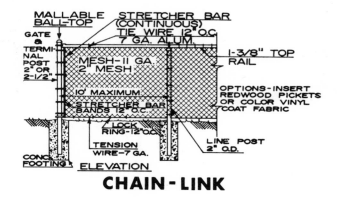

CHAIN-LINK

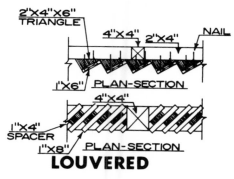

LOUVERED

Figure 6-33 Types of fences.

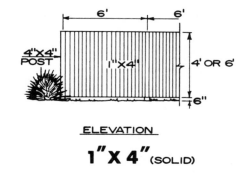

1"X 4" (SOLID)

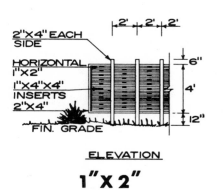

1"X 2"

SOURCE: *Landscape Development,* U.S. Department of the Interior, Field Technical Office, Littleton, Colo.

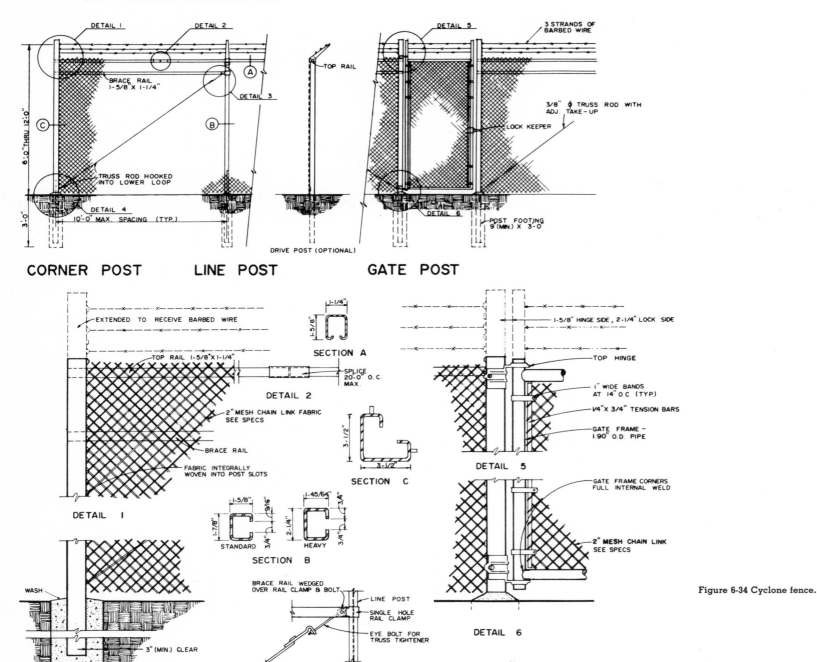

DETAIL 1   DETAIL 2

3 STRANDS OF BARBED WIRE

DETAIL 5

TOP RAIL

BRACE RAIL 1-5/8" X 1-1/4"

DETAIL 3

Ⓐ

Ⓒ

Ⓑ

3/8" ∅ TRUSS ROD WITH ADJ. TAKE-UP

LOCK KEEPER

TRUSS ROD HOOKED INTO LOWER LOOP

6'-0" THRU 12'-0"

DETAIL 4
10'-0" MAX. SPACING (TYP.)

3'-0"

DRIVE POST (OPTIONAL)

DETAIL 6

POST FOOTING 9"(MIN.) X 3'-0"

CORNER POST   **LINE POST**   **GATE POST**

EXTENDED TO RECEIVE BARBED WIRE

1-1/4"

1-5/8"

1-5/8" HINGE SIDE, 2-1/4" LOCK SIDE

SECTION A

TOP RAIL 1-5/8" X 1-1/4"

SPLICE 20'-0" O.C. MAX.

DETAIL 2

TOP HINGE

1" WIDE BANDS AT 14" O.C. (TYP.)

1/4" X 3/4" TENSION BARS

GATE FRAME – 1.90" O.D. PIPE

DETAIL 5

2" MESH CHAIN LINK FABRIC SEE SPECS

BRACE RAIL

FABRIC INTEGRALLY WOVEN INTO POST SLOTS

3-1/2"

3-1/2"

SECTION C

DETAIL 1

1-5/8"

9/16"

1-7/8"

3/4"

STANDARD

1-45/64"

3/4"

2-1/4"

3/4"

HEAVY

SECTION B

GATE FRAME CORNERS FULL INTERNAL WELD

2" MESH CHAIN LINK SEE SPECS

WASH

BRACE RAIL WEDGED OVER RAIL CLAMP & BOLT

LINE POST

SINGLE HOLE RAIL CLAMP

EYE BOLT FOR TRUSS TIGHTENER

DETAIL 6

3" (MIN.) CLEAR

CONCRETE 2500 P.S.I. (MIN.)

DETAIL 4

DETAIL 3

Figure 6-34 Cyclone fence.

SOURCE: United States Steel Corporation.

6.5 Outdoor Surfacing

No one surface will satisfactorily meet the needs of all outdoor activities. Each activity has its own surface requirements that dictate which type or types of material can be used.

In the selection of surfacing material for any outdoor area, certain qualities should be sought. These include:

Multiplicity of use
Durability
Resistance to dust and stains
Reasonable initial cost
Ease of maintenance
Low maintenance cost
Pleasing appearance
Nonabrasiveness
Resiliency
All-year usage

Obtaining the proper surface for outdoor recreation areas continues to be a perplexing problem for school administrators, play supervisors, designers, and those responsible for

TYPES OF SURFACING MATERIALS

Group	Type
Earth	Loams, sand, sand and clay, clay and gravel, fuller's earth, stabilized earth, soil and cement
Turf	Bluegrass mixtures, bent, fescue, Bermuda
Aggregates	Gravel, graded stone, graded slag, shell, cinders
Bituminous (asphalt-tar)	Penetration macadam, bituminous or asphaltic concrete (cold and hot-laid), sheet asphalt, natural asphalt, sawdust asphalt, vermiculite asphalt, rubber asphalt, cork asphalt, other patented asphalt mixes
Synthetics	Rubber, synthetic resins, rubber asphalt, chlorinated butyl rubber, mineral fiber, finely ground aggregate and asphalt, plastics, vinyls
Concrete	Monolithic, terrazzo, precast
Masonry	Flagstone (sandstone, limestone, granite, and so on), brick, and so on
Miscellaneous	Tanbark, sawdust, shavings, cottonseed hulls

maintenance. Over the years there have been significant developments in surfacing, especially under and around playground apparatus. There has been a gradual change from earth, mud, sand, and turf to bituminous surfacing, which is presently being used throughout the United States. This change has come about because of the consensus that bituminous blacktop surfacing is an improvement over other surfacing types that have proved unsatisfactory.

Turf The advantages of using grass as a surface are its attractiveness, resiliency, and nonabrasiveness and the fact that it is relatively dust-free. Such a surface lends itself very well to activities that require relatively large areas, as most field games do.

Turf is difficult to maintain in areas where usage is intensive. In regions where watering is essential, maintenance costs are high. Turf surfaces are not practical for most activities when the ground is frozen or wet and, in addition, must be given time and care to restore themselves after heavy use.

Since climatic conditions and uses should determine the species of grass selected for a particular locality, careful consideration should be given to the several varieties available.

Soils The use of earth as a surfacing material has been widespread, particularly under apparatus, primarily because it is porous and inexpensive.

Among the difficulties encountered in the use of earth as a surfacing material are dust and the tendency to become rutted. These in turn create drainage problems and relatively high maintenance costs. These difficulties can be partially overcome by mixing the earth with clay or sand. When this is done, the resulting surface is often less resilient and somewhat abrasive.

Natural soils can also be stabilized by the addition of asphalt, resin, or cement, which are the most commonly used stabilizers. The use of stabilized soils is a possibility in many areas where turf is impractical or cannot be grown.

Masonry Natural-stone slabs or blocks and manufactured brick can be used for such installations as walks and terraces where interesting and attractive patterns, colors, and textures are desired.

Concrete Concrete surfaces provide year-round and multiple usage. The costs of maintenance are very low, and the surface is extremely durable.

Bituminous Surfaces The common bituminous surface has many of the advantages sought in any surfacing material. It provides a durable surface that can be used on a year-round schedule. The maintenance of bituminous surface is comparatively easy and inexpensive. Such a surface can also be used for many different activities. When properly installed, the surface is dust-free and drains quickly. Asphalt surfaces can be marked easily and with a relatively high degree of permanence. Asphalt also provides a neat-appearing, no-glare surface that blends well with the landscape.

The disadvantages of bituminous surfaces are their relatively high installation costs and lack of resiliency as compared with some other types of surfaces. However, the high installation cost is offset by low maintenance costs.

Bituminous surfaces vary as to firmness, finish, resiliency, and durability in direct relation to the kinds and proportions of aggregates and other materials used in their mixture. Asphalt can be combined with a variety of other materials to provide a reasonably resilient or extremely hard surface. The use of such materials as cork, sponge, or rubber in combination with asphalt yields a fairly resilient surface. Aggregates such as slag or granite produce an extremely hard surface when they are combined with asphalt.

Synthetics Many different types of surfacing materials have been placed in experimen-

SOURCE: *Planning Areas and Facilities for Health, Physical Education, and Recreation,* Athletic Institute and American Association for Health, Physical Education, and Recreation, Washington, 1965.

tal use, particularly under fixed equipment. Materials such as sponge, sponge rubber, rubber mats, cork, air cell materials, and combinations in conjunction with covers of rubber vinyl, canvas, and asphaltic binder coatings are in experimental use.

Some synthetic materials appear to meet the requirements for durability. Track spikes or cleats do not leave holes in such a material; rather, the material closes around the puncture. Very little maintenance of synthetic materials is required; thus maintenance costs are low. Most synthetics have a very pleasing appearance and are available in different colors. They are nonabrasive and suitable for year-round use.

There are a number of commercially manufactured synthetic compounds such as chlorinated butyl rubber, rubber asphalt, synthetic resins, mineral fiber, finely ground aggregate and asphalt, plastics, and vinyls. They come in a variety of textures, colors, weights, and thicknesses. Most synthetic surfaces have a high degree of resiliency, which makes them desirable for many types of athletic activities. Research is needed, however, to develop a vandal-proof resilient surface.

SOURCE: *Planning Areas and Facilities for Health, Physical Education, and Recreation*, Athletic Institute and American Association for Health, Physical Education, and Recreation, Washington, 1965.

Bikeways and Trails

BIKEWAYS

In the design of any bikeway system, a number of basic considerations must be taken into account by the designer.

Bicycles and Clearances The dimensions in Figure 6-35 are by no means meant to be finite. The intention is to offer basic dimensions of the common ten-speed racing-touring bicycle and to propose certain "common-sense" design minimums that have emerged from experimentation. Designers in all cases should become aware of local public preferences in bicycle types and adjust their designs accordingly.

Bikeway Surfaces The surface of which a bikeway is constructed is perhaps the single most important feature that the designer must consider. A simple chart showing recommended materials with some basic explanations has been included to help direct the designer in considering surfaces for bikeway construction (see Figure 6-37).

Classification of Bikeways The word "bikeways" has come to be the general term describing any facility reserved for the exclusive or semiexclusive use of bicycles and related vehicles. Current literature on the subject generally accepts that bikeways may assume any of three basic forms (see Figure 6-36).

Class I This is a completely separated right-of-way designated exclusively for bicycles. Through traffic, whether by motor vehicles or by pedestrians, is not allowed. Cross flows by vehicles and pedestrians are allowed but are minimized.

Class II This is a restricted right-of-way designated exclusively or semiexclusively for bicycles. Through traffic by motor vehicles or pedestrians is not allowed. Cross flows by vehicles and pedestrians are allowed but are minimized.

Class III This is any shared right-of-way designated by signs or stencils. It designates any pathway that shares its through-traffic right-of-way with either moving (but not parked) motor vehicles or pedestrians.

Design Speeds Bicycle speed is determined by several factors, which include the type of bicycle, the gearing ratio, pavement gradients, the pavement surface type and condition, wind velocity and direction, air resis-

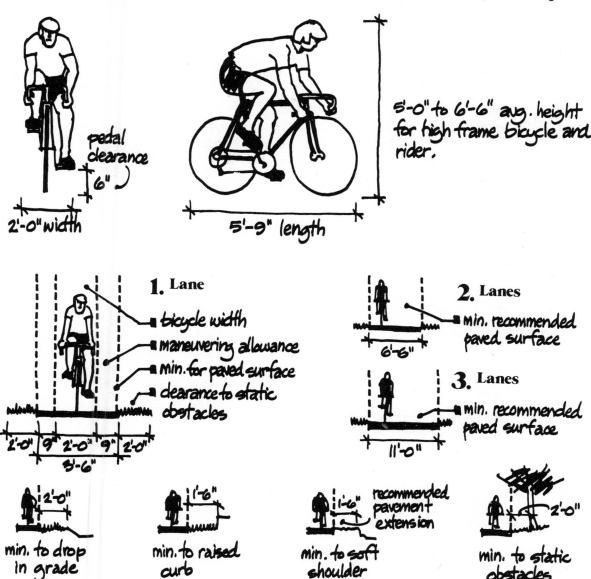

Figure 6-35 General dimensional requirements of bikeways.

SOURCE: *Barrier-free Site Design,* U.S. Department of Housing and Urban Development, 1975.

Bikeway Classifications

Class I

Bikeway   Walk   Roadway

Total separation / Dividing strip between right-of-ways on separate surfaces.

Class II

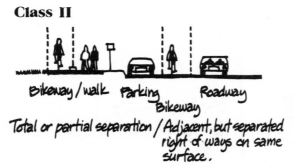

Bikeway/walk   Parking   Roadway
Bikeway

Total or partial separation / Adjacent, but separated right-of-ways on same surface.

Class III

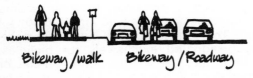

Bikeway/walk   Bikeway/Roadway

Partial or no separation / Shared right-of-way on same surface

Possible Locations for Bikeways

- Abandoned RR right-of-ways
- Electric and pipeline right-of-ways
- River banks
- Dry washes
- Beach fronts, lake fronts
- Flood control dikes and levees
- Irrigation canal banks and dikes
- Fire breaks

Intersections for Bikeways

1.

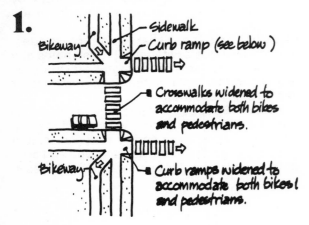

- Sidewalk
- Curb ramp (see below)
- Crosswalks widened to accommodate both bikes and pedestrians.
- Curb ramps widened to accommodate both bikes and pedestrians.

2.

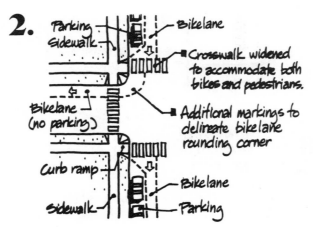

Parking
Sidewalk
- Bikelane
- Crosswalk widened to accommodate both bikes and pedestrians.
Bikelane (no parking)
- Additional markings to delineate bikelane rounding corner
Curb ramp
- Bikelane
Sidewalk
- Parking

Figure 6-36

tance, and the cyclist's age and physical condition. Although bicyclists have averaged touring speeds in excess of 30 miles per hour, a conservative speed for the average cyclist is around 10 to 11.5 miles per hour, with a range of 3 to 19 miles per hour. In determining minimum widths and radii of curvature on level bikeways, 10 miles per hour is a conservative figure for design speed.

Gradients Since cyclists may be discouraged from using a facility in direct proportion to the amount of energy and the work rate necessary to overcome any given length of grades on the facility, the importance of developing criteria based upon physiological requirements cannot be overemphasized. The following are suggested norms and maximums that should be considered when laying out a bikeway route:

Gradient (percent)	Length (feet)	
	Normal	Maximum
1.5	1600	...
3.0	400	800
4.5	150	300
10.0	30	60

Radius of Curvature At present, accepted radii in the United States vary from 6 to 50 feet. When designing radii for bikeway layouts, the designer should use the following formula. The equivalent radius of curvature as a function of velocity is expressed in the following linear relationship:

$$R = 1.25V + 1.4$$

where R = unbraked radius of curvature (in feet) negotiated by a bicycle on a flat, dry, bituminous concrete surface

V = velocity of bicycle in miles per hour

SOURCE: *Barrier-free Site Design*, U.S. Department of Housing and Urban Development, 1975.

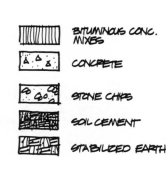

| | BITUMINOUS CONC. MIXES | |
| | CONCRETE | |

All weather, permanent surfaces:
(most widely used; highest installation costs, longest wearing life; especially good for heavy use in urban areas.)

STONE CHIPS
SOIL CEMENT
STABILIZED EARTH

Loose aggregate, compositional, natural surfaces:
(lower installation costs; high maintenance requirements, susceptible to poor natural drainage; will not stand up to continual heavy use.)

WOOD PLANKING

Wood Surfaces:
(use only when laid perpendicular to direction of travel, usually on light bridges, boardwalks, etc.)

Standard Construction
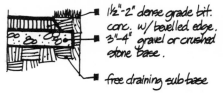
- 1½"-2" dense grade bit. conc. w/ bevelled edge.
- 3"-4" gravel or crushed stone base.
- free draining sub base

Silts & Clays
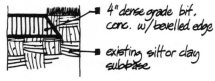
- 4" dense grade bit. conc. w/ bevelled edge
- existing silt or clay subbase

Gravels & Sands

- 3" dense grade bit. conc. w/ bevelled edge
- existing gravel or sandy subbase

Poorly Drained
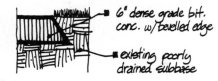
- 6" dense grade bit. conc. w/ bevelled edge
- existing poorly drained subbase

Figure 6-37 Recommended surfaces for bikeways.

- 2'-0" spacing allows cyclists to place or remove bikes from racks with minimum of effort and damage.

1. Concrete blocks w/ metal rings

2. Steel and wire hoops.

3. Wall racks (arms)

4. Sunken wheel wells w/ rings.

- Racks and stanchions that allow cyclists to lock both frame and wheels reduce casual theft.
- Consider rack and stanchion heights so that excessive cable or chain lengths are not needed to secure both frame and wheels.
- Can catch water, heels, debris, etc.

Figure 6-38 Bicycle parking.

EXAMPLE:

For a Class I bikeway with a use speed of 10 miles per hour, the "comfortable" unbraked radius of curvature is 13.9 feet.

Intersections The most effective way of avoiding conflicts between cyclists and motor vehicles where the bikeway must cross a heavily traveled roadway and heavy bicycle use is anticipated is to employ a total grade separation. This recommendation also holds true when the bikeway must cross heavily traveled intersections where significant bicycle traffic might disrupt the orderly flow of vehicular traffic.

Generally, in densely populated urban areas with little room for underpasses, providing total grade separation at intersections may be completely prohibitive from the standpoint of cost. This being the case, the designer must then route the bikeway across the roadway at grade. Some of the more typical situations are illustrated in Figure 6-36.

Parking When designing or locating bikeway parking areas, the following items should be considered:

1. Secure stanchions should be provided; that is, the bicycle frame rather than a wheel alone should be anchored, since the secured wheel can easily be detached from the frame and the rest of the bike carried off.
2. Stanchions should be located in areas where there is constant visual supervision.
3. Parking areas should be out of pedestrian pathways.
4. Parking areas should be conveniently located near cyclist destinations, adjacent to main entries where possible (preferably within 50 feet or less). If distances become too great, cyclists frequently secure bikes to the nearest available permanent object, such as railings, signposts, light posts, flagpoles, and trees.

Various types of parking are illustrated in Figure 6-38.

SOURCE: *Barrier-free Site Design*, U.S. Department of Housing and Urban Development, 1975.

TRAILS

Exclusive off-street bikeways and hiking and riding trails can be located in a number of fashions and combinations. Perhaps the greatest opportunities lie along the shoreline and along the levees or banks of flood control channels, rivers, creeks, and lakes. Other corridors can be found along railroad and power line rights-of-way and fire trails.

Trail Requirements The design of an exclusive trail is determined by the anticipated use, terrain characteristics, and safety requirements. Acceptable standards for exclusive trails are shown in Figures 6-39, 6-40, and 6-41.

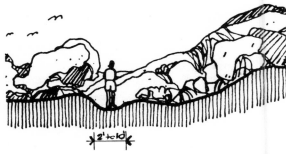

Figure 6-41 Hiking trails vary from 2 to 10 feet in width, depending on their character. The grade should be 5 percent (a maximum of 15 percent for very short distances). The clearance should be 8 feet. The surface should be firm, natural ground.

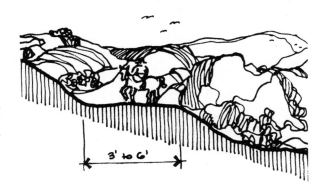

Figure 6-40 Riding trails should have a width of 3 to 6 feet. The grade should be a maximum of 5 percent (10 percent for very short distances). Clearance should be 12 feet. The surface should be natural ground (loose soil).

Figure 6-39 Bikeways should have a width of 8 to 10 feet (two-way) or 6 feet (one-way). The grade should be a maximum of 5 percent for lengths up to 1000 feet and 15 percent for very short distances. Clearance should be 10 feet. The surface should be hard, preferably asphalt.

SOURCE: *BART/Trails*, U.S. Department of Transportation.

6.7 Driveways

Widths range from 9 to 12 feet for single-lane driveways and from 15 to 18 feet for double-lane driveways. If the 9-foot width is used, it should be increased to at least 10 feet on curves.

Drainage is essential. The minimum longitudinal pitch for proper drainage is 1 percent. If gutters are used, runoffs or catch basins should be provided at suitable intervals. Underground drains should be employed if they are required by soil conditions (see Figures 6-42, 6-43, and 6-44).

Bases must be well compacted and well drained. Soft clay soil or heavy truck traffic necessitates a heavier base. Typical bases for driveways are as follows:

1. For dry construction: bank-run gravel or sandy gravel; no air pockets
2. For concrete surfaces: sandy gravel, cinders, crushed stone, slag, or other inorganic porous material
3. Crushed stone, 1½ to 2½ inches in size, rolled with a 6- to 10-ton roller

Bank-run gravel consists of stones, sand, and some clay for binder; fine bank-run gravel, of stones up to 1 inch in size; coarse bank-run gravel, of stones up to 4 inches in size.

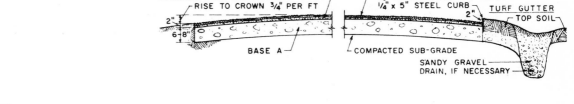

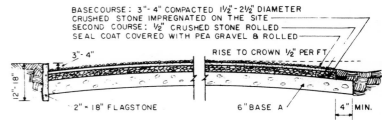

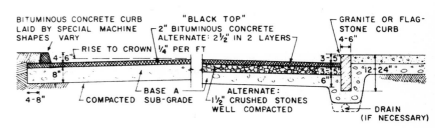

Figure 6-44 *(top)* Gravel driveway. Use calcium chloride or two coats of oil on bank-run gravel to keep surface from dusting. For heavy traffic, use two 6-inch courses for the base. *(center)* Penetration asphalt driveway. *(bottom)* Bituminous-concrete (blacktop) driveway.

Figure 6-42 Cut-and-fill grading for driveway construction.

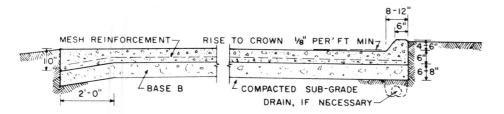

Figure 6-43 Concrete driveway. An asphalt expansion joint should be provided every 30 feet. The concrete may be covered with blacktop 1 to 2 inches thick.

SOURCE: Charles Middeleer, landscape architect; Joseph De Chiara and J. H. Callender, *Time-Saver Standards for Building Types*, McGraw-Hill Book Company, New York, 1973.

RESIDENTIAL DRIVEWAYS

The grade, width, and radius of curves in a driveway are important factors in establishing a safe entry to the garage. Driveways for attached garages that are located near the street on relatively level property need only be sufficiently wide to be adequate. Driveways that have a grade of more than 7 percent (7-foot rise in 100 feet) should have some type of pavement to prevent wash. Driveways that are long and require an area for a turnaround should be designed carefully. Figure 6-45 shows a driveway and turnaround that allow the driver to back out of a single or double garage into the turn and proceed to the street or highway in a forward direction. In areas of heavy traffic this is much safer than having to back into the street or roadway. A double garage should be serviced by a wider entry and turnaround.

For safety, driveways that are of necessity quite steep should have a near-level area from 12 to 16 feet long in front of the garage.

Two types of paved driveways may be used, the more common slab or full-width type and the ribbon type (see Figure 6-46). When driveways are fairly long or steep, the full-width type is the most practical. The ribbon driveway is cheaper and perhaps less conspicuous because of the grass strip between the concrete runners. However, it is not practical for all locations.

The width of the single-slab type of driveway should be 9 feet for the modern car, although 8 feet is often considered the minimum. When the driveway is also used as a walk, it should be at least 10 feet wide to allow for a parked car as well as a walkway. The width should be increased by at least 1 foot at curves. The radius of the drive at the curb should be at least 5 feet. Relatively short double driveways should be at least 18 feet wide and be 2 feet wider when they are also to be used as a walk from the street.

The concrete strips in a ribbon driveway should be at least 2 feet in width and located so that they are 5 feet on center. When the ribbon is also used as a walk, the width of the strips should be increased to at least 3 feet. This type of driveway is not practical if a curve or a turn is involved or the driveway is long.

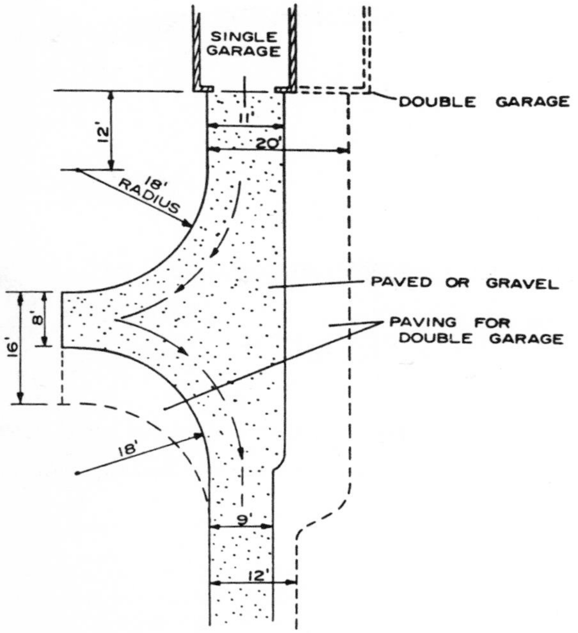

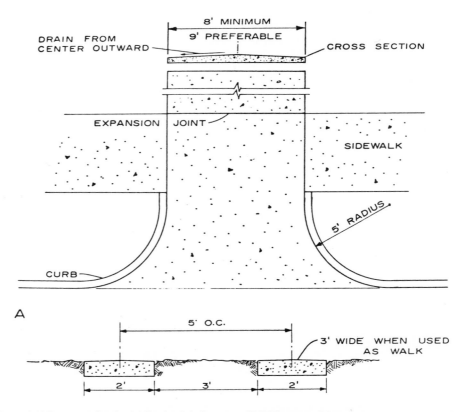

Figure 6-45 Driveway turnaround.

Figure 6-46 Driveway details. (a) Single-slab driveway. (b) Ribbon-type driveway.

6.8 Parking for the Physically Handicapped

Parking spaces of greater-than-normal width are necessary for people who are disabled and use mechanical aids such as wheelchairs, crutches, and walkers. For example, a person who is chair-bound must have a wider aisle in which to set up a wheelchair.

A minimum of two spaces per parking lot should be designed for use by physically restricted people, or at least one space per 20 cars, whichever is greater. These spaces should be placed as close as possible to a major entrance of a building or function, preferably no more than 100 feet away.

Parallel Parking Parallel parking spaces should be placed adjacent to a walk system so that access from the car to the destination is over a hard surface. Such spaces should be made 12 feet wide and 24 feet long and should either have a 1:6 ramp up to the walk or be separated from it by bollards or some other device if the road level is at the same elevation as the walk. These areas should be designated as special parking since otherwise they may appear to be a drop-off zone.

Ninety-Degree and Angled Parking Spaces designed for use by disabled people functioning with large mechanical aids should be 9 feet wide as a minimum. In addition, an aisle from 3 feet 6 inches to 4 feet wide should be provided between cars for access alongside the vehicle. It is important that there be plenty of room to open the car door entirely and, in the case of a dependent chair-bound person, that there be room for friends or attendants to assist him or her out of the car, into the chair, and away from the car.

The 9-foot standard width for a parking stall, with no aisle between spaces, does not drastically hinder semiambulant people with minor impairments, but an 8-foot width, unless used exclusively for attendant parking, is too narrow and should be avoided.

A 4-foot minimum clear aisle width should be provided between rows of cars parked end to end. The overhang of the automobile should be taken into account so that the island strip is wide enough to leave a 4-foot clear aisle when the stalls are filled. A strip 8 feet wide is a recommended minimum for an on-grade aisle, and 10 feet is a recommended minimum if the aisle is raised 6 inches above the parking level.

If the aisle between rows of cars is not at the same grade level as the cars, ramps must be provided to mount the curbs. A 1:6 (17 percent) ramp is suitable for such a short distance.

Economically, the installation of an on-grade pathway 4 feet wide is less expensive than a raised walk. Precast car stops to delineate the passage can be used provided a 4-foot-wide space between the ends of the stops is maintained to allow access to the main passageway.

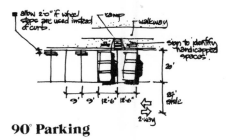

90° Parking

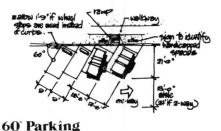

60° Parking

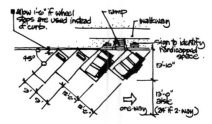

45° Parking

Figure 6-47 Types of parking.

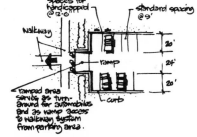

Parking Using End-Lot Access

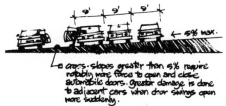

Cross-Slope in Parking Areas

Parallel Parking

SOURCE: *Barrier-free Site Design,* U.S. Department of Housing and Urban Development, 1975.

6.9 Gutters and Curbs

Designs for various kinds of gutters and curbs are shown in Figures 6-48, 6-49, 6-50, 6-51, 6-52, and 6-53.

Figure 6-48 Turf gutter or drainage ditch. Over a base of sandy gravel install topsoil and grade to smooth the contour. Apply seed and cover with glass fiber blanket held in place by steel T pins; grass will come up through the blanket. Blankets are available in a 1-inch thickness in rolls measuring 6 by 150 feet and weighing 56 pounds.

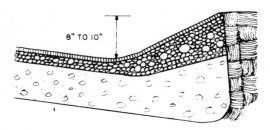

Figure 6-49 Oiled gutter for an oiled-gravel driveway.

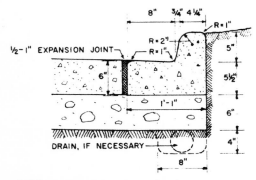

Figure 6-50 Precast-concrete gutter and curb.

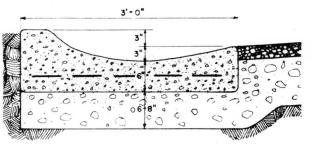

Figure 6-51 Precast-concrete gutter.

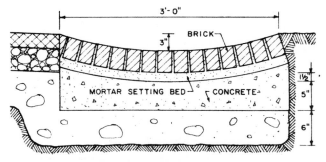

Figure 6-52 Brick gutter. Cobblestones or Belgian block may be used with similar details.

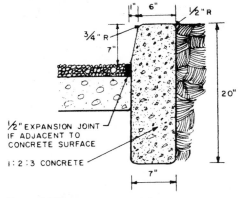

Figure 6-53 Precast-concrete curb.

SOURCE: Joseph De Chiara and J. H. Callender, *Time-Saver Standards for Building Types,* McGraw-Hill Book Company, New York, 1973.

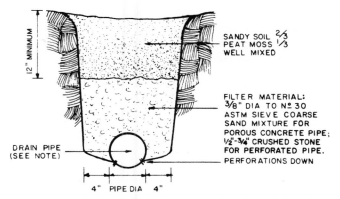

Figure 6-54 Details of a typical drain. The drainpipe may be perforated asphalt, perforated or porous concrete, or perforated galvanized-steel pipe. Under driveways use pipe strong enough to support heavy trucks. The minimum pitch for the drainpipe is 0.5 percent.

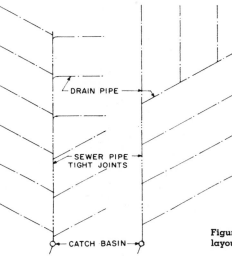

Figure 6-57 Typical drainage field layout (not drawn to scale).

DRAINAGE DETAILS

Details for the construction of drains are shown in Figures 6-54, 6-55, 6-56, 6-57, and 6-58.

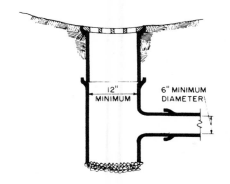

Figure 6-55 Lawn drain of concrete or vitrified-clay pipe with a standard round cast-iron grate.

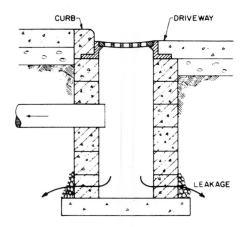

Figure 6-56 Curb inlet. The standard cast-iron grate measures 22¾ by 72½ inches.

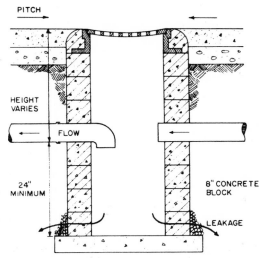

Figure 6-58 Catch basin, square or rectangular, with inside dimensions of 12, 18, 24, or 32½ inches. Use a standard cast-iron grate, light- or heavy-duty, or a sidewalk grate.

SOURCE: Joseph De Chiara and J. H. Callender, *Time-Saver Standards for Building Types*, McGraw-Hill Book Company, New York, 1973.

6.10 Retaining and Freestanding Walls

Various types of retaining walls are illustrated in Figures 6-59, 6-60, and 6-61.

Diagrams of freestanding and retaining walls are shown in Figures 6-62, 6-63, and 6-64.

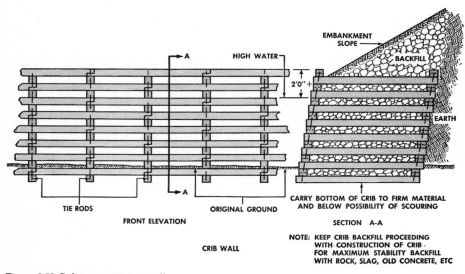

Figure 6-59 Crib-type retaining wall.

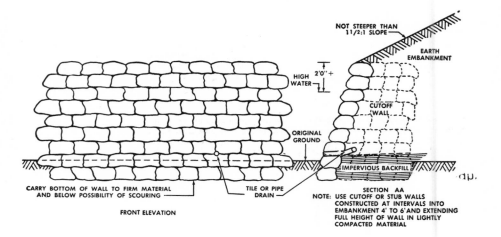

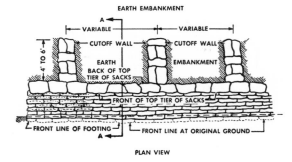

Figure 6-61 Sacked-concrete retaining wall.

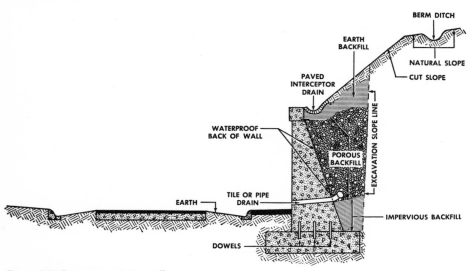

Figure 6-60 Concrete retaining wall.

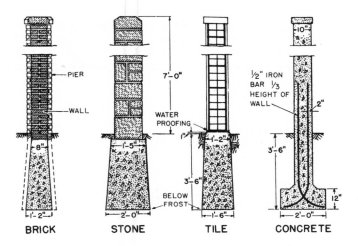

BRICK   STONE   TILE   CONCRETE

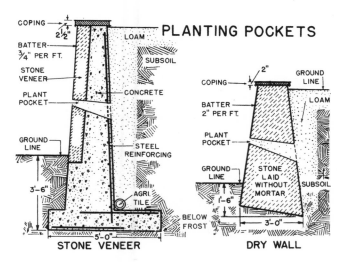

PLANTING POCKETS

STONE VENEER   DRY WALL

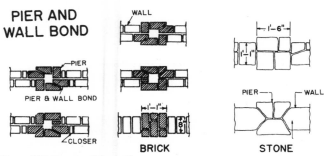

PIER AND WALL BOND

PIER & WALL BOND

BRICK   STONE

Figure 6-62 Freestanding walls.

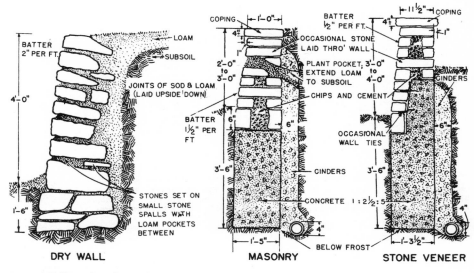

DRY WALL   MASONRY   STONE VENEER

Figure 6-63 Unreinforced retaining walls.

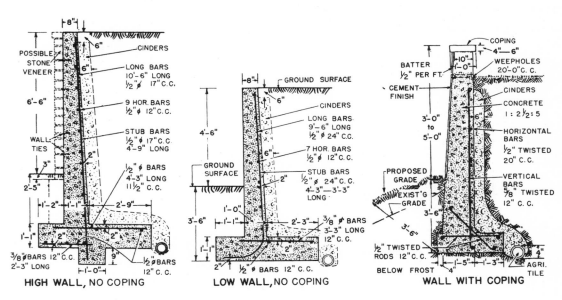

HIGH WALL, NO COPING   LOW WALL, NO COPING   WALL WITH COPING

Figure 6-64 Reinforced retaining walls.

SOURCE: *Time-Saver Standards*, 1st ed., F. W. Dodge Company, New York, 1946.

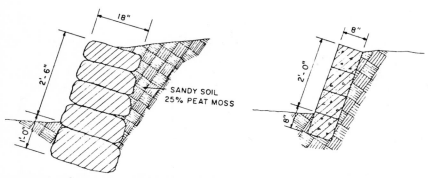

Figure 6-65 Dry retaining walls. *(left)* Stone wall. Batter 3 inches per foot in cold regions and 1½ inches per foot in frost-free regions. Spaces between stones may be filled with topsoil and plants, if desired. *(right)* Concrete-block wall; solid block 8 by 8 by 16 inches. Batter 2½ inches per foot. The wall will be slowly displaced by frost.

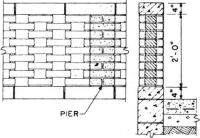

Figure 6-66 Open wall of brick. The minimum overlap of bricks is 1½ inches. Provide 8- by 8-inch piers 6 to 8 feet on center. Coping and base may be of precast concrete or cut stone.

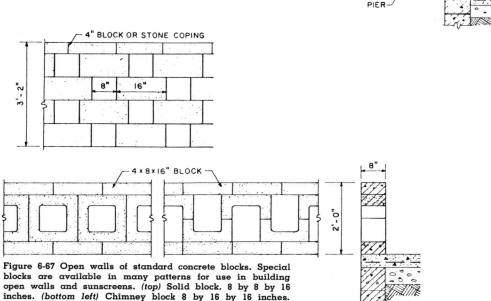

Figure 6-67 Open walls of standard concrete blocks. Special blocks are available in many patterns for use in building open walls and sunscreens. *(top)* Solid block, 8 by 8 by 16 inches. *(bottom left)* Chimney block 8 by 16 by 16 inches. *(bottom right)* Chimney block 8 by 8 by 16 inches.

Dry retaining walls are illustrated in Figure 6-65, and various types of freestanding masonry walls in Figures 6-66, 6-67, and 6-68. For the latter, foundations must extend below the frost line.

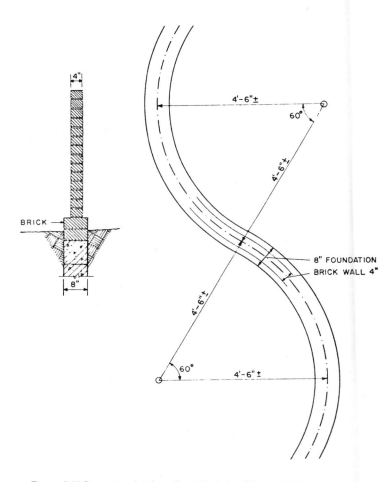

Figure 6-68 Serpentine brick wall; attributed to Thomas Jefferson.

SOURCE: Joseph De Chiara and J. H. Callender, *Time-Saver Standards for Building Types*, McGraw-Hill Book Company, New York, 1973.

6.11 Berms and Banks

Figures 6-69 and 6-70 illustrate types of berms and banks.

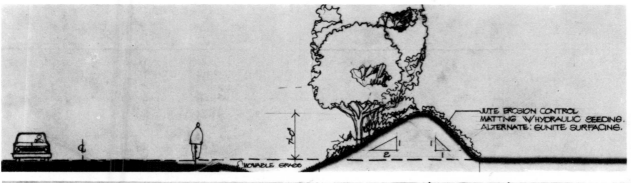

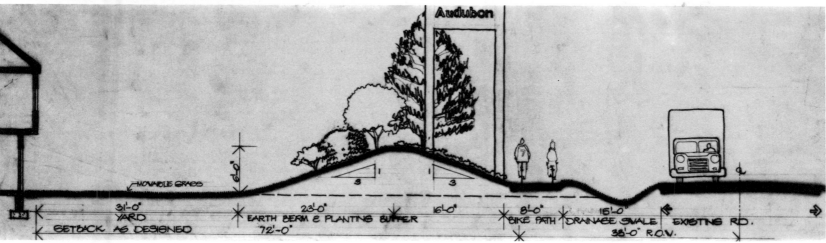

Figure 6-69 Berms.

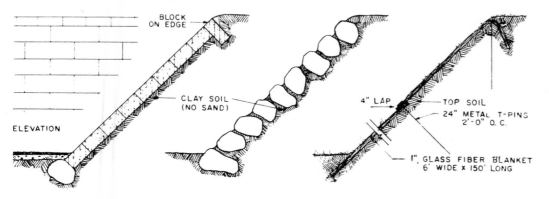

Figure 6-70 Banks. *(left)* Concrete-block riprap; solid block 4 by 8 by 16 inches, laid dry. *(center)* Stone riprap. *(right)* Grass. Sow grass seed and cover with a glass fiber blanket, held in place with T pins.

SOURCES: Schnadelbach Braun Partnership; Joseph De Chiara and J. H. Callender, *Time-Saver Standards for Building Types,* McGraw-Hill Book Company, New York, 1973.

6.12 Popular Trees and Shrubs

A number of trees and shrubs are shown with their dimensions in Figure 6-71.

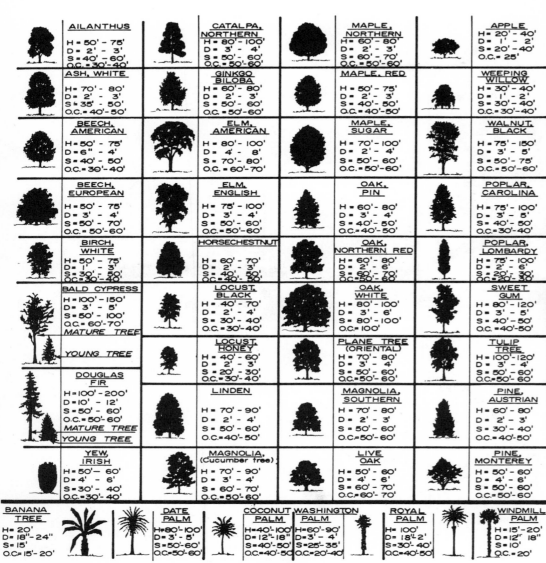

Figure 6-71 Typical sizes and shapes of various trees.

SOURCE: *Landscape Development*, U.S. Department of the Interior, Field Technical Office, Littleton, Colo.

TREE-PLANTING DETAILS

Detailed drainage of tree-planting methods are shown in Figures 6-72 and 6-73.

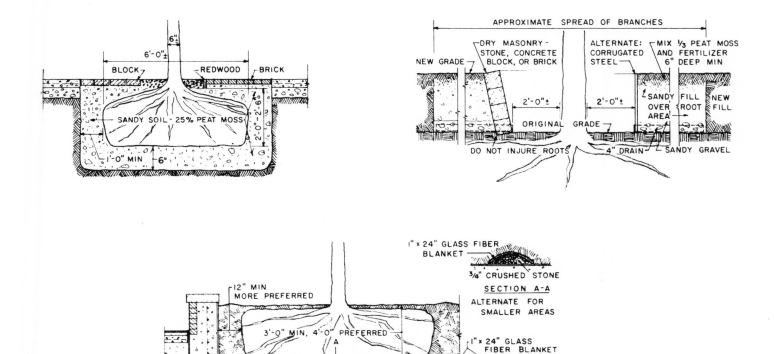

Figure 6-72 Tree roots need air. Sandy soil is porous to air; it should be mixed with peat moss to retain moisture. Do not compress the soil around trees with bulldozers or other heavy equipment. Disturb the roots as little as possible. (*top left*) Tree in pavement. Over porous backfill of sandy soil with 25 to 30 percent peat moss, lay dry paving units with tight joints. Belgian block, granite block, asphalt block, concrete block, brick, or crushed stone may be used. If brick is used, install an inner edging of 2- by 4-inch redwood. (*top right*) Tree in filled ground. Install eight to ten drain lines, placed radially around the tree. Drains may be porous or perforated pipe or agricultural tile with open joints covered by a 1-inch fiber blanket.

SOURCE: Joseph De Chiara and J. H. Callender, *Time-Saver Standards for Building Types*, McGraw-Hill Book Company, New York, 1973.

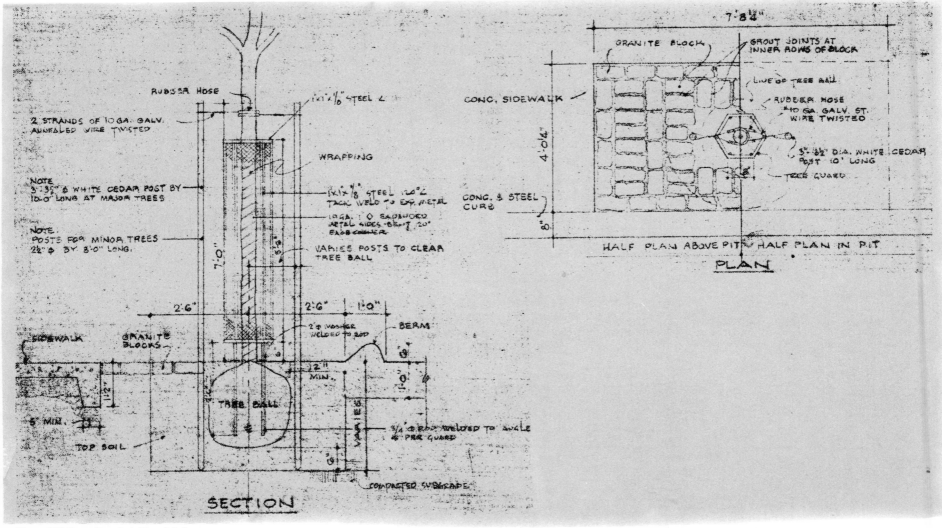

Figure 6-73 Tree pit and staking detail.

6.13 Outdoor Lighting

The purpose of site lighting is basically two-fold: to illuminate and to provide security. Lighting should be provided in areas that receive heavy pedestrian or vehicular use and in areas that are dangerous if unlit, such as stairs and ramps, intersections, or abrupt changes in grade. Likewise, areas that have high crime rates should be well lit so that people traveling at night may feel secure from attack.

The phrase "well lit" has a wider meaning than simply higher light levels. Unless light is placed where it is most useful, the expense of increasing footcandle levels is wasted. An area may need only the addition of a few lights to correct its problems, not an increase in light levels from fixtures that are too few or are poorly located.

When considering the installation or renovation of lighting systems, the designer should be aware of the following considerations:

1. Overhead lamps have the advantage over low-level fixtures of providing better economy and more even light distribution.
2. Fixtures should be placed so that light patterns overlap at a height of 7 feet, which is sufficiently high to illuminate a person's body vertically. This is a particularly important consideration now that lighting fixture manufacturers are designing luminaires with highly controlled light patterns.
3. At hazardous locations such as changes of grade, lower-level supplemental lighting or additional overhead units should be used.
4. Where low-level lighting (below 5 feet) is used, fixtures should be placed so that they do not produce glare. Most eye levels occur between 3 feet 8 inches (for wheelchair users) and 6 feet for standing adults.
5. Posts and standards along thoroughfares should be placed so that they do not present hazards to pedestrians or vehicles.
6. A minor consideration is the use of shatterproof coverings on low-level lighting where there is a chance of breakage.
7. When walkway lighting is provided primarily by low fixtures, there should be sufficient peripheral lighting to illuminate the immediate

Light Intensity

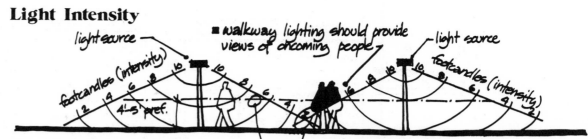

Figure 6-74

Avg. Maintained Footcandles

- Measured at average point of illumination between brightest area and darkest areas. Can be measured at ground surface or at 4-5' above walkway surface.

Min. Maintained Footcandles

- Measured on ground surface at point of least illumination.
- Note: Where intensity curves overlap, the resulting intensity is the _combined_ total of the two ratings.

Lateral Light Distribution

- Light patterns can be varied according to the needs of a particular situation. Choose the proper pattern and fixture for your specific requirements.

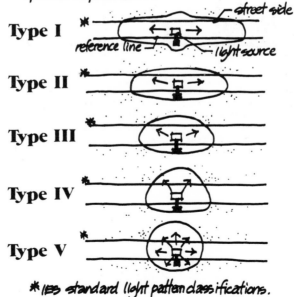

Type I
Type II
Type III
Type IV
Type V

* IES standard light pattern classifications.

Figure 6-75

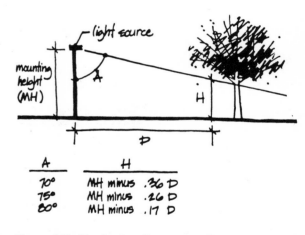

A	H
70°	MH minus .36 D
75°	MH minus .26 D
80°	MH minus .17 D

Figure 6-76 Illuminating Engineering Society tree-pruning recommendations.

SOURCE: _Barrier-free Site Design_, U.S. Department of Housing and Urban Development, 1975.

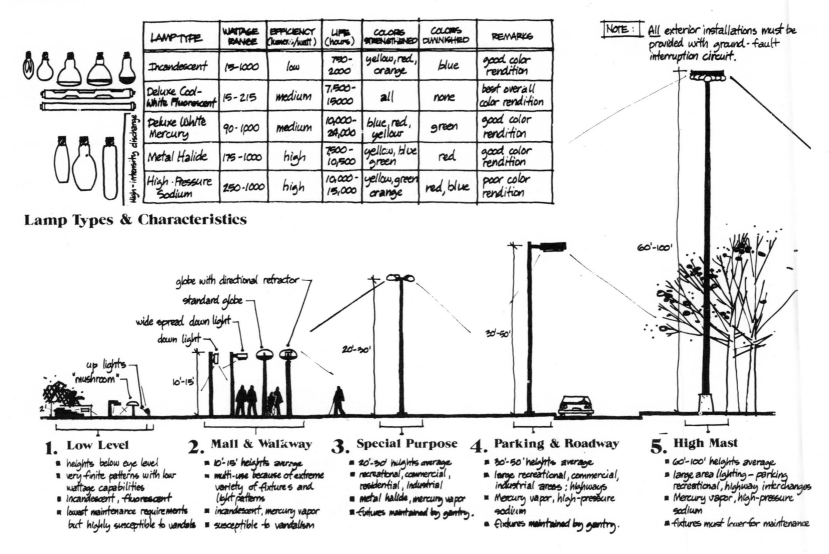

Lamp Types & Characteristics

LAMP TYPE	WATTAGE RANGE	EFFICIENCY (lumens/watt)	LIFE (hours)	COLORS STRENGTHENED	COLORS DIMINISHED	REMARKS
Incandescent	15-1000	low	750-2000	yellow, red, orange	blue	good color rendition
Deluxe Cool-White Fluorescent	15-215	medium	7,500-15,000	all	none	best overall color rendition
Deluxe White Mercury	90-1000	medium	10,000-24,000	blue, red, yellow	green	good color rendition
Metal Halide	175-1000	high	7,500-10,500	yellow, blue green	red	good color rendition
High-Pressure Sodium	250-1000	high	10,000-15,000	yellow, green orange	red, blue	poor color rendition

NOTE: All exterior installations must be provided with ground-fault interruption circuit.

1. Low Level
- heights below eye level
- very finite patterns with low wattage capabilities
- incandescent, fluorescent
- lowest maintenance requirements but highly susceptible to vandals

2. Mall & Walkway
- 10'-15' heights average
- multi-use because of extreme variety of fixtures and light patterns
- incandescent, mercury vapor
- susceptible to vandalism

3. Special Purpose
- 20'-30' heights average
- recreational, commercial, residential, industrial
- metal halide, mercury vapor
- fixtures maintained by gantry

4. Parking & Roadway
- 30'-50' heights average
- large recreational, commercial, industrial areas; highways
- Mercury vapor, high-pressure sodium
- fixtures maintained by gantry

5. High Mast
- 60'-100' heights average
- large area lighting – parking, recreational, highway interchanges
- Mercury vapor, high-pressure sodium
- fixtures must lower for maintenance

Figure 6-77

surroundings. Peripheral lighting provides for a better feeling of security for individuals because they can see into their surroundings to determine whether passage through an area is safe. Such lighting should be approached from one of two ways:

a. By lighting the area so that an object or a person may be seen directly

b. By lighting the area to place an object or a person in silhouette.

Figures 6-74 and 6-75 show recommended light intensity and distribution, and Figure 6-76 shows how trees should be pruned to avoid interference with light.

Figure 6-77 shows the characteristics of various types of lamps and recommended installations.

SOURCE: *Barrier-free Site Design*, U.S. Department of Housing and Urban Development, 1975.

RECOMMENDED LIGHTING LEVELS*

	Commercial	Industrial	Residential
Pedestrian areas:			
Sidewalks	0.9	0.6	0.2
Pedestrian ways	2.0	1.0	0.5
Roadways:			
Freeways	0.6	0.6	0.6
Major roads and expressways	2.0	1.4	1.0
Collectors	1.2	0.9	0.6
Local streets	0.9	0.6	0.4
Alleys	0.6	0.4	0.2
Parking areas:			
Self-parking	1.0	...	...
Attendant parking	2.0	...	...
Buildings:			
Entrance and doorway areas	5.0	...	...
General grounds	1.0	...	...

*Values are given in minimum average maintained horizontal footcandles.
SOURCE: *IES Lighting Handbook,* 4th ed., Illuminating Engineering Society, New York.

Lighting levels recommended by the Illuminating Engineering Society are shown in the accompanying table, and details of lighting installations in Figure 6-78.

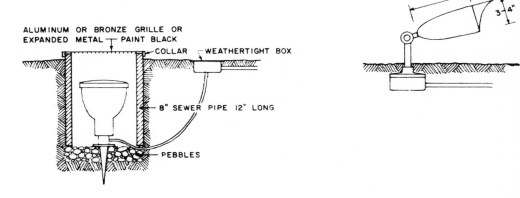

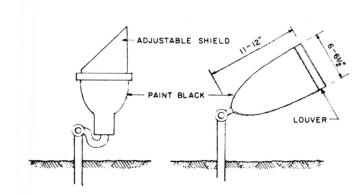

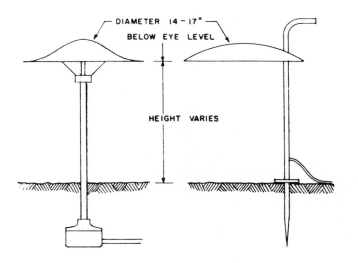

Figure 6-78 Lighting details. (*top left*) Underground floodlight to light trees; 75 to 150 watts. (*top right*) Small spotlight or floodlight to light statuary; 30 watts. (*center*) Aboveground floodlights, hidden by stones or bushes, to light trees or house; 75 to 150 watts. (*bottom*) Low-level lighting for walks or flowers; 75 watts. It may be permanent or portable.

SOURCES: *Barrier-free Site Design,* U.S. Department of Housing and Urban Development, 1975; Joseph De Chiara and J. H. Callender, *Time-Saver Standards for Building Types,* McGraw-Hill Book Company, New York, 1973.

6.14 Pools

WADING POOLS

The slope of the bottom of any wading pool should be not greater than 1 foot in 15 feet. All side and end walls should be vertical. The maximum depth of the water should not exceed 24 inches.

The complete water turnover time for wading pools should not exceed 2 hours. This turnover may be accomplished by recirculation through a filter system or by the use of an automatic valve that regulates the freshwater addition. If a recirculation and filtration system is used for a wading pool, it should be completely separate from the system serving a swimming pool.

Skimming action should be provided by means of scum gutter, deck-level, or suction-type floating weir overflows, all of which should discharge to waste. The water level should be maintained near the overflow level by means of an automatic, level regulator valve.

See Figures 6-79 and 6-80 for the design of rectangular and circular wading pools.

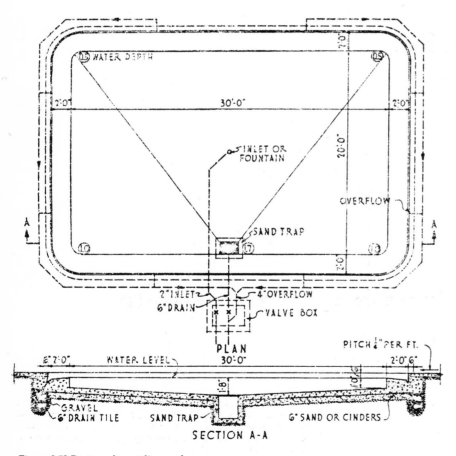

Figure 6-79 Rectangular wading pool.

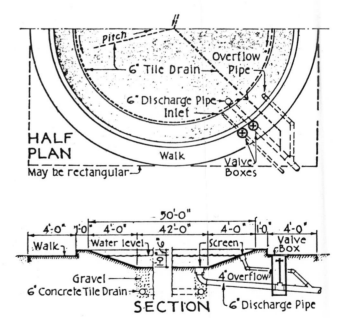

Figure 6-80 Circular wading pool.

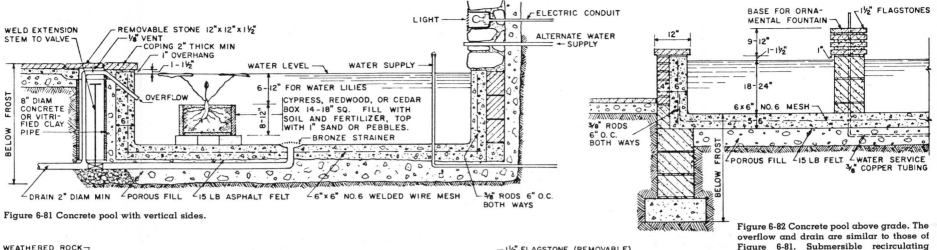

Figure 6-81 Concrete pool with vertical sides.

Figure 6-82 Concrete pool above grade. The overflow and drain are similar to those of Figure 6-81. Submersible recirculating pumps are available for fountains.

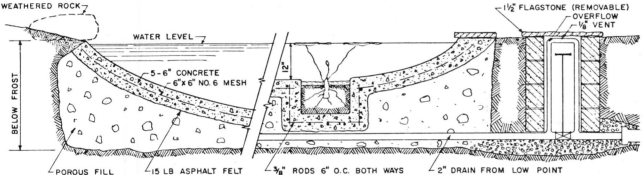

Figure 6-83 Concrete pool with sloping sides.

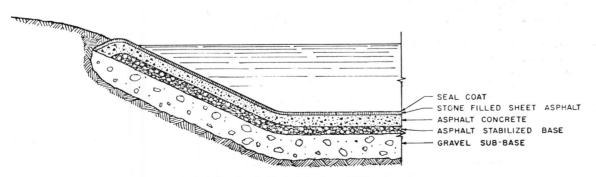

Figure 6-84 Asphalt-lined pool. [*From Asphalt Handbook, Asphalt Institute, 1960*]

POOLS AND FOUNTAINS

Figures 6-81, 6-82, 6-83, and 6-84 show the design of concrete and asphalt-lined pools. All concrete pools must be poured or sprayed in one continuous operation without joints. Inside forms, where required, must be supported from the outside and suspended. Painting the inside of the pool very dark with cement- or rubber-based paint will make the pool look deeper, improve surface reflections, and show less dirt. The water supply outlet must be a minimum of 6 inches above the surface of the water.

SOURCE: Joseph De Chiara and J. H. Callender, *Time-Saver Standards for Building Types,* McGraw-Hill Book Company, New York, 1973.

6.15 Footbridges

Designs for two footbridges are shown in Figures 6-85 and 6-86.

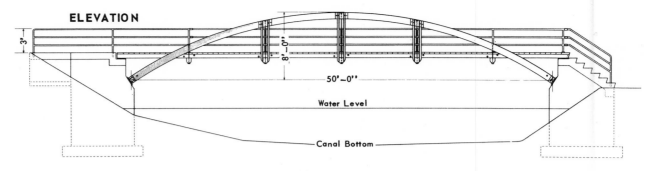

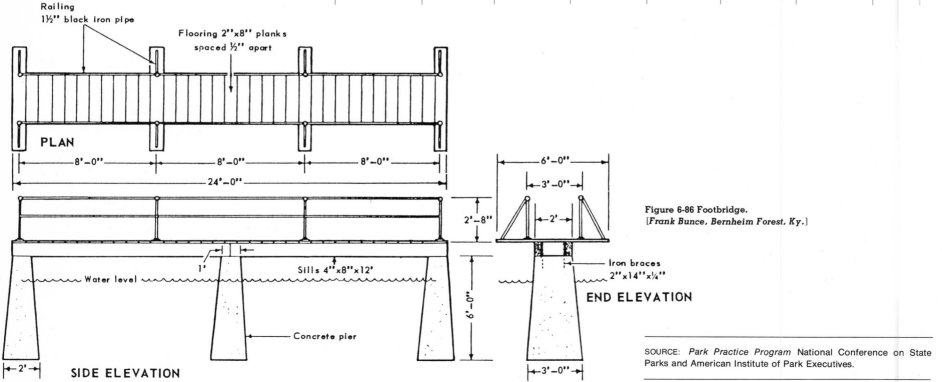

Figure 6-85 Footbridge.
[*National Park Service,
National Capital Parks*]

Figure 6-86 Footbridge.
[*Frank Bunce, Bernheim Forest, Ky.*]

SOURCE: *Park Practice Program* National Conference on State Parks and American Institute of Park Executives.

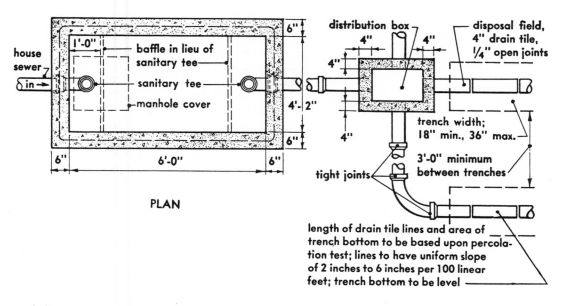

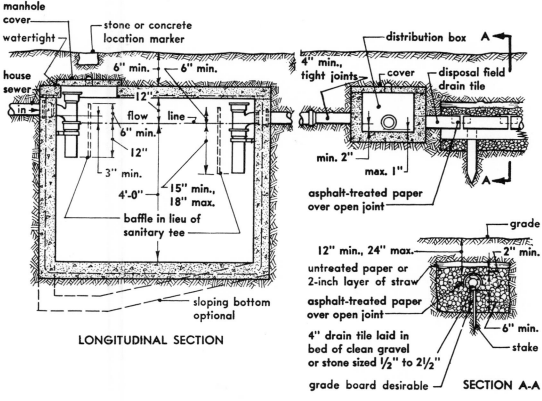

6.16 Septic Tanks and Dry Wells

ONE-COMPARTMENT SEPTIC TANK

Design for a typical 500-gallon concrete septic tank should provide adequate volume for settling and for sludge and scum storage and for access for cleaning. The structural design and materials used should be in accordance with generally accepted good engineering practice, providing a sound, durable tank that will safely sustain all dead and live loads and liquid and earth pressure involved in each case. The tank must be located so that it will achieve the minimum distances shown in the accompanying table. See also Figure 6-87, which illustrates a 750-gallon tank.

MINIMUM DISTANCES
(In feet)

| | To | | | |
From	Septic tank	Absorption field	Seepage pit	Absorption bed
Well	50	100	100	100
Property line	10	5	10	10
Foundation wall	5	5	20	5
Water lines	10	10	10	10
Seepage pit	6	6	. . .	. . .
Dry well	6	20	20	20

Figure 6-87 Concrete 750-gallon septic tank.

SOURCES: *Code Manual,* New York State Building Code Commission; *Minimum Property Standards for 1 and 2 Living Units,* Federal Housing Administration, 1974.

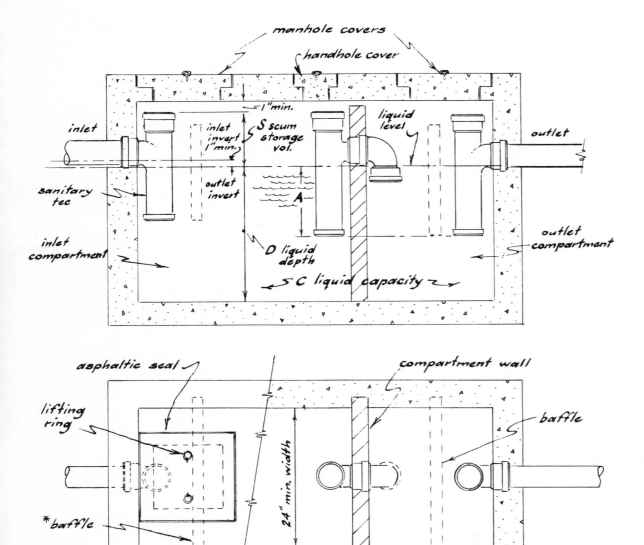

TWO-COMPARTMENT SEPTIC TANK

Liquid capacity of the tank should be based on the number of bedrooms proposed or that can be reasonably anticipated in the dwelling and should be at least as shown in the accompanying table. The design of such a tank is shown in Figure 6-88.

MINIMUM CAPACITIES FOR SEPTIC TANKS

Number of bedrooms	Minimum liquid capacity below outlet invert (gallons)
Two or less	750
Three	900
Four	1000
For each additional bedroom add	250

NOTE: These capacities provide for the plumbing fixtures and appliances commonly used in a single-family residence (automatic sequence washer, mechanical garbage grinder, and dishwasher are included).

Figure 6-88 Two-compartment septic tank. (*above*) Section. *A* is approximately 40 percent of liquid depth *D*. *D* not less than 30-inch depth greater than 6 feet shall not be considered in tank capacity. *S* is not less than 15 percent of liquid capacity *C*. (*below*) Plan. Baffles are optional to submerged inlet and outlet sanitary tee.

SOURCE: *Minimum Property Standards for 1 and 2 Living Units,* Federal Housing Administration, 1974.

DRY WELLS

Where sewers are not available for storm water disposal and where the soil and the finished surface grade are suitable, the following means of disposal may be used:

1. Dry well (size is dependent on the area to be drained and the soil absorption).
2. Dry well with additional subsurface drains where soil absorption is such that the dry well alone cannot handle the load.
3. Drainage for roof combined with drainage for surface and subsurface where the dry well is of limited capacity. The dry well is used for surface and subsurface drainage; roof drains lead to a splash block and are directed away from the dry well.
4. Splash block. When roof drains are discharged at grade, a splash block should be used to minimize soil erosion.

Figures 6-89 and 6-90 show the location and design of dry wells and splash blocks.

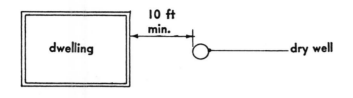

LOCATION OF DRY WELLS

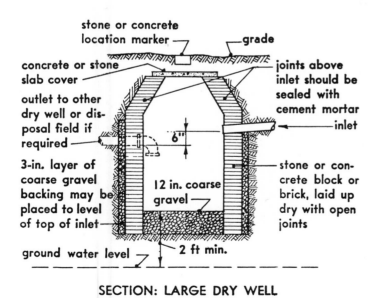

SECTION: LARGE DRY WELL

Figure 6-89

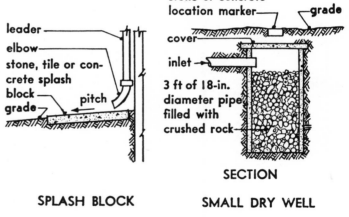

SPLASH BLOCK   **SMALL DRY WELL**

Figure 6-90

SOURCE: *Code Manual*, New York State Building Code Commission.

6.17 Inlets, Catch Basins, Outlets, and Cisterns

STORM INLETS AND CATCH BASINS

All storm inlets and catch basins should be adequate in size and design to accept and carry the calculated potential runoff without overflow. They should be constructed of durable materials that will not erode and will accept potentially imposed loads without failure.

Where inlets are accessible to small children, openings should have one dimension limited to a maximum of 6 inches. Access for cleaning should be provided to all inlet boxes and catch basins. Where inlets are located in areas of potential pedestrian use, the design of openings and exposed surfaces should be arranged to minimize the dangers of tripping or slipping. Horizontal inlet openings in paved areas should be designed to avoid entrapment or impedance of bicycles, baby carriages, and so on. See also Figure 6-91.

Manholes and Junction Boxes   Manholes and junction boxes should be spaced at optimum intervals as indicated by analysis and be provided in places where there is a particular hazard of blockage, at abrupt changes in alignment, and at junctions with mains and principal laterals.

Headwalls   Headwalls and other appropriate construction should be placed at the open ends of storm sewers to prevent excessive erosion and undermining of conduits.

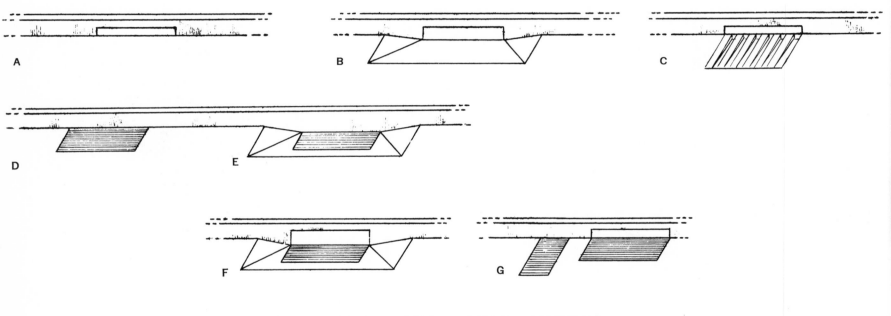

Figure 6-91 Curb inlets: (a) undepressed; (b) depressed; (c) deflector inlet. Gutter inlets: (d) undepressed; (e) depressed. Combination inlet: (f) grate placed directly in front of open depressed curb. Multiple inlet: (g) undepressed.

SOURCE: *Minimum Property Standards*, Federal Housing Administration.

SURFACE INLETS AND JUNCTION BOXES

Surface inlets should be used in low areas where surface drainage cannot otherwise be provided (Figure 6-92). They must be properly constructed to prevent washouts and silting. However, surface inlets should be avoided wherever possible. If silt is a hazard, place a silt trap (Figure 6-93) at a convenient location immediately downstream from inlet.

Junction boxes should be used when two or more main or submain drains join or when several laterals join at different elevations.

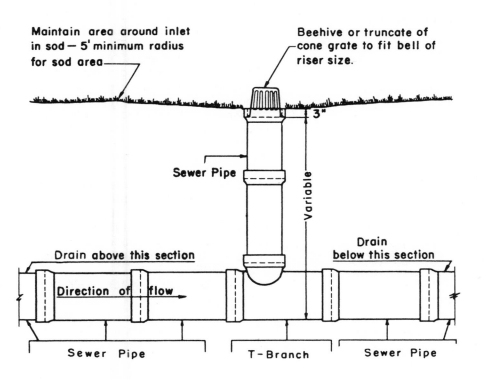

Figure 6-92 Surface inlet.

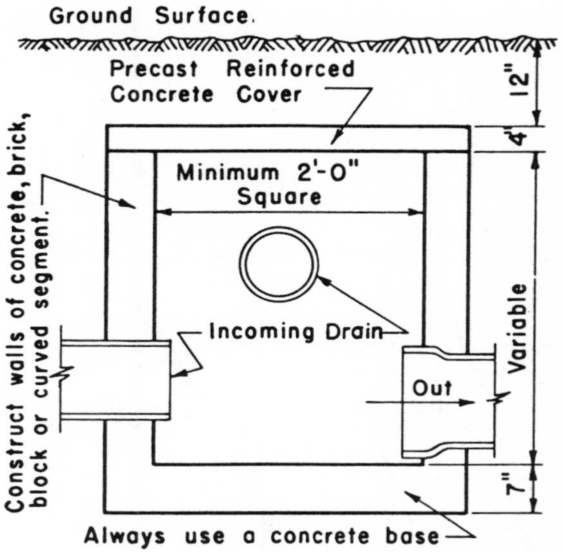

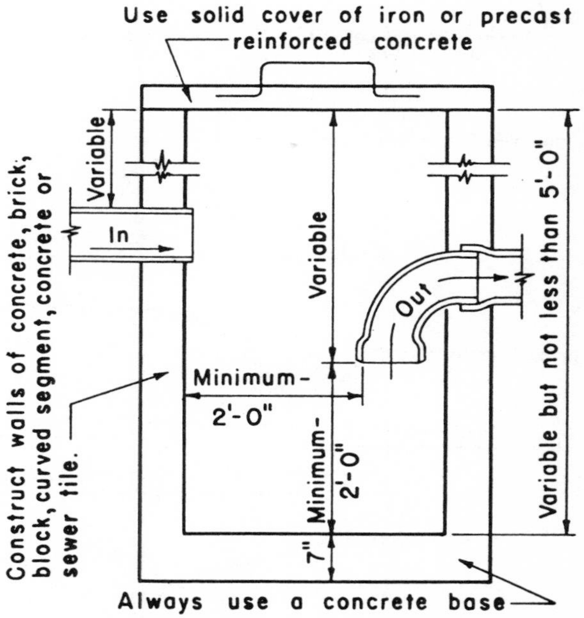

Figure 6-93 Junction box, catch basin, and silt trap.

SOURCE: *National Engineering Handbook*, U.S. Department of Agriculture, Soil Conservation Service, 1971.

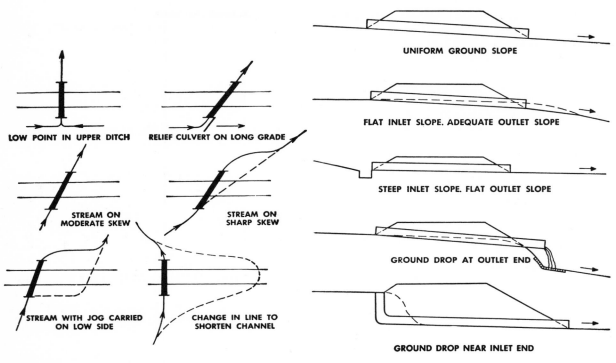

Figure 6-94 Proper location and alignment of culverts.

Figure 6-95 Proper elevation and grade of culverts.

DRAIN CROSSINGS AND OUTLETS

Culverts should be located to coincide as closely as practicable with stream alignment. The inlet should be placed where cross drainage intersects the toe of the slope so that water is not forced to travel out of its natural course to enter the opening (see Figure 6-94). Relief culverts should be provided at frequent intervals on sidehill sections to drain water to the low side, thus minimizing erosion. Install culverts at not more than 300-foot intervals on 8 percent grades and at 500-foot intervals on 5 percent grades unless paving or other ditch lining is provided.

Inlet and outlet elevations normally coincide with the corresponding streambed, ditch, or natural ground elevation at ends of the culvert. Minor variations, involving ditching to secure proper fall, are required to obtain a minimum cover of from 6 to 12 inches over the top of culvert or to increase the culvert grade to the desired minimum. When the culvert grade must be flatter than the inlet-ditch grade, a sump or a trap may be required at the inlet end to avoid silting inside the culvert. If the culvert is too high, drainage is obstructed, and undermining or scouring of the ends may occur; if it is too low, silting occurs, and the effective opening is correspondingly reduced. See Figure 6-95.

See also Figure 6-96 for illustrations of drain crossings.

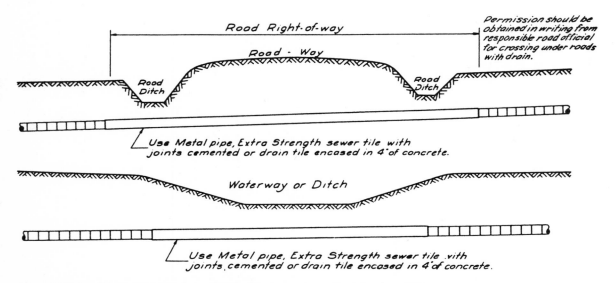

Figure 6-96 (above) Drain crossing under road. (below) Drain crossing under waterway or ditch.

SOURCE: *National Engineering Service,* U.S. Department of Agriculture, Soil Conservation Service, 1971.

CISTERNS

Catchment Area The required catchment area depends on the amount of rainfall in your area and the amount of water needed. Proceed as follows:

1. Determine your yearly water needs by using the information given below.
2. Determine the normal annual rainfall in your area from local weather people.
3. Enter the graph in Figure 6-97 with "total annual water needs" and "normal annual precipitation."
4. Read the bottom line of the graph for "area of catchment needed."

EXAMPLE:

A family of four estimates its water needs to be 200 gallons per day, or 73,000 gallons per year. The normal annual rainfall is 40 inches. From the graph the needed catchment area is 4400 square feet. If the cistern must supply only half of the family's water needs, the needed catchment area would be 2200 square feet.

Catchment Yields Each square foot of catchment area will provide the quantities of water listed below.

See also the table "Capacity of Cisterns" on page 300 and the typical cistern illustrated in Figure 6-98.

Annual rainfall (in inches)	Water available (in gallons)
10	4.2
15	6.2
20	8.3
25	10.4
30	12.5
35	14.5
40	16.6
45	18.8
50	20.8

Cistern leakage, roof washer, and evaporation will use up about one-third of the annual rainfall. These losses have already been subtracted from the numbers listed in the table.

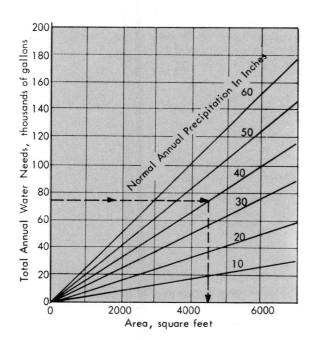

Figure 6-97 Required area of catchment.

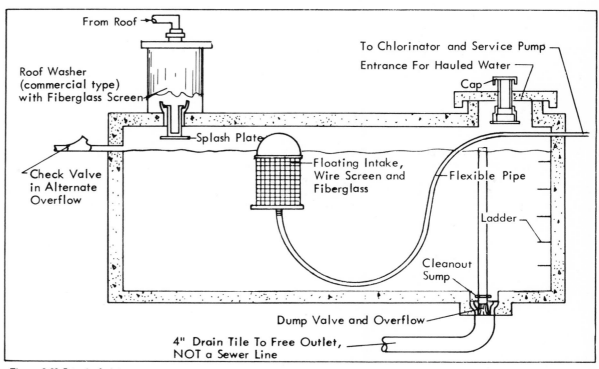

Figure 6-98 A typical cistern.

SOURCE: Reproduced by permission from *Private Water Systems,* MWPS-14, Midwest Plan Service, Ames, Iowa 50011.

CAPACITY OF CISTERNS
(In gallons)

Depth in feet	Diameter of round type and length of side of square type (in feet)													
	5	6	7	8	9	10	11	12	13	14	15	16	17	18
							Round Type							
5	735	1,055	1,440	1,880	2,380	2,935	3,555	4,230	4,965	5,755	6,610	7,515	8,435	9,510
6	882	1,266	1,728	2,256	2,856	3,522	4,266	5,076	5,958	6,906	7,932	9,018	10,182	11,412
7	1,029	1,477	2,016	2,632	3,332	4,109	4,977	5,922	6,951	8,057	9,254	10,521	11,879	13,314
8	1,176	1,688	2,304	3,008	3,808	4,696	5,688	6,768	7,944	9,208	10,576	12,024	13,576	15,216
9	1,323	1,899	2,592	3,384	4,284	5,283	6,399	7,614	8,937	10,359	11,898	13,527	15,273	17,118
10	1,470	2,110	2,880	3,760	4,760	5,870	7,110	8,460	9,930	11,510	13,220	15,030	16,970	19,020
12	1,764	2,532	3,456	4,512	5,712	7,044	8,532	10,152	11,916	13,812	15,864	18,036	20,364	22,824
14	2,058	2,954	4,032	5,264	6,664	8,218	9,954	11,844	13,902	16,114	18,508	21,042	23,758	26,628
16	2,342	3,376	4,608	6,016	7,616	9,392	11,376	13,536	15,888	18,416	21,152	24,048	27,152	30,432
18	2,646	3,798	5,184	6,768	8,568	10,566	12,798	15,228	17,874	20,718	23,796	27,054	30,546	24,236
20	2,940	4,220	5,760	7,530	9,520	11,740	14,220	16,920	19,860	23,020	26,440	30,060	33,940	38,040
							Square Type							
5	935	1,345	1,835	2,395	3,030	3,740	4,525	5,385	6,320	7,330	8,415	9,575	10,810	12,112
6	1,122	1,614	2,202	2,874	3,636	4,488	5,430	6,462	7,584	8,796	10,098	11,490	12,974	14,534
7	1,309	1,883	2,569	3,353	4,242	5,236	6,335	7,539	8,848	10,262	11,781	13,405	15,134	16,956
8	1,496	2,152	2,936	3,832	4,848	5,984	7,240	8,616	10,112	11,728	13,464	15,320	17,296	19,378
9	1,683	2,421	3,303	4,311	5,454	6,732	8,145	9,693	11,376	13,194	15,147	17,235	19,458	21,800
10	1,870	2,690	3,670	4,790	6,060	7,480	9,050	10,770	12,640	14,660	16,830	19,150	21,620	24,222
12	2,244	3,228	4,404	5,748	7,272	8,976	10,860	12,924	15,168	17,592	20,196	22,980	25,944	29,068
14	2,618	3,766	5,138	6,706	8,484	10,472	12,670	15,078	17,696	20,524	23,562	26,810	20,268	33,912
16	2,992	4,204	5,872	7,664	9,696	11,968	14,480	17,232	20,224	23,456	26,928	30,640	34,592	38,756
18	3,366	4,842	6,606	8,622	10,908	13,464	16,290	19,386	22,752	26,388	30,294	34,470	38,916	42,600
20	3,740	5,380	7,340	9,580	12,120	14,960	18,100	21,540	25,280	29,320	33,660	38,300	43,240	48,444

SOURCE: Reproduced by permission from *Private Water Systems*, MWPS-14, Midwest Plan Service, Ames, Iowa 50011.

6.18 Shoreline Protection

SEAWALLS

The distinction between seawalls, bulkheads, and revetments is mainly a matter of purpose. Design features are determined at the functional planning stage, and the structure is named to suit its intended purpose. In general, seawalls are the most massive of the three types because they resist the full force of the waves. Bulkheads are next in size; their function is to retain fill, and they are generally not exposed to severe wave action. Revetments are the lightest because they are designed to protect shorelines against erosion by currents or light wave action.

A curved-face seawall is illustrated in Figure 6-99. This massive structure is built to resist high wave action and reduce scour. The stepped seawall (Figure 6-100) is designed for stability against moderate waves. The rubble-mound seawall (Figure 6-101) is built to withstand severe wave action. Although scour of the fronting beach may occur, the rock comprising the seawall can readjust and settle without causing structural failure.

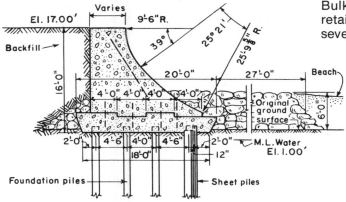

Figure 6-99 Concrete curved-face seawall.

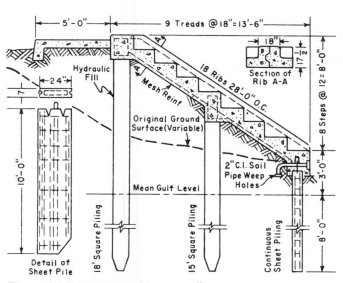

Figure 6-100 Concrete stepped-face seawall.

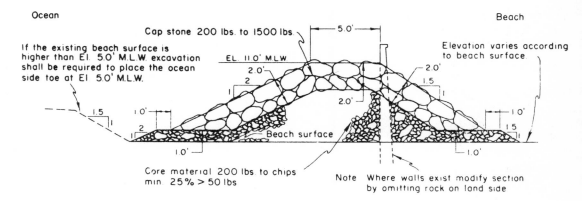

Figure 6-101 Rubble-mound seawall.

SOURCE: *Shore Protection Manual,* vol. II, U.S. Army Corps of Engineers, Coastal Engineering Research Center, Fort Belvoir, Va., 1973.

REVETMENTS

Structural types of revetments used for coastal protection in exposed and sheltered areas are illustrated in Figures 6-102 and 6-103. There are two types of revetments: the rigid, cast-in-place concrete type illustrated in Figure 6-102 and the flexible or articulated armor unit type illustrated in Figure 6-103. A rigid concrete revetment provides excellent bank protection, but the site must be dewatered during construction to pour the concrete. A flexible structure also provides excellent bank protection, and it can tolerate minor consolidation or settlement without structural failure. This is true for the riprap revetment and to a lesser extent for the interlocking concrete-block revetment. Both the articulated block structure and the riprap structure permit relief of hydrostatic uplift pressure generated by wave action. The underlying plastic filter cloth and gravel or a crushed-stone filter and bedding layer provide relief of pressure over the entire foundation area rather than through specially constructed weep holes.

Interlocking concrete blocks have been used extensively for shore protection in the Netherlands and England and have recently become popular in the United States. Typical blocks are generally square slabs with the shiplap type of interlocking joints. Joints of the shiplap type provide a mechanical interlock with adjacent blocks.

The stability of an interlocking concrete block depends largely on the type of mechanical interlock. It is impossible to analyze block stability under specified wave action on the basis of the weight alone. However, prototype tests at the Coastal Engineering Research Center on blocks having shiplap joints and tongue-and-groove joints indicate that the stability of tongue-and-groove blocks is much greater than that of shiplap blocks.

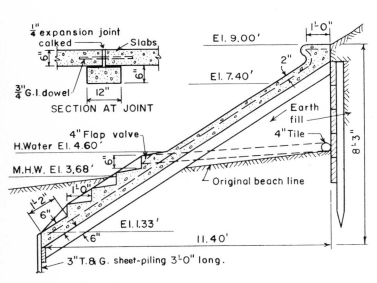

Figure 6-102 Concrete revetment.

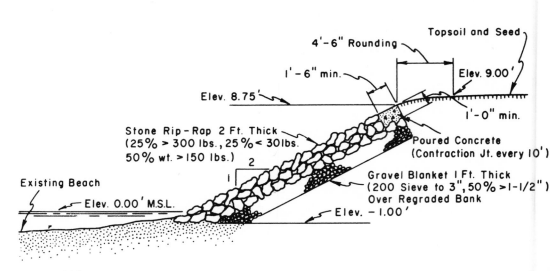

Figure 6-103 Riprap revetment.

SOURCE: *Shore Protection Manual,* vol. II, U.S. Army Corps of Engineers, Coastal Engineering Research Center, Fort Belvoir, Va., 1973.

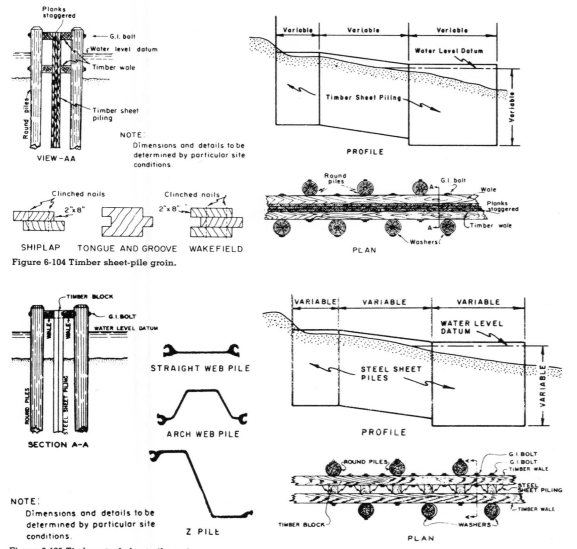

VIEW—AA

NOTE:
Dimensions and details to be determined by particular site conditions.

SHIPLAP   TONGUE AND GROOVE   WAKEFIELD

Figure 6-104 Timber sheet-pile groin.

SECTION A-A

NOTE:
Dimensions and details to be determined by particular site conditions.

STRAIGHT WEB PILE

ARCH WEB PILE

Z PILE

Figure 6-105 Timber-steel sheet-pile groin.

PROFILE

PLAN

PROFILE

PLAN

Timber Groins   A common type of timber groin is an impermeable structure composed of sheet piles supported by wales and round piles. Some permeable timber groins have been built by leaving spaces between the sheeting. A typical timber groin is shown in Figure 6-104. The round timber piles forming the primary structural support should be at least 12 inches in diameter at the butt. Stringers or wales, bolted to the piling, should be at least 8 by 10 inches, preferably cut and drilled before being pressure-treated with creosote. The sheet piles are usually of the Wakefield, tongue-and-groove, or shiplap type, supported in a vertical position between the wales and secured to the wales with nails. All timbers and piles used for marine construction should be given the maximum recommended pressure treatment of creosote or creosote and a coal-tar solution.

Steel Groins   A typical design for a timber-steel sheet-pile groin is shown in Figure 6-105. Steel sheet-pile groins have been constructed with straight web, arch web, or Z piles. Some have been made permeable by cutting openings in the piles. The interlock type of joint of steel sheet piles provides a sand-tight connection. The selection of the type of sheet piles depends on the earth forces to be resisted. Where the forces are small, straight web piles can be used. Where the forces are great, deep-web Z piles should be used. The timber-steel sheet-pile groins are constructed with horizontal timber or steel wales along the top of the steel sheet piles, and vertical round timber piles or brace piles are bolted to the outside of the wales for added structural support. The round piles may not always be required with the Z pile but ordinarily are used with the flat or arch web sections. The round piles and timbers should be creosoted to maximum treatment for use in waters with marine borers.

GROINS

Groins are classified principally as to permeability, height, and length. Groins built of common construction materials can be made permeable or impermeable and high or low in profile. The materials used are stone, concrete, timber, and steel. Asphalt and sand-filled nylon bags have also been used to a limited extent. Structural types of groins built with different construction materials are illustrated in Figures 6-104 and 6-105.

SOURCE: *Shore Protection Manual,* vol. II, U.S. Army Corps of Engineers, Coastal Engineering Research Center, Fort Belvoir, Va., 1973.

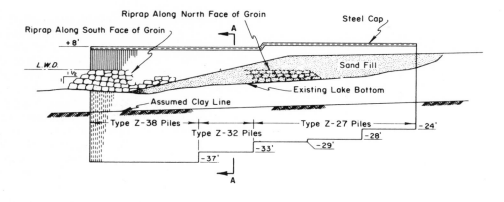

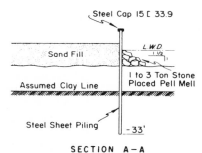

SECTION A—A

Figure 6-106 Cantilever steel sheet-pile groin.

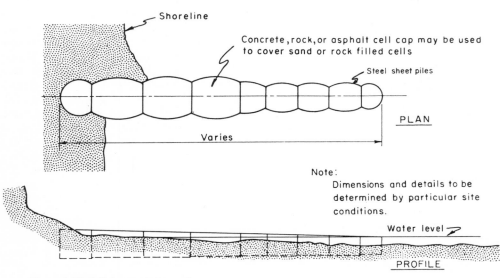

Note:
Dimensions and details to be determined by particular site conditions.

Figure 6-107 Cellular steel sheet-pile groin

Figure 6-106 illustrates the use of a cantilever steel sheet-pile groin. A groin of this type may be employed where the wave attack and earth loads are moderate. In this structure the sheet piles are the basic structural members; they are restrained at the top by a structural-steel channel welded to the piles.

A typical cellular type of groin is shown in Figure 6-107. This groin is composed of cells of varying sizes, each consisting of semicircular walls connected by cross diaphragms. Each cell is filled with sand or stone to provide structural stability. Concrete, asphalt, or stone caps are used to retain the fill material.

Concrete Groins Previously, the use of concrete in groins was generally limited to permeable-type structures that permitted the passage of sand through the structure. A more recent development in the use of concrete for groin construction is illustrated in Figure 6-109. This groin is an impermeable, prestressed concrete pile structure with a cast-in-place concrete cap.

Rubble-Mound Groins The rubble-mound groins are constructed with a core of quarry-run material, including fine material to make them sand-tight, and covered with a layer of armor stone. The armor stone should weigh enough to be stable against the design wave. A typical rubble-mound groin is illustrated in Figure 6-108.

If permeability of a rubble-mound groin is a problem, the voids between stones can be filled with concrete or asphalt grout. This sealing also increases the stability of the entire structure against wave action.

Selection of Groin Type After planning has indicated that the use of groins is practicable, the selection of groin type is based on varying interrelated factors. No universal type of groin can be prescribed because of the wide variation in conditions at each location. A thorough investigation of foundation materials is

SOURCE: *Shore Protection Manual,* vol. II, U.S. Army Corps of Engineers, Coastal Engineering Research Center, Fort Belvoir, Va., 1973.

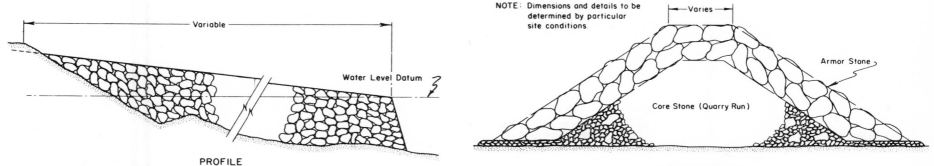

Figure 6-108 Rubble-mound groin.

NOTE: Dimensions and details to be determined by particular site conditions.

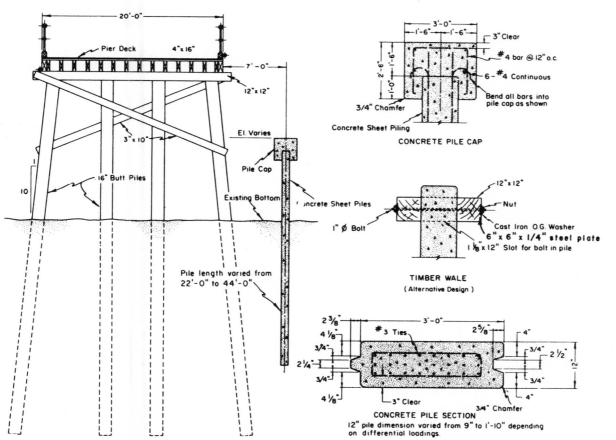

Figure 6-109 Prestressed-concrete sheet-pile groin.

essential to selection. Borings or probings should be taken to determine the subsurface conditions for penetration of piles. Where foundations are poor or where little penetration is possible, a gravity-type structure such as a rubble or a cellular steel sheet-pile groin should be considered. Where penetration is good, a cantilever type of structure of concrete, timber, or steel sheet piles should be considered.

The availability of materials affects the selection of the type of groin because of costs. The economic life of the material and the annual cost of maintenance to attain that economic life are also selection factors. The first costs of timber and steel sheet-pile groins, in that order, are often less than those of other types of construction. Concrete sheet-pile groins are generally more expensive than either timber or steel groins but may cost less than a rubble-mound groin does. However, concrete and rubble-mound groins require less maintenance and have a much longer life than do the timber or steel sheet-pile groins. The funds available for initial construction, the annual charges, and the period during which protection will be required must all be studied before deciding on a particular type.

SOURCE: *Shore Protection Manual,* vol. II, U.S. Army Corps of Engineers, Coastal Engineering Research Center, Fort Belvoir, Va., 1973.

JETTIES

The principal construction materials of jetties are stone, concrete, steel, and timber. Asphalt has occasionally been used as a binder. Some structural types of jetties are illustrated in Figures 6-110, 6-111, and 6-112.

Rubble-Mound Jetties The rubble-mound structure is a mound of stones of different sizes and shapes either dumped at random or placed in courses. Side slopes and stone sizes are designed so that the structure will resist the expected wave action. Rubble-mound jetties illustrated in Figure 6-110 and 6-111 are adaptable to any depth of water and to most foundation conditions. Rubble-mound structures are used extensively. Their chief advantages are that settlement of the structure results in readjustment of component stones and increased stability rather than in failure of the structure, damage is easily repaired, and rubble absorbs rather than reflects wave action. Their chief disadvantages are the large quantity of material required, the high first cost if satisfactory material is not locally available, and the wave energy propagated through the structure if the core is not high and impermeable.

Where rock armor units in adequate quantities or size are not economically available, concrete armor units are used. Figure 6-111 illustrates the use of quadripod armor units on a rubble-mound jetty. Figure 6-110 illustrates the use of the more recently developed dolos armor unit in which 42- and 43-ton dolos were used.

Sheet-Pile Jetties Timber, steel, and concrete sheet piles have been used for jetty construction where waves are not severe. Steel sheet piles are used for jetties in various ways. These include a single row of piling with or without pile buttresses; a single row of sheet piles arranged so that the row of piles acts as a buttressed wall; double walls of sheet piles held together with tie rods with the space between the wall filled with stone or sand, usually separated into compartments by cross walls if sand is used; and cellular steel sheet-pile structures that are modifications of the double-wall type. An example of a cellular steel sheet-pile jetty is shown in Figure 6-112.

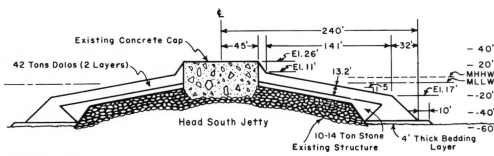

Figure 6-110 Dolos rubble-mound jetty.

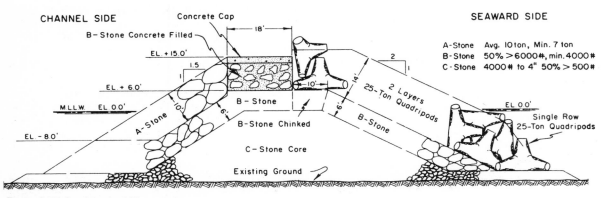

Figure 6-111 Quadripod rubble-mound jetty.

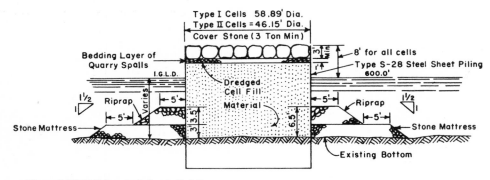

Figure 6-112 Cellular steel sheet-pile jetty.

SOURCE: *Shore Protection Manual*, vol. II, U.S. Army Corps of Engineers, Coastal Engineering Research Center, Fort Belvoir, Va., 1973.

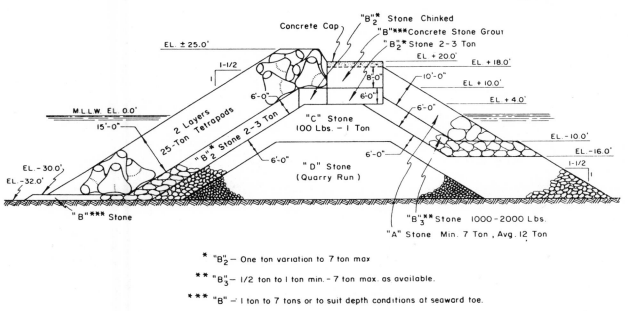

SEAWARD SIDE

HARBOR SIDE

"B"$_2^*$ Stone Chinked
"B"*** Concrete Stone Grout
"B"$_2^*$ Stone 2-3 Ton

Concrete Cap

EL. ±25.0'

EL.+20.0'
EL.+18.0'

8'-0"

6'-0"

10'-0"

EL.+10.0'

1-1/2

6'-0"

6'-0"

EL.+4.0'

M.L.L.W. EL. 0.0'

2 Layers
25-Ton Tetrapods

15'-0"

"B"$_2^*$ Stone 2-3 Ton

"C" Stone
100 Lbs.- 1 Ton

6'-0"

EL.-10.0'

EL.-16.0'

6'-0"

1-1/2

EL.-30.0'
EL.-32.0'

6'-0"

"D" Stone
(Quarry Run)

"B"*** Stone

"B"$_3^{**}$ Stone 1000-2000 Lbs.
"A" Stone Min. 7 Ton , Avg. 12 Ton

*   "B"$_2$ — One ton variation to 7 ton max

** "B"$_3$ — 1/2 ton to 1 ton min.- 7 ton max. as available.

*** "B" — 1 ton to 7 tons or to suit depth conditions at seaward toe.

Figure 6-113 Tetrapod rubble-mound breakwater.

BREAKWATERS

In exposed locations breakwaters are generally some variation of a rubble-mound structure. In less severe exposures both cellular steel and concrete caissons have been used. Figures 6-113 and 6-114 illustrate structural types of shore-connected breakwaters used for harbor protection. The rubble-mound breakwaters depicted in these figures are adaptable to almost any depth and can be designed to withstand severe waves. Figure 6-114 illustrates the use of tribar armor units on a rubble-mound structure.

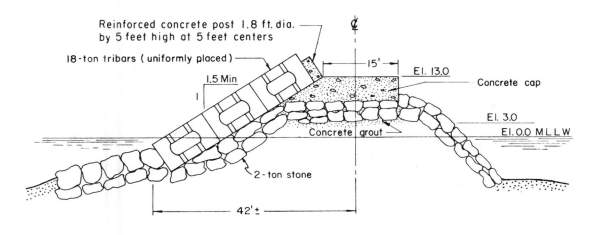

Reinforced concrete post 1.8 ft. dia. by 5 feet high at 5 feet centers

₵

18-ton tribars (uniformly placed)

15'

El. 13.0

Concrete cap

1.5 Min

El. 3.0

Concrete grout

El. 0.0 M L L W

2-ton stone

42'±

Figure 6-114 Tribar rubble-mound breakwater.

SOURCE: *Shore Protection Manual,* vol. II, U.S. Army Corps of Engineers, Coastal Engineering Research Center, Fort Belvoir, Va., 1973.

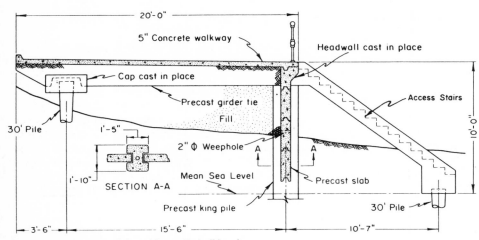

Figure 6-115 Concrete slab and king-pile bulkhead.

BULKHEADS

Three structural types of bulkheads (concrete, steel, and timber) are shown in Figures 6-115, 6-116, and 6-117. Cellular steel sheet-pile bulkheads are used where rock is near the surface and adequate penetration is impossible for the anchored sheet-pile bulkhead illustrated in Figure 6-116. When vertical or nearly vertical bulkheads are constructed and the water depth at the wall is less than twice the anticipated maximum wave height, the design should provide for riprap armoring at the base to prevent scouring. Excessive scouring may endanger the stability of the wall.

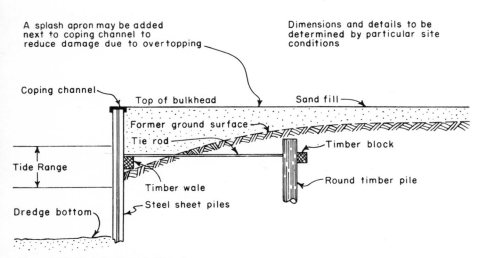

Figure 6-116 Steel sheet-pile bulkhead.

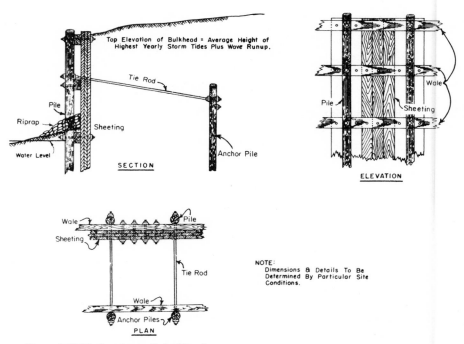

Figure 6-117 Timber sheet-pile bulkhead.

SOURCE: *Shore Protection Manual,* vol. II, U.S. Army Corps of Engineers, Coastal Engineering Research Center, Fort Belvoir, Va., 1973.

BULKHEAD WALLS

Walls of types D, E, and F are sheet-pile walls (see Figure 6-120). They generally show little settlement but at times may not be considered as permanent as walls on riprap, filled cribs, or relieving platforms. Type D, a wood sheet-pile wall, is probably the most widely used at marinas if there is a firm foundation material into which the sheet piles may be driven to the required depth. This type of wall is often the most economical. Type E, a steel sheet-pile wall, can be modified to fit many varied condiitions. In some instances it may compare favorably in cost with a wood sheet-pile wall. Type F is a steel sheet-pile wall with a concrete cap or coping. In addition to enhancing the appearance of the wall, the concrete may increase the life of the wall if it extends from above the high-water line to below the low-water line, thus encasing the area where disintegration is greatest.

Walls of types A and C have economical original construction costs but are subject to large settlements and sliding. They are often the source of future trouble and costly maintenance in recapping the walls and repairing adjacent structures. When settling and sliding are of small consequence and the encroachment of riprap or crib base does not unduly limit the use of the marina, they are recommended because of their economy. The bottom should be reasonably solid for this type of construction; otherwise the entire wall may be lost. It is suggested that the top of the riprap or crib base be built up approximately 1 foot higher than the desired grade to allow for settlement. It is also recommended that a year or two elapse before constructing the wall on the base. The walls on these types of bases can be varied as required by architectural appearance or other local conditions. The walls might be cast-in-place concrete, precast-concrete blocks, rubble masonry, cut-stone masonry, or concrete walls with stone facings and copings.

Type B, a relieving-platform type of bulkhead, consists of a concrete wall resting on a timber relieving platform supported by bearing piles. This type of wall is suitable for greater depths of water and softer underlying strata than are the sheet-pile walls.

See also Figures 6-118 and 6-119.

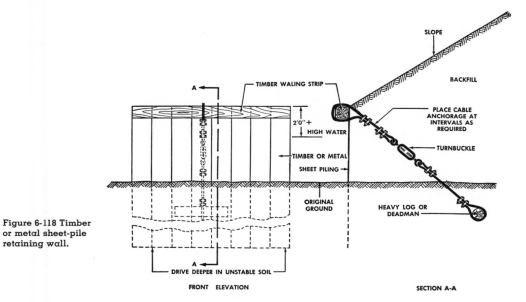

Figure 6-118 Timber or metal sheet-pile retaining wall.

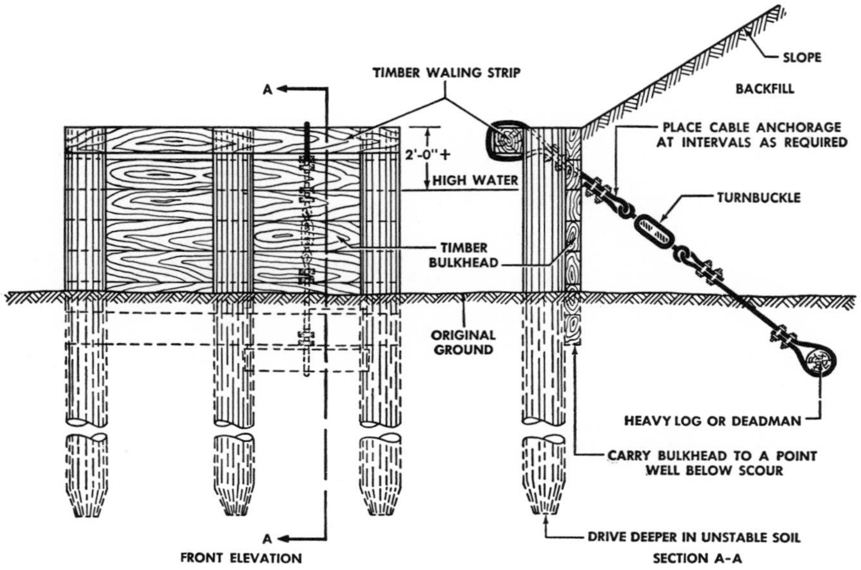

Figure 6-119 Timber bulkhead and pile retaining wall.

SOURCE: Charles A. Chaney, *Marinas: Recommendations for Design, Construction and Maintenance*, 2d ed., National Association of Engine and Boat Manufacturers, New York, 1961.

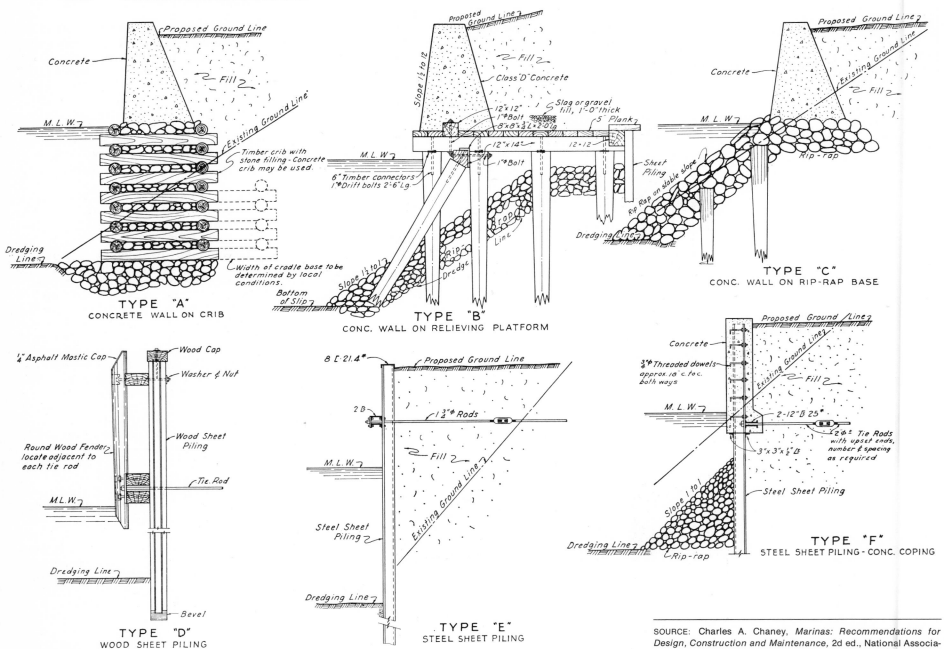

Figure 6-120 Bulkhead walls for typical pleasure boat basin.

SOURCE: Charles A. Chaney, *Marinas: Recommendations for Design, Construction and Maintenance*, 2d ed., National Association of Engine and Boat Manufacturers, New York, 1961.

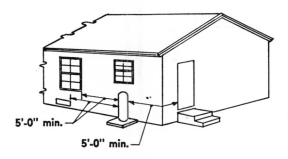

**ABOVEGROUND CONTAINERS OF
LESS THAN 125-GALLON CAPACITY**

6.19 Gas Storage Containers and Overhead Electrical Service

An aboveground liquefied petroleum gas storage container (see Figure 6-121) with a capacity of less than 125 gallons may be placed directly against the exterior wall of a building. When two gas storage container units are installed, no clearance need be provided between them.

The space where the aboveground containers are located should be arranged so that the lowest level of such space, whether enclosed or open, is ventilated horizontally to the outside air and is at least 5 feet in horizontal distance from any openable window, door, or other ventilating opening that is wholly or in part at a lower level. Such an arrangement should also be maintained for the discharge of cylinder and regulator relief valves.

An aboveground installation should be at least 5 feet from any driveway. Underground containers should be buried at least 2 feet below grade.

Overhead electrical service is illustrated in Figure 6-122.

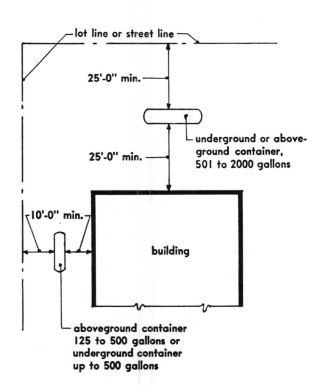

**UNDERGROUND CONTAINERS OR
ABOVEGROUND CONTAINERS OF MORE
THAN 125-GALLON CAPACITY**

Figure 6-121 Liquefied petroleum gas storage containers.

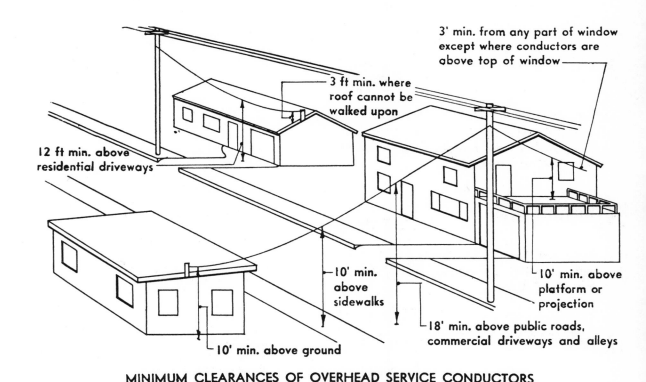

MINIMUM CLEARANCES OF OVERHEAD SERVICE CONDUCTORS

Figure 6-122 Overhead electrical service.

SOURCE: *Code Manual*, New York State Building Code Commission.

6.20 Outdoor Signs

Essentially, signs should perform three functions. They should (1) identify a place and indicate whether it is accessible to everyone, (2) indicate warnings where necessary, and (3) give routing information. (See Figure 6-123.)

1. Directional

Usually included with an arrow; are used for indication of a change in route, or confirmation of a correct direction.

2. Informational

Used for overall information for general organization of a series of elements; i.e. campus plan, bus routes, building layout, shopping mall plan, etc.

3. Identification

Gives specific location information, identifies specific items; i.e. parking lot "b", building #5, First Aid, etc.

4. Regulatory

Gives operational requirements, restrictions, or gives warnings. Usually used for traffic delineation or control; i.e. "Stop" signs, "no parking," "one way," etc.

Figure 6-123 Types of signs.

The information given on signs should always be clear and precise, and sign locations should never present unnecessary hazards for pedestrian or vehicular traffic.

Identification and Accessibility

1. Key site-related areas that should be identified by sign posting are as follows:
   a. Traffic signs announcing public rest stops with accessible facilities
   b. Public lavatories accessible to pedestrians
   c. Special car parking
   d. Directional signs for vehicles and pedestrians such as one-way street signs
   e. Signs identifying accessible entrances to buildings or facilities
   f. Informative signs on buildings
2. So that signs can be made more useful to everyone, they should be designed to be readable by all people, including the visually handicapped. This can be accomplished in a number of different ways:
   a. Braille strips can be placed along sign edges.
   b. Raised or routed letters are readable by the blind or the partially sighted.
   c. Graphic symbols are useful in transmitting messages quickly but should be avoided as the sole means of imparting information because they can be confusing to the blind.
   d. Signs that will be used by the visually handicapped must be located in a manner that first allows the signs to be recognized and, second, allows sign surfaces to be touched by the reader's hand.
   e. Signs along walkways or corridors should be set back a minimum of 18 inches and placed at a height of from 4 feet to 5 feet 6 inches.
3. The international symbol for access, the abstract man in a wheelchair, is already in extensive use in the United States. It is used to show where special provisions have been made to allow access for restricted persons.

Warnings   Textural paving may be used to warn of imminent hazards such as abrupt changes of grade, stairs, ramps, and walk intersections and the locations of special information. However, the use of textural paving as a warning device for the blind is extremely impractical because of the widely

varying nature of walkways in the country. The only effective use for such a system would be in a closed environment such as a school for the blind. Unfortunately, once away from their protected surroundings, blind persons would be vulnerable to a world full of unforewarned hazards.

Routing Information   Where it is critical that people be able to travel quickly and unhindered to their destinations, routing information should be given.

1. Hospitals, college campuses, institutions, and so on should have posted signs, lines, or arrows painted on walk systems that are accessible to wheeled vehicles, particularly if such path systems are limited in number.
2. Access to buildings with only one or two entrances that are accessible to wheeled vehicles should be clearly indicated by routing signs.

Readability   The readability of any sign is a function of many factors. In designing or choosing the format of a sign, the following points should be considered.

1. Information should be as concise and direct as possible.
2. Lettering styles and graphic symbols should be as bold and simple as possible. Fancy styles become cluttered, are time-consuming, and are confusing to read.
3. Schemes of contrasting colors with light images on dark backgrounds make signs both easier to read and more readable from longer distances.

Placement   Placement is important because wrongly located signs may present an obstacle or a hazard. Unless intended to be read by the blind or the partially sighted, they should be set far enough off a traveled way or high enough off the ground, or both, so as not to be inadvertently walked into.

See Figure 6-124 for information on the design and location of signs.

SOURCE: *Barrier-free Site Design*, U.S. Department of Housing and Urban Development, 1975.

Design and Location

- When possible, gather signs together into unified systems. Avoid sign clutter in the landscape.

- Combine signs with lighting fixtures to reduce unnecessary posts and to illuminate signs – signage can't be effective in dark areas.

- Low-level informational signs can also illuminate paving below.

- Information signs should be placed at natural gathering spots and included into the design of site furniture.

- Avoid placement of signs where they may conflict with pedestrian traffic.

- Sign location should avoid conflict with door opening or vehicular operation.

- Signs should be placed to allow safe pedestrian clearance, vertically and laterally.

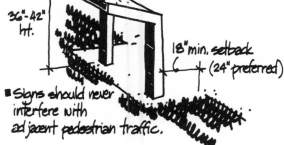

- Raised or routed letters are also helpful for the blind in reading signs.

- Informational signs should have a braille strip for the blind, often placed on edge of sign in upper left hand corner.

36"-42" ht.

18" min. setback (24" preferred)

- Signs should never interfere with adjacent pedestrian traffic.

Braille on Signs

sign

lights

BUS INFO

7'-6" min.

Roadway   4.5' min.   2' min.   Walk

Figure 6-124 Outdoor signs.

SOURCE: *Barrier-free Site Design*, U.S. Department of Housing and Urban Development, 1975.

6.21 Dimensions and Clearances for People Involved in Outdoor Activities

The data in Figure 6-125 have been gathered and condensed from a myriad of reports. Although the dimensions have been deter-mined by methods other than anatomical research, the information presented synthesiz-es the varying and sometimes contradictory recommendations published by the wide num-ber of sources. These specific dimensions best represent the collective average of the recom-mendations found in different publications. Accordingly, they should be used with the understanding that the dimensions are not finite or absolute but rather are general guidelines.

Dimensions for People Outdoors

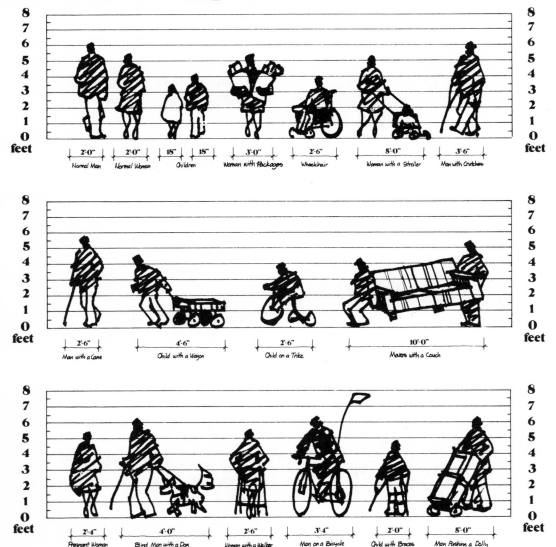

Figure 6-125

SOURCE: *Barrier-free Site Design*, U.S. Department of Housing and Urban Development, 1975.

6.22 Standard Symbols for Site Drawings

Figure 6-126 presents standard symbols that may be used in site drawings.

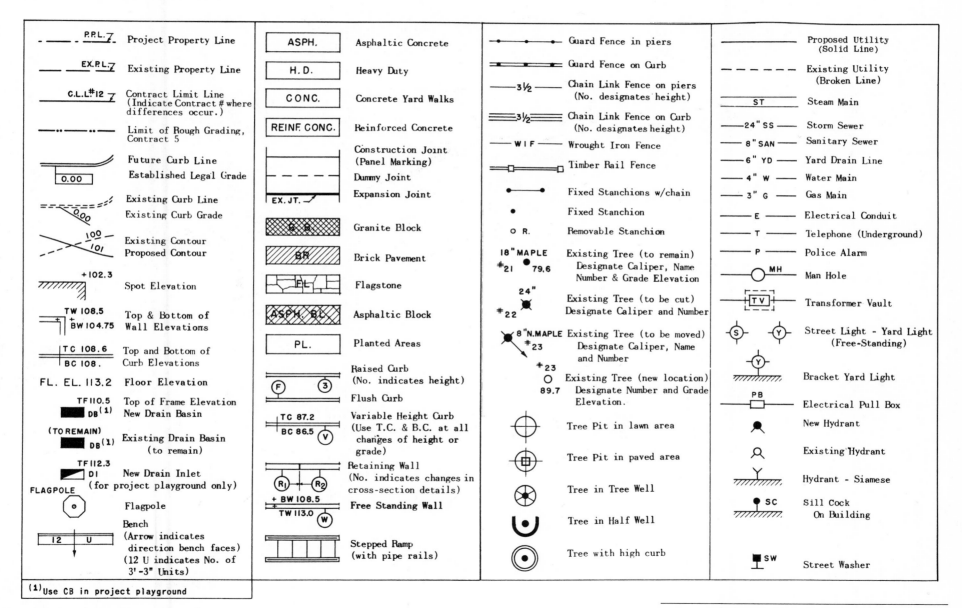

Figure 6-126 Standard symbols for site drawings.

SOURCE: *Memo to Architects*, New York City Housing Authority.

Illustrative Site Plans

The site plans presented in this section provide a small sampling of different approaches to the site planning process. In them can be seen an amalgamation of the many and varied aspects of site planning discussed in previous sections.

The town house development illustrates the various steps required to evolve properly a final design solution. It involves a typical low-density development in a suburban area.

The planned unit development shows a similar type of analysis and solution in a more heavily built-up area. Also, it illustrates various alternative approaches prior to its final scheme and even delves into typical housing types as part of the site planning process.

In addition to residential development, a school complex and a beach park development are included. Both again demonstrate the different approaches and solutions to the specific problems involved.

As previously stated, these site plans are presented not as definitive site designs but as guides to the site designer for greater awareness and understanding of the problems and their subsequent solution.

Opposite: Land Uses and the West Side Highway.
(Transportation Administration and City
Planning Commission, City of New York)

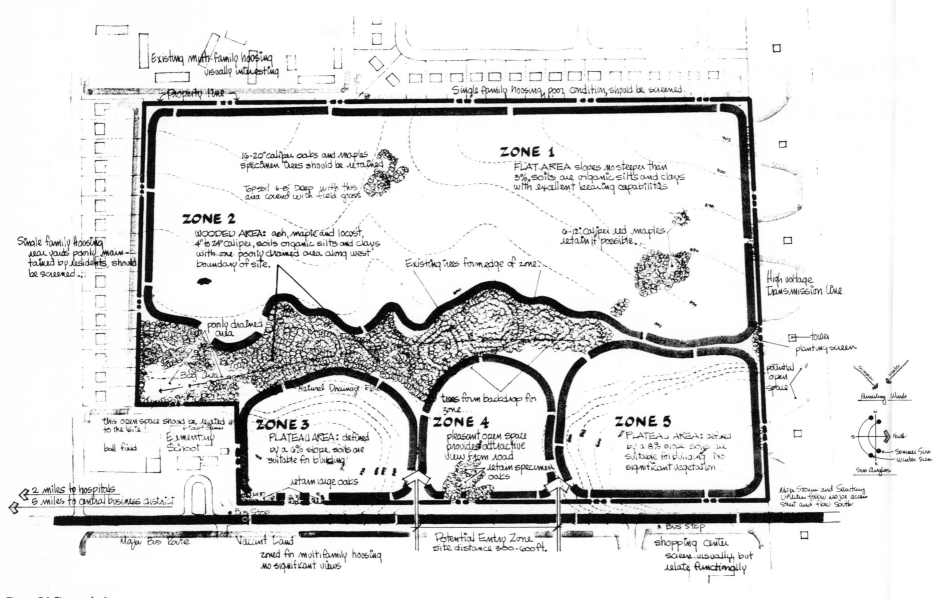

Figure 7-1 Site analysis.

SOURCE: *Townhouse Development Process*, Michigan State Housing Development Authority, Lansing, Mich., 1970.

7.1 Town House Development Process

SITE ANALYSIS AND DEVELOPMENT PROGRAM

The phase of site analysis should identify the character, structure, and potential of the site. In discovering these characteristics and relying upon them to inspire proper land use, the analyst should consider and record the items listed below. The analysis should be done on a site topographic map at a scale no smaller than 1 inch = 100 feet. The map should cover not only the site but also surrounding areas that may influence site uses and design. See Figure 7-1.

1. Contiguous land use
   Indicate type and impact of adjoining land use.
   Indicate direction and distance to community services, hospitals, shopping, and so on.
   Show public transportation route and stops.
2. Topography
   Basic topography.
   Special or unique ground forms.
   Percentage of slope.
3. Drainage
   Natural watershed (direction).
   Drainage swales.
   Bog and swamp areas.
4. Soils
   Show depth and analysis of topsoil.
   Locate soil borings and give data (this can be presented in a separate report.
5. Vegetation
   Locate and identify existing tree masses.
   Locate and identify specimen plant material.
   Indicate type of ground cover.
6. Climatology
   Prevailing wind direction.
   Sun angles.
7. Existing conditions
   Structures.
   Utilities.
   Circulation.
8. Special Features
   Lakes and ponds.
   Special land features, rock outcroppings, and so on.
   Dramatic views.

In addition to the site analysis and conceptual plan, the first phase must include a written program statement for the project. This statement provides the guidelines for development of the project and, in conjunction with the site analysis, the basis for the conceptual plan. The program should include the following:

1. Budget
   Project design budget allocated for on- and off-site improvements, residential and accessory buildings, and so on. This budget will guide and control the development of plans.
2. Time schedule
   Target time periods for completion of subsequent phases.
   Anticipated construction starting date.
3. Dwelling units
   Type of ownership or tenancy (rental, cooperative, condominium).
   Total number of units anticipated.
   Allowable site density.
   Types of dwelling units (differentiated by number of bedrooms, floor areas, and configurations) and distribution of total number of units among the various types.
   Special requirements, conditions, or features.
4. Community facilities
   Methods and requirements of project marketing, management, and maintenance.
   Management and maintenance spaces and facilities anticipated.
   Indoor and outdoor community recreation and social spaces and facilities anticipated.
5. Nonresidential facilities
   Nonresidential facilities anticipated.

SOURCE: *Townhouse Development Process*, Michigan State Housing Development Authority, Lansing, Mich., 1970.

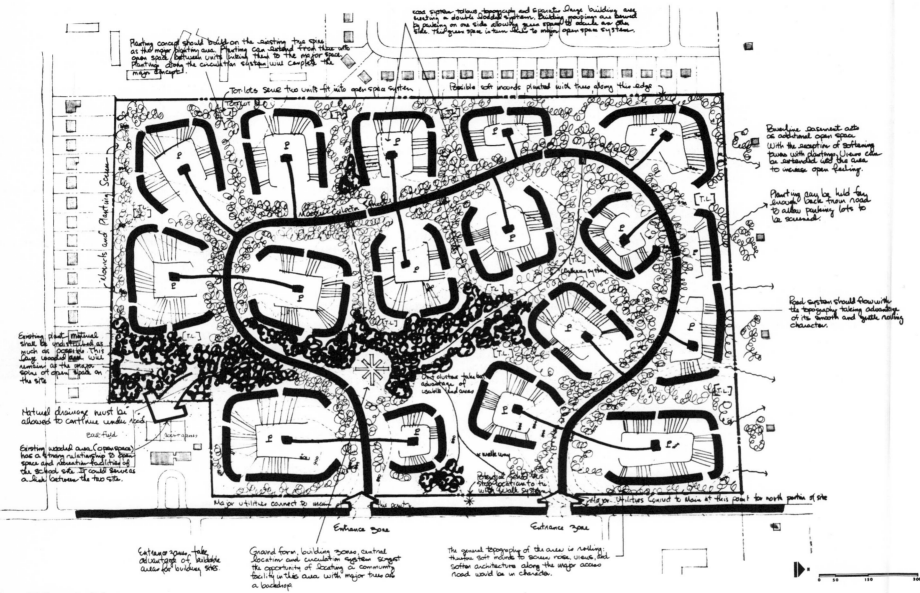

Figure 7-2 Conceptual plan.

SOURCE: *Townhouse Development Process*, Michigan State Housing Development Authority, Lansing, Mich., 1970.

CONCEPTUAL PLAN

The phase of the conceptual plan should relate in a logical manner the needs in the development program to the physical site structure as clarified by the site analysis. The conceptual plan should indicate the general building masses, circulation (vehicular and pedestrian), parking, open space, and special facilities. In general, it should convey the general intent, spatial form, and system of development. It should be prepared on a site topography base map at a scale no smaller than 1 inch = 100 feet. See Figure 7-2.

1. Structures

   Indicate location, arrangement, and general massing groupings.

   Locate any recreation or service structures.

2. Circulation

   a. Vehicular

      Show system of roads, parking, and service.

   b. Pedestrian

      Indicate general walkway system and connection to common facilities.

3. Utilities

   Indicate major trunk lines and connection points to existing utilities.

4. Recreation

   Show open space and facilities for recreational use.

   Indicate parking and service for common facilities.

5. Parking

   Location.

6. Grading

   General character.

   Mounds and berms.

   Any special grading problems.

7. Planting

   Consider existing vegetation in the development of the concept.

   Indicate the general planting concept.

SOURCE: *Townhouse Development Process,* Michigan State Housing Development Authority, Lansing, Mich., 1970.

DEVELOPMENT SUMMARY:

TOTAL ACRES
NO. OF UNITS
   1 BR
   2 BR
   3 BR
   4 BR
DENSITY
PARKING
   NO.
   RATIO

0   50   150   300

SOURCE: *Townhouse Development Process*, Michigan State Housing Development Authority, Lansing, Mich., 1970.

Figure 7-3 Schematic site plan.

SCHEMATIC SITE PLAN

Schematics should be developed from careful study and observation of the conceptual plan. The plan should refine to a more exact scale the arrangement and functional groupings of units to create a meaningful sequence of usable spaces. The specific relationship of unit arrangement, the relationship of structure to site, site grading, circulation, lighting, paving, screening, setbacks, parking, play areas, and recreation areas should be communicated in this phase. This plan should be produced at a scale of 1 inch = 50 feet where practicable. In addition to the required plan, additional sections, sketches, and study models to convey the intent should be made. See Figures 7-3 and 7-4.

1. Structures
   Location, shape, size, arrangements, and groupings.
2. Circulation
   Indicate location and materials of vehicular and pedestrian routes.
   Indicate parking–dwelling unit relationships.
3. Utilities
   Indicate general major utility layout and connections. This can be done as an overlay.
4. Recreation
   Location.
   Type of facilities.
5. Parking
   Location, material, number of spaces, and parking ratio.
6. Grading
   Resolve special and typical grade relationships.
   Indicate general grading character, proposed contours, sections, and so on.
   Show berms and mounds.
7. Planting
   Indicate character.
   Indicate screening concepts, planting relationship to units, open space, and so on with sections or sketches.
8. Lighting
   Location.
   Character (this can be shown with a catalog illustration).

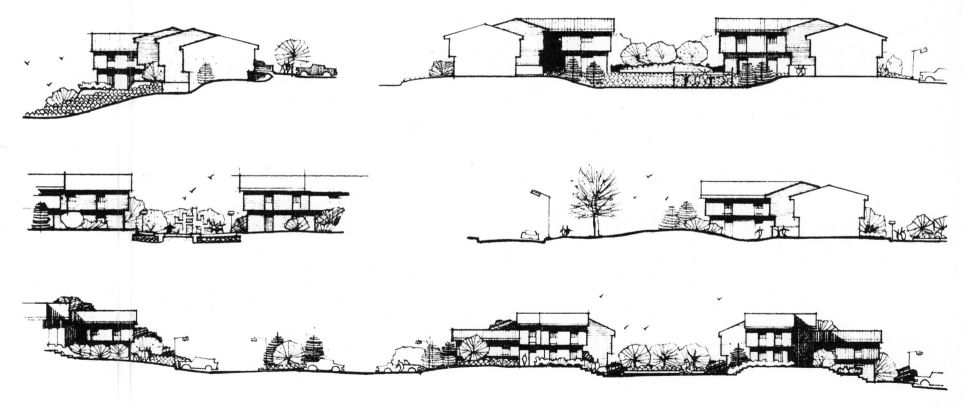

SCHEMATIC SECTIONS

Figure 7-4 Schematic sections.

SOURCE: *Townhouse Development Process*, Michigan State Housing Development Authority, Lansing, Mich., 1970.

PRELIMINARY SITE PLAN

This plan should be a detailed document of the schematic plan, refined to the point at which accurate bids can be received from bidders. It should include all elements of the site with necessary drawings and details to convey the intent. The preliminary plan should be prepared at a scale of not less than 1 inch = 50 feet. See Figure 7-5.

1. Structures

   Final location to exact scale.
2. Circulation

   Location, key dimensions, and materials of roads and walks.
3. Utility (separate drawing)

   Show all utility lines and other construction with grades.

   Locate all storm inlets, catch basins, fire hydrants, and so on, and give grades.
4. Recreation

   Locate open space or special use areas.

   Indicate play areas and equipment.

   Show equipment and facilities.
5. Grading

   Indicate spot grades, proposed and existing contours, berms, and mounds.

   Show floor grades of all structures.
6. Planting (separate drawing)

   Locate plant material.

   Indicate areas to receive seed or sod.

   Indicate plant list, showing quantity, size, and root specification.
7. Legend

   Units, density, parking, acreage, and similar information.

   Symbol key relating to drawing.

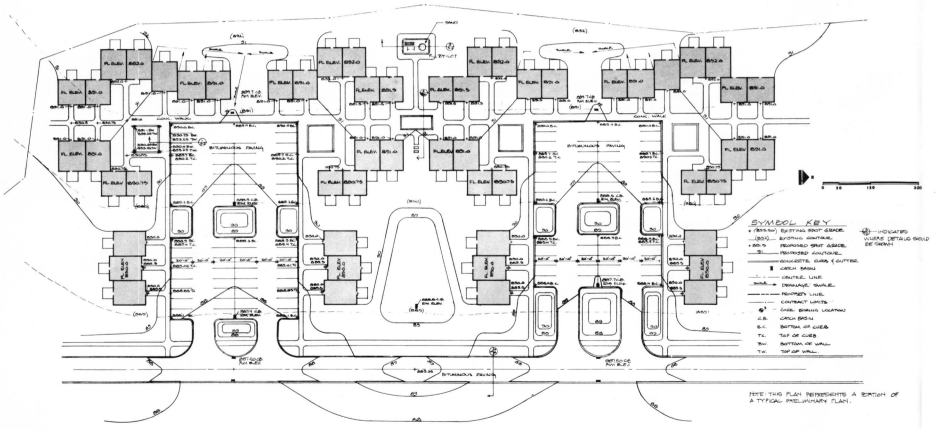

Figure 7-5 Preliminary site plan.

SOURCE: *Townhouse Development Process*, Michigan State Housing Development Authority, Lansing, Mich., 1970.

7.2 Planned Unit Development

COMPARATIVE ADVANTAGES

An actual site has been selected to illustrate the full range of site planning opportunities possible under the planned unit development amendment. The following pages show a drawing accentuating the site topography (Figure 7-7), a conventional proposal for development of the site (Figure 7-19), and four alternatives for development under planned unit development (Figures 7-12, 7-16, 7-17, and 7-18). The first two alternatives show developments of about the same density as the conventional proposal. The third alternative shows a scheme of somewhat higher density that could accommodate an increased demand for apartment units. The fourth alternative shows how a maximum number of units could be developed by using apartment houses with an urban scale but within the permissible density. A comparison of the advantages of planned unit development schemes is shown in Figure 7-6.

	GROSS SITE AREA	STREET AREA	STREET AREA % OF GROSS SITE AREA	NET SITE AREA	COMMON OPEN SPACE	NUMBER OF DWELLING UNITS	ALLOWABLE FLOOR AREA PER DWELLING UNIT	ALLOWABLE COVERAGE PER DWELLING UNIT	ALLOWABLE NUMBER OF ROOMS PER DWELLING UNIT	
1 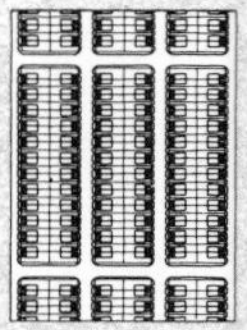	20 ACRES	6.3 ACRES	31.4%	13.7 ACRES	NONE	semi-det: 198	1400 sq. ft.	700 sq. ft.	7.5	Figures based on: typical zoning lot of 2800 sq. ft. F.A.R. (Floor Area Ratio) of .5 O.S.R. (Open Space Ratio) of 150 lot area per room of 375 sq. ft.
2 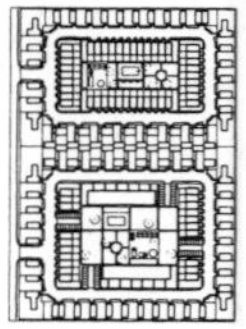	20 ACRES	5.6 ACRES	28%	14.4 ACRES	2.3 ACRES	detached: 59 semi-det: 23 townhouses: 62 garden apts: 56 total: 200	1840 sq. ft.	940 sq. ft.	9.5	Figures based on: net site area divided by number of dwelling units, and application of full bonuses resulting in: F.A.R. (Floor Area Ratio) of .575 O.S.R. (Open Space Ratio) of 120 lot area per room of 337 sq. ft.
3 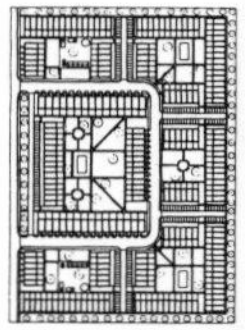	20 ACRES	4.1 ACRES	20.5%	15.9 ACRES	8.6 ACRES	townhouses: 213	1900 sq. ft.	980 sq. ft.	9.8	
4 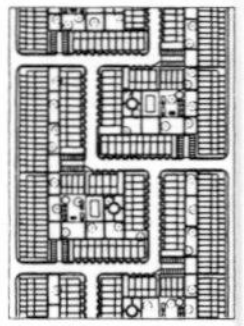	20 ACRES	5 ACRES	25%	15.0 ACRES	4.0 ACRES	townhouses: 210	1820 sq. ft.	975 sq. ft.	9.35	

Table shows land use and site utilization advantages of Planned Unit Development schemes (numbered 2, 3, and 4) over conventional subdivision scheme, 1.

Figure 7-6 Table of comparative advantages.

SOURCE: *Planned Unit Development*, New York City Planning Commission.

CONTOUR MAP

The contour map shown in Figure 7-7 accentuates the topography and water resources of the site. The high ground to the south pitches sharply and irregularly down to rather flat ground in the north.

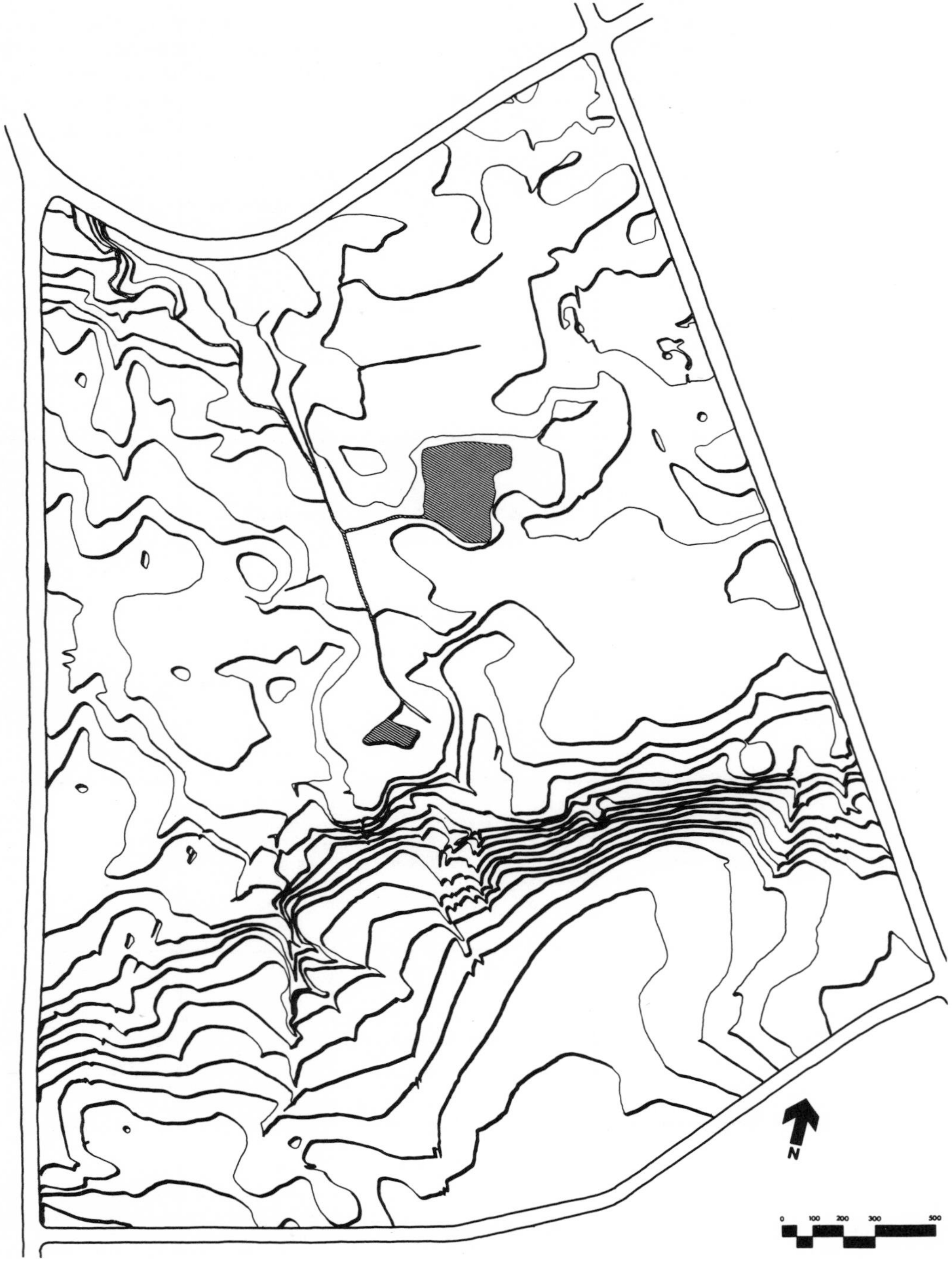

Figure 7-7 Contour map.

SOURCE: *Planned Unit Development*, New York City Planning Commission.

TYPICAL SITE DEVELOPMENT

Figure 7-8 shows a site plan of existing features, contours, including trees, ponds, and creek, and bounding roads. Figure 7-9 shows site sections, taken where indicated on the plan, with the vertical scale exaggerated by 2:1.

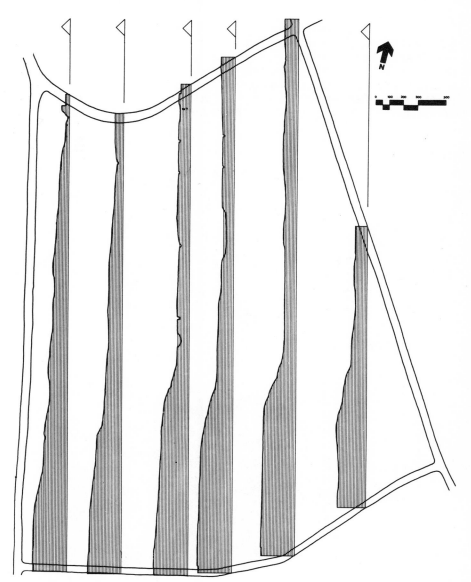

Figure 7-9 Site sections.

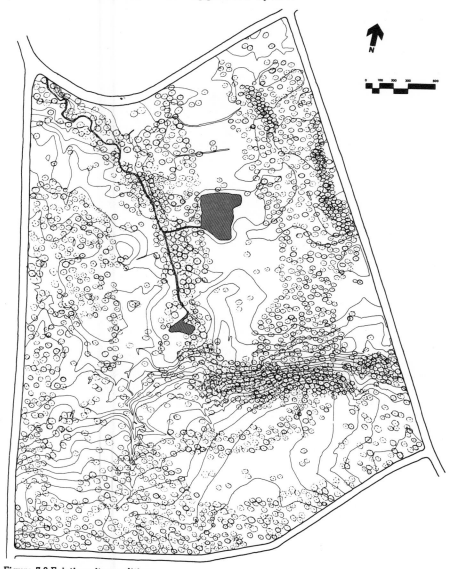

Figure 7-8 Existing site conditions.

SOURCE: *Planned Unit Development*, New York City Planning Commission.

Figure 7-10 is a preliminary street and drainage plan showing the alignment of streets and the direction of flow of storm and sanitary sewer lines. Figure 7-11 is an architectural site plan showing streets, parking, curb cuts, pedestrian ways, the placement of buildings, shopping center, and school, and open space treatment.

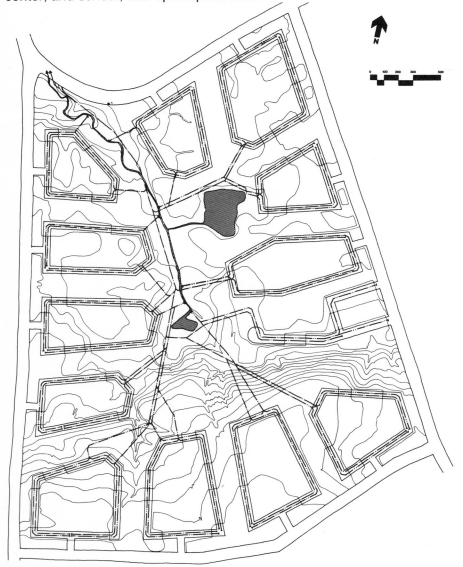

Figure 7-10 Preliminary street and drainage plan.

Figure 7-11 Architectural site plan.

SOURCE: *Planned Unit Development*, New York City Planning Commission.

TOWN HOUSE CLUSTERS ON COLLECTOR STREETS

The scheme of town house clusters in Figure 7-12 shows 1431 homes on the same site. It is characterized by a horseshoe-loop street system that eliminates through traffic, uses a minimum amount of land for streets, furnishes an enormous common open area in addition to the open spaces defined by individual clusters, and provides shopping and a school, accessible from the cul-de-sac street that enters from the eastern boundary. The strongest natural features of the site are preserved as a recreational and scenic amenity.

Figure 7-13 is an axonometric projection of one loop, that indicates the three-dimensional character of the scheme of town house clusters.

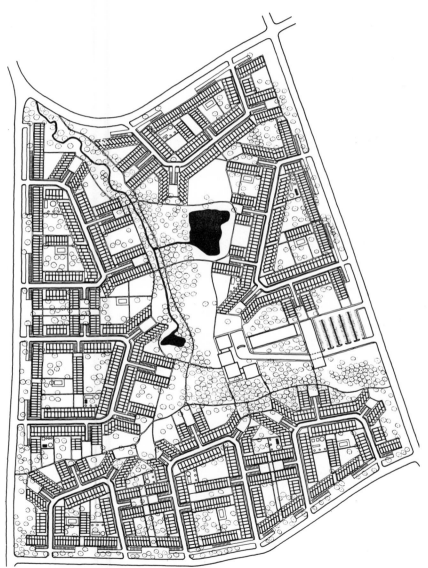

Figure 7-12 Town house clusters.

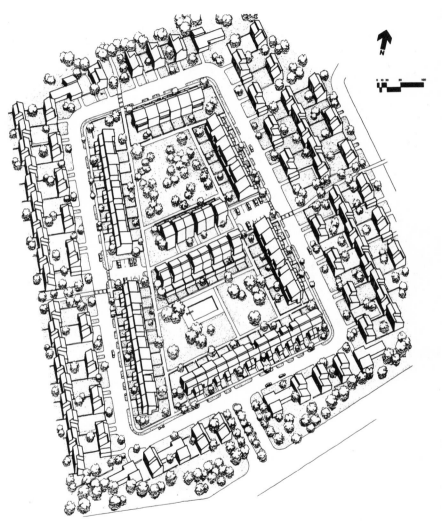

Figure 7-13 Axonometric projection of a loop of the town house scheme.

SOURCE: *Planned Unit Development,* New York City Planning Commission.

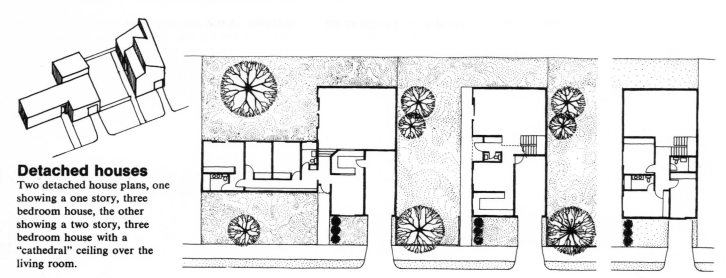

Detached houses

Two detached house plans, one showing a one story, three bedroom house, the other showing a two story, three bedroom house with a "cathedral" ceiling over the living room.

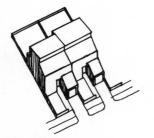

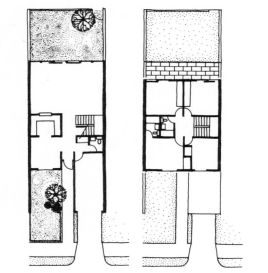

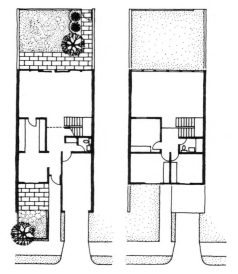

Townhouses

Two alternative townhouse plans, one showing a four-bedroom scheme in which two of the bedrooms open out onto a second story deck, the other showing a three bedroom scheme which permits a "cathedral" ceiling over the living room.

Figure 7-14

DETACHED HOUSES AND TOWN HOUSES

Figure 7-14 shows plans of the types of the detached houses and town houses to be built in the development, indicating the relationships of yards to house interiors.

SOURCE: *Planned Unit Development*, New York City Planning Commission.

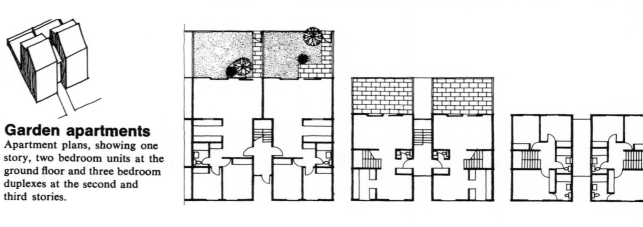

Garden apartments

Apartment plans, showing one story, two bedroom units at the ground floor and three bedroom duplexes at the second and third stories.

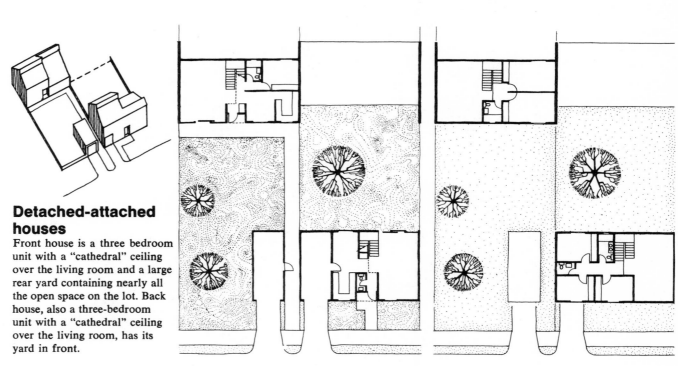

Detached-attached houses

Front house is a three bedroom unit with a "cathedral" ceiling over the living room and a large rear yard containing nearly all the open space on the lot. Back house, also a three-bedroom unit with a "cathedral" ceiling over the living room, has its yard in front.

Figure 7-15

GARDEN APARTMENTS AND DETACHED-ATTACHED HOUSES

Figure 7-15 shows plans of the types of garden apartments and detached-attached houses to be built in the development, indicating the relationships of yards to house interiors.

SOURCE: *Planned Unit Development*, New York City Planning Commission.

Figure 7-16 Varied house types on loop streets.

VARIED HOUSE TYPES ON LOOP STREETS

The scheme shown in Figure 7-16 includes a full range of house types: detached houses, semidetached houses, town houses, and town house apartments, totaling 1445 dwelling units. This mix of houses is organized around a P-loop street system in which each loop serves only the houses on it. Within each loop a sizable common open space with recreational facilities is formed, and all the loops together enclose a large parkland running along the ridge and into the center of the site. Again, school and shopping facilities are provided, and the natural beauty of the site is respected.

SOURCE: *Planned Unit Development*, New York City Planning Commission.

HOUSE CLUSTERS AND APARTMENT HOUSES

The scheme shown in Figure 7-17 anticipates changing market conditions during the course of a development time span. It assumes an initial development similar to the scheme in Figure 7-16 in the northern, lower portion of the site and then a transformation of the market into apartment units. Three- and four-story maisonette apartments perch on the crest of the ridge, backed up by six-story terraced apartment buildings. Rising out of the expanded shopping center at the south center of the site is a square apartment tower of twenty stories. A total of 2800 dwelling units is thus accommodated on the site. In addition to the surface parking shown, a sizable amount of parking is contained underneath the terraced apartments and shopping center. More open space is provided than in Figures 7-12 and 7-16, in recognition of the increased density.

Figure 7-17 House clusters and apartment houses.

SOURCE: *Planned Unit Development,* New York City Planning Commission.

APARTMENTS FOR MAXIMUM OPEN SPACE

The scheme in Figure 7-18 represents an entirely urban, apartment-type residential environment in which a maximum number of dwelling units is realized. The apartment types consist of three- and four-story town house and maisonette apartments, five-, six-, and seven-story terraced apartments, and major apartment structures stepping up from four stories to as many as twenty-eight or thirty stories, for an overall total of about 4500 dwelling units. The center of the site is the focus of the development, with extensive shopping facilities at the first-floor level of the apartment structures. The terraced structure at the south end of the center houses an elementary school. Around the periphery of the site are extensive recreational facilities as well as a considerable amount of land left in its natural state.

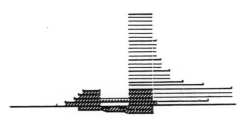

Figure 7-18 Apartments for maximum open space.

SOURCE: *Planned Unit Development*, New York City Planning Commission.

CONVENTIONAL STREET GRID

The conventional scheme for the development of the site, illustrated in Figure 7-19, shows 1427 single-family houses on about 205 acres. Houses are placed according to zoning lot requirements on a street system previously adopted by the city. The result is a disastrously barren environment, and all the natural character of the site has been destroyed.

Figure 7-19 A conventional street grid.

SOURCE: *Planned Unit Development,* New York City Planning Commission.

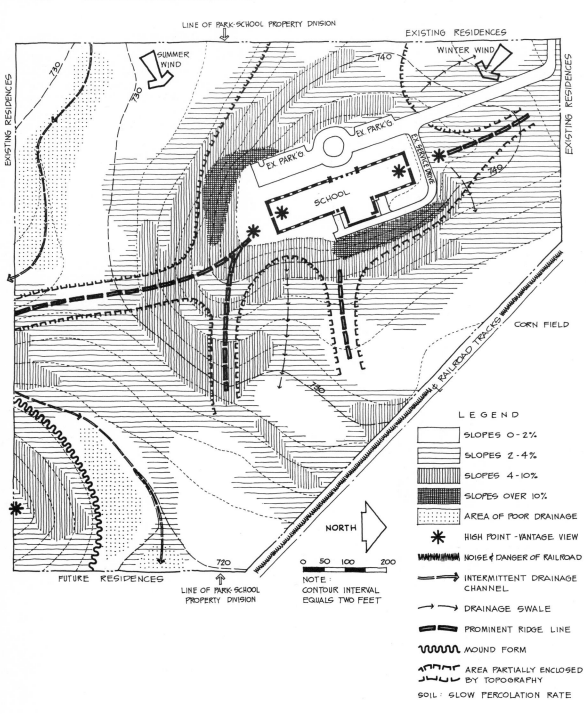

LINE OF PARK-SCHOOL PROPERTY DIVISION

SUMMER WIND

WINTER WIND

EXISTING RESIDENCES

EXISTING RESIDENCES

EXISTING RESIDENCES

EX. PARK'G

EX. PARK'G

EX. SERVICE DRIVE

SCHOOL

730

740

740

730

730

720

CORN FIELD

& RAILROAD TRACKS

FUTURE RESIDENCES

LINE OF PARK-SCHOOL PROPERTY DIVISION

NORTH

0 50 100 200

NOTE:
CONTOUR INTERVAL
EQUALS TWO FEET

LEGEND

SLOPES 0-2%

SLOPES 2-4%

SLOPES 4-10%

SLOPES OVER 10%

AREA OF POOR DRAINAGE

✳ HIGH POINT-VANTAGE VIEW

NOISE & DANGER OF RAILROAD

INTERMITTENT DRAINAGE CHANNEL

DRAINAGE SWALE

PROMINENT RIDGE LINE

MOUND FORM

AREA PARTIALLY ENCLOSED BY TOPOGRAPHY

SOIL: SLOW PERCOLATION RATE

7.3 School-Park Complex

SITE ANALYSIS

Figure 7-20 presents an analysis of a site to be used for a school-park complex.

Figure 7-20 Site analysis.

SOURCE: A. J. Rutledge, *Anatomy of a Park*, copyright © 1971 by McGraw-Hill, Inc., used with permission of McGraw-Hill Book Company, New York.

LINE OF PARK-SCHOOL PROPERTY DIVISION

EXISTING RESIDENCES

SHELTERBELT & NATURE STUDY

EXISTING RESIDENCES

EXISTING RESIDENCES

SUPERVISED PLAYGROUND

SPRAY POOL

TOT-LOT

CRAFTS AREA

SHELTER

SERVICE

INTRMDT COURT

APPARATUS AREA

TENNIS, ICE SKATING BADMINTON CROQUET HANDBALL

ADULT ZONE

EX. PARK'G.

BIKES

EX. PARK'G.

SCHOOL 3-6

ADMIN.

GYM

K-2

EX. SERVICE DRIVE

LOWER GRADES

TOT-LOT

STORY CIRCLE

PRIMARY COURT

FREE-PLAY

EXISTING RESIDENCES

AUTO PARKING

BIKES

FREE PLAY

SLED RUN

SOFTBALL

BASKET-BALL

CORN FIELD

₵ RAILROAD TRACKS

INTERMEDIATE FIELD GAMES

LITTLE-LEAGUE BASEBALL

FOOTBALL

PROGRAMMED FIELD GAMES

FUTURE RESIDENCES

LINE OF PARK-SCHOOL PROPERTY DIVISION

NORTH

0   50   100   200

NOTE: CONTOUR INTERVAL EQUALS TWO FEET

LEGEND

⇒⇒ AUTO-TRUCK TRAFFIC

⇒⇒ BICYCLE PATH

▭▭▭ MAJOR PEDESTRIAN WAY

▫▫▫▫ MINOR PEDESTRIAN WAY

········ EXISTING CONTOURS

——— PROPOSED CONTOURS

DESIGN CONCEPT—SCHEME 1

A design concept for a scheme for development of the school-park complex is shown in Figure 7-21.

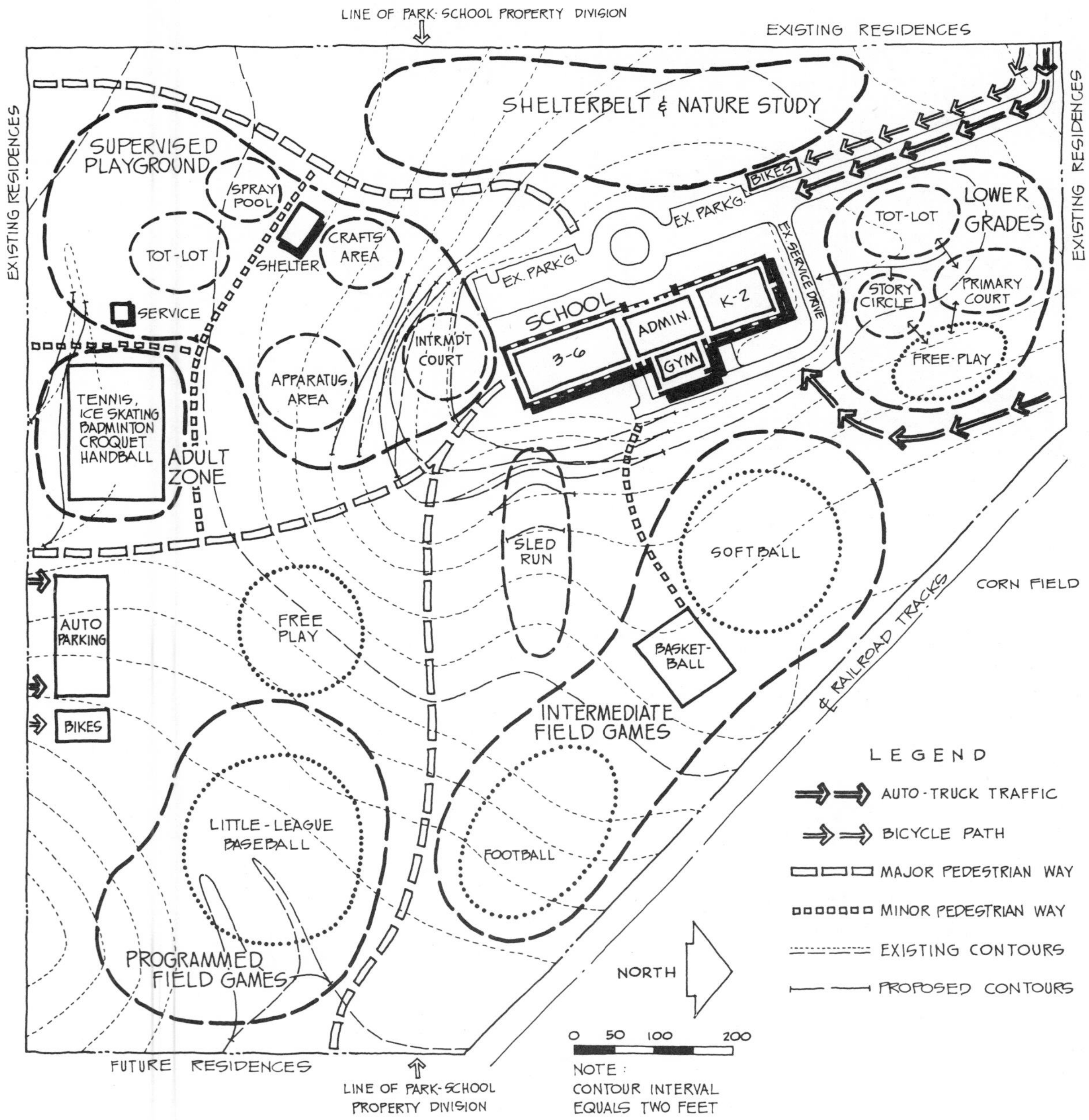

Figure 7-21 Design concept—scheme 1.

SOURCE: A. J. Rutledge, *Anatomy of a Park,* copyright © 1971 by McGraw-Hill, Inc., used with permission of McGraw-Hill Book Company.

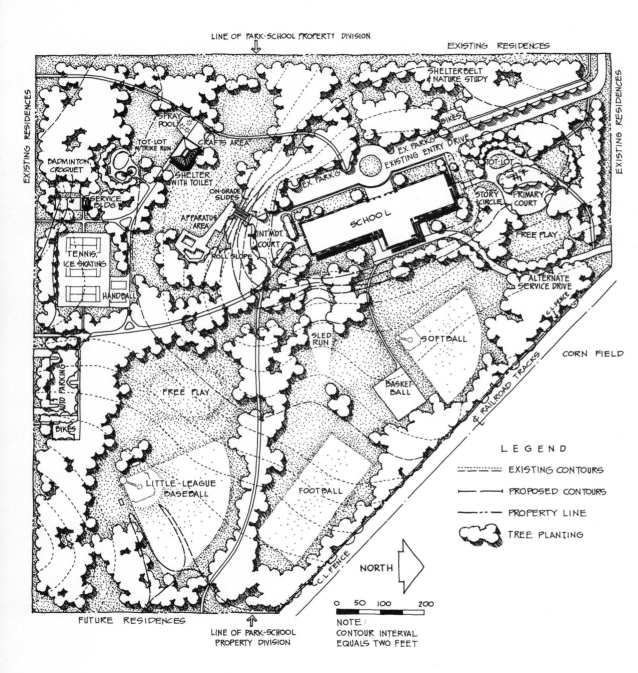

LINE OF PARK-SCHOOL PROPERTY DIVISION

EXISTING RESIDENCES

EXISTING RESIDENCES

EXISTING RESIDENCES

SHELTERBELT & NATURE STUDY

BIKES

SPRAY POOL

TOT-LOT W/TRIKE RUN

CRAFTS AREA

BADMINTON, CROQUET

SHELTER WITH TOILET

ON-GRADE SLIDES

SERVICE BLDG.

APPARATUS AREA

EX. PARKG

EX. PARKG EXISTING ENTRY DRIVE

TOT-LOT

STORY CIRCLE

PRIMARY COURT

SCHOOL

FREE PLAY

TENNIS, ICE SKATING

ROLL SLOPE

INT'MDT. COURT

HANDBALL

ALTERNATE SERVICE DRIVE

C.L. FENCE

AUTO PARKING

SLED RUN

SOFTBALL

CORN FIELD

BIKES

FREE PLAY

BASKET BALL

RAILROAD TRACKS

LITTLE-LEAGUE BASEBALL

FOOTBALL

L E G E N D

EXISTING CONTOURS

PROPOSED CONTOURS

PROPERTY LINE

TREE PLANTING

NORTH

C.L. FENCE

0   50   100   200

FUTURE RESIDENCES

LINE OF PARK-SCHOOL PROPERTY DIVISION

NOTE: CONTOUR INTERVAL EQUALS TWO FEET

SITE PLAN—SCHEME 1

Figure 7-22 shows a plan for developing the site under the scheme in the design concept of Figure 7-21.

Figure 7-22 Site plan—scheme 1.

SOURCE: A. J. Rutledge, *Anatomy of a Park,* copyright © 1971 by McGraw-Hill, Inc., used with permission of McGraw-Hill Book Company.

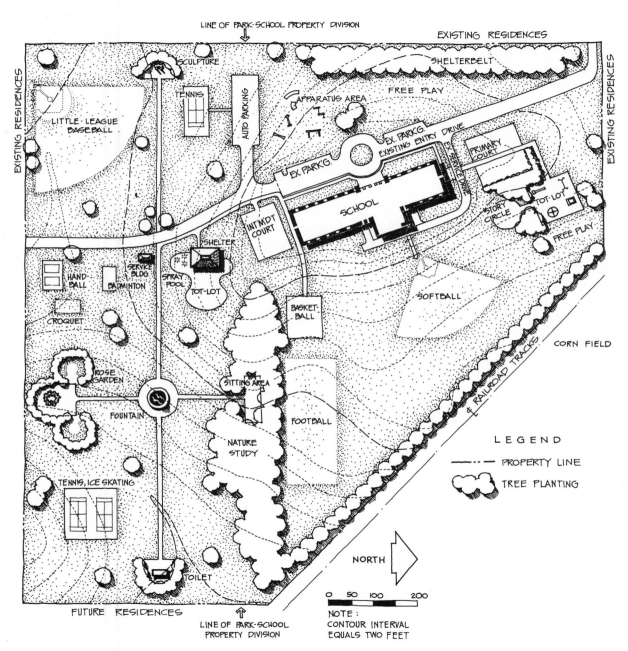

LINE OF PARK-SCHOOL PROPERTY DIVISION

EXISTING RESIDENCES

SHELTERBELT

FREE PLAY

SCULPTURE

TENNIS

APPARATUS AREA

AUTO PARKING

EX. PARK'G.
EXISTING ENTRY DRIVE

PRIMARY COURT

LITTLE-LEAGUE BASEBALL

EX. PARK'G.

SCHOOL

EX. SERVICE DRIVE

STORY CIRCLE

TOT-LOT

FREE PLAY

INT'MDT COURT

SHELTER

SERVICE BLDG

SPRAY POOL

TOT-LOT

HAND-BALL

BADMINTON

BASKET-BALL

SOFTBALL

CROQUET

CORN FIELD

ROSE GARDEN

SITTING AREA

FOUNTAIN

NATURE STUDY

FOOTBALL

TENNIS, ICE SKATING

RAILROAD TRACKS

LEGEND

—··—··— PROPERTY LINE

🌳 TREE PLANTING

NORTH

0   50   100   200

TOILET

FUTURE RESIDENCES

LINE OF PARK-SCHOOL PROPERTY DIVISION

NOTE:
CONTOUR INTERVAL
EQUALS TWO FEET

EXISTING RESIDENCES

EXISTING RESIDENCES

SITE PLAN—SCHEME 2

The site plan of a second scheme is shown in Figure 7-23.

Figure 7-23 Site plan—scheme 2.

SOURCE: A. J. Rutledge, *Anatomy of a Park*, copyright © 1971 by McGraw-Hill, Inc., used with permission of McGraw-Hill Book Company.

7.4 Beach Park Development

A comprehensive plan for a beach park development is shown in Figure 7-24, and details of the plan in Figures 7-25 and 7-26.

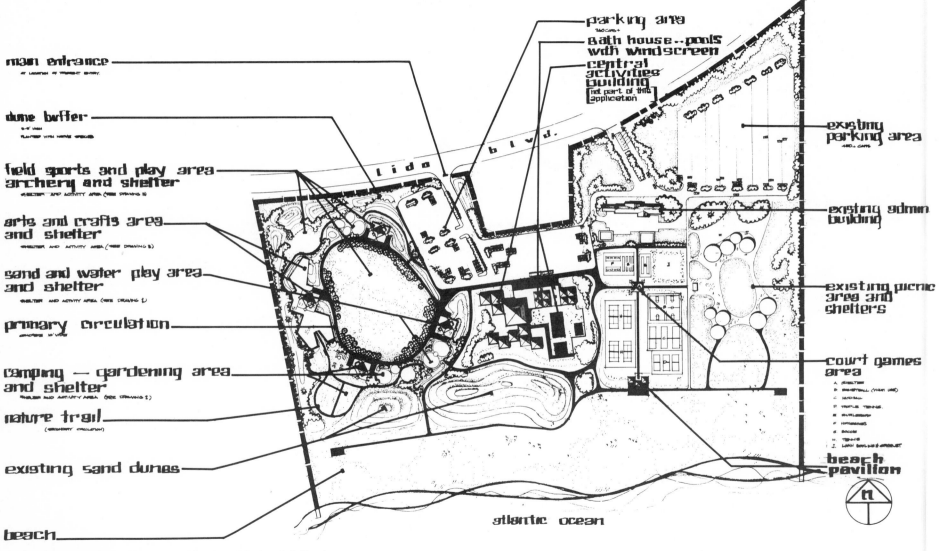

main entrance
AT LOCATION OF PRESENT ENTRY.

dune buffer
3-6' HIGH
PLANTED WITH NATIVE SPECIES.

field sports and play area
archery and shelter
SHELTER AND ACTIVITY AREA (SEE DRAWING 1)

arts and crafts area
and shelter
SHELTER AND ACTIVITY AREA (SEE DRAWING 1)

sand and water play area
and shelter
SHELTER AND ACTIVITY AREA (SEE DRAWING 1)

primary circulation
CONCRETE 10' WIDE

camping — gardening area
and shelter
SHELTER AND ACTIVITY AREA (SEE DRAWING 2)

nature trail
(SECONDARY CIRCULATION)

existing sand dunes

beach

parking area
360 CARS +

Bath house..pools
with windscreen

central
activities
building
not part of this
application

existing
parking area
440± CARS

existing admin.
building

existing picnic
area and
shelters

court games
area
A. SHELTER
B. BASKETBALL (MULTI USE)
C. HANDBALL
D. TABLE TENNIS
E. SHUFFLEBOARD
F. HORSESHOES
G. BOCCIE
H. TENNIS
J. LAWN BOWLING & CRICKET

beach
pavilion

atlantic ocean

Figure 7-24 Comprehensive plan, town of Hempstead Park at Lido Beach.

SOURCE: Planning Associates, Bohemia, N.Y.

340

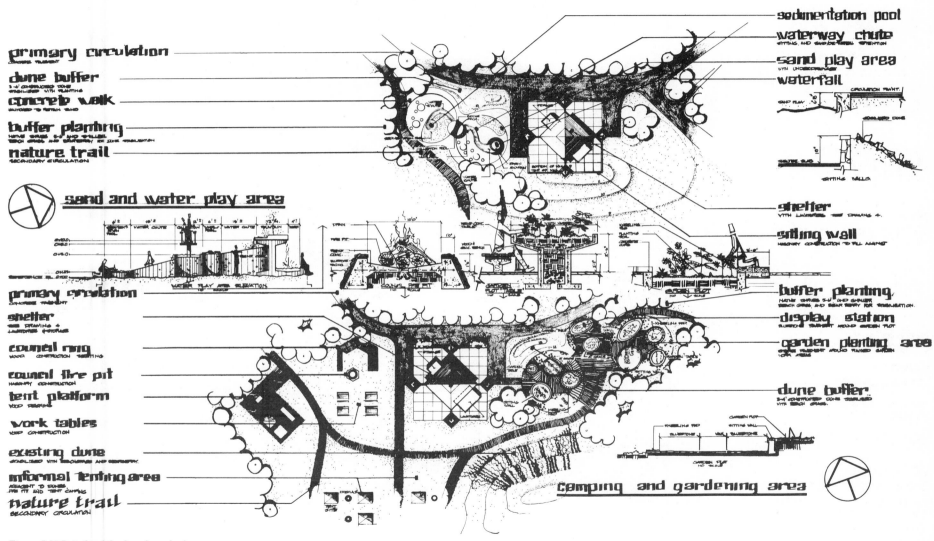

primary circulation
dune buffer
concrete walk
buffer planting
nature trail

sand and water play area

primary circulation
shelter
council ring
council fire pit
tent platform
work tables
existing dune
informal tenting area
nature trail

sedimentation pool
waterway chute
sand play area
waterfall

shelter
sitting wall
buffer planting
display station
garden planting area
dune buffer

camping and gardening area

Figure 7-25 Details of the beach park plan.

SOURCE: Planning Associates, Bohemia, N.Y.

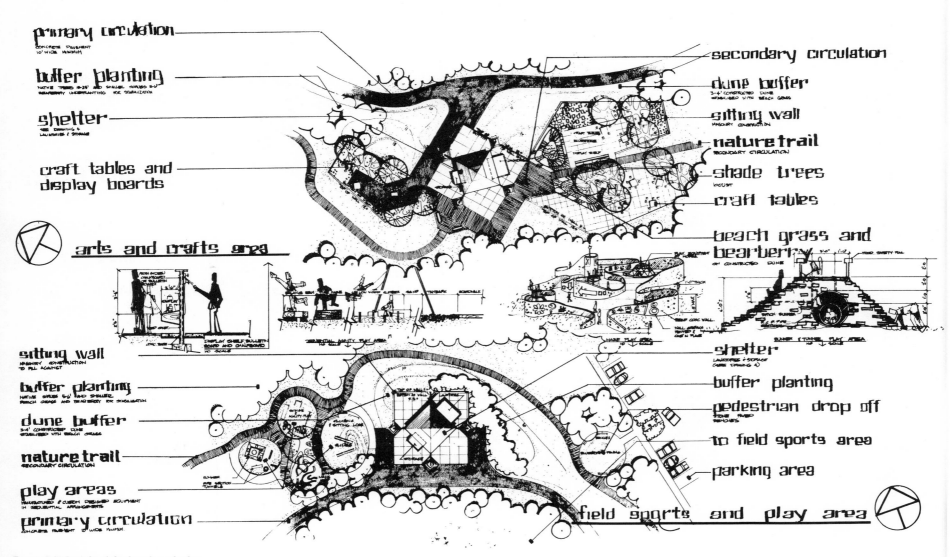

primary circulation
CONCRETE PAVEMENT
10' WIDE MINIMUM

buffer planting
NATIVE TREES 18-26' AND SMALLER SHRUBS 6-8'
BEARBERRY UNDERPLANTING FOR STABILIZATION

shelter
SEE DRAWING 4
LAVATORIES & STORAGE

craft tables and
display boards

arts and crafts area

secondary circulation

dune buffer
3-4' CONSTRUCTED DUNE
STABILIZED WITH BEACH GRASS

sitting wall
MASONRY CONSTRUCTION

nature trail
SECONDARY CIRCULATION

shade trees
LOCUST

craft tables

beach grass and
bearberry
ON CONSTRUCTED DUNE

sitting wall
MASONRY CONSTRUCTION
TO FILL AGAINST

buffer planting
NATIVE SHRUBS 5-8' AND SMALLER
BEACH GRASS AND BEARBERRY FOR STABILIZATION

dune buffer
3-4' CONSTRUCTED DUNE
STABILIZED WITH BEACH GRASS

nature trail
SECONDARY CIRCULATION

play areas
MANUFACTURED & CUSTOM DESIGNED EQUIPMENT
IN SEQUENTIAL ARRANGEMENTS

primary circulation
CONCRETE PAVEMENT 10' WIDE MINIMUM

shelter
LAVATORIES & STORAGE
(SEE DRAWING 4)

buffer planting

pedestrian drop off
STONE PAVED
BENCHES

to field sports area

parking area

field sports and play area

Figure 7-26 Details of the beach park plan.

SOURCE: Planning Associates, Bohemia, N.Y.

342

Figure 7-27 shows further plans and details of the beach park development.

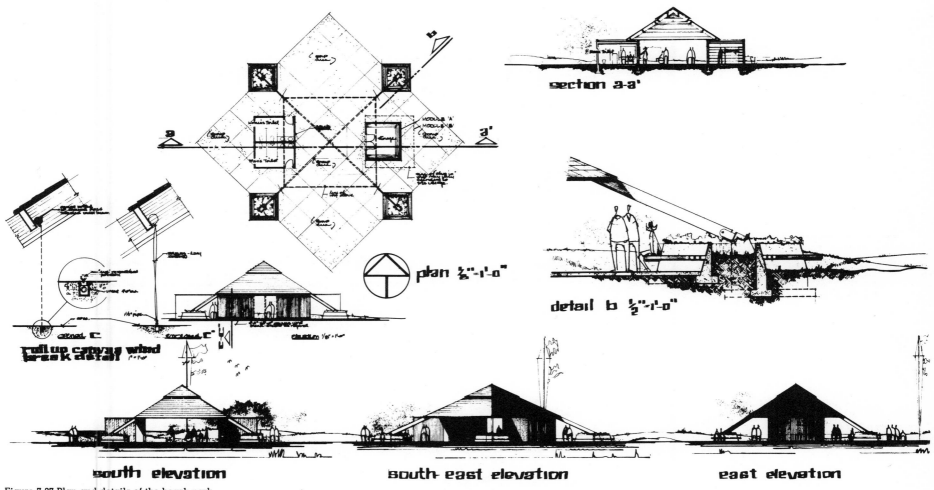

section a-a'

plan ½"=1'-0"

detail b ½"=1'-0"

roll up canvas wind break detail

south elevation

south east elevation

east elevation

Figure 7-27 Plan and details of the beach park.

SOURCE: Planning Associates, Bohemia, N.Y.

Figure 7-28 shows the plan and details for the bathhouse, and Figure 7-29 the plan and details for the beach pavilion.

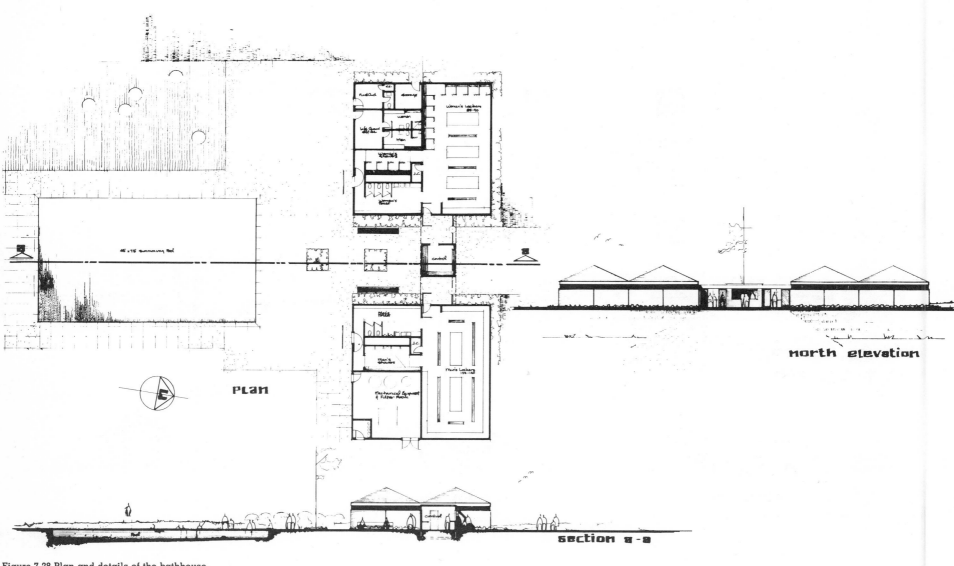

Figure 7-28 Plan and details of the bathhouse.

SOURCE: Planning Associates, Bohemia, N.Y.

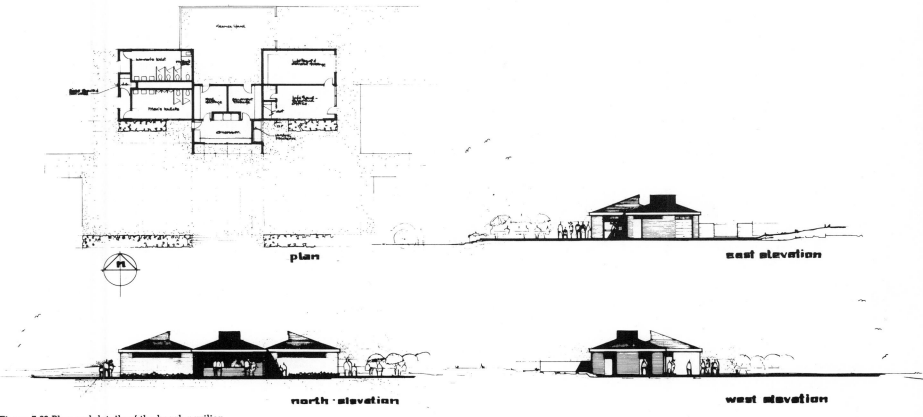

plan

east elevation

north elevation

west elevation

Figure 7-29 Plan and details of the beach pavilion.

SOURCE: Planning Associates, Bohemia, N.Y.

7.5 Mobile Home Park

Figure 7-30 shows a plan for a typical mobile home park.

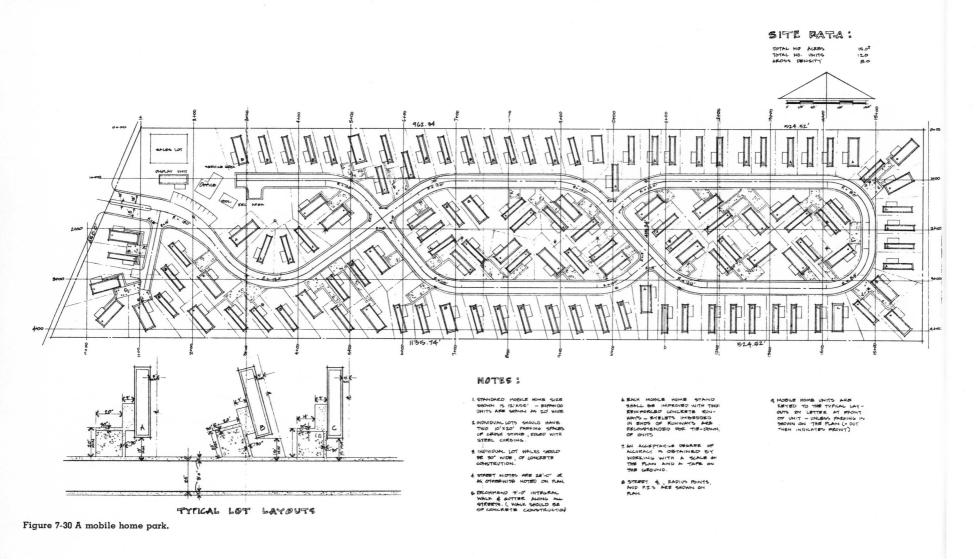

Figure 7-30 A mobile home park.

SOURCE: Mobile Home Manufacturers Association, Land Development Division.

7.6 Schematic Plan for Recreational Facilities

Planning for recreational facilities is illustrated in Figure 7-31.

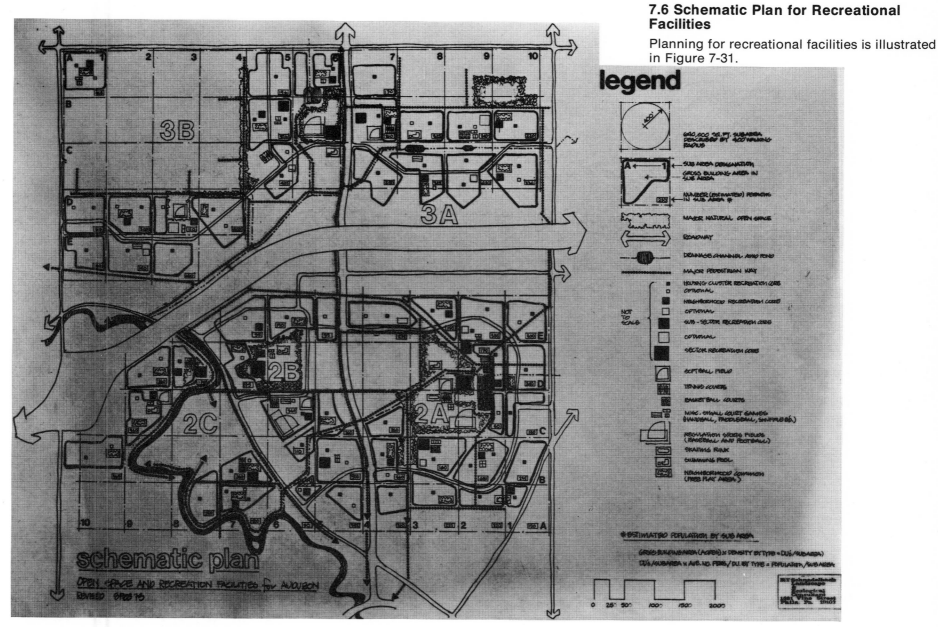

Figure 7-31 A schematic plan for recreational facilities.

SOURCE: R. T. Schnadelbach, Landscape and Ecological Consultant, Philadelphia.